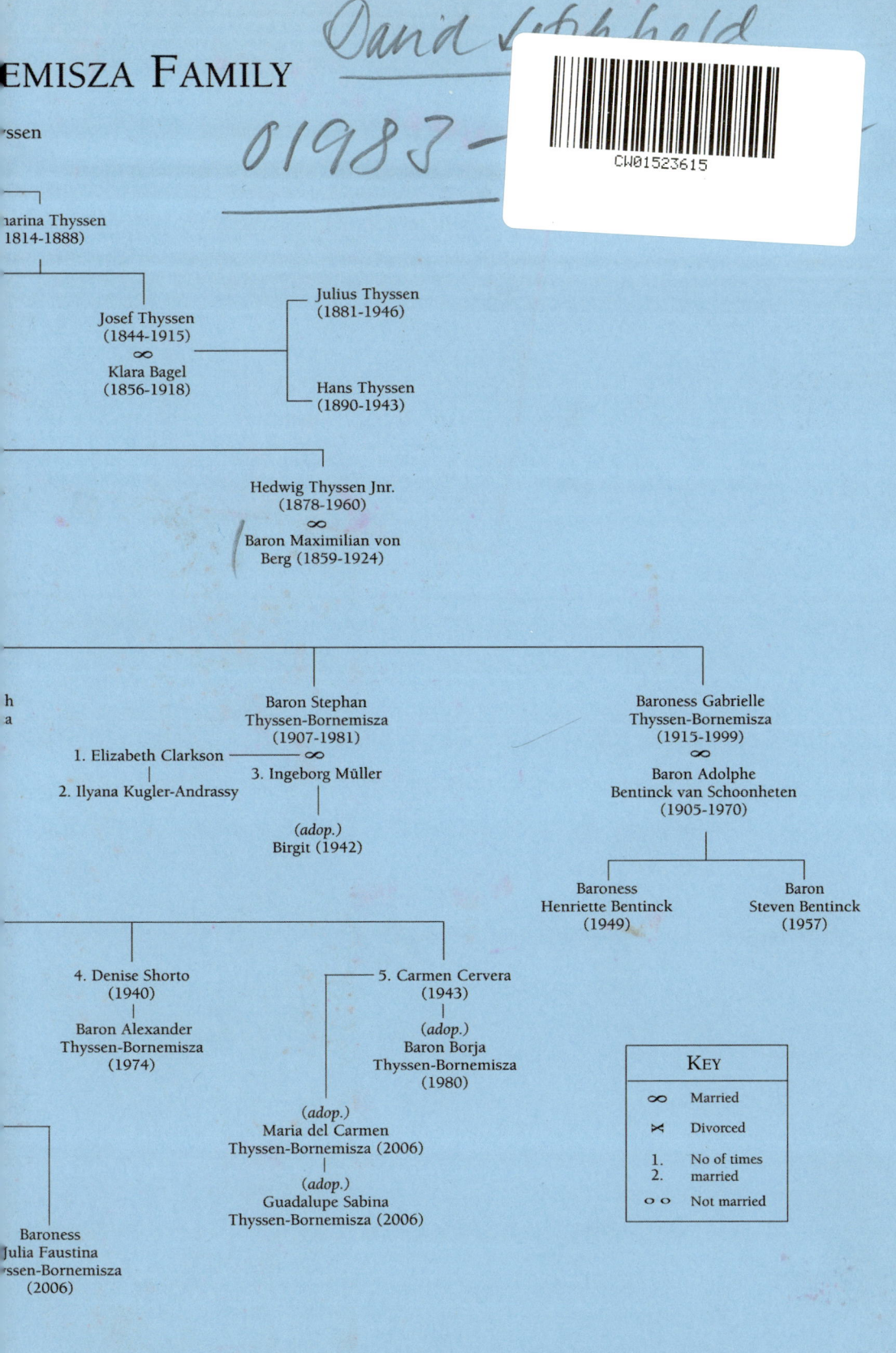

The Thyssen Art Macabre

The Thyssen Art Macabre

David R. L. Litchfield

in collaboration with
Caroline Schmitz

QUARTET BOOKS

First published in 2006 by Quartet Books Limited
A member of the Namara Group
27 Goodge Street, London W1T 2LD

Copyright © David R. L. Litchfield 2006

The right of David R. L. Litchfield to be identified as the author
of this work has been asserted by him in accordance
with the Copyright, Designs and Patents Act 1988

All rights reserved. No part of this book may be
reproduced in any form or by any means without prior
written permission from the publisher

A catalogue record for this book is available from the British Library

ISBN 10   07043 71197
ISBN 13   978 07043 71194

Typeset by Antony Gray
Printed and bound in Great Britain by
T J International Limited, Padstow, Cornwall

For Bag & Fred

Contents

Abbreviations
(Page xiii)

Acknowledgements
(Page xv)

Introduction
(Page 3)

Prologue
(Page 5)

1996 : Heini & Tita ... Lunch on the Costa Brava

Meeting in Spain, with the Baron and Baroness Thyssen-Bornemisza prior to the Thyssen *v.* Thyssen court case in Bermuda : The final chapter in the $3.5 billion legal battle between Heini and his eldest son.

Chapter I
(Page 13)

1685–1900 : 'Old' August Thyssen ... The myth of the self-made man

The Thyssens' rise to power : The birth of August Thyssen : His privileged education : His and his sister's financially motivated marriages : The vital contribution of his brother Josef : The creation of the Thyssen brothers' industrial empire : August's brilliant but ruthless business methods : The birth of his four children : The collapse of his marriage leading to a crippling settlement which resulted in the loss of ownership of his industrial empire : The arrival of the Price family.

Chapter II
(Page 33)
1900–1915 : The arrival of the Bornemiszas . . . Buying into the aristocracy

August Thyssen's status as the first German billionaire and one of the richest men in the world : The acquisition of a castle and his foundation of an art collection : His son Heinrich's purchase of the title of Baron from the Bornemisza family and assumption of the role of Hungarian aristocrat as the Baron Heinrich Thyssen-Bornemisza : The first Thyssen *v.* Thyssen court battle between father and son : Start of company's war production.

Chapter III
(Page 52)
1915–1926 : Blood & iron . . . The profits of war

The death of August's brother Josef : August's sons, Heinrich and Fritz's introduction to the business : Founding of Dutch bank : Their profitable survival of the First World War : Heinrich's flight to Holland from the communist revolution in Hungary : Development of family's anti-Semitism : Birth of Heini and separation of parents : Heini's childhood : Beginning of Fritz and Heinrich's involvement with Hitler and the Nazi Party : Founding of Heinrich's American bank : The death of August Thyssen and his dreams of a dynasty.

Chapter IV
(Page 78)
1926–1939 : Financing Hitler . . . Re-arming the Reich

Fritz and Heinrich's division of their father's financial and industrial empire : Formation and integration with United Steel Trust : Development of offshore ownership in Switzerland : Continuation of Fritz's financing of the Nazis : Opening of August Thyssen Bank in Berlin : Founding of Heinrich's art collection and acquisition of Villa Favorita : Brothers' flourishing relationship with Göring : Fritz and Amélie's membership of the Nazi Party : Heini's attendance at a Nazi school in Holland : Heini's brother Stephan's shooting of his girlfriend in Hungary : Heinrich's acquisition of a confiscated Jewish racing stables : Fritz and Heinrich's profiting from Third Reich's demand for armaments and financial services : Fritz and Heinrich's gold deposits in London : Fritz's daughter's escape from Germany to his Argentinian safe haven : Heinrich's flight to Switzerland, followed by Heini.

Chapter V
(Page 135)

1939–1945 : Banking for the Nazis… Massacring the Jews

Fritz's flight from Germany ahead of war; participation in the production of *I Paid Hitler* before arrest and return to privileged incarceration : Göring's confiscation of Fritz's industrial holdings : Heinrich's continued control of his German companies from Switzerland, including U-boat production : Heini's avoidance of German military service and increasing involvement in his father's activities : Supply of international financial services by Heinrich's August Thyssen Bank to the Nazi counter-intelligence : Stephan's work on V-rockets and armament design : Blocking of Union Bank of New York's transfer of Nazi funds to Argentina : Transfer of power from Heinrich to Heini : Margit's relationship with the SS and her part in the Jewish massacre at Rechnitz.

Chapter VI
(Page 185)

1945–1954 : Heini seizes power… Uncle Fritz escapes to South America

Heini's retrieval of German industrial assets and banks with the assistance of the Americans : Fritz's liberation and interrogation by Americans before escape to Argentina : Illegal retrieval of documents from Berlin to Rotterdam in 'Operation Juliana' : Stephan's flight from Germany to Monte Carlo and Cuba : Fritz's death : Inheritance of his fortune by his wife and daughter : Their return to Munich from Argentina to run eighty-five companies with the largest single block of Thyssen AG shares : Death of Baron Heinrich Thyssen-Bornemisza : Heini's inheritance of his father's empire after a bitter dispute with his brother and sisters : Retrieval of gold from Bank of England : Marriage to Princess Theresa zu Lippe : Her alleged affair with his brother-in-law which Heini claimed to result in the birth of Georg or 'Heini Junior' : Heini's fight for Swiss nationality.

Chapter VII
(Page 244)

1954–1967: The playboy years...
One divorce, two weddings & a panther

Heini's divorce from Theresa, resulting in a divisive and extremely expensive alimony settlement : Marriage to the sexually exotic Nina Dyer and adoption of playboy lifestyle : His divorce from Nina and marriage to Fiona Campbell-Walter : The birth of two children, only one of which is his : Fiona's affairs : Heini's rivalry with Niarchos and Onassis : Divorce from Fiona : His investment in art and loss of three banks.

Chapter VIII
(Page 285)

1967–1981: The murder of his wife's lover...
The creation of the Thyssen-Bornemisza Collection

Heini's corporate abandonment of Germany and adoption of America : His love for Diana von Buch and marriage to Denise Shorto : Indictment in Italian art smuggling : Decline in Thyssen Bornemisza Group profits : Murder of Denise's lover in New York : Peaking of Heini's art acquisitions : Heini Junior's arrival at TBG : Heini's admission to suffering from alcoholism.

Chapter IX
(Page 327)

1981–1988 : Enter Tita... The Spanish connection

Commencement of affair with Tita Cervera while divorcing Denise : Settlement including $80 million worth of jewellery removed from Villa Favorita : Creation of complex Bermudan trust ownership : Promotion of the Collection and exchange of pictures with the Russians : Heini's marriage to Tita and adoption of her son Borja : Junior's assumption of control of TBG.

Chapter X
(Page 358)

1983–1993 : By royal appointment . . . The $ 600 million art sale

Heini's first stroke : Heini Junior's curtailment of his father's excessive spending : Heini's move to Spain : Tita's assistance in selling half his art collection to Spain.

Chapter XI
(Page 395)

1993–2001 : Thyssen *v.* Thyssen . . . The $150 million court case

Family's share-out of remaining pictures and proceeds from Spanish art sale : Commencement of Carmen Thyssen-Bornemisza Collection : Heini's survival of cardio-vascular surgery and resulting coma : Tita's confrontation with Heini Junior over money owing to Heini : Tita's discovery of $350 million liquid assets held by Thyssen Bornemisza Group : Heini and Tita's action against Junior for the retrieval of the ownership of TBG, claimed to be worth $3.5 billion : The eighteen-month Thyssen *v.* Thyssen Bermudan court case estimated to cost $150 million : Collapse of the trial.

Chapter XII
(Page 432)

2001–2006 : The Fall of the House of Thyssen-Bornemisza

Heini's million settlement : His death two months later and with no legitimate male heirs, the end of the house of Thyssen-Bornemisza : Continuation of familial inheritance battles : The division and sale of TBG.

Sources
(Page 442)

Index
(Page 454)

Abbreviations

AGHütt	AG für Hüttenbetrieb Duisburg-Meiderich
ATB	August Thyssen Bank AG
ATH	August Thyssen Hütte AG
BHF-Bank	Berliner Handels- und Frankfurter Bank
BV	Bremer Vulkan AG
BVHS	Bank voor Handel en Scheepvaart
Cehandro	Centrale Handels Vereeniging NV Rotterdam
DFC	Domestic Fuel Corporation
Faminta	Familien Interessen AG
FSG	Flensburger Schiffsbaugesellschaft
GDK	Gewerkschaft Deutscher Kaiser
HAIC	Holland American Investment Corporation
HATC	Holland American Trading Corporation
HTK	Hollandsch Trust Kantoor
HTMV	Handels en Transport Maatschappij Vulcaan
IHS	Information Handling Services
MABAG	Maschinen- und Apparatebau AG, Nordhausen
NAM	Nederlands Artoilje Maatschappij
NCB	Nederlandse Credietbank
OSW	Oberbilker Stahlwerk
PRAKLA	Gesellschaft für praktische Lagerstättenforschung
PWW	Press- und Walzwerk Reisholz
RTK	Rotterdamsch Trustees Kantoor
SSEC	Seamless Steel Equipment Corporation
STEAG	Steinkohlen-Elektrizitäts AG
SUSPC	Steel Union Sheet Piling Company
TBG	Thyssen Bornemisza Group
Thyssen Lametal	Thyssen Compania Industrial y Mercantil & Thyssen Limitada Lametal, Buenos Aires
UBC	Union Banking Corporation ('Union Bank')
VBM	Vereinigte Berliner Mörtelwerke
VSt	Vereinigte Stahlwerke

Acknowledgements

The following is a list of people to whom I owe a debt of gratitude for their assistance and inspiration:

Dr Hubert Achermann, David Alexander QC, Naim Attallah, Christine Bader, Nigel Bagshaw, Jeremy Beale, Geoffrey Bell, Werner Bendix, Baroness Gabrielle Bentinck-Thyssen, Baron Steven Bentinck, Ildiko Berg, Heinz Berggruen, Sandor Berkes, Deborah Blackman, Bruno Boesch, Raquel Borrás, Emil Bosshard (†), Veronika Bosshard, D. Bourgeois, Christian Braun, Ursula Cassinone, Max Claridge, Susan Clarke, Candida Cohane, Stanley A. Cohen, Jason Cox, Michael Crystal QC, S.A.R. Infanta Doña Pilar de Borbón y Borbón, Georgia de Chamberet, Kirstin Dent, Jerome Dill, Ahmed ElAmin, Jeffrey Elkinson, Melanie Folkes, Freingruber family, Arno Gattermann, Wilhelmus Groenendijk, Claudine Groh, Dr Joseph Groh (†), Tim Gurney, Robert Ham QC, Paul Hampton, Nicholas Haslam, Dr Josef Hotwagner, Dottie Huttinger, Dr Hermann Viktor Johnen, Dr Friederich Kahlenberg, Samantha Knights, Eva Koehler, Mario König, Dr Peter Kuhlbrodt, Antje Landshoff, Stefan Landshoff, Botoa Lefé, Summer Lee Litchfield, Tomás Llorens Serra, Peter Loomes, Mairi Mallon, Catherine Mansel Lewis, Susana Manzanares, Professor Marco Marcoff, Ben Mawson, Denis Mitchell, Jeannette Mitchell, Lee Myers, Dr Adam Oellers, Elsa Oppenheimer, Howard Parker, Gregor Pickro, Anthony Price, Marie-France Railey (†), Dr Jürgen Real, Dr R. Rehli, Thomas Rendall, John Richardson, Klaus Ritter, Harold Robins, Conxa Rodríguez, Peter Rose, Jaime Rotondo Russo, Hannelore Schmidt-Engel, Dr Peter Schnyder, Heinz and Gregor Schumi, Arnie Schwarzman, Ingrid Seward, Brian Sewell, Mukta Sharma, Inmaculada Spencer, Abner Stein, Anna Maria Stirnimann, Colin Swift, Baron Alexander Thyssen-Bornemisza, Baron Borja Thyssen-Bornemisza, Baroness Carmen Thyssen-Bornemisza, Baroness Denise Thyssen-Bornemisza, Baroness Fiona Thyssen-Bornemisza, Baron Georg Heinrich Thyssen-Bornemisza, Baron Hans Heinrich Thyssen-Bornemisza (†), Baron Lorne Thyssen-Bornemisza, Claudia Thyssen-Guerreschi, Michel van Rijn, José and Silvia Vega, Gore Vidal, José Luís de Vilallonga, Baroness Marie-Claire von Alvensleben, Baroness Gloria von Berg, Archduchess Francesca von Habsburg,

Archduke Karl von Habsburg, H. von Ruette, Barbara von Stengel, Stephen Walton, Sandy Whitelaw, Dr Simon Wiesenthal (†), Peter Wilkie, Dr Stephen Wilkinson (and in Cuba: Emilio de la Osa, Jorge Fernandez, Leonardo Padura and Estela Rivas Vasquez), Harriet Wilson, Caroline Wright, Christopher Wright, Dr Waldemar Zettel, Count Federico Zichy-Thyssen and Marion Zorn. With special thanks to Robert Kearns.

*Money can have an extremely destructive effect
Especially for people who do not have any.*

Baron Hans Heinrich Thyssen-Bornemisza de Kaszón

Introduction

Baron Hans Heinrich Thyssen-Bornemisza de Kaszón was attracted by the process of commissioning biographies, which was presumably why, to my knowledge, he repeated the process six times. He also enjoyed drinking red wine while he told far from truthful stories about himself, his wives and his art collection. In all fairness, most of the writers shared his enjoyment, for 'Heini' Thyssen was a charming and entertaining man. But it soon became obvious to me that it was the finished product that he found so difficult to accept, preferring to sustain an endless process of preparation, rather than produce what he knew to be a work of fiction.

After I had completed my term of seemingly infinite invitations for 'a little more vino tinto?' and received the customary termination notice, I made it obvious that I intended to continue my book independently. Not Heini's biography, but a history of the family.

Meanwhile, yet more writers were commissioned, but when Heini finally realised that I really was continuing with my book, I was approached by his daughter with an offer of financial inducement to persuade me otherwise. When this failed, he had the Baroness re-commission me to write his biography and spend yet further time in his company, drinking ever more red wine: 'You help us with our book and we will help you with yours.'

However, the second time it was different. He started to tell me painful things about his family that he had never told me before; or anyone else as far as I know. Gradually I began to realise that Heini knew I was going to be the last member of the 'salon des refusés', because this time he would be the one who was leaving and on 27 April 2002 he did; one year after I had completed the hagiography, which remains unpublished.

I was then, theoretically, free to complete my version of the family's history. But Heini had been selective in his revelations and I still had to liberate myself from the restraints of the authorised family scenario, for dynasties have a habit of creating myths of financial and social convenience; each generation hiding the sins of its fathers and exaggerating its own achievements, while documentary evidence is dismissed, destroyed, manipulated or ignored.

One of the Thyssen-Bornemiszas' most obvious myths had been that of nationality. The severance of their German nationality and all possible connections with the country of their forefathers and source of their wealth, had no doubt encouraged Heini's collaboration with an English rather than a German writer in the telling of his family's story. I believe this was also the reason why the Thyssen-Bornemiszas had distanced themselves from Thyssen AG (now ThyssenKrupp AG) and how they had managed so successfully to conceal the extent of their personal and corporate relationship with the Third Reich.

Other branches of the family had avoided the risks associated with *Aufarbeitung* by going to ground in Argentina, Paraguay and New York and refusing to co-operate with writers of any nationality.[1]

But while Heini may have considered his final revelations and admissions to be a form of personal absolution, he could have been in no doubt as to the embarrassment they would cause, so maybe it was a legacy that he also considered a suitable punishment for his family's often unfeeling greed. There is no doubt that such embarrassment, both personal and corporate, would have appealed to the old 'capitalist agitator's' sense of humour.

---

1 *Aufarbeitung* means 'working through' and refers to Germans facing up to and dealing with their Nazi past. Another term used in this context is *Vergangenheitsbewältigung*, which means 'coming to terms with your past'.

Prologue
1996

Heini & Tita ... Lunch on the Costa Brava

*A dream is always a memory in reality,
and only reality when dreaming.*
Count Maximilian Schosberger

At 11.00 am on 17 July 1996 I received a telephone call from Spain. I was informed that Carmen Cervera, The Baroness Thyssen-Bornemisza de Kaszón, wished to speak to me. After a pause appropriate to her position, 'Tita' came on the line. After five years of silence she had apparently decided that she should help me 'tell the truth', to correct all the lies that had been told by her husband's four ex-wives and to go through all the archives with me. She said she had not told Heini because he was still under pressure from his daughter, now the Archduchess Francesca von Habsburg, not to co-operate with me. She said she would tell him that she was working with me but not straight away. She did not tell me about the family crisis, that had no doubt inspired her call, but presumably she would. She was very flattering and told me how much she liked my writing, that we should meet as soon as possible and how important it was that the real truth be told.

Marcel Duchamp described truth as 'nothing more than the accumulation of popularly held beliefs' but I felt that Tita's definition might be somewhat more personal with considerably less reference to popularity.

The following Tuesday I informed her that I would be arriving at Girona on Wednesday 28 August with a companion and I was assured there would be a car and driver to meet us at the station. That afternoon Caroline Schmitz and I left London on the 14.30 train to Paris where we boarded the overnight Talgo Express bound for Barcelona via Girona.

The Thyssens' Portuguese driver was polite, friendly and mildly formal. He drove gently through the hot dry hills of Catalonia and up the winding road leading to the remains of that sixties' playground known to millions as the Costa Brava. Like their house in Madrid, Mas Mañanas is situated in an exclusive estate; the type of estate where the very rich can feel secure in the knowledge that their neighbours' jealousy is unlikely to be financial or manifest itself in robbery or vandalism.

We were greeted warmly by Giorgio, Heini's Italian butler; a man of great elegance and style who had been with Heini, on and off, for more than thirty years. Contrary to Caroline's imagined fears of vicious Dobermann and Rottweiler guard dogs, the canine threat consisted of nothing more than a motley collection of very small but vocal dogs of mixed, poodle-ish parentage, numbering somewhere between twelve and fifteen. They rushed around us, yapping hysterically, until we were safely seated with our morning coffee on the flagstoned patio in front of the house. Then they yapped at each other.

Fifties Californian in style, the house initially appeared to be quite small but beneath the neatly trimmed lawn, which stretched to the edge of the parapet, were further levels, built into the side of the hill like closely terraced paddy fields. Far below, the deep blue sea glittered in the morning sun while the tropical atmosphere was heightened by the squawks and shrieks of Tita's early rising parrots.

The bright and colourful interior of the house is very feminine; its comfortable vulgarity a true reflection of Tita's taste rather than the impersonal skills of a decorator. There was little to suggest that this was the home of the world's 'greatest' art collector, apart from various Thyssen Collection catalogues on the coffee table and one large N. C. Wyeth landscape above the dining-room fireplace. In fact there was very little evidence of Heini's presence at all; the various mementoes scattered about being almost exclusively those from Tita's previous marriage to Lex Barker, the late Hollywood film star.

After a while, Giorgio came out to warn us that Tita might be some time. So we drank more coffee, smoked more cigarettes, explored the garden and discovered the heated fresh-water pool and cold sea-water pool in which, in the five years of regular visits, I never saw anyone swim.

Then, without warning, Heini suddenly shuffled into the room, supported by Giorgio. He was dressed in a T-shirt and shorts and clutched a small electronic device for summoning servants. He was also accompanied by an equally ancient and bad-tempered Yorkshire terrier called Juanita. Greeting us both warmly, he reminded me that it had been a long time since we had seen each other. Walking with some difficulty, his left arm obviously paralysed, he sank gratefully into a chair but did not appear to be in any pain.

Though he had degenerated physically in the four years since I had last seen him, his mind was still alert and his sense of humour very much alive. He twice asked Giorgio when 'The Baron' would be making her appearance. We chatted about the weather, Jimmy Goldsmith's chances of political success and the general state of the world without ever referring to books or family politics, apart from a brief aside when he mentioned the fact that he and Heini Junior, his eldest son, were not on speaking terms. His main source of interest appeared to be whether we were going to stay for lunch.

Heini was very pleased to hear that we were but still reassured himself with two further confirmations during our conversation. He also asked me, discreetly, what Caroline's role was. When I informed him that she was my research assistant and translator, he became somewhat uneasy. He became even more so when I told him that she was German. It would take another twelve months for Heini to feel sufficiently at ease to communicate with her in their mother tongue.

We also talked about the state of the art market and the fact that the house had been designed and built by Lex Barker. Heini explained how he had developed the property and built a separate, self-contained area for Tita, which made it fairly obvious that while they gave the impression of enjoying a close and loving relationship, physically they were leading quite separate lives.

Eventually, Tita arrived from one of the lower levels. Dressed in white cotton overalls with a conspicuous lack of decoration, she rushed across the lawn and greeted us with a huge smile and a blown kiss to 'my darling'. Apologising for her lateness she launched straight into questioning me whether Heini and I had been talking about 'the book'. Hardly pausing for breath or a reply, she explained why it was so fortunate that I was there and what sort of book was needed and why only she and Heini knew the real truth about the terrible things that other members of the family had got up to and how good it would be if I worked with them.

The conversation then shifted back to art as Tita rushed off to get me a copy of the catalogue for her latest exhibition, 'From Canaletto to Kandinsky', at the Thyssen-Bornemisza Museum in Madrid. Comprising some ninety-seven paintings, it was all rather confusing, for while the catalogue proclaimed the collection to be hers, the provenance indicated that most of the major works had previously been the property of her husband or his heirs; Heini having bought back many of the works that he had given to his children under their inheritance trust agreement.

Lunch was served on a lower terrace, under the shade of umbrella pines. Far below us small boats left white trails on the dark blue sea while a lone cicada sang his one-note song. Quiet men in white shirts and black trousers served the food. Giorgio served the wine; red for Heini, white for the rest of us. I realised why Heini had been so excited at the prospect of our staying for lunch. Guests were an excuse for him to consume a far greater quantity of wine than the single glass Giorgio normally allowed him when dining alone. Considering the amount of time Tita had invested in keeping Heini healthy, her encouragement of his indulgence was puzzling. Perhaps it was purely a reflection of her lack of sympathy with the concept of moderation. She certainly drank more white wine than he drank red, chain-smoked Marlboro throughout the meal and ate like a peasant. Her habit of preparing her own salad from a bowl of ripe tomatoes and raw garlic cloves reminded me of Onassis's habit of eating whole raw onions, like apples; particularly as an accompaniment to delicate gourmet food in expensive restaurants.

Heini asked me why I wasn't drinking red wine, so I told him: 'The last time I sat up all night drinking red wine with you in Lugano, your daughter accused me of being an alcoholic and told me that was why you didn't want to work with me any more.'

Heini giggled. Then his eyes darkened: 'She thought that you were writing a book full of terrible stories about the family that you were planning to release to coincide with her wedding and that you and your publisher were demanding one million dollars not to publish it. Maybe she and Fiona were just trying to get some more money out of me but I had already spent two million dollars on the wedding.'

I wanted to ask why he had waited four years to tell me this story but Tita was already recounting some wild allegations, which I may have been tempted to include in such a book. The main source of her stories appeared to be Heini's ex-wives, one of whom he claimed had an affair with his brother-in-law, while another he accused of sleeping with his daughter's boyfriends and of taking cocaine with Gianni Agnelli. There were also tales of a lesbian murder, paedophilia and pornography.

But when she started to recount evidence of infanticide, I politely suggested that it might not be the ideal subject for discussion over such a delightful lunch. I did not want her to frighten herself with her own revelations, so I changed the subject by informing her that I had heard rumours of betrayal in the family. Her substantiation of these rumours shocked me, not so much because of her aggressive candour but because of her confirmation of the accuracy of my informant.

Ever since Heini had officially retired from the family business and placed everything under the control of Heini Junior, he had received a fairly adequate annual income of between $13 million and $15million, being some 30 per cent of the net profits of the Thyssen Bornemisza Group (TBG) trust. Unfortunately, Heini's and Tita's fine art acquisitions had resulted in an escalating demand for the support of bank loans. On the grounds that they were threatening the capitalisation of TBG and contravening the terms of the inheritance trust agreement, which they had all signed, Heini Junior refused to assist in underwriting any further 'fund-raising'. He also refused Tita's demand for a seat on the board and a one per cent share for her sixteen-year-old son. This had led to a huge fight. Heini Senior attempted to retrieve his claimed $69 million annuity shortfall and take the reins of power.

Unfortunately, he found himself caught in his own web of ownership trust agreements and he was relieved of his position as honorary chairman leaving Heini Junior in full control. That was my informant's version of the situation. But they were family and, despite claiming neutrality, they were not great admirers of Carmen Cervera.

Having lost the first round, Heini and Tita decided they should adopt a more aggressive form of attack. On the pretext that Heini had been 'cheated' out of 'as much as fifty million; maybe more', Tita claimed that they were going to 'get it all back through the courts'.

Heini agreed and drained his glass before looking round for more.

'You're taking him to court? Your own son?'

'Of course. In September. We have to. I have five lawyers working on the case.'

Tita's eyes sparkled with excitement as she refilled Heini's glass: 'He should go to jail for what he has done.'

'And Chessy, whose side is she on?'

She answered with obvious delight: 'Heini Junior's of course.'

'She has all those idiotic Habsburgs to support,' Heini mumbled into his wine. Heini and Tita insisted that he had been supporting the Habsburgs for twenty-five or thirty years with voluntary contributions to their various political causes.

'My sister Gaby also used to give them money. Otto's brother Rudolph used to turn up personally to collect the cheque. Now they get my money through ARCH, Francesca's art preservation foundation. She has these really embarrassing fund-raising dinners where she tells people to get their money out. At one of them we walked out because she was suggesting to people that it was me who was asking them for contributions.'

Tita chimed in with her own insult: 'Juan Carlos calls them the "termites" because they have so many children. I remember when we were in St Moritz and a man came to collect the cheque. Heini had forgotten it, so Guscetti, Heini's accountant, had to bring it all the way from Lugano.'

She then rushed off to get photographs of Heini Junior and Ivan Batthyány, which, she claimed, proved that he was not really Heini's son at all, while Heini continued to nod in agreement.

'And Josi Groh, whose side is he taking?'

It was a question that initiated a long drawn out story from Tita about Groh making a pass at her in a New York porn cinema where she had gone, apparently, in search of 'American cultural experience'. She had taken Josi Groh with her because she 'really could not have gone off alone, at night, in New York with a huge diamond ring on my finger'. Waiving it in front of us, she claimed she only wore diamonds because they brought her luck. Her huge grin challenging me to reply. She then continued in more detail, explaining how Groh had told her that Heini was impotent and how he had been obliged to satisfy all the ex-wives sexually, so he had presumed she would also be needing his services.

I had to admit that my opinion of Groh, a diminutive Hungarian lawyer and one of Heini's oldest friends, was enhanced rather than diminished by the thought of him claiming the highly unlikely position of in-house stud and making a pass at Tita in a New York porn cinema. Perhaps there was more to the man than met the eye. Maybe he was just very brave because he certainly was not stupid but I could not help but remind Heini that he once told me how he fell out with the man because of his special relationship with Denise which had resulted in him assisting her in her flight from Villa Favorita. I assumed Groh was on Junior's side.

Tita's next revelation led me to believe that Heini Junior's cash control could also be affecting Heini's three surviving ex-wives' alimony. Or maybe Denise, his fourth, really was as loyal to Heini as she had always claimed to be.

'When Heini Junior resigned from the Spanish art foundation we recruited Alexander to replace him and I think Denise, his mother, is also going to help us.'

It really was like having lunch with Tita Borgia and Heini Corleoni. Only six months previously I had been told that Heini had cut off Alexander's allowance for failing to give evidence in court against his own mother in an attempt to retrieve the emeralds that Tita so coveted. But by now Heini was so inebriated that, apart from clasping my hand and telling me how good it was to see me again, it was fairly evident that our audience would have to be curtailed before he lost consciousness.

Tita appeared totally impervious to Giorgio's look of disapproval as he and a fellow servant gently lifted him from his seat and, literally, walked Heini across the lawn lifting each leg in turn and moving it forward like a life-sized marionette, while his tiny Yorkshire terrier scampered around, barking hysterically. Tita apologised for his incapacity.

'He's only like that when he's drunk.'

As we left, Giorgio shook me warmly by the hand and rather sadly said he hoped he would be seeing me again soon. I was reminded that I had recently heard how Heini had broken down in front of him one night and sobbed the question: 'What am I going to do? She's destroying the family.'

But the responsibility was doubtless Heini's rather than Tita's; familial destruction having become a tradition within the Thyssen family.

Chapter I
1685–1900

'Old' August Thyssen... The myth of the self-made man

> *Money was the instrument of their power*
> *and factories bristling with smoke-stacks*
> *were the temples of their cult.*
> Luchino Visconti

The Thyssens liked to give the impression that August was a self-made man, but he was not.

The first recorded Thyssen, Isaac Lambert, born in Germany in 1685, was an equally remarkable man, who, having lost both his parents at the age of eighteen, had succeeded in fighting and clawing his way from orphaned peasant to wealthy tithe collector for the city of Aachen. Three times married with four surviving sons and an equal number of daughters, his third wife, the widow Zinck, also contributed a good deal of the family's wealth.

The next four generations of Thyssens continued to build on his success through baking, insurance and civic responsibilities until four generations later Friedrich Thyssen married his cousin Katharina. The closeness of this relationship may have contributed to their first son, born in 1842, never growing beyond five foot one inch in height or developing an adult voice. But it did not prevent August Thyssen from becoming a legendary industrialist and one of the richest men in the world.

His progress was assisted by the fact that in 1859, his father, having gained considerable experience in banking and the burgeoning manufacturing industry, opened a private bank and foreign exchange service in Eschweiler. Of equal value to both August and his brother Josef's future success was their father's decision to provide his sons with the best and most suitable education available. Like many short people, August's diminutive stature appeared to concentrate his sense of purpose and he never seemed to be in any doubt as to what he was going to achieve or the area in which it was to be achieved.

After Catholic high school in Aachen, the seventeen-year-old August attended Germany's first Polytechnic in Karlsruhe, where he studied technical drawing, engineering, chemistry and mineralogy. In 1861 he moved to Antwerp to read international commerce and economics before returning to work in his father's bank. This would provide him with a knowledge of the mechanics of banking and corporate finance that gave him a real advantage over many of his contemporaries.

At this time there was only one area in which August needed to develop his skills if he was going to be involved in any kind of labour-intensive enterprise; that of leadership and control of a large work-force. As industry was in its infancy, first generation industrialists could rely only on the Prussian military for practical experience in this area. His father, realising its social and commercial value, paid dearly for the privilege of a commission for his diminutive Catholic son in the 28th Eifel Regiment of the Imperial Army. Fortunately for August, he was too small for combat and too well educated to be used in a subservient capacity, but after one year's service he had gained the rank of Lieutenant and the position of battalion adjutant, or administrator.

On his return from military service, August was impatient to take up the challenge of his own industrial enterprise. In 1866 he was invited to his friend Toussaint Bicheroux's wedding where his sister Balbina met Toussaint's brother. With a great deal of encouragement from August, she was led to believe that she had fallen in love; although some of her friends noticed that her attraction seemed to owe far more to the potential commercial opportunity than to romantic, human emotion.

The Bicheroux were established industrialists and August wasted no time in exploiting this fortuitous relationship by suggesting the idea of his becoming a partner in their new band iron rolling mill, while attending his sister's wedding to Désiré Bicheroux the following year.

The Bicheroux family, appreciating August's commercial expertise and his father's financial resources, were only too happy to agree to his proposal and a new company was quickly formed in which August invested 8,000 Taler and assumed the role of business director.[1] The new factory, which opened on 1 April 1867, was located in Duisburg, at the convergence of the Ruhr and the Rhine. It was also conveniently located next to the recently completed railway – a wonderful new invention that not only provided transport for coal, iron and steel but an ever increasing appetite for the same.

For the next three years, August worked for eighteen hours a day, helping to develop the Bicheroux company while learning all about the iron and steel business. While he admired the brilliance of their technical innovation, he was frustrated by their inability to appreciate his expansionist ambitions. Privately he was even more frustrated by the fact that while he undoubtedly worked a great deal harder than the other partners, he was only granted an equal share of the profits.

In 1870 August managed to sell the family his share in the company for 35,000 Taler before resigning his position, explaining that he wanted to take up a quieter occupation.

By now the Bicheroux might have been aware of August's business philosophy that to succeed in industry one either needed to 'buy the competition or cripple it', but they still had no idea that the man to whom they had offered both the hand of friendship and an entrée into the steel industry, would turn against them so aggressively.

August not only 'forgot' to tell his ex-partners that he was about to set up in competition on a nearby site in Styrum but in order to conceal his intentions he had registered his new business in Essen. Fortunately the local newspaper did not reveal the truth until three days after he had sold his share in his brother-in-law's company. August's initial actions displayed a remarkable disregard for business ethics, but so impressed was his father by his son's 'enterprise' that he invested an equal 35,000 Taler in the newly formed Thyssen & Co.

Although, to avoid the inconvenience of suffering from an attack of his son's 'fortuitous amnesia' in the future, the mistrustful Friedrich insisted they sign a formal company contract agreement, for while August was the sole shareholder and thus personally liable, he was also in an unassailable position of power. It was to be the first example of the Thyssens' paternal mistrust.

To create a fully operational iron smelting and rolling mill in six months from a piece of farm land and some outbuildings was a miracle. But August was aware that he was not the only ambitious industrialist who found this area attractive. The order for the successful supply and installation of his technical facilities had been placed with the Duisburg company of Bechem & Keetman. Having employed them months in advance to work for him exclusively, he also persuaded them to become a joint stock company. Whether they realised that he had been buying the stock before he took his seat as chairman of the board is not known but, having done so, anyone wishing to start a factory in the same area had to travel a great deal further than Duisburg to find a company capable of supplying and installing the equipment needed to present August Thyssen with any serious competition.

* * *

August was obsessed with work and money and as a practising Catholic he was quite convinced, or so he instructed his workers, that work and prayer were the same thing. As short of temper as he was of patience, he was instantly recognisable by his black frock coat, slouch hat and energetic mincing gait. August no doubt worked harder than any of his seventy workers and was proud of his motto, 'If I rest, I rust'.

In his first year of production, he managed to produce 3,000 tons of iron but he still needed more capital to finance his industrial ambitions. It was not an easy thing to obtain, for even his own family was frightened by the quantity of financial fuel needed to power August's industrial machine and it would have been all too easy to jeopardise the future of his enterprise by resorting to excessive borrowing. But not for the first time in the development of the Thyssen fortune, the problem would be solved conjugally.

There is a certain element of poetic justice in the fact that while women may have been used as a source of dynastic fund-raising during the growth years, subsequently they would prove equally efficient at the destructive redistribution of the family's accrued wealth.

The Pelzers were among the oldest established Protestant entrepreneurial families of Mülheim in the Ruhr. Considerably grander and somewhat richer at that time than the Thyssens, their lineage dated back to the fifteenth century. They had been involved in the spinning and weaving industry for a number of generations. Unfortunately, the most recent had developed a greater talent for social activity than business; particularly Hedwig, their only daughter, who at eighteen years of age was already showing signs of an enthusiasm for a style of life which hardly reflected her parents' ideals.

Despite the landowner Gustav Becker's introduction, August was less than enthusiastic. While he found the girl attractive and, despite his professed Catholicism, displayed little concern for her being a Protestant, he viewed marriage as a potential business distraction. However, her parents were convinced August was the stabilising influence their daughter needed and Mr Becker was relying on young August's success and prosperity in order to sell him more plots of his land. When the size of the dowry being offered was revealed to August, events moved with his customary speed. They were married with no great

Chapter I: 1685–1900

expense, pomp or ceremony in Mülheim on 3 December 1872; by which time the newly acquired capital was already safely invested in Thyssen & Co. and the development of the works, both in land area, plant and production, continued to grow dramatically.

* * *

In 1873, together with seventeen other Mülheim 'worthies', August founded a company to build and control the renting of workers' accommodation. One of the first and certainly the most lavish project undertaken by the new organisation was the construction of a suitable residence for the founder. It was situated, as was normally the case with the industrialists of the time, next to the factory, amidst the sulphurous air and belching chimneys. Subsequent family reports tended to exaggerate the austerity of August's existence, but 'Frogpond' could hardly have been considered a humble or understaffed 'dwelling'. Some years later his unusually indiscreet manservant, Anton Mittler, would describe the house:

> It was of medium size, set slightly back from the road in a quiet, well-tended park. Directly behind the park lay the freight depot sidings. To the left was the clerk's dining-room. Opposite were the stables, the coachman's and gardener's apartments and, adjoining these, two large areas for riding. The house was tastefully arranged, the reception rooms, winter garden, dining and billiard rooms were on the ground floor, while Thyssen's living and bed rooms and several guest rooms were on the first floor. His bedroom, which was enormous, had a large recess for its oriel window in which his writing desk stood, where he sometimes worked during the night and early mornings.[2]

But not all the Thyssens were seduced by the enormous profits to be made in such an environment. As in all dynastic stories, black sheep are needed to add colour to what could otherwise run the risk of becoming a rather grey list of ruthless industrial achievements. One of the characters who adopted this role was August's intellectually gifted, younger brother Friedrich, born in 1854. By 1872 it was already becoming obvious that Friedrich's artistic temperament was unlikely to be fulfilled by working in his father's bank or his brother's factory.

To the horror of his father, it also became obvious that there was something odd about Friedrich. He appeared to have been displaying homosexual tendencies and it was only the intervention of his mother that prevented him from being disinherited and cast out of the family with nothing. Encouraged by August, she suggested the boy be given a generous allowance and sent away to Berlin where 'his sort' were considered more acceptable and he would cease to 'bring shame on the family'. There he indulged his love of music and art, spending his summers on the Italian Riviera. His was the life of what were to become known as 'remittance boys'.

* * *

August displayed an uncanny skill and vision for the creation of the financial structure of his industrial endeavours, but his meanness and lack of appreciation for technical innovation often had a detrimental effect upon the development of his organisation. However, his ability to account for every penny and avoid waste wherever possible was also vital to the development of his manufacturing base in what could often be a volatile market. Even something as small as a discarded piece of coal or a single nail would result in a sharp reprimand and a brief lecture. It was an admonishment which August would not expect to make more than once if a man wished to keep his job.

Despite his 150 employees, the organisation and production were still entirely dependent on his input. August Thyssen entered the factory at five in the morning and would rarely leave before ten in the evening. He managed the works, planned and oversaw the development and was responsible for all sales, purchases and correspondence. But while he was more than capable of handling the business and

August Thyssen Steelworks as portrayed by Adolph von Menzel in 'Eisenwalzwerk (Moderne Cyclopen) 1872–1875'. (Copyright: "bpk/Nationalgalerie, Staatliche Museen zu Berlin/K.Göken").

administration, he had to rely on an ever increasing number of skilled craftsmen to develop and run the industrial side of his organisation.

Heavy industry was still in its infancy and August's dislike of sophisticated technology made consistency difficult to achieve and constantly susceptible to human error. The fact that the pig iron, having been delivered from the furnaces, was transported by wheelbarrow to the steam hammer gives a good indication of the crude production methods in use at this time. After being 'densified', the iron was carried to the furnaces where it was re-heated. The red-hot ingots were then manhandled through the various rolling mills to the point where a workable sheet metal had been achieved. Dust and smoke stung the eyes and choked the lungs while the intense heat sapped the strength of the strongest men and the constant percussive pounding of the steam hammer made concentration impossible. Appalling accidents were common and while August magnanimously invested part of the workers' wages in a health-care system, surgery was still as basic as the work was relentless.[3]

* * *

August had profited from the dramatic rising demand and 300 per cent increase in the price of iron and steel in Bismarck's Germany. But when in 1873 a Liberal politician warned parliament that excessive speculation was undermining the economy, there was a dramatic loss of public confidence that resulted in a rush to sell, causing stock prices to tumble. Hundreds of small businesses and banks were forced into liquidation but, by constantly reinvesting both his own and his family's money, August Thyssen's organisation continued to grow.

It was during this period that he began actively to encourage his austere, puritanical image and reputation for penny-pinching in order to reassure his creditors that their money would be safer and more profitably invested in his 'Konzern'.[4] He also encouraged the prefix of 'old' August long before he qualified for such a title, in the knowledge that most people felt safer doing business with a more mature, less impetuous figure than the real August Thyssen, whose willingness to take breathtaking and potentially disastrous, calculated risks no doubt contributed to his success.

In 1891 when the stocks and commodities market collapsed once again and the price of rolled-steel products fell by as much as 50 per cent, it seemed to have little effect on August, who was so confident that the market would recover, which it did, that he kept his nerve and ordered his managers to maintain full production so that he would be able to satisfy the forthcoming demand by drawing on his stockpiles. It was a policy that August and eventually Josef would adopt on a number of occasions and required considerable courage and a sound knowledge of economics. These tactics and their meteoric expansion often took them dangerously close to the edge of the financial abyss. The monthly financial reports that were made available to key management showing just how close they went were treated with the utmost secrecy.

* * *

While August continued to work harder than most men believed possible, he managed to spend sufficient time with his wife to assist in her creation of three sons in three years. Fritz was born on 9 November 1873, August Junior on 25 September 1874 and Heinrich on 31 October 1875. Unfortunately he appeared to lack the most basic paternal interest in his children, while there were even those who commented on the fact that only the second son, August Junior, bore any resemblance to his father. The inheritance of his father's stature was a legacy that Junior failed to appreciate.

August also profited from luck and fate and in 1875 when he was suffering from a shortage of capital, his thirty-six-year-old brother-in-law and former business partner, Désiré Bicheroux, fortuitously died and left his wife Balbina most of his considerable fortune, which she immediately invested in her beloved brother's business, remaining loyal to him for the rest of her life. Only two years later, August's father died and Josef, who had been working for him, transferred their inheritance of some 230,000 Taler into the Konzern. Both Balbina and August's mother also invested their inheritance in the company.

Josef followed his brother's example by marrying a rich woman. Klara Bagel came with a dowry of some 15,000 Marks, most of which was rapidly transferred to the coffers of Thyssen & Co. Klara came from a French Huguenot background, which represented respect for work and family business traditions. Her loyalty to both her husband and August would prove invaluable and considerably greater than that of her sister-in-law, Hedwig.

* * *

August appreciated Bismarck's government, because he created a fertile environment in which Thyssen & Co. would continue to thrive. However, while August may have lionised the Protestant, Prussian Bismarck for his creation of such an industrially encouraging environment, he was singularly unimpressed by the Prussian, feudalistic social elite, which so attracted his wife.

While adopting a somewhat Calvinistic mode of dress and marrying a Protestant, August was still theoretically a practising Catholic with sympathies towards the Centre Party, which did not, however, include any appreciation of the party's support of the trade unions.[5] He also failed to appreciate the fact that the number of socialist seats in the Reichstag would rise over the next few years from two to thirty-five.

While August's ruthless attitude to business would become increasingly obvious, he encouraged appreciation of his high moral tone. A fine example of this new order of industrial feudalism was the 'Reglement für die Meister und Arbeiter des Walzwerkes von Thyssen & Co. in Styrum', a notice to his workers, approved by the mayor of Mülheim, as to how they were expected to conduct themselves.

The Mannesmann archivist Lutz Hatzfeld recorded some of the details:

> Thyssen demanded a 'business attitude' for relations with superiors and obedience without question. Threats or insults could be punished by the manager with immediate sacking. The normal notice period was fourteen days for both sides. There was only one point where Thyssen failed to put his foot down. Paragraph 2 prohibited the 'consumption of alcoholic beverages during working hours and in general on the works premises'. Whoever was found drunk, involved in fights etc. could also be sacked immediately. But it was just a fact that none of these men, who had to work under the very difficult conditions, would come to work without a bottle of spirits. Alcohol consumption was the cause for accidents and disputes. It threatened the security of the workers, the smooth running of the plant and peaceful cohabitation of the family entities. But the worst thing was that even the best and most punctual worker was not prepared to renounce alcohol consumption at work. This is something that all industrialists had to accept. This works regulation of 1871 did not contain any regulations for the protection of minors and no ban of child labour.[6]

August's expectations of his workers was very simple and straightforward. He expected them to abide by the 'Reglement', work very hard with the minimum of waste in time or materials, and produce as much as their engineer managers could get out of them. For this they got paid an agreed weekly wage.

For the 'Meisters', the rewards were greater but far more complicated.[7] They were also far more directly capitalistic and performance-based; the production calculation taking into account the amount produced per head of labour, per shift, per Mark of wage paid and salary awarded. These Meisters were expected to act as sub-contracting entrepreneurs rather than production or workshop supervisors of their respective departments. By the beginning of the 1890s,

'Betriebschefs', or production managers, would be responsible for the marketing of their products as well as the manufacturing. Trading was also encouraged between co-ordinating departments and the Chefs 'held responsible for running their department as "self-sufficiently" and as commercially successful as possible'.[8]

Bonuses were also awarded for exceeding targets, while those who underperformed would be 'brought to account'; as would those who failed to appreciate quality and the importance of customer satisfaction. For August constantly emphasised the importance of reputation: 'We ask you to work and to fulfil the wishes of the customers with the greatest care, for this is the only way in which we will succeed to gain a reputation and to maintain the planned expansion of the factory completely and continually.'[9]

August expected total commitment to the Konzern from his managers and it was a commitment that often included personal sacrifice. Failure to abide by this philosophy was considered totally unacceptable. In order to minimise the risk of social or political challenges to managerial endeavour, August insisted on quite extreme investigation of any potential candidate's social status and political leanings.

* * *

In the winter of 1879–80, world trade recovered. Helped by the restart of railway expansion in North America and Bismarck's introduction of protective trade tariffs, German steel production would double to surpass the British by the end of the century.

On 18 April 1879, Josef Thyssen finally joined the company but there was never any doubt that August continued to hold the reins of power and despite their increasingly equal responsibility for the success of Thyssen & Co., Josef was never awarded more than 25 per cent of the equity of the Konzern.

There was no doubt that they were a perfect team. It may have been the fire and energy of August's ambition that was responsible for the meteoric growth of the organisation but it would not have been possible without his brother's total commitment to the efficiency of their administration and money management.

As the only two shareholders, the brothers were fortunate in being able to reach agreement on matters of policy with minimal delay. It was this flexibility and speed that often gave August such an advantage during his aggressive acquisitions and rapid reaction to market forces.

* * *

If August Thyssen had an Achilles' heel, it was social and he could not have chosen a wife less well-fitted to share his life. Being young, rich, attractive and sexually active, Hedwig was welcomed into the highly developed Prussian spa society, which was full of good-looking, aristocratic fortune hunters.

But Hedwig had given him three healthy sons, which encouraged August to overlook his wife's various failings. It was the arrival of their only daughter in 1878 which finally cracked the foundations of their relationship, as August became increasingly suspicious that he was not the father. But for another four years, no doubt aware of the cost of divorce, he continued to ignore his wife's behaviour and accept the situation. Then, in 1882, Hedwig had a miscarriage in which August had played no part and he immediately filed for divorce. It was only after their divorce was finalised in 1885, that his wife would unofficially confirm her daughter's illegitimacy.[10]

* * *

While August was busy divorcing his wife and rejecting the world of court society, another family of industrialists arrived in Germany, equally determined to adopt it. The Price family had already made their industrial fortune before they, like many other wealthy Americans, arrived in Europe with the sole intention of buying their way into the aristocracy. It was pure coincidence that, having successfully done so, they in turn would eventually sell their aristocratic status to August's socially ambitious son Heinrich.

Louise Price was one of five sisters from Philadelphia who came to Europe on an aptly named 'grand tour'. Born on 14 March 1865 in Ellerslie Hall, Delaware, she would mature into the most dreadful old snob and appalling anti-Semite with an extremely colourful imagination and scant regard for modesty. She later recorded her reminiscences of a world far removed from 'old' August's forest of belching chimneys:

> My mother's father, Samuel Harlan, founded the steamship company Harlan & Hollingsworth in Wilmington, Delaware. He was of British descent, as was my father's forefather, Thomas Price, who had come to America with the first Welsh settlers in about 1690. At the time we sailed to Europe, grandfather Harlan was seventy-six. In addition to our parents and grandfather, there was his valet, an extraordinary mulatto named Charles.[11]

At the time they sailed from New York on the White Star liner *Republic*, Louise was fifteen years old and already boasting of having had exactly fifteen boyfriends. Her sisters Margaret and Susie were older while Annie and Maisie were younger and they were considered by Louise to be 'five pretty young heiresses from an upper-crust American family'. They had first landed in England and after

The American heiress Louise Price and the Hungarian Baron Gabor Bornemisza on their wedding day.

a short stay in London, the elder sisters were shipped off to Dresden to study music, languages and painting.

They then moved on to Vienna, where they stayed for the winter; living in considerable style at the Grand Hotel, where Louise's mother had gas lighting installed throughout the entire suite of rooms. But while they revelled in the luxury, glamour and culture of Imperial Europe, there was little doubt as to the intention of their visit. They wanted titles and titles wanted them.

A box at the opera remained the prime source of contact for potential suitors and it was not long before Louise had spied 'an extremely handsome young Hungarian Hussar officer who kept his eyes fastened on me night after night'.

His name was Baron Gabor Bornemisza and he was indeed extremely good-looking, but obviously Louise's mother had her heart set on someone a little further up the social ladder and persuaded her daughter to wait a while.

'I was only sixteen when my father dragged us off to Baden-Baden. There we remained until the autumn and had a most enjoyable summer. In those days, Baden-Baden was a very gay spot. The Prince of Wales always favoured it with his presence and racing week was a reunion for the smart set.'

On their return to Vienna later in the autumn, the dashing and persistent Baron Bornemisza proposed to the impassioned Louise and they agreed to elope if her father failed to give them permission to marry. But father eventually agreed, presumably awarding the Baron a very generous dowry as well as his daughter's hand in marriage; for without one it is unlikely there would have been the other.

Louise Price married Baron Gabor Bornemisza on 16 June 1883 in Vienna. Then, after the ceremony, they had 'a jolly wedding breakfast at the Hotel Sacher', before departing by train for Prague and Dresden. After a short honeymoon, they returned to join her husband's regiment at Nagy Szeben in Transylvania.

Meanwhile, her sisters continued to enrich the Austro-Hungarian Empire; Susie married Captain Alexander Socec, also in Vienna, while Maisie married Baron Max von Berg, who would subsequently become the second husband of Hedwig Thyssen, August's illegitimate daughter. Only Annie Price would succeed in achieving full royal status when she became the wife of Prince Ardeck and took on the title of Her Royal Highness Princess Ardeck of Hesse Barchfeld.

For the next twenty-five years, while the Bornemiszas raised three daughters, Mae, Margit and Matilda, their life would continue to revolve around a fairly strict and utterly predictable court social life of country-house parties, hunting parties, visits to spas in the summer and cities in the winter; the grand balls being the pinnacle of this intense social activity.

Such was the size of the Austro-Hungarian court that Louise was rarely at a loss for a title when describing her friends. The title of Archduke was officially conferred to all sons of the Emperor of the House of Habsburg during Emperor Franz Joseph's reign. There were also several Archdukes who ranged from the Emperor's cousin, Archduke Joseph, to his second cousin, Archduke Rainier. 'Austria's idiot Archdukes' was Bismarck's scornful dismissal of the Habsburg nobles. August Thyssen was somewhat more extreme in his opinion.

* * *

While the great courts of Europe were dancing their last cadenza and the dawn was still breaking on August Thyssen's empire, he achieved a crucial step in his ambition for total industrial self-sufficiency when, in 1883, with the support of the Sal. Oppenheim Bank, he acquired a majority shareholding in the Duisburg coal-mining company Gewerkschaft Deutscher Kaiser (GDK). Having finally become president of the company, he not only continued to increase coal production but also initiated the building of a steel and rolling works right next to the mines. Within the next thirty years, this plant would become one of the largest industrial complexes in the world and the basis of the August-Thyssen-Hütte and, eventually, Thyssen AG.

By 1889 Thyssen & Co. comprised an estimated 34 million square metres of coal fields, making the Thyssens the biggest mine owners in Germany. Within ten years they would also be the country's largest steel producers.

One of August's more ruthless moves was his entry into heavy engineering. Having bought sufficient shares in Jordan & Meyer to qualify as chairman of the supervisory board, it took him four years to guide the Mülheim-based engineering company into liquidation, rid it of the redundant founders and incorporate it as a department of Thyssen & Co. to become the second largest tube manufacturer in Germany.

By now the Konzern was employing a work-force of 2,305, including a considerable number of children. Many of the workers were from Pomerania, East Prussia, Poland and Lithuania. They were considered foreigners and not welcomed by the local population. With their limited knowledge of the German language, the presence of these outsiders caused considerable xenophobic hostilities. Newspapers reported on the shortage of living space and the overcrowding of houses with boarders. They failed to mention the constant presence of smoke, soot, coal dust, sulphurous fumes and the pollution of the rivers.

For the workers there was little time or opportunity for the luxury of being able to concern themselves with the environment. They remained entrapped by the Thyssens' policy of supplying, and owning, all the workers' needs 'on-site'. The store, baths, canteens and lodging houses were all a man had time to need.

* * *

The financial settlement between August and his wife would take even longer to finalise than the divorce, while Hedwig spent the intervening years frequenting the various fashionable spa resorts, paid for by her ex-husband. He even paid for her servants, not all of whom were as limited in their services as their title might have suggested, including a chauffeur who, according to Heini, spent more time in his grandmother's bed than he did in her car.[12] Meanwhile, friends of Hedwig's blamed August's reluctance to make a financial settlement on his meanness and constantly reminded her how much of her family's money had been invested in his mines and factories.

Eventually, as part of her settlement, August had to agree to a pledge of property transfer to their children which meant that, theoretically, they now owned the family business. They were also each offered an index-linked annual allowance of some 3,000 Marks and their mother 6,000.[13] Thus her lawyers had not only guaranteed Hedwig's and her children's financial future, but also ensured that none of August's possible future offspring could make any claims on the inheritance structure of the Konzern.

But August had lost none of his business guile when it came to negotiating the settlement, and he managed to persuade Hedwig that he and his brother should retain overall control and remain sole shareholders until death, while Josef's 25 per cent share was unaffected. Predictably, August did not see fit to transfer the business over to his sons until shortly before his demise.

'Old' August Thyssen (second left) with a group of friends after a visit to the pit face.

The final agreement was not reached until 6 May 1887, after which Hedwig went to live in Wiesbaden with an annual apanage which had by then been negotiated up to 60,000 Goldmarks. The fact that she apparently made no attempt to be awarded custody of her children reflected her lack of interest in retaining much in the form of maternal status.

Unfortunately, August's aggressive ambition, so admired by his siblings, had done little to endear him to his children. They would remain more influenced and attracted by their mother's light-hearted, indolent snobbery than their father's cold commitment to the work ethic. A particularly unpleasant aspect of his relationship with his sons was the fact that while Fritz proved the most receptive to his father's will, August would make it painfully obvious that he did not like the boy. He even instructed his managers to 'teach the boy some discipline'. He also observed: 'Fritz's character is unpredictable and he all too easily falls under the influence of strangers.'[14]

While Fritz suffered the appalling treatment with quiet but determined fortitude, Josef took pity on him and eventually managed to persuade August to allow Fritz to continue his studies at university in Liège, London and Berlin; though whether he completed any courses or passed any exams was never confirmed.

The four times married Hedwig Thyssen née Pelzer pictured in 1928.
(photo: Hamm, Bruxelles).

Meanwhile, recognising the sharp intelligence and natural abilities of his middle son, he chose 'kleiner August' as heir to the crown of the Thyssen industrial 'dynasty'. But much to his father's disappointment, August Junior chose to reject his obvious favouritism and grew increasingly rebellious.

August's youngest son Heinrich managed to avoid his father's dictatorial criticism and quietly attended to his university studies in Munich, Berlin and Heidelberg where, in 1900, he gained his doctorate in chemistry (not, as often claimed, philosophy) from the Faculty of Natural Sciences and Mathematics, by which time his father was the eighth richest man in Germany.[15]

In 1883, Klara and Josef's first son Julius was born, nine years before their second son Hans. They responded well to their strict upbringing and were taught to hold their uncle August in

Chapter I: 1685–1900

Josef Thyssen, the often overshadowed co-founder of the Thyssen Konzern

Josef's wife Klara Thyssen (both photos: courtesy of Ursula Cassinone).

total awe and respect and appreciate work as an extension of their religious faith; there never being any question that they would eventually assume their place in the family firm. While August became increasingly disillusioned with the behaviour of his own children, his respect and affection for those of his brother grew. In an attempt to inspire his children, he would even use their cousins as an example. But as his alienated offspring considered themselves to be socially superior, it had little effect.

* * *

The Thyssens were beginning to display increasing signs of social ambition and appreciation of a more extravagant lifestyle and after August's divorce, when Josef and Klara had finally moved into their new villa, more and more of the Thyssens' social occasions took place there, including winter and summer balls organised by Klara.

While August still enjoyed the convenience of his villa 'Froschenteich', his children's friends and even his own social contacts were becoming increasingly vocal in their questioning as to why a man in his position should continue to live in the grounds of the factory, amid the noise of the steam hammers and shunting yards. Finally, to the considerable relief of his children, August grudgingly agreed to at least consider looking for somewhere more suitable. But this did little to improve his relations with them.

While Fritz constantly strove to obtain his father's respect, it became obvious to everyone except 'old' August that he was deeply disliked by possibly his only legitimate son. In 1898 he made yet another attempt to persuade August Junior to assume a loyal and responsible position in their company, by granting him collective power of attorney and a 'suitable post' in the Berlin office. Unfortunately, Junior's appreciation of Berlin had absolutely nothing to do with industrial endeavour. He was far more impressed by the glamour of the Imperial Court. But to gain an entrance would take all August Junior's guile and considerable quantities of the family fortune to overcome his social disabilities of stature, religion and lack of aristocratic status. He even managed to successfully blackmail his father into giving him yet more money by threatening to spread detrimental rumours on the Berlin stock exchange and canvassing various banks with information concerning his father's finances.

Later, when the boy's colourful love life became the subject of public attention and he became engaged to an actress, the old man appeared to lose all reason and started an incapacitation proceeding against Junior on the grounds that he was mentally ill. The yellow press responded enthusiastically with the headline 'Thyssen *v.* Thyssen' and a lot of dirty linen was washed in public. Meanwhile, the medical report from the sanatorium, where 'old' August had had him committed, failed to reveal anything of sufficient importance to justify Junior being detained. He retaliated by supporting the cause of striking miners in his father's mines and what started as a highly effective retaliatory act soon developed into a genuine sympathy and long-term support.[16] This included his painting slogans on the factory walls, with no attempt to disguise his handwriting, when he wrote in huge letters: 'Piss off Thyssen.'

Meanwhile, when Fritz became engaged to Amélie zur Helle in 1899, August made it obvious that he was completely opposed to the marriage and even suggested that Amélie came from a family with some form of hereditary disease. Fritz had always been loyal to his father's opinions, but in affairs of the heart he proved to be capable of far greater resistance to his will.

The same year, while their mother was re-marrying for the fourth and final time in her constant quest for social advantage, her daughter Hedwig met and married Baron Ferdinand von Neufforge for entirely social reasons. Having obtained the title of Baroness, Hedwig would eventually sue him for divorce and then, when he sued her for alimony, accuse him of only marrying her for her father's money. It eventually proved to have been an extremely expensive indulgence; the courts awarded the Baron a comfortable income 'in perpetuity'. It was a situation which failed to amuse 'old' August but remained a constant source of amusement for the rest of the family, until they inherited the responsibility for paying the Baron's apanage.

* * *

Fortunately, the Thyssens' industrial fortune had little difficulty in continuing to finance the increasing demands of their social ambitions. In 1899, GDK turned over 46.9 million Marks and dwarfed Thyssen & Co., which still managed to generate some 34.6 million Marks.

Meanwhile, the machine engineering workshops became even more independent as they achieved market leadership in Germany, and the number of auxiliary departments grew rapidly as a result of both operating and market demand. Many of these departments would eventually be spun off as independent firms, while an international chain of Thyssen trading agencies would handle sales and marketing both for their own products and others. This policy would continue to prove its value, and many of the other major companies would follow August's example, but he was thirty years ahead of them by the start of the twentieth century.

GDK was primarily conceived both as a supplier of coal and semi-processed material for Thyssen & Co. and as an independent and complementary producer of low value, heavy structural steel and formed iron for the open market. By the turn of the century, GDK represented a completely integrated steel works situated directly on top of the coal and adjacent to one of the largest inland harbours in the world, at Alsum on the Rhine. It combined a group of collieries, which pioneered mining construction techniques at unheard of depths in a very dangerous area where, in 1899, 3,600 miners produced 1.2 million tons of coal.[17]

GDK had grown to the size of a city. It dominated the Ruhr like some vast manifestation of Dante's inferno; reverberating to the percussive pounding of the steam hammers, the scream of steel wheels and the roar of the blast furnaces, as the flames from the gas flares and the glow from ribbons of red-hot steel lit up the night sky and reflected off the columns of grey steam and black smoke. Speech was impossible and men communicated by hand signals while, thousands of feet below them, half-naked miners lay on their sides in the darkness and hacked out the coal to fuel the blast furnaces and steel mills above.

1. The Taler (or Thaler) was the German unit of currency that preceded the Mark, which was introduced during the consolidation of the German Empire in 1871.
2. Wessel, p. 31.
3. August Thyssen implemented a health insurance scheme for his workers on 9 October 1871 (see ibid., pp. 116 ff.).
4. 'Konzern' is a German generic term for a large firm or commercial organisation.
5. 'Calvinistic' is used here to describe a lifestyle, rather than a religious adherence, in order to express the qualities of stoicism, determination, austerity and asceticism, while hinting also at August's somewhat uncompromising and disapproving attitudes.
6. Wessel, pp. 114 ff.
7. 'Meister' is German for 'foreman'. It denotes a master craftsman who as such is in a privileged position.
8. Fear, p. 117.
9. ibid., p. 56.
10. In 1916, Heinrich Thyssen lodged a statement with his lawyer Dr Jacke in Berlin which read: 'My father recently told me under four eyes in his study when we were talking about family matters, that Hede is not his child. He said that he had his suspicions at the time of the divorce but that he was only convinced of it later on, and that my mother confirmed to him that his suspicions were correct. He added that he did not know whether my mother would still be prepared to confirm this now, but that she did in fact give him a confirmation following the divorce . . . My father said he hinted at Hede as to who her real father is and that he didn't think she was so stupid as to not understand him. My father added that in view of these circumstances, Hede would not receive any more than the legal share, which he thought would be understandable. I told my wife about my conversation with my father the same evening. On our trip back to Rohoncz I am writing all this down, because I have a funny feeling that this confession could become important at some later stage.' (Source: TBG Archives).
11. Memoirs of Louise Bornemisza-Price (Bentinck Archives).
12. Author's interviews with Hans Heinrich ('Heini') Thyssen-Bornemisza (†), 1990–2000.
13. To determine the contemporary value of currency, consult the Economic History Services on http://www.eh.net.
14. Wessel, p. 50.
15. The title of Heinrich's dissertation was 'On the hydrazide of a-Thiophencarbon acid'.
16. August Junior's bank statements show monthly contributions to the Mülheim charitable institution Caritashaus. (TBG Archives).
17. In 1888, Thyssen had set up a drilling company, Schachtbau Thyssen GmbH, which meant that he could profit from sinking his own mine shafts.

Chapter II

1900–1915

The arrival of the Bornemiszas...
Buying into the aristocracy

*A noble person by nature is much more
than some nobleman by birth.*
Fortune Cookie

At the turn of the century, August Thyssen was fifty-eight years old and very, very rich. He was also reaching that stage in life when he wanted to command respect for his spectacular achievements. He wanted some manifestation of his dynastic ambitions that would give him a measure of immortality. But as he got older, his offspring, and particularly August Junior, appeared either increasingly unfit or unprepared to fulfil his dreams. In July 1900 he wrote: 'I feel more miserable than I have ever before felt in my life . . . I see all my hopes destroyed because my children want to – and will – make the most unworthy and unbelievable use of my achievements.'[1]

Despite August's opposition, on 18 January 1900 Fritz and Amélie were finally married. It showed remarkable resilience on the part of Amélie that she was prepared to have anything to do with the organisation after the treatment she had received from August, let alone commence married life by living in a house in the middle of the old man's smoke and soot-laden industrial empire.

Meanwhile, having gained his doctorate in Germany, Heinrich suggested to his father that he should go to England for further studies at London University and Cambridge. He did not tell him that both were establishments where he could enjoy an extremely sophisticated social life with minimal involvement in lectures or exams. For Heinrich, it was the perfect cover for the son of an incredibly rich German industrialist who wished to relinquish his past and reinvent himself as an English 'gentleman'. Unbeknown to his father, Heinrich had already rejected the idea of becoming involved in industry and had set his sights on a career in the diplomatic service. It was an ambition known only to his mother and his great friend and mentor, Eduard Freiherr von der Heydt, heir to the famous Bankhaus von der Heydt.[2]

But Heinrich was not the only member of the Thyssen family developing a new persona. In 1900 Emil Kirdorf persuaded 'old' August, as a matter of technical and scientific interest, to go with him to see the Paris Exhibition.[3] The appearance of the by now legendary industrialists caused considerable excitement and for the first time in his life, August felt free to bathe in the glow of admiration. He openly accepted the public attention and social popularity that immense wealth brings, while the creative extravagance of the exhibits had a profound effect on him.

The excitement of Paris at the turn of the century was artistic, not industrial, and the city was alive with radically new fine art in the form of both painting and sculpture. When August was taken to the studio of Auguste Rodin, whose sexual activity was almost as famous as his remarkable sculpture, it was no doubt the first time he had seen so many naked females. Even more shocking was the knowledge that women such as the Duchess of Choiseul, Lady Warwick and the Countess Anna de Noailles were being treated with casual sexual familiarity by the master. It was a memorable experience for 'old' August.

On his return from Paris it soon became apparent that he was about to abandon his image of self-denial and austerity. In Mülheim, he announced to his astonished family that he was going to move and intended to start looking for a house more in keeping with his achievements. Possibly a Schloss and perhaps something even more ambitious than the Krupps' Villa Hügel. The fact that he made the announcement at the beginning of yet another downturn in Germany's economy was in itself a provocative reminder of his immense personal wealth.

* * *

The economic slump at the turn of the century was sudden and severe, despite Admiral Tirpitz announcing Germany's naval build-up of thirty-six battleships and proportional investment in other areas of military expansion. Unfortunately for Germany's industry, this was offset by the legacy of Bismarck's new, more liberal economic policy, which included the removal of import duties, thus opening up the market to cheaper imports.

The recession not only reduced the price of steel, but also led to a stock market frenzy which depressed the value of securities. This had a detrimental effect on Thyssen's use of securities as collateral and banks nervously resisted the granting of increased credit facilities.⁴ By the end of 1901, the Thyssens could no longer meet their payments and asked creditors to delay their claims.

Rescue arrived in the unlikely form of the Prussian state. A major consumer of coal, it had relinquished its last mines around the middle of the century only to fall victim to the private sector's ever-increasing prices. But in March 1902, August sold them six coal fields for 'over 37 million Marks' or '58 million Marks', depending on who you believe.⁵ It cured the Thyssens' liquidity crisis and presented them with a net profit of some 7 million Marks.

During this long period of almost constant expansion and investment in the iron and steel business, there was one area which the brothers had failed to secure: that of obtaining a source of their own iron ore. Like many of his other moves into integrated production, August admitted that they came to the iron ore question rather late, although he had already secured participations in Russia, Norway, Algeria, Morocco and India.

But the ore fields of Lorraine were the most coveted prize, and when August decided to seal the gap in their line of manufacturing firms, he did it better than anyone else, for his ambition was not just to obtain the ore, but to have the facility to turn it immediately into steel.

Within four years, August and Josef raised over 85 million Marks to form Stahlwerk Thyssen, purchase the ore fields and commence construction of the steelworks at Hagendingen in Lorraine, which, despite the enormous investment, remained 100 per cent family-owned. German, European and American newspapers predicted that it would be the best-designed, most modern steel factory on the continent. The Thyssens also had their own private railway with 360 km of tracks, 2,300 wagons and 54 locomotives for the transport of their own goods.

In 1911, the vast Hagendingen steelworks was finally completed, but by this time the French were beginning to be justifiably concerned, and articles started to appear in their press warning of 'a foreigner exploiting our valuable ore sources' and 'The German Danger', and even accusing them of 'invasion'.⁶ In fact, August's expansion policy had already spread way beyond Europe.

*　　*　　*

August had not forgotten his own personal plans. Quite soon after the sale of the mines to the Prussians and the resulting profit, he had asked Conrad Verlohr to make enquiries regarding a certain Schloss Landsberg, which had been the summer residence of Freiherr Ignaz von Landsberg-Velen auf Steinfurt. On 12 October 1902, August wrote to Verlohr: 'Your information regarding Landsberg delighted me. I find the location in the hills desirable.'⁷

Landsberg Castle.

The purchase contract was signed on 11 April 1903 and 380,000 Marks changed hands. Situated in the wooded hills above the village of Kettwig, Landsberg was still close to the Thyssens' industrial heartland and, having made the decision to adopt a more extravagant lifestyle, August commissioned the Hanoverian architect Otto Lüer to renovate the building accordingly.

In fact, there was to be virtually nothing of what could have been described as original left. It was a restoration policy that would become familiar in the Thyssen family. In keeping with this policy, a young historian was commissioned to create a provenance and history of what little remained. Designed in the style of the era, with the Landsberg coat of arms on the cover, the slender volume was not on sale to the general public, but was presented to guests so that they could show their friends where they had been.

The interior decoration was assigned to A. Bembé Company in Mainz, which had developed a reputation for lavish decoration and furnishing of passenger liners. The excessive costs of the whole venture took most people's breath away. But it was August's first-floor personal quarters, or part of them, that remained a subject of gossip and speculation.

After passing through his grey marble, abattoir-style bathroom into a large, cheerless, dark bedroom containing a small four-poster bed, past a short passageway leading to a small private chapel, the visitor headed through his even darker and more oppressive study, complete with a carved ebony cabinet model of a blast furnace and dark embossed leather wall covering. From the study, another door led into a contrasting adjoining room in the form of a large, light, extremely feminine bedroom, complete with huge double bed and chandelier. From this room, extravagant double doors led into an outrageous, brilliantly coloured and romantically extravagant bathroom that had excited August at the Paris Exhibition.

Neither the bedroom nor the adjoining bathroom appeared on the original plans for the interior, and, judging by their style and proximity to August's quarters, they were unlikely to have been used by anyone other than the most intimate of female guests. One young lady who was an occasional guest of the sixty-two-year-old industrialist was Maria Fromen. Maria also spent a part of her time living in a small villa in Kettwig, where August was known to have visited her. Another regular visitor was Fräulein Rosa Metzger, a young friend of his daughter's who had accompanied Hedwig Junior to Sunday lunch at the castle and stayed for supper and breakfast.

* * *

When August finally moved into Landsberg, it was without his family but accompanied by his valet, Anton Mittler, and the coachman, Josef Grewe. Also employed were 'a housekeeper and a housemaid as well as a forest guard and a head gardener, who were assisted by other workers according to the season of the year. There was also a stable boy, who used a team of horses to work in the forest and the garden. The room of the valet, Anton, was located opposite August's bedroom.'[8]

August may have changed his lifestyle in a very dramatic manner, but his dress remained the same: 'His favourite colour suit was black, and his favourite piece of clothing, especially when he was older, was a frock coat. In his later years, his clothing had to be made to order, as the wing collars and cuffs had gone out of fashion.'[9]

On Sundays and holidays, August's relatives were often invited to lunch with their families, as well as the directors with their wives. There were also regular social events, often related to the Konzern, which were described as enjoying a distinguished atmosphere and which, contrary to popular belief, were often very lavish. According to the banker Hjalmar Schacht:

> Although August Thyssen tried to make the most modest impression in his personal dealings, he knew, on the other hand, how to make a magnificent impression. Well-groomed parks surrounded the castle, the peacocks which strutted around waking us early in the morning with their piercing voices. The dinner, the servants, the table setting, all had the form of a true grand seigneur.[10]

The 'aristocratic side of the family', as Hedwig and her children referred to themselves, were not impressed by their father's new home, which they

Heinrich Thyssen, travelling.

considered a fake, made even worse by his use of the original owner's name and coat of arms.

Since the departure of Hedwig, both the Thyssen brothers relied upon Josef's wife Klara to organise the social events in both their houses. But Klara was not without her own social agenda. Nor for that matter was her husband. This was illustrated by the fuss they raised when their sons announced their plans to marry the daughters of local businessmen whom they considered of insufficient social status. August's admiration for Klara never diminished, although, despite his approval of the way in which she had raised her two sons, it failed to present them with any particular advantage within the Konzern, where his own children continued to be favoured.

* * *

Although hindered in his attempts to gain entry to the diplomatic service by his lack of social position, Heinrich was sufficiently well-equipped financially to purchase a share of someone else's aristocratic status. In an ironic reversal of fortune, the Baroness Louise Bornemisza née Price, had found herself financially disadvantaged as, with both her parents deceased, the source of revenue that had supported both her and her husband's extravagant social life had come to an end. Having decided on a course of action, Louise wisely chose Margit, whom she described as the most attractive but least intelligent of her three daughters, to advise: 'You had better marry a rich man.' Fortunately, there was just such a thing looming on their horizon.

According to the gossip columns of the time, in 1905 Heinrich Thyssen had been fleeing from England to escape a breach-of-promise case being brought against him by a ballet dancer, when his red Daimler broke down just outside Bad Homburg and, as if by some miracle, he met and fell desperately in love with the beautiful Margit, who, after barely three weeks of courtship, accepted his hand in marriage.[11]

It was far more likely that one of Heinrich's social advisers had informed him of the presence in town of a Hungarian Baron with three unmarried daughters, no son and a financial crisis; the main attraction, apart from the undoubted beauty of one of the young daughters, being the possibility of access to a baronetcy. At this time, such a thing was possible through the female line by the devious and questionable practice of adoption. Apparently the Austro-Hungarian court was as desperate for funds as the Bornemiszas. It would appear that, for a suitable consideration, a certain Prince Lieven offered to make the introduction and broker the meeting, marriage, adoption, baronetcy and change of nationality.

Margit Bornemisza, daughter of Louise Price, soon to be the first Baroness Thyssen-Bornemisza. (photo: Brückner, Sopron/Hungary).

As Margit's father had no male heirs, the plan was for him to adopt his son-in-law, who could then, theoretically, inherit the title and Hungarian citizenship. Along with his approval of the adoption, Heinrich would also need the agreement of Emperor Franz Joseph I to grant him the Bornemisza de Kaszón rights, name and coat of arms, as well as the title of Baron, for him and his descendants. It would all cost a very great deal of Thyssen money, which was presumably why everyone was prepared to overlook the fact that if everything went according to plan, Heinrich would actually be married to his own sister.

* * *

While Heinrich was entering the incestuous world of 'faux aristocracy', his father had been taking the first steps in an unlikely cultural relationship. Heini would claim that August had always been interested in art, but the few pictures hanging on the walls of Landsberg Castle were decorative copies; hardly the type of works that could form the basis of a collection.

But in 1905, August was again reminded of Rodin's existence by a series of exhibitions at various German art centres where his works caused considerable sensation, for despite their titles and apparent religious and mythological subjects, they were in fact extremely erotic. For August, they no doubt reminded him of the heady visit to Rodin's studio in Paris.

Although he was loath to admit it, even to himself, the only factor that had prevented him commissioning some work had always been the cost, for Rodin's sculpture was not cheap. But it was to the old man's credit that he appeared to appreciate the genius of Rodin's work and on 15 September 1905, when the German poet Rainer Maria Rilke became Rodin's secretary and started to remind August of his previous promises to purchase, he succumbed. In December of that year, he finally commissioned the first three marbles for an astonishing FrFr 50,000.

The first works arrived on 27 April 1906 at Landsberg. August was so overcome that the following day he wrote Rodin a letter informing him of his pleasure; but the chance of August developing a close friendship with Rodin was curtailed when he explained that he was having difficulty understanding the works and asked Rodin to prepare what he called 'explanatory notes'.[12]

It was all rather embarrassing. Rodin avoided the problem by getting Rilke to prepare three short texts, but they were in the form of poetic observations rather than an explanation of the meaning of the pieces. It was obviously not what August had in mind, and it did not help poor Rilke when August replied to him personally. Rodin discovered the letter and immediately fired Rilke for establishing direct contacts with his clients.

Subsequent generations of Thyssens, particularly those involved in collecting fine art, would talk of the very special relationship that developed between August and Rodin, but there is little evidence of such. In fact, most of their correspondence, which was not always polite, good-humoured or respectful, usually concerned payment terms and responsibility for the cost of transport and insurance.

Another matter that particularly concerned August was his realisation that Rodin, having created a 'maquette' in wax or clay, would have his 'executor' reproduce as many marble, bronze or plaster copies as he saw fit. It was a dangerous situation for a man as avaricious as Rodin and obviously a cause of considerable concern to a man as distrustful as August, who repeatedly tried to get Rodin to reassure him of the exclusivity of the work he was buying.

Their letters demonstrate a penny-pinching lack of dignity on both sides. A particularly embarrassing example of this was when, on hearing of Rodin's ill health, August wrote to his secretary and asked what would happen to his unfinished commission in the event that Rodin was unable to complete the work and what sort of discount he could expect if it had to be completed by another sculptor. He even asked for details of any cut-price works (presumably also unfinished) that might be available. But their often quite aggressive correspondence would continue until 1911 when August took delivery of the final, seventh marble.[13]

The FrFr 145,000 which he had paid for the sculptures over six years would be the cause of considerable financial discomfort and frustration and, despite his immense pride in the works, August never bought another piece of sculpture or even another painting. However, his investment would prove to be the start of what was eventually claimed by the old man's grandson to be the world's largest private art collection.

One of August Thyssen's seven Rodin marbles (photo: R. Gerling, Duisburg).

* * *

On 3 January 1906, with meticulous planning, the German Heinrich Thyssen married the half-Hungarian, half-American, Baroness Margit Bornemisza de Kaszón in Vienna. Still disappointed that her daughter was being financially obliged to marry a commoner, Louise had managed to raise some enthusiasm for the wedding when she realised that it could be quite a grand affair.

Fritz Thyssen was one of their witnesses but, predictably, August Senior did not attend. Although he claimed to be suffering from ill-health, he apparently disapproved of the manner in which his son was obtaining aristocratic status.

But the other reason he may have failed to attend was due to the presence of August Junior, who spent most of the time, much to the amusement of the younger generation, teasing the Hungarians for the operatic extravagance of their costumes. Few of those who criticised his behaviour would have realised that had it not been for his pressure on their father, it was doubtful that there would have been sufficient money available to Heinrich for the Thyssens and the Bornemiszas to have entered into such a mutually beneficial relationship. For all his apparent irresponsibility, it was largely as a result of August Junior's persistence and his mother's compliance that they had all received such generous settlements.

Meanwhile, the bride's mother tried to concentrate on the social rather than the financial content of the proceedings:

The evening before the wedding, our dear friends Sir Frederic and Lady Duncan, then residing in Vienna, gave a large soirée for the wedding guests. It was a brilliant social gathering. The older ladies from Hungary, with their magnificent tiaras and jewellery and as pretty a set of bridesmaids as could be found, enhanced the beauty of the evening. One of the guests, an officer of the Guard of Hussars from Berlin, had begged to have the privilege of accompanying the prettiest of the bridesmaids. This was the young Countess Ily Czaky, one of the great beauties of Hungary. Perhaps out of jealousy or only for the fun of playing a trick on the German officer, after the soirée, the younger men offered to show the stranger the night life of Vienna. This outing was fatal for him. He was too tight the next morning to appear at the marriage ceremony and we only regretted the absence of his beautiful and decorative uniform.

This statement, for all its light-hearted charm, reflected her disdain for Germans, particularly those with no title. Fortunately, the wedding would more than compensate by fulfilling her obsession with Hungarian rhinestone hussars:

The Hungarian men were arrayed in their Magnate court costumes; each one a complete picture in itself. Our old friend Count Paul Szapary, then Governor of Fiume, had arrived for the occasion, looking stunning in cloth of gold and ruby velvet with sable fur. He put his valet, almost as gorgeous as his master, in a red and gold Hussar uniform, on the box of the bride's carriage.

After the marriage ceremony there was the usual wedding breakfast, held at the Hotel Bristol. The bridal couple departed for Budapest where the wedding festivities were to be continued as the Hungarian relatives insisted also upon celebrating the event in their own country. After the departure of the young couple we still gave a dance at the Hotel which lasted through till 8 o'clock in the morning. Everyone was in high spirits and I played the piano in accompaniment to the band.

The next day, or the same day, the whole party travelled down to Budapest. This novel idea of carrying on the wedding celebrations in another city amused the foreign guests immensely. Count Szapary, then president of the Park Club, gave us a beautiful reception and our cousin, Count Karl Kornis, and other relatives, gave similar entertainment. The poor bridal couple was glad when the marriage festivities were over at last and they could leave for Venice. After the conventional bridal trip, they joined us at San Remo on the

Riviera where we spent the remainder of the winter together. The following autumn they also joined us in Vienna.

* * *

It was said, probably by Louise, that the young Margit threw her wedding ring out of the window on their wedding night because she could not believe her new husband was only prepared to pay her parents a monthly apanage of RM1,500 .[14] Subsequently, it was increased before the more bizarre part of the marriage was entered into:

> Not having a son ourselves, the decision was made that my husband should adopt his son-in-law, Henry Thyssen. He had to undertake the complicated formalities necessary for the adoption. The prominent Hungarian ministers being very good friends of my husband's, they were most kind in their efforts to aid my husband in his wish, and his initiative in going direct to the Emperor led to expedient action.

On 22 June 1907, after eighteen months of social and financial negotiation, Heinrich finally achieved that which he obviously considered appropriate, aristocratic status, when he received a heavily sealed and ribboned testimonial proclaiming such from Emperor Franz Josef I:

> We wish to confer upon you the title and the coat of arms of your adopted father, our Chamberlain Baron Gabor Bornemisza de Kaszón. Your descendants of both sex will also be Barons and Baronesses and you should seal your letters with red wax and you will enjoy the advantages that come with the title before courts and assemblies and everywhere else too.[15]

However, the question of whether a formal adoption ever took place remained open to conjecture. Certainly, the papers proving such were never produced, even when later required for legal purposes. But from now on, Heinrich Thyssen would be known as the Baron Heinrich Thyssen-Bornemisza de Kaszón.

Louise would no doubt have preferred not to have had to go through such a degrading arrangement to enable this German commoner, whom she insisted on referring to as 'Henry', to inherit their aristocratic title. However, she perked up a bit when Heinrich bought a 5,000-acre estate in Hungary with a 365-room castle for them all to live in and adopted Hungarian nationality.

Louise claimed castle Rohoncz dated back to the thirteenth century and had in 1503 been owned by the Bornemiszas. However, in the future there would be

A bleak Rohoncz Castle; the Thyssen-Bornemisza country seat.

complaints from the grander side of the Bornemisza family concerning the Thyssens' use of the family name, while Josi Groh, a Swiss-Hungarian solicitor who would act for Heini, was more specific: 'Bornemisza de Kaszón was a simple man. He was not from the Bornemisza family that were regents of Transylvania during the Turkish rule. His real name was Csutak and he only became a Chamberlain after the Thyssen money had arrived.'[16]

* * *

For the next few years Margit remained in the castle and bore 'Henry' a son, Stephan, and two daughters, Margit and Gabrielle. Stephan Thyssen, an extremely intelligent and good-looking child, born on 26 July 1907, would be treated appallingly by his father while his younger brother Heini, born subsequently in Holland, commenced a life-long campaign of character assassination against him from an early age: 'Stephan was a very sickly child and had to be fed artificially for several years. He was a very nice boy, but he also suffered from behavioural problems later on. He stole money from the servants and did stupid things.'

There may have been an element of truth in his accusations, but apart from jealousy and the fact that, as the eldest son, Stephan could have been expected to have enjoyed certain inheritance advantages, it was difficult to understand why Heini insisted on revealing damaging details of his brother's life. It was certainly not something his sisters were ever subjected to, despite far greater cause.

Having established his new identity as a Hungarian Baron, Heinrich would spend less time at the castle and more time travelling, ostensibly on business. He also spent an increasing amount of time in Berlin where he kept a permanent suite at the new grand Hotel Adlon.

During his brief stays in the castle, Heinrich seems to have been determined to subject his son Stephan to a life of constant corrective punishment. This included locking him in cupboards and banishing him to deserted and desolate parts of Rohoncz Castle. Heinrich's behaviour was so extreme that it is difficult not to believe that he actively disliked the boy. The possibility of Stephan enjoying a happy childhood was also limited by the foreboding and depressing atmosphere of the castle. It was a vast, grey-stoned, Kafkaesque monolith, which had been designed to be used as a barracks, rather than as a home and a place for small children. Stephan in particular found it terrifying.

Only a few years after Margit had given birth to a daughter, also named Margit, it became obvious this attractive, bright and lively child was to be subjected to a similar regime. While the young Stephan had found little protection in his unresponsive mother, his sister would suffer increasingly as her mother began to develop a jealousy of her adolescent daughter's attractive appearance. Thus Margit was terrorised by both parents. Heini remembered her being forced to spend days with a sign round her waist saying 'I am a liar', and the staff being encouraged to become involved in her punishment by refusing to speak to her.

* * *

August Thyssen never denied his wealth, only the specific amount of his personal fortune which, in 1908, was estimated to be in the region of RM75 million, although the company profits that year alone were RM265 million. Meanwhile August Junior had little trouble convincing various banks that his inheritance entitlement was also RM75 million and that he could borrow accordingly.

By 1910, August Junior's debts had reached a sufficient level for an aggrieved creditor to initiate bankruptcy proceedings against him for RM11 million. There was even evidence to suggest that the aggrieved creditor may have been his own father. 'Old' August, no doubt encouraged by highly paid legal advisers, initiated the Thyssen family tradition of attempting to settle family grievances in open court. He even offered Junior a yearly allowance of RM130,000 if he renounced his inheritance. But Junior refused, so August tried to get his son placed under guardianship. But that also failed, so the case continued with endless claims and counterclaims; a process that appealed to Junior's highly developed sense of humour and somewhat overactive intelligence.

The boulevard press loved it; particularly in 1912 when the old man celebrated his seventieth birthday and was described by the *Frankfurter Zeitung* as the first German billionaire.[17] Also when, after ten years of continuous court action, the case was brought to a halt by the death of the adjudicator and the whole procedure had to start all over again. Junior even wrote some articles about the case for the small paper *Roland von Berlin* and was jailed for one month for libel after blaming the manager of his Rüdersdorf limestone and cement works for his debts and challenging him to a duel.

Eventually, 'old' August, no doubt aware that the Konzern would have to pay for the entire court action as well as his son's extravagance, was persuaded to give in and settle Junior's debts.

Apart from the continuation of financial hostilities between August and Junior, there was another good reason for the old man's increasing ill humour. News in 1907 that he was ill and in need of hospital treatment spread very rapidly in the Ruhr area while its effect in reducing the value of related equity on the stockmarket was quite dramatic. The official version of the story was that the sixty-five-year-old August had been suffering from a nasal growth for some time, which had eventually become extremely uncomfortable. It was just as likely that he simply disliked the size and shape of his nose and for purely cosmetic reasons decided to indulge in recent advances in plastic surgery. But he then suffered from the reverse; a new nose that was far too sharp and pointed. With little choice but to accept the disastrous result, this then became the official face of 'old' August Thyssen.

Despite his three-week Norwegian convalescence cruise, inspired by the Emperor's enthusiasm for Nordic waters, his humour did not improve: 'I was neither pleased with my sea-sickness nor with the throng on the ship. The younger elements on board made the night seem like day, and no sense of order was respected.'[18]

Meanwhile, August's ill health and the family's fear that he might not survive surgery had resulted in yet another crisis as questions of ownership and inheritance were once again raised by his sons. Unfortunately, the wording of the divorce settlement was unclear and it too became the subject of family argument. An independent legal report was prepared which, to the annoyance of the sons, not only confirmed August's claim of control, but suggested he could also claim ownership. Not surprisingly, this situation encouraged further legal action and remained a continuous source of aggravation between father and sons.

* * *

Fritz remained the most loyal of August's children and would create minimal personal or corporate problems until 1923. Compared with his siblings, even his marriage remained remarkably free of drama or complication; the birth of Anita, their only child, in Bonn on 13 May 1909 being achieved with little fuss or commotion. That did nothing to diminish August's criticism concerning the length of time it took Amélie to present him with a grandchild and her failure to produce a son.

While 'old' August continued to devote much of his time to the celebration of his new way of life and continuation of his family battles, the Konzern proceeded with its relentless programme of modernisation and growth. German military development provided an ever-increasing demand for production. A Thyssen financial statement in 1912 listed the value of the Konzern's assets as RM 562,153,182, while according to their own records, the value of Josef's shares now amounted to some RM40 million and August's RM122 million. It qualified them as two of the richest men in the world and their children, potentially, among the most financially fortunate.

The Thyssen works now comprised Thyssen & Co. Mülheim, Maschinenfabrik Thyssen & Co. Mülheim, GDK Hamborn-Bruckhausen, GDK Dinslaken, AG für Hüttenbetrieb Duisburg-Meiderich and Stahlwerk Thyssen Hagendingen. At that time, GDK used 4.5 million tons of coal to produce 839,000 tons of raw steel and 755,000 tons of rolled steel a year. The Konzern employed a total of 26,000 workers, and by now Germany was the world's third most successful industrial power after Britain and the USA.

By 1913, war seemed inevitable despite the fact that the protagonists were all related and had all, King, Kaiser and Tsar, pledged everlasting friendship and good relations with each other within the previous seven years. Nor had it stopped the arms race between Britain and Germany or the latter's voicing of its aggressive intentions.

The Emperor had already communicated his plans of conquest to August and asked for his support and assistance in canvassing other industrialists to participate. Apparently, in return for their contribution to his war effort, he promised they would be rewarded with conquered land in Australia and Canada.[19]

As August was already profiting from the Emperor's military ambitions, he displayed appropriate enthusiasm and, based on his massive ore interests in Lorraine, advised 'we must go with France against England', but in truth his international industrial expansion was by this time hugely successful, and he was not entirely confident that the Emperor's plans were without risk.[20] He would soon be asking his banker friend Hjalmar Schacht: 'But how will it be if we do not win the war?'[21]

Not only had he already created a trans-Atlantic shipping line to transport iron ore from neutral Brazil, but he also formed an offshore, Rotterdam-based company to own the fleet, including his Rhine tugs. The expansion of coking stations in Rotterdam, Antwerp, London, Newcastle, Cardiff, Naples, Genoa, Algiers and Port Said would have been difficult to describe as anything other than an attempt to profit from the forthcoming war through neutral Holland.

Vulkan GmbH had been founded by GDK to run the Thyssen fleet of Rhine tugs and barges. In 1910, Handels en Transport Maatschappij Vulcaan was set up as its Dutch subsidiary, based in Rotterdam.[22] It quickly became independent and took over the river shipping operations. It also operated the Thyssen ocean-going vessels and traded internationally in bunker coal and iron ore, while Vlaardingen, also in Holland, a large site on the Nieuwe Waterweg, was acquired and made into a major private port.

* * *

Some British politicians suggested that Britain, and later the USA, went to war as a means of resisting the formation of a Franco-German industrial alliance. Considering August's preference for combining with France against Britain, which he no doubt shared with other industrialists, it was a difficult theory to refute. Even Ramsay MacDonald claimed that the British government's eventual declaration of war was nothing more than 'prejudice against a very strong commercial rival' and resigned as leader of the Labour Party in protest.[23]

But for the fortunate Thyssens who, apart from Josef's son Hans, would not have to participate actively in the Great War, the conflict was only ever referred to as a commercial opportunity. There are certainly no indications that any of them would ever consider, let alone regret, the appalling cost in human lives. As 'the lamps were going out all over Europe' August was enjoying nothing more life-threatening than a cure in Badgastein, one of his favoured spas, where the lamps burned as brightly as ever.

Meanwhile, his son Heinrich displayed minimal interest in becoming any more involved in the Konzern or the war than was absolutely necessary and responded with uncommon haste by arranging a document issued by the Hungarian Legation in Munich advising border controls to facilitate his passage by chauffeur-driven, private car (complete with faux diplomatic registration number HG 222) to and from Hungary. Something he could wave at the guards as he roared across the Austrian border while lesser mortals were subjected to hours of questioning and searching.

Heinrich's brother Fritz responded to his sense of romanticised patriotism by polishing his buttons and boots and galloping off to war. But he managed to avoid becoming involved in any life-threatening activity by accepting the position of general's adjutant or administration officer. Less than a year later, when things were beginning to look a good deal more dangerous, it cost 'old' August a great deal of money to buy Fritz out and have him returned as a cavalry captain with an Iron Cross and a 'debilitating lung disorder'.

* * *

In order to take maximum advantage of the Emperor's plans, Matthias Erzberger, Minister of Finance and spokesperson for Germany's heavy industry, was invited by the Thyssens to join the board of GDK. In turn, August joined the industrial committee of the Reich War Ministry which decided that heavy industry in the occupied territories should avoid competing with German industry.

Up until the outbreak of war, apart from plates, pipes and boilers for the navy, there had been minimal direct production of armament within the Konzern. But once war had been declared, production of grenade cases, large diameter shells, shell cases, gun turrets and barbed wire grew so rapidly that full capacity was

Workers posing for Thyssen sales catalogue.

achieved by 1915. It was an activity that Heini and the Thyssen-Bornemiszas would strenuously deny; particularly regarding the profits that they subsequently enjoyed. In fact, by 1918, practically the whole Konzern was fully engaged in war production with the manufacture of 5 million mines, various artillery pieces and their supports, mortars, grenades and such-like.

GDK expanded quickly, with the number of employees quickly increasing from 3,500 to 24,000, of whom 8,000 were women. As war progressed, more and more prisoners of war and women were made to work, but as they were less productive, more of them had to be employed.

But as the appalling loss of life continued to rise, the spirit of the German people deteriorated and they began to realise the pointlessness of the conflict that they had been dragged into. The power of the Prussian aristocracy was eroded and began to be replaced by unions' and workers' councils. The number of strikes increased and socialism started to threaten the independence of the Thyssens and other industrialists.

1 Wessel, pp. 36–37.
2 Eduard's father was Baron August von der Heydt, a Ruhr banker who had been Commerce Minister from 1848 and later Finance Minister. August Thyssen had long since been doing business with the von der Heydt Bank.
3 Emil Kirdorf was the other 'grand old man of the Ruhr'. Since 1873, he had been the Director of the Gelsenkirchener Bergwerks AG and after the Great War formed the Rhein-Elbe-Union with Hugo Stinnes.
4 According to Fear (p. 159): 'August Thyssen admitted to his friend Carl Klönne at Deutsche Bank that Thyssen & Co and GDK were operating for years with RM30–40 million worth of short-term debt.
5 Fear, p. 160 and Pritzkoleit, p. 39.
6 Willing, 3 February 1968.
7 Baumann, p. 34.
8 Ibid., p. 38.
9 Ibid., p. 41.
10 Hjalmar Horace Greeley Schacht was a personal friend of August Thyssen. In the 1920s he was President of the Reichsbank and from 1934 onwards Minister of Economics.
11 Pritzkoleit, p. 58.

12 The correspondence between August Thyssen and Auguste Rodin is held at the Musée Rodin in Paris as well as at the Thyssen archives in Duisburg and Monte Carlo. Most of it has been published in the catalogue *From Canaletto to Kandinsky, Masterworks from the Carmen Thyssen-Bornemisza Collection*.
13 The titles of the Rodin sculptures bought by Thyssen were: 'Young Girl Confiding in Isis or Nature', 'Athen(a)'s Death or The Lamentation on the Acropolis', 'Christ and Magdalene', 'The Birth of Venus or The Aurore', 'The Dream or The Kiss of the Angel', 'Visit to the Doctor' and 'Psyche'.
14 Willing, 27 January 1968.
15 Bentinck Archives.
16 Author's interviews with Dr Joseph Groh (†), 1995–97.
17 Willing, 10 February 1968.
18 Wessel, p. 190.
19 *New York Times*, 14 April 1918.
20 Franz Jungbluth's recollections of 1912 (Wessel, p. 42).
21 Wessel, p. 206.
22 See for instance the strictly confidential report compiled by the Trading with the Enemy Department in February 1947, p. 27 (National Archives, Washington, DC).
23 Moore, p. 210.

Chapter III

1915–1926

Blood & iron... The profits of war

*By brooks too broad for leaping
The lightfoot boys were laid.*
A. E. Housman

On 15 July 1915 an event took place which should have devastated August Thyssen. His seventy-one-year-old brother Josef was killed in a shunting accident in the firm's railway marshalling yard. For thirty-six years Josef and his family had devoted their lives almost exclusively to the Konzern; his 25 per cent holding in the organisation failing to reflect his contribution to the creation and maintenance of the Thyssen empire. Not only are there remarkably few details available of exactly how the accident occurred, but there also appear to have been a suspicious lack of familial honouring of his memory. There is no evidence of a lavish funeral. Obituaries were minimal, with no record of an eulogy by August or of any attempt to create any kind of memorial, while all Josef's personal files were disposed of.

Even the behaviour of August's sons, particularly Fritz and Heinrich, displayed little in the way of respect or family loyalty. Josef's stake in the business was divided equally between Hans and Julius, who entrusted their cousin Fritz with the safeguarding of their shares, so that Fritz Thyssen for all practical purposes would control 62.5 per cent of the Konzern. In the autumn of 1915, August brought all his various companies together into one central joint stock company with all the shares held by the family. A supervisory board was formed with August as the president and including Fritz, Heinrich, Hans and Julius. But their inheritance of board membership expressly excluded Josef's sons from any actual power of direction.

From this point on, Fritz and Heinrich, who had as little loyalty and affection towards each other as they did for their cousins, became the key figures in the overall direction of the Konzern. Fritz concentrated on the more politically charged, heavy industrial side and Heinrich on the cleaner and more socially acceptable areas of banking, logistics and services.

* * *

On 20 December 1915, the Baroness Margit gave birth to Gabrielle, her second daughter and as far as her father Heinrich was concerned, the one child with whom he would develop a close relationship. For the following thirty-two years Gaby would be referred to by her father as 'Baby' and in his letters as 'my dearest darling Baby'. But she only enjoyed the first three years of her childhood at Rohoncz Castle before the Habsburg Empire collapsed and with it her mother's and grandmother's entire world.

By 1916 August had also begun to realise that his German holdings might be under threat if Germany were to lose the war. He obviously considered it time to put his recovery plan into place, distance himself from all the politicians and generals responsible and prepare for the renewal of international business. This he did by making conciliatory overtures to Britain and America. An early example of his sophisticated public relations appeared in Britain's *Daily Mail* newspaper:

> If the managing director of some big British shipping concern could be appointed as Ambassador in Berlin or the head of a large Rhenish-Westphalian factory be installed at the Court of St James's, Anglo-German relations would be permanently on an amiable footing . . . We want peace. We do not desire to develop our industries by war. It is true that a few of our ammunition manufacturers wish for a long war, but they do not speak for Germany. In peace, our relations with America are always most friendly and we want them to continue friendly after the war.[1]

As the German forces retreated, they were ordered to sabotage French and Belgian factories, industrial plant and mines, leaving Germany in a strong industrial position, while generals refused to admit to their nation's defeat and Matthias Erzberger was chosen as a civilian sacrificial lamb to head the German delegation which was to sign the Treaty of Versailles on 28 June 1919. Fritz Thyssen set in motion a particularly unpleasant betrayal in order to distance the Konzern from their previous profitable relationship with Erzberger, whom he now considered a Jewish traitor. Erzberger was later shot while on holiday in the Black Forest. The assassination was discovered to have been the responsibility of the Germanic Order, a post-war, right-wing organisation financed by people of similar political and financial position to Fritz Thyssen.

* * *

Leaving the country in the throes of revolution, Kaiser Wilhelm II went into exile in Holland, where he was the guest of the Duke of Bentinck and often visited by Eduard von der Heydt (the close friend of Heinrich Thyssen-Bornemisza whose daughter Gabrielle would eventually marry Baron Adolphe Bentinck). Within days of the abdication, all twenty of the German monarchies were abolished, bringing down the centuries-old kingdoms, grand duchies, duchies and principalities 'like a great house of playing cards'. The Austro-Hungarian Empire had also ceased to exist, but this did not prevent the Thyssen-Bornemiszas still insisting on being referred to as Hungarian aristocrats.

The year 1919 marked the beginning of their loss of Hungarian citizenship, when they fled from the 'Red Menace' of Bela Kun and his nationalisation of the great estates under his communist government. According to Heini's sister Gaby, the family actually reached the safety and comfort of Landsberg Castle by a no more life-threatening method than a first-class railway carriage, but their mother still wrote a highly imaginative and revealing account of the family's dramatic escape, entitled *Six Weeks Under the Red Flag*, which included many examples of the Baroness Thyssen-Bornemisza's extreme views:

> Most of the agitators and the heads of the Bolshevik formations were Jews, common looking Jews with devilish expressions, who lived more or less by unfair means and managed to get the lower class of labourers entirely into their power through their violent and ferocious eloquence. The Jewish doctor was declared head of the dictatorship. Like all Jews in Hungary he had, up till now, not received much consideration from his fellow citizens and revenged himself as soon as he came into power. If money was needed on the farm, the head steward had to go to the dictator's office, where he had to show the list of bills the estate had to pay, and only then did the impudent Jew sign the authorisation by which the money could be drawn from the bank. Nuns and priests who remained true to their vocation were most cruelly treated. During this dreadful period, it was known by the British Legation in Vienna, that a lot of corpses were found floating in the different ports of the Danube.[2]

In fact, Bela Kun's revolution was accepted as being virtually 'bloodless' and there was no evidence to support Margit's claim that the Thyssen-Bornemiszas' lives had been threatened. By the end of 1919, Bela Kun's Republic was overthrown and for the following twenty-five years Hungary bore a semblance of the old regency under the dictatorship of Admiral Horthy, who according to Heini was greatly admired by his father. But under the Treaty of Trianon in 1919 the Habsburg territories were divided and Rohoncz found itself positioned in the new Republic of Austria.

Having expended so much time, effort and money in becoming a Hungarian aristocrat, Heinrich was not amused to find himself a resident of Austria but he claimed to have subsequently retained his Hungarian citizenship, while the castle and the surrounding town would in future be known by their German title of Rechnitz. Although the family visited the castle for summer holidays and Heinrich used the woods for hunting, he would never live there again.

*   *   *

'Old' August had been careful to avoid revealing that he had taken steps to protect the Konzern prior to 1914 for fear of being accused of unpatriotic or even traitorous activities. Officially the Bank voor Handel en Scheepvaart NV was registered in Rotterdam in July 1918 by two Dutch bankers. However, the bank appeared to have been in Thyssen hands prior to 1918; Fritz would later admit that August had bought it 'discreetly' in 1910, a date which he then modified to 1916, insisting it was the result of his father's concern for the course of the war.[3] Due to the fact that Holland retained its neutrality throughout the war, the bank could be used to protect the Konzern by ownership of shares.

After the war, the Allies discovered the Thyssen connection with BVHS and froze their accounts. But having settled in Holland and taken charge of the bank, Heinrich also used his purported Hungarian nationality in order to wrest control of the customer accounts, including those of the Thyssens. In due course he would reallocate the shares of BVHS: 37.5 per cent for himself and Fritz and 12.5 per cent for Julius and Hans. Heinrich's success in transposing the Konzern's identity from German to Dutch would ensure the organisation's survival and avoidance of reparation payments through two world wars, despite the fact that Heinrich continued to hold a German passport (no. 2136 issued at the Germany embassy in Vienna on 17 April 1919), a fact that Heini would subsequently strongly deny.[4]

While they had undoubtedly contributed enormously to Germany's war efforts, August even successfully managed to claim compensation from the Reich for his losses, which in 1920 were valued at RM87.7 million, while his steel works and ore mines in Lorraine were valued at RM246 million during 'preliminary compensation proceedings'.[5]

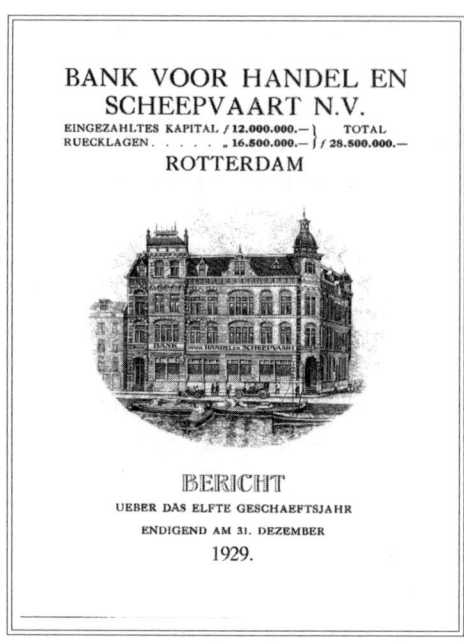

The Thyssens' first off-shore banking facility.

So despite the loss of some of his foreign resources, particularly those in France, August still had a fully functional organisation and was in a very much better situation than many of his competitors who had borrowed too heavily and assumed Germany was going to win the war. His ability to trade in foreign currencies through BVHS would also prove a vital advantage during the forthcoming hyper-inflationary period.

* * *

It was no time to be celebrating any form of financial achievement as the socialist threat to German industry and the Thyssens' way of life was increasing day by day. For while the Emperor had been busy involving Germany in an arms race and war, he had ignored and often opposed most forms of social reform and even supported repressive measures. The mood of the people was one of deep and aggressive dissatisfaction. Capitalism was under threat from armed rebellion against the social, political and economic order. The most immediate cause of people's anger and frustration lay with the upper echelons of society who, having dragged them into a war, now seemed unable or unwilling to protect them from an inflationary spiral and the shortage of food which was rapidly developing into a full-scale famine.

The Thyssens' main concern was that the workers' councils had already managed to reduce working hours from ten to eight and they were now trying to nationalise the mines, so when a radical suggestion of creating a Rhenanian Republic was made, Fritz persuaded his father to lend his support.

In December 1918, a group of industrialists including August and Fritz Thyssen met at the Hotel Fürstenhof in Dortmund to discuss the possibilities. When a waiter later reported their conversation, they were arrested by the workers' and soldiers' council of Mülheim and transported to Berlin, where they were incarcerated in the Moabit prison. But the case against them was dismissed; the official reason given was that it had not been possible to prove they had

Chapter III: 1915–1926

committed any high treason against Germany.

The whole experience did little to improve August's already failing health but it did persuade him the time had come to hand over more control to his sons. The general unrest also strengthened Fritz's phobic reaction towards socialism and served to fire his political ambition.

* * *

Heinrich's decision to take up residence in Scheveningen had been made considerably more acceptable by the presence of his friend Eduard von der Heydt, who was Legation Councillor at the German Embassy in The Hague from 1915 to 1919. It was the type of position that made Heinrich extremely envious but at least he could profit socially from Eduard's circle of diplomatic friends.

Scheveningen was originally a fishing village, but, with the increasing popularity of the beach as a fashionable area for recreation, it soon became accepted as the smart, coastal district of The Hague, the seat of Holland's government. It was a peaceful area full of large houses, hotels and embassies, striped sun-awnings and tennis courts. As the Netherlands still had a monarchy, the capital was host to a thriving aristocratic and diplomatic community. This

Margit (centre), summering at Rechnitz, with her four children, circa 1927.

milieu suited Heinrich and Margit and enabled them to continue enjoying their imperial style of life with like-minded people. There was even a small Hungarian community with whom Margit would form a strong and extremely close relationship.

Their large house may have lacked the grandeur of Schloss Rohoncz, but the Thyssen-Bornemiszas compensated for it with lavish social expenditure. One of Heinrich's closest friends was Prince Hendrik, Queen Wilhelmina's German husband, who came to see him often. The style of their entertaining was so extravagant that even their new English chums, Lord and Lady Marling, the British ambassador and his wife, were prepared to accept their assumed mantle of Hungarian aristocracy, regardless of the fact that the Baron and Baroness shared at least part of their surname with one of Germany's best-known industrialists.

However, one particular house-guest of the time appeared to be under no illusion as to where the Thyssen-Bornemiszas had come from and why they were there:

> We scattered refugees from all over Europe met in that little haven of rest and clung together through those long months when the peace terms were being drawn up. Though the Thyssens, I suppose, could hardly be considered refugees. Owing to their father's foresight, they were able to save most of their money as they had transferred much of their capital to Holland before the war. As a result they were able to keep a very fine house at The Hague and entertain lavishly.[6]

Soon after the brief 'Bolshevik Revolution', the Baron and Baroness, refusing to accept the new Austrian title, returned to their 'beloved Rohoncz', though rarely for very long or together. Heinrich would visit in the autumn for the hunting season, while Margit would return for some two or three months during the summer. From time to time she would also be joined by her various children with their nannies and governesses. Much as she enjoyed the social life of The Hague, Margit was in her element playing the role of 'Queen of Rohoncz', where she reigned supreme over her large staff and played hostess to her many house-guests and those of the local population whom she considered socially worthy.

* * *

While his son and daughter-in-law were avoiding the German post-war tidal wave of revolution, destitution and starvation, 'old' August continued to be incensed by the social and political unrest and demanded the use of force in intervention. He wrote letters to the Reich government requesting 'greater police and military protection against the Communists as well as compensation for the losses from the revolutionary upheavals'.[7]

Unfortunately this desire to destroy the forces of communism fuelled the rise of yet another extreme political movement. With the influence of Lenin and Trotsky spreading across Europe, Benito Mussolini was creating Italy's Fascist Party while in Germany, the seeds of fascism were being planted in the para-military Freikorps who were also busy 'protecting' the public against the communists. Their enthusiasm in Berlin during the month of March 1919 resulted in the shooting of between twelve and fifteen hundred 'enemies of the state'.

As August became older and less mobile, his social extravagance waned and was replaced by an obsessive concern with the dynastic future of the family, manifest in a constant stream of letters. But many of his letters appeared to be more a result of his general dissatisfaction than any genuine attempt to communicate:

> Fritz is demanding with all his force that Julius and Hans are to keep their participations with minimum power and influence which I think means he wants them to relegate some of their positions. I will work against him with all my force in this respect. I wish I were dead because of all these frictions, which in the past came from August Junior, and are now initiated by Fritz.[8]

In a letter to his grandson Stephan he obviously considered the fact that the boy was still only twelve years old to be totally irrelevant: 'The new taxes in Germany will apparently eat up 75 per cent of big fortunes, so that only 25 per cent will remain for the owner.'

The demand for increased tax was a cause of constant distress. This was understandable as, under the Kaiser, tax had been almost non-existent. Thus the effect of a sudden demand for a 65 per cent wealth tax was predictable. The old man even managed to infect his entire family for generations to come with his violent aversion to the payment of tax. As with many very rich families, tax avoidance and evasion would become a major contributing factor in the eventual downfall of the Thyssen dynasty.

* * *

In September 1919, the old man's correspondence began to reflect more disturbing opinions. In a letter to Heinrich congratulating him on his courage in returning to Rechnitz, he wrote:

I am so happy for you that the farmers in Rohoncz turned out to be so loyal as to beat up the Communists and their friends. I hope it will be a lesson to them for many years to come. If at all possible, one should exclude Jews like the ones there from business on a permanent basis in order to chase them away. I will leave Baden-Baden soon and return to Landsberg. Here everything is totally overcrowded and they say that the trains cannot accommodate all the people who wish to travel. I don't say too much if I say that half of the guests here are Jews.

However, 'old' August was a man blessed with a far greater degree of pragmatism than conviction. By 1923 he would be telling Heinrich about his problem persuading an apparently reluctant Fritz to continue doing business with a Jewish pipe-dealer; something August Thyssen obviously considered an unavoidable evil:

Now Fritz says he also wants to resign from his position at Thyssen & Co if I continue dealings with Mr Nussbaum . . . He is the biggest tube trader in Germany and also has an important position in Hanover, so that the mayor and other important people mix with him at his home. The tube business has many Jews among its dealers. I agree that we drop our desire to participate in this business, but sometimes he asks us for one million kilos of tubes in one go, and I would like to continue to supply this man.[9]

In a subsequent letter from August to Heinrich, Fritz's anti-Semitism was revealed even more clearly. Yet again, the problem was the industrialists with whom Fritz was trying to make it impossible for the Konzern to do business:

His main problem seems to be the fact that Herz and his partner are Jewish, which I don't find agreeable either, but the fact is that all businessmen in Borislaw are Jews, so there is really no choice, to be honest . . . I sometimes think that Fritz's antipathies against the Jews are unjustified . . . The whole of the southern German trade is in Jewish hands and we simply cannot do without it.[10]

* * *

Baron Heinrich Thyssen-Bornemisza considered himself a gentleman and a cut above those involved in trade. More often than not, his brief visits to Holland were made, not to interfere with the smooth running of the bank but in order to visit friends and avail himself of various diplomatic 'conveniences' which would ease his progress through strife-torn Europe. In 1920 he had visited the Hungarian legation in The Hague to make a Christmas donation of DK100,000 and received privileged documentation.

Although he was officially resident in Holland, Heinrich was already spending an increasing amount of time separated from his wife and staying at the Adlon Hotel in Berlin or visiting various fashionable resorts. By 1920 their marriage had become a sham, although their relationship remained largely amicable, while Heinrich already had a mistress called Lisa Abel, who was the daughter of a night porter. Apparently, she had been walking on the beach near Scheveningen when she overheard Margit complaining to one of her friends about her husband's lack of sexual prowess. Lisa then passed this information on to Heinrich who was furious. So much so that on his next visit to Scheveningen he made sure that his wife remained under no illusion as to his sexual vigour.

Shortly afterwards, the servants noticed that the Baroness was taking alternate hot and cold mustard baths; something women of the time did in order to terminate a pregnancy. When the Baron heard what was happening, he immediately ordered her to stop and allow her pregnancy to run its course. The result of his insistence was the birth of another son, Hans Heinrich Thyssen-Bornemisza or, as he became known, 'Heini'; a nickname given to him by his unappreciative mother which in German signifies a wimp or the runt of a litter.

There was no doubt as to 'old' August's desire for a second generation male heir or that he was capable of financially pressurising Heinrich into agreeing to create a 'spare' in case Stephan failed to survive or proved unsuitable. There was also no doubt that Heinrich despised his first-born son, whom he already considered unsuitable and so needed little persuasion to provide a replacement. Baroness Margit would have had little choice in the matter if she wished to receive a generous alimony settlement, as she appeared to be already enjoying a close personal relationship with a Hungarian diplomat called Janos Wettstein. Judging by the generally clement relationship which continued to exist between the Baron, the Baroness and Wettstein, the financial arrangements appeared to suit everyone.

* * *

As 'old' August was now eighty years of age, the logistics of the inheritance were becoming of increasing concern. Despite the basic terms of his will having been agreed, when family interest in the old man showed any sign of flagging, he would either threaten some alteration of his intentions or complicate some existing agreement. Sometimes it was just a reminder of his power after death. It was a habit that would be repeated by future generations with ever-increasing levels of complication in direct proportion to the number of lawyers involved.

By 1922, August was obviously becoming increasingly worried that Heinrich's social habits, indulgences and aspirations were hardly conducive to the inheritance of an industrial dynasty, and his advice took a distinctly personal slant. Having accused him of excessive enthusiasm for champagne and liqueurs, he then charged him with lacking the knowledge and attitude to ever become a successful industrialist. He lashed out with what he considered a serious insult: 'You, Heinrich, are only a banker.'

It was an insult that was lost on Heinrich, who had no desire to be considered an industrialist and was far more concerned with the commencement of the hunting season. 'Old' August was further incensed when he realised that his son had by-passed Landsberg on his way to Austria without even bothering to stop and 'pay his respects'.

Having failed to exact an appropriate response from his son, he tried to canvass his support for the Konzern against the escalating problems posed by the workers:

> I am well, but our situation here goes downhill with giant steps. The iron and coal prices are being put up again today, also the salaries for workers and employees. The government says yes to anything the masses want, and so wages and salaries are constantly increased and the prices too, which are spiralling up into unlimited heights.

He went on to warn Heinrich of the 'tragedy for Germany' threatened by the reduction of the working day from ten to eight hours and the introduction of workers' councils in all enterprises with more than twenty employees. He also spoke with obvious annoyance of the new law requiring two members of the workers' councils to be members of the supervisory boards.

But none of these problems was of the slightest concern to Heinrich, as they had little effect on his banking business or the Rechnitz hunting season and if 'old' August's threats had any effect at all, it was to persuade Heinrich to extend his stay, well away from strife-torn German industry.

In a letter dated 15 December 1922 to his brother, Fritz made it quite obvious that he, too, was only marginally irritated with their father's behaviour: 'The relationship with father is very difficult again, because he makes trouble everywhere with his old-fashioned views, which is something that irritates people in general.'

But Fritz could also not resist having a little dig at his brother's medical condition, which was obviously alcohol-related: 'I hope your gout attack is now over.'

*   *   *

'Old' August's patriarchal relationship with workers and management, which has often been exaggerated, had all but disappeared and he was finding it increasingly difficult to know how to deal with the social, political and financial changes in the nation. This was obvious in one of his letters to Heinrich in 1922: 'I share your view that we will end up like Russia. I fear I am getting too weak and I have nobody to help me and am normally standing here alone. We have become too soft and nobody has the courage to state their opinion. Only a collapse can bring about a change, but not only for the top, for the lower levels also.'

Having been arrested during Berlin's communist revolution in December 1918, 'old' August was somewhat guarded in expressing his political views in a letter. But the old man was doubtless aware that the country was very close to civil war and he predicted that only an even greater crisis could prevent the country's slide towards self-destruction.

The announcement of this even greater crisis was made in July 1922 when Germany informed the French that they could not afford to continue paying the war reparations, due to hyperinflation. The situation was aggravated by rumours that the French and Belgians were planning to invade the Ruhr causing the Mark to go into free-fall.

On 11 January 1923, the rumours were confirmed and 100,000 French and Belgian troops marched into the Ruhr to take coal and other raw materials in place of Marks. Having informed the French troops that he had no intention of co-operating, Fritz was arrested with five other directors to be tried by a military tribunal in Mainz where he told the court: 'I am a German and I refuse to obey French orders on German soil.'[11]

As a result, seven ultra-reactionary Berlin organisations sent Fritz congratulatory messages and it became apparent that Fritz's plans were somewhat more ambitious than the encouragement of passive resistance. He was not alone among industrialists willing to take extreme action, including the formation of their own military corps.

Seventy-five thousand men and women in nine Thyssen coal mines and steel plants throughout the Ruhr area came out on strike as a protest against Fritz's arrest. Crowds burnt copies of the Treaty of Versailles and Fritz Thyssen returned to Essen, believing himself to be a German hero. Although there were massive public protests, they were nationalistic rather than supportive of Fritz but it had given him a taste for public veneration and for politics; his subsequent claim to have been exclusively responsible for organising the passive resistance and thus saving the Ruhr industries indicating his appreciation for the value of political exaggeration.

This outpouring of nationalism against a common foe was exploited by a more dangerous figure. On 27 January 1923, Adolf Hitler and 6,000 SA men assembled in Munich for the first Nazi Party rally and called for the repeal of the Treaty of Versailles, the removal of the French and Belgian troops, and the elimination of communists, liberals, Jews and traitors. His message and that of the National Socialist Party was enthusiastically received by his supporters and the swastika was accepted as a symbol of the new extreme nationalism.

* * *

While the old man's inability to accept graceful retirement was a source of considerable aggravation, fortunately for the family fortune August never lost his gift for financial opportunism and counteracted the problems of hyperinflation by printing his own money. Not a forgery of national currency but an internal unit of payment that could be used in the company stores, canteens and lodging houses. One of his self-promoted anecdotes concerned his visit to the Deutsche Bank, where Director Schlitter asked the old man: 'Herr Thyssen, we have so much of your scrip in our tills. What is to become of it?'

For a few moments, August appeared to be deep in thought. Before standing up to leave, he replied: 'You're quite right Herr Schlitter, what is to become of it?'[12]

There was another popular story concerning an industrialists' meeting at a hotel in Elberfeld where Ernst Poensgen found August outside and refusing to enter, with the excuse that: 'I can't go in there, Herr Poensgen. The cloakroom attendant has just demanded seven million Marks from me.'[13]

The possibility that he failed to comprehend the effects of hyperinflation is a great deal less likely than his faking incomprehension, so that someone else would pay for his hat and coat. But as always, there were contradictory stories. When he heard that Conrad Verlohr, one of his most trusted and successful financial advisers, was due to retire after thirty-five years of faithful service and had lost his entire life savings, August awarded him a monthly pension of RM3,000 (revalued), which would of course also have assured his discretion.

* * *

By June 1923, £1 was worth Mk600,000, by September Mk15 million and by November Mk20 billion. But in view of the value of their shares and their offshore banking arrangements, the hyperinflation had presented fewer dangers to the Konzern than to many other organisations, a situation for which August was quietly grateful: 'The only good thing is that our shares have increased in the opposite direction to our debts through the fall of the Mark and the increase in the value of the foreign currencies, a balance that has saved us.'[14]

This private admission was in fact a quite dramatic understatement, as their facility for paying off huge debts with very small quantities of foreign currency was extremely profitable.

Meanwhile Fritz was beginning to develop friendships with like-minded people. In October 1923, his friend Heinrich Class, the imperialistic, anti-Semitic President of the Pan-German League, suggested he went to Munich to talk to Field Marshal Erich von Ludendorff, the First World War hero and Nazi sympathiser, whom Fritz had already met during the war at his father's Landsberg estate. It was Ludendorff who would in turn introduce him to Adolf Hitler, who revealed to him his plans for the overthrow of the Weimar Republic. According to Heini, Fritz considered that the Republic's 'weakness' was responsible for 'leading Germany into anarchy'.

It is likely that they also discussed other people whom they considered responsible for Germany's downfall, including communists, liberals and Jews, for by this time, Hitler's opinions had been expressed at numerous public gatherings in the three-and-a-half years since his first appearance at the Munich Hofbräuhaus.

Although Fritz was far too much of a snob to welcome an ex-corporal as the country's future leader, he was sufficiently impressed by his ideas to present Ludendorff, who was helping to finance the Party, with 100,000 Goldmarks for what he must have been aware was to fund the overthrow of the state government of Bavaria.

As the date for the planned beerhall putsch grew closer, Hitler's paramilitary thugs demonstrated their Führer's methods by beating up political opponents, ransacking the socialist *Munich Post* newspaper offices and attacking Jews and their businesses. On 6 November 1923, 1,000 Jewish shops were looted in Berlin.

Hitler's coup d'état failed and he was sentenced to five years in prison. By February 1925, Hitler, who was released after only six months in jail, was back in Munich encouraging 4,000 Nazi Party supporters to continue the struggle. On 8 July 1925, part one of *Mein Kampf* was published, and from that moment on it would be quite impossible for anyone, particularly Fritz, to claim innocence of Hitler's ambitions.

The failure of Hitler's putsch had done little to diminish Fritz's political ambitions although his credibility was damaged when the Konzern's business methods were revealed in the Paris-based magazine *Oeuvre*. It made clear that while rules imposed by the German government had made the export of capital by the ordinary person practically impossible during the inflationary period, large companies had easily avoided these controls: 'The Reich is ruined, that's clear. But the German magnates are rich. They have billions in good currency, gold in foreign bank accounts. Why not seize these assets and use them for the reparation payments?'

The authors detailed the methods used, such as false invoicing through Swiss and Dutch banks and the billing of pseudo-clients in Berlin. The writers did not specifically name the Thyssen organisation as being guilty of this style of trading but it is obvious that they would have been among the candidates referred to as 'German industrialists'.

By now the *New York Times* had picked up on Germany's trading anomalies and expressed astonishment 'that a country professing starvation and bankruptcy is America's major importer of cotton, copper and meat products'.

* * *

While the Thyssens continued to exploit every financial opportunity, Fritz decided, for the moment, to join the upper-middle-class, ultra-conservative DNVP party. Heinrich would also become involved with the Nazis, although he was far more discreet concerning both his personal and corporate financial affairs. His discretion was evident in his incorporation of the Union Banking Corporation of New York in 1924 which would in due course provide financial services for the Nazi Party.

This extremely private, transatlantic banking facility was instituted with the help and assistance of his friend William Averell Harriman (four of the directors were partners in Brown Bros Harriman) and the Chase National Bank, although the $400,000 capital stock came from Bank voor Handel en Scheepvaart. Harriman himself did not serve on the board but designated a number of his associates, including Prescott S. Bush, George W. Bush's grandfather.

At the same time, Heinrich also incorporated a whole string of companies in America and South America through his holding trust Rotterdamsch Trustees Kantoor via BVHS and the Union Bank.[15]

But even though it was obvious that Germany was leaking capital, the Americans refused to co-operate in stemming the flow. In January 1924, *Deutsche Allgemeine Zeitung* reported: 'American members of the commission investigating the flight of capital from Germany have met with President Coolidge and Secretary of State Hughes. The result of this meeting was that it was considered impossible to seize the foreign assets of German capitalists and that an investigation of American banks would be illegal.'

Instead, the Dawes Plan was accepted and a loan of $200 million was made by America to stabilize the German economy, while the Mark was pegged at four to the dollar.

* * *

Despite the fact that the Konzern appeared to be returning to some form of normality, 'old' August's bad humour remained undiminished and his letter writing as prolific as ever. He reacted with considerable displeasure to Heinrich's demands for representation by BVHS on Thyssen supervisory boards:

> I cannot communicate with your bank managers; it is absolutely impossible. I think it would be questionable if we wanted to send a German banker to Holland, and it is no doubt even less possible for you to send Dutch bankers to leading supervisory boards in Germany. They would immediately start fighting and very soon be thrown out. I thus have to urge you not to press your men onto the board of the mines. That would deeply threaten the German overseas business, particularly as there is no German person in your bank.

He then continued to voice his theatrical intransigence concerning Fritz: 'It seems that we will have to split permanently for the rest of this life.'

Meanwhile, Fritz appeared to have inherited his father's enthusiasm for letter writing and a slightly more arrogant ill-humour, particularly towards Heinrich:

> You seem to think that the assets entrusted to you are being well looked after while the ones in my care are not. I refuse to let you represent my interests in Holland and elsewhere if you don't have the same trust for my work and sphere of influence. This concerns not only the papers, which bear my name, but also those that you are administrating as a trustee. The way the bank has acted repeatedly lately is also not to my liking at all.

August also displayed continuing concern for Heinrich's health, though whether this was genuine or a manifestation of 'old' August's even greater anxiety that Heinrich might drink himself to death and thus leave the whole Konzern in the hands of his hated brother is a matter of conjecture. He also appeared to be unaware of Heinrich's separation from Margit:

It's too bad that your gout and your stomach pains are not going away. Maybe you should stop smoking and drinking heavy wines and liqueurs. I recommend that you drink tea. Black coffee is much too heavy for you. I want you to concentrate only on your health in the near future. I think you should live in Rohoncz for a while. In fact, I would really like to live there for a short time just with you, Margit and the children. Don't go to the doctor when it's too late, like Stinnes did. You must save and maintain the company. Nobody else can do it.

His dislike of Fritz had become so intense that the old man seemed quite determined to take it to his grave and beyond: 'When I die, I shall be buried in a simple grave in Kettwig's cemetery. Please make sure Fritz doesn't come to my grave.'

God only knows how 'old' August might have reacted if he had been told that one day he and Fritz would be sharing that same grave.

* * *

The Konzern was now valued at RM657 million (nearly as much as the entire Dawes Plan budget) and most of the Thyssens' liquid assets were in Holland but, despite entreaties from his father, Heinrich was ill-disposed towards reinvesting BVHS capital in the Konzern. So it was decided to seek funds from New York where there was no shortage of American banks keen to invest in German industry. The $11.2 million raised in 1924 went to consolidate the short-term debt of the Konzern held by Dutch and German banks and circa $2.4 million to complete the modernisation of the mines.

Goldman Sachs had already brokered a loan for Krupp and certainly pitched for the Thyssens' business but would later respond to questions concerning their financial support of Germany's re-armament by claiming that all their records were destroyed in a fire in 1950 at their New York headquarters.[16]

While Fritz intended to take credit for the deal, in fact it was Hans Thyssen who had accompanied Director Rabes to New York. Not that he received any thanks for their success due to the fact that he took his wife with him. Obviously 'old' August considered this a crime against the Konzern which, according to yet another letter to Heinrich, should be punished with nothing less than banishment: 'Apparently, Hans is completely dominated by his wife and his mother-in-law. Her parents recently received a cheap house from Thyssen & Co. through my mediation and goodwill. I have now written to him that, unfortunately, I will have to reclaim the house.'

The diligent Hans, son of Josef Thyssen. *Gertrud, wife of Hans Thyssen (photos: courtesy of Ursula Cassinone).*

* * *

The old man's constant oscillation between loving and hating his sons and nephews appears to have increased as he got to the end of his life, while his obsession with extravagant wives and distrust of women in general remained constant:

> Fritz, who has done a lot of good work for the lowering of the overheads, has, unfortunately, together with his wife, a bad habit of spending and this has given his many inferiors and neighbours a very bad example. Before I die, I shall make a renewed attempt to restrict drastically his needs and those of his family and I will ask him to refrain from travelling together with his wife and daughter, the costs of which are unaffordable for either himself or us.

August even criticised his own extravagance by complaining about the cost of the upkeep of Landsberg which he claimed to be RM10,000 per month and that he could not possibly afford to continue paying for the castle unless his son helped him. He suggested that Heinrich and his family might wish to join him in living there. Finally, August tried to instil guilt in Heinrich by claiming: 'I want to lead a quiet and retired life and not be a burden to anybody.'

He seemed to have forgotten that none of his sons showed any indication of liking their father and had absolutely no intention of allowing him to become a burden on them.

It was also obvious from his letters that his devious and grasping nature showed no signs of diminishing. Its effect was not limited to his own family:

> Yesterday I went to see Baron Fürstenberg at Schloss Hugenpoet and his family. His oldest son has visited the Berlin banks to get a loan of RM500,000, which he didn't achieve, it seems. The Baron has a lot of land, c.4–5,000 acres, 2,300 of which alone are here in Kettwig. He has eight children, all of whom do nothing else but smoke, hunt and travel and get visits from their numerous relatives. Sooner or later they will be finished. We could get a lot of cheap land from him for our ATH.
>
> I think you should make the loan, alone or with America, at 10–12 per cent, and of course against the properties as a security. I told him that you had probably made a big loan of RM5 million to Prince Pless, which he found very interesting indeed. As my income is small, I would like to arrange a little commission, but only if you are alright with that.

* * *

Meanwhile, the question of which son was to replace 'old' August as head of the Konzern remained unanswered. Unable to choose between Fritz and Heinrich, both of whom he obviously considered unworthy and unsuitable, he would probably be left with little choice other than to hand over the reins of power to them both.

The threat of Hans and Julius assuming any positions of power were seriously curtailed somewhere between 1923 and 1925, when, according to official records, they both contracted severe encephalitis; the long-term effects of which were advancing paralysis. This led to the gradual reduction in their managerial responsibilities, while their share in the Konzern continued to be represented by Fritz and Dr Carl Härle, the executor of 'old' August's will. Many years later, Heini even alleged that Hans and Julius had contracted syphilis. This habit of stigmatising members of the family perceived as possible rivals for inheritance remained one of the more unpleasant characteristics of Heini's personality.

But the fact that the Konzern would develop in a way that made dual control between Heinrich and Fritz a practical solution was the result of organic growth rather than design. 'Old' August and his fellow German industrialists had often considered forming a similar organisation to the United States Steel Corporation to enable them to compete on more equal terms. But it was not until 1925 that the leading German steel companies met to plan the creation of an equivalent steel trust, to be known as the United Steelworks. Krupp would subsequently withdraw, while the Thyssen family, in the form of Fritz, would be the largest private shareholders.

While August and Fritz had been supportive of the plan, Heinrich had always been sceptical, due to the necessary corporate transparency that would inevitably result from such a development. In view of the nature of his banks' business, it was an understandable concern. However, he also appreciated the possible advantages, so he decided to use the situation as an opportunity to divide the concern in a way that he considered to be in his best interest.

He started by demanding permanent ownership of their banking shares and repayment of all BVHS loans in return for his co-operation. Other areas that he wanted to form part of his half of the Konzern included gas and water, shipping and shipbuilding. Heinrich also insisted that their undeveloped coalfields were withdrawn from the negotiations.

His father appeared to have genuinely mixed emotions about the trust. While realising the financial wisdom of such a move, he would obviously have preferred to have had sons capable of developing the Konzern in his image. But the old man's decision to join the steel trust was also the result of his anger resulting from the outcome of the war and apparent determination that Germany should try again: 'We will not allow ourselves to be crushed. We will rise up again if not this generation then the next.'[17] And: 'Germany cannot be without a great iron industry if it wants to be a major player. It has to have the facilities to create an army, make planes, a navy and ammunition by itself in a war.'[18]

* * *

With only seven and a half months left to live, blind in one eye, nearly blind in the other, partially paralysed and in generally poor health, 'old' August's ill-temper showed no signs of improvement. Even this close to the end he seemed determined to make sure there was still no love lost between father and son by once again insulting Heinrich's wife: 'You should keep your wife on a short lead. She seems to be a big money waster.'

He also saw fit to remind Heinrich that they were unlikely to get any immediate respite from their father's constant criticism and that he intended to 'stand at the helm until my dying breath'. A dying breath that was unlikely to come too soon for either of his weary sons.

The one area where the old man displayed some form of positive human emotion concerned his grandchildren, or, to be more specific, his grandchild, for he now, pointedly, only ever referred to one. Having persuaded Heinrich to create a second, fitter son, it was typical of 'old' August's ability to infuriate that he constantly referred to Heinrich's despised first son Stephan in quite fond and, by his standards, positive terms. He obviously enjoyed the boy's company and happily accepted his habit of inviting himself to stay. It was unusual behaviour for an eighteen-year-old whose youthful interest and exceptional intelligence both delighted and invigorated the grumpy old man but caused Stephan's father considerable unease. He tried to guide August's interest away from Stephan and gain approval of his favoured son Heini but neither the old man nor the young boy displayed any great enthusiasm.

* * *

Having refilled my glass, Heini sank back on his sun-lounger, crossed his thin brown legs and delicately pushed his tortoiseshell-framed sunglasses back up his nose: 'I remember a photograph we took with my grandfather when I was four and a half years old, at The Hague. Gaby and my parents are also in it. I was forced to wear clothes I didn't like. I remember my grandfather taking me on his knee.'

As Heinrich and Margit had decided to separate before Heini had even been conceived, it is difficult to believe that some five years later 'old' August was not aware of the situation. He no doubt also knew of his son's reasons for having such a photograph taken. What is perhaps more difficult to explain was the reason why Heini never gave me any indication of affection or even mild appreciation of his grandfather's existence or his achievements. This attitude appeared to have been part of Heini's life-long denial of his German roots: 'I am not German and have never lived in Germany. I had been there once or twice to see Uncle

Heini on the steps of a bathing machine on the beach at Scheveningen.

Fritz, and once to visit my father and Maud in Berlin. However, I do not really know the country at all. I lived in Holland and in Austria until the age of nineteen. In fact I have never been to Germany for pleasure, only for business, and I never stayed longer than necessary.'

Heini's sense of identity was not improved by the fact that he remained largely abandoned and rejected by his own parents:

> I hardly knew my parents when I was a child. Certainly I very rarely saw them, but my sisters always said I was very lucky not to. I was baptised in The Hague by my uncle, the Bishop of Szombathely, a Hungarian town near the Austrian border. When he arrived, he was accompanied by Janos Wettstein, my mother's lover who was the Chargé d'Affaires from the Hungarian Legation at The Hague.

With little or no contact with his parents, brother and sisters, the objects of Heini's affections were limited to his nanny, school friends and the house at Scheveningen:

> On the ground floor were the living room, the dining room and the kitchen. The first flight of stairs went up to my parents' and sister's bedrooms, and on the second floor there were my bedroom and that of my nanny. There was also a gallery full of flowers protected by glass like a conservatory. The playroom was in the basement, with a wonderful electric train set. One of my childhood weaknesses. At the back of the house were a tennis court and a garden, where I could satisfy another of my childhood hobbies, climbing trees. I think I climbed all the trees in that garden, either as a pastime or to overcome my fits of temper by hiding from others. You couldn't see the sea from my bedroom but the nearby

Heini's beloved governess Edda Volz striking a pose with the aid of a world-weary donkey.

The self-indulgent Baron Heinrich Thyssen-Bornemisza.   *Heini's favourite aunt Ilda, who did little to hide her unrequited love for his father.*

lighthouse transformed the room every night into an ideal place for dreaming. On foggy days, I could hear the sound of the horn which seemed to absorb all the normal sounds.

The brief moments when Heini's parents were present were usually the result of some social occasion: 'My first contact with high society came about through our nannies' curiosity. It was with them that I watched the arrival and departure of guests. I was fascinated by their clothes, the music and sound of the conversation. I usually fell asleep in my nanny's arms after I had finally tired of looking for my parents and following their progress through the party.'

Gradually he began to appreciate the importance of certain guests by using the reaction of the staff as a social barometer: 'These receptions were especially talked about when Queen Wilhelmina and her husband "Henry" attended. "Henry" was a close friend of my father and also knew the Duke of Windsor. I met the Duke myself in 1950. He was nice. On these occasions, the nannies didn't leave their observation posts until the Queen left.'

According to Heini's sister Gaby, who was five years his senior, the most talked about social event was the attendance of Adolf Hitler at one such dinner party, which would also be the first public evidence of their father's discreet association with the Nazis. It was partly as a result of such socialising that both the Nazi Party and the Dutch royal family would become clients of Heinrich's international banking services.

* * *

The social life at their house in The Hague became less active as Heinrich and Margit drifted further apart and her relationship with Janos Wettstein developed. Margit's sister, Aunt Ilda, remembered Heini's plight with particular sympathy:

> Heini was very frail as a child, very thin and not talkative. He loved to play with engines and mechanical toys, but I don't think that The Hague was a happy place for him. While his father, whom I liked very much, was busy fulfilling his many obligations and responsibilities, my sister went in for too many social distractions. The four children were not much considered, as selfishness prevailed, although appearances still had to be kept up. Little Heini must have felt this tragedy of his parents, and must have felt rather isolated with his nurse.[19]

Meanwhile, Heinrich would be quite prepared to profit from his wife's new relationship in order to maintain his questionable Hungarian nationality. Wettstein also assisted in obtaining freedom of passage documents from the Royal Hungarian legation for Heinrich travelling as a 'diplomatic courier'. Also acknowledged by the Swiss and the Czechoslovakian legations in The Hague, they enabled him to travel between Holland and Hungary, via Germany, Switzerland and Czechoslovakia with diplomatic immunity.

Towards the end of 1925, while his various banks and industrial holdings were left in the capable hands of his managers, Henrik Kouwenhoven in Holland and his brother-in-law Cornelis Lievense in New York, Heini's father was displaying a number of disturbing symptoms as a result of his increasing alcoholism. Letters to Margit are entitled 'Blue', 'Palace Hotel Fourth Dimension' and signed 'Henry Ghost'. The Palace appeared to be the hotel in St Moritz which he tried to convince Margit was some form of sanatorium: 'If you dance till late in the night, the fresher you feel the next morning [. . .] Even the champagne becomes a healthy tonic [. . .] My nerves have improved very much and I am thinking to leave my lofty whereabouts [. . .] The care is quite wonderful. [. . .] In four weeks' time, I will let you know more.'[20]

* * *

Heini with his parents, his sister Gaby and 'Old August' in the garden at Scheveningen.

Finally, on 4 April 1926, 'old' August, the legendary steel baron and co-creator of both the Thyssen and the Thyssen-Bornemisza family fortunes, returned to his maker. He was attended until the last, not by any of his children but by Jula Thyssen, his nephew Julius's wife. A distant relative, Franz Jungbluth, described the funeral:

> August Thyssen died aged eighty-three on Easter Day at Schloss Landsberg. A few days later hundreds of cars filled the Ruhr valley. On the hill up to the castle miners in their uniforms stood in rows, draped in black with their lamps lit. In the great hall of the castle stood the closed coffin, surrounded by flowers and candles; a sculpture by Auguste Rodin at its head. The Archbishop of Cologne appeared, consecrated the coffin and delivered an address about the deceased. The hearse waited in the castle's yard, drawn by four black horses which were draped with black sheets and wore black plumes on their heads.
>
> Behind the coach walked a solitary figure in a frock coat and a top hat; this was the coachman who had always driven him for August Thyssen had never personally owned a car. Then followed the three sons, Fritz Thyssen, August Thyssen Junior, and Baron Heinrich Thyssen, behind them the grandson Stephan with his guardian, then a column of further nephews and cousins and then an endless column of managers, workers and unrelated

industrialists. It went to the cemetery in Kettwig, where the coffin was once again consecrated by the local priest and, following the wishes of the deceased, given over to the earth.

1 *Daily Mail* report quoted in *New York Times*, 21 October 1916.
2 de Kaszón, pp. 11 ff. Also author's interviews with Baroness Gabrielle Bentinck-Thyssen, 1995–98.
3 Interrogation of Fritz Thyssen by Ralph S. Spritzer of US Military Intelligence, dated 21 June 1947 (National Archives, Washington, DC).
4 Report of the Office of Military Government for Germany (US), Property Control & External Assets Branch, Wiesbaden, 7 May 1948 (ibid).
5 Uebbing, p. 27.
6 Extract from unidentified book (Bentinck Archives).
7 Fear, p. 261.
8 The correspondence between August Thyssen Senior and his sons is held at the TBG Archives in Monte Carlo as well as at the ThyssenKrupp AG Archives in Duisburg.
9 Letter from August Senior to Heinrich, dated 21 July 1923.
10 Letter dated 30 July 1923.
11 Schneider, p. 7.
12 Wessel, p. 208.
13 Ibid.
14 Letter from August Senior to Heinrich, dated 6 June 1923.
15 Among the companies were Holland American Trading Corporation and Holland American Investment Corporation, established on 8 July 1926.
16 Author's correspondence with Jason Cox and Peter Rose at Goldman Sachs in New York, 1996–97.
17 *Manchester Guardian*, 2 June 1925.
18 Letter from August Senior to Heinrich, dated 26 September 1925.
19 Memoirs of Princess Matilde Sapieha-Bornemisza (Bentinck Archives).
20 Letters dated between February and October 1925 (TBG Archives).

Chapter IV

1926–1939

Financing Hitler ... Re-arming the Reich

He who pays the piper calls the tune.
Proverb

The unfortunate thing about death, for those not directly involved, is that it so often brings out the worst in people, when the dignity of grief is replaced by the ugliness of greed. The money 'old' August had intended to leave to his secret lady friend Maria Fromen to enable her to secure a controlling interest in her company, provoked an angry letter from Fritz to Heinrich: 'The matter is very unfortunate and will be detrimental to the memory of our father, if it gets out. As things stand, it is impossible to continue with this; the only thing that's left to do is to bury it somehow, without creating too much news.'[1]

What was particularly unpleasant about the brothers' attitude was that they saw fit to blame someone else for their gross lack of generosity:

> As far as Schloss Landsberg Foundation is concerned, you know already that I have told Dr Härle that I cannot talk to him directly as an executor of father's testament, as I am highly critical of his behaviour during the creation of this testament. I really don't think that our father, if he had still been master of his mind, would have left most of his estate to the Rheingau Canned Foods Factory.[2]

Somehow, Fritz and Heinrich managed to overrule their father's wishes so that Maria Fromen failed to receive August's bequest and as a result her company went bankrupt in 1929 leaving her penniless. There is no record of either Heinrich or Fritz having compensated her for her exclusion from the will. Maria Fromen would not be the only victim of Thyssen lack of consideration. According to subsequent reports, August's loyal old housekeeper was left nothing and, rather than face destitution, threw herself into the Rhine.

They also went against the old man's wishes concerning his 'simple' burial at Kettwig churchyard and soon commissioned an extremely lavish mausoleum in the grounds of Landsberg Castle where he was moved five years later and members of the family, including his despised son Fritz, were later buried next to him.

* * *

Meanwhile it was difficult even for those very close to the old man to tell exactly how much he had been worth; a situation not helped by the fact that he instructed that all his papers should be destroyed after his death. Although he was undoubtedly one of the richest men in the world, most of his wealth had been invested in the Konzern.

On 1 April 1926, shortly before August died, six German steel companies including the Thyssen Group had combined to form the Vereinigte Stahlwerke AG (VSt) or United Steelworks. It was founded with a starting capital of RM60,000, later increased to RM800 million. American banks such as the Chase, Chemical Bank, National City Bank, J. Henry Schroeder and Dillon Read played a large part in financing such an ambitious project. Later they would prove unwilling to admit their involvement in supporting what was to become such a major part of the Third Reich's war machine.

Worldwide, the United Steelworks was now the second largest national coal and steel company after the US Steel Corporation. An American investment prospectus announced: 'The Thyssen works are the core of the Steel Trust. If one wanted to rebuild them from scratch, one would need a capital of 256 million dollars or 1 billion Marks.'

That did not include the Thyssens' coal mines, which an American expert claimed to be the biggest of their kind in private hands in the world. The Steel Trust employed 200,000 workers and was the second largest private organisation in Germany after IG Farben. It was inevitable that it would assume the political status of a major power bloc and that Fritz Thyssen, in his position as president of the supervisory board, representing a controlling stake of 26 per cent, should acquire a dangerously powerful political position.

During the Weimar period, VSt assumed a reactionary role, opposing any economic steps taken by the Republican government that were inconvenient to heavy industry, by threatening the dismissal of thousands of workers. The complex was also able to exert considerable pressure on its work-force due to its ownership of some 67,000 workers' dwellings.[3]

The United Steelworks played an important part in the political events that brought National Socialism to power in Germany and would subsequently be accused by the Allies of 'consistently giving their full financial support to the militarily-minded National Socialist Party.'[4]

Although Heini liked to claim that the setting up of the United Steelworks signalled the end of any co-operation between Fritz and his father, there were still many areas where ties between the brothers remained. When Heinrich sold his brother his share of the companies which were to be taken into the Steel Trust, he did so in exchange for RM55 million worth of United Steelworks equity. In return, Fritz retained Florins 750,000 shares in BVHS. Their cousins also remained connected to the Steel Trust via Fritz, whose holdings were divided with 60 per cent for himself, while the brothers Hans and Julius, held 20 per cent each. Despite his reported illness, Hans was also voted on to the supervisory board of the Trust.

While Heinrich much preferred the more gentlemanly pursuit of banking than the grime and toil of heavy industry, he wisely chose to follow his late father's advice to 'retain an interest in coal, a treasure of incalculable worth', and constructed a new coal mine at Walsum. The mine was situated north of Hamborn on the Rhine, in the immediate neighbourhood of Thyssen Gas and Waterworks, free from any ties with the United Steelworks and the coal syndicate. Heinrich's investment in the mine was a fortunate decision for future generations of the Thyssen-Bornemisza family.

Meanwhile, it would remain difficult to establish exactly who owned what, partly because of the size and complexity of the Konzern and partly because that was the way the brothers liked it.

Some years later, an official, simplified explanation of the brothers' separate organisations would start with:

> On the one hand there was Fritz Thyssen's partnership in the United Steelworks, into which he had incorporated the Friedrich Thyssen coal-mining division and the August Thyssen Hütte steel division. On the other hand there was the private concern of Baron Heinrich Thyssen-Bornemisza, comprising the following companies: Oberbilker Steelworks AG, Press- and Rolling-Works Reisholz AG, Bremer Vulkan Shipyard, Flensburger Ship-building Company, the August Thyssen Bank, the Thyssen Gas and Water Works, with the coal mine at Walsum as a division, a limestone quarry east of Berlin with a majority shareholding in a cement works and various coal fields. Finally the Bank voor Handel en Scheepvaart, which in turn held the shares of various Dutch shipping lines and trading companies.[5]

* * *

Having allowed a suitably respectful period of time to elapse since the demise of 'old' August, the Baroness Margit and the Baron Heinrich Thyssen-Bornemisza finally agreed not to a divorce, as would have been expected, but to a separation. It would be another six years before their divorce was finalised. The effect upon their children was negligible, as they would see little less of their parents in the future than they had in the past. Only the ten-year-old Gaby would experience any change in her situation as she spent an increasing amount of time travelling with her father. But Heinrich's devotion to Gaby transcended the accepted level of paternal affection and there appeared to be something deeply unnatural about the intimacy of their relationship.

Presumably in anticipation of his relocation and ignoring the fact that inheritance trusts are not recognised in Switzerland, in 1926 Heinrich asked Director Kouwenhoven to set up the Kaszony Family Foundation in the Swiss canton of Schwyz. The foundation's purpose was to safeguard and maintain the family fortune while minimising Heinrich's exposure to tax and exchange control. While he continued to use his Dutch bank as his holding company, there was little evidence to suggest that Heinrich spent much time in Holland and even less at his various industrial concerns. He was the antithesis of his father; rarely visiting any of his industrial sites personally, relying on his executives for all personal contact. This low-profile style of operation was the opposite of his brother's and suited both the style and content of his business practices and associates. He was more than happy that Fritz's high-profile behaviour attracted so much attention and kept the spotlight well away from his own activities.

Meanwhile, only August Junior possessed the courage and creative appreciation really to indulge his inheritance and immerse himself in the true, decadent spirit of the Weimar Republic. But while Junior revelled in the seedy adventure of Isherwood's Berlin, he also enjoyed

Heinrich travelling alone with his 'Dearest Darling Baby' Gabrielle in 1930.

Stephan (centre) and Prince Ruspoli (right) admiring August Junior's (left) new Hispano-Suiza.

a life of ultimate extravagance. He still stayed at the Adlon Hotel and bought his suits from Luttmann. His Cartier cigarette cases, Tonnel visiting cards, Leinen-Peuch shirts, cravats and silk underwear all came from Paris, while his Hispano-Suiza came from a dealership in Biarritz. But regardless of his inheritance and his various financial safeguards, Junior appeared quite incapable of living without debt and remained constantly pursued by people to whom he owed money.

It was inevitable that a close friendship would develop between Stephan and his favourite Uncle August. Despite their age difference, they shared considerably greater intellectual ability than either Heinrich or Fritz, while August Junior also retained sufficient wealth to contribute to his nephew's adventures. Unfortunately, they also shared a propensity for disaster and, eventually, tragedy.

In the mid-1920s, Stephan managed to get his father to allow him to study in America, where he had obtained places at Harvard University and the Massachusetts Institute of Technology. Much to the amusement of his uncle August, he also managed to fall in love with and marry an eighteen-year-old Texan girl. It took his furious father three years, countless lawyers and even his customary Hungarian diplomatic assistance to get the marriage dissolved.

Meanwhile, August Junior found a somewhat less taxing means of amusing himself. In 1927, Alfred Hugenberg, the extreme right-wing media baron, had invested in UFA, the legendary movie company, which he intended to use as a tool for political propaganda. Hugenberg, who would later serve in Hitler's first cabinet, persuaded his friend Fritz Thyssen to invest in and serve on the supervisory board of the film company. August Junior was quite used to being confused with his father or brothers and usually found it to be of little advantage other than to extend his credit, but the chance of visiting America as a movie mogul was too great an opportunity to miss and he was soon the toast of New York.

He received an even warmer welcome in Los Angeles, where he and his travelling companions, Count Oppersdorff and Prince Ruspoli of Italy, discovered just how many attractive young American actresses were willing to be extremely hospitable in return for the chance to be considered for parts in German movies. When Fritz was informed of his brother's behaviour, he was livid and immediately contacted the film company's New York office and ordered them to inform the press of his brother's deception. But the press found their new German movie mogul's exploits far more entertaining and newsworthy than Fritz's denial and never ran the story.

* * *

Fritz was doing little to assist his own political role in Europe. Having been forced to resign by his fellow industrialists from the Franco-German Conciliation Committee due to his arrogant behaviour, he continued to make unpopular statements: 'France seems to think that they can keep Germany down on its knees while they arm themselves up to their eyeballs.'[6]

Meanwhile, the *Frankfurter Zeitung*, wrote: 'This paper, in turn, cannot agree that Mr Thyssen's resignation is such a big thing. We know this man and know that one can be sure that he will commit a faux pas each time he comes out of his cosy industrial field and gets into the public arena. He would be well advised to stay out of such public matters in the first place.'

Fritz's arrogance would prove equally unproductive in his dealings with the tax authorities. They had accused the Konzern of not paying taxes between the various companies during the period from 1924 to 1928. The Thyssens claimed the transactions in question were internal transfers and won their case. Then, the authorities started to investigate the foreign ownership of the Konzern and accused the Thyssens of keeping disorderly company records. Although they still failed to convict them of any offence, the tax authorities sensed something was amiss, particularly in the case of Fritz, and decided to continue their long-term investigations until they had sufficient evidence to bring an action.[7] It was an investigation that would last for twelve years, terminate his political ambitions and have a profound effect on his life and that of his family.

Meanwhile, the Thyssen brothers continued to develop their political sympathies on a visit to Italy in February 1927, which was reported in the *Frankfurter Zeitung*: 'The well-known industrialist Fritz Thyssen has gone to Italy accompanied by his brother [Heinrich], following an invitation by Mussolini.'

It would be one of the few occasions when the intensely private Heinrich would reveal his political sympathies in a public display of his acceptance of a fascist dictatorship. Later the same year, Heinrich bought the Bank von der Heydt which was situated at Behrenstrasse 8, close to the Reichstag in Berlin, while Fritz extended their South American interests by founding the Thyssen Lametal company in Buenos Aires.

* * *

In 1928, in response to an attempt by the government to increase workers' wages and reduce working hours, the Ruhrmeisters denounced the government for squandering the Dawes Plan reparation loan on social luxuries and responded by locking out 225,000 workers for four weeks. Americans also began to panic about their own economy as share prices soared. Even Great Britain, until 1925 the richest country in the world, had 10 million working-men living in conditions of abject poverty. The Thyssen family, however, continued to live by a different set of rules and fortune. They increased the capital of the August Thyssen Bank from RM 500,000 to RM 16 million, while continuing to call it the Bank von der Heydt until 1930. The names of Fritz and Heinrich remained absent from the board. Only Hans Thyssen was voted on to the supervisory board where he remained until 1941, continuing to negotiate American loans.

Heini always claimed that in 1928 his father had predicted the Second World War. He said he had explained there was this madman called Hitler, whom his Uncle Fritz was already involved with, who would be responsible for the war, and that they would have to move, as Holland would no longer be neutral. He thought they might move to Switzerland. While it was highly unlikely that he would have bothered to explain such a thing to a seven-year-old child, the plan sounded plausible as Heinrich was already spending an increasing amount of time vacationing in various Swiss resorts and his friend Eduard von der Heydt had recently invested in the palatial Villa Monte Verità in Ascona.

Fritz and Amélie had also begun to spend time in Switzerland, though for less pleasurable reasons. Their daughter Anita, an attractive girl who was still only nineteen years old, had contracted polio and spent long periods of time recovering in a sanatorium in Leysin.

* * *

This period heralded the commencement of Eduard's encouragement of Heinrich's art collecting. Eduard was a cultured man who had been collecting since his youth and was aware that due to the state of both the German and subsequently the US economy, there were many formerly wealthy people, particularly Jews, who were desperate to sell their art treasures. With Heinrich's susceptibility to his influence, von der Heydt also appreciated the commission he could make in encouraging his friend's investment.

Despite his father's fascination for the work of Rodin, Heinrich had inherited little aesthetic appreciation, nor had he ever displayed any great interest for cultural activities in general. He appeared unaware or unappreciative of the Weimar 'renaissance' and the Bauhaus school of architecture and design under Walter Gropius and Ludwig Mies van der Rohe; or of the theatre of Max Reinhardt; the writing of Thomas Mann; the movies of Fritz Lang; of painters such as Paul Klee and Wassily Kandinsky, and particularly the Expressionists such as George Grosz, Max Beckmann and Otto Dix, arguably Germany's most important twentieth-century artistic movement. Culturally, it was a very exciting time to be in Germany, but Heinrich considered himself more of a sporting man. He did, however, appreciate the investment potential of buying on a falling market and the social advantages of being considered an art collector.

First Eduard introduced him to his dealer, Rudolf Heinemann, a young German Jew from Munich who worked in an art gallery but would eventually become the creator of Heinrich's collection. Then, in order to give him some semblance of knowledge, Eduard also introduced Heinrich to the art historians Bernard Berenson and Max Friedländer. They were a formidable team, although the former introduction was a somewhat double-edged sword, as it had been Berenson who had financed a school for forgers and invented the 'art' of cataloguing or the creation of provenance. He introduced such phrases as 'the work of an anonymous German master', 'attributed to' and 'from the studio of'.

Unfortunately, the temptation to off-load extremely suspect paintings on a man with more money than knowledge appears to have been too great for his various advisers and dealers. Heinrich Thyssen-Bornemisza was soon the proud owner of a generally appalling collection of largely over-restored paintings, many of which suffered from questionable provenance and very few of which were masterpieces. Fortunately, the value of a few would more than compensate for the many which, in his son's opinion, would have satisfied his father: 'My father only collected art as an investment and a way of moving money.'

There was certainly no evidence to suggest that Heinrich ever considered his 'lack-lustre' collection to form the basis of what was to become one of the world's best known private art collections. Nor that it would honour his contrived family name with a far greater degree of immortality than that resulting from their industrial or banking activities. To finance his collection, Heinrich raised a loan through BVHS, using various financial instruments to cloak the ownership of the paintings, thus avoiding tax as well as foreign exchange controls.

To avoid being accused of taking advantage of the devastating financial suffering of the time, including that resulting from the increasing persecution of Jews, Heinrich and subsequently his son wanted people to believe that he had started to become involved with art when he moved to Hungary in 1906 and therefore called it the Schloss Rohoncz Collection. In fact, he did not start buying pictures until some ten years after he had ceased to live in the castle. Apart from one or two paintings, which he hung on the walls of his suite at the Adlon Hotel in Berlin and a few in his house in The Hague, the paintings were left in storage at the various points of purchase.

The first painting listed in the Thyssen-Bornemisza archive was purchased in 1928, not 1906 as Heini would later insist. It was a landscape painted in 1635 by Jan Lievens, a friend of Rembrandt, and entitled 'Rest on the Flight into Egypt'. Its provenance failed to explain who might have owned it between 1635 and 1928. Subsequent purchases by the Baron would continue to be noteworthy for their lack of provenance.

The 'experts' may have established the title and date of 'The Madonna and Nursing Child' painted in 1525, but they honoured the artist with no more specific identity than 'Anonymous Netherlandish Master'. The same could be said of 'Portrait of a Woman', which was listed as having been painted in 1480 by an 'Anonymous German Master'. What is perhaps more surprising is that such inconsequential pictures remained in Heinrich's collection until two generations later, when they were accepted as part of the Thyssen-Bornemisza Collection in Madrid.

* * *

By 1928 Fritz was beginning to feel increasingly politically frustrated. Italy, Portugal and Spain were already in the hands of right-wing dictators, while Germany had striking workers, a collapsing economy and communists rioting on the streets of Berlin. When, at the behest of Emil Kirdorf, Rudolf Hess approached Fritz, he readily agreed to assist in the financing of the Brown House, the new Nazi headquarters in Munich.

Although it is doubtful that he ever expected to be repaid, Fritz offered to act as guarantor for a RM350,000 loan. As the loan was made through the discreet financial channels of the family's Dutch bank, few people would have been aware of his contribution. Although Fritz's account was anonymously coded 'QQ1', his brother would certainly have been aware of any such arrangement. There was no evidence of any objection on the part of Heinrich or indeed Albert Vögler, the right-wing director general of the United Steelworks, who was at that time on the supervisory board of BVHS. So it was that Fritz became one of the Party's principal financial supporters.

Fritz's next financial assistance, or the one he admitted to, had less to do with the Party and more to do with Hermann Göring's personal self-aggrandisement. Göring lived in a very small apartment in those days and, according to Fritz, 'he was anxious to enlarge it in order to cut a better figure. I paid the cost of this improvement.'[8] This gift consisted of three payments of RM 50,000 each.

The initial meeting and the contributions heralded the start of a long and close relationship with Göring, a relationship that contributed to the survival of both Fritz and his family. It was also due to the Reichsmarschall that the structure of the United Steelworks and the Thyssens' controlling interest would survive the war. Göring also got on well with Heinrich, with whom he shared an enthusiasm for horseracing, and, along with the President of the Reichsbank Walther Funk and the German counter-intelligence division or Abwehr, became a major customer of the August Thyssen Bank.

Although they supported the Nazi Party, the brothers' commitment to the ideology of Nazism was less powerful than their devotion to self-interest. This was evident in Fritz's movement of his capital offshore at the same time that he was investing in the Nazi Party. As they became increasingly privy to the Nazi Party's intentions, the Thyssens realised that the Netherlands, where they held most of their securities, would provide insufficient protection. While Heinrich moved funds and securities into his Swiss foundation 'Kaszony', Fritz was slower in relocating his capital to his Swiss foundation 'Familien-Interessen AG' (Faminta) in which he placed RM 35 million of his Dutch equity in 1929.[9]

In view of his 'Hungarian nationality' these kind of defensive financial logistics were not a major problem for Heinrich, but for a German national like Fritz it was far more dangerous and attracted the attention of Mr Jansen, a tax inspector and Mr Brill, a foreign exchange controller. However, they were constantly frustrated by his reluctance to supply them with the necessary

The August Thyssen Bank in Berlin which was used by Göring and the Nazi party before its destruction during the Second World War.

details. Brill later pointed out that the investigation proved conclusively that Fritz Thyssen was cloaking his foreign capital and that he created the Pelzer Foundation as yet another financial instrument in Switzerland when matters grew too risky for him in Germany.[10]

However, his movement of capital exposed him to other dangers. When Friedrich Flick started to buy shares in steel trust companies, Fritz Thyssen found himself with insufficient funds in Germany to stop Flick becoming the largest shareholder in the United Steelworks. But worse was to come. Flick's financial position was not strong enough to withstand the worsening financial crisis and he in turn was forced to sell his shares to the government, giving the state the controlling interest in the Steel Trust.

In three years, Fritz had in effect taken the Konzern to within an inch of nationalisation and 'old' August's worst nightmare. This created another incentive for Fritz to assist Hitler's claim to the chancellorship, as there was little chance of the then Reich Chancellor Heinrich Brüning and his Minister of Finance, Dr Hermann Dietrich, selling him back the government's controlling interest in the United Steelworks. Hitler and Göring, on the other hand, intimated that they would reward his support by doing so.[11]

* * *

Events on Wall Street on 24 October 1929, when the American stock market collapsed and the Great Depression began, did not have a particularly detrimental effect on either the Thyssens or the Thyssen-Bornemiszas. In fact, both Heinrich and Eduard von der Heydt profited from the collapse, as suicidal Americans in search of cash were forced to sell pictures. Between 1929 and 1933 the Russians were also selling art as a means of propping up their economy.

Heinrich's most active periods of acquisition were between 1928 and 1930, when he bought some 187 works and from 1931 to 1938, when he purchased 87. The latter period coincides with Hitler's ascension to power, the escalating persecution of the Jews and the appropriation of their assets. Heinrich's investments were not limited to painting. Carpets, furniture and other objets d'art were also included in his sights. Accompanied by Heinemann, Heinrich attended auctions for dissolved Jewish collections, such as the one organised in Berlin by Ball & Graupe in March 1931 for the collection of Erich von Goldschmidt-Rothschild.

Meanwhile Heini remained happily ensconced in Holland while his brother Stephan was studying in America, Gaby continued her travels with her father and Louise Bornemisza-Price was organising a suitable match for Heini's elder sister Margit. For four years they lived together at Prinz Eugen Strasse 68 in Vienna, before the twenty-one-year-old Margit's marriage to the appropriately handsome Hungarian aristocrat, Count Ivan Batthyány de Németújvár on 17 June 1933.

Louise Bornemisza continued to organise the social elevation of the family by introducing the Hungarian Count Gabor Zichy de Zich et Vásonkeö to Anita, the daughter of Fritz and Amélie, whom he married in 1936. The Count could hardly be described as 'dashing' and was known in the family as 'Piggy Zichy' but he was capable of siring two sons, who, while accepting the inheritance of his title, would assume their position in the Thyssen dynasty and the fortune that went with it.

* * *

Heini continued to share the house in Scheveningen with the cook, butler, driver and gardener who became his surrogate family: 'The cook was a Russian lady and her meals were very heavy, nothing exotic. The driver had a huge moustache and he later married Countess Bentinck and became a relative of my sister.'

Being deprived of his parents, Heini formed a particularly close relationship with his governess Edda Volz. This was hardly surprising as she became his adopted mother and looked after him from birth until he left home at the age of eighteen: 'She was born in Ulm and was hired during my mother's pregnancy. She had a strong personality but was also very generous and warm-hearted. Not too tall or pretty, she didn't wear a uniform and enjoyed dressing up to go out for walks with me.'

Heini was also fortunate in enjoying the small German school, the Deutsches Realgymnasium, in The Hague, which he started to attend on a regular basis when still only four years of age.

'It had a nice atmosphere and I liked my classmates. Because many of the

Chauffeur Buijnk, who would later marry into the Bentinck family, with Heini, Nanny Volz and Gaby in their father's Daimler Benz.

children came from diplomatic families, there were various nationalities and in the beginning there were about twenty pupils to a class but later, with the introduction of racist measures, we ended up with six to a class.'

Heini admitted that, in the early days, he found the discipline of school life valuable in taking his mind off his family's absence:

> I used to get up early in the morning and go to school. Then I would return for lunch and leave again for school in the afternoon. Usually, I cycled, apart from the time following the kidnapping and murder of the Lindbergh baby when all the parents became paranoid. During that time, the driver took me to school in a huge black Hispano-Suiza (later understood to have been a Daimler Benz), which I hated. I felt very self-conscious sitting there all alone in that enormous car. Fortunately, it didn't last too long and I could go back to peddling my regular twenty-minute journeys four times a day.
>
> I remember when the bicycle became too small for me, I wrote to my father at the Adlon Hotel in Berlin and asked him for a new one. He refused and said: 'Why do you only write to me when you need something?' I think the staff bought it for me in the end. I never had the feeling of being a wealthy child and I have always appreciated the value of money. My father, who gave me a very modest monthly allowance, probably instilled that in me. With it I started a stamp collection.

It was at this point in his life that Heini met a girl who was to become his first love and lifelong friend. A beautiful linnet of a girl, Hannelore Schmidt was nicknamed Pusch. It was an endearment that failed to reflect her strength and energy. Pusch loved her father and inherited his life-long passion for racing cars but unfortunately he spent all his own and then all his wife's money, on Bugattis, which eventually led to her divorcing him: 'During the divorce they decided to send me away, so that I wouldn't be traumatised. My parents were friends with Leni Riefenstahl and she suggested they send me to Forte dei Marmi in Italy for the summer.'[12]

It was a suggestion for which Pusch was eternally grateful to Riefenstahl, particularly when it became a regular feature of her life: 'Every year, between May and October, I would go and stay in Italy. Meanwhile, in 1928, my mother went on to marry Baron van Linden whom she had met in Wiesbaden. Together, they moved to The Hague and that's where I met Heini at the Deutsches Realgymnasium.'

Having both been largely abandoned by their parents, a sympathetic bond quickly developed between the two children. Heini recalled:

> We always liked the coincidence that both our parents had divorced, or in my case separated, when we were six as it brought us closer together. Also, just like me, after Hitler came to power, Pusch had a little problem with the morning salute. One morning she still hadn't finished her banana before the teacher arrived and she said 'Heil Hitler' while still holding the banana! She had to write something on the lines of, 'You mustn't salute the Führer with a banana in your hand' a hundred times. When we had lunch together we often repeated the joke. We looked at each other and one of us would salute the other while still holding an apple or an orange or banana; anything edible.

*   *   *

While Hitler remained little more than an amusing distraction for Heini and his friends, Uncle Fritz continued to encourage and support the Nazi Party and Adolf Hitler's increasingly more violent election campaign. Fellow industrialists even claimed to have requested a severing of support for the Nazi Party in view of his tactics. They would later claim that Fritz Thyssen had been the only member of their group who financially supported Hitler. But during the period 1928–33, German industrialists distributed at least RM5 million of political donations and it was highly unlikely that some of these funds would not have gone to assist a political party that was promising to crush communism, stop the payment of reparations and re-arm their country.

Flourishing in a soil rich in financial and political discontent, Hitler's National Socialist Party came second in the 1930 German elections, increasing their representation in the Reichstag from 12 deputies to 107. There was uproar when the new deputies arrived at the opening of the Reichstag in September in Nazi uniform. However, this did not affect the Thyssen brothers' involvement; according to Heini, they hosted a celebratory dinner for Hitler at Schloss Landsberg the following month. There Hitler thanked them for their support and assured them of his.

* * *

While those affected by the international turmoil continued to sell their art collections, Rudolf Heinemann had little difficulty in encouraging Heinrich to increase his investment and further exploit the market. But regardless of his expenditure, the identity of many of the artists remained suspiciously vague. 'Landscape with Drinking Peasants' (c.1630) was only 'attributed' to Adriaen Brouwer. The somewhat grander title of 'Master' was regularly used to add importance to an anonymous artist's work as in 'Master of the Sala Capitolare Dell'Abbazia di Pomposa', who apparently created 'The Crucifixion' in 1320 – a painting whose only provenance was that it surfaced in a Viennese private collection in 1924.

In other cases, the artist's identity appeared to be more specific than the identity of the painting. Three El Grecos were purchased in surprisingly rapid succession in 1930: 'Mater Dolorosa', followed by 'Christ with the Cross', while 'The Immaculate Conception' surfaced in Budapest. Seventy years later, investigations concerning the authenticity of yet another 'Mater Dolorosa' inherited by Gaby revealed the existence of five versions of the same painting. Predictably, Heini would later claim he owned the original.[13]

Meanwhile, some paintings continued to create endless and expensive confusion. While Heinrich was delighted with his Rubens, 'Saint Michael Overthrowing Lucifer and the Rebellious Angels', he was less so when it was later attributed to the 'artist's workshop'. Many years later Heini redressed the painting's reputation by having it re-attributed to Rubens.

But the most amusing acquisition that his father made during his frenzied collection creation was also one of its few genuine old masters. When he had heard that Goudstikker of Amsterdam had obtained a Rembrandt from a private Russian collection, he immediately agreed to buy the work 'sight unseen'. What had inspired Rembrandt to paint such a picture is a great deal more difficult to imagine than Heinrich's reaction when he realised that he had invested his money in a picture of a fat naked cherub entitled 'Cupid Blowing a Soap Bubble.' When he first saw the picture, he described it as 'effeminate, romantic nonsense', but, regardless of the subject matter, there was never any doubt as to its authenticity.[14]

In 1933, Heinrich bought his second Rembrandt, 'Tobias and His Wife', from the same Dutch dealer for Dfl 17,500. On his death, like the 'Cupid', it was inherited by his beloved 'Baby' who, in a rash moment, agreed to sell it to the Rijksmuseum in Amsterdam for $1.5 million. When in 1979 it became obvious that the painting was worth considerably more, the museum's curator Simon Levie had to apply considerable pressure to persuade Gaby to fulfil her promise.

The fact that the two most authentic Rembrandts in the Thyssen Collection should have both been sold without him being given the opportunity of acquisition would be a source of considerable frustration to Heini, since his retained works by the artist remained a source of persistent criticism.

* * *

By 1930, Heinrich had acquired a collection of some 187 pictures and was persuaded to hold an exhibition. For a man who had always appeared so determined to avoid public scrutiny, it seemed a strange decision and Munich, Hitler's power base, an even stranger choice of venue. But Munich would certainly have been safe from the predictable communist reaction to such extravagance, at a time when many people were having difficulty feeding their families, let alone appreciating Baron Thyssen-Bornemisza's art collection.

It was Heinemann who suggested that a major exhibition of the pictures at the Munich Neue Pinakothek would assist in authenticating them. He realized that the respect for the name Thyssen in Germany and the cultural reputation of Munich would encourage a more positive reaction from both the local and international press, than in Switzerland. Then, having convinced the public that he was a serious, knowledgeable collector, the Baron announced his intention to loan his collection to the people of Düsseldorf for twenty years. The aim was to convince the public that his collecting was an act of philanthropy and that he was saving the pictures for the German nation.

The *Sonntagspost* newspaper gave the normally secretive Baron a sympathetic hearing in which he illustrated his lack of respect for the truth by claiming: 'I relied on my own taste and always made the purchases personally without a scholarly adviser.'

Apparently the only assistance he received was from the Pinakothek:

It often happened, for example, that I saw a masterpiece that I liked, but whose quality I could only assess by getting on the train and hurrying to the Pinakothek in Munich with the impression of the picture in my mind, in order to study and compare an acknowledged work of the highest quality by the same painter. Not until I was convinced that the painting I wished to acquire was of the same, or close to the same quality as the museum picture did I make the decision to purchase.

Finally, he struck an altruistic attitude: 'Although the pleasure of collecting is something very personal, I well understand the unwritten law that obliges one to make first-rate examples of past periods of art available to the public.'[15]

After the show, which lasted for six months, the *Mittag* newspaper of Düsseldorf carried an article which gave the impression that the town was expecting to be chosen as the new home for the collection: 'Baron Thyssen wants his collection to be maintained permanently for the benefit of the public at large and from the start he has envisaged the town of Düsseldorf as a location, for obvious reasons, because this is the base of his industrial empire.'[16]

Presumably they had forgotten that Heinrich Thyssen was now a Hungarian Baron.

The naivety of the paper was quite touching as they continued to celebrate their forthcoming good fortune and the Baron's generosity: 'Fortunately, we are able to inform you that the loan of these pictures over twenty years, temporarily agreed, would not have any financial disadvantages for Düsseldorf, so that the joy to the town, to have its wish come true, especially in these times, is doubly understandable. It's almost as if a miracle were happening.'

As other towns heard of the Baron's indecision concerning the future location, they in turn approached him and asked to be considered. On being informed that they would be considered, the local newspapers proceeded to write reviews of the collector and his collection, each one more glowing than its predecessor. It was an extremely effective means of obtaining press coverage and one that Heini would use again when he was brokering a deal with the Kingdom of Spain sixty years later.

But not all the critics were convinced the collection was worthy of museum status, while Heinrich found it impossible to accept the inevitable criticism of his collection. Even the title of the exhibition was criticised and in a letter to his wife Margit from the Grand Hotel in Lucerne, he wrote: 'People make so many difficulties. They are angry that "Schloss Rohoncz" is better known than their socialist "Rechnitz". With the exhibition, I have a lot of bother. Every day I get letters and articles and not all of them are favourable.'[17]

Heinemann's art-dealing friends were also extremely concerned, as Heinrich began to consider moving his investments into something less subject to critical analysis, and feared that they might be in danger of losing a major client. They appeared to come to the conclusion that, if they were to save their reputations and a rich source of revenue, it was time to enhance the collection with some higher quality paintings.

But Eduard von der Heydt, the man responsible for introducing him to the art business, who also wished to continue receiving commissions on Heinrich's art investments, had a secret weapon. Her name was Maud Feller and the time had come to introduce her to Baron Heinrich Thyssen-Bornemisza. Young, athletic, blonde and beautiful she was built for the jazz age. Sexy and extrovert she was the toast of Berlin where she worked for a small art gallery and was known to be capable of selling a man a blank canvas for the price of a Bugatti.

Born Else Zarske, in Thorn, East Prussia, she was the illegitimate child of Minna Zarske. Grandmother, mother and daughter had moved together to Berlin. There they were joined by Sergeant Feller whose name Maud adopted, becoming: 'The beautiful butterfly Ilse Maud Feller. One of the most beautiful and elegant women of Berlin.'[18]

Art was not the only thing Eduard wanted to sell Heinrich. He also had a good friend, Prince Leopold of Prussia, who was suffering from severe financial difficulties and needed to sell his house, the Villa Favorita on Lake Lugano in Switzerland.

* * *

Heinrich's short temper, which was not improved by his excessive drinking, may have contributed to his constant badgering of his eldest son Stephan. Having made little secret of his dislike for the boy, Heinrich spitefully interrupted his studies in America and demanded his return to Hungary to take part in military service.

Perhaps he wanted to use Stephan's military service as a further confirmation of his family's Hungarian status. If that was the reason, it was an act of extreme selfishness that would lead to tragedy. Stephan's acquiescence to his father's wishes is clear from a letter he wrote to Heinrich's lawyer, Dr Fritz Jacke, while still studying at Washington University: 'I am happy to join the Hungarian army to serve my country and obey my father's wishes. Please tell me ASAP when I can come, as I have to inform the immigration authorities here well in time.'[19]

In a letter from the Grand Hotel in Lucerne, Heinrich also saw fit to explain to Margit the conditions he intended to impose on Stephan to minimise his chances of enjoying life on his return to Europe:

He is not allowed to live in Rohoncz as before. When you are with him alone, he may go out shooting with Szera only for sport and his health, but not if there are guests there. Should I hear that he is treated differently by you or he does it himself, I should not allow Stephan to come to Rohoncz anymore. I shall not invite him to return until I am convinced that he gets on in the right way.

Heinrich apparently thought this 'improvement' would take many years: 'Until now I have not got the impression that he has improved at all. He can't bluff me anymore. He did it enough before. I want to make it clear that I will only allow his presence in Rohoncz now that he is, with your help, getting into the army.'

*   *   *

On 30 December 1931, Margit and Heinrich signed a formal agreement to divorce. Negotiations for the agreement remained surprisingly cordial; both Margit and Heinrich even staying at the same Hotel Bristol in Vienna. It was soon agreed that Margit would retain ownership of Czaitha, a sub-estate of Rechnitz, and receive a yearly apanage of Dfl 24,000 regardless of her future marital status, a sum which would increase to Dfl 30,000 if Heinrich remarried. Margit was also given the right to reside at Rechnitz to the same extent she had done so far, while Heinrich accepted full financial responsibility for the children's education and their allowances.

Meanwhile, Stephan had arrived back from America and with the speed befitting a Thyssen had fallen in love with the beautiful, young Hungarian Baroness Marie Foerster. It was a match that bore all the hallmarks of a Louise Bornemisza introduction. But their mutual attraction was to be cruelly curtailed. A letter from his mother Margit to August Junior revealed the full horror of their tragic story:

> I went to see Stephan in the military hospital for the mentally ill where he was lying in a barred cell. He had been at his woman's bedside until she died. Then he lost control and was in such a state that four doctors had to take hold of him and strap him down onto a bed where he was calmed down using the strongest of injections. I will make sure that the legal procedures, which are unavoidable after such a death, will have a positive outcome, as indeed Stephan has been pronounced not guilty following the inquiry. Thanks to God it was not his pistol and he wasn't shooting. His poor bride had a

weakness for pistols and she took it with her on this trip. Her mother was also with them. After six bullets had been fired, one cartridge became stuck. As they were both handling the gun, it went off. The shot wound was not fatal. It went into the stomach and out the other side. The problem was that there was no doctor available as it was Easter Monday and so Stephan had to drive the poor girl himself sixty kilometres on bad roads to the hospital where she was operated on and died the next day.[20]

Margit also pointed out that despite sending several telegrams to Stephan's father, she had received no response. Heini displayed no greater respect for his brother by insisting the gun belonged to Stephan and that he had been responsible for the girl's death. He also spoke of his brother's next relationship and his 'surprisingly rapid' recovery for a sensitive young man who had undergone such a traumatic experience: 'When he was finally released, he started seeing Helena Kugler-Andrassy, known as Ilyana. She was very kind to him and they decided to get married on 24 May 1932 in Budapest. My father was very much against their marriage because she was a rather lowborn Hungarian who worked in a patisserie.'

Despite his disapproval, Heinrich awarded his son a surprisingly generous annual allowance of RM30,000.

*   *   *

In January 1931 a meeting took place between Fritz Thyssen, his friend and banker Hjalmar Schacht, Adolf Hitler and Joseph Goebbels in the Berlin apartment of Hermann Göring; the same apartment whose enlargement and improvements Fritz had paid for. Hitler, who arrived after dinner in full Nazi uniform, rather than become involved in a conventional conversation, further surprised all present by subjecting them to an impassioned speech. Goebbels wrote in his diary: 'Thyssen is of the old school. Great. A capitalist,

Stephan in Hungarian military uniform shortly before the shooting of his girlfriend.

but one can put up with business leaders like this. His wife is very nice and pleasant.'

The meeting took Schacht one step closer to becoming Hitler's Minister of Finance and Fritz and his fellow industrialists forged even closer links with the Nazi Party.

By January 1932, Fritz's enthusiasm had resulted in an invitation to Hitler to address the Industry Club at the Park Hotel in Düsseldorf. Having spent two-and-a-half hours promising the gathering anything that would gain their support in the campaign for his Party's supremacy and his position as Chancellor, the elite of Germany's industrialists reacted with 'frenetic, long-lasting applause'. Fritz's closing address included the phrase 'Heil, Herr Hitler' which created quite a stir.[21]

The *New York Times* reported his increasingly extreme opinions. Apparently, Fritz said he found sufficient reason for supporting Hitler in the fact that he had roused in the country a new spirit of nationalism that was essentially healthy and necessary and served as a bulwark against communism. He believed that the choice, not only for Germany but for Europe in general, lay between communism and fascism and he preferred fascism: 'I regard a fascist state as one that in a crisis will take the measures needed to bring order and then restore economic freedom when the crisis passes.'[22]

The day after his address to the Industry Club, Hitler was once again invited to Landsberg Castle as a guest of Heinrich and Fritz, who continued to contribute financially to the Party and eventually joined in 1933; surprisingly, two years after his wife Amélie.[23] Von der Heydt also became a Party member in 1933 while Fritz eventually succeeded in becoming a member of the Reichstag, a Prussian state councillor and a member of the German Economic Council, claiming it had been at Hitler's request, although it was far more likely to have been Göring's.

But Hitler's socio-political policies had not been the only ideas to attract Fritz's attention. That same year, 1932, Fritz was introduced to the teachings of the Viennese philosopher and sociologist Othmar Spann. This converted him to the concept of a corporate state with clearly divided classes. The Nazi Party pretended to be in agreement and commissioned him to set up an institute for 'corporatisation'. In fact, Hitler was deeply suspicious of Fritz's motives and after he came to power instructed the Gestapo to keep him under surveillance.[24]

* * *

Chapter IV: 1926–1939

Fritz's financial support and promotion of Hitler, his assumption of public office and membership of the Party were all obvious manifestations of his commitment to the Third Reich. But in the long term, Heinrich's less public involvement, at least commercially, if not socially or politically, would be far greater. However, this did not stop him creating a safety-net, in case the Führer's plans failed to fulfil his promises.

A part of this safety-net was the creation of yet another Swiss foundation; this time for the control of the ownership and inheritance of his art collection. Like many of his endeavours, it involved him personally in remarkably little effort.

Baron Eduard von der Heydt, Heinrich's mentor, with Eddi von Strunckhofen, a Nazi acquaintance (photo: Max Kluge, Berlin).

While Heinrich was busy divorcing one wife and gaining another, BVHS bank director Henrik Josef Kouwenhoven and solicitor Ede Homme Heida went to see the notary Albert Reichlin in the Swiss town of Schwyz again and set up the Rohoncz Family Foundation on 3 February 1931.

The foundation was to contain SwFr 50,000 plus ownership of all the paintings. The object was to protect the inheritance rights of the male heirs of the founder. It was also to keep the collection together and in the ownership of the Thyssen-Bornemisza family. The applicable law was to be Hungarian law. As long as the founder lived, he alone was to make all the decisions, including that of disinheritance. If an heir was to get married and set up his own household, he could get twenty-five pictures on loan to decorate his or her house. The duration of the foundation was to be 100 years. If sales were made, the mention 'From the Schloss Rohoncz Collection' was to be made.

* * *

Eduard von der Heydt's introduction of Heinrich to Maud Feller had been extremely successful. Maud had not only succeeded in encouraging Heinrich to start collecting again, but had also persuaded him to buy Villa Favorita and take

Maud Feller, the second Baroness Thyssen-Bornemisza and the toast of Berlin. (photo: Binder).

Chapter IV: 1926–1939

Villa Favorita, the Thyssens' Swiss refuge on the shores of Lake Lugano,

her as his bride. When they were married in Berlin in 1932, society columns announced her marriage with regret: 'Berlin society has lost the beautiful, witty and very much liked Maud Feller and with her one of the most precious personalities of the time.'

Villa Favorita was prepared for their arrival. According to Josi Groh, Maud's taste and style 'made Villa Favorita what it is now. She had a very good taste. She went to England to study and literally followed Heinrich around to encourage him to buy pictures.'

It was Maud's personal magnetism that persuaded men to believe she was so capable of affecting everything she touched with such style and glamour. As far as Villa Favorita was concerned, there was not a great deal of opportunity to change very much, apart from their private quarters, as Heinrich bought the villa with everything still in place. It is also unlikely that Maud had much interest in such an antique interior as, following their marriage, she would almost immediately start denigrating her new husband by referring to him as the 'fusty old museum director'.

Heini, who had already been introduced to and impressed by his new stepmother in Berlin, remembered the history of Favorita, the fake Renaissance-style villa, with academic precision:

My father bought it from Prince Leopold of Prussia for the equivalent of SwFr 3.8 million. He bought the Villa by selling one painting – a large Watteau, 'The Clown', which is now in the National Gallery in Washington.

Leopold had built the staircase and the wings on the right and left. My father added the gallery. He bought the villa furnished and decorated, complete with the English drawing room and the Gothic Hall. The Prince had 900 cypresses brought from Italy by train to line either side of the kilometre long drive. Nothing changed and the original contents remained in place: the paintings, curtains, settees, beds, armchairs, carpets and tapestries, silver and chandeliers, the piano, the sideboard, vases, dishes, linen, mirrors and clocks, a Fiat truck, an Isota Fraschini car, a library with 3,257 books, 68 vases in the garden, lovely animal sculptures, statues of warriors and goddesses, gnomes and a statue of Hercules and the Lion.

Heinrich had not only managed to create questionable nationality and title but had bought two aristocratic country seats which had no connection with the Thyssen family and a collection of art and antiquities with which he had no affinity. He did not even appear to be motivated to permeate the villa with his own identity, or equip it with any tribute to the industrial source of his wealth.

By the time his pictures started to arrive at the villa from storage, the Third Reich was in power and it would have been quite impossible for Heinrich, regardless of his dual nationality and Dutch residency, to have moved some 300 paintings out of Germany without permission. This may explain why Heinrich left no evidence of the logistics of such a transfer and why Heini remained remarkably hazy concerning any details.

As his father did not start building the separate picture gallery until 1936 and, according to his Hungarian manservant Sandor Berkes, it would remain unfinished until 1940, it seems highly unlikely that, as Heini claimed, his father opened his picture gallery to the public in 1937. The idea, let alone the reality, of having the public trudging through his private art gallery would have been an anathema to his father.

While the Nazi authorities

Maud and Max on Lake Lugano.

appeared quite prepared to authorise Heinrich's movements, the Swiss required a degree of reassurance. This included confirmation by his Bank voor Handel en Scheepvaart that he had ample funds to support himself and a diplomatic letter from Heinrich to the Federal Foreigners' Police in Berne stating: 'Please be notified herewith that the undersigned agrees that he will not exercise any political activities in Switzerland, just as has been his custom so far in Holland and elsewhere.'[25]

* * *

With a new young wife encouraging the continuation of his investment and a suitable palace in which to hang his paintings, the Thyssen-Bornemisza Collection began to grow once again.

The exact details of the growth are confusing for while Heinrich continued to purchase works, the number of paintings he bought as part of the contents of the villa are unspecific. Certainly, records indicate that, by the end of the war, his collection contained a total of 542 paintings.

What is clear is that Heinrich was still sold a lot of rubbish but at least he was now also sold a higher percentage of genuinely good paintings and even the occasional masterpiece. Whether he knew the difference is doubtful but Maud and Heinemann certainly did. The latter needing little persuasion to move from Munich to Lugano and accept the position of curator. He made it his business to source most of the works that the Baron acquired during the following six years.

Even the authenticity of many of the masterworks that he purchased is open to question, for faking and forging was as common then as it is now. A more destructive practice was that of over-enthusiastic restoration or over-painting, to the point where some works in the Thyssen Collection had developed a distinctly 1930s look about them. This was particularly evident in the 'Portrait of a Man' by Rogier van der Weyden; a picture which, like many others, would eventually be demoted to 'attributed to van der Weyden'.

Heinrich was also still encouraged by his friend Baron Eduard von der Heydt, who lived close by in Ascona, where he had a big collection of modern and Asian art; although his house, Monte Verità, was better known for his guests' 'modern' habit of wandering around naked than for the magnificence of his paintings. Von der Heydt would eventually be accused of having been profitably involved in selling Jews safe passage into Switzerland for a fee of up to SwFr 300,000 per head.[26]

At 12.40 pm on 30 January 1933, a short statement was made to the German public: 'The President of the Reich has proclaimed Mr Adolf Hitler as Chancellor.'

During the months that followed, the Reichstag was burnt to the ground, Hitler pushed through the Enabling Law permitting him to rule by decree, the Nazi Party ordered the boycott of Jewish businesses, opposition parties were banned, racial purity legislation was introduced and concentration camps established.

Neither Heinrich nor Fritz voiced any opposition or concern regarding Hitler's actions, as they profited from their investment in the Nazi Party. At a meeting at the Reichs Finance Ministry on 24 October 1933, Heinrich's and Fritz's friend Hjalmar Schacht fulfilled the Nazi leaders' promise by agreeing to the return of the controlling shares in the United Steelworks back into the hands of Fritz Thyssen, his brother Heinrich and their collaborator, Albert Vögler. The honorary chairmanship of the supervisory board was given to the eighty-six-year old Emil Kirdorf, holder of the golden Party badge, a distinction accorded only to early Party members.

*   *   *

The year after Heinrich married Maud in Berlin, his ex-wife Margit married her lover Janos Wettstein von Westersheimb in Dresden on 12 July 1933. Heini did not seem to think that being presented with two new step-parents in consecutive years had very much effect on his life:

> Everything stayed the same as it was. If anything, I saw them more often, especially from 1932, when my father bought Villa Favorita in Lugano and I used to visit my mother in Prague and in Berne, where she lived with Wettstein, who was a member of the Hungarian delegation. I also used to visit Rechnitz where my sisters used to spend their summers. I never went there with my parents, only with Nanny Volz. The castle had a chapel with an organ in it. I got up one night and went and played it. I frightened everyone to death. It was like the Phantom of the Opera.
>
> I spent winter holidays with my father in Davos where I started skiing quite late, when I was thirteen or fourteen years old. Previously I had preferred to ice-skate, which was a very popular sport in Holland because of the canals. When they froze over you could skate from town to town.

Despite being theoretically Hungarian and resident in Holland, Heini was obliged to celebrate Hitler's rise to power when his school marked the event with various celebrations and quasi-religious rituals. These included the unveiling of a portrait of the Führer which was a dangerous undertaking in a school full of rebellious teenage students, particularly Heini who was acutely aware of his privileged position:

Heini pursuing 'Kraft durch Freude' or Strength through Joy.

> I sabotaged all those festivities of the Nazis by doing something really silly. I was very thin so after school I could climb through a window and turn the portrait upside down. It had been hung above a sort of altar hidden by curtains. The next morning they had this unveiling ceremony when they played Beethoven, pulled the curtains back and there was Hitler standing on his head. There was also supposed to be an accompanying picture of the school's Hitler Youth leader but I had put that in the loo. Well, there was a terrible scandal because they knew I was responsible but they couldn't do anything about it because they also knew my Uncle Fritz was financing Hitler.

In 1933 the whole system of the school changed. The headmaster was replaced by a typical Nazi German. After that we were all subjected to ideological indoctrination. I remember having lessons in Theory of the Races or 'Rassenkunde' in German. In the end of term exams I recommended something stupid like marrying several times to improve the strength of the race and as a punishment I had to write out a whole text about the multiplication of flies.

While making light of his Nazi education, Heini insisted: 'My nurse was very anti-Nazi and used to have heated discussions with my Uncle Fritz when we went to visit him in Munich.'

But he remained subject to intense indoctrination. A school journal of the time, complete with swastika and eagle on the front cover, reminded students of the fact that Germans should be proud of having been given back their country and honour the brave men responsible. It contained subjects for students' essays which included 'Class consciousness and class snobbery' and 'The German expatriate as a member of the German Volk community'. They were also reminded that Jews were no longer considered German citizens.

> I had a close friend called Rafael Birnbaum who was Jewish and had a hunchback and a crippled leg. One of his uncles was chief rabbi of the Berlin synagogue and in 1933 he was thrown out of the school. He was very bright and before he left we often used to do our homework together. He also collected stamps. After Rafael left, I still used to go and see him and play chess and chequers at his home. His family was always very kind and welcoming to me. We also used to go walking in the sand dunes together and discussed politics a lot. During our chats by the sea, we plotted how to kill Hitler. He wanted to use my Uncle Fritz to get close to the Führer, and we weighed up our different options of how to kill him.

Unfortunately, it did not happen that way round.

> When we said good-bye to each other I remember him saying that the Nazis were going to exterminate all Jews, including his family. They had nowhere to go. I tried to cheer him up and could not really believe that anything so

Heinrich Thyssen-Bornemisza (second from left) and his party on the same camels featured in the photographs of everyone who was anyone in Egypt at the time.

inhumane could happen. I told him not to believe in the alleged massacres and at the same time tried to convince myself. How could human beings do such a thing?

Josi Groh remained cynical about the relationship between Heini and Rafael: 'I really don't remember Heini ever talking about it before about 1983 when he suddenly cropped up. Around that time, Heini started to become anti-Nazi. In the thirty, forty years that I was involved with him before that I never once heard him talk about this school friend.'

He was convinced Heini used the somewhat exaggerated story to improve his image and that of his family around that time when he was promoting his collection in America.

Heinrich on vacation in Sudan with his somewhat better presented guide.

There had certainly been no reluctance on the part of his father to leave his son to be educated at a school where Jews were persecuted and pupils were encouraged to wear the Hitler Youth uniform.

In fact, Heini admitted that his father never even visited the school and when the Hitler picture scandal occurred, was busy hosting an extremely lavish Nile boat-trip for a large party of his friends before moving on to the Sudan to shoot elephants.

* * *

Having been encouraged to believe that he was going to be involved in shaping the policies of the Party by Hitler's agreement to the formation of Fritz's Institute for Corporate Affairs, he soon realised that Hitler had no intention of allowing the institute to assume any real power or influence. With his customary lack of diplomacy or appreciation of timing, Fritz decided to criticise Hitler and accuse him of breaking his promise at the very moment that Hitler was planning to slaughter Ernst Röhm and his SA officers in the bloodbath that became known as 'The Night of the Long Knives'. It was no doubt due to Göring's support that Fritz survived with little more than the immediate closure of his institute and a private admonition from Hitler: 'I never made any promises. I've nothing to thank you for. What you did for my movement you did for your own benefit and wrote it off as an insurance premium.'[27]

It was hardly surprising that after such a humiliation, Fritz decided to go to Argentina where he had plenty to do preparing his safe haven. But Göring had advised him to repair his rift with Hitler by flattery and, during his visit, Fritz did not hesitate to extol Hitler's virtues in the Buenos Aires press, in particular the dramatic drop in Germany's unemployment. Only twelve months after their disagreement, on 20 April 1935, Fritz would even send Hitler a telegram wishing him happy birthday and thanking him for his great concern and action on behalf of Germany. Hitler's reply was minimal, returning the wire with a simple message written on the reverse: 'Thank you for your good wishes etc. Adolf Hitler'.

* * *

It was typical of the Thyssen brothers' different characters that while Fritz had been trying to use his financial support of the Nazi Party to establish his own political status, Heinrich would be quietly taking advantage of the Jewish persecution to obtain a stud farm and racing stables. The Jewish paper manufacturer Moritz James Oppenheimer had been arrested by the Nazis in 1933 and forced to sign a declaration of bankruptcy. He then spent some time in jail and eventually died in hospital on 4 May 1940. The official story was that he committed suicide, using poison he found in the hospital, although his surviving daughter-in-law Elsa Oppenheimer said he was executed.[28]

On 23 November 1933 Heinrich's company Hollandsch Trust Kantor

Stephan and his uncle August Junior, the brains and black sheep of the family, in Berlin, c.1928.

Chapter IV: 1926–1939

bought the Erlenhof estate on his behalf from Oppenheimer's liquidators; all the land, buildings and a collection of particularly valuable horses for RM160,000. Heini, who would eventually inherit his father's equestrian interest, also failed to show any remorse or concern for the way in which his family acquired the Erlenhof stud farm near Bad Homburg: 'It still exists today. My father also had racing stables for his racehorses at Hoppegarten near Berlin and used to go there regularly. He was very successful. Though not immediately.'

This statement was somewhat questionable as the horse Nereide alone won RM100,000 in the first year of Heinrich's ownership. It was also interesting that horseracing in Germany continued throughout the war and only in 1945 was the Derby cancelled.

Eventually the Thyssen-Bornemisza family would sell most, but not all of the stud for DM 12 million to the Rothenberger tool manufacturing family, while the Thyssen-Bornemisza Group retained some of the land for infinitely more profitable housing development.

* * *

After his Austrian tragedy, Stephan had asked for a job in Seismos GmbH, a small company owned by his Uncle Fritz, which specialised in the engineering and geophysics involved in mining and oil exploration. Dr Waldemar Zettel, the brilliant scientist and spokesman on the history of Seismos, remembered the period with the clarity and pride of a mentally agile ninety-four-year-old:

> He just wasn't sufficiently committed. He was too busy living 'à la carte'. He was a playboy. I didn't like him at all. The Thyssen people sent him to Seismos to get rid of him. One of the directors, Dr Trappe, introduced me to Stephan. He told me: 'The people in Mülheim have sent him so that he should learn to work'. Trappe didn't like him either. They were too different. Trappe was a very earnest scientist, whereas Stephan was more of a 'Lebens-künstler', a bon vivant. Although there was no doubt that he was a highly intelligent and charming man.[29]

Heini's cousin Barbara von Stengel remembered Stephan with considerably greater generosity: 'I only remember Stephan from when I was a child. He was totally different from all the other people. He was purely a scientist and was not in the slightest interested in his father's inheritance. He was constantly studying things and writing books. He and Ily used to live on this beautiful estate near Hanover called Einbeck.'[30]

For a man who appeared from his letters to be so vulnerably sensitive,

Stephan managed to generate considerable ire among both his elders and his contemporaries. In the case of Dr Zettel, there may have been a degree of professional jealousy for there was no doubt that Stephan was involved in, or responsible for, an instrument of very considerable scientific value. But it was the proportion of his input that Dr Zettel questioned:

> Stephan Thyssen joined Dr Alfred Schleusener's department where he was said to have invented the 'Thyssen-Gravimeter', an instrument used for oil prospecting, which won a prize at the 1937 Paris Exhibition. My personal opinion is that it would be best to say that Thyssen and Dr Schleusener invented it together. I think the reason they called it Thyssen-Gravimeter is that Thyssen sounds better and it was of course a famous name in Germany.

Dr Zettel left the company shortly afterwards to join the newly formed 'PRAKLA'. He claimed that this had originally been created by Göring at the specific instructions of Hitler after Stephan 'had refused' to carry out the type of work required by the Nazis, as he believed it would damage Seismos's export market; for despite Heini's insistence that his brother had been a close friend of Sepp Dietrich, Martin Bormann and Heinrich Himmler, they all realised the value of foreign currency. There was certainly evidence that the family's Bremer Vulkan shipyards also went to considerable trouble to hide their military work from their merchant marine export customers.

Another member of the staff of Seismos who found Stephan difficult to work with was the administrator Klaus Ritter, whose father Curt Ritter worked for the August Thyssen Bank. Ritter thought Heini's accusations concerning Stephan's friendship with Dietrich, Bormann and Himmler were highly unlikely: 'He may have had Nazi friends, but not those guys. He was a snob, I think that's a good word to describe him. I cannot imagine he was a friend of those people. They were not the people that he liked. He liked people of a much higher social level.'[31]

Ritter also remembered the events that led up to the change of ownership of Seismos from Fritz to Heinrich: 'In 1936, a dissatisfied client from Essen sued Seismos for compensation for an explosives accident in which Stephan had been involved. Fritz Thyssen was extremely angry about the whole affair and held his nephew responsible. One week later he gave Seismos to his brother saying: "Take your son and your problem with it".'

The vitriolic Heinrich displayed no greater appreciation of his son's talents and also blamed him for the whole 'mess'. He even blamed his wife for 'not making any efforts to have a positive influence' on his character.

But as a result of Stephan's value to the Reich, he continued to work for

Chapter IV: 1926–1939

Seismos, while his wartime activities would prove to be very much at odds with the generally accepted account.

*   *   *

By now Maud and Heinemann's efforts to increase the quality of Heinrich's art collection were beginning to bear fruit. In 1934 he bought 'Family Group with Negro Servant' by Frans Hals which was recognised to be a 'sublime masterpiece' and one of the collection's incomparable paintings. It was of such quality that it made up for many, though not all, of his disasters. In 1935, Heinrich made another fine purchase, 'Santa Catharina of Alexandria' by Caravaggio, which was only allowed to leave Italy after his acquaintance Mussolini gave his permission. Heini remembered the sale price: 'My father bought it for $14,000, which was a ridiculous price for one of the best Caravaggios that exist in the world. Nowadays, it is worth between $50 and 60 million.'

The same year, Heinrich bought, or was persuaded to buy, a painting of far greater importance, not only because of the artist and the provenance, but most of all due to its subject. Acquired from Princess Diana's grandfather, the Earl Spencer, Hans Holbein the Younger's 'Portrait of King Henry VIII of England' is the only 'national icon' in the whole collection. Heinrich also bought another exceptional work from the estate of Otto Kahn, 'Young Knight in a Landscape' by El Vittore Carpaccio. Many years later Heini would come to be particularly appreciative of the painting: 'It was the most important picture in Otto Kahn's collection but he lost 10 million dollars in the collapse of Wall Street, so he had to sell it and my father bought it for $250,000.'

Another painting purchased around this time would become Heini's favourite: ' "Portrait of Giovanna Tornuabuoni" by Ghirlandaio came from the Morgan Library Collection. This is my favourite picture. There is not a spec of dust on it and it has never needed to be cleaned.'

This comment revealed a dangerous obsession shared by both father and son; that of excessively cleaning and eventually ruining many paintings.

Meanwhile, the authenticity of many of Heinrich's purchases remained questionable. In 1935 he bought two Goyas and a Velàzquez, 'Portrait of Maria Anna of Austria, Queen of Spain', an appalling portrait, which would have embarrassed even the lowliest of forgers. To attribute it to Velàzquez was to pollute the reputation of a genius. To sell it to Heinrich was to insult the man. Even the author of the 1992 official Thyssen-Bornemisza Collection catalogue was forced to question the painting: 'Critics are not unanimous in cataloguing this work among his originals.'[32]

Heinrich also bought a painting subsequently claimed to have been the work of Piero della Francesca, although his son Heini would finally admit that 'Portrait of Guidobaldo da Montefeltro' was an extraordinarily optimistic attribution: 'Yes, it's true. I'm not sure about my Piero della Francesca. It would of course be nice if it was really by his hand.'

* * *

Meanwhile, Maud Feller, who was undoubtedly the most glamorous thing that ever walked into Heinrich's life, walked out of it with an equal degree of style only three years later. She would have appreciated Elsa Maxwell's theatrical account of her exit:

> While Maud von Thyssen constantly played with Alexis Mdivani in Paris, von Thyssen, for once forgetful of his beautiful wife, was in Berlin devoting himself to Hitler. While Alexis was making love to Maud, von Thyssen was making cannon for Adolf. He was so busy making guns that he left his wife to her own devices. How near to marriage they got, no one will ever know. It was understood that she would go back to Berlin and try to make her jealous old husband give her freedom. So Maud and Alexis drove to Palamos and spent gloriously happy days there. In one thing Baron von Thyssen had showed vast generosity to his young wife. He had covered her with jewels more magnificent than even a Mdivani could conjure. She had taken these jewels with her. The final night of her visit came. She had missed the day train, but Alexis had promised to drive her across the French border into Perpignan, where she could catch the late train. They sang flamencos as they flew through the dark night.[33]

Many years later, Heini continued the story while sitting on the beach in front of the La Gavina Hotel in S'Agaro on the Costa Brava where Maud and Alexis had stayed the night before they set off. They had enjoyed an early supper by the pool with cocktails and champagne, which would doubtless have left them slightly 'squiffy':

> I still remember it all happening because I was on summer holiday in San Remo with my father at the time. They had been staying at the hotel while they visited the painter Sert and his wife Russie Mdivani at Mas Juny, their property near Girona. On the night of 1 August 1935, Alexis was driving Maud to the Girona train station in a recently acquired Rolls-Royce convertible which he had obtained as part of the settlement from his ex-wife, Barbara Hutton.

Chapter IV: 1926–1939

A kilometre before the village of Albons they hit a bump in the road at high speed, which threw the car in the air and on to its side. The windscreen almost decapitated Alexis who was killed instantly. Maud was thrown clear but suffered two broken legs, facial and head injuries. She was taken to the clinic of Doctor Coll in Girona while Mdivani's body was taken to 'Mas Juny' where Russie and Salvador Dalí watched over him, because Sert was away in Venice.

A newspaper account claimed that the Baron Thyssen-Bornemisza arrived at the hospital and visited Maud several times a day, although she later denied this unlikely story. Apparently she could not speak for a while due to her injured tongue but wrote a note enquiring about the Prince's condition. She also claimed that she had been carrying $180,000-worth of jewellery in her luggage and that it was no longer there. It was not long before lawyers were involved in compensatory claims for cosmetic surgery and the value of the missing jewellery while Heinrich filed for divorce in Hungary, citing Prince Mdivani as co-respondent. Eventually, the Mdivani estate settled Maud's claims, while Heinrich had to pay her lawyers' fees and her debts. He also agreed an alimony settlement of a one-off payment of RM600,000 and a monthly pension of RM1,300.[34]

* * *

Due to the well-publicised extent of the family's vast wealth and news of Heinrich's pending divorce, it was only a matter of months before Maud had been replaced by another determined, potential bride. In the spring of 1936 Gunhilde von Fabrizius, daughter of a retired German cavalry colonel, swept across the Croisette and in through the doors of the Carlton Hotel in Cannes with her Scots terrier 'Gipsy'. There can have been few other reasons why a young, single girl would move into such a hotel for several weeks other than to present herself to one of the richest men in the world. So it would hardly have been a surprise to Gunhilde when they bumped into each other on 9 March 1936. Apparently, she recognised him from his similarity to August Thyssen Junior whom she had met in similar fashion at Claridges in Paris. Unfortunately, while Junior was no doubt more fun to be with, he only 'married' for one night at a time.

Three days later, Heinrich sent her flowers and a note saying how he had sacrificed an hour of golf in order to find them. It was hardly the most seductive introduction but Gunhilde was not going to be easily discouraged. So it was that the affair began and continued in secret, until Heinrich got his divorce from Maud.

On 15 November 1937, they were finally able to get married in Berlin before taking up residence at Villa Favorita. Thus Gunhilde had become a very rich woman and would remain so for the rest of her life.

Cynics suggested that, on their wedding day, the immensely wealthy, sixty-two-year-old Baron Heinrich Thyssen-Bornemisza was persuaded by his young bride to make a new will. Seven months later, in June 1939, he made another will with a second addition, and a third one month later. He then wrote a first codicil in October 1940. Then he started all over again with a new will signed and dated in Lugano on 11 December 1941. In fact, he was later discovered to have been staying in Zurich on that day, so the will was invalid as was an additional codicil made in 1946. The two last documents were lodged in a safe at the Swiss Banking Corporation in Lugano.

Margit's sister, Aunt Ilda, who retained a lifelong unrequited love for Heinrich and a conviction that she would have made him a far better bride than her sister, was quite horrified: 'I could never understand why he chose this rather ugly specimen of a human being. She derived from some impoverished German family and had a small singing career in Paris night clubs.'

By 1938, she was quite convinced that Gunhilde was trying to kill her beloved Heinrich: 'Henry was drinking far too much. His face was red and bloated. I had a feeling that his wife wanted to finish him off with drink, as she always kept his glass full.'

* * *

By 1936, the United Steelworks' rearmament production was flourishing and they had declared a 3.5 per cent dividend in response to a 25 per cent increase in steel production, while in private Göring was already discussing war preparations with Fritz, referring to it as the 'A-case'.

Heinrich's mining management at Walsum had been displaying equal 'diligence'. Since 1933, the development of his coal mines was stepped up energetically and more than 1,000 unemployed miners had been given employment. There was a surprising lack of concern on the part of the Reich that the mines were not German-owned or that the development finance came through a Dutch bank with loans of Dfl 19 million and RM6 million.

While the brothers continued to assist in rebuilding Germany's war machine, they also spent a considerable amount of time and effort insuring against the possibility of Germany losing the war. For anyone who had lived through the First World War, it was a realistic attitude. Most of their movement of assets offshore was obviously intended to safeguard their own financial well-being.

However, some of it was also designed to assist in achieving the Nazis' ambitions.

A particularly obvious example was the Thyssens' investment in gold. Between 1931 and 1933, their Union Banking Corporation in New York purchased in excess of $8 million worth of gold bullion of which $5.78 million worth was sent by boats to England in 1936. While the gold would remain a useful reserve in case Germany lost the war, there is also evidence to suggest that Heinrich used it as foreign banking security for the Reich throughout the war, although Heini initially claimed that it was used by his father to fund anti-Nazi activities.

The eighteen-year-old Gaby Thyssen-Bornemisza on holiday in Switzerland.

* * *

In 1936, the Baron Heinrich Thyssen-Bornemisza met his Hungarian Sancho Panza who helped him live out the last eleven years of his bibulous, aristocratic, cultural fantasy. Having met at a Rechnitz hunting party where he was working for Count Szechenyi, Sandor Berkes became the Baron's chauffeur, manservant and companion. He was also an excellent horseman.

The same year, Heinrich commenced the addition of a new wing to Villa Favorita to house his ever-expanding art collection. Under the guidance of Rudolf Heinemann, he also installed a conservation laboratory, which was a dangerous convenience in view of his enthusiasm for 'restoration', although the whole project would take another four years to complete.

In 1937, Rudolf Heinemann compiled the first comprehensive catalogue of the Schloss Rohoncz Collection. It was printed in Switzerland and gave Villa Favorita as the address of the collection, although the language was German, despite the fact that Ticino is an Italian-speaking canton. Apart from the photographs of the paintings, the information was limited to the title and the name of the artist. All other information concerning size, minimal provenance, exhibitions or bibliography was contained in a separate volume.

Meanwhile, Fritz returned to Argentina where he spent sixth months developing his estates and corporate interests. On his return to Germany, he was once again questioned by the tax and foreign exchange control authorities concerning his foundation Faminta AG and his Argentinian assets, which he would eventually explain with customary selfless nationalism:

> As German industrial leader I am of the opinion that the promotion of exports is of utmost necessity in spite of the steadily growing difficulties owing to political conditions. As far as I am informed, my opinion in this respect is shared by the competent authorities. I am therefore particularly grateful to the administration of Faminta AG for supporting my endeavours to increase German exports considerably.[35]

But the authorities remained unconvinced and frustrated by their inability to obtain from Faminta any details of Fritz's affairs. Finally, they requested a full audit while Fritz threatened to refer the matter to Hermann Göring, for whom his daughter Anita was now working as a private secretary.

By comparison, Heinrich was far less financially threatened, although a considerable amount of creative organisation was needed to stay that way, including justifying to the Ticino tax authorities their miraculously conservative SwFr 12,500 annual tax calculation. Despite the fact that Heinrich was still spending a considerable amount of time in Berlin, it was something he had no wish to advertise, as it may have had a detrimental effect on his Swiss residency status; essential for both his personal and financial protection. This was evident from a letter from Roberto van Aken, his Lugano-based Dutch lawyer: 'Your "provisional residence permit" for Ticino has expired. I think you should not only extend it but in fact go for permanent residency here. I have now spoken with the relevant authority, and it seems it can all be done very quickly.'

On 18 November 1937, three days after they were married, Heinrich and Gunhilde were issued with Swiss foreigners' passes; this was two days after receiving a letter from the Mayor of Berlin thanking Heinrich for a transfer of RM 2,000 from August Thyssen Bank which was to be used 'for needy people in the capital'.

* * *

Although he must have been aware that war was inevitable, Heinrich appeared to have made no provision for the safety of his children; even his beloved Gaby. According to Pusch, the looming war and lack of parental concern had little effect on Heini or their enjoyment of each other's company, which was rapidly

Chapter IV: 1926–1939

Gaby (left), Heini and his first love, 'Pusch' on the beach at Viareggio.

developing into much more than a casual friendship. There were also an increasing number of diversions that they were now old enough to enjoy.

One of the first artificial ice-rinks was opened in The Hague in 1936 and Heini and Pusch used to go there every Wednesday and Saturday, either to skate or to watch ice-hockey matches. But what he really enjoyed doing was 'cruising' in a hired, red MG sports car. Unfortunately, he was still only sixteen when the required age to obtain a driving licence was eighteen, so he had to pay an older friend to get the car. Then he and Pusch drove around the streets of Scheveningen so everybody could see, admire and envy them. These excursions were apparently made even more glamorous by the fact that Pusch took her black cocker spaniel along. She remembered how, once, their car stopped on the boulevard right in front of several very crowded cafés and, to their great embarrassment, somebody shouted, 'Ah, that's the car that costs Dfl 2.50 an hour.'

Heini's fondest memory was for the summer of 1937, when they became lovers:

> She was my first love and, at 16, I would have done anything to impress her or just to be by her side. In the summer of 1937, Pusch was staying at a friend's house in Forte dei Marmi and I was at a hotel in Viareggio, with my mother, Janos Wettstein and nanny Volz. Although we spent a lot of time

Der Stellvertreter des Reichskanzlers
  Der Adjutant
von Tschirschky u. Boegendorff.

Berlin W 9, den 9. Aug. 1934.
Lennéstr. 9

Lieber Baron T h y s s e n !

    Bis heute ist es mir leider beim besten Willen infolge meiner augenblicklich besonders starken dienstlichen Inanspruchnahme nicht möglich gewesen, Ihnen für die grosse Überraschung zu danken, die Sie mir mit der Übersendung des Zigaretten-Etuis bereitet haben. Ich habe mich über dieses selten schöne Geschenk riesig gefreut, und es wird mich immer an den siegreichen Tag des Hamburger Derby erinnern.

    Ich hoffe, dass wir uns in Wien später öfter sehen werden; vielleicht kann ich Sie auch einmal in Ungarn besuchen.

    Mit nochmaligem herzlichsten Dank für Ihre grosse Freundlichkeit und mit den besten Grüssen

                Ihr stets ergebener

S.H.
  Herrn Baron T h y s s e n ,
    Karlsbad/Tschechoslowakei.
      Grand Hotel Pupp

Letter from Hitler's aristocratic adjutant to Heinrich thanking him for an extravagant gift.[36]

together and she came to lunch at the hotel, or I went to the beach, it was never enough. I never wanted to leave her. So one night I filled my bed with clothes so that Edda wouldn't notice I had gone and slipped out to catch the train to where Pusch was staying. I got in through her window and stayed all night with her.

When it was time to leave I couldn't get out of the window because their chauffeur was sitting on the wall smoking a cigarette. Pusch couldn't stop laughing but eventually he went back inside and I left. Gianni Agnelli was also spending the summer nearby. He used to take her for rides on the crossbar of his bike and she talked about him far too much as far as I was concerned. I think that was the first time I really felt jealous of anyone.

Unlike Heinrich, who left his children to their own devices, Fritz and Amélie encouraged their daughter to form a close relationship with Hermann Göring, a relationship that only came to the attention of the press when he married the actress Emmy Sonnemann. According to the *Prager Montagsblatt*: 'Emmy had a very ambitious rival in Anita Thyssen who, in 1933, had been very eager indeed to be married to Göring.'

Newspaper reports also accused Fritz Thyssen of egging his daughter on, because he wanted to have a loyal observer among the Party leadership. Heini thought it was far more likely to have been her mother Amélie who encouraged Anita: 'Amélie was a very nationalistic German. At the time, it could have been confused with Nazism, which I suppose it probably was. She was certainly friendly with all those people.'

With Göring's assistance, Fritz would arrange for Anita's escape ahead of the war, despite subsequently claiming that she and her family had been with him when he eventually fled Germany; a myth which has been maintained to this day by ThyssenKrupp AG.

According to Heini, Anita and her family were taken to Argentina by the German navy:

> They went on a German naval vessel that was visiting Argentina. Fritz could have easily gone with them, but he decided to stay. He was not very bright. I think he suffered from delusions of grandeur and saw himself as a statesman. A sort of national hero. The idea of sneaking off quietly didn't appeal to him and it certainly wouldn't have been an option as far as Amélie was concerned. Even Anita had to be convinced that she could better serve the Party in Argentina before she was prepared to leave.

Nationalsozialistische Deutsche Arbeiterpartei
Gau Hessen-Nassau

Gaugeschäftsstelle:
Frankfurt/M., Gutleutstr. 8-12, Schließfach 1636
Girokonto 6221 Nass. Landesbank, Frankfurt/Main
Telefon: Sammelnummer 30381
Postscheckkonto: Frankfurt/Main 53003

Kampfzeitungen des Gaues:
"Frankfurter Volksblatt" Frankfurt/Main
Neue Mainzerstraße 8, Telefon 28232
"Hessische Landeszeitung" Darmstadt
Saalbaustraße 19, Telefon 2445

Kreis Obertaunus
Amt für Volkswohlfahrt
Ortsgruppe Dornholzhausen
Bankkonto:
Nass. Landesbank, Bad Homburg v. d. H.

Dornholzhausen i. Ts., den 22.1.37

Herrn A.v.Borcke.
Berlin-Hoppegarten

Sehr geehrter Herr v.Borcke.

Wohl edwas verspätet, aber deshalb nicht minder herzlich, möchte ich Ihnen im Namen meiner Ortsgruppe danken für die Spende von 250 Rm. Ich kann Ihnen versichern, dass es diese Weihnachten für uns eine grosse Freude war unsere bedürftigen Volksgenossen ein schönes Fest in jeden Hause zu bereiten. Ich bedaure dass Sie nicht einmal stiller Beobachter sein konnten, es macht doch viel Freude helfen zu können am rechten Platz. Habe das Geld zum Ankauf für dringende Gegenstände verwendet, und einen kleinen Rest für den 30. Januar aufgehoben. Sollten Sie nun im Februar oder März nach hier kommen, so bitte ich mir bescheid zu geben, wann ein Besuch bei Ihnen angenehm, damit ich Ihnen an Hand der Quittungen von den Einkäufen Spenden-Quittungen geben kann. Die eingekauften Sachen sind von mir als Sachspende auf Ihren Namen Gestüt Erlenhof durch Herrn v.Borcke an den Kreis ge= meldet worden.

　　　　Für dass Jahr 1937 wünsche ich Ihnen und dem Erlenhof
　　　　recht guten Erfolg.

　　　　　　　　　　　　　　　Heil Hitler!
　　　　　　　　　　　　　　NSV.Ortsgruppenamtsleiter

N.S.D.A.P.
Amt für Volkswohlfahrt
Ortsgruppenamtsleitung Dornholzhausen i. Ts.

Rudolf Lotter

Letter from the local Nazi Party to Heinrich's stud farm manager thanking him for a financial contribution.[37]

Heini was non-committal concerning the exact date of their departure, but Barbara von Stengel claimed: 'Federico was born in 1937, then the following year, 1938, Anita left for Argentina with her son and Count Zichy, her husband. Her second son Claudio was born there in 1942.'

* * *

Heinrich's determination to hide his German nationality and holdings beneath a Dutch-Hungarian veneer sometimes resulted in the development of farcical situations, as in the case of his horse breeding.

After Maud's reluctance to pay an outstanding personal debt led to litigation, the Baron's ownership of the Erlenhof stud farm was examined in court and the Union Club, Germany's horse breeding and racing establishment, were questioned concerning their member's ownership of fifty thoroughbred mares. The club confirmed their understanding that 'the Baron owns 37 of the registered thoroughbred mares of Erlenhof and receives 10 per cent of the race earnings as a breeder's fee'. Unfortunately, his lawyer had denied this, insisting that the stud and the horses were owned by a faceless corporation. This resulted in the club president being obliged to question Heinrich's ungentlemanly behaviour: 'Apparently, your lawyer has stated that the Erlenhof horses are not your property. The racing authorities, however, have not confirmed this

Göring and Heinrich celebrating victory at Hoppegarten in 1938. (photo: Zinsel, Darmstadt).

statement. Such a denial on your part would have consequences concerning your membership of our club. Please contact me as soon as possible.'

The club appeared to have forgotten that the Baron, gentleman or no gentleman, was a man of such vast wealth that he could easily afford to close down the country's premier stud and racing stables and put all the horses out to grass. He was also aware of the damage this course of action would do to the club's international reputation; so that was exactly what he did and, in June 1938, the club president was forced into a deeply embarrassing climb-down:

> Having received your statement, I have passed it on to the other gentlemen and can assure you everything is settled. I was horrified to hear that the owner of Erlenhof, namely Erlenhof GmbH, had given the order to dissolve the stables. We would all find this absolutely terrible, as you have done so much for the sport. Nobody here could possibly accept such a situation.

While Heinrich's appalling behaviour had won him few friends, his money had undoubtedly bought him victory over the Union Club but, later that year, it would also contribute to his personal embarrassment. On his return from Berlin to Switzerland, Sandor Berkes was driving the car when they were stopped by German border guards, and the Baron 'was molested terribly'.[38]

The nationalistic guards would have known exactly who Heinrich was and the source of his fortune and would have been irritated by his rejection of German identity and use of a Hungarian diplomatic passport. It was not helped by his arrogant insistence that he was a Hungarian aristocrat and expected to be treated as such. So the guards decided to punish him for his lack of commitment and loyalty to the fatherland by subjecting him to a full body search in front of his manservant. It was a shame that Heinrich did not see it as typical of the tragic degradation that was being suffered by millions of people across Germany; people for whom escape was impossible and a drive across a Swiss frontier an unobtainable dream.

The whole experience must have been particularly galling in view of the fact that he had been returning from a day at the races, where, in the privileged company of Reichsmarschall Göring, he had enjoyed the satisfaction of watching his horse win. He would have been even more angry if he had known that Göring's imitation of his indignity could be guaranteed to reduce Hitler to hysterics for some time afterwards.

As a result of the incident, Heinrich never returned to Germany, while Hitler's actions also prevented his return to Rechnitz. On 14 March 1938, Hitler marched into Vienna at the head of his troops and announced to jubilant crowds

Margit Junior at Rechnitz Castle fifteen years before the Jewish massacre.

that Austria would henceforth be part of the German Reich. In response, Heinrich gave his castle and the estate to his daughter Margit as he had no wish to be seen owning any property in what was now Germany.

Margit was delighted. She was even more delighted when the castle was sequestered by the SS as a staff college and recreation centre for Hitler's elite. While her husband repaired to his family's estate in Hungary, Margit chose to remain in Rechnitz and spend the war in a castle full of young officers with stables full of horses. For the local population, particularly the Jewish community, the situation would end in terrible tragedy; one that the Thyssen-Bornemiszas would never speak of.

* * *

Another area that they would try and draw a veil across was the manufacture of armaments. Heini would always insist that while his family made steel that was no doubt used in the manufacture of weapons, they were not directly involved, but Robert Kabelac, a manager at Bremer Vulkan, Heinrich's shipyard, told a different story:

In 1938, we finished the first of three ordered Hansa ships, which in 1939 was overhauled to become a K16 cruiser called 'Atlantis' that was to become quite famous in the war. The ship stayed 631 days at sea without coming into port and sank 19 enemy commercial ships. It was sunk on 22 November 1941 by the English cruiser *Devonshire*.

Now began my regular travels to the Navy High Command in Berlin. A mobilisation plan was being drawn up and in case of war Bremer Vulkan was to build mine searching boats. Director Esser didn't like this at all, as during World War One, Bremer Vulkan had built U-boats. We still had many engineers and workers from that period working with us at the time. So Esser wanted to build submarines instead. It also meant we could build the engines ourselves. During the negotiations with the authorities, I managed to get the orders for Bremer Vulkan changed.[39]

So Bremer Vulkan would become one of the largest builders of U-boats; an activity which they would continue throughout the war. But when confronted with this fact, Heini would grumpily change the subject or claim loss of memory.

August Junior, having ruined his niece's wedding.

As a result of the unfortunate 'incident', the impending war and Heinrich's deteriorating mental and physical health, he would be largely confined to Villa Favorita for the rest of his life, while his various German, Dutch and even American companies continued to profit from the Third Reich.

The Baron would also become increasingly alienated from his wife, friends and family. Even his relationship with Gaby, his 'dearest darling Baby', had been gradually cooling as she grew older and lost her 'little girl' appeal. He also found her developing interest in other men annoying. When she was seventeen years of age, Gaby had developed a relationship with Prince Ratibor, which Heinrich managed to put a stop to on the grounds that he was too old and only after her money, which was no doubt an accurate, if somewhat ironic, observation.

Gaby was obviously sorry to have lost the power of her attraction over her father and was reassured by his approval of her subsequent engagement to Baron Adolphe Bentinck, whom they had met together in St Moritz; possibly through yet another introduction by Eduard von der Heydt. According to Heini, it was 'a marriage of convenience for the Bentincks who had no money'. Heini also seemed to think Adolphe may have been homosexual; an echo perhaps of stories of homosexuality in the family's past when, in the seventeenth century, the Dutch page boy Hans Willem Bentinck came to England with William of Orange and was rewarded for his loyalty with the title of Earl of Portland. Apparently he had shared William's bed when the Stadholder was sick with small-pox; it being believed at that time that an increase in physical heat eased the suffering of the victim. As a result of this somewhat dubious physical congress, enemies of the King were quick to resort to the 'foulest kinds of slander'.

Adolphe Bentinck was an adviser to the Dutch Minister of Finance in The Hague and, although Heini claimed he was 'not one of my favourite people', he would prove to be of inestimable value in reclaiming the Thyssen-Bornemisza fortune after the war. In 1939, Adolphe entered the diplomatic service and was sent to Budapest as Chargé d'Affaires, which was a convenient coincidence for Heinrich. He and Gaby stayed there until 1940, when they were posted to Cairo, a city that was as sympathetic to the Reich as it was to the Allies. There they would stay until 1946 while his gratefully received dowry continued to gather interest in the Royal Dutch bank in Scheveningen.

Gaby's marriage on 1 September 1938 was one of the last opportunities for the entire family to gather before the outbreak of war and gave August Junior the opportunity to voice his opinion concerning the relationship between marriage and prostitution and Adolphe's financial inducement. Heini was probably the only person present who found it amusing:

> My uncle August made all the elegant guests deeply embarrassed by giving a speech in which he said, 'So Gaby is getting married and here we all are, toasting the occasion. But the only difference between this celebration and that of him taking a prostitute for the night is the length of time the union lasts.' He did not seem to appreciate the irony of the fact that it was Adolphe who was getting half a million florins from my father for marrying my sister Gaby, or that he would never again have to spend another penny of his own money.

Gaby's wedding to Baron Adolphe Bentinck (centre), including Amélie Thyssen (second left front row), Baroness Gunhilde Thyssen-Bornemisza (fourth right front row), next to Baron Bentinck Senior and Louise Price (second from right). 'Piggy' Zichy (extreme left second row), next to Count Ivan Batthyány, August Junior (fifth from left) below Stephan Thyssen-Bornemisza and to the left of Margit Batthyány, next to her Anita Thyssen, Baron Eduard von der Heydt (fourth from right) and Fritz Thyssen (extreme right).

August Junior's outspoken behaviour appealed to his nephew as much as his lifestyle. Both appeared to have had considerable influence on the impressionable young man:

> My uncle had a large income which permitted him to live in style in Paris, where he was known as the White Wolf. He left behind a reputation as a playboy that was still remembered when I used to go to Carroll's in the 1960s. He lived on biscuits, smoked 120 cigarettes and drank one and a half bottles of whisky every day. He was very funny and extremely provocative. He used to say anything that came into his head, spoke very loudly with a strong Rhenanian accent and had a very coarse sense of humour.

* * *

By now Heinrich's collecting had slowed considerably and in 1938 he apparently purchased only one picture. It was a magnificent panel by Hans Memling with 'Young Man at Prayer' on one side and 'Marian Flowerpiece' on the reverse. Originally part of a diptych, the work possessed a provenance as impressive as its subject matter, though its early history was obviously lost in the mists of cultural pillage. Heini Thyssen said it was the last painting that his father bought. He also claimed Rudolf Heinemann left to work for Knoedler in New York as a result of a quarrel with his father. No mention was ever made that, as a Jew, he may have begun to feel somewhat insecure working for a German with social and business links with the Nazi Party; though this would not prevent him from returning to do business with the Thyssen-Bornemiszas after the war, prior to which a somewhat surprised Berkes, in addition to his other duties, had accepted the role of curator.

The claim that Heinrich ceased to buy and sell paintings in 1938 is contradicted by the records which show that pictures moved between Paris and Switzerland during the war and that by 1945 Heinrich had purchased or otherwise obtained another 218 works of art. A post-war Swiss police report also revealed that Heinrich travelled frequently to Paris throughout the war, a fact strenuously denied by himself and subsequently by his son Heini.[40] It is a reminder that the Paris auction houses such as Hotel Drouot continued to do business throughout the occupation, handling art which had often been confiscated by both the Vichy French and the Nazis, through dealers such as Karl Haberstock and Julius Böhler, who are known to have sold paintings to Heinrich Thyssen-Bornemisza.

* * *

After Hitler had taken Austria, and six months before he invaded Czechoslovakia, Heini completed his schooling in Holland:

> I passed my Baccalaureat in March 1939. At the ceremony, Gluck's *Iphigenie on Tauris* was played, followed by a gramophone record of one of Hitler's speeches which sounded like a dog in a kennel. This was followed by a typical Nazi song and a speech I delivered on behalf of the successful candidates. Then there was more music, a speech by the headmaster, a Brandenburg concerto and the Dutch and German national anthems. The whole effort was put on for only six pupils, as everybody else had either been expelled or returned to Germany.

In September, despite the fact that the war had already started, Heinrich saw fit to send his son to work at his bank in Rotterdam. The Dutch staff were

The three Thyssen Brothers: Heinrich, August Junior and Fritz, at Villa Favorita in September 1938.

embarrassed and obviously not a great deal pleased, as it appeared to them that Heini had been sent to spy on them:

> The staff just ignored me. They showed no sign of being servile or condescending or even friendly towards me. Just total indifference and coldness. I didn't know that the bank belonged to my father or that it was the holding company for all his other companies. I just took my bicycle to the station every day and there I took the train. I would have a sandwich for lunch, return on the train and ride my bicycle home. I got paid Dfl 300 every month and I never asked any questions, although I was somewhat puzzled because there were so many Thyssen accounts there. But I just knew my father wouldn't have told me anything about them, even if I had asked. He would have accused me of impertinence.

Then, on 20 November 1939, two months after the start of World War Two, Heini was finally summoned to Switzerland by his father, not to Lugano, but to Berne: 'There I was due to meet my mother and stepfather. Everything was very complicated because I had difficulty in getting a proper visa. As my passport was Hungarian, they could only give me a student visa for three weeks.'

Heini also insisted that despite being the son of one of the richest men in the world, and having been taken to school in a car to avoid the risk of kidnap, he was allowed to make the trip from Holland to Switzerland completely alone, with barely a hundred Francs in his pocket, during a period when a major European conflict had just started. Heini refused to remember the emotional departure from his beloved Nanny Volz, which would have been expected after eighteen years of an intensely close relationship; presumably due to the guilt generated by his having abandoned her.

Neither of his parents had been keen to take responsibility for the safe-keeping of their son, his father flatly refusing to have him in Lugano which, much to Heini's relief, obliged him to stay with his mother and Wettstein at the Royal Hungarian Embassy in Berne: 'Suddenly, I was enjoying the most incredible social life because I was invited to attend all the social functions at the embassy, and it was very easy to forget that Europe was at war.'

* * *

But Heini's safety was still not assured. Switzerland was not prepared to give Heini or his father limitless safe haven unless they took Swiss nationality, and that was complicated by Heinrich's rapidly deteriorating relationship with Gunhilde. According to the Swiss Political Department in Berne, in 1939, Heinrich Thyssen-Bornemisza filled in an application for naturalisation in Switzerland but at the last minute was obliged to refrain from filing it. Apparently, he was worried that under Swiss law Gunhilde would have been entitled to far greater inheritance rights than under Hungarian law.

That winter, Heinrich asked Gunhilde for a divorce, but she refused to co-operate and booked herself into a clinic for treatment for an ulcer. When she returned, he would not allow her back into the Villa and she had to move into a local hotel. He then refused to return any of her belongings until she agreed to the divorce. But Gunhilde successfully commenced proceedings against him, and he was forced to return her clothes and possessions. She also successfully demanded financial support as he had initiated the separation.

Meanwhile, Heinrich tried to file for divorce in the local Lugano court, until they informed him that they lacked the jurisdiction to divorce foreign nationals under foreign law. So Heinrich went to Budapest where his lawyers had discovered a new law that said that couples who had lived apart for more than five years could be divorced if one of the partners wished to do so. But he would have to wait until 1944 until these conditions would be met.

Gunhilde, having been so badly treated, refused to give up what she considered her legal share and spent the war preparing her claim with the assistance

Gunhilde von Fabrizius, the third Baroness Thyssen-Bornemisza and Count 'Piggy' Zichy.

of her lawyer, Dr Robert Goldstein. It was he who would claim that far from being 'poor', Heinrich's pre-war fortune amounted to some SwFr 1.2 billion, while Gunhilde supported this claim with a whole series of business accounts from BVHS, which showed Dutch assets of considerably more than Dfl 100 million.

Gunhilde would not only outlive Heinrich, but also outsmart both father and son. Heinrich's behaviour towards her was an unfortunate example of his meanness and arrogant pride while his attitude towards Maud was no better. A private detective, hired by the Baron in July 1939, reported on his ex-wife's unauthorised use of his questionable title:

> Mrs Feller is breaching the agreements that were reached concerning use of name. She was using the name Baroness Thyssen-Bornemisza in two shops in Zurich and at the hairdressers at Hotel Baur au Lac. The Engadin Express newspaper also ran her name under the list of foreigners residing at the Palace Hotel in St Moritz as Baroness Maud Thyssen of Zurich.

* * *

In May 1939, the Düsseldorf Foreign Exchange Control Office, under instructions from Berlin, started making renewed enquiries into Fritz Thyssen's affairs with what appeared to be considerable success. Their report indicated their possession of the latest information concerning his movement of funds.

Fritz's Faminta assets had been transferred to another Thyssen foundation, the Pelzer Foundation, also based at Glarus in Switzerland, but administrated in Rotterdam. It was ascertained that BVHS bank had RM44.5 million claims in the United Steelworks while Fritz Thyssen had his own participation and controlled a large part of the stock which he received from Heinrich Thyssen-Bornemisza. The investigators also established that in 1936 Fritz Thyssen had repurchased stock of the United Steelworks from the Reich with the financial aid of BVHS, while between 1936 and 1938 there had been co-operation between BVHS, the United Steelworks and August Thyssen Hütte to cover up Fritz Thyssen's flight of capital to Faminta, which confirmed the financial intimacy between the brothers' affairs.[41]

While Heinrich remained safely beyond the jurisdiction of the investigation, Fritz's justifiable paranoia increased still further when Hitler decreed the evasion of foreign exchange control to be a capital offence. He also realised that since Göring's setting-up of his Reich Works Hermann Göring, he had effectively become a competitor with little motivation to protect Fritz or his controlling interest in the United Steelworks. It was not a reassuring thought and supported Fritz's claim to have finally realised the true nature and intent of the political force that he had helped bring to power.

He was on holiday in Badgastein in the Austrian Alps when, on the evening of 31 August, he received an official telegram instructing him, as a member of the Reichstag, to attend a meeting of members in Berlin the following morning. He claimed to have immediately sent Göring a telegram informing him that he would be unable to attend due to ill health and the impossibly short notice. Whatever form of travel he used, like many other Reichstag members who were enjoying their seasonal holiday, he could not possibly have arrived in time. What is perhaps less likely is his claim that in his telegram he also explained his opposition to the invasion of Poland and the inevitable war that would follow.

The following morning at the Opera House, where the Reichstag meeting was being held, the seats 'conveniently' left vacant by absent members were soon filled with representatives of the Nazi Party. Predictably, they reacted with wild enthusiasm to Hitler's speech informing them that the invasion of Poland had, in fact, already started. Or as Hitler put it: 'We are shooting back.'

He also broadcast a warning: 'In the same way as I am prepared to offer my life at any moment for the German people and for Germany, I expect the same thing from everybody else. Whoever believes that he can oppose this national requirement, be it directly or indirectly, will fall . . . Whoever is not with me is a traitor and shall be treated as such.'[42]

Fritz later claimed that he fled in reaction to this speech because at the time he believed Hitler had seen his telegram and, in response, was referring to him personally. It was hardly surprising that he considered it time to leave Germany, which he did by the simple expedient of instructing his chauffeur to cross the border into Switzerland for lunch.

1   Letter dated 12 May 1926 (TBG Archives).
2   Letter from Heinrich to Fritz, undated (probably 26 April 1926) (ibid).
3   Today's merged company of ThyssenKrupp AG still owns some 51,000 apartments in the Ruhr area (*Frankfurter Allgemeine Zeitung*, 2 October 2003).
4   Imperial War Museum/GED, p. 2.
5   'The history of the Thyssen Family and their activities', a speech given by Heini Thyssen-Bornemisza in Divonne 6 June 1979.
6   *Frankfurter Zeitung*, 29 December 1926.
7   Report from Max Guttmann, Joint Special Financial Detachment Office of OMGUS, Control Commission for Germany (British Element), Düsseldorf, to Mr Constant and Mr Fattakos, re Report on Baron Heinrich Thyssen-Bornemisza, Interrogation of Obersteuerinspektor Jansen and Zollamtmann Brill, dated 27 August 1946 (which revealed that investigations had taken place against Fritz, Hans and Julius Thyssen personally on account of tax evasions committed from 1919 to 1939). Also, report by Joseph Nachtsheim on the findings in the tax files of Fritz Thyssen and Julius Thyssen, Mülheim/Ruhr, regarding participations in BVHS, Vulcan, Vulcaan Coal and Dunamis, dated 28 May 1946 (both National Archives, Washington, DC).
8   F. Thyssen, *I Paid Hitler*, 1941, p. 131.
9   See for instance Joint Special Financial Detachment, US Group Control Council, Control Commission for Germany (British Element), Düsseldorf, Memorandum from M. Guttmann to Ens. E. F. Rains, re Fritz Thyssen's flight of capital to Switzerland and Holland, dated 10 December 1945 (National Archives, Washington, DC).
10 Report from Max Guttman, 27 August 1946 – see note 7.
11 Report by the Joint Special Financial Detachment, US Group Control Council, Control Commission for Germany (British Element), Düsseldorf, Max Guttmann to Ens. E. F. Rains, re 'The National Socialist Revolution' and the Vereinigte Stahlwerke Majority, dated 1 December 1945 (National Archives, Washington, DC).
12 Author's conversations with Hannelore Schmidt-Engel ('Pusch'), 1998-2004.
13 In 1969, Gaby Bentinck-Thyssen donated her painting of the 'Mater Dolorosa' to the Chiesa Parrocchiale church in Porto Cervo, Sardinia, where any knowledge of its existence is now denied.
14 The painting was sold at Sotheby's London in 1995 by Heinrich's grandson Steven Bentinck for £3.5 million.
15 *Sonntagspost* article, reprinted in the Sotheby's catalogue for the sale of the Bentinck-Thyssen Collection, held in London on 6 December 1995.
16 Front-page article on 8 January 1931.
17 Letter dated 2 September 1930 (TBG Archives).
18 Willing, 6 April 1968.
19 Letter dated 11 July 1930 (TBG Archives).
20 Letter dated probably April 1931 (German Federal Archives, Berlin-Lichterfelde – File August Thyssen Junior).

21 Eglau p. 134 and Baumann, pp. 60/61.
22 *New York Times,* 10 March 1932.
23 Eglau, p. 208.
24 Willing, 30 March 1968 and Baumann, p. 63.
25 Letter dated 1 June 1932 (Swiss Federal Archives).
26 Bower, p. 68.
27 Ashby Turner, p. 339.
28 Author's interviews with Elsa Oppenheimer, 1995.
29 Author's interviews with Dr Waldemar Zettel, 1997.
30 Author's interview with Barbara von Stengel, 1998.
31 Author's interviews with Klaus Ritter, 1997.
32 Pita and Borobia, p. 586.
33 *Cosmopolitan* Magazine, December 1938.
34 Pritzkoleit, p. 61.
35 Letter from Fritz Thyssen to the Foreign Exchange Control Office in Düsseldorf re Faminta AG, dated 7 June 1939 (National Archives, Washington, DC).
36 The letter dated 9 August 1934 from The Adjutant von Tschirschky und Boegendorff in Berlin to 'His Excellency' Baron Thyssen in Karlsbad (now Karlovy Vary) reads:

> Dear Baron Thyssen! Due to my extraordinary workload at the moment, I have unfortunately, despite my best endeavours, so far been unable to thank you for the wonderful gift of a cigarette case with which you surprised me so greatly. This very beautiful and rare piece has delighted me tremendously and it will always remind me of that victorious day at the Hamburg Derby. I hope that we will later meet often in Vienna; perhaps I could also visit you in Hungary sometime. Once again many thanks indeed for your great kindness. With best regards. Yours faithfully. Von Tschirschky.

37 The letter dated 22 January 1937 from Rudolf Lotter of the National Socialist Workers' Party, district of Hesse-Nassau, local chapter of Dornholzhausen, Office for public relief, to Adrian von Borcke in Berlin-Hoppegarten reads:

> Dear Mr von Borcke. It is somewhat belated but no less from the heart that I, in the name of my local chapter, wish to thank you for your donation of RM 250.
> I can assure you that it was a great joy for us this Christmas to be able to arrange a beautiful celebration in each house for our needy members of the community. I regret that you could not witness this in person, as it does bring so much pleasure being able to help in this way. I have used the money to buy urgently needed goods and have kept a small amount back for 30 January (*anniversary of Hitler's assumption of power*). Should you come here in February or March, please let me know when it would be convenient for me to visit you so that I can give you the receipts for the purchases. I have notified the district of your donation under the name of Erlenhof, Mr von Borcke. I wish you all the best for the year 1937 and plenty of success for Erlenhof. Heil Hitler!

38 Author's interviews with Sandor Berkes, 2000.
39 Robert Kabelac's memoirs (TBG Archives).
40 Letter from Mr Tinguely, Intelligence Chief of the Fribourg cantonal police forwarded, to the Federal Political Division in Berne, dated 9 August 1946 (Swiss Federal Archives).
41 Spot report compiled by Max Guttmann on 14 December 1945 concerning the ownership of Bank voor Handel en Scheepvaart, written using two folders confiscated at August Thyssen Hütte Gewerkschaft (Gewerkschaft Preussen) in Mülheim/Ruhr, which contained Fritz Thyssen's declarations on 23 May 1935 about Rotterdamsch Trustees Kantoor made in a discussion of taxes to be paid by Faminta, towards an investigator of the tax collecting authorities (National Archives, Washington, DC).
42 Schneider, pp. 20–1 and F. Thyssen, *I Paid Hitler*, 1941, pp. 33 ff.

Chapter V

1939–1945

Banking for the Nazis...
Massacring the Jews

To save your world you asked this man to die.
Would this man, could he see you now, ask why?
W. H. Auden

'They say that we made a lot of money out of war. In fact, the exact opposite happened to us. The First and Second World Wars were financial disasters for my family. In the First World War, we lost all our industries in France and in the Second everything that wasn't confiscated by the Germans was taken by the Allies.'

From quite an early age Heini developed the ability to create his own reality when that which existed or had existed proved unpopular or inconvenient. It was a talent he had inherited from both his Uncle Fritz and, to a lesser degree, his father. The Second World War offered considerable encouragement for the exercising of this ability.

By 1942, Heini's retrospective denials would already have been proved hollow. While the minutes of the meetings in Switzerland, attended by Heini, his father and their German directors, gave a minimum of precise financial information, they reported overall profitability with the steel manufacturing division posting a 2 per cent dividend and a RM5 million reinvestment, while Thyssengas posted a 6 per cent dividend on profits of RM2 million. BVHS reported a Dfl 3 million surplus while the August Thyssen Bank continued to trade profitably in Berlin and confirm the credit-worthiness of the 'armament enterprises' at Heinrich's Flensburg shipyard.[1]

The most immediate wartime problem was the shortage of workers, as 26 per cent of the work-force were already serving in the armed forces. By 1943, Heinrich's Walsum mine was using forced labourers at a ratio of two to every one German; a record in German mining.[2]

Despite his absence, Fritz's corporate liquidity was equally healthy. The enormous United Steelworks trust ruled over 75 per cent of Germany's ore reserves, 50 per cent of its coal reserves, 200,000 workers, 60,000 dwellings, 52 square miles of property, a railway network from Paris to Königsberg, fourteen harbours and 219 power stations. Less well publicised was the fact that Fritz's steel division, August Thyssen Hütte (ATH), built nine POW camps and seventeen forced labour camps which, according to the questionable authorised figures, in 1944 housed 2,800 POWs and 2,800 forced labourers.[3] Despite Heini's subsequent denials, both his father's and his uncle's organisations continued to use a high proportion of slave labour to profit from the conflict. In 1938/39, ATH turned over RM 467,752,000. By 1942/43, despite Allied bombing, the turnover had decreased by less than 10 per cent.[4]

* * *

Fritz liked to give the impression that his flight from Germany had been the result of an impulsive reaction and that he had been accompanied by his family. In fact, his passport contained visas for America and Argentina where he had transferred SwFr 40 million and he had already overseen the flight of his daughter's family to South America.[5]

When Fritz refused to return to Germany, rather than seize his property for the Reich, Göring's response was to place Fritz's German holdings, including the 20 per cent stake in the United Steelworks and the entire August Thyssen concern valued at RM200 million under the trusteeship of the state of Prussia which Göring controlled. But it soon became apparent that Fritz had little to fear from the confiscation of his property, as Göring authorised various mutual friends and business associates to look after it.

Albert Vögler took over as President of the Supervisory Board of VSt, while Josef Terboven, the Gauleiter of Essen, and the banker Kurt Freiherr von Schröder of the Nazis' premier banking house J. H. Stein in Cologne, were appointed trustees of Fritz's fortune. They were assisted by Otto Steinbrinck, formerly General Director of the Flick concern.

However, Fritz's 25 per cent participation in the August Thyssen Bank in Berlin, with which both Göring and the Party continued to do business, was sold to his brother Heinrich.

Another member of the family affected by the confiscation was his sister, Hedwig, who until that time had been enjoying regular interest payments on the RM3 million held by Fritz on her behalf. Hedwig made a claim against Fritz but Baron von Schröder informed her that any recompense was impossible, as the state was not liable for any creditors. Hedwig then displayed an inspired appreciation of the distribution of power within the top echelons of the Reich by approaching her friend Emmy, the wife of Hermann Göring, for assistance. In response to her approach, in 1942 Göring repaid Hedwig her RM3 million from Fritz's confiscated interests.[6]

Some considered Fritz a traitor. Others saw his flight and the subsequent sequestering of his holdings as some form of self-sacrifice. Many years later, the German journalist Thomas Rother would write: 'Fritz Thyssen is the only German industrialist who did not profit from Hitler's war.' However, this overlooked the fact that all Fritz's various companies continued to trade and manufacture under the control and guidance of men of far greater commercial acumen. The result was that his fortune not only survived but flourished.

* * *

Having heard nothing from Göring, on 20 September 1939 Fritz had sent him another memorandum via an employee who subsequently decided against presenting the memo to Göring on the grounds that 'the language was too violent'. Fritz was also informed that the original telegram he claimed to have sent Göring was never received and if he was prepared to return to Germany, Göring would guarantee his safety.

But Fritz still had a far greater fear of the consequences of tax and foreign exchange revelations than confidence in any guarantee of safe passage by Göring, so he proposed impossible conditions; demanding that his memo be made public in Germany, so that everyone would appreciate his opposition to Hitler. His posturing had little effect and on 4 February 1940, Fritz and Amélie Thyssen were stripped of their German citizenship.

Fritz responded with critical letters to Hitler and the Interior Minister of the Reich but, due to his criticism of the present German regime, Fritz's presence was causing the Swiss considerable embarrassment and they readily agreed to the somewhat questionable British suggestion, supported by the French and Portuguese, that he should be offered freedom of passage to South America. The British also arranged a meeting with Sir William Firth from the Bank of England who wanted to come to some arrangement concerning the gold, which Fritz had deposited in London through the Swiss Pelzer Foundation. Apparently, he told Firth that he could do nothing without his mother's consent, which was unlikely to have been true, as the gold was under the control of Heinrich's Union Banking Corporation of New York. But it ensured his safe passage to Brussels where he persuaded his eighty-five-year-old ailing mother to sign various financial documents. She died on 21 April 1940; the situation regarding the gold remained unresolved.

Having failed to receive any response from Hitler or Göring, at the beginning of April 1940 Fritz gave copies of the letters to the international press from the Crillon Hotel in Paris. He was also approached by an American agent and publisher called Emery Reves who did not have to try very hard in persuading him to write or at least dictate his memoirs. It would prove a fortuitous piece of propaganda against both Hitler and communism but did nothing to improve Fritz's relations with the Swiss or his brother, who feared his own arrangements would be compromised.

By now the international press had started to respond to Fritz's outbursts and the Exchange Telegraph Press Agency broke the story that Fritz Thyssen had admitted to having provided the Nazi Party with RM62 million over a twelve-year period.[7] The *New York Times* reacted to his excuses with considerable scepticism:

> It would have been better if Fritz Thyssen had talked of the responsibilities he shirked in 1932 and 1933 when he and many of his fellow captains of industry trafficked with a movement whose sworn aim was the destruction of German liberties ... If Herr Thyssen's voice was ever raised against these things while he still lived in Germany, the fact is not on record.[8]
>
> He says that he protested in November 1938 because the Jews were being 'robbed and tortured' and because a 'vulgar pamphlet' against Catholics had been distributed in Düsseldorf. One wonders whether Thyssen had any eyes or ears in the preceding years of Nazi growth. 'My sole error', he wrote to his former leader, 'was that I believed in you, Adolf Hitler, the Führer and in the movement that you led'. His real error was in compromising with evil in the hope of saving his own millions. The world will waste little sympathy on such a man.[9]

On his return from Paris, the Swiss avoided the embarrassment of any involvement in his inflammatory political comments by denying him re-entry and Fritz and Amélie headed to Monte Carlo, where they installed themselves in the Hotel de Paris; closely followed by Reves. The next three weeks involved nothing more strenuous than enjoying extended late spring lunches at some of the finest restaurants on the Côte d'Azur, while an assistant recorded Fritz's fanciful excuses for his multi-million-Mark investment in Hitler. These formed the basis for his book of memoirs, entitled *I Paid Hitler*, published in 1941. Although Fritz later distanced himself from the book, it seems highly likely that he paid Reves to write it and arrange its publication.

Chapter V: 1939–1945

Following France's defeat, Fritz and Amélie moved to Cannes from where it could only have been a matter of time before they would be returned to Germany; yet they made no move to escape. Fritz undoubtedly preferred the glamour and political excitement of life on the Vichy-controlled Côte d'Azur to the anonymity of Argentina, while Amélie no doubt hoped that some form of negotiated settlement could be arranged and they would return to re-establish their privileged position within the Nazi Party.

On the 26 December 1940, six months after the Franco-German armistice, they were arrested by the French police and handed over to the Gestapo, who took them back to Germany; not, as popularly reported, to incarceration in a concentration camp, but to the comparative comfort and safety of Doctor Sinn's private clinic in Neubabelsberg, on the outskirts of Berlin.

* * *

Having arrived in Switzerland on 21 November 1939, there appeared to be some disagreement as to what papers Heini was travelling on and why he enrolled at one university and then four months later moved to another. It would subsequently transpire that in 1939 Heini had no passport of his own, his name being entered on his father's dubious Hungarian passport. So it seems likely that while Wettstein would eventually arrange a limited diplomatic passport for him, he had escaped from Holland with nothing more than identity papers and a letter from the Hungarian legation in Berne, where he was obliged to take up residence.

Heini never mentioned the four months he spent at Berne University and one can only assume that he was enrolled there to qualify him for the student status he needed to remain in Switzerland. But Berne was a German-speaking university and Heini quickly realized the unwanted attention a Thyssen would attract in such an establishment: 'The German Chargé d'Affaires in Berne, Herr Birbrach, who represented the

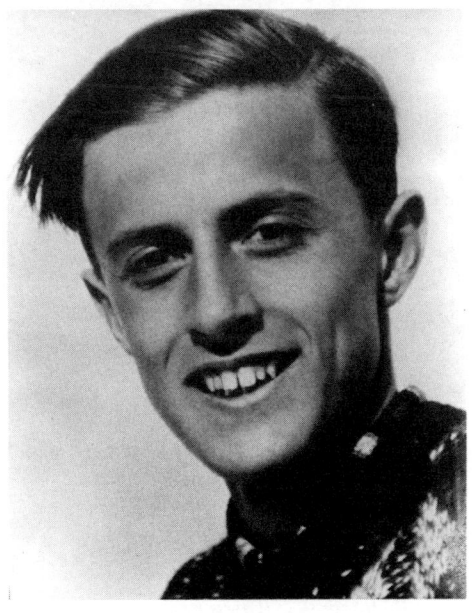

Heini in Switzerland, having escaped recruitment by the SS in 1939.

National Socialist Party, had advised my father to enlist me in the SS or risk confiscation of all his plants and facilities in Germany.'

According to Heini, he never suffered from any questioning by his fellow students concerning his uncle's public support of Hitler or why he had fled from Holland, due to the fact that, 'We never discussed it. I had no problems. I was Hungarian.'

In March 1940, Heini enrolled at the French-speaking University of Fribourg and, apart from occasional visits to his father in Lugano, he only returned to Berne at the weekends, when he could continue to enjoy a diplomatic lifestyle.

> I was happy that my mother and father were living in Switzerland. I was also happy that the Hungarian Embassy became my home. Here I learned what 'social life' really meant when I mixed with ambassadors, politicians, royalty, intellectuals and artists. It was an ideal environment for an inexperienced young man to acquire the necessary social skills to mix in these circles.

Despite spending more time in the company of his mother, their relationship failed to develop any genuine warmth or affection. His reclusive father appeared equally unable or unprepared to develop a healthy paternal relationship: 'We used to go for long walks from the Villa, down the hill to the Hotel Splendide but he often suffered from gout, so it took hours. He was also not a very talkative man, so I usually accompanied him in silence.'

His occasional conversation hardly encouraged Heini to develop an appreciation of family or even a respect for women:

> He used to say: 'Variety is the spice of life' and 'The best aphrodisiac is another woman'. He had a girlfriend called Elena Medicina and used to take me with him to San Remo to see her. Her friend was quite pretty and

Janos Wettstein in full dress uniform leaving a reception at the Royal Hungarian embassy in Berne.

Chapter V: 1939–1945

Heinrich, Margit Junior, Ivy Batthyány and Heini escaping the rigours of war at the Palace Hotel in Davos (photo: Caspar, Davos).

we used to go to the casino where the orchestra played fantastic tangos. We danced together and I kissed her. When she started smoking a cigarette, I also took one to look older and appear more independent. I remember clearly that she smoked Chesterfield cigarettes. I took a few puffs and felt quite sick.

To the annoyance of his father, they could not get to St Moritz during the war, as it was too far from Lugano and

> we would have had to go via Italy, which would have been far too dangerous. So we went to the Palace Hotel in Davos. He went for walks and I skied early in the morning from 8 to 10 o'clock. Then, I went for a walk with him till noon and we had lunch together. In the afternoon, I took him to a 'thé dansant' and then I'd have a nap. I went out every night with Teddy Stauffer to have a good time and afterwards I slept with a pretty Danish girl.

* * *

Heini's life was a long way from the horrors of war; a fact that he had no desire to be reminded of, particularly by letters from his abandoned girlfriend who had her dreams of studying journalism in Rome shattered by the war and her love for

Heini shattered by his insensitivity. On 28 November 1939, Pusch wrote him a letter in green ink in response to his in more conservative blue:

> I don't quite understand what you mean by the sentence 'don't be sad because of the past, that's over now'. But if this means that you want to draw a line under your time in The Hague, under all our experiences, then that line is really drawn very straight, abruptly and hard. You know that it took me a very long time to fall in love with you. How is it possible that you should want to finish with one sentence everything that united us?
>
> It was so much more than a friendship. We lived a piece of life together and we got on right until the last day. Why, then, do you want to turn this temporary good-bye into a final separation? Yes, people do change, but not as quickly as that and not without a reason. And if so, it would be a weakness which I could never have expected from you, Heini.
>
> Go now, to your university, to your many ambassador's daughters and to your nice visits to Lausanne. I hope you will not have to endure that which you have made me go through.

There was no evidence to suggest that Heini ever sent her a conciliatory letter, while his wonderful new social adventures in Switzerland did not improve poor Pusch's humour. But she carried on writing to him despite the fact that he advised her not to: 'Last week we couldn't go to the beach because of mines. Enemy airplanes were above the northern part of The Hague and we heard the thundering of the "Flak" guns for a whole hour.'

Meanwhile, Heini continued with his regular visits to the glamorous, French-speaking Lausanne, which was home to the socially and financially privileged refugees and

Heini and Ivy enjoying the company of the Palace bear.

accompanying courtesans of Spain, Italy and other European nations. There he came to meet the Count of Barcelona, father of the future King of Spain Juan Carlos, who lived at the Hotel Royal.

* * *

Heini liked to give the impression that he led the life of a carefree young student and knew nothing of his father's business but in fact, from April 1941, he was obliged to attend the regular board meetings with his father which occurred not, as he later admitted, once a year but every three months, in Lugano, Flims, Zurich and Davos. The German directors Dr Wilhelm Roelen and Heinrich Lübke also attended these meetings. From time to time, they were joined by SS-Brigadeführer Baron Kurt von Schröder, the trustee of Fritz's confiscated industrial holdings.

Heini would later deny that his father played any part in arming the Third Reich and said that if his organization did, it was without their knowledge. But the minutes of these meetings, many of which were approved and signed by Heini, make it clear that he must have been aware of Bremer Vulkan's U-boat production, coal exports to Switzerland and the use of slave labour in its extraction. He would also have known that his father's other companies, Seismos, Press and Rolling Works Düsseldorf-Reisholz and Oberbilker Steelworks were all engaged in the manufacture of weapons and weapon parts.

For Heinrich to control such an organisation from the safety and anonymity of a neutral country required the assistance of a manager of exceptional loyalty, and the Dutch Henrik Jozef Kouwenhoven was such a man. He was the most powerful manager and director in Heinrich's organisation, who also shared intimate knowledge of Fritz's financial dealings. Kouwenhoven was on the board of BVHS, ATB and the Union Banking Corporation in New York and a trustee of both Heinrich's Kaszony and Fritz's Pelzer Foundations. He was an infinitely more talented businessman than Heinrich and had shared the responsibility with Eduard von der Heydt of creating much of his business strategy and financial instruments. He was also unique among the management in accruing considerable personal wealth in the process.

In 1940, when Fritz's fortune was confiscated and the Germans invaded Holland, Kouwenhoven was put under intense pressure to reveal details of the Thyssens' financial arrangements. Initially, he remained discreet, but when Heinrich made the decision to replace him with two German directors and move all the securities, including those of the Dutch monarchy, to the August Thyssen Bank in Berlin, Kouwenhoven became more co-operative with the authorities;

particularly when he was reminded that he could also be incarcerated. Heini resented what he considered a betrayal:

> The Germans found out about our tax evasion through Kouwenhoven who double-crossed us. My father always insisted that he and his brother were never mixed up in business together but they had agreed that my father would buy gas from Uncle Fritz's blast furnaces and sell him water to cool the steel. In the deed of separation between the brothers in 1930, it was agreed to overvalue the water and pay the profits in Holland to avoid German taxes. Unfortunately, Kouwenhoven belonged to a Protestant sect, which decreed that their adherents could not lie. So he was telling all sorts of stuff, in fact all the truth about the accounts of my uncle and those of my father and how they were organised. That was why he was replaced on the board of BVHS by Lübke and Roelen in 1942. The latter was a well-known figure, very nationalistic but not a Nazi. He helped us avoid further inspections and prevented the assets from returning to Germany.

A Dutch newspaper would eventually publish a more realistic explanation:

> In autumn 1942, Dr Kurt Bockamp ordered that the shares which lay in the vault of BVHS, including those of Queen Wilhelmina, should be transported to Germany. Ostensibly, the move was necessary because of the threat of an Allied invasion and bombing attacks. But the Dutch director of BVHS, Mr Kouwenhoven, correctly saw it as an attempt to plunder the bank and tighten the German grip on the Dutch economy. He protested vehemently and was then dismissed from his post by the trustee of the general Thyssen conglomerate, the Düsseldorf resident, Dr Wilhelm Roelen.[10]

Wilhelm Roelen was a man in the mould of 'old' August, a *Wehrwirtschaftsführer* or leader of the wartime economy, who described the Thyssen enterprise in 1943 as 'of vital importance to the war effort and victory'.[11] An equally loyal manager, Robert Kabelac, who was also awarded the status of *Wehrwirtschaftsführer*, continued to run Heinrich's Bremer Vulkan shipyard with total dedication and loyalty to the owner: 'At the shipyard we had by now managed the beginning of the change to war production. I seem to remember we delivered three U-boats in 1940.'

Over the next three years, they would deliver a further 68 U-boats and supply 178 diesel engines.

* * *

Perhaps the most surprising reaction to the outbreak of war by any of the family was that of Stephan Thyssen-Bornemisza who continued his work with Seismos. For a man with ample financial means and a legitimate Hungarian passport, it is significant that he chose to remain in Nazi Germany. Heini insisted that Stephan had friends among the Nazi hierarchy but he also supported Dr Zettel's claim that his brother had been only involved in the peaceful development of instruments and machinery for export to the foreign oil industry. However, after the war, evidence emerged strongly indicating that Stephan's design skills had not been limited to peaceful activities and that his relationship with the Reich may have been professional as well as social.

At some time during the war, Stephan divorced Ilyana Kugler-Andrassy and in 1946 married Ingeborg Müller, a divorcee with a daughter called Birgit. Many years later, between 1956 and 1960, Baroness Ilyana registered the following patents at the German Patent Office:

> Cartridge case for mortar shell, propelling charge cartridge for mortar shell, smoke charge for missiles, bolting of the base piece of a mortar shell tube with a base plate, wing stabilized mortar, mortar shell, mortar missile, explosive charge with various speeds of detonation for mortars and a device for the adjustment of the heightening angle of an infantry mortar.[12]

Stephan and his third wife Ingeborg. (photo: Prestel-Hofmann, Hanover).

It is unlikely that a girl who had only ever worked in a patisserie should take up a career as a weapons designer. It is far more likely that these designs were in fact the work of Stephan. This theory is supported by the fact that during the war he would also become involved with a second company that manufactured armaments, including parts for V-rockets.

The other Thyssens who stayed in Germany were Hans and Julius who ironically had accepted Fritz as nominee for their shares in the United Steelworks. Once the Prussian state had confiscated Fritz's holdings, Hans and Julius, having settled their outstanding RM 12 million tax demand, were invited by Hermann Göring to sell their shares of Thyssen & Co. for a rate that gave them a RM 54 million return which they then invested outside the Thyssen conglomerate before dying in 1943 and 1946 respectively.

While Göring may have initiated the sale for his own profit, it would prove extremely fortuitous for his friends Fritz and Amélie Thyssen and the subsequent return of their sole ownership of the Thyssen organisation in Germany. Meanwhile, through continued pooling of investments, Hans and Julius's descendants, while abandoning careers in industry and adopting the professions, would still eventually come to own 75 per cent of the equity of the mining industry in the Duisburg area.

* * *

Having enrolled at Fribourg University, Heini took up lodgings on the fourth floor of a guest house on Boulevard de Peyrolles, run by Miss de Meyer, a sixty-year-old spinster. There he met and formed a lasting friendship with Luís Villegas, a Spaniard whose father was military attaché in Rome. He also met a young Calvinist called Edouard Gueydan and an Austro-Hungarian American called Count Janos Palffy who would introduce Heini to Princess Theresa zu Lippe, the girl who was to become his first wife.

> My father gave me SwFr 500 a month, which was quite a lot but I had to pay everything with that: my rent, my books, my clothes, travel and tuition fees. I wasn't any better off than the other students, although I did have a car. It was a small Fiat which was fortunate because petrol was very scarce. However, through the Hungarian Embassy, I received twenty litres per month. There was a relaxed friendly atmosphere at the guest house and above all we liked practical jokes. Miss de Meyer was always worried about the glass in the front

door of the house and never tired of telling us to be careful shutting the door. Luís came back from his holidays with some sheets of metal that could be made to sound like breaking glass. We tried them out at breakfast one morning and Miss de Meyer went white. Those sheets were the bane of her life for quite a while.

Heini did not actually gain any academic qualifications while he was at university but he did achieve one objective, which, apart from avoiding becoming involved in the war, justified his stay in Switzerland: 'I met Joseph Groh, a Hungarian who would later become one of my legal advisers. He was in the year above me, studying Law. Later we would work together for many years and his knowledge of Hungarian law would be particularly useful in the execution of my father's will.'

Unlike Heini, Josi Groh was academically gifted or perhaps he just worked harder for, having gained his doctorate in Switzerland, Groh returned to Budapest where he gained a further degree in Hungarian law before becoming actively involved in the war and finally returning to Switzerland. Meanwhile Heini was enjoying a less productive but no doubt more enjoyable series of romantic adventures. 'I went out with a Dutch girl who was the daughter of a chocolate manufacturer and a few years younger than me. We used to go out for drives in the country but the first time we tried to make love and started undressing I discovered I was covered in red spots. I had measles! That put an end to that.'

Despite his somewhat puny physical stature, there were a lot of girls in Fribourg who no doubt found the heir to one of the world's largest industrial fortunes extremely attractive. One of them, Rita Troesch, came from a wealthy Swiss family that made kitchen and bathroom appliances:

> She was madly in love with me although she was eight years older and already divorced. The whole relationship was very physical. She taught me how to make love and it was a wonderful experience. Our affair lasted for two years and I often took her to my mother's place. One day, in the middle of the war, her mother threw a dinner party in the best restaurant in Berne with caviar and champagne. She stood up and announced that they were celebrating my engagement to Rita. I told her that I couldn't get engaged because I was too young and was only a student. She was furious.

* * *

But Heini's behaviour was also somewhat more anti-social than he cared to

Heini's student days in Fribourg.

admit and failed to impress the Swiss authorities. This was made clear in a report from the head of police in Fribourg to the Federal Police in Berne in response to Heini's application for Swiss nationality on 9 August 1948: 'We are doubting the degree of assimilation of the claimant Hans Heinrich Thyssen-Bornemisza who stayed in Fribourg from May 1940 to April 1946. His behaviour, especially when in the street, gave rise to complaints and several protests, mainly from the public.'

These included complaints about his wastage of fuel by driving his car at high speeds through the streets, how he ferried young girls about, made fun of the local guards and police with Nazi salutes and played his gramophone loudly on the balcony in order to annoy the neighbours. The report continues:

> The behaviour of the young Thyssen is 'sovereignly unpleasant'. He has this idea that because he holds a diplomatic passport he can scorn the basic laws of courtesy towards the people of his host country. From a political point of view, we don't have any indications as to a political involvement of the young Thyssen. He is also unknown in the legal registers here. Please review the above and make your own judgement as to whether the integration of this gentleman in our midst would be of any advantage to our country.

While Heini played with the girls and annoyed the neighbours, Pusch was witnessing the war first hand. Her harrowing letters to Heini concerning dead and wounded soldiers were as close to any military action as he would ever get. While obviously desperate to escape, she realised that for her it would now be quite impossible. 'War is a terrible nonsense. Sometimes I really get mad about it and am very sad that this war has taken away so much from me. I am not even allowed to visit my father any longer. This is how strict and complicated the regulations are now concerning traffic between Germany and Holland.'

The German invasion of Holland took five days. Then, because Pusch had learned shorthand, she was ordered to serve in the German naval administration. From Heini's reply, it was obvious that, despite the threat to the lives of his friends, Nanny Volz and the servants at his home, he considered the war to be little more than an unfortunate irritation. Pusch was not at all impressed: 'You write about this awful war that it is "old, annoying and boring". Frankly, I cannot understand that. Don't you have any eyes and ears in your head? Well, of course, it is probably difficult to appreciate the misery from the Waldhotel in Flims.'

* * *

Having been returned to Germany, Fritz and Amélie were treated with remarkable lenience considering his public condemnation of Hitler. After a brief stay at a Berlin hotel, on 9 January 1941 they were finally interned in a private sanatorium on the outskirts of the city in Neubabelsberg, where they would remain for two-and-a-half years.

In reality, their 'incarceration' appears to have been more a form of mild custody which imposed no serious inconvenience, apart from the fact that they were not allowed to leave. Certainly, their life at the sanatorium appeared to involve them in few discomforts apart from the threat posed by allied bombs. It was reported that they enjoyed many privileges and were even permitted free contact with family and business associates.

When a fellow inmate, a Swedish woman of mixed German and South African parentage, was allowed to return home in 1943, she relayed her experience and revealed to journalists the relatively comfortable conditions under which the Thyssens lived:

> The sanatorium is directed by Dr Richard Sinn. Only about a quarter of the inmates are genuine mental cases. Another quarter have been put away by relatives while the remaining half are refugees and 'guests' of the Gestapo who could afford to pay the very high fees demanded by the proprietor. Thyssen and his wife are allowed some liberty of movement. They go into Berlin most days in a hired car and usually have lunch at the Hotel Bristol.

The car was driven by Fritz's chauffeur, while Amélie had been permitted to keep a maid with her. 'Thyssen seems to be anxious to escape from his concentration-camp deluxe, but his wife, who is a very hysterical woman, begs him continuously to do nothing rash.'

The source declared him to be 'completely out of touch with what is really going on in Germany, and content to keep his promise, made to the Gestapo when he was handed over by the French police, not to discuss politics or to have any dealings with his former associates'.[13]

* * *

Towards the end of 1941, Fritz's book, *I Paid Hitler*, was published in Britain and the United States, where it received unanimous criticism:

> It is with a feeling of distrust and disgust that one puts down these memoirs of the once powerful German industrialist who financed Hitler for many years. Here, as in many other personal confessions, the explanations obscure rather than clarify. His answers are often unbelievable and sometimes obviously untrue. A great industrialist with a minimum of brains. A devout Catholic whose mouth was filled with religion while he dressed and armed the storm troopers and subsidised anti-Semitism for higher reasons. That he finds fault with the German people and makes them more responsible for Hitler than he was, at least by implication, adds merely the last stomach-turning touch to his performance.[14]

The book certainly bore all the hallmarks of Fritz's typical self-delusion. One prime example concerned his involvement in the First World War: 'Until the last day I shared the sufferings and the hopes that animated all the soldiers at the front.' In fact, he was only in the army for one year during which time he served as a non-combatant administrator, some distance from the front.

He also claimed: 'I have spent my life among workers.' This was quite untrue. Fritz had previously admitted to lacking affinity with the workers and never displayed the slightest desire to spend any more time in their company than was absolutely necessary: 'I had not as much time as my father to occupy myself with the workers. I didn't have my father's way to talk with the men either and I did not enjoy their confidence to the same degree.'

He then claimed to have single-handedly 'organized the passive resistance in its entirety', making no mention of the equal if not greater contribution made by either the trade unions, other industrialists or indeed the government of the time.

Fritz admitted that *Mein Kampf* 'revived the insane aspirations of the Pan-Germans' but then insisted 'not even the most rightist circles in Germany ever took such hysterical ideas seriously'. As a supporter of the Pan-German League and a member of the Nazi Party, who used to give copies of *Mein Kampf* to his friends while ploughing vast amounts of money into helping the author achieve his ambitions, one would have to assume Fritz took it very seriously indeed.[15]

As an avowed anti-Semite, Fritz's most hypocritical statement concerned the financial debt of gratitude Germany owed the Jews. 'No one knows better than I, an industrialist, what services were rendered by Jews to the German national economy after the war. It was thanks to these Jews that medium and small enterprises were able to obtain from the American banks the necessary loans for their re-equipment.'

He went on: 'The Simon Hirschland Bank at Essen, for instance, obtained loans to the amount of at least fifty million dollars for the small and medium establishments of our region. It was this bank which negotiated the important American Krupp loan in collaboration with another Jewish bank, Goldman Sachs & Co. of New York.'

* * *

In May 1943, Fritz and Amélie were moved to Sachsenhausen 'concentration camp', although in their case the term was misleading. While thousands of people died there under appalling conditions, the Thyssens continued to suffer from nothing more than terminal boredom. They were assigned to one of the four, undecorated, simple houses that had been built for important detainees. Once again they were afforded quite remarkable privileges. They even had a small garden where they used to take tea with friends. They didn't have to work or wear prison clothes and shared the same food as the SS officers.

It appeared that Fritz Thyssen's imprisonment had very little adverse effect on the profitable running of the United Steelworks. He also managed to keep in touch with his daughter in Buenos Aires and control his Argentinian investments through Heinrich Blass of Credit Suisse.[16] American intelligence sources were also of the opinion that Hermann Brassert, a relative and business associate of Göring, for whom he made frequent trips to Switzerland, acted as a courier between Fritz, Amélie and Anita, as did a Mr Bausch.

Various new directors joined the supervisory board of VSt and when Albert Speer took charge of the Reich Ministry for Armaments and War Production in 1942, he and the new chairman of the United Steelworks, Walter Rohland, adopted Landsberg Castle as their headquarters. There they organized an appropriate social programme which included chamber music *soirées*, social gatherings and even 'a lively summer party'.

The United Steelworks soon became the largest producer of military hardware with its many divisions making gun barrels, shells and gun components, the most important being Hanomag, which produced guns from 8.8 cm to the largest railway guns and in the range of 10.5 cm to 12.8 cm. Anti-aircraft guns and ammunition accounted for 50 per cent of the total production. Besides a large capacity for shell production, they were especially well equipped for the production of sintered iron driving bands for shells.[17] They were also the largest manufacturers of 3-ton half-track vehicles. Another arms producer within the trust was the Bochum Cast Steel Manufacturers, the oldest and one of the strongest competitors to Krupp in the field of artillery.

Total VSt turnover in 1943/44 amounted to well over RM 4.2 billion. The turnover for August Thyssen Hütte fell from RM 468 million in 1938/39 to RM 393 million in 1940/41 and rose again to RM 417 million in 1942/43, none of which had anything to do with Fritz Thyssen. The alterations were largely affected by the previously mentioned labour and raw material shortages. In 1939, August Thyssen Hütte employed 22,000 people and in 1943/44 its suprastructure VSt employed 300,000 people.

The Trust also incorporated a number of trading companies, some of very great importance. Total turnover for all the trading companies in 1943 was RM1 billion. One of them, Thyssen Eisen und Stahl AG, turned over RM 137 million in 1942/43 up from RM 121 million in 1938/39.

* * *

It is ironic that while it was Fritz who made all the noise about his part in bringing Hitler to power, he would actually have remarkably little involvement in the war, despite the fact that he remained in Germany, while his brother, who stayed safely hidden away in Switzerland, would continue to aid and abet the Nazi war machine.

The immaculately dressed Sandor Berkes spent more time delighting in his good fortune in sharing the Baron's safe-haven than concerning himself with his master's involvement in the creation of guns and submarines. But he remembered the war-weary German directors' regular visits to Villa Favorita:

> After the Baron had written a letter to Hitler complaining how his people had treated him, he didn't go to Germany anymore but the directors of his companies came here. For instance, there was the general manager, Mr Roelen. He was a very simple man but very, very nice. He was like a father. Once when he arrived, his shoes looked dreadful and he asked me if I could have them resoled for him. He and his colleague arrived here looking like travelling journeymen.

It is difficult to imagine what must have gone through the directors' minds when they visited the Thyssens in the luxurious tranquillity of their lakeside palace, knowing that they would soon be returning to work twelve to eighteen hours a day, under appalling, life-threatening conditions, to ensure the uninterrupted profitability of the Thyssens' Konzern. Meanwhile, Sandor continued to arrange the Baron's life with loyalty and dedication: 'During the

Chapter V: 1939–1945

war, there were hardly any people here at all. I looked after the car as well as the house. I did everything. I even gave him his insulin injections.'

Apart from visits from Heini, his managers and lawyers, Berkes had been the old man's sole companion:

> In the mornings, between 10 and 1 o'clock, he would spend time with me alone in the gallery. I think he found it a pleasure to train me to look after his paintings. Then he would have lunch. Sometimes with me and sometimes alone. He would say, 'Are you staying for lunch?' and I would say, 'No, I'm sorry but I can't. My wife is at home with our baby.' 'But you stayed yesterday!' 'Well, yes, but that's why I can't stay today,' I replied.
>
> Afterwards he would have a nap. Then I would return at 4 o'clock and we would walk into town. Sometimes we would take the electric tram. If I returned from lunch five minutes late, because I had taken a telephone call, he would always point out that I was five minutes late but if I had to wait for him he would always apologise. He expected discipline both from himself and from others. He also demanded peace and quiet. When he was reading on the terrace, the gardeners had to stay away from anywhere he might see or hear them.

* * *

For Heinrich the meetings offered a brief but welcome respite from his solitary existence. For Heini they were a convenient opportunity to get to know both his father and his business. But in late May, when the mimosa was in full bloom and champagne could be taken on the terrace above the lake, Roelen and Lübke, having escaped from a country being destroyed by war, would no doubt have derived a great deal more pleasure from their visit than either Heinrich or Heini.

The minutes of their five-day meeting in May 1941 reveal coal deliveries from Heinrich's Walsum mine to Switzerland through the intermediary of the Swiss Bank Corporation in Zurich. It was also agreed that changes to the supervisory board of August Thyssen Bank would take place following the sale to the Baron of his brother's 25 per cent share in the bank by Göring. Obviously, Heinrich was fully aware of his brother's incarceration yet continued to do business with the Nazis, which was presumably why no harm came to Fritz despite his histrionics. It was then noted that 18,000 Pengö had been transferred from the Pest Bank in Budapest to pay Gunhilde's alimony. There was also a note to remind everyone that their mother, Madame Neuter-Pelzer, had died in Brussels in April 1940 and that he had failed to attend her funeral. The fact that there was no mention of her death or the funeral in his personal diary reflected his lack of personal attachment.

The meeting of August 1941 lasted four days and took place in Flims. The first item on the agenda was about considerable capital increases within the utilities divisions followed by news that the gas supply negotiations between Thyssengas and the Dutch authorities were 'expected to be concluded very soon'.

Presumably the personal fortunes of the BVHS-managers Wilhelm Roelen and Heinrich Lübke also improved, as they were voted on to the supervisory board, although the bank was also assigned some minimal degree of Reich control by the assignment of a 'special envoy for special economic matters in the form of Director Dr Mojert at the Reichs Commissary in The Hague, with whom contact will be maintained'. The bank was also reported to be enjoying 'a gross surplus of Dfl 6 million of which 10 per cent are to paid out as dividends and the board is to receive shares in the profits of 3 per cent'.

Meanwhile, Heinrich continued to care for the family financially with Margit at Rechnitz receiving a fixed annual remit of RM 30,000 'plus RM 18,000 as a "flexible" contribution for maintaining the castle and a loan of RM 400,000', while the SS remained in residence.

* * *

The regular business meetings continued to be held in Switzerland and by the end of 1941 Heini was signing the minutes both on his own behalf and on behalf of his often inebriated father, while their horse trainer, Adrian von Borcke, reported to the Baron directly from Germany in a remarkably light-hearted frame of mind.

> After yesterday's racing I was cornered by Aunt Olala. She told me that Gunhilde is now back in a hotel in Lugano and asked what it was that she had done. Of course she hadn't done anything, but you are such a terrible man, who needs a new woman every two years, and the two years were up. Oh, what a Don Juan you are! We all hope that Peace may come soon and I shall then be looking forward to meeting with you again, dear Casanova.

Von Borcke also gave somewhat more serious news concerning the performance and earning abilities of Heinrich's most directly profitable investment in Jewish persecution. The 'Erlenhof stud' Figaro had won RM 8,500 in two races in Hoppegarten, RM 1,500 in Dresden and RM 1,000 in the Wilamowitz race. Six other horses had enjoyed similar success. But he appeared to be far more

Margit Batthyány-Thyssen collecting prizes for the Erlenhof racing stables in Vienna in 1942. (photo: Menzendorf, Berlin)

interested in gossiping about Gunhilde and their mutual German friends than discussing breeding, training or racing.

> I'm sorry that the information I got from my manicurist didn't prove to be accurate. I do hope to be able to find out something more worth your while in the near future. It seems that Gunhilde and her sister are putting out all sorts of rumours, but of course now I don't know what's true and what isn't.
>
> I had two very nice days in Munich. I did not see your brother August. I only heard that he is better now and also that Gretl Holzner has arrived back in Munich. It seems that this young lady also fears she would not get anything otherwise. As I entered the Regina, my heart sank into my trousers when I saw Pucky Solms behind a newspaper. I am very sorry to hear that your health is poorly. Let's hope Peace comes soon and calmer times and then we will all feel better again, won't we? I will be going to Obergurgl in the Oetz Valley for my winter sport. I think I will meet Karlchen Kleist there. Maybe I can find something out from him. I am often thinking of our poor Baby. She will be twenty-five this year. You probably don't hear much from her either.

* * *

As Heini learned his father's business, Pusch continued to remind him of their romantic past and her war-torn present with increasing candour:

> In the mornings, I wake up quite quickly, even if it has only been four hours since I 'made nonsense' with someone from the navy. Are you in love? If this question seems to be too indiscreet, of course you don't have to answer it. But I think we are friends enough to tell us our respective adventures without blushing any longer. The guy from the navy is called Jonny and I like him a lot. Jonny and I often go to the cinema and eat out. He loves Zarah Leander. All in all it can be said that we also made a lot of 'nonsense'.

Heini appears to have been more discreet concerning his 'nonsense', but there was plenty of it, as this letter from one of his French-speaking conquests in Fribourg reveals:

> My amour Chéri. How can I thank you for the lovely flowers. I give you a mouth to thank you, my body to recompense you and my spirit and heart to love you. Are you happy? I had a hectic day. Our house maid left us just before the holidays, so I'm having to replace her until Tuesday. But I have lots of energy, which could be dangerous for you when you come back. I only think of you. You will never know to what degree I belong to you. I am alone again tonight, but it does not bother me. I listen to rhythmic and voluptuous tangos. A hot Argentinian voice cradles my nostalgia.
>
> I have your picture in front of me. I am trying to find out what it is I like so much in you. The sensual mouth, the wolf's teeth, the laughing eyes . . . I don't care about your former life. My own life has been so empty, flat, stupid. Fortunately, you have come and given it a sense of direction. When you come back, I will be going mad and I will bite your tongue so hard that not much will be left of it. But don't worry. I am sending you my most tender kisses for your 20th birthday and for Easter, falling on the same day. I love you deeply and wish to remain your wife forever.

Pusch eventually married Jonny, who miraculously survived service as a U-boat captain. But he would find peace far more difficult to adjust to than war and died in 1961, leaving her to bring up their two sons alone. Despite their differing fortunes, Heini remained in touch with his mercurial first love for the rest of his life.

* * *

From Heinrich's point of view, *I Paid Hitler* was a welcome and successful means of turning attention away from himself and towards Fritz and when the

Chapter V: 1939–1945

American press finally realized, in July 1941, that the Thyssen family owned their own bank on Broadway, it was Fritz, not Heinrich whom the *New York Herald Tribune* held responsible when they announced:

> Hitler's Angel has three million in New York bank. A sort of nest egg for Thyssen or perhaps some of his high-placed Nazi friends when the present troublesome days are over. Maybe it was money sent here for safekeeping on behalf of Göring, Goebbels, Himmler, or Hitler. Many think the rift between Fritz Thyssen and the Nazis was not at all genuine.

As of January 1941, the officers and directors were said to have included: 'President: Cornelis Lievense. Treasurer: Walter Kauffmann. Directors: C. Lievense, E. Roland Harriman, H. D. Pennington, P. S. Bush [of George and George W. fame], H. J. Kouwenhoven, Ray Morris and J. G. Groeninger'.

The Treasury Department, possibly motivated by the press coverage, appeared to be struggling to obtain sufficient information to freeze the bank's assets. Cornelis Lievense, the Dutch managing director, remained insistent that the bank was Dutch and 'all the shares are owned by BVHS, but held nominally by Averell Harriman of New York'.[18]

They eventually discovered that Baron Heinrich Thyssen-Bornemisza, 'a Hungarian citizen living in Holland', also held a substantial interest. This partially explained why Heinrich insisted he was still living in Holland rather than Switzerland but it did not explain why the Department was so slow in making the obvious German connection, especially when they discovered the name of Lievense on the board of directors of August Thyssen Bank AG in Berlin. Perhaps it was the power and status of the directors or the delicacy of the situation, as at that time the US had at least $475 million invested in Nazi Germany.

Mr Lievense stated that several months after the war started, in the

Louise Bornemisza-Price's arrival in America for a short stay in 1941.

```
                    UNITED STATES DISTRICT COURT
                       DISTRICT OF DELAWARE
                           WILMINGTON
JUDGE'S CHAMBERS


                                              June 4, 1941.


        TO WHOM IT MAY CONCERN:

              I am familiar with the families
        of Price and Harlan who were residents of Wilmington,
        Delaware for many generations.

              Matilda Louisa Price now Baroness
        Bornemisza is a descendant of these families
        and has no trace of Jewish blood in her veins.

                              Yours very truly,

                                    [signature]
                              ─────────────────────
                                 John P. Nields,
                           United States District Judge.
```

Worrying evidence of American judiciary's compliance with Nazi policy of racial purity.

winter of 1939/40, he received a telephone call from Mr Kouwenhoven from Rotterdam in which the latter said that 'whatever the ownership of the Dutch bank had been, there was now no longer any German interest and had not been for quite some time'. This telephone conversation allegedly arose in connection with certain difficulties experienced 'with various companies and holdings whose ownership could be traced through BVHS'.

One such organisation, the Steel Union Sheet Piling Company, was even believed to be an affiliate of VSt, the German steel union. But according to Mr Lievense, all funds received by the Union Banking Corporation (except dividends and coupons) had come only from BVHS. He said he had no knowledge of funds held for account of Fritz Thyssen and that UBC had its principal banking account with Brown Bros. Harriman and Company, New York, but also carried inactive accounts with Chase National, Guaranty Trust and National City Bank.

But the Union Bank also held shares in sixteen Argentinian companies for Fritz Thyssen while ongoing investigations began to uncover many more assets than the 'ranch and a few cows' that he would later admit to.

Finally, on 15 September 1941, the Foreign Funds Control Division of the US Treasury discovered that in 1931 the August Thyssen Bank of Berlin had an account at the Union Bank containing $1,000,923.25 and that both payments and receipts that year had totalled $17,467,805.40; many of the transactions having been in gold. It was also discovered that the bank had been acting as proxy shareholder for German and Argentinian companies. Finally, Erwin G. May, the Treasury Attaché, stated in his recommendation: 'For reasons previously given in this report, and from information which I have received in interviews with European bankers now in the United States, I am of the belief that BVHS represents German interests and German capital.'[19]

Having discovered a paper trail from Germany to Argentina via Holland and New York, the Treasury recommended that the Union Banking Corporation, Holland American Trading Corporation, Domestic Fuel Corporation and the Seamless Steel Equipment Corporation should all be blocked as both Dutch and German companies. All of them worked out of the Union Banking Corporation offices at 39 Broadway, a company whose existence and location Heini would subsequently try to deny. Lievense then wrote to Brown Bros. Harriman on Wall Street asking for a favour: 'We would greatly appreciate it if the Treasury Department would reconsider their decision and allow you to block our accounts as Dutch as heretofore instead of German.'[20]

But by now America had entered the war, favours were in short supply and the British Embassy was working with the US Treasury in an effort to trace the Thyssens' Argentinian fortune and its control. By 1943 they would come to value Fritz's total holdings in Argentina at some $50 million and discovered Fritz, Amélie and Anita's Übersee Trust (Liechtenstein) and that it was administered by Credit Suisse in Zurich. Then there was Colamina SA, the holding and management company for their Argentinian interests, and the 3,000 shares of Colamina which belonged to Übersee Trust and were deposited with the Buenos Aires branch of the National City Bank. They also discovered ArgPs 750,000 on deposit in the Buenos Aires branch of the Bank of London and South America.[21]

As an increasing amount of information came to the surface, it became obvious that either the British or the Americans had a mole in Credit Suisse who continued to leak them information and documents.

* * *

By the time Amélie and Fritz had been subject to their first experience of life in a concentration camp, their nephew had become involved in building them. Throughout the war, Stephan continued to work for Seismos and kept his apartment in Hanover and his country retreat at Einbeck. But at some time between 1941 and 1942, no doubt as a result of the increased allied bombing, the decision was made to move the company to Barbis in the Harz mountains. But Stephan's move to the Harz was motivated by a far more sinister purpose.

Around this time, he had also taken on the position of chairman of the supervisory board of MABAG, situated in the same district as Seismos' wartime premises. The company built and repaired the machinery and tools used to sink mine shafts but they also specialised in the building of petrol storage installations. Although there was no direct relationship with Seismos, there appears to have been some major investment by Heinrich through either BVHS or the August Thyssen Bank, which would have justified Stephan's position as chairman; for despite his scientific talent, he had so far displayed little in the way of management skills.

With the development of the aviation industry, MABAG installed an increasing number of fuelling facilities and with the onset of war, orders for the Luftwaffe increased dramatically. In addition, between 1940 and 1944 the company would also produce 3,000 mortars per month, which may have explained the patents lodged by Stephan's ex-wife after the war. But the main reason for MABAG being in the area had been their work in the creation of a vast network of caves and tunnels in the Kohnstein mountain near Nordhausen equipped with tanks and pumps in conjunction with IG Farben. This would become the Reich's main fuel-oil storage depot as well as the site of its most ambitious weapons system.

From February 1942 onwards, the Armaments Minister Albert Speer recommended all possible support for the development of rockets. This represented massively ambitious armaments manufacturing plans and a great deal more work for MABAG, who, under the control of the Wehrmacht, were now also producing turbo fuel pumps for the V-rockets. The programme no doubt also involved Heinrich's company Oberbilker Steelworks, described in a 1944 official report as 'the most modern special armaments plant, especially for submarines, air force, ammunitions, etc'. They were also reported to have been engaged in the manufacture of parts for 'aerial torpedoes'.[22]

The work required massive amounts of manpower both for the dangerous tunnelling into the mountains and for the engineering and industrial work:

Chapter V: 1939–1945

As early as 28 August 1943, Dr Ing Hans Kammler, the SS-Brigadeführer responsible for all the SS's building works, authorised the arrival of the first prisoners from the Buchenwald concentration camp. External branches of the big concentration camps were built close to the production areas. In this instance 'Dora', the external branch of Buchenwald, was built at Niedersachswerfen just north of Nordhausen. At the end of October 1943, more than 6,000 prisoners were in the sleeping caves in the Kohnstein and by the end of the year there were more than 10,000 forced labourers from Russia, Poland and France.[23]

MABAG had also been involved in equipping the Dora caves and tunnels which by 28 October 1944 held 32,532 prisoners and had gained its independence from Buchenwald, becoming the 'independent concentration camp Mittelbau'. In all the camp would hold 60,000 prisoners of whom 20,000 were worked to death.

While Stephan's surviving wife and daughter persistently refused to comment on his wartime activities, Heini denied all knowledge of MABAG or any involvement by either his father or his brother, despite his insistence that the latter had a close relationship with the SS. Only Pusch appeared to remember Stephan's involvement with the company but any attempt to remind Heini during our long lunches at Mas Mañanas was met with an extremely grumpy denial and what appeared to be a veiled threat that her constant insistence might have a detrimental effect on his continued financial generosity.

* * *

While Gunhilde may have motivated Heinrich to prepare his first will, Gaby always claimed it to have been largely Heini's determination that resulted in his achieving the status of his father's sole heir, as specified in his fourth will, written in December 1941:

> My sole heir will be my youngest son Hans Heinrich. My children Stephan, Margit and Gabrielle will only receive the obligatory share, namely in such a fashion that they are not co-heirs but will receive half of the monetary value of the legal share of the inheritance in money, which as far as possible should remain invested in the enterprises and can only be withdrawn over time, in accordance with the wishes of all concerned.

Heinrich did not consider there to be one woman in his life who deserved any particular financial reward as a mark of his affection. Not even his 'darling

Baby child', and certainly not his third wife:

> I am excluding my former wife Gunhilde, from whom I have not yet been legally divorced but with whom I am living 'in separation of the common table and bed' from any share in this inheritance. Should the Budapest court assign her a monthly payment, then my main heir Hans Heinrich will have to meet this obligation. He will also be responsible for the maintenance of Villa Favorita, Villa Mita, etc.

A Hungarian court had awarded Gunhilde SwFr 2,500 per month in alimony, while Heinrich had said that his assets in Germany and Holland were blocked, so that no money at all came from there at first, and later only RM1,000 per month in all. Heinrich's plea for the payment to be reduced was rejected because he was deemed to be capable of affording it. When Gunhilde asked the Lugano court to increase the sum, she was told that these were war times and everybody had to scale down their aspirations. It said that the luxurious trips she used to enjoy with her husband would no longer be possible, even if they were still married.

* * *

By 1942 many Germans realised that victory could not be considered a foregone conclusion and that many millions were going to die before the senseless carnage was brought to an end. For the Thyssen family, the war remained only a minor irritation. Despite the increasing bombing, Amélie and Fritz still enjoyed lunches at the Hotel Bristol while Heinrich may have felt some cause for anxiety when Britain declared war against Hungary. But he still enjoyed his champagne and the reassuring success of his racehorses. For Heini, apart from quarterly business meetings, there remained little interruption in either his pursuit of pleasure or its enjoyment.

There was only one other occasion when he was obliged to make a family commitment on behalf of his father:

> I wasn't given any choice. It was 1942, in the middle of the war and my father told me I had to go to Landsberg for my grandfather's 100th birthday commemoration. My father sent me because, he said: 'I don't want to be represented by Stephan.' I had papers that said I was a member of the diplomatic corps in Berne, so I crossed the border without any difficulty despite the strict controls. I wore a black suit and carried a suitcase full of chocolate and cigarettes.

Chapter V: 1939–1945

163

All of our company directors were present, together with members of the family and several lawyers. There was no one from the SS or the SA. Everybody was in black suits. I was only twenty and the idea of returning to Germany in the middle of the war worried me.

I was afraid they would keep me there. I left straight after the commemoration. My grandfather's lawyer, Dr Härle, was there. He was a very tough man and ended up having a quarrel with my brother Stephan and shouting at him, 'You're just here for the money and there's nothing left for you to inherit'. My brother's behaviour was rather sad as he did have financial problems at the time but then Uncle August died and left him all his money. I took the night train back to Switzerland which passed through Cologne at ten o'clock. At midnight there was a big bombing raid on Cologne and the station was destroyed.

* * *

Despite Heini's denial that his family profited from the war, according to the quarterly reports, his father's various businesses remained profitable, while the use of forced labour facilitated their continued expansion: 'The Walsum coal mine yield is increasing with the number of workers, most of whom are by now foreigners. The authorities know how much capacity still lies dormant and we can surely count on their support if we want to extend operations.'[24]

The balance sheet for 31 December 1941 showed a Thyssengas profit despite the fact that corporation tax had been increased from 20 per cent in 1938 to 50 per cent in 1941. It was also announced that Bankhaus Stein in Cologne was to do the audit, as 'they already know pretty much everything'; a telling remark that reflected the intimate relationship that existed between the Third Reich and the Thyssen-Bornemiszas.

But for their loyal managers, life became increasingly less comfortable and a great deal more dangerous. Robert Kabelac at Heinrich's Vulkan shipyard remained remarkably positive, even under attack:

On 9 April 1942 the fourth attack on Bremer Vulkan took place with 35 phosphorus fire bombs. Three submarines were holed but the fires could be quelled easily. Nobody died and production was unaffected. The fifth attack came on the night of 26 June with 211 'Stabbrand' bombs; at least that's how many were counted. Still, production continued without being affected.

On 27 August we had just come back from holiday when the sixth attack happened. It was the most daring attack ever flown. It was a beautiful

Saturday and a lot of Vegesack people were on the beach road. We were working in the garden. No alarm had been sounded. Suddenly a big, twin-engine airplane appeared, gliding at 50 metres height over the beach road with suppressed engines. There were sharp detonations. The Flak started firing wildly, but they didn't hit anything. The plane was already gone. Those people who were on the beach road were able to look straight up into the open bomb bays. Later, it was said the plane was of a new type; all made of wood which made it difficult to detect.

The planes were de Havilland Mosquitoes; the same plane flown by Count Mieczyslaw Pruszynski, a Polish pilot flying with the British Royal Air Force who was soon to become the lover of Heini's sister, Gaby.

Gaby and her husband Adolphe (Dolf) stayed in Cairo for six years from 1940 to 1946. He had an excellent reputation as a diplomat and was well-liked. So much so that fellow diplomats tended to overlook his wife's outrageous behaviour. In a confidential report on the various diplomats and their wives, the British Ambassador limited his description of Gaby to one word. Apparently he considered her 'decorative', although he no doubt also appreciated her extravagant hospitality. She did not help her husband's diplomatic career by developing a close relationship with the supremely decadent King Farouk, a man with a particularly exotic sexual appetite.

Long after the war was over, Gaby retired to bed on the island of Mallorca with her beloved Siamese cat 'Pussy'. Lying back on the pillows dressed in a fake leopard-skin top and camel-hair slacks, she still remembered her years in Cairo with an enormous grin and admitted, 'I was very naughty.' With particular affection she remembered the Gezira Club, the Turf Club and the St James Club. She was also a regular visitor to Shepherd's Hotel and her favourite, the Continental, from where Dolf would often be obliged to retrieve her.

According to her friend Marie-France Railey, Gaby's parameters of 'naughtiness' during the war were somewhat more liberal than most people's:

> There was a time when Dolf had to go away for a while. I think he went to South Africa. Anyway, he was very worried about leaving Gaby alone so he asked some friends to look after her while he was away. Well, no sooner had he gone than she also disappeared. When he returned two weeks later he had to get the military police to help him find her. Eventually they traced her to a hotel used for military rest and recreation where Gaby had spent the entire two weeks that Dolf had been away, sexually entertaining a random selection of young officers.

Chapter V: 1939–1945

It was while they were in Cairo that Gaby first met Count Pruszynski recovering from wounds received during the Libyan campaign.[25]

Gaby was heartbroken when the war was over and she and Dolf had to leave Egypt for London.

* * *

Undoubtedly the most important corporate event in 1942 was the decision to transfer ownership of all the shares of Heinrich's various companies and those belonging to the Dutch royal family from BVHS in Rotterdam to the August Thyssen Bank in Berlin, ostensibly for 'reasons of security'. It was an ironic situation for a man who had spent so much time and energy distancing himself from Germany.

While Heinrich had been hiding in Switzerland, cloaked in a Hungarian nationality and a Dutch residency, it was all too easy to forget that he was a German and that for ten years his factories, mines and banks had been working for Hitler and the Third Reich. But now, as the tide of war began to turn, both he and the Nazi leadership began to feel increasingly insecure, and keeping all his stock in the ownership of a Dutch bank was not improving their state of mind, regardless of the fact he had replaced the Dutch management with Germans.

It probably did not occur to Heinrich or his associates that one day Berlin, still considered the very heart and soul of the German Reich would be overrun by Russians. The worst they could imagine was another armistice; the August Thyssen Bank would no doubt continue to trade and presumably Heinrich expected to move back into the Adlon Hotel.

The placement of the shares into the same bank that held Göring's accounts would have also reassured the Reichsmarschall and Heinrich's brother Fritz, who appeared to have been kept informed of such events. He may even have been aware that the labour exchange in Saarbrücken had been asked by the new board member of the United Steelworks, Hans-Günther Sohl, to supply 'another 2,400 Russian POWs' and that the Gauleiter in charge had encouraged 'the use of Russian civilian workers especially in view of the newly incorporated territories'.[26]

While the Thyssens continued to profit from the suffering of others, an event occurred that was to be one of the few instances when they suffered any personal cost from the conflict. On 28 August 1942, Kurt-Ferdinand August Thyssen, son of Julius, a corporal in the artillery and one of the few members of the family to become directly involved in the fighting, was killed on the eastern front. Heinrich gave no indication of remorse or concern when his management delivered the news as a minor part of their otherwise positive reports.

He also displayed little surprise that, in the middle of a war, with their population decimated by allied bombing, the city of Düsseldorf should not be concerned with more pressing matters than the need to reassure Heinrich that with his assistance they still intended to promote themselves as an 'art town'.

The Erlenhof stud management also seemed totally unconcerned by the fact that while they were breeding and racing horses for the prime purpose of gambling, the Wehrmacht was suffering the most terrible defeat at Stalingrad, with appalling casualties on both sides.

Judging by the letter from Count Theo Seherr, Union Club president, his only concern was the continuation of the financial support the club was still receiving as a reward for turning a blind eye to Heinrich's dishonesty and he assured him what a splendid fellow most of the members thought he was.

> Dear Baron Thyssen, In the name of all our members, many congratulations to the spectacular success of your colours at the 'Grosser Preis of the Reichs Capital'. Your stud Ticino is no doubt a horse that once again is very much superior to others. Everybody in Hoppegarten and in our Club was very sad that, because of the war, you could not be here yourself. Of course everybody understands. We had a dinner with eighty gentlemen and I proposed a toast for you and your stables. We are of course particularly grateful that you are supporting our club so well during this war and allow us to keep up certain standards.

While the Baron's champagne continued to flow at the Union Club, according to his managers the transfer of stock from Rotterdam to Berlin proceeded with the inevitable complications involved in the ownership restructuring of an already immensely complicated organization:

> The basic request for the moving of assets has been submitted to the Berlin authorities. They have already approved the sale of the following from BVHS to Thyssenbank: RM 2.7 million Bremer Vulkan shares, RM 1.6 million Flensburger ship building shares and RM 3.2 million Thyssenbank shares.

In their quarterly report of August 1942, Messrs Roelen and Lübke displayed an appreciation of the financial conditions imposed by war: 'The valuation is to be based more on the reality of today and the graveness of tomorrow rather than the yields of yesterday.'

Chapter V: 1939–1945   167

But while 'the Thyssenbank group is convinced that the lodging in Berlin is necessary for security reasons, in particular in view of the second front as discussed', they were concerned that the 'restructuring' might reveal certain irregularities, particularly under the heading 'Powers of attorney and declarations': 'BVHS is raising concerns because of Baron Thyssen-Bornemisza's debt and because of the situs of the family foundation [in Switzerland] and the general difficulties and opacity of things.' The report continued:

> The only auditing firm that has been contacted is the Amsterdam firm of Klynveld Kraayenhof, which is accepted by both The Hague and Berlin. The following important German papers are not lodged with Thyssenbank as yet: RM 2.4 million Bremer Vulkan shares, RM 7.2 million Thyssenbank shares, RM 4 million PWW Reisholz shares and RM 1.5 million Flensburger ship building shares.

Around the same time the US Alien Property Custodian finally took over the Union Banking Corporation in New York and closed this conduit for the transfer of Thyssen and Nazi funds to Argentina.[27] Heinrich's loyal team obviously considered it inadvisable to discuss this matter openly, choosing instead to concentrate on their mining successes: 'Coal production has exceeded 3,000 tons a day. A total production of 1 million tons this year seems feasible. The local authorities have written to congratulate us on this success. We will have a gross surplus of RM14 million this year. This means profits of RM3 million.'

At the following meeting in Lugano on 4 May 1943, a particularly interesting report was made concerning Seismos: 'Big investment was made to keep up with technical and scientific progress. The works were visited by the relevant authorities and have found unrestricted praise. With the agreement of the relevant authorities some assets have been transferred to Thyssenbank.'

There is something deeply suspicious in the wording of this report and its lack of transparency suggests that it refers to the Thyssens' investment in Hitler's development programme for a miracle weapon of mass destruction through Seismos, MABAG and Oberbilker Steelworks.

*   *   *

While the management and workers ran the Thyssen banking and industrial Konzern, the largely absentee family enjoyed an increasingly surreal existence. On 13 June 1943, August Junior died at the Hotel Continental in Munich where he had been living for some time. Confined to a wheelchair, he had often been seen being pushed around by Ilyana, Stephan's ex-wife. His personal physician Geheimrat Stupler had apparently become suspicious of the circumstances surrounding his death and insisted on carrying out an autopsy, but when he opened up the coffin, he found not the body of August Junior but the body of an anonymous young soldier. What was even more surprising was that none of the family appeared to be particularly shocked or requested there be any further investigation. According to Heini, the lid was screwed back on and the dead man buried, while a death certificate was issued for August Junior, claiming him to be 'missing'.

Heini thought he may have been killed in an air-raid which had resulted in insufficient identifiable remains, and given that the undertaker had no wish to bury an empty coffin he had filled it with an anonymous corpse, of which there was no shortage. But it was also possible that August had been murdered and his body replaced to avoid incriminating evidence. While he had the reputation of being a man of considerable intelligence, his lifestyle, particularly the sexual side, had always proved unacceptable to everyone in the Thyssen family except Stephan who had been the only male member of the family for whom August Junior had any time. It was thus hardly surprising or suspicious that he should leave him his not inconsiderable fortune.

August Junior was not the only mysterious death in the family. While Edda Volz could not be considered strictly family, she had certainly fulfilled the role of Heini's surrogate mother. A report by Heinrich's executors dated 20 July 1953 states that Nanny Volz died on 16 November 1943. No details were given of how she might have died. Pusch was quite convinced that Volz was Jewish, while Heini always insisted that she was a Protestant and, over the years, developed what appeared to be a perfectly feasible, if highly unlikely, account of her demise, for which there was no supporting evidence:

> In 1940, Holland was occupied by the Germans. My nurse Edda Volz hated them. During the occupation, she collaborated with the Resistance and carried out acts of sabotage. But she was so upset by the unhappiness they had caused that she committed suicide by gassing herself in her room in our house in Scheveningen. She couldn't stand the idea that the Germans had conquered Holland and it looked like Hitler would stay for ever, which meant that I would never return. It was something unacceptable to her. Her death was one of the greatest losses of my life.

Yet at the time there was no evidence of even the most basic mark of respect for her death either by Heini or by any other member of the family.

* * *

Chapter V: 1939–1945

By 1944 German forces were retreating, towns and cities were subjected to ever increased bombing and the Allies were about to invade the Normandy beaches. The August Thyssen Bank in Berlin had been severely bombed and was only continuing to function due to the loyalty of the staff who were prepared to work from the vault and one small office. The Reich was sufficiently impressed to present Director Lübke with a medal for his sterling work.

Exactly whom the Thyssen management were trying to reassure at the Walsum mine when they decided to erect a prominent plaque featuring Goethe's words, 'That which you inherit from your fathers, receive it in order to keep it', was unclear. They talked of it being 'a message of thanks and warning', but for the few remaining German workers it would have done little more than remind them that those who inherited the mine had not been near the place since well before the war started. Regardless of Goethe's advice, Heini was displaying remarkably little concern for the coal mine that he would inherit from his father:

> I met Elaine Keller in Davos towards the end of the war. She was very sporty and we skied together. She wanted to go to bed with me straight away and we got a room near the Palace Hotel. We made love together and she enjoyed it. One night, she offered to let me sleep in her room, as her father was leaving early the next morning. At the crack of dawn, he knocked on her door to say good-bye. She pretended to be asleep, but he insisted and she had to open. I didn't have time to get dressed and had to hide behind the cupboard stark naked. Her father came in and must have noticed my ski boots that were lying at the foot of the bed.
>
> Then, he saw me behind the cupboard, and went completely berserk. He started hitting me and I ran out of the room naked. I raced down the corridor, scared stiff that someone would see me. Fortunately, I managed to find a towel in the toilet, which I wrapped around my waist. My room was at the other end of the hotel. As I was a student at the time, I only had one ski suit, which I'd left in her room together with my boots.
>
> I had to spend several hours in my room until Elaine got the maid to bring me my clothes. Later on, she phoned me and told me her father was in an absolute state. I had to tell him we were getting engaged, and she suggested we could break it off a week later. I simply had to do something to save the family honour. She assured me she wouldn't take advantage of my promise. I agreed to go along with the plan and we got engaged at a dinner in Geneva. Two weeks later, we broke it off, saying we didn't get on with each other.

Shortly afterwards, on 15 March 1944, Princess Theresa zu Lippe decided to abandon the dangers of Austria for the comfort and safety of Lausanne where Count Janos Palffy introduced her to his friend Heini. It was a fortuitous introduction as Prince Bernhard of the Netherlands was her uncle; a genealogical qualification that would assist Heini in his inheritance: 'She was only nineteen and I was twenty-five. She was a tall Austrian girl with a beautiful smile but a little bit chubby.'

Theresa would not have remained smiling for long if she had heard Heini describing her as either chubby or Austrian as the family had also gone to some trouble to assume protective Hungarian nationality, which should have been a familiar enough concept to Heini.

After the war, when she applied an equal amount of time and trouble to dropping her Hungarian nationality and joining Heini in gaining a Swiss passport, his solicitor Roberto van Aken wrote a particularly persuasive letter to the Berne police department:

> Mrs Therese Thyssen-Bornemisza is a member of a branch of the house of Lippe, which has been living in Austria for 300 years and acquired Austrian nationality. During the 'Anschluss' of Austria to Germany in 1938, her family refused to take on German nationality, as it would have been automatically the case, and had itself naturalised in Hungary. As her family fought off the danger of becoming German with all the means that were in their power, it would be wrong to use her Hungarian nationality to her detriment. This background information should not make people think that the person in question tends to change her orientation like a candle in the wind.

Regardless of van Aken's recommendation, the Swiss were no doubt fully aware that Theresa's interest in Swiss nationality was purely for her convenience, while Heini seemed equally aware that that was the basis for the whole relationship:

> I wasn't really in love with Theresa, nor do I think she was in love with me, because later I found out that she was already having a relationship with my brother-in-law Ivan Batthyány. She had heard about me from her father who knew me. I didn't have much money at that time, but it was well known that I would inherit a fortune. In those days, Austrian aristocrats didn't have a penny and in their eyes I was very wealthy.

Father Gueydan, Heini's friend and the man who was to adopt the mantle of the Thyssen-Bornemiszas' private priest, claimed Heini's father was less philosophical about the union. He questioned her morals and predicted she

Chapter V: 1939–1945

would create problems for the family. One thing that has over the years become undeniable is the web of accusations, which their relationship would seem to have encouraged. Tita, Heini's fifth wife, subsequently claimed Father Gueydan told her: 'Ivy and Theresa had devised a plan. He would marry Margit and she would marry Heini and together they would control the Thyssen fortune.'[28]

* * *

According to Heini, 1944 was also the year when his father handed him the reins of power though he would admit his father only made this decision in the belief that, despite his cloaked ownership and assumed nationality, he could still face retribution from the Allies. Having had his son dutifully sign the minutes of the quarterly business meetings and finally wrest control of the organisation from his frail old father, Heinrich thought he could claim ignorance and diminished responsibility for his support of the Nazi Party and abuse of various human rights, or at least his condonation of such. But Heini also learned to avoid any accusations of involvement by the simple expedient of lying:

> I had no knowledge of my father's business or training of any kind. I had never discussed business with my father. We would talk about a picture, a pretty girl he had met, or that my tie was ugly or something like that. His German managers came twice during the war and I think they talked about Thyssengas while I was just sitting there. I had a vague knowledge that my father had something to do with a gas company in Germany but I didn't really know anything. Maybe I'm just stupid.

Heini also claimed that the power of attorney granted him by his father only referred to assets outside Switzerland, which did not really make a great deal of sense as ownership of all his father's holdings came under the umbrella of the Swiss Kaszony Family Foundation of which his father remained the founder, sole board member and sole beneficiary. Presumably Heinrich, as befitting the Thyssen character, did not entirely trust his own son despite his insistence on having inherited only the highest possible moral values:

> The Thyssen coat of arms bears the following inscription, which is our motto, 'Virtue transcends wealth'. [In fact it was the Bornemisza coat of arms whose motto was blatantly unsuitable for the Thyssens.] My parents and I have always respected this principle and they passed it on to me together with the firm belief in ethical behaviour. I think the most important thing in life is

irreproachable behaviour founded on integrity, personal dignity and good education.

* * *

While the Thyssen-Bornemiszas and their lawyers began to plan a damage limitation strategy, including entering into discussions with the Reich's Economy Ministry concerning claims for war damages, they were becoming increasingly concerned that after more than four years, the Baron had still failed to gain his divorce from Gunhilde, thus increasing the possibility of her succeeding in claiming a widow's inheritance rights. On 30 May 1944 his lawyer Roberto van Aken had written to Dr Sztehlo Dezsö, his counterpart in Budapest, voicing his concern. Unfortunately for Heinrich's protection of the family fortune, the allied bombing of Dr Dezsö's home and invasion by the Germans presented him with far more pressing concerns than alimony and divorce proceedings, as Russian tanks headed towards Budapest: 'Enemy bombs have hit our house twice. Everything is destroyed. We hear that it is possible to send "love goods" parcels from Switzerland to individual addresses via the Red Cross.'[29]

There was no record of van Aken having responded to Dr Dezsö's destitution or having been in any way concerned that Budapest was about to be the location of one of the bloodiest and, for Hitler, the last decisive battle of the war. Although, to be fair, most of the city's residents displayed an equal lack of concern; going about their last-minute Christmas shopping as the Russian T-34s rumbled up to the tram terminus in the western suburbs.

No doubt of far greater concern to Heinrich was a letter he received from Mrs Richard Haniel von Rauch, a gossipy German national living in Davos:

> Two weeks ago, in Ascona, I met a long-standing good friend, who told me that she has met Baroness Gunhilde many times over the last few years and that the Baroness has told her and others repeatedly that she has no intention whatsoever of agreeing to a divorce from her husband. She said that he has already had three strokes and would surely 'croak' soon and then, according to Hungarian law, she would be an heir. If need be, I am prepared to repeat this statement under oath before a court of law.

* * *

Meanwhile, the Swiss were beginning to prove somewhat less sanguine towards those connected with Nazi Germany and van Aken was forced to address problems somewhat closer to home: in this case the Federal Foreigners' Police in

Chapter V: 1939–1945

Berne who were suddenly refusing Heinrich's manager Dr Roelen entry into Switzerland:

> As the permanent legal representative of Dr Heinrich Thyssen-Bornemisza senior, I can tell you that Dr Roelen has been coming to Switzerland for several years every three months for reporting purposes. In most cases, Dr Roelen has met with Baron Thyssen-Bornemisza senior at the latter's domicile in Castagnola. Dr Guido Solari of the Federal Foreigners' Police knows about this.
>
> The Baron is not able to go personally to Mülheim/Ruhr for the meetings due to health reasons. Amongst other things, they have to talk about questions relating to the import of coal from the German Reich into Switzerland. Baron Thyssen-Bornemisza would be very glad if Dr Roelen's entry request could be cleared as soon as possible, as in the past.[30]

But even more pressing problems were looming. On 28 December 1944, the Swiss, either bowing to allied pressure or ingratiating themselves with the winning side, announced that all Hungarian, Slovak and Croatian assets in Switzerland had now been blocked by a decree of 20 December. It was the type of ruling that would keep the Thyssens' solicitors and accountants busy and justify the existence of Heinrich's Swiss-based Kaszony Family Foundation.

By now the end of the conflict was only a matter of months away and it was not only the Swiss whose loyalties began to change, particularly when allied intercepts revealed that Swiss banks, especially Credit Suisse, had been regularly transferring German loot and gold to Argentina. By 30 October 1945 Allied Law number 5 would be approved in Berlin, confiscating all German property in Switzerland. Before that, Argentina had been obliged to start tightening up its control of what the *New York Times* referred to as 'axis firms':

> The first measure taken specifically against a German firm in Argentina suspected of having contributed money for espionage or other activities on this continent was taken today when the government by decree appointed a manager-delegate to act as co-administrator of the blacklisted company Thyssen Lametal SA ... The measure is justified by the fact that the company between 1937 and 1943 had paid $250,000 to persons whose identity it has been impossible to establish. The recipient of the money, it is believed, was the German Embassy [in Buenos Aires].[31]

It was not long before the Argentinian government had taken even more extreme action:

The vast German industrial and commercial consortium of Thyssen Lametal has been seized and nationalised by the Argentine government. The companies have been under government control for some time. The government today deprived them of the right to be legally represented before Argentine courts.³²

Although the action appeared Draconian, it was to have remarkably little effect on the Thyssens' fortune or their ability to continue operating from Argentina.

* * *

On 8 October 1944 Heini and his father succeeded in having their last management meeting with Dr Roelen in Lugano. There had apparently been a previous meeting on 20 July between Heinrich's representatives and people from the Reich Economy Ministry, Finance Ministry, Exchange Control Authority and the Reichsbank, and a second meeting with various directors at the Dutch foreign exchange institute at which certain 'debt restructuring' had been agreed.

The discussion was extremely complicated, but it appeared that the Reich had agreed to ease the foreign exchange restrictions on Heinrich so that the debts of BVHS could be 'balanced out' with the accrued income from his various German companies. What was not revealed was exactly why the Reich, which was on the verge of collapse, should have bothered to agree to such a thing unless they were expecting to continue to do business with the Thyssens in the future. There also appeared to be little doubt that the Dutch intended to continue doing business with Germany.

For some of Heinrich's loyal managers, the end of the war was somewhat less academic. Roelen's story was an amazing example of his spirit and determination in contrast to Heini and his father's indolent lack of concern. Unfortunately Roelen's failure to appreciate basic human rights overshadowed any admirable qualities he may have possessed regarding corporate responsibility.

At 2 pm on 27 March 1945, there was news that the allied front had reached the Emscher canal between Walsum and Hamborn. Roelen spent the night in the cellar of the administrative building writing out a summary on the Thyssengas group's position. At 12 noon on 28 March, allied troops passed the water tower. Roelen ordered everything to be prepared to start again with the normal running. He sent a driver to Schloss Landsberg with orders to ensure that August Thyssen's crypt was put back into an honourable state. Roelen's first goal then was 'to restart work in the enterprises in order to get the masses off the street'.³³

While Roelen's loyalty undoubtedly lay with the owners, he proved quite capable of transferring his apparent allegiance from the Third Reich to the Allies within twenty-four hours; this was five weeks prior to Germany's capitulation. All offices were transferred from the cellars back to their old sites and by 9 am the next day he was already attending a meeting with Allied Military Governor Colonel Grass. Water, electricity, coal and gas were priorities and Grass confirmed he would give Thyssen Gas and Waterworks the necessary authorisations to start working.

While fighting continued, Roelen travelled with an American major to inspect the various Thyssen installations. Having curtailed looting by both Germans and Americans, Roelen ascertained that energy creation at Walsum could start within one week. Unfortunately, although Roelen no longer owed his allegiance to the Nazis, his attitude towards forced labour and its use by the Konzern appeared to show no sign of change: 'On 3 April, the first problem was to get rid of the foreign labour, in particular of the Russians, who, under the protection of the occupation forces, have become a nuisance in both the town and country. The Governor has assured me he will see to it that they are assembled and deported.'

It soon became obvious that Roelen had little more concern for the German workers' welfare than he had for that of the foreigners: 'Miners at Neumühl are saying they can't work more than eight hours underground because they don't have enough to eat. But enterprises which will only perform average outputs will die. The bad pits will die and the workers either die with them or work ten hours instead of eight.'

He added that all companies were devoid of funds and were awaiting allied help; but that potential creditors only saw destroyed works, a market that was unclear and prejudice against German products. If on top of that the work-force was not prepared to give of its best, then there was really no hope at all. He gave no indication whether any support or responsibility could be expected from any of the Thyssens.

* * *

While the reinstatement of the Thyssen mining and heavy industry may have been considered 'dirty work', it was a great deal safer than that involving Heinrich Lübke, the director of the August Thyssen Bank in Berlin in 1945.

Having transferred most of his securities from Holland to Berlin, in 1945 Heinrich Thyssen-Bornemisza's management were now faced with the problem of getting them back out again. The bank found itself, not as Heinrich might have hoped, in the relative safety of the American sector but in the Russian zone of Berlin where Heinrich Lübke, the bank's director, would have had difficulty staying alive, let alone concerning himself with the bank:

> During the last weeks of the war, Dr Roelen sent a lorry to Berlin, with the intention of taking assets out of the safe of ATB and returning them to the West. I thought long and hard about this, and finally took the decision to send the lorry back empty; a decision that was not made easily. But since 20th July 1944, my telephone was being tapped and in my last conversation with Dr Roelen I was not able to explain my decision to him, which I'm sure he could not understand. But since the middle of March 1945, the Gestapo came to see us daily at Behrenstrasse . . . If a lorry had come to the bank and had been loaded with securities and other deposits, the bank would have been closed and the employees would have had to face serious reprisals.[34]

Lübke could see no point in taking this excessive risk: 'It is not difficult to reprint shares that have been destroyed.'

The theoretical end of hostilities only served to increase the dangers presented to Heinrich Lübke, Curt Ritter and the other managers trying to protect what remained amid the ruins of the bank:

> At the end of April 1945, the Russian military ordered all the banks to prepare statements of their activities. I decided to do nothing. However, Mr Ritter decided otherwise. Without wanting to criticise, it has to be said that the Russians only became aware of the bank's activities through his report. On Sunday, 13 May 1945, a car came to my flat in Berlin with a Russian lieutenant, his adjutant, a Polish woman and Mr Ritter. The lieutenant ordered me to accompany him to the bank and open the safes. Client and bank safes were examined, suitcases opened and the tills cleared of money. The safe doors were then sealed and I gave the safe keys to the lieutenant.

According to Lübke's statement, for the following ten days, the Russians, in the presence of the managers, continued systematically to ransack the bank. Having examined the list of clients, they concentrated their investigation on former members of the Nazi Party. But Ritter had in fact already removed vital documents and securities from the bank without informing Lübke. When the Russians realised important documents were missing, it suited Ritter to infer that, as the key holder, Lübke had been responsible. Heinrich Lübke and the signing-clerk Kurt Schlessiger were arrested by the Russians on 22 May 1945 and taken to the concentration camps of Jamlitz and Buchenwald.

Schlessiger failed to survive the imprisonment and died in Buchenwald while

Lübke was only able to return to his family after five years. Quite remarkably, after a brief period of recovery, he rejoined the bank's employment and expended considerable effort to achieve its reopening for business in 1952. He died in 1962, two years after retiring.

Meanwhile, Robert Kabelac probably displayed more common sense than loyalty in refusing the Gestapo order to blow up the Bremer Vulkan dockyards ahead of the allied occupation. He also displayed more consideration for the forced labour than Roelen:

> In the evening of 4 May we heard the news about the capitulation of the German army in north-west Germany. I decided to assemble all the men. I informed the confidants of the foreign nations' forced workers that I wished to restart production and that it was up to them whether they wanted to work or not. The intermediaries told me that most of them wanted to return to their homeland without delay. I recommended they didn't go abruptly but orderly, with their papers brought up to date etc. and some payment. Then my wife told me that she had seen the first Americans while out shopping. For the first time in 2,074 nights, we could go to bed knowing that no bombs could drop on us. In Bremen, 22,000 soldiers and 5,500 civilians had been killed during this war.

* * *

While Heinrich's directors risked life and limb to save his Konzern, the end of the war had remarkably little effect on the general well-being of Heini and his father. But for Aunt Amélie and Uncle Fritz it began to appear increasingly unlikely that they would survive the monster which they had helped create. As this part of their story is largely their own account and cannot be substantiated, its accuracy is questionable. Fritz's subsequent interrogation by allied intelligence would illustrate his vivid imagination and propensity for altering the facts to suit his purpose.

In February 1945, there were apparently serious fears that Sachsenhausen would soon be overrun by the Russians, so the VIP prisoners were moved to Buchenwald. Fritz seemed to think that Himmler had a personal interest in preserving them for use in some political deal with the Allies. In reality the SS probably intended to use them to bargain for their own survival, rather than any higher political purpose.

Whatever the real reason, from this point the conditions of the Thyssens' incarceration would change dramatically. Herded into an isolated barracks with fifty other detainees, they were encircled by 3-metre-high walls and guarded by twelve members of the SS. Yet Fritz and Amélie still managed to travel with twelve heavy leather suitcases while their friends, the Stauffenbergs (relatives of Claus Graf Schenk), were apparently accompanied by a pile of huge trunks; far removed from the pathetic personal possessions that the prisoners in the main camp had arrived with.

It is inconceivable that Fritz and Amélie were unaware of the atrocities that took place in the camps, yet there is no record of their regret or concern, either at the time or subsequently.

By now, their guards were becoming nervous and had taken to wearing civilian clothes and burning their documents. They were also increasingly friendly towards their charges, which did not stop the rumours that all the prisoners were going to be shot.

Within two months they were moved once again. This time to Dachau where they met up with other similar VIP prisoners. But regardless of their status, by now they were reduced to sleeping on straw mattresses while listening to the rumbling of bombs and artillery. Within two weeks they were off again to Reichenau concentration camp near Innsbruck, via Rosenheim and Kufstein. The unhappy group included Hjalmar Schacht, Prince Leopold of Prussia and Prince Philipp of Hesse, Leon Blum, Prince Xavier von Bourbon-Parma, a group of Hungarians, including Admiral Horthy, Bishop Piquet, the Dutch Foreign Minister, some Russian generals, the Italian partisan general Ante Garibaldi, a nephew of Churchill who had been arrested in Yugoslavia, the Stauffenbergs, Gördelers, von Hofackers, von Hammersteins and Hoeppners.

On 29 April 1945, they apparently reached their final destination, Niederndorf, in the Southern Tyrol. Everything came to a head when the SS guards were ordered not to allow the approaching Americans to rescue the prisoners alive. Then one of the prisoners, Colonel Bogislav von Bonin, escaped and telephoned his friend the Chief of the German General Staff, General Röttiger, to explain their position and his fear that they were all to be shot. Röttiger immediately ordered another aristocrat, Captain Wichard von Alvensleben, who was only 20 kilometres away, to go to the aid of the prisoners. The following day, Alvensleben formed an assault party of ninety-five men and overpowered the SS.

Another, less heroic, report said that the soldiers had discovered the SS-men drunk in a bar and while they were all pointing their guns at each other and quarrelling as to who was responsible for the prisoners waiting outside on the bus, two Americans arrived in a jeep and everyone surrendered. After that the prisoners were held in a local hotel before being transferred to the US-base in

Capri; where the Russians would soon report them to be 'sunning themselves on the beach'.

The Thyssens had been incarcerated for four and a half years, but due to his unabated arrogance and lies, it would be almost the same amount of time again before Fritz Thyssen stopped paying for his support of Hitler. In Amélie's case, it would remain questionable whether she paid or profited.

* * *

Heini always discouraged interest in Rechnitz by insisting that at the end of the war the family castle had been totally destroyed by the Russians and nothing had been left except the Thyssen-Bornemisza name on a row of pews in the local church. Other members of the family reinforced this story. Heini also gave the impression that his sister was rather ineffectual and totally dominated by her husband, while everyone seemed very vague concerning Margit's whereabouts during the war. Only the Hungarian Josi Groh told a different story.

> During the war, the castle in Rohoncz was occupied by the SS. The young officers used to go riding with Margit and say, 'When the Russians come we'll all ride together to Switzerland.' At the end of the war she helped many of them escape, including one who was her lover. She kept him in a small apartment above a bar in Lugano.

Groh also insisted that the Russians had totally destroyed the castle. In fact, quite a lot of the original castle remains standing. Josi Groh also missed out some of the far more damming revelations.

A small municipal park in the town of Rechnitz contains not only a memorial to local soldiers, but also a memorial to the large number of people who died either as the result of persecution or their use as forced labour during the war; including Josef Hotwagner, a schoolteacher from Kitzladen.

A local innkeeper who knew both the Thyssens and the Batthyánys admitted that terrible things had happened five days before the Germans' defence of the castle against the Russians, which had resulted in a large number of Jews being massacred. There was also evidence that incriminated Countess Margit Batthyány-Thyssen and her husband.

Josef Hotwagner Junior had only been eight years old when the Russians fought the occupying Germans for possession of his town but his father was already incarcerated in a concentration camp:

> My father was headteacher at the primary school in the community of Kitz-

laden and after 1938 he was moved around several times as a punishment. He and a few other people in Rechnitz and the surroundings were supporting members of the families of people who had been murdered by the Nazis. My father was arrested in August 1941 and accused of high treason. He was taken before the criminal national court in Graz and was given a ten-year prison sentence. He was to serve his time in Straubing which was an external camp of the Dachau concentration camp. The prisoners had to perform heavy work and my father became very ill with tuberculosis. He was freed by the Americans at the beginning of May 1945 and taken to a hospital. But he died there on 3 July 1945.

Josef also confirmed eye-witness reports that both Countess Margit Batthyány, the owner of the castle, and a number of high-ranking Nazi and SS officers had been amongst the residents of Rechnitz Castle. Margit's husband, Count Ivan, had a famous stud farm at Körmend across the border in Hungary where he spent much of the war. But on the night of 24 March 1945 he was also 'in residence' at the castle. There were also others present who had been living there for some time. During 1944 and 1945, huge fortifications had been built as protection against the Russians. Thousands of people were forced to work on these fortifications including Hungarian Jews. Many died from exhaustion and hunger. Hundreds were also shot dead in a very arbitrary fashion. Ironically it was the Batthyánys who, in the seventeenth century, had first settled a Jewish community in the 'Tabor' part of town, opposite the castle.

The man responsible for the construction of the fortifications was Ortsgruppen-Leader Franz Podezin, a Gestapo civil servant. The Thyssen-Bornemiszas' estate manager, Hans Joachim Oldenburg, could also have been described as Podezin's assistant. People in Rechnitz claimed that Oldenburg had been Countess Margit's lover, but it seems more likely that it was Podezin whom she took to Lugano with her after the war before helping him escape to South Africa. Oldenburg, whom Heinrich had enlisted to run the estate, had originally been an employee of Thyssengas.

But before she left, with the Russians already fighting at Szombathely, only 15 kilometres away, and the SS preparing to do battle at Rechnitz, the Countess decided to host a party at the castle on the night preceding Palm Sunday. Under the headline, 'The Rechnitz Murder', the *Oberwarter Zeitung* newspaper would later describe the party as an 'orgy ball' and a *'danse macabre'* to which thirty or forty people were invited. The party started at 9 pm and lasted until dawn, with a great deal of drinking and dancing.

In order to provide the guests with additional entertainment, around midnight some 200 half-starved Jews, who had been working on the town's fortifications but were announced to be unfit for further work, were delivered by lorry to Kreuzstadel, a piece of land within walking distance of the castle. Podezin then invited fifteen of the more senior guests to a store room where they were given weapons and ammunition and invited to take part in a slaughter: 'Let's go and kill some Jews!'

The Jews were then forced to strip naked before being shot by the drunken party guests, who then returned to the castle where they continued to drink and dance.

Apparently, Franz Podezin had been in the habit of locking Jews in the castle cellars for minor offences before taking them out at night and shooting them. Local people reported the Countess Batthyány deriving considerable enjoyment from witnessing these barbaric acts.

Following the party, guests were heard bragging and even exaggerating about the previous night's appalling atrocity; one Stefan Beiglböck claiming: 'Last night we killed three hundred Jews. I slew six or seven with my own hands.' The bodies of the victims had been buried by fifteen of the Jewish prisoners saved for the purpose. The following day they were kept in a barn close to the local abattoir before being shot that evening by Oldenburg and Podezin.

Five days after the killing, the Russians reached Rechnitz and for three days the SS defended their position while the eight-year-old Josef Hotwagner, his mother and grandparents hid in their wine cellar. By the time it was safe enough to escape, the castle was ablaze. But although the Russians were blamed, Josef was insistent that there was evidence to prove that it had been razed in order to destroy incriminating evidence. Two local men, who tried to put out the castle fire at the time, were shot dead by the Germans.

In the wake of this atrocity the ruined town of Rechnitz inherited a terrible legacy of mistrust, bitterness and guilt. Witnesses were murdered or died in 'accidents'. Houses were burned down and a local police inspector who opened an investigation was transferred to another county. Beiglböck was eventually found guilty and received a sentence of twenty-five years. Although Podezin was named as the main instigator, culprit and ringleader, the court was told that he had fled to South Africa.

After the war, the ruined castle and the remaining land was sold off in plots but Heini's sister eventually returned to build a hunting lodge on the 'Hirschenstein', near Rechnitz, where she continued to entertain friends during the hunting season. No legal action was ever taken against the Count or Countess Batthyány, who died in the 1990s and were buried in Lugano. The location of the grave of the 200 Jews murdered at Rechnitz was never revealed.³⁵

Heini died before being confronted with his sister's appalling activities, but he had previously told the Spanish writer José Luís de Vilallonga:

> One must play the game. We live in a capitalist economy, which has its own rules to survive. In my family, we have always thought it normal to be considerate and show respect to the workers. During the war, a group of big industrialists employed Jewish deportees in their plants and made them work like slaves. When they became ill or too weak to work, they were sent to the concentration camps and to the gas chambers. Not only did we have nothing to do with this, but we were persecuted by the Nazis as well.

1 From the minutes of company meetings for the Thyssen-Bornemisza group of companies held in Flims, Davos, Lugano and Zurich, between 1939 and 1944 (TBG Archives).
2 Memo dated 21 July 1947 from Ralph S. Spritzer to Gerard A. Weiss, Chief, Alien Property Custodian Section, Finance Division, Office of Military Government US, re the American Thyssen Companies etc., p.7, quoting a report made by the foreign exchange control office (National Archives, Washington, DC).
3 Uebbing, p. 264.
4 Imperial War Museum/GED, p. 29.
5 Supplement to the substantiation of the verdict in the proceedings against Fritz Thyssen, made at Königstein/Taunus. Critical examination of the report made by Investigation Branch, Finance Division HQ, RB Düsseldorf 318 HQ CCG BAOR 4, British Military Government, compiled by reporting investigator H. R. Priestley, dated 5 April 1949, Appendix 1, p. 8 (Public Record Office, Kew/UK, Ref. FO 1046/451).
6 Pritzkoleit, p. 57 and Account Land Preussen, originating from the accounts of Fritz Thyssen/BVHS/Pelzer Foundation, Appendix 5 to H. R. Priestley's report dated 5 April 1949 (National Archives, Washington, DC).
7 British Legation in Berne to William Strang, dated 16 October 1939 (Public Record Office Kew/UK, Ref FO 371/23011).
8 *New York Times*, 10 February 1940.
9 Ibid, 5 May 1940.
10 Articles entitled 'Operation Juliana' in *NRC Handelsblad* on 1 and 3 June 1991, by Gerald Mulder, Cees Wiebes and Bert Zeeman.
11 Schneider, p. 23.
12 Ibid, pp. 1–2.

13 From the Press Reading Bureau in Stockholm to the Central Department, Foreign Office, memorandum addressed to the Political Intelligence Department, dated 5 April 1943 (Public Record Office, Kew/UK, Ref FO 371/34429).
14 Franz Hoellering in *The Nation* magazine.
15 The fact that Fritz Thyssen used to give copies of *Mein Kampf* to his friends has been alleged by Eglau. During his denazification proceedings, Fritz Thyssen said that he had never even read the book.
16 Memo from Walter W. Ostrow, US Treasury Representative based in Berne, to Mrs Rella R. Schwartz, Acting Director, Foreign Funds Control, US Treasury Department, dated 6 October 1948, concerning a report by the Swiss Compensation Office (National Archives, Washington, DC).
17 Imperial War Museum/GED, pp. 23 ff.
18 Memorandum from Mr Erwin G. May re Information received from Mr Lievense, President of the Union Banking Corporation, dated 1 August 1941 (National Archives, Washington, DC).
19 Letter from Erwin G. May, Treasury Attaché, Treasury Department, to John W. Pehle, Assistant to the Secretary, Treasury Department, dated 15 September 1941, p. 31 (ibid.).
20 Letter from C. Lievense, President of the Union Banking Corporation, 39 Broadway, New York to Brown Brothers Harriman & Co, Wall Street, New York dated 28 November 1941 (ibid.).
21 British Embassy, Washington DC, to Irwin Seibel, US Treasury Department, Foreign Funds Control, Washington DC, dated 21 April 1942 (ibid.).
22 Memorandum from Ralph S. Spritzer to Gerard A. Weiss, Chief, Alien Property Custodian Section, Finance Division, OMGUS, concerning the American Thyssen companies, quoting a report made by the foreign exchange control office, p. 7, dated 21 July 1947 (ibid.).
23 Bornemann, pp. 45–69.
24 Minutes of a meeting held at Villa Favorita in Lugano on 30 March 1942, attended by Dr Wilhelm Roelen, Heinrich Lübke, Baron Heinrich Thyssen-Bornemisza and his son Hans Heinrich ('Heini') Thyssen-Bornemisza.
25 Author's conversations with Marie-France Railey (†), 1996.
26 Letter from the Reichs Association Iron, Unter den Linden 10, Berlin, to the General Representative for the sourcing and distribution of iron ore in the territories of Luxembourg, Lorraine and Meurthe & Moselle in Metz, signed by Sohl, copied to A. Krupp, Dr Rohland a.o., dated 14 August 1942. (Imperial War Museum, Duxford/UK). Later, Hans-Günther Sohl became chairman of the August-Thyssen-Hütte, a post he held from 1953 to 1973. His successor at the renamed Thyssen AG was Dieter Spethmann.
27 Vesting order no. 261, executed on 20 October 1942 by the Alien Property Custodian Leo T. Crowley re Holland-American Trading Corporation and Vesting order no. 248, executed on 5 December 1942 by Francis A. Mahoney, Secretary of the

Executive Committee of the Alien Property Custodian Office to the Secretary of the Treasury, Washington DC, re Union Banking Corporation (National Archives, Washington, DC).

28 Author's interviews with Baroness Carmen Thyssen-Bornemisza, 1996–2000.
29 Letter from Dr Deszö to Dr van Aken, dated 27 December 1944 (TBG Archives).
30 Letter dated 31 July 1944 (ibid.).
31 *New York Times*, 21 December 1944.
32 Ibid, 17 May 1945.
33 Confidential report concerning reconstruction, written by Dr Roelen, for the attention of the partners, dated 27 March to 20 April 1945 (TBG Archives).
34 Report by Heinrich Lübke, Director of the August Thyssen Bank in Berlin, about the events immediately after the German capitulation, written down upon his release from Russian incarceration on 16 June 1950 (ibid.).
35 For the account of these events in Rechnitz/Austria at the end of the Second World War, I am indebted to Dr Josef Hotwagner, who also supplied me with excerpts from a 1970s document called 'Resistance and persecution in the Burgenland, 1934–1945' and a 1980s series of articles in the *Oberwarter Zeitung*, entitled 'The Rechnitz Murder'.

Chapter VI

1945–1954

Uncle Fritz escapes to South America ...
Heini seizes power

*Rich bad boys
get better presents
than poor good boys.*
Anon

The Second World War resulted in the deaths of 55 million people. But for Heini Thyssen-Bornemisza and his father, the end of the war was of little consequence apart from facilitating the reopening of the shorter Italian route to St Moritz which enabled them once again to indulge in the social extravagance of their favourite winter playground.

One late summer evening, when we were strolling through the gardens of Villa Favorita, I asked Heini if he could remember the war ending. He seemed genuinely puzzled by the question.

'No. Should I?'

Yet when I suggested that his life as a student might have been considered somewhat decadent compared with many others at the time, he became quite grumpy at what he obviously considered an accusation rather than an observation. He also managed to avoid any feelings of guilt by denying any connections with Germany.

'But you must have known that one day you would have to return to Germany? It was still your grandfather's country. That's where your family's fortune was created and where it was still being maintained. That was where you and your father were also intending to be buried.'

'But I never came from Germany, so how could I "go back" there?'

Then he giggled, and taking my arm he said: 'Although I suppose you could say, I would be dying to go back there.'

Heini's black humour did not alter the fact that it was in Germany that his father's managers and workers had had to fight for the survival of what would become the Thyssen Bornemisza Group.

Initially, the workers at Bremer Vulkan were reduced to making axe heads and lighters. Later, they started repairing trains and then converting and repairing ships. But as the winter of 1945/46 developed into one of the coldest on record, the workers' situation worsened due to lack of coal, food and shelter. Robert Kabelac struggled to get the shipyard back on its feet and avoid reparatory dismantlement, yet he remained resolute and did not complain.

Meanwhile, Wilhelm Roelen took responsibility for the rest of the Group and, despite his apparently enthusiastic contribution to the Nazi war effort, was recruited as an adviser to the occupying powers' North German Coal Control, while continuing to send regular reports to Villa Favorita and staying in touch with the rest of the Thyssen family.

By 1948, Bremer Vulkan alone had amassed orders from the Allies to a value of DM 11.25 million. By November 1949 it got the authorization to build ships and soon there was full employment at the yard which continued until Kabelac's retirement in 1960: 'The Korean War started in 1950, then there was the Suez crisis in 1956. These were the main "economic stimuli" for our yard's prosperity.'

The Thyssen-Bornemisza family displayed a much greater concern for their bombed-out bank in the Russian sector of Berlin than their functioning shipyards in Bremen; although it was not the bank itself that they were worried about, so much as the documents that had been stored in the strongrooms. These comprised not only the share certificates for much of the Thyssen-Bornemisza companies but also the records of their dealings with the Third Reich. Initially, Heinrich's peace of mind was not reassured by a communication from bank director Curt Ritter informing him that the Soviet Banking Commissar considered 'the Baron' a German and had realised that many documents had already been removed.[1]

Had the Russians been aware of either Ritter's political status as a former Nazi Party member or his responsibility for the illegal harbouring of documents, he would certainly have been arrested and probably shot. However, Heinrich was so relieved by Ritter's removal of the only accurate record of the full extent of the Thyssen-Bornemiszas' financial support of the Third Reich, that he even managed to get a note to him 'expressing his appreciation for Ritter's initiative'.[2] It is the only record of his ever having formally thanked an employee.

* * *

Chapter VI: 1945–1954

While Heinrich continued to enjoy the safety and anonymity of Switzerland, Hermann Göring, his friend and business associate, was being interrogated by allied intelligence. In June 1945, he admitted to having received large contributions of cash from Fritz. He also confirmed having bank accounts with the August Thyssen Bank in Berlin. But despite his admission that Himmler was 'frequently requesting large sums of foreign exchange to be used abroad for the purpose of intelligence', no connection appears to have been made by allied intelligence between Heinrich Thyssen's Berlin bank and the movement of Nazi funds.

When Göring was asked what he thought about Thyssen, there appeared to be no question as to which one of the brothers was being referred to, which makes it difficult to believe the transcripts have not been edited:

'I always liked Thyssen very much. Thyssen was generous and interested in things, but then in 1939 he left the country, without reason, and actually became a traitor to Germany by giving the French government details about German supplies of oil and about industry. When Thyssen was handed over by the French, I took the side of Thyssen. I kept him out of prison and instead he and his wife were put in a sanatorium. I used my influence for many years so that Thyssen could stay in the sanatorium, but I think in the last year he was taken by the SS. In any other country like America or England Thyssen would have been condemned to death.'

'Was it because of your own personal power that you were able to save him?'

'Yes, I thought that Thyssen had not committed treason knowingly.'

'Did he do it as a means of undermining Hitler's regime?'

'I think that Thyssen was not aware of what he was doing.'[3]

* * *

By June 1945, correspondence shows that Heini was coming under increasing pressure to respond to the directors' demands for his father's presence at the factories. In a letter to Theresa, he wrote:

We have received a lot of news from Holland, Belgium and Germany concerning our businesses. They are all doing rather well, but the people there are demanding that we go there. My father, of course, doesn't want to know about it and I cannot do anything on my own account from here, because the things belong to him.[4]

The main reason for his increasingly alcoholic father's lack of enthusiasm for visiting his assets was his fear of being held responsible for his collaboration with the Nazis. But Heinrich and Fritz would both manage to avoid being held to account on the same level as Alfried Krupp and Friedrich Flick, who, having remained in Germany as German citizens, would be made figureheads of allied retribution against German industry at the Nuremberg war trials. According to Wilhelmus Groenendijk, who was part of the Thyssen Bornemisza Group financial management from 1957 to 1986: 'Both Heinrich and Fritz were listed as war criminals. But from the Netherlands, we managed to get their names brought further down and down on that list until we were able to claim that the assets were in fact allied property.'[5]

The British military government's commandeering of the United Steelworks in August 1946 would prove to be the start of the industrial recovery of Fritz Thyssen's Konzern. Despite their stated intention to transform the German steel and coal industry into a publicly-owned organisation and punish the Thyssens for their support of Hitler, the British chose Dr Heinrich Dinkelbach, a close friend and confidant of Fritz and leader of the original United Steelworks administration, to become head of the new Steel Trustees Administration. With Dr Roelen acting in Heinrich's interests as an adviser to the North German Coal Control, both branches of the Thyssen family were thus well represented in the re-establishment of Germany's industrial power.

* * *

In 1946, the Swiss altered the conditions under which Germans could enter Switzerland and for SwFr 200,000 they could officially buy temporary residence. Lugano was particularly popular. In the town's luxury hotels and villas, escaping Nazis took up residence and paraded around town in expensive cars. Many soon took the favoured KLM flights to Argentina and Brazil, for which tickets were easily available through the Swissair offices. For a while, Lugano became the departure lounge for those awaiting passage to longer-term safe havens. Meanwhile, Heini and his father decided to escape from the summer humidity of the lake-side town to the cool alpine meadows of Flims, where Heini temporarily inherited Sandor Berkes's role as his father's manservant:

> After a lot of effort, I have finally managed to get my father up. He is really completely helpless. The only thing missing now is that I should have to blow his nose for him. Here it is rather cold and cloudy and a lot of the people are awful, unfortunately. A few pleasant tennis-playing acquaintances are helping

me over that. But the business and my father are also giving me lots to do, as he is unable do anything for himself.

At this point, Heini even managed to persuade his father to write, or wrote on his behalf a very sketchy reply to a letter from Roelen but with little in the way of a positive response or any indication that either of them had any intention of leaving the safety of Switzerland. What Heinrich did not tell Roelen was that he had already instructed his son to visit both Germany and Holland, but perhaps he was aware that mail was being intercepted and examined by the Allies.

Meanwhile, Roberto van Aken arranged the necessary documents for Heini, who still had no passport and had been travelling on questionable identity papers. First Heini called on Janos Wettstein who managed to persuade his various 'royal' Hungarian contacts to collaborate. They supplied a certificate from the 'royal' Hungarian General Consulate in Zurich 'confirming' Heini's Hungarian nationality which read:

> The consul general of Hungary certifies, on the basis of documents presented to him, that Baron Heinrich Thyssen-Bornemisza senior acquired Hungarian nationality on 4 December 1906 by naturalisation (File/decree: 130220/906). His son, Baron Hans Heinrich Thyssen-Bornemisza, born on 13 April 1921, has been a Hungarian subject since birth.[6]

Van Aken was particularly pleased with the wording: 'I even think it is better that they are talking of "naturalisation" rather than adoption because the naturalisation into Hungary through adoption has happened en masse during the last years before the war and was finally outlawed.'

Of course, Hungary was in the process of becoming a communist state and even Heini realised that beyond a certain theatrical effect, there would be little validity in any documents supplied at this stage by any 'royal' Hungarian Embassy. Even the American intelligence services received a negative response when they approached the Hungarian Ministry of the Interior concerning Heinrich's nationality.

* * *

Despite the grandiose documentation, Heini felt somewhat insecure about his application for a Dutch visa and decided to seek the assistance of a cousin of his brother-in-law, Baron Bentinck, called Dick van Karnebeek, who had recently taken up a position as secretary at the Dutch Legation in Berne. Unfortunately, in order to impress Karnebeek, he made the bad decision of taking Theresa with him, which had quite the opposite effect to that which he intended:

Dear Heini. I was unpleasantly surprised to see you come to me this morning with a German. If you weren't Dolf's brother-in-law, I would have asked Princess zu Lippe to leave. I cannot believe how you could have the lack of delicatesse and the nerve to come to the Dutch Legation with a German after all the misery and suffering that my country and its people have had to endure at the hands of these dirty pigs. Have you learned nothing in this war? How could Princess zu Lippe be so imprudent as to accompany you? One has to be German to have such an elephant's skin.

Even for you, as a Hungarian, it is doubtful whether you can be accorded a visa under the present circumstances, but if you insist on bringing a German when you come to the Dutch Legation, I will in future see myself forced to report this to my government. You asked me this morning if there was hatred in the Netherlands against the Bosch. Well, what do you think, after all we had to suffer from their hands? The hatred is terrible and you will have to be aware of this if by chance they will allow you to go to Holland. Good-bye, Heini, and don't act again like you did this morning in your ignorance. Think what you are doing in these current times.

It did not seem to cross Karnebeek's mind that he was addressing the grandson of Germany's legendary steel baron. Fortunately for Heini, Karnebeek's accusations failed to affect his eventual success in obtaining the necessary documents to facilitate his free moment in and out of Holland. Meanwhile, Heini felt compelled to remind him: 'Princess zu Lippe is a Hungarian subject, like myself. I cannot see a problem with her going to the Dutch Legation since Hungary has never been at war with Holland. She also has less German blood than her uncle in direct line, Prince Bernhard, Chief of the Dutch Resistance.'

It was ironic that while Heini had been spending so much time and effort getting out of Switzerland and into Holland and Germany, according to van Aken, his sister Margit appeared to have little difficulty getting out of Austria and into Switzerland. Van Aken gave no indication how he knew she had entered Switzerland in July 1945 or that he had any knowledge of the terrible atrocity in which the Countess Batthyány had been involved.

* * *

Having survived their liberation and further incarceration on the island of Capri, Fritz and Amélie were finally returned to Germany where Amélie was freed to go and stay with Fritz's sister Hedwig, while her husband was taken to Internment Camp 75 at Kornwestheim. From there he was soon transferred to

Chapter VI: 1945–1954

the Seventh Army Interrogation Centre at Kransberg, where Clifford Hynning of the US Group Control Council, Finance Division, initially interrogated him. Four and a half years of incarceration by his fellow countrymen, followed by re-arrest by the Americans, had had little effect on Fritz's arrogance or his ability to be economical with the truth. He denied that the return of the controlling interest in the United Steelworks by the Nazi government between 1933 and 1936 had been in any way connected to the financial contribution he had made to the Party. He also insisted that his contribution had been far less than was reported:

> The total amount I paid to the Nazi Party and its affiliates in any one year may have been a little over RM50,000; certainly not as much as RM75,000. I do not remember whether I made larger contributions in 1934 than in 1933. I have no idea where the *New York Times* got the figure of RM3 million, which they quote me as saying I gave to the party in the year 1932 alone.

In answer to questions concerning his South American interests, he admitted to the existence though not the ownership of Thyssen Lametal, while denying any Nazi political connections and insisting that the only money that went to Argentina was through an endowment belonging to his daughter and administered by Credit Suisse.

The questioning was not very skilful or tenacious and often rather vague, giving Fritz ample opportunity to invent, evade, lie and deny. His few regrets were exclusively personal. He gave no indication of any sympathy for the millions who had been killed and made very little mention of the Jews, save for a small slip when referring to President Hindenburg's invitation to Hitler to assume the role of Chancellor: 'Hindenburg was in a very difficult situation. He was the President of Germany with a bunch of Jews.'

Fritz persistently denied he had any commercial interests, bank accounts or safe deposits outside Germany. However, he did admit to the existence of a Swiss trust called the Pelzer Foundation, which he insisted had been set up by his mother for the exclusive benefit of the family, but pointed out that he was prevented from giving any financial details due to 'a secret arrangement I made with the British government through Sir William Firth, former president of the steel works in Wales.' Fritz then claimed that he had persuaded his mother to sell the British the Pelzer gold in order 'to undo the Nazis', which was a complete fabrication but one that his interrogators appeared quite prepared to accept.[7]

* * *

In November 1945, the Americans questioned Emmy Göring, the wife of Hermann, to little effect. In fact, the only time she did not appear to be deeply bored by the whole proceedings was when she was asked: 'Can you explain how a man of your husband's means acquired paintings and sculptures, works of art, amounting to $500 million?'

To this question she no doubt quite truthfully answered: 'I did not know that these purchases were so valuable.'

The interrogator's attention then turned to Gisela Limberger, Göring's secretary. Apparently, less than a month before the end of the war, the SS had removed all her files, bankbooks and records, which severely limited her factual recall. But she could still remember that Göring kept money in the August Thyssen Bank, where 'he just kept piling up bigger and bigger balances'.

On 10 October 1945, Curt Ritter had already admitted to the Americans the following accounts and balances of the Görings that still existed at the August Thyssen Bank: Hermann Göring: RM 926,530; Emmy Göring: RM 4,175; charity account: RM 63,455; war fund account: RM 52,583; special account: RM 1.5 million; and savings account: RM 1.3 million. Considerably larger amounts had already been transferred to Argentina.

Meanwhile, Gisela Limberger told how Göring had decided to flee Berlin on 20 April rather than die in the bunker with Hitler and had sent her to the August Thyssen Bank to retrieve his securities. This proved impossible, 'because they were in a safe or elsewhere'. Limberger may or may not have known that Ritter had already removed all incriminating evidence, including Göring's securities but her interrogator appeared to have little interest in pursuing this line of questioning. By this time, the various US and British intelligence agencies knew that Heinrich Thyssen-Bornemisza owned the August Thyssen Bank and that he had been involved in acting as an international service for the German counter-intelligence and various Nazi leaders. Yet remarkably little emphasis was placed on this fact during the interrogation of any of the detainees, including his brother Fritz.

Meanwhile, the Foreign Economic Administration in Washington had gathered considerable information concerning Fritz's financial interests in Argentina, including the fact that the implicated Soteria AG of Maienfeld, Switzerland was Thyssen-owned and that Dr Ernesto Aguirre was the president of Thyssen Lametal in Buenos Aires which had nine branches throughout Argentina. They found this to be 100 per cent owned by Cehandro of Rotterdam, which in turn was 100 per cent owned by VSt Düsseldorf, while all transactions

Chapter VI: 1945–1954

were in actual fact channelled through another cloaking vehicle called Themis Finanzgesellschaft based in the Swiss town of Zug.[8]

* * *

Although Curt Ritter's work had already proved to be of inestimable value, his Nazi past was beginning to present problems in the re-establishment of the Thyssen-Bornemisza holdings. In a letter to Heinrich he explained that the Russians, unlike the British or the Americans, were being extremely tricky:

> Despite all certificates of good conduct, the damn party membership is holding up many things. The bank is still closed. The supplementary supervisory board at Berliner Mörtelwerke has finally been registered with the Courts according to my wishes, but as a former party member I was rejected by the Magistrate. Red Berlin is not very co-operative at all.
>
> For Rüdersdorf we urgently need a special power of attorney that allows us to continue to administrate all the assets which are, as you know, entered into the commercial court register under the name of Bank voor Handel en Scheepvaart. Based on Order 124 of the Russian Authority, the central administration of German industry is making additional problems as it wants to declare Rüdersdorf an abandoned property because the owners are not personally present.[9]

The last statement may have been an indication that Ritter's loyalty was tested to the limit as he was having to ask the Baron to send him food, while being obliged to address his letters to the Palace Hotel in St Moritz.

* * *

When Germany was defeated, the Dutch government seized BVHS while the former Dutch manager, Henrik Kouwenhoven, who had been replaced by German management during the war, returned to support the Dutch government's claim. Heini, through his advisers Jakob Kraayenhof and P. W. Kamphuisen, would enter negotiations with the Dutch government in an attempt to retrieve his father's Dutch bank and holding company. Kamphuisen was a lawyer who was also in charge of Akzo, a major Dutch chemical company with very large investments in Germany. Kraayenhof was a well-known accountant who, according to Heini, enjoyed the additional qualification of working for both the Dutch Queen and Royal Dutch Shell.[10] Heini also had three other advantages. The first was his brother-in-law, Adolphe Bentinck, the Dutch diplomat. The second was Theresa's connections to the Dutch royal family. It also helped that

Curt Ritter was holding a considerable quantity of Queen Wilhelmina's stock and bonds in Berlin.

While Heini began to work with his father's management to retrieve their Dutch and German assets, the Swiss media began to reveal the part that the Thyssens had played in siphoning money out of Germany into South America. In November 1945, the *Neue Zürcher Zeitung* ran an article entitled 'Camouflaged German interests in Argentina', implicating Soteria AG, the Vulcaan group of Rotterdam and its main shareholder, Dr Heinrich Thyssen-Bornemisza. If the newspaper had intended to elicit a response and generate some panic, the article certainly had the desired effect. Roberto van Aken reacted so quickly that, having taken Heinrich's instructions, his letter to the newspaper arrived within 48 hours: 'My client must protest most vehemently against the malevolent inventions and untruths in this article. My client has been a Hungarian national since 1906, so there can be no question in his case of camouflaged German interests.'

By this time, even Fritz's interrogator was beginning to wake up to the fact that there may have been some connection between his prisoner and his brother, Heinrich Thyssen-Bornemisza. When asked, Fritz insisted they were 'not on good terms'. The two brothers indeed continued to take every opportunity to give the impression that they disliked each other in order to disguise the fact that their business empires had remained interlinked. Fritz also claimed that his only connection with the August Thyssen Bank was through a company called 'Thyssen Bank AG' and that he knew nothing of friends' admissions that he had told them how his brother helped Göring get money out of the country: 'My brother who lived in Switzerland controlled the August Thyssen Bank and I was not on the administration board although I know that Göring had an account there.'

But US Intelligence was becoming suspicious of Heinrich's nationality claims and issued a directive: 'Heinrich Thyssen-Bornemisza's nationality must be specially examined on the basis of Hungarian, German and Dutch laws.'

* * *

The US Treasury investigation into the Thyssens' affairs was often much more efficient than that carried out by military intelligence. In a preliminary report, investigators took very little time to unravel the complicated ownership structures: 'The whole attempt at camouflaging failed, as it became widely known in Argentina that Thyssen Lametal was not Swiss-owned but German.'

Then, having established who owned the company, they also concluded that it had been trading with Germany through the United Steelworks' subsidiary

Chapter VI: 1945–1954 195

Steel Union Sheet Piling of New York. But the report made little of Sheet Piling's procurement of raw materials for the Nazis or its connection with Heinrich's Union Bank.

Thyssen Lametal's political activities in Buenos Aires were also investigated and it was found that:

> In a letter to VSt on 2 July 1941, Thyssen Lametal requested permission to purchase a real estate property belonging to the German School Association, which had been offered to Thyssen Lametal by the local Nazi party ... The German Embassy strongly recommended the sale, as did the local Party leadership.
>
> It is obvious that any political activities Thyssen Lametal engaged in were chiefly of a secret nature, and that therefore there does not exist any documentary evidence ... All secret files of VSt were destroyed prior to the arrival of American troops in Düsseldorf on the order of the German counter-intelligence service ... Evidence has been uncovered in the case of Brazil, when two VSt agents were actually apprehended and convicted of espionage, receiving long-term prison sentences.[11]

Once again, no connection was made with Heinrich and his August Thyssen Bank despite US intelligence in Germany having already established that the Abwehr had reportedly used the bank to pay its worldwide network of agents throughout the war.[12] The Allies would also, somewhat surprisingly, fail to respond to their undoubted knowledge that the Thyssens' facilities had been used as a means of moving not just their own but also other private German money out of Europe and into Argentina. There was also every reason to believe that the funds included gold which Josi Groh insisted Eduard von der Heydt, the bank's original owner and Heinrich's closest friend, had obtained from concentration camp victims.

Meanwhile, both the British and American investigators remained unconvinced by Heinrich's claims of Hungarian nationality. On 4 December 1945, Max Guttmann, who was investigating the Thyssen-Bornemisza family and its Dutch connections on behalf of US Financial Intelligence, stated in one of his reports:

> It is likely that the property of Heinrich Thyssen-Bornemisza, originally derived from the August Thyssen part of German heavy industry, was maintained and enlarged by continued ties to Fritz Thyssen and to the United Steelworks respectively. Insofar as this property helped to establish the Nazi regime, financed German re-armament and profited from German

war spoils, it must also be used for paying German reparations, regardless of the nationality of the holder.

* * *

While the various intelligence agencies were gathering increasingly incriminating evidence against the Thyssens and the Thyssen-Bornemiszas, Heini's much-needed protective assistance arrived at Villa Favorita in the small but perfectly qualified form of Josi Groh, his student acquaintance who was returning from the eastern front. 'By the time Josi arrived back in Switzerland he had lost everything. So I gave him a room in the tower without telling my father, who was still alive at the time. With his knowledge of Swiss and Hungarian law he was very useful to me. He was extremely intelligent and helped me a great deal.'

Today, Heini Junior remains in little doubt that 'without Josi Groh, there would be no Thyssen Bornemisza Group'.[13]

The Hungarian quickly realised that if he wanted to enjoy a comfortable future as Heini's legal secretary, his immediate task was to assist him in retrieving his father's industrial and commercial holdings by establishing his Hungarian nationality. He would then have to help Heini evade the allied reparation claims and finally weather the family's inheritance challenge. Gunhilde, Heinrich's estranged wife, was also still working towards an alimonial demand of half his estate. His reliance on Hungarian law to protect himself from her claims would be another area where Groh's knowledge would prove invaluable.

Heini invented many entertaining stories concerning Josi Groh. But there was one that Groh liked enough to support its authenticity, although probably more for its theatrical content than its accuracy:

> During the divorce battle with Gunhilde, Josi had a problem with a particular point of Hungarian law. The problem was that we didn't have a Hungarian law book to consult, so Josi went to the Hungarian Consulate in Zurich that was already communist and tried to consult the book. He was told they didn't have it. However, he had to go to the toilet at the Consulate and instead of toilet paper, they only had pages torn out of a book. By an incredible coincidence, he found the paragraph of the book he had been looking for. The communist Consulate used royal law books as toilet paper! So I won a particular part of the divorce and inheritance battle because of the fact that Josi had had an urgent need at that precise moment.

* * *

The nationality question was complicated because Heini not only needed to prove that both he and his father were Hungarian with full Hungarian passports but also that his father was no longer German. He was not helped by the fact that while he did not have a passport, his father had four, two German and two Hungarian; all of which had been issued at The Hague. Passports had also been extended at embassies or legations of questionable legitimacy. Josi Groh could remember one such extension being obtained in Madrid. Apparently, General Franco did not recognise the communist regime, so a 'royal' Hungarian Ambassador was encouraged to continue representing his fictitious country and issuing 'royal' passport extensions. There is no evidence that other European countries questioned this arrangement.

It is not surprising that there seems to have been little agreement in the whole matter of nationality. Heini's sister Gaby was convinced that their father was stateless at the time of his death: 'My father had a Hungarian passport until the last war, until Hungary finally became an Iron Curtain country, I believe in 1944. His passport was withdrawn by the new Hungarian officials in Berne and the Swiss gave him a stateless passport.'

Although Gaby's grasp of reality might have been tenuous, there is reason to believe that she was correct in her belief due to a Hungarian nationality law that deprived citizens of their nationality if they remained outside the country for more than ten years. As the wife of a diplomat, Gaby would certainly have been in a position to know about such things.

However, there remained convincing evidence that Heinrich never lost his German nationality.[14] But regardless of the contradictions, if Heini was to use Hungarian nationality to retrieve and protect the family fortune, he still needed to get himself a Hungarian passport. Unfortunately, Hungary under Soviet occupation was unlikely to have been

Margit Senior with her second husband, Baron Janos Wettstein, in Karlsbad.

sympathetic towards a German capitalist whose only justification of Hungarian nationality was by imperial decree.

Eventually, with considerable assistance from Janos Wettstein, and a generous contribution to diplomatic funds, a certificate of Hungarian nationality was issued to Heini by the embassy in Berne in January 1947, which was only valid for six months. It was renewed continuously until the booklet was full. But there was still some element of doubt, even in Josi Groh's mind, as to whether Heini ever really enjoyed legitimate Hungarian nationality.

* * *

As Heinrich's health deteriorated, Groh began to anticipate the enormous inheritance problems that could result from the invalidity of the Kaszony Foundation, which Heinrich had formed to hold his estate. Fortunately, at this point in time it appeared to be in nobody's interest to mount a challenge and risk freezing the entire family fortune, so ownership of the Thyssen Bornemisza companies continued to be anchored to a powerless organisation. Heini also decided to increase his control of his father's will by replacing the existing executors with himself, Roberto van Aken and Jakob Kraayenhof.

The old man did not appear to have been given a great deal of choice in this matter and from this point in time Heini, who was obviously growing up very quickly, placed himself firmly in control of his inheritance. Even Heini Junior would subsequently admit that 'over time the old man's will became more and more positive in favour of my father to the detriment of everybody else'.

The executor problem had been a great deal easier to solve than the one that still existed in Holland, where BVHS was sequestered by the Board for Administration of Enemy and Collaborators' Property, or Beheer Institute, and the only way to overrule the Dutch was by a mixture of blackmail and diplomacy. But threatening to reveal the extent of Dutch collaboration with the Nazis was a dangerous policy that would require exceptional diplomatic skills. Fortunately, Heini was about to profit from the return from Cairo of his Dutch diplomat brother-in-law, Dolf Bentinck who, from 1946 to 1950, became Councillor Minister in London.

Meanwhile, Jakob Kraayenhof, Heini's Dutch accountant, would also play a vital role in rebuilding the Thyssen Bornemisza group of companies. Josi Groh would generously admit: 'Mr Kraayenhof really was the main planner of the recovery after the war, together with Dr Stappert and Professor Mann.'

* * *

Chapter VI: 1945–1954

With American policy and financial investment dominating the rebuilding of Europe, the spring of 1946 was an opportune time for Heini to visit New York. One of the major reasons for his visit, apart from the retrieval of their US assets, was to raise money to finance the recovery of his father's empire. At that time the organisation was still under allied control and with various members of his family demanding money, lawyers and accountants to pay and a future bride to impress, Heini needed cash. He had, also, only recently discovered that his father had financed the creation of his art collection with a Dfl 32 million loan which BVHS was demanding be repaid.

To achieve his aims, Heini decided to recruit the services of Sullivan and Cromwell, the legal power-base of the future US Secretary of State, special adviser on reparations and architect of America's anti-communist Cold War policy, John Foster Dulles. There is little doubt that, in his involvement in First World War reparations, Foster Dulles had already had dealings with the Thyssens. Certainly his brother Allen Dulles, the Berne-based head of the Office of Strategic Services, which by 1947 had metamorphosed into the CIA, had already met Heini. In fact, he had introduced him to a wealthy young Swiss-based American lawyer called Henry Hyde, who, Heini would later admit, was also working for the OSS and was assisting in their policy of fighting communism by getting German industry back on its feet.

Henry Hyde had a great deal more to offer than a political agenda and a law degree. The grandson and namesake of the founder and first president of the Equitable Life Insurance Company, Henry spoke fluent French and German and had a penchant for art and intrigue. It would also eventually be revealed that, as well as being a friend of the British spy Biffie Dunderdale, model for the fictional James Bond, he himself would also become a distinguished spymaster. Heini would be given little choice but to take him into his confidence.

I remember one particular hot sunny afternoon on the terrace in Sant Feliú, when Heini had drunk sufficient red wine to answer the question that I had drunk sufficient to ask: 'Was Henry Hyde aware that the August Thyssen Bank and the Union Bank were used by the Nazi Party to move money to South America?'

Heini raised his hand to his forehead in the customary manner that signalled the onset of amnesia, but this time he paused and slowly lowered his hand. After a few minutes of silence while he stared out to sea, he replied: 'Yes. He was astonished. He said, "My God. I'm defending a Nazi." Of course that wasn't true. Just because the banks did things for Nazis didn't mean the owner of the banks was a Nazi.'

'How did Hyde find out?'

'I had to give affidavits about the history of the bank. I was not secretive. I was sure everybody would know everything anyway, so there was no point in hiding things . . . SCHTOPP! Now!', Heini suddenly screamed at an ancient brown poodle that was peeing on a pot-plant already yellow from previous assaults.

Heini was not being entirely honest but after a few more glasses of wine he became even less so: 'It was Kouwenhoven's fault. He went to the US and did his big denunciation of our family as being fascist. The bad thing was that Kouwenhoven also represented Fritz. I don't know, it might be pure imagination, but I think he did it to divert blame from himself for having been involved with Fritz.'

* * *

As Stephan and Margit tried to organise their own safe-havens and Gaby prepared for her move to London with Dolf, they all became increasingly concerned with their financial positions and their brother's control of their father's fortune. Their mother Margit appeared to offer a sympathetic ear to her various children. In fact, while admitting to Heini's aggressively superior attitude, she obviously favoured his control of the family fortune. In February 1946 she wrote to Gaby advising her to accept Heini's 'acting on behalf of his father in protecting the interests of the family, as open conflict would lead to "chaos" which would profit only the state and the lawyers'. She also claimed to be puzzled by Stephan's apparent inability to leave Germany and enter Switzerland.

Meanwhile Stephan seemed to be naïvely optimistic that he could 'sort everything out' concerning the family fortune, while warning Gaby: 'Here in Germany we can forget about Papa's assets. Of course, I always assumed that in order to save everything, Papa had acquired Swiss nationality.'

Gaby obviously gave Heini some indication of their brother's concern and his intended arrival in Switzerland, for within a matter of days Stephan was visited in Hanover by a rather mysterious Austrian lawyer, Dr Erwin Lowatschek. While Stephan seemed quite prepared to accept that Lowatschek had been authorised by Heini to look after the financial affairs of the family and keep the relations between the siblings on a very tight basis, it seemed more likely that Heini had hired him to keep Stephan out of Switzerland. If so, he certainly succeeded. Stephan continued to be refused entry into Switzerland and wrote constantly to his mother informing her of his suspicions concerning who may have been responsible for initiating the refusal.

Chapter VI: 1945–1954 201

Heini must also have secured a degree of protection for both his brother and the organisation as there is no evidence of Stephan ever being questioned concerning his wartime activities in either Seismos or MABAG.

* * *

According to US intelligence, in May 1946 Wilhelm Roelen, on behalf of the Thyssen Bornemisza Group of companies in Germany, submitted claims to the Allies for war damages amounting to RM 35 million. By October compensation payments had already commenced with Oberbilker Steelworks receiving RM2 million. What the Allies did not know at the time was that from the safety of Switzerland, Heinrich had also claimed damages from the Reich in 1944, when the Thyssen-Bornemisza Konzern had been authorised to file applications for compensation to the same extent as Reich Germans. Apparently, for these purposes Heinrich Thyssen-Bornemisza was classified as a *Volksdeutscher* or a person of German descent living abroad.[15]

While Roelen used allied funds to facilitate the recovery of the Konzern in war-torn Germany, Heini used the funds he had raised in New York to celebrate his engagement to Theresa. On his way to Holland, he had stopped in Paris to have a suit made for his wedding and a wedding-dress for Theresa. He even bragged about his credit of SwFr 140,000 while revelling in the new social status afforded him by his introduction to Theresa's friends and relatives:

> In Paris I had lunch with Comtesse de St Leon, Comtesse de Cerisy, Princess Cassaigne Polignac, Comtesse d'Elbée and Monsieur Hurbe. My wedding will probably take place at the end of August, after which we want to go to Spain and in October we will be going to America for two to three months.

But he was also aware that the continuation of his good fortune would need a degree of 'attention to business'. Entering Holland to negotiate the release of BVHS presented few difficulties but Heini had yet to gain permission to enter the British sector of Germany, so a degree of subterfuge was needed which Katherine Coert, the wife of Dr J. Coert Junior, remembered in considerable detail:

> It was my husband who had suggested Heini pose as his driver, using the passport of Hartmann, his real driver. Apparently it was very funny, because they had a flat tyre and as my husband was a major, it would have looked very suspicious if he had been seen changing the wheel while his driver watched, so Heini had to do it himself. Something he had certainly never done before. Then my husband left him at the Thyssen headquarters in

Duisburg for two or three days. While he was there, the British Military police arrived and the factory managers had to hide Heini in a cupboard.[16]

In fact, Heini thoroughly enjoyed the whole adventure while not forgetting the purpose of his visit, particularly in view of the situation in which he found the Konzern, which he revealed to his sister Gaby:

> We have not been confiscated in Germany. Each enterprise has been given a production officer who controls production; that's all. We enjoy a priority position concerning material supplies for reconstruction ahead of all other German companies. The English are deeply impressed with our works and our activities.[17]

* * *

Heini liked to give the impression that the reason for his clandestine journey to Germany in 1946 had been to retrieve the shares proving his father's cloaked ownership of BVHS and Holland American Investment Corporation through certificates that were still locked up in the partially destroyed August Thyssen Bank in Berlin. When he had drunk sufficient vino tinto, he would tell his least accurate but most entertaining version of the retrieval in which, dressed as a Dutch soldier and assisted by a Russian General's Polish mistress, he had taken part in a daring, moonlight raid amid the ruins of Berlin to remove the contents of the strongroom under the noses of the Russians.

In fact, Heini was fully aware that the shares and records were being held by Curt Ritter, awaiting illegal removal from Berlin and return to Holland. A somewhat more accurate, if less entertaining, version of the sequence of events would eventually also appear in a Dutch newspaper. But while the paper accepted the involvement of BVHS, it chose not to mention that the Thyssen-Bornemiszas owned the bank and that it was partly their shares that were being retrieved. The actual retrieval was done with the help of the Coerts, father and son, and the plan was known as 'Operation Juliana' after the Dutch Queen's daughter.

> On 24 August 1946 Coert Junior, a Dutch reserve officer, appeared at Ritter's house with a military truck and driver. The cargo was loaded aboard and legalised by imposing-looking transport documents from the Dutch Military Mission. Two days later, Ritter heard from Dirk Swart that the transport had reached Holland without any difficulty. Ironically the problems began only when the adventurous part of 'Operation Juliana' was over.[18]

Chapter VI: 1945–1954

While the consignment was still under way, it apparently occurred to Coert Senior that they would have to gain the permission of directors Kouwenhoven and Groeninger before the shares could be returned to BVHS bank. But having strongly objected to the original transfer of the shares to Berlin, both had voiced even stronger objections to the planned return for what they considered to be the Thyssen-Bornemiszas' convenience. When they were suddenly faced with a *fait accompli*, the trustees refused to accept the consignment until they had consulted The Hague; so until further notice the bundles had to be stored at Coert's father's house in Rotterdam.

While certain junior members of the government tried to encourage them to keep quiet about the whole affair, Kouwenhoven and Groeninger sent a letter to the Dutch Minister of Economics in which they warned:

> The removal from Russian territory of securities of which a Hungarian subject, who is probably still classed by the Russians as an enemy, regards himself as the ultimate owner, remains, as does the provision of assistance in obtaining the custody over those securities, a highly irresponsible act towards a nation with which we are not on a footing of war.

The Minister was left with little choice but to inform the Ministers of Finance and Justice, although, due to the fact that the shares had included the property of the Dutch royal family, it was unlikely that they would have been unaware of their removal from Germany and return to Holland. Mr Lieftinck, the Minister of Finance reacted with appropriate indignation and on 7 November 1946, requested the head of the customs investigation service to investigate the occurrence of smuggling and 'if necessary confiscate the securities concerned'. But by this time too many people were implicated and a serious political scandal needed to be avoided. Lieftinck backed down almost immediately when certain highly-placed individuals made him aware of the consequences of his intended actions.

While the newspaper admitted that one of the 'highly placed individuals' was 'Baron Bentinck, the London-based Dutch diplomat, who was married to the daughter of Heinrich Thyssen-Bornemisza', they apparently decided to avoid revealing the identity of the other members of the original raiding party. Wilhelmus Groenendijk eventually acknowledged:

> Civilians were not allowed into Germany, but managers in Holland wanted to know what had happened to their property, so representatives of Unilever formed a Dutch military mission together with managers from Royal Dutch Shell, Philips and Akzo. The man in charge was Dirk Swart, who worked

for Philips and was given the honorary rank of Colonel. He later became a manager of the Thyssen-Bornemisza Group.

The knowledge that major Dutch companies had combined to carry out an illegal act from which they, the Thyssen-Bornemiszas and their own royal family would profit was not something the Dutch government wished to advertise. So the shares were permitted to be quietly moved back into Bank voor Handel en Scheepvaart. While the bank officially remained sequestered by the Dutch, no one seemed in any doubt that it was only a matter of allowing a respectable amount of time to elapse and a suitably impressive Dutch board to be recruited before the sequester would be lifted and the bank returned to the Thyssen-Bornemiszas.

* * *

On 29 August 1946, the twenty-four-year-old Hans Heinrich Thyssen-Bornemisza, 'a Hungarian student, living in Fribourg', married the twenty-one-year-old Theresa Amalia Francesca Elisabeth Anna Maria Princess zu Lippe Bisterfeld Weissenfeld, 'a Hungarian student, living in Lausanne', born on 21 July 1925 in Vienna, daughter of Prince Alfred Lippe and Princess Lippe née Francesca Anna Maria Countess Schönborn-Buchheim.

Heini claimed his father was so against the marriage that he refused to attend the wedding, which took place in Lugano. In truth, he had not encouraged him to attend, due to the fact that his father was becoming increasingly anti-social. Whether, as Heini insisted, his father really tried to convince him that the Princess was only marrying him for his money, is open to conjecture. In fact, a far greater incentive for the marriage was the Princess's connection to the Dutch royal family which Heini would readily exploit in his retrieval of his father's fortune.

It was only after their union had served his purpose and he needed to justify his divorce that Heini, in a manner remarkably similar to his father, started to criticise Theresa. He accused her of behaving like an empress and treating him like a socially inferior upstart. But his sister Gaby suggested Heini was in turn jealous of his brother-in-law, Count Ivy Batthyány's, aristocratic status and title. It was this festering jealousy that no doubt eventually lead to Heini's accusing Theresa and Ivy of having an affair, claiming that his sister Margit had discovered them locked in a passionate embrace 'in the drawing room', although this allegation was never substantiated.

Shortly after his wedding, Heini organised a meeting with his sisters at Villa Favorita to discuss the family's financial arrangements. His sisters' suspicions that Heini had taken full control and had no intention of seeking their approval

Chapter VI: 1945–1954

The wedding of Princess Theresa zu Lippe Bisterfeld Weissenfeld and Baron Hans Heinrich Thyssen-Bornemisza de Kaszón.

of his decisions, were confirmed by his refusal to supply them with even basic information, including copies of the powers of attorney granted him by his father. Margit's solicitor made it obvious that his client was not prepared to accept Heini's omnipotence, but to little effect.

Subsequently, Margit, Gaby and Dolf prepared an application for an incapacitation order for their father and suggested his affairs be controlled by a family council consisting of Baron and Baroness Bentinck and Heini and Theresa; no mention was made of Stephan. Their belief that Heini would share power was at best naïve, as he had absolutely no intention of relinquishing the control already granted him by his father of the Kaszony and Rohoncz foundations, which owned all of the foreign assets and his art collection.

Heini then bribed his sister Margit, who unlike Stephan appeared to have had little difficulty in entering and remaining in Switzerland, into supporting his opposition to the request for guardianship by transferring to her his monthly student allowance. Margit excused her change of heart by blaming Gunhilde who could use an incapacitation order to invalidate an imminent court judgment and eventually claim a widow's legal portion of their father's fortune.

But Heini was still concerned that his brother might choose to oppose him. As the eldest son, Stephan could certainly claim a legal advantage. The easiest short-term protection was to keep him out of Switzerland by leaking rumours of Nazi affiliations to the Swiss authorities. On hearing the insinuations, Gaby wrote to van Aken:

> I just received news from a Swiss friend who said that some information has been lodged with the foreigners' police in Berne against my brother Stephan, saying that he was a member of the SS. His request for a Swiss visa has been denied on the basis of this information. I must insist that the information against my brother is absolutely false.[19]

But Gaby's claim failed to convince the Swiss authorities who continued to refuse Stephan a visa. Meanwhile, Margit and Gaby continued to complain about Heini's dictatorial attitude and financial control, while his mother claimed she had not seen or heard from him since he married. When not travelling, Heini remained in an apartment in Zurich with Theresa and her extended family while his father remained at Villa Favorita, with only Sandor Berkes for company.

In fact, the only person Heini really wanted to see was Gunhilde who continued to avoid the service of divorce papers by remaining constantly on the move; evading Roberto van Aken even when he pursued her to Milan.

* * *

In the autumn of 1946, William Averell Harriman, ex-US Ambassador to London and Moscow and a founding director of the Thyssens' Union Bank in New York, returned to the US to take up the post as Secretary of State for

Commerce. Henry Hyde had suggested to Heini that it might be a good time for him to visit New York again. This resulted in one of Heini's favourite anecdotes concerning his last-minute cancellation of a KLM flight which crashed at Schiphol killing all on board. But while getting into the US may not have been as life-threatening as getting there, a letter accompanying his visa application illustrated van Aken's willingness to lie on Heini's behalf: 'From the advent of the Nazis' rise to power, and particularly from 1938 on, Dr Heinrich Thyssen-Bornemisza's Dutch corporations were directed with the definitive purpose of minimising the Nazi rearmament efforts.'[20]

He went on to emphasise the rift in the relationship between Heinrich and Fritz, apparently due to the latter's involvement with the National Socialist Party.

Heini's return from New York resulted in yet more imaginative anecdotes:

In those days planes used to stop for fuel at Gander in Labrador. We were all allowed off the plane to refresh ourselves and while I was in the toilet, I fell into conversation with a Dutchman. He asked me what I did and when I told him I was in banking he said, 'Me too', and during the rest of our flight we continued to get better acquainted and I told him about my banking interests in Holland and the problems I was having retrieving them. He told me he was involved with the Dutch government and that he might be able to help me one day, but that it would be a good idea not to tell people about our conversation or even that we had met.

Heini insisted the man he met in the toilet had been Lieftinck, the Dutch Minister of Finance, and that a year or two later Lieftinck had summoned him to Holland and as a reward for his discretion had made him a remarkable offer. Apparently, the Dutch government was prepared to consider the loan his father had taken out to buy his paintings as 'covered by pre-war dividends to be taxed at 10 per cent'. But Heini claimed to be suffering from such an extreme shortage of funds that he was unable to take advantage of his offer. So Lieftinck responded with even greater generosity. 'He said the tax claim could be covered by dividends paid on our Royal Dutch Shell shares. It was incredible. What he was actually doing was to cancel my father's debt leaving me with sufficient money to buy my brother's share in the bank.'

While there is no reason to doubt the accuracy of this remarkable financial arrangement, it appears likely that Heini invented the circumstances of his meeting because he did not like to admit the contribution made by Adolphe Bentinck's close relationship with Lieftinck. Regardless of who was responsible, it is unlikely that the Dutch public would have appreciated the fact that they were subsidising the Thyssen-Bornemiszas' art collection.

* * *

On his return, while discussing passports and visa with his 'Uncle Janos', Heini inadvertently revealed the true purpose of his visit to New York. Apparently, a group of Americans had made a serious offer to buy the entire Konzern. Heini's negotiations with the Americans were not limited to companies he had yet to inherit. According to one of his internal memos, they had also discussed the possibility of obtaining Fritz's property in his absence. But Heini was being very naïve in assuming such plans could succeed. Regardless of the fact that Fritz was under house arrest, with the support of his wife, daughter and loyal ex-Party members, he never stopped devising ways to retrieve what they considered their birthright. It was an endeavour in which, eventually, Fritz's family, particularly Amélie and Anita, would be extremely successful. Meanwhile, the cloaked ownership of his international holdings continued to be relentlessly investigated by various US intelligence agencies.

Heini would later claim that the reason for the failure of his plan was his father's insistence that they remain independent of the big publicly owned steel works. Nevertheless, he would eventually admit that he and his American friends had tried to get a 25 per cent stake in the August Thyssen Hütte complex, but had been fought off by a lawyer called Dr Robert Ellscheid, who was representing his uncle Fritz.

When asked why he thought he had been prevented from buying into what would eventually become Thyssen AG, Heini said:

> I am not in Germany considered in those circles a real national German. I didn't study in a German university and haven't been in a German student corps. All these people have had the same background. In the Ruhr, they are very nationalistic Germans. If you are not one of them, you are out. I find it very difficult for them to say to me that I cannot be part of the Ruhr. Because, if you are in the Ruhr, everything is Thyssen, Thyssen, Thyssen. So it's a bit ridiculous for me to have nothing to do with it. I cannot even form a company under the name Thyssen. I have to call it Thyssen-Bornemisza. Legally, they have the name Thyssen.

He also eventually revealed the US company behind the attempted take-over: 'Louis Carl Loeb had worked for the Metallgesellschaft in Germany but left before the war and founded Loeb Bros, which now belongs to American Express.

He was a stockbroker but he also traded metal and commodities. I met him through his partner, Palmer Dixon, who was a friend of Henry Hyde, my lawyer.'

While Heini continued to plot against his Uncle Fritz, Stephan planned to take legal action against his brother's control of the family fortune. But before he had a chance to take such action, he and his sisters were rendered powerless when, on 3 December 1946, their father signed a power of attorney that not only reinforced Heini's and van Aken's powers, but also specified that only Heinrich had the power of revocation. It is debatable whether the old man knew what he was signing. There was certainly no evidence of a doctor having been present, while a psychiatric report prepared earlier in the year had pronounced Heinrich to be 'incapacitated' and suffering from, among other debilitating problems, 'pathological suggestibility'.

* * *

Meanwhile, the US Trading with the Enemy Department tried to prove Heinrich's ownership of BVHS, ATB and various Dutch trading companies. They were obviously unaware that the Rotterdam branch of Price Waterhouse & Co. had already established this fact in December 1939 for the British Consul General after Heinrich had opened an office for the English Vulcaan (London) Company Ltd.

The investigators did manage to conclude that the buying of Fritz's 25 percent share in August Thyssen Bank, after the confiscation of his assets, illustrated the close business relationship which existed between Göring and Heinrich. They also accepted the fact that the share capital in BVHS of Dfl 12 million was held by three Dutch companies, all of which represented Heinrich's interests and one of which administered not only BVHS but also the Pelzer Foundation and Faminta AG, a fact that also confirmed the continued business connection between Fritz and Heinrich Thyssen.

But the Department also seemed quite prepared to accept Heinrich's immunity as a Hungarian national despite the fact that another department of US intelligence had already established his German nationality.

The External Assets and Intelligence Branch of US Intelligence also concluded: '[The removal of the securities from the August Thyssen Bank with the aid of the Netherlands Military Mission] has obviously violated the terms under which [the individual Dutch officers] were accredited to the Allied Control Authority in Berlin.'[21]

Yet no action was taken and the gradual liberation of Heinrich Thyssen-Bornemisza's industrial and financial empire continued.

In March 1947, the influence of Adolphe Bentinck and Theresa's father over

August Thyssen-Hütte AG, Dbg.-Hamborn (484 Mill. DM/ca. 34 %)
bei Thyssen AG Beteiligungen = Gräfin Anita de Zichy, ca. 4 %)
bei Fritz Thyssen Vermögensverwaltung AG =
Wwe. Amélie Thyssen)

Niederrheinische Hütte AG, Duisburg, Organvertr. (55,2 Mill. DM / 96 %)
Westfälische Union AG für Eisen- u. Drahtindustrie, Hamm, Organvertrag (25,2 Mill. DM / 100 %)
Wireholt Investment Ltd, Toronto (2 Mill. can. $ / 100 %)
Donald Roper & Wire Cloth Ltd, Hamilton / Ontario
Wirex Precision Wire Manufacturers (Pty) Ltd, Vanderbijlpark / Transvaal (130 130 £ / 100 %)
Bau-Stahlgewebe GmbH, Düsseldorf (5 Mill. DM / 31,15 %)
Kampenwand Seilbahn GmbH, München (1 Mill. DM / 87,5 %)
Müro AG, Kriens / Schweiz (120 000 sfr / 16,67 %)
Hexagonal GmbH, Düsseldorf (20 000 DM / 14 %)
Haus der Drahtseilindustrie GmbH, Essen (300 000 DM / 12,02 %)
Lehrwerkstatt Altena GmbH, Altena i. W. (50 000 DM / 5 %)
Westfälische Wohnstätten AG, Dortmund (18 Mill. DM / 4 %)
Lennewerk Altena GmbH, Altena i. W., Organvertr. (2,5 Mill. DM / 100 %)
Eisenwerk Steele GmbH, Essen-Steele, Organvertr. (1 Mill. DM / 100 %)
Rheinisch Westfälische Kalkwerke AG, Dornap (35 644 800 DM / 2,7 %)
Rheinische Wohnstätten AG, Dbg.-Meiderich (21,6 Mill. DM /4 %)
Westdeutsche Wohnhäuser AG, Düsseldorf (21 Mill. DM / 3 %)

Deutsche Edelstahlwerke AG, Krefeld, Organvertrag (55,2 Mill. DM / 94,4 %)
Vereinigte Edelstahl AG, Glarur / Schweiz (100 %)
Marathon Fine Steels Great Britain Ltd, London (15 000 £ / 100 %)
Marathon Staal N. V., Rotterdam (150 000 hfl / 100 %)
Marathon Edelstahl Verkaufs-Gesellschaft mbH, Wien (500 000 S / 100 %)
Acciaierie DEW S. p. B., Mailand (100 Mill. Lire / 100 %)
Marathon Speziality Steels, Inc., New York (10 000 $ / 100 %)
Marathon Fine Steels Canada Ltd, Toronto (40 000 can. $ / 100 %)
Marathon Edelstahl AG, Zürich (320 000sfr / 98 %)
Marathon S. A., Paris (120 000NF / 97 %)
Doeror Marathon Ltda, Santiago de Chile (64 500 Esc / 74 %)
DEW Hammerwerk Werdohl GmbH, Werdohl (20 000 DM / 100 %)
Marathon Export-Gesellschaft mbH, Krefeld (45 000 DM / 100 %)
Hochfrequenz-Tiegelstahl GmbH, Bochum (200 000 DM / 100 %)
AEG-Elotherm GmbH,Remscheid (1 Mill. DM / 50 %/ 50 % bei AEG)
Sinterstahl GmbH, Füssen (1 Mill. DM / 50 % / 50 % bei Metallwerk Plansee AG, Reutte / Tirol)
Continental Titanium Metals Corporation SA (= Contimet), Luxemburg (10 Mill. lfr. / 50 % / 50 % bei Titanium Metals Corp. of America, New York)
Marathon Argentina Aceros Finos y Especiales S. A., Villa Constitution (300 Mill. Pes. / 50 % / 50 % bei „Acindar" Industria Argentina de Aceros S. A., Buenos Aires)
Rennanlage Rhein-Ruhr GmbH, Essen (1 Mill. DM / 20 %)
Blankstahlmaschinen GmbH, Düsseldorf (100 000 DM / 5,5 %)
u. a. kleine Beteiligungen

Thyssen Industrie GmbH, Dinslaken, Organvertrag (7 Mill. DM 100 %)
Thyssen Industriehandel GmbH, Dinslaken (20 000 DM / 100 %)
„Thyssen-Verkehr" GmbH, Dbg.-Hamborn (20 000 DM / 100 %)
Handelsunion AG, Düsseldorf (46 Mill. DM / 51,8 %)
Heinrich August Schulte Eisenhandlung GmbH, Dortm., Organvertr. (20 Mill. DM / 100 %)
Rheiner Eisenhandlung GmbH, Rheina (1 Mill. DM / 100 %)
Bölling & Co GmbH, Hagen i. W. (412 000 DM / 100 %)
Christian Sede GmbH, Minden (300 000 DM / 100 %)
G. A. Schlichter GmbH, Münster i. W. (200 000 DM / 100 %)
Eisen- und Stahlhandel GmbH, Frankfurt a. M., Organvert (15 Mill. DM / 100 %)
Jos. Hupfeld GmbH, Wiesbaden (3 Mill. DM / 100 %)
Bucher & Mayer GmbH, Stuttg.-B. Cannstatt (600 000 DM 100 %)
Stahlunion Export GmbH, Düsseldorf, Organvertr. (7 Mill. DM 100 %)
Thyssen-Export GmbH, Düsseldorf (25 000 DM / 100 %)
Schrotthandel vormals Albert Sonnenberg GmbH, Düsseldor Organvertr. (4 Mill. DM / 100 %)
Willi Heine GmbH, Hamburg (450 000 DM / 100 %)
Berliner Eisen- und Stahl-GmbH, Berlin, Organvertr. (2,4 Mi DM / 100 %)
Röhren- und Roheisen-Großhandel GmbH, Frankfurt a. M., O ganvertr. (1 Mill. DM / 100 %)
Stückblechkontor GmbH, Düsseldorf, Organvertr. (1 Mill. DM 100 %)
Düsseldorfer Metallwerke GmbH, Düsseldorf, Organver (700 000 DM / 100 %)
Bicken & Co GmbH, Essen, Organvertr. (500 000 DM / 100 %

Eisen, Stahl und Röhren AG, Zürich (700 000 sfr / 50 %)
The Stahlunion Company, Ltd, London (21 000 £ / 50 %)
N. V. Nedexímpo von 1949, Amsterdam (980 000 hfl / 50 %)
Montan Selbstversicherungs-GmbH, Düsseldorf (100 000 DM / 16,5 %)
Bergbau- und Industriewerke GmbH, Düsseldorf (20 000 DM / 8,75 %)
Rasselstein AG, Neuwied (56 Mill. DM / 50 %)
Tolas-Vertretungs-AG, Zürich (700 000 sfr / 50 %)
Lametal Union S. A. Comercial e Industrial, Buenos Aires (23,972 Pes / 43,2 % / 14,2 % bei Handelsunion AG)
Armco-Thyssen Breitband-Verarbeitung GmbH, Dinslaken (2,5 Mill. DM / 50 %)
Rheinische Kalksteinwerke GmbH, Wülfrath, Organvertr. (25 Mill. DM / 32,5 %)
Dolomitwerke GmbH, Wülfrath, Organvertr. (12 Mill. DM / 25 %)
Harzer Dolomitwerke GmbH, Wülfrath (1,6 Mill. DM / 90 % / 10 % bei Rhein. Kalksteinwerke)
Sterchamolwerke GmbH, Wülfrath (800 000 DM / 50 % / 50 % bei Rheinische Kalksteinwerke)
Barbara Erzbergbau AG, Düsseldorf (15 Mill. DM / 25 %)
Ruhr Consulting GmbH, Düsseldorf (4 Mill. DM / 25 %)
Vereinigte Ton- und Quarzitbetriebe GmbH, Siegen (1,2 Mill. DM / 25 %)
Bergbau- und Industriewerke GmbH, Düsseldorf (20 000 DM / 21,5 %)
Montanzement-Vertriebs GmbH, Düsseldorf (35 000 DM / 14,3 %)
Rennanlage Salzgitter-Ruhr GmbH, Salzgitter (500 000 DM / 11 %)
Thomasphosphatfabriken GmbH, Düsseldorf, (100 000 DM / 10 %)
Thomasmehl-GmbH, Köln (1 Mill. DM / 8,33 %)
Rheinische Wohnstätten AG, Dbg.-Meiderich (21,6 Mill. DM / 10 %)
Westdeutsche Wohnhäuser AG, Düsseldorf, Organvertr. 21,6 Mill. DM / 6 %)
Gesellschaft für Teerverwertung mbH, Dbg.-Meiderich, Organvertr. (18 Mill. DM / 6,5 %)
und einige kleine Beteiligungen
Kraftwerk Hamborn, Duisburg-Hamborn (Miteigentum: 50 %)
Gemeinschaftsbetrieb Eisenbahn u. Häfen (E. b. R.), Duisbg.-Hamborn (Miteigentum: 33 1/3 %)

Phoenix-Rheinrohr-Konzern

Phoenix-Rheinrohr AG Vereinigte Hütten- und Röhrenwerke, Düsseldorf
(276 Mill. DM / 52 %) bei Fritz Thyssen Vermögensverwaltung AG = Amélie Thyssen)
Friedrich Thyssen Bergbau AG, Duisburg-Hamborn, Organvertr. (50 Mill. DM / 50 %)
Rheinische Kalksteinwerke GmbH, Wülfrath, Organvertr. (25 Mill. DM / 32,5 %)
Dolomitwerke GmbH, Wülfrath, Organvertr. (12 Mill. DM / 25 %)
Wuragrohr GmbH, Wickede Ruhr, Organvertr. (4 Mill. DM 100 %)
Lindener Eisen- u. Stahlwerke GmbH, Hannov.-Linden, Organvertr. (3 Mill. DM. 100 %)
Vereinigte Rohrleitungsbau GmbH, Düsseldorf, Organvertr. (3 Mill. DM / 100 %)
Phoenix-Rheinrohr International GmbH, Düsseldorf, Organvertr. (3 Mill. DM / 100 %)
Phoenix-Rheinrohr Eisen- u. Röhrenhandel GmbH, Mülheim Ruhr, Organvertr. (20 000 DM / 100 %)
Rhein-Plastik-Rohr GmbH, Mannheim, Organvertr. (1 Mill. DM 50 %)
Westdeutsche Wohnhäuser AG, Düsseldorf, Organvertr. (21,6 Mill. DM / 9 %)
Silika- und Schamottefabriken Martin u. Pagenstecker AG, K.-Mülheim (3,45 Mill. DM / 50 %)
Emscher-Lippe Bergbau AG, Datteln i. W. (30 Mill. DM 51 %)
Langmatz GmbH, Berlin-Spandau (1,5 Mill. DM / 51 %)
Blohm & Voss AG, Hamburg (20 Mill. DM / 50 %)
Handelsunion AG, Düsseldorf (46 Mill. DM, 35,3 %)
Barbara Erzbergbau AG, Düsseldorf (25 Mill. DM / 25 %)
Rheinische Wohnstätten AG, Düsseldorf (21,6 Mill. DM 20 %)
Wehag Westdeutsche Haushaltsversorgung AG, Bochum (6 Mill. DM / 2,25 %)
Westfälische Wohnstätten AG, Dortmund (18 Mill. DM / 1 %)
Ruhr Consulting GmbH, Düsseldorf (4 Mill. DM / 25 %)
Phoenix-Rheinrohr France S. à. r. l., Paris (100 000 NF/ 90 %)
Officine Meccaniche e Fonderic A. Bosco S. p. A., Terni-Ital. (171 Mill. Lire / 55 %)
Phoenix Industris Ltd, Vancouver / Canada, Holding (100 %)
Phoenix Industrial Overseas Investments Ltd, Vancouver / Can., Holding (100 %)
Big Inch Pipe Corporation Ltd, Calgara / Canada (100 %)
Alberta Phoenix Tube & Pipe Ltd, Edmonton / Can. (7 Mill. can. $ 100 %)
Canadian Western Pipe Mills Ltd, Port Moody / Can. (5,2 Mill. can. $ / 100 %)
Phoenix Rheinrohr Corporation, New York (100 %)
u. einige kleinere Beteiligungen

the affairs of BVHS were evident by the involvement of Crown Princess Juliana's husband Prince Bernhard. The Prince, whose political and commercial honesty would subsequently be questioned, supported the termination of government control and recommended its replacement by a supervisory board including two of the Queen's confidants, the former mayor of The Hague and an ex-Minister for the Navy, to reinforce the Dutch character of the bank.

By now the British had been made aware of 'Operation Juliana'. The Foreign Office reacted by accusing the Dutch of protecting German interests while the American commander in Berlin, General Lucius D. Clay, also forwarded his comments about the affair to the State Department. But neither London nor Washington took any further action. By mid-1947, the Dutch government even issued a formal import licence for the smuggled securities, thus retrospectively legalising the transaction.

* * *

While the reclamation of Dutch property from a German bank could be made to seem acceptable, assisting in the reclamation of the property of a German exile from a German bank that had supported the Nazi Party was definitely not. So before his father died, Heini desperately needed to prove his father was Hungarian, not German. Having vainly tried to commission Professor Hans Oppikofer, a Swiss academic in Zurich, to confirm Heinrich's nationality claims, Josi Groh wrote to his colleague Dr Dajkovich in Budapest suggesting that he forge the necessary documents.

Back in Switzerland, Joseph Szall, Secretary to the Hungarian Legation in Berne, prepared a document confirming Heinrich's Hungarian nationality. Szall also confirmed Heinrich's loss of German nationality, but this was a somewhat pointless exercise as it could serve as nothing more than an opinion. The situation would have been somewhat more complicated if the Adlon Hotel had not been burnt to the ground in 1945 and with it all evidence of the residential suite that Heinrich had retained throughout the war. According to Heini, it had actually caused his father some problems with the German tax authorities when they discovered a picture from his collection hanging on the wall of the suite. Apparently, this proved residential status and thus German tax liabilities, which led to protracted, secret negotiations.

Around the same time, in answer to a letter from US intelligence, Curt Ritter

◄ *Corporate inheritance of Fritz Thyssen's heirs, Amélie and Anita (source: Pritzkoleit).*

confirmed his position as a director of the August Thyssen Bank from 1927 until March 1946 as well as Lübke's and Roelen's regular visits to the Baron in Switzerland throughout the war to keep him informed concerning his various financial and business interests in Germany. In answer to questions concerning the Nazi officials who had accounts with the bank, Ritter confirmed those held by Reichsmarschall Göring, Economy Minister Funk and Secretary of State Körner. Apparently Göring and Funk also had safe deposit boxes in the bank.[22]

By now there could have been no doubt that US intelligence were fully aware of Heinrich Thyssen-Bornemisza's German nationality and his international financial arrangements with the Nazi Party. But any reference to the Union Bank of New York remained conspicuous by its absence.

*   *   *

On the morning of 26 June 1947, Sandor Berkes called Baroness Gaby in London. 'I asked her to come. She said, "I don't think it's that bad. I have spoken to the doctor." I said to her: "Please come." She arrived in Lugano at half past eleven. At twelve her father died. So she still just managed to see him. He died in the big bed. Countess Margit, Ivy, Baby, Theresa and Heini were there and I was holding his hand until it became cold.'

Fifty-three years later, Sandor still chokes back his emotion when remembering the moment, for the old man had been his life, and when Heinrich's body was removed from the local churchyard in Lugano some five years later, to be interned in the family mausoleum at Landsberg Castle in Germany, Sandor bought the Baron's original burial plot for himself.

Gaby was probably the only member of the family to suffer any genuine grief, but it was an emotion for which Heini held little sympathy. He was far too busy for such indulgences as, armed with the key to safe-deposit box no. 434 and accompanied by van Aken, he headed for the Swiss Bank Corporation in Lugano to retrieve his father's will.

Having read out the contents to his astonished sisters, Heini then passed the documents, dated 1941 and 1946, to van Aken who publicly announced them before the court by notarial instrument on 1 July 1947. Heini had not only been awarded five-eighths of his father's estate but he was also in full control of the eighths awarded to each of his siblings, thus effectively giving him full power over their inheritance. It was hardly surprising that Gaby and Dolf should have immediately sent copies to their attorney, Dr Züblin, who replied with his blunt analysis: 'Such a set-up as this belongs more into the time of the feudal law of the early Middle Ages and goes so much against our Swiss legal understanding and laws that I personally would not hesitate for a moment in declaring these decrees as unacceptable for any decent human being.' He also advised them to 'seek the adjustment of the quotas, ideally to one-quarter for your share, or failing that a compromise solution' and added: 'I don't think that either the Gunhilde problem [technically, she qualified as Heinrich's widow, as the official Hungarian divorce ruling did not come through until a week after Heinrich's death] nor the tax difficulties are reasons for you not to contest the will. On the contrary, today you have nothing to lose.'

In Dr Züblin's opinion there were also contributing legal and technical reasons for challenging the wills. He considered the 1941 testament to be invalid due to incorrect dating and lack of witnesses, while he recommended contesting the 1946 testament due to the fact that 'it was obviously dictated to the Baron who was not in a fit state to make a will'.

The result of Heini's determination to retain his position as sole heir would be five years of fighting and a deeply divided family, while the only beneficiaries who appreciated their legacies with grace were Berkes and his wife with their SwFr 30,000 and the head gardener with his SwFr 15,000. The forester, Czerer, accepted a plot of land at Rechnitz, while Buijnk, the chauffeur, received Dfl 12,000.

* * *

Meanwhile, Heini had even managed to prevent his brother's attendance at the funeral by continuing to ensure he could not obtain the necessary visa. What is perhaps more sad is that there is no evidence that his father ever made any request to see his eldest son or even displayed any enthusiasm for getting him out of Germany, while Heini continued to encourage enmity: 'You know, everyone hated my brother.'

Stephan got angry when he finally realised not only who was responsible for his visa problems but that he was now being held to account for being his father's son:

> I have finally found out about my visa. There are no concerns at all from the allied side. The problems are entirely retraceable to Heini and Roelen. These two are the ones that I owe all my exit problems to. The only concern remaining now, brought up by the Financial Division in Berlin, is that I am my father's son. It is said that the whole situation with the fortune is still so unclear, that there have been orders from London not to let any members of the family exit Germany for the time being.
>
> Dolf should now try to explain to the relevant offices in London that I

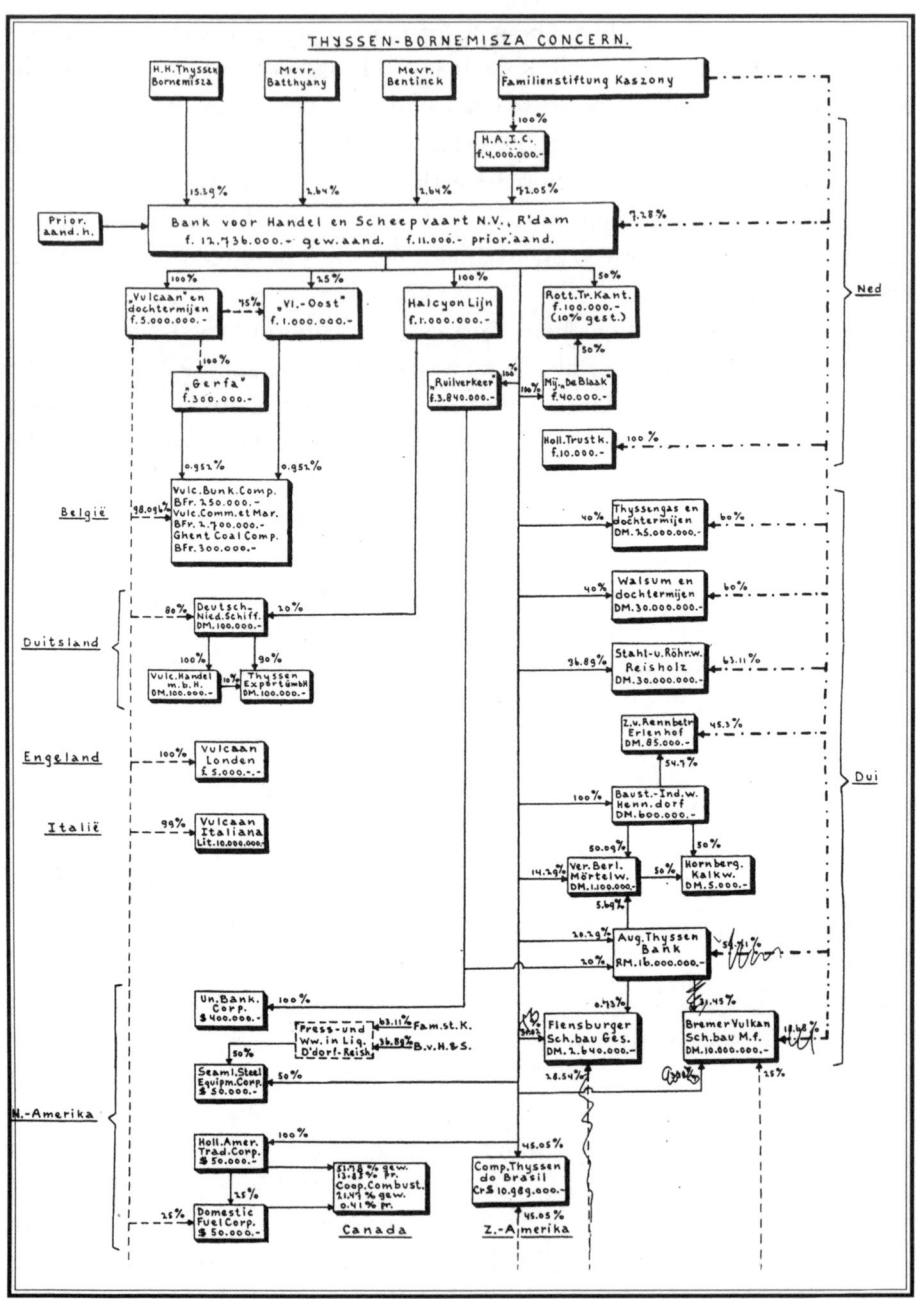

The corporate inheritance of Heini and his siblings.

have only been apportioned a legal share, so that I in no way can endanger the possible English interests concerning Papa's assets. However, it seems that Heini's name is mud here. I hope you will be able to help. It's not very good news and I am seeing this as a major interference into my personal freedom, since I have absolutely nothing at all to hide, was never a German and am only interested in science.[23]

But even if Heini was as greedy and dishonest as his siblings claimed, there was little that they could do while challenging their father's will but accept that, for the moment, their financial future lay in the hands of an arrogant twenty-five-year-old with very limited business experience, who was easily influenced by his legal advisers. On the other hand, there could be no argument concerning the complexity of what lay before him. His father's inheritance consisted of the art collection and of all the possessions, enterprises and businesses in Holland, the two Germanies, England, Canada, North America, Brazil and Argentina dealing in coal, gas, electricity, steel, pipes and machinery, banking, shipbuilding and shipping.

Due to the complexity of ownership and the aversion to the payment of tax which Heini had inherited from his forefathers, the work involved in getting this network of companies and banks back under the name of Thyssen-Bornemisza was immense. But despite using his in-laws to help him achieve this ambition, Heini had no wish for them to remain involved in the management of the Konzern and, regardless of the outcome of the challenge to his father's will, he also had no intention of his siblings remaining as shareholders: 'My sisters were married to such idiots and intriguers I couldn't possibly work with them. I knew that I was going to have to buy off the family.'

Heini also knew his actions would almost certainly destroy any remaining family unity, particularly when they realised that he also wanted their share of his father's art collection. But what concerned him far more was his nationality, for despite obtaining an extension to his Certificate of Hungarian Nationality, he had yet to prove his nationality conclusively or that of his father, whose will had been prepared in accordance with Hungarian law.

Luckily for Heini, Henrik Kouwenhoven, the one man most determined to reveal the truth concerning Heinrich Thyssen-Bornemisza's German identity, died suddenly while visiting his brother-in-law, who was the manager of the Union Bank in New York. Heini had become worried about him making public accusations of German ownership and Nazi connections; accusations that could also have proved embarrassing for the Dutch: 'I thought he was in a dangerous frame of mind and persuaded the Beheer committee, the Dutch government administrators, to recall him. When he received their telegram, he had a heart attack and died.'

Heini would later admit that Kouwenhoven's death was extremely opportune for both his American partners and the Dutch government.

*   *   *

While the family commenced their lengthy fight over their inheritance, Gunhilde continued to battle for her rights as Heinrich's widow. Raising funds by syndicating her case, she formed a share company with her lawyer, with whom Heini claimed she was having an affair. But his accusations were also a reaction to her courtroom revelations, which, while no doubt exaggerated, contained a damaging degree of accuracy. She accused the family of knowing that their father had been mentally ill, which was why they had him interned in a clinic in 1946:

> On the main square of Lugano he showed his tongue to an old acquaintance. At the Hotel Waldhaus in Flims he hit a young boy on the chest. He spat at other children. He pinched the servants in public and ran into them violently. He relieved himself repeatedly in the public restaurant and wherever else he felt the need, such as the corner of his own room. After his son's wedding, his family took him back to Favorita. Since that time, two guards disguised as butlers were permanently at his side.[24]

Meanwhile, Heini continued to prevaricate over the preparation of inventories and Margit discovered that many of the more valuable paintings had been removed from the gallery. Apparently, this had been carried out under Heini's instructions in order to reduce the claimed value of the collection from SwFr 25 million to SwFr 4.7 million prior to a visit by the tax inspectors.

While opposition to the terms of the will and distrust of Heini grew, there was also an increasing concern with the personal allowances, which Heini constantly delayed paying in order to illustrate his power, punish their lack of compliance and remind everyone that, regardless of the will's validity, he alone could decide when and how much they should receive.

Baron Adolphe Bentinck continued to help Heini, albeit to his own and his wife's advantage and often to a questionable degree, considering his position as a member of the Dutch diplomatic service. But his efforts did little to gain any appreciation or improve Heini's opinion of either Dolf or Gaby: 'Bentinck wanted to lay his hands on Gaby's one-eighth share of the inheritance. I objected, especially as they were company shares. It was very unpleasant! Gaby was extremely disappointed when the will was disclosed. She thought she had been my father's favourite and bore me a grudge.'

While Gaby had enjoyed an extremely special relationship with her father and had no doubt been disappointed by her lack of appropriate treatment in his will, it had little to do with financial reward. As she had sufficient to maintain an appropriate standard of living, Gaby had little interest in the accumulation of money. As a rather elegant old lady, lying back on her pillows with 'Pussy' delicately drinking from her glass of water, she would react to questions concerning Heini's manipulation of the will with a shrug and a wave of her hand in a gesture of weary acceptance. To the question of why Heini wanted more than anyone else, she would laugh and with no hint of malice, give the logical answer: 'He was greedy. He always wanted more.'

In a letter to his accountants Klynveld and Kraayenhof, Heini confirmed that he had been financially favoured, even before any inheritance resulting from the will:

> I have received the following gifts from my father: Through a deed of 1 October 1943, he left me his part in the inheritance of his mother, which he received through Stephan's renunciation, although I have not received this to this date. He also left me a Ford 1939, a Rolls-Royce 1926 and a Horch 1934. At the beginning of 1946, I was given power to use a loan of SwFr 200,000. On 7 September 1946, I received SwFr 500,000 as a wedding gift. On 1 September 1946, he had assigned me an annual apanage of SwFr 30,000.

* * *

With his father dead and Hungary now under a communist government, there was little advantage in Heini trying to maintain his questionable Hungarian nationality and every reason for him to apply for Swiss citizenship, so, in October 1947, van Aken wrote to the Political Department in Berne applying for Heini to become Swiss. In so doing he made great play of both the financial and cultural advantages to Switzerland: 'It will only be possible in the long run to keep the collection of paintings at Lugano if the founder's property outside Switzerland, which is invested in the Kaszony Foundation, can be at least partly safeguarded, so that sooner or later funds from the foreign assets may be received here.'

Despite the fact that they must have been aware that the Thyssen-Bornemiszas' intention was the protection of their German assets from allied retribution, the Swiss accepted van Aken's thinly veiled argument. They were even persuaded to instruct Mr Burki of the Swiss Delegation in Berlin to contact the British authorities and assure them: 'The information received from Berne is that Thyssen was Hungarian on his death. His successors, now Hungarians, have applied for Swiss nationality and will enjoy that nationality in a short time.'[25]

The Swiss were equally protective of Fritz Thyssen and when the Americans became threatening in their approach towards the Swiss Compensation Office, they terminated their co-operation, arguing that they did not have sufficient reason to give details of Fritz's Swiss companies and foundations as the Allies could not prove that he was still a German.[26]

From time to time, Fritz and Amélie must have appreciated the irony in the fact that it was Hitler's withdrawal of their nationality followed by the Americans' initial confirmation of their statelessness that was saving their German fortune.

But while the Swiss and the Dutch had been prepared to accept the Thyssens' protective claims, the British were not. G. S. Bailey of Trading with the Enemy Department, who had contacted R. C. R. Goodchild at the Foreign Office in London, informed him that;

> The Kaszony Foundation was set up to support the family members and maintain the inherited family fortune. The Foundation is an alias for Baron Heinrich himself. During the war, the Baron retained directorships in German industry and was keeping in touch with his financial and business interests in Germany which may entitle Trading with the Enemy Department to regard him and his Kaszony Foundation as enemies at common law.[27]

In a letter from Property Control Branch to the British Foreign Office, they also stated:

> One cannot escape the conclusion that although the case is being presented through the Swiss and Dutch governments, it is in fact being organised by the Thyssen family, itself ex-enemy, in a calculated attempt to save the family fortune, largely acquired in Germany and one which actively supported the German war effort, for which simple evidence is available.[28]

* * *

Keeping the collection in Lugano was complicated by the siblings' discovery that the Rohoncz Art Foundation was legally invalid and their demand that the collection be broken up and shared between them, although Heini would still inherit the largest share; a share that would form the basis of the Thyssen-Bornemisza Collection.

To encourage the paintings' exhibition, the Swiss tax authorities reminded Heini that any pictures not available for public display would be subject to taxation, which resulted in his decision, in January 1948, to open the gallery to the public 'for a day or two a week'. Van Aken appreciated the public relations potential and prepared an appropriate guest list of local worthies, dignitaries and political figures whose acceptance of Heini as a Swiss citizen would prove valuable. On 19 January, a somewhat guarded review appeared on the front page of the *Neue Zürcher Zeitung*:

> It is a truly princely gallery of southern character. Twenty-six rooms, some big, most of them small, corresponding to the bourgeois picture format prefered by Heinrich Thyssen-Bornemisza, all with skylights and artificial lighting. No expense has been spared for the marble doorframes and floors. The fabric-covered walls present a good background for the paintings, which are currently still placed much too close together.

But the reviewer was careful to avoid reference to the authenticity or quality of the paintings, apart from the Franz Hals which he described as 'a masterpiece of world renown' and Carpaccio's 'Young Knight' as being 'a fantastic Italian equivalent of first class quality'.

Although Heini was pleased with Lugano's reaction to the collection, in 1948 neither he nor his family had any idea that art would come to assume such a prominent place in his life.

At around the same time, another event took place of far greater, immediate importance. The sequestration was to be lifted, the Dutch control of the Bank voor Handel en Scheepvaart and the Holland American Investment Corporation returned to the Thyssen-Bornemiszas and Heini promised Margit, Gaby and Stephan 'the shares will soon become available to the estate for our disposal'. Judging from the balance sheets, the financial situation appeared favourable. BVHS had tax-free reserves of Dfl 32.5 million and Vulcaan NV had tax-free reserves of Dfl 19 million. Even the impressive new board, which the Dutch had insisted upon, seemed to please Heini – at least socially:

> On the whole, it was a very pleasant group which included Dr de Monchy, the former mayor of The Hague, who was well-known for his resistance work during the occupation of Holland; Dr Albarda, a former secretary general at the Dutch Finance Ministry; Dr Hintzen, a leading Rotterdam

economist; Professor Kamphuisen, Director of AKZO; Dr Coert, and Dr Six Bart, a former member of staff of Prince Bernhard as well as Dr van Elden, the European representative of Standard Oil and Dirk Swart of the Philips works at Eindhoven. All of these people became personal friends, as they worked for me for many years. I knew their families and we often had dinner together.

* * *

Finally, Heini's American lawyers recommended that Stephan be assisted in his endeavours to leave Germany where his continued presence was becoming a danger to Heini's denial of a connection with the country. They also conveyed their concern to their friends at the CIA. This led to pressure being applied to the allied authorities in Germany, which resulted in Stephan and his family suddenly being allowed to leave, in March 1948, not for Switzerland where they could also have been a source of embarrassment but for Monte Carlo; although even there their presence continued to annoy Heini. 'They lived at the Metropole Hotel for a while, when they were still quite well off. They went out to gala dinners every night in a white dinner jacket and evening gown. My brother's butlers had to wear white gloves, because Stephan and his wife were afraid of catching diseases.'

Unfortunately for Heini, his brother found Monte Carlo an extremely agreeable location and he displayed no enthusiasm for moving any further or certainly not before he had challenged his father's will. The challenge came the very same month when Margit and Stephan questioned the validity of both family foundations and threatened to mount a challenge unless Heini agreed to their terms. They also questioned the terms of the division of the art collection which gave Heini the right of first choice. In a letter, their lawyer Professor Vinassa stated that there were unexpected complications in the valuation of the paintings: 'Dr Nathan said that some paintings are so questionable that a more detailed examination of them will have to be carried out, possibly with a quartz lamp, in order to ascertain whether they could be forgeries or have been painted over.'[29]

He also mistrusted Heini's distribution of the collection: 'He is too insecure, inexperienced and immoral.'

* * *

On 12 May 1948, the four heirs, including Stephan, all met at Villa Favorita for a conference to discuss the inheritance. For four days the tone of the negotiations varied from occasional civilised discussion, through mainly heated argument, to hysterical fury. It took five days before his siblings realised that Heini was

Chapter VI: 1945–1954

serious when he warned that if they did not at least accept the validity of the will he would immediately stop paying their allowances. He pointed out that this might result in some difficulties in retaining their solicitors' enthusiasm. He also reminded them that it was he and he alone who had been awarded the power both to retrieve the family fortune and to distribute it. It was, as Heini said, 'a compelling argument'.

Three days later, they all met at the notary's office in Zurich where they signed an agreement that:

> The estate of Heinrich Thyssen-Bornemisza shall be distributed: $^1/_8$, $^1/_8$, $^1/_8$ and $^5/_8$, in kind and as soon as possible. The assets and liabilities of Kaszony and Rohoncz shall be included in the estate and the siblings recognize definitively and irrevocably the validity of the will of 11th December 1941 and the codicil of 1st May 1946 and shall do so even if Gunhilde is successful in her challenge.

While their mother gracefully accepted the continuation of her apanage, the siblings agreed that the Kaszony Foundation would remain the administrator of their joint assets for a period of at least ten years. The following week they returned to sign another agreement concerning the distribution of 542 paintings whose proportional value was based on a points system. One of the prime conditions, which would affect the future of the collection, and eventually Heini as a collector, was that up until 1 January 1959, he had to be given the first option to buy any inherited picture that his siblings wished to sell.

Of the available 532 paintings, ten having been withdrawn altogether, Heini was to get 363, Stephan 33, Margit 31 and Gaby 104. In addition, Margit and Heini agreed to share half each of the Frans Hals family portrait, although it would not be long before she sold him her half plus fourteen other pictures, all of which would eventually become part of the Thyssen-Bornemisza Collection in Spain. In view of the questions that had been raised concerning the authenticity of certain paintings, it should have come as no surprise to Margit that her 'Young Girl in an antique costume', purported to be by Vermeer and apparently bought by Heinrich in 1930 from Cassirer in Berlin, was in 1952 discovered to have been painted by Hans van Meegeren, the famous Vermeer forger.

By 1987 only 73 of Gaby's 104 paintings would be accountable for, 57 of which would be sold at Sotheby's in 1995 for £7.25 million by her son. Only three of her paintings were recorded as having been bought by Heini, two of which were later included in the Spanish collection. The third was the 'Crucifixion', attributed to a painter from the circle of Sir Anthony van Dyck, which Heini purchased from Sotheby's at the 1995 sale of the Bentinck-Thyssen Collection for only £17,000 and immediately re-attributed to the master himself.

While the squabbling over the pictures continued, in May 1948 Stephan agreed to accept SwFr 800,000 in exchange for ceding his claims in the collection of paintings and art objects to his brother Heini. Having also recovered the fortune left to him by August Junior, Stephan continued to enjoy a particularly lavish if somewhat bizarre lifestyle. There can have been few millionaire exiles in Monte Carlo at the time who, having returned from a night at the casino, continued working on a scientific paper entitled 'Oscillatory Sliding Friction or The Frictionless Bearing', while his white-gloved butler mixed soothing cocktails. It was hardly surprising that by 1948 Stephan's exceptional standard of living should have imbued him with sufficient confidence and well-being to prepare another small volume with the none too modest title 'The Explanation of Life', which he dedicated to the legendary German physicist Max Planck.

*   *   *

The recovery of the Thyssens' classic symbol of wealth would epitomise the ease with which immense wealth shields the owner from retribution. On 22 July 1948, Heini Thyssen, assisted by Hardman, Phillips and Mann, a firm of solicitors which gained considerable notoriety for reclaiming German fortunes, commenced his claim against the British Crown for approximately £2 million, or two-thirds of the value of the gold deposited in London by his father and uncle shortly before the outbreak of war. He did so under the premise that he was a Hungarian whose gold had been deposited with a Dutch bank, namely the family's BVHS.

Heini was claiming the value of 585 gold bars and coins which had originally been shipped from New York to London; although in more biblous, anecdotal moments he liked to claim that the gold had been flown to London from Frankfurt by private plane and that one of the bars had 'fallen out' over France: 'The funds were destined to support a potential anti-Nazi government made up of Generals Goerdeler, Beck and Canaris.'

Much as Heini enjoyed telling this story, its lack of authenticity was supported by the fact that it was never used as evidence in court, by either side. Meanwhile, according to the British Board of Trade, his uncle Fritz claimed the £1 million value of the remaining 318 gold bars deposited in the name of his family foundation, the Pelzer Foundation. Little is known of the process concerning Fritz Thyssen's eventual retrieval of his gold or the equivalent value.

It is difficult to believe that despite the brothers' industrial and financial support of the Nazi Party, they would be given the opportunity of suing 'the enemy' for the return of their gold deposits. It was even more remarkable in view of the fact that of all the Allies, the British had displayed the least inclination to accept any branch of the Thyssen family as anything other than 'the enemy'. The Economic Warfare Department of the Foreign Office had made even stronger accusations: 'The Baron's non-German claims have been a complete "frame-up" designed precisely to meet the present situation.'

Dolf's attempts to intervene appeared to have only raised the level of their scepticism: 'Bentinck's intervention is purely a personal one inspired by his relationship to Thyssen.'

The only member of the family to suffer the direct effect of this increasingly aggressive British attitude, according to the Foreign Office, was, ironically, Stephan.

> Nobody can have any doubt that all Thyssens are tarred with the same brush, that they all played major parts in assisting the German war effort and that claims not to have done so are mere eyewash. I see no ground for granting favours to such people or for changing, at the present time, our decision not to let Stephan loose in Switzerland, from where the Heinrich Thyssen interests are controlled. This may not please Bentinck, but that seems to me totally immaterial.[30]

* * *

Before Fritz could devote his attention to gold retrieval, he had yet to go through the process of German 'denazification'. The first attempt in 1947 had been delayed when Fritz's defence lawyer Dr Robert Ellscheid shared the prosecutor's concern about the fitness of Thyssen to stand trial. When the proceedings began in August 1948, Amélie was firmly by his side and during the six weeks of the proceedings she did not miss a single hour in court. But despite the fact that it took two days to read out the indictment, it soon became obvious that it contained little new evidence and that, in the words of the *New Yorker*, the prosecutor was acting as more of a 'consoler of the accused than a bloodhound'. He even appeared to accept Fritz's claim to be 'the poorest man in Germany'.

Having already incriminated himself through the statements contained in his book *I Paid Hitler*, his defence counsel sought to prove it was a fake which Fritz claimed never to have even read. They went on to introduce dozens of witnesses and sworn witness statements that apparently confirmed their client's fine character, opposition to fascism and lack of anti-Semitic feelings. The court then accepted his Nazi support as being that of a 'political error' by a man 'who had not acted out of reprehensible motives' but, perhaps most remarkably, that he would 'never do it again'.[31]

He was accused of having paid RM 100,000 to Hitler and Ludendorff and also of giving RM 150,000 Reichmarks to Göring and of helping Hitler carry out the 1923 beerhall putsch.

On 2 October 1948 Fritz was declared a 'minor Nazi offender' and ordered to surrender 15 per cent of his German assets as a penalty. The value of his property was not disclosed but it was of little consequence, as there was no evidence of his ever paying the fine. The seventy-four-year-old Thyssen accepted the verdict and did not appeal against it. His reaction was to smile and say: 'I am satisfied. I am satisfied.'[32]

Within a matter of days, Fritz had applied for permission to leave Germany. But there was still opposition from the Inter Allied Reparation Agency in Frankfurt and as part of Germany's post-war reparations the Allies started to dismantle Fritz's factories. It was a situation that Heini, who still harboured ambitions for the takeover of his uncle's industrial holdings, was prepared to expend considerable energy opposing. Advised by John Foster MP in London, he even prepared a statement for the British press in an attempt to gain some degree of sympathy, pointing out that the dismantlement could have a detrimental effect on the whole European economy:

> August Thyssen Hütte was founded by my grandfather, inherited by my uncle and taken over by VSt. It is the largest establishment of that kind in Europe. Although our group is not directly interested in VSt or ATH, the dismantling would mean great loss to our companies in Germany as well as in Holland. Thyssen Gas und Wasserwerke are economically in close connection with ATH. The commerce, transport and turnover in ore, which were of great importance in Rotterdam, will shrink considerably. It is also objective that the whole European economy would suffer very much. The Economic Cooperation Act 1948 of the American Congress requests that production establishments in Germany, which could help to rebuild Europe, should be left in their country. I hope that the Dutch government will enter a protest against the pulling down of these works. I think it would be advisable to render the British population attentive to the contradiction between the aim of the Marshall Plan and the dismantling of August Thyssen Hütte.

* * *

At the same time, Heini continued to forge closer links with the US while still attempting to resolve the problem of his nationality status. At an inheritance meeting with a notary in Zurich, he had presented his Swiss driving licence as proof of identity. Further evidence that he lacked a passport is contained in minutes of a meeting with Henry Hyde in America:

> Heini has identity papers, but no passport documents. Hyde stressed the necessity of establishing for Heini a practice and a record of getting visas to come to the USA with a view to eventually obtaining yearly visas. Heini is currently in the USA with a visa granted on the strength of his Swiss identity papers.

It was not only Heini's nationality, that presented a problem to the American interests, but also his brother's history of Nazi involvement in Germany: 'Hyde suggested some attempt should be made to get Stephan out of Heini's enterprises. Heini informed there is such a plan. Stephan has agreed to relinquish his interests in the enterprises for $1 million. He has been paid part of this in pictures and other property.'

On 20 November 1948, Roberto van Aken was appealing against the Berne police department's refusal to grant Heini and Theresa Swiss nationality. As in the original application, he again reminded them of the advantages to the country of having Heini and his wife as citizens. It was an argument that Heini would dangle over Lugano's head for the next forty years:

> If Baron Thyssen can become a Castagnola burger, he will feel even closer to this property and there would be a guarantee, which should not be underestimated, that the collection will remain in our country. If he was to be naturalised, he thinks that this would give him the strength to keep the centre of his business activities in Lugano. He would then not have any reason anymore to find a home somewhere else and exhibit his art collection there.

* * *

In December 1948, Fritz and Amélie were given permission from the Americans to leave Germany and take up temporary residence in Brussels. Meanwhile, British intelligence warned that Fritz would take the opportunity of using his move to Brussels to regain control of his foreign assets. These suspicions were confirmed when, soon after his arrival at the Hotel Astoria, they learned that the lawsuit brought against the Belgian Office des Sequestres for the release of his Belgian assets had been decided in his favour, based on his claimed statelessness since 4 February 1940. Fritz had apparently won the Belgians' co-operation by promising to invest his Swiss Francs in Belgian property and base his operations in Brussels; a promise which was remarkably similar to that which Heini made to the Swiss concerning his fortune.

The decision by the Belgians to release his assets coincided with the release of Faminta AG funds by the Swiss; a coincidence that caused American intelligence some difficulty in reconciling with the fact that, throughout his interrogation, Fritz had insisted he had 'no external assets'.

Fritz then made a tactical error when he filed an application for the retrieval of his German property which re-awakened the Allies' interest in his affairs and he was forced to return to Germany for further questioning by the Americans. The main bone of contention remained his external assets whose existence he could no longer deny. But he insisted Law 53, which demanded the declaration of all foreign assets, only applied to German nationals and that: 'I even had an American passport at that time. I had a passport for stateless persons.'[33]

He also said that he was just a 'poor old man' whose memory had been affected by Strophantine injections that he had received for his heart condition and would say anything to get an exit permit; which was one of Fritz's few accurate statements. But by now the investigators were better informed concerning Fritz's assets and his various cloaking instruments including Faminta AG, although he still continued to deny that he used it as a Swiss safe haven for his foreign assets.

The Americans also displayed an increased interest in his contravention of German tax and foreign exchange laws after unearthing a report into his financial dealings that had been carried out in Germany in 1939. The document was important, because it not only reinforced the real reason why Fritz left Germany but also illustrated his special relationship with Göring who, on Fritz's forced return to Germany in 1941, had solved the problem of his friend's foreign exchange irregularities by dissolving the foreign exchange investigation office.

This damning evidence had no effect on Fritz who just denied all knowledge of the contents of the report. He even started to deny things he had already admitted.

* * *

With the communists' rise to power in China, Soviet control of Eastern Europe and successful development of atomic weapons, the Americans were increasingly determined that the Marshall Plan should succeed in rebuilding Western Europe. This resulted in a curious contradiction, in that it made the pursuit of reparations counter-productive; a situation that would prove advantageous for both Heini and Fritz.

In a letter to Heini from the comfort of New York, Jakob Goldschmidt seemed quite optimistic that American pressure would triumph:

> I have learned that August Thyssen Hütte is a special target for dismantling and that the French in particular desire this plant in way of reparations. It is one of the most unbelievable economic crimes that I can imagine. But I think it probable that we will be able to change the decision. I have spoken to several people in Washington and will meet again with Rudolf Heinemann, maybe together with Mr Hyde.[34]

Meanwhile, the ex-Reichswirtschaftsführer Roelen would appear to have no qualms (and vice versa) in assisting the Jewish banker Jakob Goldschmidt in his attempts to acquire Fritz's August Thyssen Hütte steel division for the Thyssen-Bornemisza group of companies by lobbying Senator Malone in Washington: 'I read with great joy that you have become interested in the dismantling question. August Thyssen was a friend of Carnegie and Schwab. America alone can avoid the spread of Marxist nonsense in Europe.'[35]

There was a certain chilling familiarity about the use of right-wing anti-communism to assist German industry.

*   *   *

Seemingly unconcerned with either Heini's attempts to take over his industrial holdings or their dismantlement by the Allies, Fritz continued with his plans to leave Europe. In 1949, Fritz once again applied for a visa to enter Belgium and, despite British misgivings, the Americans allowed him to leave Germany. Inexplicably, the Belgian Custodian's Office had decided not to appeal against the release of Fritz's funds and no sooner had Fritz reached the safety of Brussels than Pierre Ansiaux, a prominent Belgian lawyer, presented a formal protest:

> This is the protest of his client Fritz Thyssen, of treatment which he claims to have received last May in endeavouring to leave Wiesbaden for his present residence in Belgium ... Fritz Thyssen states that he was refused permission to return to Belgium from Germany, unless he should sign the following declaration: 'I hereby certify that I am familiar with Military Government Law 53, which prohibits the disposition of any property at my disposal in Belgium without licence by Military Government.' Fritz Thyssen states that he took this declaration under duress, declares that its terms are contrary to the truth and concludes 'the manoeuvre of which I was victim and the

measures taken against me have a meanness and a childishness worthy of totalitarian states'.[36]

There is no evidence of any immediate response but it was the start of a whole series of aggressive and potentially litigious actions.

Then there was a demand from the leader of the Social Democratic Party in Germany to 'stop the dismantling of the August Thyssen plant in Duisburg-Hamborn immediately . . . This is not a dismantling but complete destruction and scrapping of the factories . . . Today in the suburb of Hamborn alone there are 3,000 men without employment because of dismantling and the existence of the entire city is endangered.'[37]

The British were also coming under increased pressure. The future Prime Minister Harold Wilson, then at the Board of Trade, wrote a number of ineffectual letters, one to Stafford Cripps concerning Heini's gold, which in November 1949 had yet to be successfully reclaimed:

> If it is your considered opinion that Thyssen's heirs should on no account be allowed to benefit from his fortune in the United Kingdom, I think this is the preferable procedure, unless the Foreign Secretary, who must be consulted, sees some objection. In the meantime, we are under continual pressure to announce our decision to the solicitor acting for the Dutch Bank, John Foster, who made a very strong protest against the delay which he represented as most unjust to his clients.[38]

Unfortunately, the Foreign Secretary was having some difficulty making a decision as the Foreign Office was still under no illusion as to the identity and nationality of the owner of BVHS and thus the gold: 'There is evidence that the German authorities still regard Heinrich Thyssen-Bornemisza as retaining some form of German nationality.'[39]

Meanwhile, even under the assumption that the Baron enjoyed Hungarian nationality, British investigators added the damning verdict: 'The fact that the Thyssen family was so heavily involved in the early fortune of the Nazi party, in the rearmament of Germany and, during the war, in the productions of arms and munitions is adequate reason for treating their property differently from the property of other Hungarians resident in Switzerland.'[40]

* * *

At the same time, Heini was still meeting with some resistance from the Swiss concerning his nationality application. Not only was his bad behaviour as a

Chapter VI: 1945–1954

Fribourg student still fresh in their memory but they also appeared far more knowledgeable about his father's financial and industrial relations with the Third Reich than they publicly admitted. This was evident in a letter to the Federal Council:

> We question whether it is still too early for this naturalisation to be carried out. If it became known, it would probably cause a sensation in certain circles, not the least because of the activities and the position of his late father ... He is apparently heir and nominal head of the Thyssen works. These are and shall remain German enterprises. The name Thyssen has a connotation today that makes it, in my eyes, impossible to grant the Swiss citizenship to the head of the Thyssen works.[41]

But three months later, on 6 December 1949, the Federal Department of Justice and Police wrote to van Aken, 'We are now in a position to grant the demand', and for a sum of SwFr 103 ('because of the considerable amount of paperwork involved') Heini got the right to claim Swiss naturalisation. The dramatic change of heart was never explained but it seemed highly likely that American pressure had been applied. There was certainly no doubt that Swiss immunity was a major contributing factor in the preservation of the Thyssen-Bornemisza fortune.

* * *

Even better news came on 22 November 1949, when, after considerable US pressure, the dismantlement of August Thyssen Hütte was halted and the recommencement of production confirmed in an agreement between the German Chancellor Konrad Adenauer and the Allied High Commission. While Roelen was transmitting his good news to Heini, Fritz and Amélie were encouraged to slip out of Belgium and headed for Argentina, where they arrived before anyone realised they had left.

With a long sea voyage ahead of them and their first free Christmas and New Year to celebrate in ten years, they filled their time, not with deck quoits and champagne, but by writing additional material for Fritz's book *I Paid Hitler*. They also planned retribution against the Americans whom they blamed for their incarceration and Germany's pre-war rearmament. Ironically, while the US may not have liberated them in the way they expected, they were certainly the most enthusiastic supporters of Germany's reconstruction. Without America's support, it was also unlikely that Fritz and Amélie would have been able to leave Europe. But this knowledge did nothing to diminish their vitriol:

In my opinion, the Nuremberg trials were conducted mainly to find someone to blame for Hitler's war policy. It would have been very embarrassing for the Americans to have to admit that they had supported the German rearmament from the very first, because they wished for a war against Russia. Germany is still suffering today, but her people have a great history behind them and will never forget that this history and their past give them the right to believe in the future.[42]

While Fritz settled down in Argentina under Juan and Evita Peron, the new Dutch board members at BVHS remained aggressively protective of Heini's organisation and were even prepared to lie on his behalf, claiming that:

The pre-war ownership and control of the Thyssen-Bornemisza group has never furthered the aggressive designs of the German National Socialist Party. From 1920 on when Heinrich first acquired holdings in his father's enterprises, he never lived in Germany. Unlike his brother, he never carried out any political activity at any time on behalf of the National Socialist Party or gave any aid to it. Finally, like the German companies in the TBG, he was personally considered as unfriendly to the Third Reich.[43]

As the Dutch gave the impression that they were fighting for the survival of a vital part of their economy, Heini, who had finally been awarded Swiss citizenship in March 1950, was collecting insurance money on his nine Dutch-registered merchant ships, which had been sunk by the German navy. Ironically, at the same time his Bremer Vulkan yard, which had in all probability built the U-boats responsible for sinking those ships, delivered its first 15,000-ton tanker.

* * *

Heini's organisation of his inheritance and establishment of his ownership rights were progressing satisfactorily while his managers were gradually reactivating the Thyssen Bornemisza group of companies. His sisters had little choice but to accept their brother's control of their inheritance, while Stephan's acceptance of Heini's terms was as inevitable as Gunhilde's eventual settlement.

But the one area where Heini was vulnerable was in his marriage which had deteriorated to the point where a separation was inevitable. He would later insist that his suspicions concerning Theresa's relationship with his brother-in-law had been reinforced when he discovered that while he had been away on business in Holland, Theresa and Ivy had set off to Paris together. Heini claimed

Chapter VI: 1945–1954

that he only learnt that they had gone to Paris when they became involved in a motorcar accident. But it was indicative of his waning interest in his wife that he admitted to being more concerned with the cost and inconvenience of having to return to Lugano.

In the summer of 1949, shortly after Heini had announced his intention to commence divorce proceedings, Theresa informed him that she was pregnant. No doubt aware of the effect the birth of a child could have on his wife's alimony entitlement, Heini denied responsibility, claiming that his brother-in law, Ivy Batthyány, was the father, although he would later contradict this claim. But the pregnancy had remarkably little effect on the couple's increasingly separate lives or Heini's development as a playboy.

With his unprepossessing appearance and fragile body, Heini was physically ill-equipped to assume such a role, but he was all too aware of the physical attraction of wealth. However, it also had certain disadvantages: 'As I became more aware of the attraction of my wealth, I had to learn to be more careful, more questioning of people's motives.'

He overcame this problem by socialising with people of similar privilege: 'I met a lot of people in St Moritz. People like Theo von Portago, Cadaval, Duca di Sangro and Andrea Badrutt. Theresa was elected Miss Corviglia Club. The first winner was an American girlfriend of mine. We used to go to moonlight parties at the club, which were great fun.'

Despite his claimed misgivings concerning people's motives, Heini cultivated a habit of using conspicuous evidence of his money in the form of gifts to attract favour. He even made cash offers to women in return for their sexual co-operation; a habit that he had picked up from his favourite Uncle August Junior. However, as he had little respect for the presence of accompanying husbands or boyfriends, it was a habit that could also lead to violent reactions.

On 19 March 1950, Theresa gave birth to Georg Heinrich Alfred Gabor Thyssen-Bornemisza de Kaszón and almost immediately Heini initiated divorce proceedings, although it would take four years to reach a mutually acceptable settlement.

During this period, Theresa remained in residence at Villa Favorita and appeared remarkably loyal to her husband, while the increasingly absent Heini somewhat cynically and perhaps unfairly insisted that it was purely a ruse to accentuate his responsibility for the breakdown of their relationship.

I decided that if I was to be accused of behaving like a selfish bachelor, I might as well enjoy the privilege; which enraged Theresa. I remember a

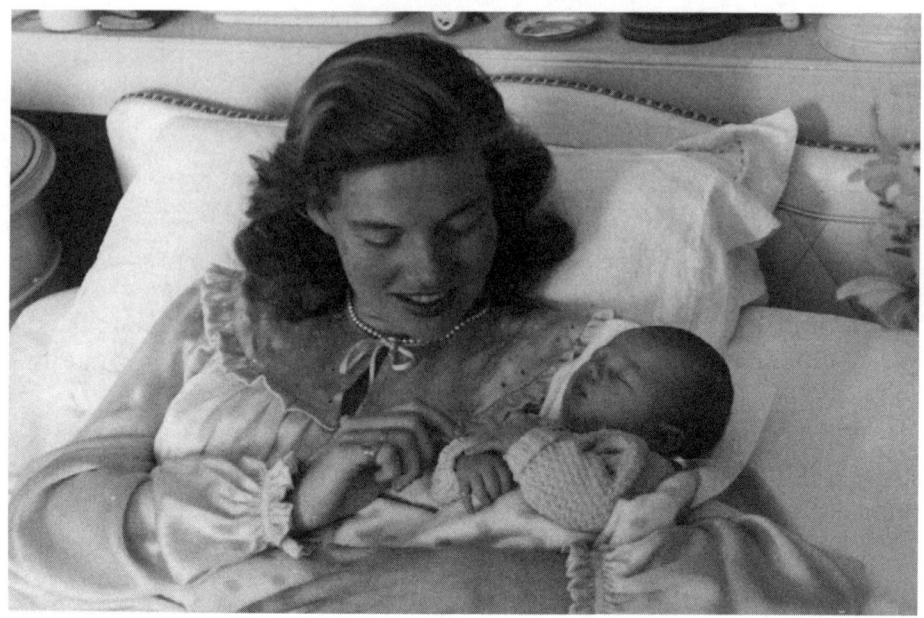

Princess Theresa with Heini Junior.

fancy dress ball in Venice given by Carlo Beisteguci, a Mexican billionaire, who wanted to inaugurate the Labia Palace, which he had just bought. I refused to go. Theresa went with her father and friends. I thought such a lavish ball was in bad taste after the war in a place like Venice, with its communist mayor.

So he stayed in Lugano with a friend called Pierre de Malleray. 'We were at a loose end and I knew this very pretty Danish model in Milan so we called her up and she agreed to have dinner with us. We went to fetch her and then we all went for dinner at the Villa d'Este. She looked gorgeous. We had a wonderful dinner and all drank quite a lot.'

Unfortunately, while driving her back to Milan in his Jaguar, Heini spun off a bridge in the pouring rain and crashed the car on to its roof 5 metres below. While they all miraculously survived, he was left with a fractured cervical vertebra. Heini made the mistake of not seeing a doctor immediately and continued driving and playing tennis despite the pain until he became completely paralysed: 'I could no longer walk and had to wear a corset for a long time, before I went to see a back specialist in New York called Doctor Kraus. He got me to do ten minutes of exercises a day which were a mixture of yoga and Swiss Army exercises.'

Chapter VI: 1945–1954

The only subsequent manifestation of this cure was Heini's habit of standing on his head to enliven what he considered boring social gatherings.

* * *

While he developed his role as a playboy, Heini's legal team continued to negotiate an inheritance settlement with Stephan. As well as an annual allowance, this included the allocation of 'cash, shares and bonds to the value of Dfl 4,340,000, $1,666,500, RM 42,670,840 and £800'. As advised by Henry Hyde, in June 1950, Stephan sold Heini 2 per cent of his share in HAIC in return for Dfl 100,000 Royal Dutch Shell shares and stated: 'For reasons known to the executors, I do not wish to remain involved with BVHS. I think things would run much more smoothly for you and Dolf etc.'

In 1952, there were indications that Stephan had already received RM 2.5 million plus $167,000 from the Kaszony Foundation and $1 million for his paintings. By now, it also appeared that he had been paid a total of Dfl 5 million for his HAIC shares, which may have included shares inherited from August Junior and SwFr 1.2 million for his German interests. There was a further arrangement whereby he received a monthly payment of DM 650 until a total of DM 100,000 had been paid.

Stephan also continued to provoke his brother concerning his suspension as managing director from Seismos and demanded a compensatory position with Thyssengas: 'I should get a new position at Thyssengas, as Scientific Expert or Foreign Business Director, with a monthly salary of at least DM 2,000.'[44]

After further negotiations, Heini agreed to pay Stephan a pension for life, starting on 31 December 1954 and running through 31 December 1973, which was to comprise twenty payments of SwFr 38,000 each. But then, on 7 August 1952, his lawyer, a weary Dr Papa, wrote to Heini:

> As foreseen, Stephan cannot agree to your proposal. Today he sent me a telegram, 'Offer unacceptable as SwFr 250,000 lower than minimum offer of 15 July'. His proposal is certainly not exaggerated namely SwFr 600,000 now, SwFr 600,000 in one year and twenty annual payments of SwFr 133,000 each. It would be the last transaction between you two brothers and I am sure you don't want it to go wrong.

* * *

A final settlement between the brothers was never achieved, as Stephan's demands continued to change while Heini rarely paid what had been agreed

Stephan with his wife and daughter and Rafael Silva, his solicitor, in their suite at the Hotel Nacional in Havana.

when he had agreed to pay. There was also a long silence before the surprising news that, on 7th March 1951, Stephan and his family had arrived in Cuba and taken up residence at the Hotel Nacional.

Around the same time, following further investigations into the Rechnitz atrocity, Margit Batthyány moved to Montevideo in Uruguay where Heini visited her:

My sister Margit had bought an estate near the river and I went to see her. I think I stayed for two or three months. I also went to Punta del Este, a beach resort there. It was considered a South American Switzerland and a sort of refuge in case the Russians invaded Europe. People were keeping their money there as they considered it to be safe.

Uruguay was also next door to Argentina and particularly Buenos Aires, where both Heinrich and Fritz had the headquarters of their South American interests. Heini had also opened an account with Banco di Montevideo, which in 1953 would show a balance of $133,150.66.

Stephan's reason for leaving Monte Carlo and moving to Havana was somewhat less political or economic. He did not stay in hotels so much as live in them and when the Metropole had informed him they were closing the hotel for refurbishment, he wrote to the management that even after three years he had no wish for his suite to be redecorated and refused to leave. When they threatened to call the police and have him forcibly ejected, Stephan reacted by moving with his family to Havana, a city with ample gambling facilities, controlled at the time by the Mafia, many of whom also had their residential suites at the Hotel Nacional. Stephan and his family would remain at the hotel for twelve years and although they lived an extremely private and reclusive life, they are still remembered by long-standing members of staff, including Jorge Fernandez, the night manager:

He always dressed very elegantly. He spoke little to other guests or the employees but was always extremely polite and considerate. Thyssen, his wife Inge and his fifteen-year-old daughter Birgit only allowed the staff to enter their rooms in order to clean. The daughter's Austrian governess was one of the few people they allowed into their two suites and one double room. All the furniture was theirs, as were the paintings, the drapes, various porcelain ornaments and other valuable objects. One of the rooms was used as a library for 'the Baron' where he studied and carried out his research. They never went to the Hotel restaurants to eat relying instead on the room-service waiter who took the meals to their door but was never permitted to enter.[45]

They also had a black Rolls-Royce, which, according to Jorge, was

> an old coupé that was always kept in immaculate mechanical condition. He used to drive it along the seafront on Sundays and sometimes his wife would drive it to the beach with her daughter. They spent a lot of time playing tennis, golf and swimming, had no visitors, rarely left the hotel and had no social life, although there were rumours of an affair between Inge and the hotel's manager, William Land.

Emilio de la Osa, who was the manager of the poolside 'cabanas', said: 'They had their own, permanent cabin. It had a small room with a sofa and two chairs plus a toilet. No one ever went near their cabin. They were very scrupulous with their personal objects and if anyone touched their towels, they would have to be changed.'

De la Osa contracted Pepe Aguero, the Cuban tennis champion, as their tennis coach. Sometimes, he would also play golf with their daughter Birgit: 'They were very fond of her and I had to be very careful because The Baron was also very jealous.'

When the weather was bad, they would sometimes invite Emilio to tea or call him on the phone and most days he gave them Spanish lessons for almost two hours.

> Whenever I raised the subject of the past or anything that touched on the war, they would change the subject, so I never learned anything about their past life, or their family, and I always got the impression that they were hiding something. They told me they were Austrian, not German, and they never used the surname Thyssen. Instead they used Bornemisza de Kaszón.

Stephan's SwFr 175,000 apanage from Heini would have easily covered his annual bill from the hotel while Emilio calculated that he had considerably more than $100 million in capital and said that from time to time they would visit Monte Carlo or New York where they also had residential suites in suitably grand hotels.

> The only business they did in Cuba was playing the Paris, London and New York stock markets. Each of them, including the daughter, had their own 'runner' or agent and competed to see who could make the most money. He once told me that he was not able to spend all the money he made on the stock market.

* * *

On 16 May 1950, the allied military government of Germany acknowledged that the former owners and creditors of the coal, iron and steel industries would be compensated. One year later, Konrad Adenauer finally pushed through what became known as the 'Montan Vertrag' contract, which permitted the release of assets and paved the way for the major industrial shareholders to return to the Ruhr.

In 1948, in an effort to stabilise the currency, the revalued Deutschmark had replaced the Reichsmark. For every RM1,000 people had in the bank, they got DM 65. But people with VSt-shares, or any other legitimate shares, received liquidation certificates worth DM 3,055 for every RM1,000 worth of shares. It was as a result of this policy that Amélie and Anita effortlessly multiplied their fortune and so dramatically contradicted Heini's claim that the Thyssens only lost money as a result of the war.

Understandably, many of the less fortunate Germans were extremely upset by this situation. Allied investigators also remained unconvinced of Fritz Thyssen's innocence despite the German Restitution Agency in Duisburg claiming that 'the court knew him to be a victim of Nazi persecution'. But when Fritz Thyssen died of a heart attack in Martinez near Buenos Aires on 8 February 1951, their claimed Nazi persecution did not inhibit Amélie and subsequently Anita from abandoning Argentina and returning to Germany. Not to the heartland of their industrial legacy or to Fritz's eventual resting place at Landsberg Castle but to Bavaria – the birthplace of the Nazi Party.

Despite Germany's agreement and the Allies' intention to prevent fresh undesirable concentrations of power, it soon became obvious that this was not going to happen. Between June 1951 and May 1953, twenty-three new steel companies were formed, including the successor to August Thyssen Hütte. However, through careful purchase and exchange of shares in the new companies, by the end of the decade, the Thyssens managed successfully to re-establish ownership control. They were not unique among German industrialists in applying this technique to regain their power.

Using the DM 300 million worth of shares that was divided and inherited equally between her and her daughter, Amélie Thyssen then set up a new holding company called 'Fritz Thyssen Asset Management AG', into which she brought her new shares. Her daughter Anita created a similar vehicle for her inheritance, which was called 'Thyssen Participations AG'. The majority of Amélie's shares were in August Thyssen Hütte, while Anita held a minority interest but together they held a controlling interest of 58 per cent. By 28 July 1952, all allied production restrictions for ATH would be lifted and the Thyssens would be finally returned to their position of industrial might.

It was ironic that Fritz Thyssen had originally only owned 26 per cent of the United Steelworks but now his widow and daughter owned over 40 per cent of the admittedly smaller group of companies. Although the plan had no doubt been put together by management loyal to the family and sympathetic to their political views, it was the Allies, encouraged by Chancellor Adenauer, who had facilitated Amélie's and Anita's control of 25 per cent of Germany's entire steel industry. In the process they had, as one journalist pointed out, become considerably richer than Barbara Hutton, the heir to the Woolworths fortune.

* * *

It was now some fifteen years since Gunhilde first walked into the Carlton Hotel in Cannes. Finally, on 7 April 1951 in Lugano, in front of three Swiss arbitration judges, she got what she had gone there for. The capital sum of SwFr 150,000 was payable in one final and unconditional payment on 1 July 1951 and not reclaimable if she remarried or died. Her annuity would be SwFr 24,000 and DM 8,400 per annum, to be paid in monthly instalments. The obligation to pay the index-linked annuity would not terminate until the widow's death. In the event that she remarried it would continue to be paid without alteration.

By Thyssen standards it may not have initially seemed a great deal of money, although Heini may not have thought so had he known Gunhilde was going to live for another fifty years, by which time the value of her annuity had risen to SwFr 48,000 and DM 72,000. Considering Gunhilde had only lived with Heinrich for eighteen months, it was a remarkable reward. She must be admired for her initial appreciation of the financial potential of the will, the skill in her campaign direction and her tenacious determination.

Three months after Gunhilde had won her settlement, Heini gained some comfort from winning his father's case against the British Crown for the retrieval of his gold. On 30 July 1951, in London's High Courts of Justice, Judge Devlin finally gave his judgment: 'The amount due to the plaintiff was the sum of £2,224,367 6s. 11d.'[46]

The major factor contributing to the success of his claim was his lawyers' ability to convince the court of the legitimacy of Heinrich's Hungarian nationality. Heini's lawyers also pleaded that the British Crown should pay interest for the disputed period when the gold was held on the assumption that he was German. Devlin agreed and the sum awarded included four and a half years' tax-free interest.

On 27 June 1952, having decided there no longer existed any danger in his father being judged a German, Heini had his father's body transferred from a churchyard in Lugano to the family mausoleum at Landsberg Castle in Germany.

The next piece of the Thyssen-Bornemisza recovery jigsaw to fall into place was the August Thyssen Bank, which had been cut off from the rest of Germany during the Russian blockade of Berlin between 1948 and 1949. Thanks to the tireless efforts of Heinrich Lübke, the bank was able to re-open for business on 30 January 1952. The bank was never fully investigated by allied intelligence. The Americans had every reason to discourage the exposure of a Nazi banking system which would have implicated other international banks, including some of their own. With John Foster Dulles as Secretary of State and Heini's connections with the CIA through Henry Hyde, there was every reason for them to discourage any form of embarrassing investigation; especially 'under the noses of the Russians'.

It appeared for a time that Heini would even manage to have some of his US holdings unblocked. Once again it had been facilitated by Foster Dulles and his supporters who considered the confiscation of German property in America to be an immoral, un-American, communist plot. But the attempt was foiled when President Eisenhower vetoed their Return of Property Bill in August 1954.

* * *

With Gunhilde and Stephan now almost entirely out of the picture, the finalisation and agreement to the contents and terms of the inheritance, or what was now known as the 'Family Agreement', should have been concluded within a very short time. But the reality was that the Thyssen-Bornemisza family inheritance was never really finally agreed and continued to be a source of conflict. The main reason for this was Heini's determination to retain the unity of the Thyssen Bornemisza Group, rather than facilitate the process of inheritance by dividing it up. Heini also wanted total control of the Group and, to achieve this ambition, in 1952 he finally persuaded Stephan, Margit, Ivy, Gaby and Dolf to sign the 'Kaszony Agreement', which agreed to Kaszony's continued joint administration of the following, hugely simplified, solely owned assets:

a. Dfl 872,000 shares in BVHS
b. Dfl 4 million shares in HAIC
c. RM 21 million shares in Thyssensche Gas und Wasserwerke
d. RM 4 million shares in August Thyssen Bank
e. RM 14.3 million shares in Press- und Walzwerk Reisholz
f. 37.5 per cent mining shares

He then persuaded Bentinck and van Aken to resign from the foundation, leaving Heini as the sole board member and trustee of an organisation that still had no legal identity. But if everyone concerned wished to continue to profit from the Group, they were obliged to accept.

As the Thyssen Bornemisza Group was constantly changing and minimising its taxable value, it is difficult to calculate the value of individual inheritances. But to live to the standards they adopted, Margit and Gaby would have needed to inherit a cash value of some $150 million each, in the days when $1 million was sufficient to guarantee a life of luxurious indolence. Theoretically, Heini would be entitled to six times this amount, but due to his various loans and the ever-increasing value of the art collection, the exact amount of his inheritance was even more difficult to calculate. Estimates vary from $1 to $3.5 billion dollars. Stephan's haste to settle for cash cost him dearly, his total payments amounting to 'only' around $20 million.

It may or may not have occurred to Margit and Gaby at the time that, having been bought out, Stephan transferred his share of the Kaszony Foundation profit to Heini who, as sole trustee, then saw fit to adjust his proportional dividend so that his sisters' one-eighth share remained unaffected, while his own increased to six-eighths. As an example of these proportional rewards, in 1952 Margit and Gaby received SwFr 435,000 each from the Kaszony Foundation, while Heini received SwFr 2.8 million.

* * *

The only two organisations that Heini had yet to liberate were his steel manufacturing companies, whose control had been in the hands of the Allies' Combined Steel Group since 1946. Obviously, his people had been working towards the lifting of the control and on 15 June 1953 a decree was issued by the Allied High Commission for Germany formally confirming the lifting of their control.[47]

There is no indication of any further control or the results of any investigation into the factories' war records or the status of the owner. It must have been of considerable relief to Heini that he had finally completed the retrieval of the entire Thyssen Bornemisza group of companies without any investigations or public revelations concerning his father or his business practices. But his respite would be short-lived, as he entered another, far more dangerous and ultimately more expensive theatre of combat. That of courting a new wife before he had completed a financial settlement with the old one.

1 Minutes of meeting of unidentified person with the Russian Banking Commissar on 14 May 1945 (National Archives, Washington, DC).
2 Minutes compiled by unidentified person, entry for 20 September 1945 (ibid.).
3 Allied interrogation of Hermann Göring, 2, 3 and 25 June 1945 (ibid.).
4 Letter from Heini Thyssen-Bornemisza to Princess Theresa zu Lippe, dated 25 June 1945 (TBG Archives).
5 Author's interviews with Wilhelmus Groenendijk, 1997. According to Safehaven report no. 463, Berne dated, 20 December 1946, Fritz Thyssen had been held for a while 'in the custody of the 7742nd Guard Company at the International Military Tribunal, Nuremberg' (National Archives, Washington, DC).
6 Public Record Office, Kew/UK, Ref. FO 837/1158.
7 All from the following: US Group Control Council (Germany), Office of the Director of Intelligence, Field Information Agency, Technical Intelligence Report no. EF/Me/2, Report no. 2, Examination of Dr Fritz Thyssen by Clifford Hynning, Finance Division, dated 4 September 1945 (Public Record Office, Kew, Ref. FO 1046/40); Seventh Army Interrogation Center, APO 758, Preliminary Interrogation Report of Fritz Thyssen, dated 8 October 1945 (National Archives, Washington, DC) and Interrogation of Fritz Thyssen in Oberursel, dated 23 November 1945 (ibid.).
8 Letter from Walter A. Rudlin, Chief, Intelligence Service Staff at the Foreign Economic Administration in Washington, to Lt. Colonel Tom B. Coughran, Civil Affairs Division, War Department, Washington, re Interrogation of Fritz Thyssen,

Chapter VI: 1945–1954

Swiss Thyssen interests and Latin American interests, dated 18 October 1945 (ibid.).
9 Letters from Curt Ritter to Heinrich Thyssen-Bornemisza, dated 2 October 1945 and 26 January 1946 (TBG Archives).
10 Jakob Kraayenhof's firm Klynveld, Kraayenhof & Co. became Klynveld, Main, Goerdeler and finally KPMG in the 1980s, one of the big four accounting firms in the world.
11 All from a preliminary report on Thyssen Lametal Buenos Aires, by Fred Stevens, US Treasury Investigator, to Captain I. Roth, dated 21 December 1945 (National Archives, Washington, DC).
12 A memorandum from Albert Bender at the Foreign Department, External Assets and Intelligence Branch, to Mr Wesley Haraldson, dated 28 May 1947 would reveal: 'It is requested that you approach the Office of the Soviet Political Adviser to secure permission to interrogate, in Berlin, Heinrich Lübke, Manager of the August Thyssen Bank. This interrogation is essential in assisting the Swiss authorities to prosecute Baron van der Heydt for aiding the Abwehr in transmitting funds from Switzerland to German agents abroad. Heinrich Lübke acted as the intermediary between the German Abwehr and Baron von der Heydt. He travelled regularly between Germany and Switzerland, transporting espionage funds.' (Ibid.).
13 Author's conversations with Georg Heinrich Thyssen-Bornemisza, 2003.
14 For instance, letter from the President of the Police, Department II, 60.5/53 (Thyssen), Tempelhofer Damm 7, Berlin, to the solicitor Dr Albert Stappert, Benrather Strasse 12–14, 22A Düsseldorf, concerning the nationality of Dr Heinrich Thyssen-Bornemisza, born 31.10.1875 in Mülheim/Ruhr, dated 9 April 1956 (TBG Archives).
15 Trading with the Enemy Department, to Economic Warfare Department, Foreign Office: Note on the Kaszony Foundation, the nationality of Baron Heinrich Thyssen and the ownership and control of Press- und Walzwerke AG, Düsseldorf, dated 4 November 1947 (PRO, Kew/UK, Ref. FO 371/65381).
16 Interview with Katherine Coert in 1988 (TBG Archives).
17 Letter dated 21 June 1946 (Bentinck Archives).
18 Based on a series of articles entitled 'Operation Juliana' in *NRC Handelsblad* on 1 and 3 June 1991, by Gerald Mulder, Cees Wiebes and Bert Zeeman.
19 Letter dated 21 October 1946 (Bentinck Archives).
20 Undated file note (TBG Archives).
21 Secret intra-office memorandum from Herbert Sorter, External Assets and Intelligence Branch, to Albert Bender, Chief, External Assets and Intelligence Branch, concerning the removal of securities from the August Thyssen Bank, Berlin, with the aid of the Netherlands Military Mission, dated 21 February 1947 (National Archives, Washington, DC).
22 Statement by Curt Ritter made in Berlin on 25 June 1947 (ibid.).
23 Letter from Baron Stephan Thyssen-Bornemisza to his sister Baroness Gabrielle Bentinck-Thyssen, dated 4 August 1947 (Bentinck Archives).

24 From a decision by the Appeal Court in Budapest concerning the divorce between Heinrich Thyssen-Bornemisza and Gunhilde Emilie Asta Edith Marie Amanda de Fabrice, dated 8 August 1947 (TBG Archives).
25 Letter from the Chief of the Finance Division to the Control and Decartelisation Branch, Economic Sub-Commission, HQ Control Commission for Germany, Berlin, British Army on the Rhine, dated 29 October 1947 (Public Record Office, Kew/UK, Ref. FO 1039/816).
26 James Gantenbein, Chief, Economics Branch, Office of Political Affairs, OMGUS Berlin, to Samuel M. Rose, Associate Chief, Property Control and External Assets Branch, Property Division, dated 15 July 1948; Samuel Rose to James Gantenbein re Swiss Interests of Fritz Thyssen dated 23 July 1948 and Fred E. Hartzsch of OMGUS, Property Division, to E. J. Cassoday, dated 27 March 1949 (National Archives, Washington, DC).
27 Letter dated 4 November 1947 (Public Record Office, Kew/UK, Ref. FO 371/65381).
28 Letter from the Director of Property Control Branch to G. B. W. Woodroffe, Foreign Office, dated 18 November 1947 (Ref. FO 1039/816).
29 Letter from Professor Walter Vinassa to Baroness Gabrielle Bentinck-Thyssen, dated 29 April 1948 (Bentinck Archives).
30 R. C. R. Goodchild to Mr Villiers on Stephan Thyssen's exit permit, dated 22 November 1947 (Ref. M13/415). Foreign Office, Economic Warfare Department to Baron A. W. C. Bentinck, Netherlands Embassy, London, dated 25 November 1947 (Ref. FO 837/1158) (both Public Record Office, Kew/UK).
31 Eglau, p. 295.
32 *New York Times*, 3 October 1948.
33 Interrogation of Fritz Thyssen in Wiesbaden on 4 and 5 May 1949 by Messrs Harry Harry R. Priestley and Bruno Meyer (both HQ Investigation Branch, Office of the Financial Adviser, Düsseldorf), Robert Pollard and Rudolf Nathanson (both Department of Justice, Overseas Branch, Munich) and Herbert Sorter (Property Control and External Assets Branch, Investigation Section, Wiesbaden) (National Archives, Washington, DC).
34 Letter from Jakob Goldschmidt, New York, to Heini Thyssen-Bornemisza, dated 13 May 1949 (TBG Archives).
35 Letter from Dr Wilhelm Roelen to Senator Malone in Washington, dated 20 July 1949 (ibid.).
36 Confidential memorandum from Hugh Millard, Chargé d'Affaires, American Embassy, Brussels, to the Honorable Secretary of State, Washington, re Protest of Fritz Thyssen at alleged duress imposed by passport authorities at Wiesbaden, dated 30 June 1949 (National Archives, Washington, DC.
37 Letter from Kurt Schumacher to the Honorable John J. McCloy, High Commissioner, IG Farben Building, Frankfurt, dated 19 August 1949 (ibid.).

38 Letter from Harold Wilson at the Board of Trade, to Stafford Cripps re Heini Thyssen-Bornemisza's gold in London and his attempts to retrieve it, dated 7 November 1949 (Public Record Office, Kew/UK).
39 Letter from A. N. Halls to Mr Kinna MBE, Foreign Office, Downing Street, dated 24 June 1949 (ibid., Ref. BT 271/574).
40 Ibid.
41 Memoranda from Mr Riesen and colleagues to Federal Councillor von Steiger, dated 20 September and 26 September 1949 (Swiss Federal Archives).
42 'My Life', by Fritz Thyssen, Brussels, 9 June 1949, p. 20. This was included at the back of a 1996 reprint by Federico Zichy-Thyssen of his grandfather's book *I Paid Hitler*.
43 Memorandum of BVHS entitled 'Deconcentration of the Thyssen Bornemisza Group under military government law 75', dated 3 January 1950 (TBG Archives).
44 Letter from Dr Baron Stephan Thyssen-Bornemisza to Dr Joseph Groh, dated 29 April 1952 (ibid.).
45 Local investigation in Cuba organised by Dr Stephen Wilkinson and carried out by Señor Leonardo Padura in 1998, whose interviewees were Emilio de la Osa, Jorge Fernandez and Estela Rivas Vasquez.
46 Bank voor Handel en Scheepvaart NV *v.* Slatford and another, Queen's Bench Division, Judge Devlin, July 1951 / October 1952. The figure is given in the currency denomination used at the time, i.e. including shillings and pence.
47 Order issued by the High Commission for Germany, Combined Steel Group, to Family Foundation Kaszony in Schwyz, Bank voor Handel en Scheepvaart NV in Rotterdam, Baustoff-Industriewerke Hennickendorf GmbH, Press- und Walzwerk GmbH, Stahl- und Röhrenwerk Reisholz AG (all in Düsseldorf), dated 15 June 1953 (Public Record Office, Kew/UK, Ref. FO 1029/81).

Chapter VII
1954–1967

The playboy years...
One divorce, two weddings & a panther

*Spoil the child, spare the rod,
open up the caviar
and say Thank God.*
Noël Coward

Heini was thirty years of age when he accepted an invitation from a Russian friend to a reception near l'Étoile in Paris in 1951. But six years of sexually repressive marriage and the development of his role as a playboy had done nothing to prepare him for the new world of decadence into which he was about to be led.

There were two women who caught his eye that night, a blonde and a brunette. He later discovered the blonde to have been Kim Novak but it was the exotic brunette, Nina Dyer, who recognised the multi-millionaire Baron Heini Thyssen-Bornemisza and made the decision to seduce him.

Heini, whose Catholic upbringing made it difficult for him to accept the concept of lust, was convinced it was 'love at first sight'. A middle-class English girl with a string of lovers of both sexes, Nina was an occasional swimwear model, who was well known in Cap d'Antibes and a regular habitué of Carroll's, the legendary Parisian gay nightclub. She introduced Heini to an entirely different stratum of society: the so-called 'beautiful people'. At this point in his life, apart from the members of the Corviglia Club, whose only qualification for membership was their wealth, his wife's friends had dominated Heini's social life.

'Theresa only mixed with aristocrats like the Hohenzollerns and the Württembergs. She was a snob and thought actors and models were common. Nina was more of a celebrity than Theresa. She was in the papers long before we got married, because of her affair with General Franco's brother in Cannes.'

Heini would have been well advised to have delayed his affair or practised a degree of discretion until he had agreed to the terms of Theresa's alimony settlement. But he seemed determined to flaunt his new relationship with Nina. Theresa was also in possession of a great deal of knowledge concerning his family's wartime activities and post-war recovery exploits which would result in his being left little choice but to accept many of her alimony demands. What would prove to be the most effectively punishing of these demands was an inheritance agreement entitling the four-year-old Georg to a 25 per cent advantage over any subsequent heirs. This would eventually give him an effective controlling interest in the entire group of Thyssen-Bornemisza companies.

Of far less importance was an immediate annual allowance of SwFr 30,000 which would be paid into a savings account with the Swiss Bank Corporation in Zurich for twenty-six years. Although it was not part of the contract, on Georg's eighteenth birthday Heini would also lodge $500,000 in an account for him with the Union Bank of Switzerland.

Having agreed to Theresa's custody, Heini was also obliged to concede that in order to protect the interests of Georg, Theresa should be granted approval of all corporate policy that might affect her son until his thirtieth birthday – this apparently being the age at which such aristocrats were accepted as independent adults. It gave the Princess zu Lippe quite astonishing power. As well as securing her son's future, Theresa also ensured that she would remain financially secure for the rest of her life. From May 1954, when her divorce was made absolute, she received an index-linked yearly apanage of SwFr 150,000 until 1968 when it was reduced to SwFr 100,000 from then on. The result of the index-link was an increase of the amount to SwFr 211,208.90 by 1975 and to SwFr 399,109.00 by 1997.

Within five years, Theresa had also achieved a social status which she no doubt considered more befitting by marrying Friedrich Prinz zu Fürstenberg, who came complete with a castle in Southern Germany and a highly successful brewery. But being Catholics who wished to have the approval of their Church for their actions, Heini and Theresa applied jointly to the Ecclesiastical Court in Rome for their divorce to be given the status of an annulment. Unfortunately, the judges were unanimously unimpressed with many of their claims. Initially, Heini insisted there had never been any divorce proceedings in his family but withdrew the claim when it became obvious that the judges knew this to be untrue. He also claimed he and Theresa had enjoyed 'regular relations without any difficulties' but that, as he was infertile, the child could not possibly have been his.[1] There was even evidence to suggest that their marriage may never have been consummated.

Heini entering his playboy period with Nina Dyer at the Hotel du Cap d'Antibes in 1953.

But none of these admissions and suggestions appeared to have any effect on the surprisingly friendly relations which all parties would continue to enjoy. This was evident in a letter from Heini to the Prince: 'Dear Fritzi, Thanks for your Christmas greetings. I will drink all my bottles of Fürstenberg Pils to your health.'

Heini's friendship also extended to the Prince's brother, Crown Prince Joachim, at Donaueschingen Castle: 'Dear Jocki, Thanks for lending me your nice white Mercedes to drive to Werenwag Castle. Look forward to your visit to Lugano sometime. Unfortunately, I don't have such a nice car here.'

Meanwhile, Theresa would apparently remain happily married to Prince Friedrich for the rest of his life, bearing him two daughters and a son, while Heini reacted to the Church's intractability and subsequent refusal for him to be made a Knight of the Order of Malta with scurrilous and highly unlikely stories about the Pope.

Chapter VII: 1954–1967

The Thyssens have actually done a great deal for the Church. By mistake, I once received a letter addressed to the Pope. My name was written on the envelope, but it contained a bank statement for His Holiness. The envelopes were probably mixed up. I kept the letter, reasoning that I didn't have to return mail that is wrongly addressed. The bank statement, from Banca di Roma, was addressed to the Pope personally, and concerned a $500 dividend that he had received from a US manufacturer of contraceptive pills.

* * *

After an outrageously adventurous three-year relationship, during which time Heini should have learned that the twenty-four-year-old Nina Dyer was unlikely to adapt to the role of wife, they were married in Colombo on 23 June 1954, less than one month after his divorce from Theresa had become absolute.

We flew there by Comet, the world's first jet passenger plane. I remember my aunt Amélie coming to see me shortly before I married Nina. She was convinced I was heading for another disaster and offered to merge our companies providing I cancelled the marriage. She reminded me that the combination of our holdings could result in the creation of Europe's largest and most powerful industrial conglomerate but I was very much in love with Nina and refused to listen. I don't regret the marriage but I do regret not merging our companies.

Heini claimed to have married Nina because he felt sorry for her, as she was 'all alone in life apart from her mother. She couldn't have children and had tried to commit suicide several times.' But an anti-capitalist leaflet that was widely distributed among the Walsum miners claimed: 'In Mr Thyssen's prenuptial agreement with his second wife Nina, there is a paragraph stating explicitly that she can continue to have "close relations" with the French actor and male model Mr Christian Marquand.'

Heini denied the arrangement but admitted that after the marriage Nina had tried to negotiate the retention of her lover's services in a *ménage à trois*. When Heini refused, she told him, 'I've never been interested in you sexually. I only married you for your money', but their marriage continued, as did her relationship with Marquand. 'Nina was very unstable, insecure and constantly unfaithful but everyone liked her. She was very kind and generous.'

She was also very demanding. When her mother died, Nina told Heini that her stepfather had killed her. He wanted to inherit her estate in Ceylon where

Nina had spent her childhood, so he faked a car accident. Nina claimed he drove the car into a tree in such a way that her mother was killed while he escaped unhurt. Josi Groh enriched the story by insisting that Heini promised Nina he would 'fix it' and that the man had subsequently been found dead. Whether his murder had anything to do with Heini is unknown but it certainly enabled Nina to inherit her mother's estate.

* * *

Life with Nina never assumed any kind of normality, either before or after their marriage.

> Nina and I spent a lot of time in France. We lived at the Queen Elizabeth Hotel in Paris for a year with two panthers and six dogs, all in one hotel suite. The management didn't find it very amusing. It was somewhat complicated and the stench was appalling. I wonder how I survived in that zoo for a whole year. To get to the bathroom, you had to push your way through the pack of dogs who would all start barking.

Heini gained almost as much pleasure from retelling the stories of his wife's outrageous behaviour as he did from taking part.

> As you can imagine, the chambermaids loved it. I had to take the animals out at six every morning; first the panthers, then the dogs. There was certainly little chance of being mugged when I went out with the panthers. They were always with us when we travelled and Nina played with them as though she were a panther herself. She refused to have their claws cut and her arms, shoulders and back were full of scratches and scars.

According to Sandor Berkes, this was despite the fact that Nina used to wear leather when she played with them, while Heini appeared to get his masochistic pleasure from the cost of their damage: 'Not only did they cause a sensation wherever we went but I also constantly had to replace mauled carpets, torn curtains, broken furniture and ripped sheets, not to mention the other rooms I had to pay for because people refused to live next to us. Although they never complained to us personally.'

Heini obviously found this immensely amusing and enjoyed the media attention regardless of the effect it might have had on his credibility as an industrialist and banker. Even when the 'zoo' was reduced to a mere 'three dogs', they made headlines in *Der Spiegel* magazine: 'Heinrich Thyssen (34) arrives in

New York with his wife Nina Dyer (24). In the hotel Ambassador their three dogs Sou, Suki and Bambi got a room each to recover from the trip.'

Having been forced into a position of corporate responsibility at such an early age, Heini now revelled in his delayed rebellion: 'It was very exciting. One moment I was in a very serious business meeting to do with the coal mines etc. and having to work very hard and read lots of papers, and the next moment I was taking a plane to Paris or Cannes to meet up with Nina to be frivolous and let off steam.'

Perhaps influenced by the panthers, Heini also began to gain a certain satisfaction from participating in their trail of destruction: 'I remember smashing up a whole room at the Carlton Hotel once because I was furious about something. That was so much fun! We spent a whole summer in the Carlton before we moved on to the Eden Roc. It was a frivolous life but it was also very exciting.'

Pausing mid-sip, Heini turned to me and commented: 'It's a pity I didn't know you then. We could have had so much fun.'

* * *

Up until this time, Heini had displayed little interest in art apart from in its value as part of his inheritance and the opening of the gallery to the public as a means of avoiding taxes. But slowly and carefully, Rudolf Heinemann was encouraging his active participation. Despite the climate of post-war austerity, the opening of an exhibition of Dutch art at the Royal Academy in London in 1952 was a smart event, which opened Heini's eyes to the social advantages of exhibitions. Even more socially seductive was the opening of a prestigious exhibition at the Metropolitan Museum in New York three years later, for which Heini had lent his Holbein, 'Henry VIII', and three other old masters.

While purchasing works from his siblings, he had also been encouraged to invest in the occasional addition to his collection and in 1956 made what he liked to consider his first important acquisition. It was 'Portrait of a Young Man' by Francesco del Cossa. While it may not have caused a great deal of excitement in the international art market, it attracted sufficient attention and flattery to encourage Heini to consider himself an 'art collector'. It was a label he found more socially acceptable than 'industrialist', while Josi Groh insisted that the 'art business was the only business that ever really attracted Heini' or for which he ever really developed any aptitude. Despite describing it as 'the dirtiest business in the world', its cavalier style of operation undoubtedly appealed to him.

* * *

By 1955, Heini's lack of attention to business was beginning to concern his management. Despite taking over as president of the supervisory board of the August Thyssen Bank on 4 June 1955, there was no evidence of any increased enthusiasm for becoming involved in the organisation of the bank's affairs. In December of the same year, a branch of the bank was opened in Düsseldorf. In view of the isolation of Berlin within Germany, it had become necessary to open another branch in order to maintain business relations with the bank's clients. The Düsseldorf branch became so successful that one year later the board had decided to invest in larger premises and the base capital had risen from DM 8 to 16 million. But once again, according to Josi Groh, Heini had very little to do with it, although Josi was also more than capable of retrospectively increasing his own responsibility for business success and reducing his involvement in failures and disasters. 'The ATB was the only bank after the war that didn't have any compensation claims, so it was technically able to work. All the other banks in Germany were bankrupt. I reorganised the branch in Düsseldorf together with Mr Kredit.'

Although Heinrich Lübke had nearly lost his life for the good of the August Thyssen Bank, Groh saw no reason for his efforts to be recognised. 'Lübke had been in a Russian prison camp after he was captured at the end of the war. I remember him showing us his wounds. But he only did it because he thought he deserved a bigger pension.'

However, Josi Groh also made another revelation of far greater importance when he stated: 'We also had branches in Buenos Aires and Rio de Janeiro.'

It would be another forty years before a declassified State Department memorandum of December 1946 revealed that: 'Swiss bankers used diplomatic pouches to smuggle Nazi gold and securities to Argentina, including a £3 million retirement fund for Hermann Göring. Joseph Goebbels placed $1.3 million in a safety deposit box in a German-controlled bank in Buenos Aires.'[2]

Heini's reaction to the suggestion that the August Thyssen Bank in Buenos Aires may have been involved was somewhat more extreme than that concerning the Union Bank of New York. He categorically denied all knowledge of the South American branches.

* * *

While the management of the Thyssen-Bornemisza group had been attending to business in Heini's absence, Amélie and Anita Thyssen had been planning the final part of their ultimate move to cloak their holdings in a veneer of philanthropic respectability, in the style of the great American robber barons, by setting up a charitable foundation called the Fritz Thyssen Stiftung. This 'foundation for the advancement of science' served to reduce their liability to inheritance, income and wealth tax and, by holding one-third of their shares in August Thyssen Hütte, avoid the accusation of an excessive concentration of power. It also distracted people's attention away from how much of the rebuilding of the Thyssens' industrial empire had been paid for with both allied and German public money.

At the same time as the charitable Fritz Thyssen Foundation was being created, Amélie was closing the family's Pelzer Foundation because 'the conditions which brought my late husband to set it up have long since vanished'.[3] Her confidential admission of Fritz's sole responsibility for the formation of the Pelzer Family Foundation, which had succeeded in protecting their fortune from both allied and German seizure, directly contradicted Fritz's declaration to allied intelligence. When Amélie subsequently realised that the Pelzer Foundation was likely to have exposed her to tax liabilities in Switzerland, Holland and Uruguay, she became quite incensed and abusive towards the trustees, exposing her seemingly limitless fiscal hypocrisy.

* * *

Of perhaps even more concern than Heini's ever-increasing lack of involvement in the running of his Konzern was his lavish expenditure, not only on his extravagant lifestyle but also on gifts: 'It was Nina who introduced me to the excitement of buying large gems. There was something wonderfully decadent about buying her outrageously extravagant presents. I adored her and in the early days I could refuse her nothing.' This included a beautiful plantation-style house built on a piece of land known as Alligator Head at Port Antonio in Jamaica. But when Nina started to give Heini's presents to her lovers and their fights became violent, Heini began to question the future of their relationship.

When Nina realised that it was all about to end, she decided to go shopping and on 14 April 1956, she spent FrFr 2.4 million at Balenciaga. Four days later she spent a further FrFr 2.25 million francs at Jacques Fath. Two days after that she ran up a bill of FrFr 1.75 million francs at Christian Dior. Givenchy even sent Heini a letter expressing concern both about the rumours of their imminent separation and what they suspected as her obvious determination to spend as much of his money as possible before Heini could close her accounts. Jewellers were also the subject of her attention although Van Cleef and Arpels appeared more concerned that her $1 million worth of jewellery was adequately insured.

The Düsseldorf branch of the August Thyssen Bank.

By 3 July, Heini's patience snapped and he filed for divorce. Despite his insistence that he was still in love with Nina and that without her liberating influence he would never have truly been capable of appreciating art, it is evident that the split was acrimonious. Initially he tried to recover the fortune in jewels that he had bought for her. He also hired private detectives to establish her promiscuity. It seemed a rather pointless exercise, although the Colonial Investigating Bureau in Kingston, Jamaica, did manage to establish that the Sunset Lodge Hotel in Montego Bay, where she had stayed, was frequented by 'rich sodomites and homosexuals'.

Such evidence had little effect on Nina's alimony and after barely two years of marriage, she was awarded SwFr 500,000 on divorce, SwFr 250,000 six months later and SwFr 250,000 after one year. She also kept the apartment in Paris, the house in Jamaica, all the jewellery and an El Greco, while Heini settled her bills with Balenciaga, Dior, Hermes, Givenchy et al. There was also a further FrFr 3,862,000 to cover 'miscellaneous' expenses and FrFr 20,000 towards her legal costs.

However, she was obliged to renounce her title, although this was hardly a hardship as, like Theresa before her, Nina was soon to become a Princess when, in 1957, she married Saddrudin Khan. His family also pleaded with him to reconsider his decision but he refused and forfeited his inheritance of the position of Aga Khan. They were married in Geneva and Heini was invited to the wedding.

In 1962 he divorced her after she ran off with a doctor who used to control her by supplying her with drugs. She also lived in Jamaica for a while with two dykes who treated her like a slave and kept her on a chain. Then she went back to Paris where I saw her a week before she committed suicide. Her last lover was a young shopkeeper who was married and had children. They had planned to go to the Côte D'Azur together but at the last minute he told her he was not going to leave his wife. It gave her a shock. She saw that she was losing her hold over men.

Having received huge alimony settlements from both Heini and Saddrudin Khan, Nina was by this time extremely wealthy and still possessed a great deal of jewellery. No one appeared surprised when Heini encouraged the rumour that Nina had been murdered for her money by one of her lesbian lovers.

The Herald Tribune announced Nina's death, describing her as an international glamour model, who had 'pushed herself from obscurity as a model into international society at the age of twenty by means of a bikini and two Pekinese dogs'.

On the same day, they also announced the death of Porfirio Rubirosa: 'Another member of the Parisian smart set, the Dominican playboy and diplomat was killed when his powerful Ferrari smashed into a tree in the Bois de Boulogne'.

* * *

Having recovered from the rigours of life with Nina, Heini returned to the less challenging world of St Moritz. While it may have been considered predictable that Heini should return as a weekend playboy to this more familiar world, it was considerably less predictable that within a matter of months he would yet again be proposing marriage, this time to a girl he met on the train from St Moritz to Zurich. 'She was going to visit her parents in Berlin where her father was serving in the British Navy as a Rear Admiral.'

Fiona Campbell-Walter was from a middle-class, Anglo-Scottish family who had combined her father's surname with her mother's maiden name for increased social effect. Like Nina she was also a model but because she modelled couture gowns rather than swimwear, she was awarded the more respectable qualification of 'mannequin'. Remarkably elegant and strikingly beautiful, she was the photographer Cecil Beaton's favourite and voted one of the three most beautiful women in the world by the painter Pietro Annigoni. She had already appeared many times on the covers of *Vogue* and *Life*.

By the time they got to Germany, Heini claimed to have been in love with Fiona who was living in Paris and engaged to an Italian playboy called Ernesto. Apparently, he had bought her a Ford Thunderbird and she was waiting for it to be delivered. But by the time she got back to Paris, having realised that Heini was one of the richest men in the world, she was also in love. Having accepted his present of a Ford Thunderbird, which Heini had managed to procure on the black market while her boyfriend was still waiting for his to arrive from America, Fiona also accepted Heini's proposal of marriage. When Roberto van Aken heard that Heini was engaged to be married and had already started buying presents, he found it difficult not to betray a degree of panic. In his letter recommending a pre-nuptial agreement he wrote:

> On special request I shall be glad to be at your disposal this week or at any time thereafter, by day or night, should you need me. An agreement can be made whenever and wherever you like, at the villa, or in Josi's home and will take only a few minutes. At any rate it would be advisable to sign the agreement before the marriage has taken place.

It was perhaps indicative of Heini's decision to re-establish his commitment to business that he took van Aken's advice and on 25 August 1956 a contract of property separation between Fiona and Heini was drawn up, read out and signed in the small drawing-room on the second floor of Villa Favorita.

*   *   *

Three weeks later, Heini married Fiona Campbell-Walter in Castagnola's small town hall to the muted fanfare of mainly British press. According to Heini: 'Fiona was not insecure like Nina but she loved attention and publicity while her mother loved to see her daughter in the newspapers and magazines.'

Heini did not appreciate the intrusion and the media were disappointed by the lack of ceremony and extravagance, a policy which he had adopted out of respect for his special relationship with the cantonal tax authorities. 'Any sign of luxury was conspicuously absent. Her dress, made by a local dressmaker, was of her own design and whilst glasses of champagne were served, there was no evidence of a buffet.'

However, they cheered up when the value of her pearl necklace was revealed as 'an estimated £40,000.' They also appreciated the Thunderbird when 'they drove off in the Baron's dove-grey American roadster'.[4]

It soon became apparent that Heini had no intention of repeating the intensity of his previous relationship and expected little more from Fiona than a decorative presence; something she accepted with scant regard for modesty: 'He had the fastest plane, the best motor-boat, the most precious paintings. Of course he had to have the most beautiful woman.'

Heini displayed an equally appreciative acceptance of Fiona's cerebral shortcomings:

She wasn't very intelligent but she would talk endlessly in that wonderful dark brown voice of hers. One day, when we were driving she asked me a question and I didn't answer. I said, 'You've got such a sweet, charming voice, you can't expect me to listen to what you are saying as well. Just talk to me'. I like beauty. It fascinates me. She had a fantastic figure, although she looked better dressed than naked. No woman has ever impressed me with her intelligence. I have been attracted to them socially but it is mainly beauty and physical attraction that I am interested in.

Age and experience have taught me that when it comes to women, one should not fall madly in love, travel with them, trust or spoil them too much. One should, however, show jealousy. Women like that. Although I am capable of dismissing directors, negotiating difficult deals and suing large companies, when I am with a woman, I give in to all her whims and act like a weak and insecure student. It may be a reaction. My marriages did not last long, but at the beginning, I was always sincerely in love.

Meanwhile, according to Heini, Fiona took her role as the 'Baroness' extremely seriously: 'Like Theresa she believed the title had been created expressly for her and had nothing to do with me.'

But while Heini attended to business, Fiona had no intention of reducing her social activity:

Fiona was heavily into socialising, especially in St Moritz with Caprice and Andrea Badrutt, the Niarchos's, Gunter Sachs, the Agnellis' and Dewi Sukarno. She enjoyed St Moritz so much that I finally agreed to build a house there. But every time she organised a party for us to go to, so I still had to go out. The result was that I was too tired to feel like making love. When you get older and tired, you start having problems. You should take it easy instead of going out all the time.

Heini was thirty-five years of age.

* * *

While Heini was trying to satisfy the demands of both his management and his new young wife, his brother had to cope with an entirely different set of problems. In 1956, while Fidel Castro and his band of revolutionaries launched their second unsuccessful attempt to overthrow Fulgencio Batista, Stephan must have been the only multi-millionaire in Cuba who was more concerned about the decorators.

Once again Stephan and his family had found themselves subjected to a hotel manager's insistence on the refurbishment of the rooms. According to an article in the Cuban society magazine *Bohemia*, written by Carlos Castanada, which was remarkably sympathetic to his plight, Stephan was both a respected and appreciative guest who had been forced by the management to become 'a refugee in his luxury suite on the seventh floor'.

Apparently, he and his family had barricaded themselves in their rooms 'with enough biscuits and water to survive for three days'.

Having already survived for five days without water, electricity or room service, Stephan and his family continued to defy the management who wanted them to move out to facilitate the installation of three bathrooms and air conditioning. The manager, Mr Vaughn, who justified the development by the demands of modern tourism, accused the Baron of holding up progress and threatened to starve him out. In response, the Baron accused Vaughn of converting the hotel into a 'Motel Nacional', and reminded him: 'I am only interested in being able to study and think in peace and quiet.'

Castanada obviously appreciated Stephan's rebellious behaviour and pointed out:

> The Baron is not an arrogant noble as some wish to portray him. He is a scientist who has fallen in love with Cuba and who doesn't recognise any titles other than those from Zurich University and the Massachusetts Institute of Technology. He is reserved and lives in his little world of suite 712, his books, his paintings and the blue of the sea. It's the contradiction of the century.

When the work started on the hotel's conversion, Stephan claimed $30,000 vibration damage to his paintings. Then, the hotel changed its strategy and a solicitor, a notary, an administrator and a policeman forced open the door and demanded immediate payment of the current week's bill of $700. As it was a Saturday, and the banks were all closed, they assumed their refusal to accept a cheque would leave the Baron unable to meet their demand and give them sufficient grounds to evict him. What they did not foresee was the fact that the Baron always kept a considerable quantity of cash in his suite and had no difficulty paying the bill, while informing them: 'I have no intention of moving unless I am forced to by official Cuban regulations and as a citizen of this country I expect foreigners to comply with the rule of law.' This referred to Mr Vaughn's American nationality.

Heini flew to Cuba with Fiona to try and persuade his brother to leave, but

Stephan refused. He even stayed during the revolution and assisted in the hotel's survival while Cuba became the first socialist state in the Americas.

When all the banks closed in 1959, the management approached Stephan with a request to loan the hotel some cash to tide them over the crisis. Apparently, he immediately agreed and presented them with $250,000 in crisp new bills. Some weeks later, when the money was returned by the specific permission of Fidel Castro, Stephan was appalled to discover the returned bills had already been in circulation. To a man who was almost as obsessed as Howard Hughes with cleanliness and the avoidance of germs, their acceptance was quite out of the question.

When Stephan finally arrived in Palm Beach in 1961, there was still no evidence that he had been under any pressure to leave Cuba or that he intended to stay away permanently. He and his family had been in the habit of making periodic visits to Europe and America and, as was their normal practice, they had left everything at the hotel including his black Rolls-Royce, whose wheels had become embedded in the sun-softened tarmac before the revolutionaries presented it to the British Ambassador. He also left a number of paintings, which Heini later reclaimed through the Swiss Embassy, and thousands of dollars-worth of jewellery. But the suspicions of the staff, initiated by a Jewish guest who had publicly accused Stephan of being a murderer, were confirmed, when they eventually discovered among his belongings an iron cross and an SS-officer's uniform folded neatly in a suitcase.

* * *

The Korean War, the closing of the Suez Canal and the Arab-Israeli wars all presented massive opportunities to ship owners, especially in the tanker business and for those with the facility for building and repairing their own ships. Heini enjoyed all these advantages but he failed to exploit his privileged position, allowing his rivals Aristotle Onassis and Stavros Niarchos to forge ahead and become owners of the world's largest private shipping fleets. As they never ceased reminding him, neither of them had been born with Heini's advantages or his available development capital. With his aunt Amélie soon to own a controlling interest in the giant Blohm & Voss, Germany's other major shipyard, there had been little to stand in the way of their combining their resources and becoming the world's most powerful fleet owners, except Heini's lack of business acumen and inability to avoid personal involvement:

After the war, Mobil Oil wanted to build five large tankers of 45,000 tons each with me. I told them that it was impossible unless they invested money in my Bremer Vulkan plant. I also worked out a way of keeping two places for myself in the shipyard. Mobil Oil sent a delegation with several experts and the general manager for Germany who was the former captain of a German submarine during the war. They wanted me to give up my two places in the shipyard.

There was a dinner party which I attended with Fiona. During the evening the manager of Mobil Oil told us that he had been stationed in La Spezia in Italy during the war and that they used to sink English ships just for fun. Fiona was furious. The dinner came to an abrupt end and I refused to give them the places in our shipyard, which they wanted. They left in a rage and the captain didn't even apologise. But they were unable to find another yard so they had to come back to us.

In 1957, Bremer Vulkan celebrated its 150th anniversary and it became obvious that Heini still harboured ambitions of inheriting all or part of his aunt's industrial empire. Considering the number of times Amélie had threatened her daughter with disinheritance and promised to leave everything to her nephew, it could hardly have been considered an unrealistic ambition and did nothing to improve his relations with his cousin Anita or her sons Federico and Claudio. At the launching of Amélie's ship *Fritz Thyssen* from her Blohm & Voss yard, Heini made a revealing speech:

> In the time of the Sputnik, we have to prove that we are not only a country of the economic miracle but also one that can produce a scientific miracle. Young scientists and technicians have to show us how we can produce more, cheaper. Therefore I would once again like to say how important it would be for our companies to work together. I think the Thyssen family has proved time and time again that it will not let itself be carried away by the stream of time. Sail well, *Fritz Thyssen*!

* * *

The shipping business obviously excited Heini. It was extravagant and glamorous but he lacked the financial courage and acumen needed to rival the likes of Niarchos or Onassis, who refused to accept him as a serious competitor. But he still enjoyed the social status of being a ship owner and Fiona displayed considerable enthusiasm for the then fashionable activity of launching ships. It was one of the few industrial events that profited from the presence of a beautiful woman who could easily attract international media attention while smashing a bottle of champagne across the bow of her husband's latest launching. Much to the annoyance of the Greeks, with her naval background, undoubted beauty and ability to perform for the cameras, Fiona succeeded in transforming Heini's image as a ship builder.

But perhaps the most conspicuous manifestation of their rivalry occurred in 1957 when Stavros Niarchos purchased the French Impressionist art collection of Edward G. Robinson for $2.5 million. Not only was it a sound investment but it assured Niarchos of an enormous amount of publicity which undoubtedly affected Heini's determination to create a superior collection to that of his competitor, in size if not quality.

Meanwhile, the Greek ship owner's image remained tarnished by his investment in cheap, war surplus 'Liberty' ships, while Heini hardly ever bought second-hand and usually had his ships built in his own yards. Starting with small vessels of around 10,000 tons, they gradually increased in size from 26,000 tons to 38,000, then on to 70,000 and 160,000 tons. At one point he would claim the total tonnage of his fleet to exceed one million tons but it all went wrong when he tried to build two 315,000-ton super-tankers in Portugal. Unfortunately, they were not very well built and were sold on by the shipyard when Heini refused to accept delivery. Far more successful were the two refrigerated banana boats he had built at Gdansk in Poland which were chartered by a firm in Ecuador that shipped the fruit to North America.

Niarchos would soon be operating more than eighty tankers among his fleet, while Heini's fleet never rose above twenty-six vessels of mixed use and his rival never ceased teasing Heini for his choice of land-locked Switzerland as a country in which to base his shipping company: 'Have you met my friend Heini Thyssen, he runs banana boats out of Switzerland.' For Niarchos, who was not a man who laughed easily, it was a great source of amusement.

Heini's shipping company, Suisse Outremer, did indeed have offices in Zurich but this was due to the fact that in his tax and nationality deal with the Swiss, Heini had promised to base his business within their country. In fact, apart from his various holding companies, his shipping business would represent the only active fulfilment of his promise.

* * *

While the Thyssen-Bornemiszas continued to negotiate for the remaining share of their inheritance, the Zichy-Thyssens had stayed relatively free of legal conflict. But in July 1957, Fritz's seventy-eight-year-old sister Hedwig went to court against Amélie. She claimed that due to the German currency reforms, her inheritance had become relatively worthless, while Amélie and Anita were now two of the richest women in the world and owed her DM 2 million in compensation. As Amélie had accepted Hedwig's hospitality at her home on the Tegernsee lake during Fritz's post-war incarceration, it was an indication of her lack of generosity that she had refused to compensate her sister-in-law. This was despite the fact that prior to his death, Fritz had assured Hedwig that he would pay her more money.

Amélie's refusal to honour this commitment may have been affected by Hedwig's illegitimacy, but in 1961, before a judgment could be achieved, Hedwig died leaving Amélie to direct her inexplicable embitterment towards her own daughter whom, in the true spirit of 'old' August, she would continue to threaten with disinheritance in favour of her nephew Heini.

According to Heini, Anita's sons, Federico and Claudio, felt sufficiently threatened to initiate a smear campaign against him, while her lover, Guillermo Winterhalder, made a conciliatory approach, insisting that the boys' derogatory accusations should be considered nothing more than unfortunate, youthful outbursts. He suggested they should not be taken seriously and that Anita, in particular, was doing everything in her power to reunite the family. For while Amélie and Anita had signed an inheritance agreement, Winterhalder and Anita were aware that it could still be reversed.

Apparently, Amélie's legal advisor, Dr Ellscheid, had been somewhat more forthright, advising his client that any such disinheritance on her part could lead to the disintegration of the entire Fritz Thyssen complex.

In fact, it seems quite likely and entirely in character that Heini would indeed have been encouraging Amélie to make him her sole heir. The profits from his Walsum mines would have certainly impressed her. Most of the mines could hardly hide the fact that they were now making remarkable, albeit state-sponsored profits. For the first time since the end of the war, the shareholders of the Ruhr mining companies pocketed dividends of an average 6.9 per cent in 1957, while the press revealed that Heini was taking 12 per cent dividends from his Walsum mine.

While the mine's exceptional profits had a great deal more to do with the hard work and diligence of Wilhelm Roelen than any input from Heini, it no doubt improved his image in the eyes of Amélie, which he capitalised on in his speech at her eightieth birthday. It was another subtle suggestion that the two families' Konzerns should be combined, couched in an unlikely claim for family unity:

Chapter VII: 1954–1967

You, dear aunt, helped Fritz through terribly difficult times; the reward was the reconstruction of the works. But there are new storm clouds, as we eternally have to battle against the powers of nature and man. The danger coming from the East has brought the European states somewhat closer. Only a tight Europe can survive and as it will comprise more people than America, it means the works units will have to become bigger. The Thyssen family has overcome past disputes and has become friendlier towards each other again. But we should do more than that and actively work together. We must do as our forefathers did from whom we have inherited so much. I hope this day will help us surmount past anger and prejudice, old injustices and mistakes. Happy birthday!

* * *

The avoidance of tax liability continued to dominate Heini's business policy, even in the running of the Erlenhof stud farm, which it would have been safe to assume was a sporting activity with little justification for state support. But it was with considerable ill humour that Heini reacted to an appeal from the Directorate for Thoroughbreds and Racing that, as Erlenhof had billed DM 500,000 in winnings and breeders' fees for 1958, Heini should admit to a profit in his tax return.

In a letter of 21 May 1958, Chales de Beaulieu very politely told Heini that since the Directorate had, six years earlier, managed to negotiate an agricultural

M.V. Fiona, *named after his third wife, and the latest addition to Heini's Swiss-based shipping company.*

style of tax status dependent on two consecutive years of losses, not one of the German studs had admitted to a profit. Apparently the tax authorities had warned Beaulieu 'in no uncertain terms' that they would cancel the arrangements unless they were presented with some admission of profit. Beaulieu insisted: 'Mr Breskes, the Chairman of the Directorate, therefore asks you urgently to see to it personally with all the powers at your disposal that the draft year end report for 1957 for Erlenhof GmbH be amended and be submitted to the tax authorities in a more positive form.'

Heini's sense of injustice was amplified by the fact that he and Fiona, apart from their attendance at the more fashionable meetings and their introduction to the Queen at Ascot, had, unlike Ivy and Theresa, no interest in the breeding or racing of horses. Unfortunately, he still insisted on dictating policy. This situation was compounded by the fact that his sister Margit, who continued to lease the stud and control the day-to-day running while investing millions in the acquisition of further studs in Norway, Kentucky, Ireland and France, considered herself an expert. Despite spending much of her time in South America, she insisted on overruling Adrian von Borcke, the legendary trainer who had been largely responsible for the success of the operation.

This soon resulted in negative stories appearing in the press. Heini was infuriated and unwisely chose to hold von Borcke responsible, although by this time Heini and Margit were already planning to replace him and even ordered him to train his own replacement. In a rather petulant manner Heini reminded von Borcke that he was still waiting for a promised report resulting from the 'long trip you made through South America to study racing and race courses'.

Like many trainers, von Borcke's protection against such owners was a highly developed sense of humour combined with the skilled use of imperceptible insolence:

> It would be great if you could wait a little longer, because your cousin Anita has in fact invited my wife Erika and I to go to San Roberto. I hope you have nothing against it and I thought we could go at Christmas and New Year by boat. We would be back at the end of January. On Friday I am flying with Orsini to Oslo. I hear from Margit that Fiona and you will be coming, which I am very glad about.

But none of them bothered to turn up to what they no doubt considered an unfashionable race meeting and Heini reacted grumpily to the headlines announcing Lester Piggot's victory on Erlenhof's Orsini with a curt telegram to von Borcke: 'About time too.'

Heini's mood lifted with the news that he had finally succeeded in his claim of DM 20,712 plus DM 666 interest as wartime damage compensation for the military use of Erlenhof. It was yet further insult to the heirs of Moritz James Oppenheimer whose claim for compensation in 1948 had been so strongly denied by Heini's lawyers:

> Erlenhof GmbH has expressly challenged the compensation claim from every legal point of view and particularly explains that it acquired the assets of the Erlenhof stud farm from the official receiver in the administration of the bankrupt property of the late M. J. Oppenheimer at a fair price and that there had been no misappropriation of the property which would allow the case to be treated in accordance with the compensation laws.[5]

The injustice was compounded when Emma Neuhof-Oppenheimer and her children were forced to withdraw their claim for restitution and obliged to accept a derisory settlement offer of DM 28,500 in 1953. But there would be some poetic justice after 1962 when von Borcke was fired and the front page of *Sport-Welt* announced Baron Thyssen-Bornemisza's sacking of the 'very popular trainer' who had given the Baron's father his first Derby win with Athanasius in 1933, his first year of ownership.

With the loss of von Borcke and the brilliant combination of Oskar Schmidt and Orsini, the stables went rapidly downhill. New trainers arrived from Chile and Argentina, but under Heini and Margit's ownership, Erlenhof fell to twentieth position of importance among German studs. Heini became increasingly determined to obtain planning permission for development of the land for housing and in 1978 the first of three major fires took place. During the third fire in 1988, several horses died and the police who had proved the fires to have been started deliberately, warned Heini and Margit that any further fires would result in criminal proceedings against them.[6]

*　*　*

While Baron Adolphe Bentinck had been of inestimable value in assisting Heini to reclaim the family fortune and continued to protect his wife's share of the inheritance, his political and diplomatic career was occupying an increasing proportion of his time. In 1956, he accepted the post of Deputy Secretary General of NATO before becoming Dutch Ambassador to London in 1958. Meanwhile Gaby had been enjoying a series of independent relationships. Having already given birth to a daughter Henriette in 1949, in 1957 Gaby had a son, Steven ('Steffi') who, judging from their correspondence, her Romanian lover, Ion

Ratiu, obviously considered to be his responsibility. 'Darling Gaby, We have each other, imperfect though it is, for keeps and we have this lovely boy whom we must help grow into a fine, self-sufficient man.'

Ratiu was a dapper, softly-spoken, handsome man, whose genteel demeanour did not always work in his favour. He was unflatteringly known to his countrymen as 'Mr Bow Tie' because of his English style. He was also married to Elizabeth Pilkington, the glass manufacturing heiress, with whom he had two sons.

Heini had permitted Ratiu to stay with Gaby in the 'Baby Home' at Villa Favorita but he did not approve of their relationship, particularly when, in Gaby's absence, he discovered Ratiu paying court to other women in the nearby Hotel Splendide. He even made a play for Josi Groh's wife. But what really annoyed Heini, who had also 'made a go for Claudine Groh', was Ratiu's use of his sister's money to subsidise his London-based Regent Shipping Line. He was relieved when, after a ten-year affair, Gaby finally left Ion Ratiu, who remained in contact with Steffi, while she re-established her relationship with the Polish aristocrat, Count Mieczyslaw Pruszynski.

* * *

On 7 July 1958, Fiona gave birth to her first child, Francesca Anna Thyssen-Bornemisza de Kaszón. Following months of extravagant preparation and enormous cost, Dr Rochat delivered the 7lb 5oz baby in his Monchoisy clinic in Lausanne. It was an unremarkable event apart from the fact that Francesca would remain the only child for whom Heini would admit responsibility, although he could not remember being present at his daughter's birth or making much contribution to her childhood: 'I must confess that her arrival had very little effect on my life. I continued to devote a great deal of my time and energy to business matters, leaving Fiona to look after Francesca and enjoy her independence.'

But Fiona had not married one of the richest men in the world to sit at home with a baby and within a very short time her craving for excitement and attention resulted in her enthusiastic return to a rich social life.

* * *

Heini had never experienced any difficulty convincing himself that sitting on the jetty of his house in Jamaica with his toes in the water was anything but a devotion to business; particularly when he was considering his tax position and paying his lawyers to share his concern. Roberto van Aken did not seem to be in any way surprised that while Heini was relaxing in his own private tropical paradise with one of the most beautiful women in the world, his new daughter and sufficient staff to ensure minimal expenditure of energy, he should be concerned with possible changes in his Swiss tax arrangements.

However, van Aken did admit that his personal friends at the local cantonal tax office had warned him that, due to federal pressure, Heini might indeed be obliged to revise his tax agreement. He did not remind Heini that it was the Swiss who had saved the family fortune; but he did point out that they had for some time been prepared to accept the fact that his 'stated' personal fortune had been SwFr 1,050,000 and his annual income SwFr 50,000 when they knew full well that the real figures were SwFr 37,000,000 and SwFr 3,300,000 respectively. Obviously, this exceptionally generous agreement could not last for ever.

Baron Adolphe Bentinck with Henriette and Steven.

Van Aken was well aware that the better equipped people are to pay their taxes, the less prepared they are to pay them and that the world is full of people who profit from the often dangerous and usually expensive activity of tax avoidance. Around this time, two specialists, Robert Genillard and Eric Pfaff, had visited Heini in Jamaica. It was in response to their advice that Heini discovered Bermuda, where in 1961 his new personal accountant, Riccardo Guscetti, incorporated Favorita Shipping. Heini would also choose Bermuda as the inheritance trust headquarters for his Thyssen-Bornemisza Group. This tropical paradise would eventually become the site of the family's most extravagant conflict.

* * *

Heini was still on the island when a particularly puzzling scandal occurred. Even though the headquarters of the August Thyssen Bank had been moved from East to West Berlin, it could hardly have been considered an ideal location for a bank and regardless of the money that the West German government pumped

Portrait of Fiona by Cecil Beaton for Vogue (copyright: Condé Nast Publications).

into Berlin by way of subsidies, it was difficult to explain the bank's success. In 1960, the August Thyssen Bank's annual accounts reported an increase in the balance from DM 684 million to DM 758 million, while the turnover was said to have risen from DM 46 billion to an astonishing DM 52 billion.[7]

Heini was staying at the Coral Reef Club when he received the news from Dirk Swart in Holland in October 1961, two months after the erection of the Berlin Wall, that evidence of a loss-making fraud by three of the bank's management had been uncovered. Heini would later claim the bank's losses to have been DM 60 million while sometimes his estimate rose as high as DM 800 million. But the true loss appeared to have been a far less spectacular DM 20 million, which could hardly have supported his claims of bankruptcy.

On 8 November, Heini and his directors were invited to attend a meeting with the Bundesbank in Frankfurt. Heini did not appear to have taken the matter very seriously and claimed to have attended wearing a Hawaiian shirt and Bermuda shorts due to the fact that he had flown directly from 'Jamaica' where he had no winter clothes. But having agreed to a DM 18 million loan from BVHS, to cover the banks' losses, no one seemed particularly concerned or prepared to explain why a bank that had been turning over DM 52 billion could not absorb the loss.

Heini's friend David Rockefeller, while marginally sympathetic, also expressed minimal concern: 'What a shame that you have had so much trouble because of the dishonesty of three employees in your bank. Please let me know if there is anything further we can do to be helpful.'

Meanwhile, Wilhelmus Groenendijk, who had been summoned to Berlin to clear up the mess, gave an equally confusing account of what had happened that included Berliner Handelsgesellschaft's receipt of a post-dated cheque from ATB that somehow led to the discovery that the bank had been involved in the financing of arms deals with Algeria, while Heini insisted that 'they spent money developing an automatic whisky chair, which raised a glass to your lips when you pulled a lever'. Even the judiciary appeared reluctant to take the matter seriously and none of the managers received sentences which involved them serving longer than six months in prison.

As a consequence of 'these breaches of trust', it was decided at a general meeting in November 1961 to move the headquarters of the bank from Berlin to Düsseldorf and to close the Berlin branch. To Heini, the August Thyssen Bank in Berlin had been a constant reminder of his father's financial involvement with leading Nazis and the Nazi Party and the longer it existed the more likelihood there was that someone would publicly reveal its wartime activities. There also appeared to have been some suspiciously high profits which may not have withstood scrutiny. But the next chapter in the bank's history was even more confusing.

In 1962, 50 per cent of the share capital of ATB was transferred to the Berliner Handelsgesellschaft in Frankfurt (the original recipient of the post-dated cheque that had initiated the scandal), thus creating the Berliner Handels- und Frankfurter Bank (BHF-Bank). Meanwhile, the bank continued to grow with further branches being opened in Duisburg and Walsum, both of which were in the Ruhr, close to Thyssen AG. It was also noticeable from the bank's annual reports that both the chairman of the board of Thyssen AG and the chairman of the supervisory board of the Thyssen Bornemisza Group retained their seats on the advisory board of the bank.

Ten years later, the remaining 50 per cent share in the August Thyssen Bank would be transferred to the BHF-Bank, yet the denial of any financial connection between Thyssen AG and the Thyssen Bornemisza Group would continue, despite Heini's eventual replacement on the board of BHF-Bank by his son Georg and the fact that the bank continued to make loans to Heini. The Thyssens, in one form or another, were involved with the bank until 28 March 2003, less than one year after Heini's death, when both his son Georg and Dr Stein of ThyssenKrupp AG suddenly and simultaneously resigned from its board.

BHF-Bank has persistently refused to comment concerning their relationship with ThyssenKrupp AG, the Thyssen Bornemisza Group, and particularly the August Thyssen Bank and its Nazi past, claiming that their historical archives 'do not go beyond the 1950s'.[8]

ThyssenKrupp AG refused to grant access to their archives or even comment on the existence of such incriminating records of the Thyssens' financial collaboration.

* * *

Heini liked to give the impression that by this time he was already a major art collector but in the twelve years between 1955 and 1966 he would purchase only 108 paintings. The term 'major collector' would assume a greater degree of accuracy when his rate of acquisitions later rose to an average of one painting a week. However, the fact that included among these paintings would be works by El Greco, Tiepolo, Titian, Canaletto, Zurbaran, Fragonard, Rubens and Palma Il Vecchio certainly convinced the old master dealers of his value as a client.

But not all Heini's artistic investments were purchased on the open market. Ever since 'old' August's purchase of his Rodin marbles, they had remained at

Chapter VII: 1954–1967   269

Landsberg Castle where, as the property of the Landsberg Castle Foundation, they had been carefully stored and protected throughout the war. At the end of hostilities there was no practical reason why the old man's wishes could not have been complied with and the marbles put back on display for the family's enjoyment; 'old' August having specified in his will that Landsberg be retained and preserved for that purpose. But since its use by Albert Speer and the Nazis, none of the family was disposed to either visit the castle, except for business meetings or family funerals, or spend money on its upkeep. However, Heini somehow managed to convince the foundation's board that his purchase of his grandfather's six Rodin marbles was a charitable contribution. The sixth was in fact only removed later by Heini from its place in the burial chamber after Amélie had, at her request, been laid to rest at Fritz's side.[9]

*   *   *

In 1961, Rudolf Heinemann managed to increase both the status and legitimacy of Heini's collection by the organisation of the National Gallery exhibition in London, 'From Van Eyck to Tiepolo. Pictures from The Thyssen-Bornemisza Collection'. With no mention of Rohoncz, this would also serve to re-brand the collection. The inclusion of Holbein's 'Henry VIII' guaranteed both public interest and media coverage while the director, Philip Hendy, excused himself by saying that the catalogue had had to be completed in less than a month and so had resulted in the production of 'a simplified catalogue, which is intended merely as a guide for the general public'. Thus Heinemann yet again avoided unwanted scrutiny of many of the paintings' questionable provenance.

By 1961, Heini had yet to invest in any work by nineteenth- or twentieth-century painters, giving the impression that he agreed with his father's claim that 'art finished in the eighteenth century'. In fact, Heinrich had invested in a considerable number of nineteenth-century works including seventeen by German painters, all of which Heini had quietly disposed of after the war. But in 1961, he bought a painting for what he would insist were 'political, anti-Nazi reasons'. While this may or may not have been the reason why he attended the Ketterer auction in May at the Villa Berg in Stuttgart with his 'beautiful young wife', it certainly was not the reason why he paid a record DM 39,000 for 'Young Couple', by the German expressionist Emil Nolde, whose work, along with fellow artists of the same school, had been banned by the Nazis for being 'degenerate'. The art dealer and Heini's new friend, Roman Norbert Ketterer, was delighted: 'It was an absolute world record at the time. There was a tremendous uproar in the auction room. Everyone sprang up in order to see who was paying so much for a Nolde. The press, radio and television reported the new record. It was so exciting. I'll never forget it.'[10]

Neither would Rudolf Heinemann who had accompanied Heini to the auction. Apparently, having enjoyed a good lunch, Heini had already dozed his way through most of the proceedings before Heinemann gently nudged him in the ribs and quietly asked him if he was intending to purchase anything. Heini's head raising from his slumbers was perceived as a bid by the auctioneer and the price continued to rise. Heini's head bounced off his chest two or three more times before he finally awoke to discover he had paid a world record price for a painting. But he was understandably confused how such a comparatively low price could be considered a world record, until he discovered he had purchased a watercolour.

*   *   *

The resulting publicity for Heini and what was still generally referred to as the Rohoncz Collection encouraged him to continue to invest in more 'Modern Masters' by Chagall, van Gogh, Heckel and Beckmann. He would also purchase a further twelve paintings by Emil Nolde.

It would not be the last time that an action beyond his control would influence his purchase of a painting. Many dealers were equally astonished when, in 1963, Heini purchased 'Brown and Silver I' by Jackson Pollock. At the time it was considered extremely avant-garde. It was also totally out of character and at odds with anything else in the Rohoncz Collection.

When Heini was originally shown the painting at Toninelli Arte Moderne in Milan he had no intention of buying and was only viewing it as a curiosity. But when it was explained to him that Pollock's death in a car crash in 1956 was caused by the artist's mistress treating him to oral sex while he tried unsuccessfully to concentrate on driving the car, Heini had to have the painting.

He continued to enjoy the process of buying both old and modern works of art but it would be many years before he would admit that his motivation had little to do with his aesthetic appreciation. For some time his increasing interest in the international art market was largely the result of his rivalry with Onassis and Niarchos, that would at times result in gladiatorial auction duels which, Ketterer delightedly admitted, could prove so costly for the buyer. 'When two fanatical art collectors come together at an auction, prices can easily climb over and above real values.'

This rivalry intensified when it became obvious how much the ruthless business methods and savage charm of the Greeks attracted Fiona. To her delight, Heini responded in 1963 by replacing his leased Cessna with his very own Lear Jet. Thus they became founder members of a new social elite which the media christened 'the jet-set', while Fiona claimed: 'That jet made Stavros Niarchos green with envy, until he got one too.'[11]

* * *

After the August Thyssen Bank crisis not only had Gaby and Margit demanded more regular and reliable figures from Heini but they went as far as insisting that financial controllers from the by now hugely successful Thyssen AG (which until 1973 was still officially called August Thyssen Hütte) sit in on their family meetings. While this may have reflected their lack of faith in Heini's honesty and his managerial abilities, it may also have been another indication of the financial connections between Thyssen AG and the Thyssen Bornemisza Group. Whatever the basis for such an arrangement, Heini appeared to have had little choice but grudgingly to agree, although it did nothing to improve his relationship with his brothers-in-law.

This threat to his independence and increasing demand for transparency encouraged Heini to settle his sisters' inherited proportion of the Kaszony Family Foundation and in December 1961, he offered them Dfl 45 million each, plus a direct participation in Thyssengas of 12 per cent each. It was to be known as the Thyssen-Bornemisza Family Inheritance Agreement.

A rather poignant telegram from Maud Feller, once considered the most beautiful and elegant woman in Berlin, to Heini at 'Thyssen Chalet' in St Moritz indicated that Maud may also have considered it a propitious time to renegotiate her apanage but it was probably more the result of her inability to cope with her financial affairs: 'It's a scandal the way you are having your presence denied when I phone. Do you think that everybody has as much money as you do? The hotel is closed, I have no food, no telephone, no water, no money. You have SwFr 20,000 in your cellar; I don't even have SwFr 50 per week. It's no way to carry on.'

But while there may have been a degree of self-interest motivating his actions, Maud had in fact continued to receive Heini's financial support since his father's death. Meanwhile, van Aken, with some justification but little chance of success, suggested that Maud be put under guardianship.

In April 1963, Stephan woke up to the fact that another agreement was imminent and in a letter from Coconut Row in Palm Beach, optimistically requested a renegotiation of his share, his argument being that his original agreement had only been provisional. But Heini's rejection was resolute and in September of the same year, seventeen years after the death of their father, the Thyssen-Bornemisza Family Inheritance Agreement was finally signed between Heini and his sisters. In settlement of their shares in HAIC, BVHS and Press and Rolling Works Reisholz, Gaby and Margit each received a cash payment of Dfl 32.75 million, which was Dfl 12 million less than the previous year's offer. Heini justified this reduction by saying that there had been a downturn in the economy and even managed to convince them of their good fortune that the payout was so generous.

In addition to the cash they also retained 12 per cent of Thyssengas, 12 per cent of Walsum and shares in Bremer Vulkan and the Flensburger Shipbuilding Company, which continued to give them yearly dividend payments. But it would still be another twelve years before they received the final cash balance from the sales of Thyssen Gas and Waterworks and the Walsum coal mine. For the mine alone they received DM 15 million each, while overall Margit and Gaby each received around DM 60 million for relinquishing the majority of their interests in the Kaszony Family Foundation.

* * *

Meanwhile, Heini and his management continued to put together a deal whose success he would claim to have determined his eventual severance from his involvement in German industry and sale of all his German holdings. The main purpose of the deal was to profit from the piping, distribution and sale of Dutch natural gas to Germany. To this end Heini sold half of the capital of his company Thyssen Gas and Waterworks for DM 55 million to the Netherlands Petroleum Company (NAM) in which Esso and Shell each held 25 per cent of the shares. They also agreed to construct a pipeline from Holland to Duisburg in order to supply the Thyssen network which had originally been developed by 'old' August for the distribution of gas from the Ruhr coking plants.

The deal provided an excuse for bibulous celebrations:

> Details of the deal were worked out in Bonn where each country had a mission. We then had a big meal followed by cigars dipped in rum and lots of brandy; it was absolutely disgusting. I got very drunk and spent the night in a small room. I woke up the next day with a terrible hangover. We finally got the licence and I went to Haarlem to sign the contract.
>
> The next morning, I had a meeting with my managers and some of the Ruhr directors. It was followed by a big luncheon attended by the representatives of Germany's industry. The night before, I had taken my executives out on a spree as we had a hard day ahead of us and were likely to encounter heavy criticism. We went to a nightclub and got back very late. I

told them to look absolutely exhausted at the meeting and to stutter and stammer so that hopefully we would be treated sympathetically but we were still accused of having betrayed Germany by signing the contract.

Although an attempt in 1964 by the Ruhr industries led by Hans-Günther Sohl of Thyssen AG to prevent the sale of Dutch gas to Germany failed, it certainly succeeded in increasing Heini's injured pride resulting from his failure to gain control of Thyssen Hütte; a situation that was exacerbated by the fact that, as a member of the founding dynasty, Heini found himself being accused by 'mere management' of having betrayed Germany.

A special assembly was convened in Düsseldorf to promote German coal, which I had to attend. I told them I was in favour of the combined use of gas and coal for greater efficiency which made them very angry as they thought the importation of Dutch gas would be a disaster for the German coal industry. Herr Dütting, the head of the German coal sector, who was also Secretary of State, stood up and raised his glass toasting 'This is to the destruction of Mr Thyssen'. I told him I hoped he had enough strength to destroy me and he died shortly afterwards from a heart attack.

Eventually a compromise was achieved when, in 1965, Shell and Esso announced that they would also acquire a 25 per cent interest in Ruhrgas, a company owned by thirty-three of West Germany's principal coal and coke producers and a further 25 per cent of the German natural gas industry. But it did little to improve Heini's relationship with German industry with which, despite his claims to the contrary, Heini was still involved through his mines and steel manufacturing companies.

*   *   *

Heini claimed that Fiona liked to justify her and her mother's constant striving for publicity by insisting they were only doing it to improve his image. It was their efforts in 1962 that had resulted in Alan Whicker, the British celebrity documentary-maker, devoting a whole TV programme to the 'Model Millionairess, Fiona Thyssen'. The first thing Heini knew about it was when he stepped out of his Lear Jet to be embraced by Fiona who whispered in his ear, 'Be careful what you say and don't swear. I'm wearing a microphone for a TV documentary.'

What she did not tell him then was that she was also pregnant by another man.

While the media continued to shower Fiona with attention, she was listed as one of the eight most elegant women in Europe and a subject of a major photo report only a few weeks before the birth of her son. But her somewhat hypocritical quotes to the press already indicated that the relationship was not going well.

> Villa Favorita is like a super-duper hotel. Heini locks himself in his office and is unaware of the tremendous number of people who visit us. We have little privacy, let's face it. At Lugano, I have no social obligations of my own. I didn't want to have a big house in Paris. I didn't want to be the leader of the international set. I didn't want to be one of the ten best-dressed women. The thing is not to be too intelligent. Everything goes much easier. When Heini and I are out and he is flirting abominably with someone, I eat and drink and dance and pretend not to notice. But when we go home, I make a scene.[12]

In fact, both Heini and Fiona had been involved in other relationships from early in their marriage.

> While Fiona cheated on me, I was seeing Diana von Buch and Paola de Liège, who is now the Queen of Belgium. Paola was very bored in the Belgian court and I was not her only flirt. Fiona gave a dinner for Paola's husband Prince Albert of Belgium in St Moritz which Theresa also attended. So there were two Baroness Thyssens and I was flirting with another woman. Prince Albert was totally confused asking who was who and how it all fitted together.

By the time the Whicker programme was screened in May 1963, Heini and Fiona were already living separate lives with Fiona spending an increasing amount of time in St Moritz. Heini was convinced the child she was bearing was not his, despite a subsequent blood test: 'I'm sure the doctor was bribed to tamper with the sample and say I was the father.'

On 15 June 1963 in Lausanne, Fiona gave birth to a son, Lorne Johannes. Initially, Heini and Fiona behaved as if they were leading a happily married life and even said they were planning to have more children. In press interviews Fiona insisted that after a life of breathtaking extravagance she was 'still very much the down-to-earth British girl' she had been when she married Heini seven years previously:

> I don't differ very much from the average British mother, other than the fact that the children can travel with me everywhere. We are a close-knit family. We always have lots of guests coming and going and my husband's business associates to entertain. Villa Favorita is a beautiful spot for the children and they love it. I'm quite sure Chessy and Lorne will not be spoilt by wealth. I think one of the most rewarding things for a woman is being a mother.

Heini appeared to have been able to chose when to forget his own infidelity. He also realised that there was a certain continuity in the promiscuous behaviour of all his wives. He was quite philosophical in accepting responsibility for their behaviour, although his explanation also suggested a certain degree of misogyny resulting from their inability to satisfy each other sexually.

Francesca's first exposure.

Our relationships gradually deteriorated to the point where living together became unpleasant and difficult. You cannot change people and I made the mistake of thinking I meant everything to them. Furthermore, none of them had a wonderful character, full of patience, understanding and determination. Fiona was not insecure. She was stupid, good-natured and ravishing. She listened to Kapi Badrutt's advice about how one should enjoy life and started travelling on her own. Eliette, Herbert von Karajan's wife, and Barbara Goalen were also partly responsible. Fiona and Barbara once went to Rome and made a bet to see who could sleep with the most men. They were like spoiled children, spoiled by life and especially by me. It may be partly my fault because I was completely absorbed by my work and my companies. I suspected that Fiona was having a fling with other men but I wasn't aware that she was having an affair with anyone in particular.

While neglect may have been a contributing factor to the breakdown of his relationships, it was more the result of Heini's short attention span than of his commitment to business and his motivation was certainly more emotional than material:

I gave my wives everything I could and made them feel they played an important role in my life. To me fidelity represents more than a purely physical concept. I am talking about women who stop confiding in you and being your friend and who forget that you both made a commitment and have common interests. I am talking about loyalty. Once that has disappeared physical infidelity follows as a consequence. I always knew when my wives were no longer faithful and from then on, they meant nothing to me. I lost all emotional interest in them and detached myself without suffering too much. I had never tried to force anyone to love me or share my life. I cannot live alone. I have to have someone to love.

Fiona later claimed her decision to file for divorce in January 1964 was the result of Heini's affair with Diana von Buch rather than her relationship with the American film director Shelley Reynolds or her subsequent admission that he was her lover, Lorne's father and the man she wished to marry.

Predictably, it was only a matter of time before Fiona was explaining to the press her reasons for their divorce. She blamed his neglect on the pressure of his work while complaining: 'I was there to be shown off as the lovely wife, in the right jewels and the right clothes.'

She also claimed that they had been trying to patch things up, while admitting that she may also have been over-indulging in excessive nightlife.

* * *

Of far greater concern than any emotional accusations or admissions of responsibility was the settlement. Considering the irrefutable evidence of

Heini with Fiona and Francesca in St Moritz.

Chapter VII: 1954–1967 277

Fiona's promiscuity, her life-long, index-linked annuity seemed remarkably generous. For despite the pre-nuptial agreement, Fiona received sufficient reward for her to remain comfortably rich for the rest of her life, or as long as she remained single. An act of alimonial generosity that succeeded in both continuing to control his ex-wife's life while symbolising her ex-husband's financial virility:

> In Fiona's case, the divorce was more complicated because she had the Nepal emerald which I had bought at Arpels. It was a wonderful emerald. She had participated in the purchase of the necklace by contributing some of her jewels. When we divorced, I would have had to return the value of the jewels to keep the necklace. Instead, I gave her my chalet Chesa Alcyon in St Moritz which she sold to Gianni Agnelli. In Theresa and Nina's case, I was the one who filed for divorce but with Fiona it was the other way round because she wanted to marry someone else and I agreed. However, Shelley didn't marry her in the end; he only wanted to be Baroness Thyssen's lover, not her husband.

Through her Delphina Trust (Liechtenstein) Fiona was to receive within ten days of the decree absolute a payment of SwFr 2 million. Within twelve months, a second payment of SwFr 820,000. After twenty-four months, an annual index-linked annuity of SwFr 120,000, payable in advance, during her lifetime or until remarriage. In case of Fiona's remarriage, Heini was to make a final lump-sum payment to her trust of SwFr 1.2 million if she remarried within five years, SwFr 1 million if she remarried within five to ten years, and SwFr 800,000 if her remarriage took place within ten to fifteeen years. She was also to be paid an additional index-linked annuity of SwFr 24,000 per annum from 1966 to 1973 and one of SwFr 12,000 per annum from 1973 to 1988.

Then there was the jewellery; the campaign medals of any financially successful divorce. Fiona received fifty-six items amounting to $1.5 million in value. These included a necklace of forty-seven pearls with platinum clip worth $150,000, one marquise diamond ring weighing 25.53 carat with platinum mounting and two baguettes at $165,000, as well as one platinum-mounted emerald and diamond necklace with matching bracelets worth $580,000.

Fiona was also awarded a bullfighting painting by Goya that no doubt reflected her attraction to bullfighters, although it was to remain in the gallery, a Monet which she was entitled to sell, and a sculpture by Marino Marini.

While Fiona was to retain custody of the children, Heini was awarded visiting rights amounting to a maximum of three months a year; a privilege which he was unlikely ever to have fulfilled. He was to pay maintenance of

SwFr 1,000 per month for each child, up to their full twenty-fifth year, plus medical and illness expenses exceeding SwFr 2,000 per year, as well as education costs in excess of SwFr 500 per month each.

Heini also consented to Fiona's continued use of his title, which seemed a somewhat hollow act of generosity because as a Swiss citizen even his own use of the title was questionable.

* * *

While Heini liked to give the impression that he had accepted financial responsibility for Lorne, despite both he and Fiona accepting the fact that Shelley Reynolds was the father, it appeared that Fiona actually remained insistent that Heini was Lorne's father until after their divorce settlement. Meanwhile, Heini hired an astonishingly inept private detective to trail Shelley in the vain hope that he could prove him to be having an affair with his wife.

Finally, on 11 July 1964, according to the *Daily Express* in London, they announced their divorce in appropriate style from the bridal suite at the Hilton Hotel in Madrid. Fiona had just broken off her fiesta holiday at the Pamplona bull festival. He drank whisky, while she drank vodka. The impression they gave was one of casual, almost light-hearted acceptance of the inevitable. But having escaped, this time accompanied by her children on yet another holiday, to Alligator Head in Jamaica, it soon became apparent that Fiona was far from happy with her settlement. Particularly when Heini was quoted in the press as being proud of having achieved a settlement so 'cheaply'. Later he admitted she had expressed her true feelings in numerous letters to him. 'Basically, Fiona felt bitter and resentful and genuinely believed she had been badly treated, claiming that the settlement put her on a level with second-rate divorced actresses. She was particularly dissatisfied with the children's allowances when compared to that of children from comparable homes and argued that Francesca would be forced to curtail her friendships with her wealthier friends.'

Heini's friends and rivals also fuelled Fiona's dissatisfaction. Specifically Stavros Niarchos who could not resist claiming to be astonished that Heini had failed to provide Fiona with a suitable home or sufficient funds to enable her to exist without having to work for a living. There had also been comments concerning the conspicuous absence of her emerald necklace, whose enforced return had particularly hurt Fiona.

Heini admitted that he had blamed her for the divorce, although, as she pointed out, he had in fact instigated the initial move by telling her that he was in love with Diana von Buch. But he found it less easy to admit that Fiona, with considerable justification, had also accused him of being immature, vindictive, lacking a sense of responsibility and all too ready to blame others for his own shortcomings.

Heini was far prouder to reveal Fiona's admission that he possessed enormous charm when necessary, which no doubt contributed to the fact that, contrary to her post-divorce predictions, their friendship survived and Fiona remained remarkably loyal to Heini for the rest of his life.

* * *

Despite her claimed financial deprivation, Fiona appeared to have little difficulty in continuing to socialise with her customary extravagance. The following year she was reported to be enjoying dinner with John Galbraith at the fifteen-room apartment of Jackie Onassis on New York's Fifth Avenue, before attending an exhibition with Gianni Agnelli and going on to the Dove restaurant on Third Avenue which Jackie had transformed into a discotheque. In a magazine interview she admitted her difficulty in adopting a more austere lifestyle: 'Of course when you have been living at a certain standard for seven years you can't just stop living that way. I must have the best car, the best food, the best clothes if life is to be possible.'

In the same interview she also revealed her abhorrence of 'prudish men' and her even more revealing choice of antidote. 'I think if I ever found out that I had married a prudish man I would become a hooker.'

In 1967, while still only thirty-five years old, Fiona became the nineteen-year-old Alexander Onassis's, 'mistress, mother and priest confessor'.[13] His father was deeply disapproving of the relationship and made no secret of the fact, while Heini, who Aristotle considered to be in some way responsible, displayed remarkable sympathy. 'It was a beautiful story but ended tragically when Alexander died in a plane crash. Fiona was distraught and I always felt that her various personal problems developed as a result of her grief.'

This apparently generous reaction did not prevent Heini from displaying considerable hypocrisy when accusing Fiona of neglecting Francesca, flirting with her boyfriends and developing an increasingly decadent lifestyle. 'As she grew older, her behaviour got worse rather than better. She eventually did some really awful things and became completely immoral'.

While they remained genuinely fond of each other, it was Fiona's final act of commitment that Heini considered her ultimate and most unforgivable betrayal: 'She joined Alcoholics Anonymous and gave up drink and drugs, which transformed her but now she has become evangelical and preaches to everyone about

Fiona Thyssen in 1972 (photo: Henry Clarke, copyright: Condé Nast Publications).

the evils of drink. People who give up drink always seem to do that. It is so hypocritical.'

As Heini happily drank himself into pleasurable oblivion, Fiona gained the maximum advantage of her settlement by remaining single, sober and delightfully grand, wintering in Switzerland and summering in Greece. She also repaid her debt to society by capitalising on her experience, becoming a highly effective counsellor, working not with the rich and famous but the sons and daughters of the local population in Gstaad who succumb to the collateral chemical and alcoholic temptations.

* * *

Although Fiona always insisted that Heini's relationship with Diana von Buch had been a contributing factor in their divorce, he preferred to give the impression that he first met Diana in 1966.

> Still in her twenties, she lived in Florence and studied in Geneva. I remember she loved gambling and even though I hated it, I agreed to take her to the Campione Casino. Her father was fairly rich but she turned pale when she realised she had lost Fr Fr 20,000. She said how terrible it was and wondered how she was going to tell her father. I told her not to worry, that while she had been playing I had stolen one of her chips and got everything back in one game. But she just said, 'Fantastic, then let's go back and play some more.'

In fact, it was not gambling that he hated. Despite his theory that the rich prefer to lose because 'any idiot can afford to win', Heini hated losing.

But Heini was undoubtedly in love with Diana, while an added attraction was her father who lived in Argentina and ran Siemens, the German electronics giant, in South America. Unfortunately, despite Heini's lengthy courting, both his romantic and business plans suffered a serious setback when Diana refused to marry him. Her reason being almost more upsetting to Heini than her refusal. She said, 'Heini, I couldn't possibly marry you. You're far too rich. I would make your life a nightmare. I'd always be trying to get you to give all your money away to the poor or build hospitals or finance revolutions.'

Heini also admitted that while he got on very well with her father, the latter was very much against his daughter marrying a man who was nearly twice her age, particularly one who had already been married three times. However, for Heini her refusal only increased her attraction and he was furious when she suddenly left him to marry someone else. 'She got married to an Italian called Mauri who was a publisher and much smaller than her. She also had the bad manners to go out with him while she was still going out with me. To make matters worse she even married him in Lugano. Then she became a leftist and got involved in mysticism which I find a bore.'

* * *

Diana von Buch may have left Heini with a bruised ego but she also left him with a legacy which would have considerable influence on both the appearance of his paintings and Heini's development as an art collector. The Princeton and Columbia-educated Marco Grassi had returned to his native Italy to study fine art restoration at the Uffizi Gallery and the Central Institute in Rome before opening his own studio in Florence. It was there that he met Max von Buch and his daughter Diana, who introduced him to Heini.

> One day, she asked me whether a friend of hers could show me something. The friend turned out to be Heini Thyssen-Bornemisza. Obviously, I was familiar with his collection, which I'd seen several times. In fact, his father had even bought some of the works from my grandfather. Heini and Diana came to the studio and he was carrying a wooden polychrome renaissance bust under his arm. I immediately thought it was a fake, which put me in a difficult position. I had only just begun my career as an art restorer and was very honoured by the visit of one of the world's most famous collectors but I asked him for time to examine the work and prepare an appraisal.[14]

A week later Marco took the bust and the bad news to Lugano.

> I summoned up enough courage to tell him the bust was a fake but he still offered me the job of curating his collection. It was an incredible, if somewhat surprising offer. I told him I still had a studio in Florence, which I wanted to retain, and a number of matters that I would have to settle first. To my astonishment Heini agreed to all my terms and I started work almost immediately. I alternated between staying at the guest house in Lugano and my own studio in Florence. I didn't see a lot of Heini because he was hardly ever at home. At 1 o'clock Giorgio, the butler, used to bring me a sandwich and at 2 o'clock, I'd return to work. There was a huge amount of work to do because nothing had been touched for so long. It was a unique opportunity.

For Heini, who had minimal knowledge of painting or restoration techniques, to allow a thirty-year-old, zealous picture restorer free rein with minimal instruction or control was also a typically rash act.

* * *

Amélie's numerous suggestions that she was considering fulfilling 'old' August's dreams of a Thyssen steel dynasty by leaving Heini her vast Konzern had always been more of a threat to her own family than a serious promise to his. His lack of attention to business, playboy lifestyle and disrespect for the 'fatherland' prevented her from making such a commitment. She had also never fully

Chapter VII: 1954–1967

forgiven his and the Americans' attempts to seize Thyssen Hütte while Fritz remained incarcerated under US control.

Despite only being a Thyssen by marriage, Amélie had more of the true spirit of determination of 'old' August than any other member of the extended family. She had ruthlessly achieved a quite remarkable reconstruction of much of his Konzern while amassing an equally impressive fortune. On 25 August 1965 she died at Schloss Puchhof aged eighty-eight, and it was no doubt her indestructible family loyalty that ensured that her daughter, the Countess Anita Zichy-Thyssen, with whom she had squabbled for years, would be her sole heir and return from Buenos Aires to Munich doubly rich and twice as powerful while retaining little interest in anything or anyone apart from her many dogs.

Around the same time Arndt von Bohlen und Halbach, son of Alfried and the last Krupp, gave up his shares in his family Konzern in return for an income of $12 million per annum and spent the rest of his life, some twenty years, 'in a whirl of rhinestones and spangles', accompanied by his mother Anneliese, reigning over a court of young men until he died of an AIDS-related illness in the spring of 1986.[15] Ten years later the two legendary Konzerns of Thyssen AG and Krupp AG would unite under public ownership.

1 Lugamen nullitatis sententiae, Nullitatis matrimonii et dispensationes super ratio (De Lippe – Von Thyssen-Bornemisza), Sacra Romana Rota, 1968 (TBG Archives).
2 Article by Tom Rhodes entitled 'Nazis smuggled gold in Swiss diplomatic bags' in *The Times* (London), November 1996.
3 Letter from Amélie Thyssen-zur Helle at the Hotel Splendide in Lugano to Dr Heida and Dr Sanders, Board of Pelzer Family Foundation, 19 February 1958 (TBG Archives).
4 *Daily Express*, *Tanfield's Diary* and *Sheffield Telegraph* (all 17 September 1956).
5 Agreement between Paula Spiegler, née Oppenheimer, Dr Walter Oppenheimer and the Erlenhof Stud and Training Stables, Bad Homburg, 13 January 1953 (Bentinck Archives).
6 *Frankfurter Rundschau*, 25 January 1988, and *Taunus Kurier*, 6 January 1994.
7 Year end report 1960 regarding August Thyssen Bank, dated February 1961, signed by Messrs von Schwartzkoppen and von Tümpling (TBG Archives).

8   BHF-Bank merged with the Dutch ING-Bank to become ING-BHF-Bank in 1999 but was sold on to the Sal. Oppenheim Bank in 2004, a bank which has a history of co-operating with the Thyssens that stretches back to August Thyssen's acquisition of Gewerkschaft Deutscher Kaiser in 1883 (see Chapter I).
9   The seventh marble, 'Psyche', had been a gift from August to Fritz and is believed to have remained in the Zichy-Thyssen family.
10 Ketterer, p. 168.
11 Interview with Ronald Handyside, *Nova* magazine, 1965.
12 Interview with Susan Barnes, *Sunday Express*, 5 March 1961.
13 Fraser et al., p. 323.
14 Interview with Marco Grassi, 1988 (TBG Archives).
15 Schifano, p. 371.

Chapter VIII
1967–1981

The murder of his wife's lover ... The creation of the Thyssen-Bornemisza Collection

*Nothing sedates rationality
like large doses of effortless money.*
Warren Buffett

Unlike 'old' August, Heinrich's relationship with his workers was very straightforward. He refused to have anything to do with them; that was a task for his management. His lack of interest in his employees was matched only by his chosen ignorance concerning the mechanics of industry. It was an attitude Heinrich seemed to have successfully instilled in his son, who despite his apparent social ease and claimed socialist sympathies often echoed his father: 'One shouldn't get sentimental – it's not a good idea. I never visit a plant and avoid personal involvement, especially with the workers. Businessmen should take objective decisions, like financiers who buy and sell things without seeing them.'

So Heini was deeply unimpressed when, in 1969, the Social Democrats came to power in Germany under the leadership of chancellor Willy Brandt. But he was presented with an opportunity to minimise his relationship with the new regime by selling his Walsum coal mines to Ruhrkohle AG, a trust of nineteen companies set up as part of the federal government's endeavours to unite German coal production.

Prior to the sale, Heini had decided to avoid confrontation by appearing sympathetic with the socialists and giving the impression that his father had only operated coal mines at Walsum as a magnanimous act of employment opportunity for 6,000 miners; the daily output of 12,000 tons of coal being a mere by-product. No mention was made concerning profit or even the financial incentives involved in selling the mine, although his emotional claim to the miners' union loyalty was, even by Heini's standards, somewhat theatrical:

Union representatives explained that they were uncertain about working conditions under the German government and that they wanted the mine to remain in my hands. I was deeply moved and it was one of the rare occasions in my life when I cried. I stood up with tears in my eyes and a lump in my throat and walked out of the meeting.

What he failed to mention publicly was that the family retained 37 per cent of the mining rights in the area between Walsum, Dortmund and the Dutch border in case the political climate and market forces should encourage his reinvestment in coal mining some time in the future.[1]

The only other remaining piece of his grandfather's legacy and connection to his uncle's side of the family that Heini was prepared to admit to would also be affected by his unwillingness to remain involved in labour-intensive industry under a socialist government.

In 1965, a rationalisation had been carried out, which resulted in a 50/50 partnership between Thyssen AG and the Thyssen Bornemisza Group in Heini's Reisholz engineering company, then employing 8,000 people. Then, in 1973, when Mannesmann acquired Thyssen AG's interest, Heini decided to sell them his group's shares in Reisholz as well. It would be the end of his involvement in German heavy industry.

Typically, having agreed to attend a meeting of the various board members, lawyers and accountants to negotiate the price and conditions, Heini drunkenly agreed the price 'over a few drinks at the bar' with one of the Mannesmann directors, while everyone else waited patiently and pointlessly in the conference room:

> When I told the others that we had reached an agreement, they were shocked and started protesting: 'That's impossible. You don't know the details or the technology involved.' I told them I had agreed and the rest was up to them. We didn't give a damn about the details and had a few more drinks to celebrate as it had gone so well.

Heini remained hazy concerning the actual price that had been agreed. He liked to give the impression that the Group was considerably richer as a result. While there was no doubt it was, the asking price had actually been DM 90 million which had been decreased by DM 37 million by the time Heini got off his bar-stool.

He was even less keen to advertise the losses that the Group had sustained since 1965 when he had made a contradictory and inexplicable DM 25 million investment in Pintsch Bamag, a privately-owned, Frankfurt-based machine engineering company, which manufactured cranes, containers and other industrial installations. By 1967, the company's losses had nearly doubled, while Heini's overall policy of withdrawal from heavy industry and commitment to investment in fine art and gems was being encouraged by the new Baroness Thyssen-Bornemisza.

* * *

Born in São Paulo to a wealthy Brazilian banker father and a Scottish mother, Denise Shorto was the only one of Heini's five wives whom he conceded to be intelligent. After school in Montreux and college in America, she claimed to have studied art and literature at the Sorbonne for three years before further studies in Geneva. By then Denise spoke Portuguese, English, French, Italian and Spanish but after such an academic education she and her sister Penny had developed a surprising reputation as 'good-time girls' with a penchant for outrageous behaviour and 'fast living'. Their taste for very rich men and knowledge of press manipulation certainly appear to have been more than equal to that of Fiona. European newspapers, who were quick to appreciate her more fashionable, Bardot-like appearance, were soon comparing them: 'You would think the term "kittenish" had been coined expressly for her. Not a classical beauty [like Fiona] but "undeniably sexy".'[2]

Denise's appearance may have belied her intelligence but Heini's intended bride was still not appreciated by his mother, who considered the twenty-five-year-old, fake blonde 'sex-kitten' socially inferior to her son. Only Fiona gave the relationship her rather superior, public blessing: 'Denise is a very sweet and lovely girl. Both my children like her, so it's all very easy.'[3]

Unfortunately for Heini, he would fail to appreciate the inaccuracy of Fiona's description until after the wedding, for while Denise could undoubtedly have been considered 'lovely', she possessed an explosive temper of sufficient magnitude to successfully neutralise any degree of 'sweetness'. But by 20 November 1967, London's *Daily Express* had already announced their engagement, although they admitted: 'The wedding date is secret.'

Heini was quite certain where and when he first met Denise, although less so who he was with at the time.

> I first met Denise in 1967 in Gstaad. I was with a Syrian, or maybe she was Lebanese friend called Nana Niri or Zana Mousi. She was engaged to Franco Soldati, a friend of mine, who lived in Buenos Aires. She was

gorgeous. We went to Gstaad together for a big dance that the Shortos were giving. The mother and children had rented a whole restaurant. I went along as a gate-crasher. She wanted to know if I had already been married four times and I said only three. The next day, I sent her flowers; then I started going out with her.

Denise soon agreed to Heini's proposal of marriage but there was some delay while she refused to sign a pre-nuptial agreement. Eventually, in the naïve belief that 'being rich already Denise would be less financially demanding than my previous wives', the infatuated Heini accepted her refusal and after eleven months of gift-laden 'courtship' but only twenty-three days of engagement, the press were once again summoned to Lugano, on 13 December 1967, for the exchange of Heini and Denise's wedding vows.

Following the familiar complaints by the press at the brevity of the ceremony and subsequent lack of extravagance, the happy couple left for a two-month honeymoon and tour of the Far East in his Lear Jet. Heini always insisted that, despite the Vietnam War, they spent part of their honeymoon in Saigon, which seemed highly unlikely although the Swiss federal authorities had once suggested that he had been approached by a Russian agent with a view to being enlisted as a spy, an activity which would have certainly amused Heini and befitted his self-styled role as 'capitalist agitator'.[4]

They also visited the small island of Ilo Ilo to celebrate Vice-President Lopez of the Philippines' ruby wedding anniversary. There, Heini continued to indulge his anarchic sense of humour:

> When the celebrations were over, the Vice-President asked me whether he could return to Manila in my jet. The plane was already full, and we had to squeeze in his bodyguard with his machinegun and ammunition. Nevertheless, we managed to take off and I remember asking Lopez if he wanted us to provide his friends with an unforgettable memory of our departure. My pilot was highly skilled, but also great fun. He climbed the plane high up into the clouds and then dived back down towards the airport in complete silence with the engines closed down. As we came back over the runway, he slammed the throttles forward and re-ignited the engines, which made the most incredible bang. Looking back as we climbed up and away, you could see lots of terrified people lying on the ground. It was totally irresponsible and immensely satisfying.

* * *

It would not be long before Heini discovered that his marriage to Denise involved an expensive relationship with almost the entire Shorto family. Having inherited various Brazilian business interests, it seemed logical to develop their potential through his new family's connections. One such interest was a real estate company, Companhia Thyssen do Brasil, which had been founded by his grandfather:

> It consisted of warehouses for storing steel. But São Paulo had expanded so much that, by 1967, the warehouses were close to the centre of the city and worth a great deal of money. We sold them for millions of dollars, which unfortunately disappeared into the Coca-Cola business of my brother-in-law, Roberto Shorto, and I never saw the money again.

The 'business' consisted of the Coca-Cola concession for north-eastern Brazil, owned by the Shorto family. Initially, they had asked for $100,000 to bail out their financially troubled organisation. But having supplied the necessary capital injection, Heini soon discovered the cause of their financial difficulties: 'The mother was helping herself to company funds. I was pumping money in at one end and she was taking it out at the other.'

The besotted Heini honeymooning with Denise Shorto, the fourth Baroness Thyssen-Bornemisza.

Heini decided to buy the family out for $8 million and invest a further $20 million in development. Unfortunately, they decided they wanted more money and the whole deal collapsed. Heini lost his original investment and his valuable real estate, yet for some inexplicable reason he continued to do business with his brother-in-law Roberto and the family. But according to Heini, accusations of spectacular dishonesty would result in ever-increasing litigation for the entire period of his marriage to Denise and beyond.

* * *

During the breaks in their global travel schedule, Heini and Denise often preferred to return, not to the tranquillity of Villa Favorita but to the rich social life of St Moritz, a location they continued to share with Herbert von Karajan, Stavros Niarchos, Gianni Agnelli, the Italian helicopter manufacturer Agusta, the Aga Khan, the Shah of Iran and anyone else who could afford to land their private jets at the nearby Samaden airfield.

Heini also shared the resort with two ex-wives and their families. Although he had little respect for family responsibilities or interest in children, the pressure of their demands was increasing, particularly in the case of Heini Junior for whom his relationship was contractual.

> Heini Junior did well at school and Theresa and I were present when he received his diploma in 1968. Afterwards, we had lunch with him at the Hotel Vierjahreszeiten in Munich. Later, when he went to university in Zurich, I would see a bit more of him, although his mother was always between us. However, I think I spent more time with him on the whole than my father spent with me.

This was certainly not true in the case of his daughter Francesca, who would often be abandoned during school holidays by both her mother and her father. In comparison, the attention paid to Heini Junior was all too obviously disproportionate. If anything, the forty-four-year-old Theresa's protective relationship with her son increased, after her second husband, Prince zu Fürstenberg, died in 1969. Despite having had a further three children, the major concern in her life became her nineteen-year-old son Georg (Heini Junior) and his future control of the Thyssen Bornemisza Group. Meanwhile, Denise, unencumbered by the time-consuming inconvenience of children, adapted well to her new role as Baroness and wife to one of the richest men in the world and gave the press the impression that she had been born into her privileged position:

In Lugano, I always discuss the menu with the chef. I also love flower arranging. Then I might go for a ride in a motorboat or go shopping in Milan. I love Givenchy, Courrèges and Saint Laurent. It takes three weeks at the Paris couturiers to choose my spring clothes but I also use boutiques, as it's not so time-consuming.

Denise was also rapidly gaining a reputation for extravagance with her husband's money and legendary meanness with her own, whereas Heini remained capable of displaying both generosity *and* meanness. The latter was often difficult to detect when disguised with polite forgetfulness. This was evident from instructions he gave Groh on returning from a trip to India: 'I owe the Maharaja of Jaipur $14,120 but let's only transfer the money once he asks for it.'

But for those whose co-operation and subsequent discretion were of significant value, Heini suffered no such memory lapses. Such was the case with Franz von Marosy, the last remaining 'royal' Hungarian Ambassador to Spain, who had assisted Heini in confirming his fictitious title, Hungarian nationality and passports:

> My dearest Baron, I am deeply touched by your generosity and thank you from all my heart for your patronage, which enables me to continue the activities of this last and only free-Hungarian embassy for a little while longer. Our time knows few such truly seigniorial gestures and I appreciate your nobility, which is certainly also witness to your Hungarian blood. You have given me courage and trust in humanity again. As far as the transfer is concerned, it would be best if you could arrange it to my account at Credit Suisse in Zurich. God bless you and your family.[5]

* * *

There is little doubt that Heini enjoyed flying round the world in his Lear Jet with his new 'sex kitten'. But his constant absence and excessive drinking were beginning to become a source of considerable dissatisfaction among his directors. In 1969 his board of management began to demand that some form of corrective action be taken. Having overcome Heini's reluctance, they commissioned McKinsey & Company, the management consultants, to report on the state of the Thyssen Bornemisza Group, naïvely believing that the consultants would support them in their decision to persuade Heini to stand down. McKinsey upset their plan by including a damning criticism of the management, to which Heini reacted by firing the entire board. The situation became even more farcical when he was told that it was not within his power to make such a decision without the authority of the supervisory board.

Fortunately for Heini, the president of the supervisory board, Mr Meynen, the president of Akzo and former Minister of Defence of the Netherlands, who had been responsible for hiring McKinsey, decided, after a glass or two of whisky at the BVHS fiftieth anniversary dinner, to reverse his decision and authorised the sacking of the managers. According to Wilhelmus Groenendijk, this resulted in a boardroom fistfight.

Apart from their justified criticism of the management, McKinsey's appraisal of the Group's policy and results gave little cause for optimism. One of their first conclusions was that 'the highly complicated legal-financial-ownership structure of the Group has given rise to undue emphasis on tax and legal – rather than commercial and economic factors in decision making'.

The board probably did not need to be reminded that past Group performance had been poor, the management lacked effectiveness, outlook for current businesses was unpromising or that the substantial task facing management required 'a major top-level commitment to change'.

The report's observations concerning turnover and profitability were even more damning. It pointed out that most gains had been the result of acquisitions rather than internal trading, while overall profits of TBG had declined since 1960. Apparently, 'by nearly any measure, the Group's performance compares unfavourably with other large groups and the average performance of industry in general'. It also exhibited 'few generally accepted concepts, institutions, systems or skills'. In short, it was a shambles. The report also accused the management of defensively preserving rather than creating wealth, to the point where 'the Group is faced with a problem of unusual proportions. Performance is declining and has reached unacceptably low levels.'

While the consultants admitted that a sale or merger would be the most obvious cure, they accepted the fact that this course of action would be unacceptable to Heini. It was suggested that 'Baron Thyssen should withdraw entirely from direct involvement' (this being one of the few opinions which they shared with the management). He should then 'concentrate on leading long-term Group development rather than participating on the boards of operating companies'.

It is interesting that McKinsey also recommended the appointment of Josi Groh to serve on the 'strategy and policy committee', presumably to keep an eye on Heini, who was to chair the committee. He was the only other person, apart from Heini, who was named in the report. But perhaps the most important recommended appointment was that of an executive vice chairman 'to serve as Chairman and make important decisions in Baron Thyssen's absence'. This was the role which Heini's son Georg would eventually fill.

It was hardly surprising that McKinsey's suggested short-term aims were to 'stop the profit drains quickly', to 'negotiate the sale, as in Walsum and Thyssengas, of several units of the group' and to 'systematically and energetically identify new business areas to invest in'.

On the last page there was a somewhat puzzling recommendation: 'Establish, in specific terms, the role and position of BVHS and ATB in the new structure.'

It was the only reference to banking in the whole report.

* * *

The following year, what was left of August Thyssen Bank was amalgamated with BHF-Bank, while the banking interests of Bank voor Handel en Scheepvaart were sold to Nederlandse Credietbank, which in turn would be taken over by the Chase Manhattan, a bank with previous connections to the Thyssens and the Third Reich, having kept their Paris branch open throughout the Nazi occupation with impunity.[6]

This move out of banking affected the end of any further 'investment' in Pintsch Bamag and resulted in the company's liquidation and losses to TBG of DM 70 million. With the takeover of BVHS by the Credietbank, the group needed a new holding company and on 31 December 1970, the Thyssen Bornemisza Group NV was officially formed. However, it did little to protect 'Heini Thyssen, the forty-nine-year-old aging playboy' from media criticism, while 25,000 Pintsch Bamag creditors waited for their claims amounting to DM 200 million and 4,000 employees faced an uncertain future.

The Hamburg newspaper *Welt am Sonntag* stated: 'Heini Thyssen does his own thing but is business-wise not very professional. Most of his money comes from the Thyssengas AG, which originates in the gas and water works created by his grandfather August and which makes profits through the sale of Dutch natural gas.'

Der Spiegel qualified him as a 'billionaire' but accused him of 'selling important pillars of his grandfather's empire in order to support his lavish lifestyle'.

Even the rather conservative economic paper *Der Volkswirt* reproached him for having 'early capitalist attitudes', because 4,000 employees at one of his enterprises were confronted with 'the unidentifiable arbitrariness of a single person'.

Attention was also brought to the August Thyssen Bank scandal and the sale of Bank voor Handel en Scheepvaart. Finally, the media were unimpressed with his building of two 12,375-ton ships in East Germany:

> He said he gave the orders to the GDR because the prices and conditions were more favourable there than in his own shipyards. Yet he received practically all the dividends from his West German and international companies in Holland tax-free, because according to Dutch law, dividend income and the profits from multi-national holding companies from sales in Holland are free of tax.[7]

Heini's personal absence from Germany and preferential tax situation in Switzerland was also examined and his arrogant reactions recorded: 'Why should I go anywhere else when I am doing so well in Holland and Switzerland?'

Meanwhile, his New York doctor, R. E. Rees-Pritchett, gave Heini little cause to celebrate. No doubt torn between losing a valuable patient either by the unpopular diagnosis or the ravages of alcoholism, he diplomatically pleaded with him: 'You still have evidence of a fatty liver due to excessive alcohol intake. You drink more alcohol than is desirable. Once again I would urge that you reduce your alcohol consumption substantially, ideally you should give up alcohol altogether, until your test returns to normal and then resume alcohol to a limited extent, such that your liver test will remain normal.'

* * *

Heini's art collecting was also proving unsatisfying, as he finally realised that he was not so much collecting art, as paying for pictures that someone else was choosing: 'On many occasions Rudolf Heinemann sold marvellous works of art to museums without ever offering them to me. As is true of all dealers, he decided beforehand who should buy what. I am grateful for his years of association and his advice but I am a man who likes to make his own decisions.'

But what really angered Heini was that he was being sold second-class goods, although he later admitted that he was generally not prepared to pay the 'super' prices required to get the best, museum-quality paintings: 'Price is my prime consideration when buying a picture, followed by condition.'

However, apart from 'Sunset – Laura, the artist's sister' by Edvard Munch, which, Heini claimed, 'I bought myself', he continued to allow Heinemann to dictate to him, possibly because he lacked the knowledge and confidence to decide for himself. Even at auction Heini usually had others bid on his behalf.

In the case of a collection of prints by Toulouse-Lautrec that came up for auction at Kornfeld and Klipstein in Berne in 1973, Roman Ketterer even managed to get Heini to agree to let him bid without restriction, telling him:

> You can trust me that I will stop when the price is no longer reasonable. But you have to understand that you might regret it for the rest of your life if you now fail to get a piece just because you remain a few thousand Francs under the final bid. You have to buy these pieces. Never again will you be able to acquire examples of such quality, such a good state of preservation and such a beauty of colour.[8]

Simon de Pury, Sotheby's auctioneer and subsequently Heini's curator, seemed quite prepared to endorse the concept that bidding for a set of prints with someone else's chequebook was an act of selfless heroism:

> These pieces are still today the most beautiful and rare masterworks of graphics that one can imagine. They form one of the many highlights of the Thyssen-Bornemisza Collection. They were acquired during bidding matches that count amongst the most exciting that I ever witnessed. Since then, I have been able to attend most of the auctions in the world. But I still believe that the fight between Roman Ketterer and Harry Fischer will remain for me the most exciting event that I have witnessed in the auction scene.[9]

Heini was also reminded that the dealers' powers extended beyond the salerooms when he bought, 'Autumn landscape in Oldenburg' by Karl Schmidt-Rottluff from a friend: 'Ketterer, who was my usual dealer, wanted to sue him for interfering in his business. I told him that if he filed a suit against my friend, I would never buy anything from him again.'

What Heini failed to mention was that Ketterer had already accepted the picture on assignment when Heini decided to negotiate directly. Despite his posturing, Ketterer's threat appeared to have worked as the name of his gallery still appears in the painting's provenance.

In spite of the control affected by his dealers, Heini managed to acquire some important works. In 1967 there was a nude by Chagall as well as a Boucher, although its Rothschild provenance impressed Heini more than the painting itself. In 1968, he also acquired 'The Madonna and Saints with Saint Rosalina of Palermo' by Bartolomé Esteban Murillo, which illustrated his concern with price: 'It is one of the best Murillos but this painter wasn't in fashion when I bought it, so it was relatively cheap. It's a great picture.'

He also bought 'The Yellow Flowers' by Henri Matisse, which mysteriously disappeared from the records of the collection, with no indication that it had been sold, given away or lost, and 'Young Girl Seated in an Interior' by Auguste Renoir. Valued at $700,000 when it was eventually inherited by Alexander, it seems unlikely to have been genuine.

* * *

In 1969, he bought another Tintoretto of the same subject as the previous year, 'Portrait of a Senator', from his sister Margit, perhaps in the hope that at least one of the two would be genuine. Almost the most expensive work Heini ever bought was 'Crucifixion Group with Mary, Saint John and Angels' by Ugolino di Nerio; the purchase was followed by the panel's illegal export from Italy. In May 1969 it was reported that Baron Thyssen and seven others were accused by Italian customs police of 'illegal export of italian art' valued at $500,000. The accusations followed an investigation by Rudulfo Siviero, the head of a special state unit created shortly after the war to trace and return works of art taken by foreign troops. Included among the seven accused were the seventy-year-old Florentine art dealer Arturo Grassi and his two sons, Marco, an art restorer, and Luigi, also a dealer. Heini was accused of complicity in the clandestine export of two works of art, the Ugolino 'Crucifixion' and 'Madonna and Child with Saint Catherine and Angels' by Francesco di Giorgio Martini.

Due to the potential embarrassment to the Italian art-dealing establishment, which had been involved in the illegal export of art for years, the investigations proceeded at a snail's pace and it was not until 14 March 1972 that the *New York Times* reported: 'One of Switzerland's best-known businessmen was indicted on charges of having smuggled art treasures.'

Their value had by now risen to $1 million. Meanwhile, *Welt am Sonntag* claimed that the extent of the smuggling included some twenty works over a period of seven years and that Grassi senior had admitted: 'Thyssen bought the fourteenth-century decorated woodcarving "Christ's Descent from the Cross" from me for DM 140,000. He sent an estate car to Italy for the dismantled 'Christ' and we reconstructed it in Lugano.'

The paper noted the discrepancies with the Baron's own testimony: 'I bought the two works in Switzerland and therefore do not see why I should have to return them.'

Heini even tried to introduce an element of sarcasm into the proceedings when he said: 'I hope that none of the pictures in my gallery was painted in Switzerland. They were all painted abroad. I buy the stuff in Switzerland and the United States, but how it gets there I don't know. I can't check all that.'[10]

Despite the fact that everyone was prepared to admit that the pictures had been removed from Italy without permission from the relevant authorities, Heini claimed: 'They couldn't come up with definite proof, so the case was suspended.'

The fact that Heini made a number of generous, voluntary contributions to the Italian establishment might have affected their judgment: 'In 1972, I restored some of the frescos in the San Marco convent. When the flood broke out in Florence, I also donated millions of lira to various flood relief organisations and art foundations in the town.'

In addition, he donated computers and environmental control machinery for the Vatican's Sistine Chapel and built them a huge laboratory and workshop for the restoration of their statues.

Meanwhile, Marco Grassi blamed the whole affair on his brother's vengeful American ex-wife, while Heini insisted that 'the whole thing will blow over and people will forget'; which they did.

Soon the painting was being referred to by the fine-art establishment as 'The Thyssen Ugolino'.[11]

* * *

On the evening of 7 March 1970, at the Dutch Embassy in Paris, an event took place which would result in the emergence of a new black sheep in the family.

Wishing to speak to Baron Adolphe, Steven Bentinck had been knocking on his door for some time. Family protocol forbade him from entering his father's room without a reply but eventually instinct overcame manners and he entered, only to find his father dead on the floor. Frightened and shocked he returned to his room and 'waited for his mother's screams', which came all too soon and 'lasted for years'.[12]

With the death of his surrogate father and the absence of his real one, the confused thirteen-year-old was left in the doubtful care of his scatty and often hysterical mother. While being expected to assume the role of 'the man of the family', he was constantly and contradictorily reminded how he was still 'only a child', while his mother's lovers and Steven's hated uncle Heini all tried to act as mediators.

The resulting chaos was evident in the two wills Gaby made in Lugano in 1970. The first made her children 50/50 heirs with the proviso 'if something happens to me, Steven should be looked after by my daughter and her husband. He should go to an American school, as is his wish.' But only five months later, she signed another will with somewhat contradictory conditions: 'My son Steven should be my main heir, my daughter is to get her obligatory share. If something happens to me, Steven should under no circumstances be looked after my daughter and her husband.'

Dolf's death also left Gaby's vast fortune with minimal protection or control apart from that given by a steady stream of advisers; both professional and amateur. Two months after the death, presumably in response to an adviser's suggestion, Gaby requested a list of her participations, which Heini wearily supplied:

> Thyssengas AG: DM 3.12 million shares; Niederrheinische Gas- und Wasserwerke GmbH: DM 600,000 participation; Bremer Vulkan: DM 2.1 million; Flensburger Schiffbau: DM 205,000. These are all administered by Kaszony where you have furthermore ⅛ of mining shares Friedrichsfeld and Hiesfeld and ⅛ of 37.5 per cent salt fields Bruckhausen. Your participations also include ⅛ in the estate under administration of Hollandsch Trust Kantoor, namely Erlenhof stud farm and two villas in Dahlwitz-Hoppegarten. Finally, there is ⅛ in the assets under administration of Maatschappij Francesca, namely 37.5 per cent share in plots Kirchhellen and Bottrop and 37.5 per cent share in fields ex-Lohberg and Hiesfeld.

Heini also advised her to 'generally limit the amount of people in whom you put your trust and do not change them if they have only made one mistake'. The latter being a reference to his sister's capricious relationships with her lawyers and accountants whose professional advice she was in the habit of challenging. His own involvement remained perfunctory, since he no doubt wished to distance himself from the inevitable financial disasters. He offered her the use of his tax specialist to reduce her exposure and pointed out that her Ludmilla Foundation, which held SwFr 47 million of her assets, might consider reducing the twenty-eight different banks involved. But while world leaders honoured Baron Adolphe Bentinck, Heini displayed a total lack of personal concern.

It was hardly surprising that the death of their cousin, Ivy Batthyány Junior, aged thirty-six, in a plane crash the same year would give rise to an equal lack of response. The only genuine affection shown by the Thyssen-Bornemisza children even for their own parents remained the extreme intimacy between Gaby and her father. The lack of affection for their mother Margit became particularly evident on 17 April 1971 when she died in Locarno. The family archives contain no record of any funeral arrangements, obituaries, letters of condolence or any other evidence of either formal or personal regret or sorrow. The only correspondence between her sons concerned Stephan's request to convert his share of her considerable inheritance into a pension for himself and, following his death, for his wife and daughter. From then on, Stephan received from Heini $5,200 per month plus expenses as and when required while continuing to write his research papers on 'fundamental geophysical advancements', which he regularly sent to his brother, who continued to ignore them.

* * *

While Heini may have been better advised to concentrate more effort on his role as an industrialist, he increasingly immersed himself in more rarefied areas of investment. But he was beginning to realise that jewellery, which lost half its value on purchase, could hardly be considered a sensible option, especially when it became part of his ex-wives' alimony. So he decided, with considerable encouragement from Denise, to become involved in the apparently more glamorous and 'potentially' more profitable activity of investing in gemstones. Major players do not buy finished stones; they invest in uncut gems and gamble on the alchemistic skills of master cutters.

> In 1972, I bought a rough diamond from which I expected to get two 50-carat or one 70-carat stone. Then, when Fred Horowitz went to Cartier, I was persuaded to have it cut there. I was always fascinated by the cut and shape of stones and had long and heated discussions with Fred. But the resulting single 108-carat, blue-white, $50 million stone was a complete and wonderful surprise.

Due to the fact that Cartier had been responsible for its creation, it became known as the 'Cartier diamond' and so impressed Denise that she chose to adopt it as her own. For some reason, this failed to deter Heini and in 1976 he invested in another brick-sized rough diamond in conjunction with Horowitz.

Out of this monster came a 170-carat, pear-shaped solitaire, which Heini christened the 'Star of Peace'. Unfortunately, its size was not matched by its quality. Bucherer of Lucerne rather uncharitably described it as being 'not a first-class stone. It is in fact very badly cut, slightly brown, though flawless. Only its size of 170 carats is rare.'

Even the passing of time failed to increase the Star's value and in 1982, having managed to keep it away from Denise, he allowed himself to be persuaded by Andrew Crispo, the notorious New York art dealer, to let him sell it through his gallery. After a while, it became obvious that Crispo, who would later be accused, though not charged or convicted, of having been involved in a horrifying, sado-masochist gay murder, was using the stone to attract people to his gallery and may have been in no hurry to achieve a sale. Heini's displeasure was increased when Solomon Lipner, who had obviously been commissioned without his knowledge, tried to sell him his own stone for $10 million, $7.4 million more than Heini's own insurance valuation. But it was not Heini's anger about this outrageous price hike that caused him to cancel his arrangement with Crispo and retain the stone but female persuasion. Predictably, having been set as a pendant 'encircled by 102 brilliants and nine rubin-navettes', the 'Star of Peace' eventually found its way into his fifth wife Tita's jewellery chest.

The fact that his indulgence in precious stones invariably profited only his wives did not seem to be of any particular concern to Heini who continued to enjoy the acquisition of both gems and jewellery while accepting the fact that they could hardly have been considered investments. Like many of his peers, he was motivated by the gems' success as conspicuous symbols of his wealth.

* * *

Although he still largely ignored the recommendations of the McKinsey report, Heini did make what in the short-term appeared to be an appropriate commercial decision when, in 1972, he approved the recruitment of Gerard Bernard Huiskamp as the new general manager of TBG. Huiskamp, who had formerly worked for Shell and Hill Samuel Bank in London, was probably responsible for saving the Thyssen-Bornemisza family firm. His method, which consisted of selling off large parts of the Group, could hardly have been considered ground-breaking but it did raise DM 400 million worth of cash and securities to invest in more profitable organisations.

As Huiskamp prepared to invest in the US, Heini seems to have viewed the Group's recovery as an encouragement to maintain his extravagance. Spurred on by the news that, in 1973, the leasing of his Lear Jet had actually made him a net profit of SwFr 435,000, Heini had been persuaded to build himself a motor-yacht, which also presented a profitable potential by means of

Heini doing his Lex Barker impression on board Hanse.

chartering. It would be christened *Hanse*: 'It had two 1600-horse-power engines, as well as facilities to transform salt water into drinking water. I enjoyed the idea of having a yacht but the nicest part was designing the boat and having it built.'

The undertaking turned into a nightmare. The idea for the boat came from the head of Bremer Vulkan, Hans Martin Huchzermeier, who convinced Heini that they could fund the boat's construction with state subsidies for which they formed a special company, Geestse Shipping Company. But their plan backfired when *Der Spiegel* ran a story headlined, 'Private boat built with monies from the state.' Then, to the amusement of his Greek ship-owning friends, Heini discovered that he suffered from a fear of being at sea. He preferred to disguise it by blaming his lack of enthusiasm on his guests' boredom:

> Being on a boat is not much fun, because one always goes to the same places. I swim a lot so I don't mind, but the others just stay on board and tend to get bored. You go for a walk in the port and then you return to the boat, because the food is usually better than the local restaurants. You do that once or twice and you have seen it all. One is much better off in a villa where you can go on excursions, see museums, other villages, etc. Obviously, a boat has the advantage of isolating you from the crowd, until you enter a port, but then there is the problem of finding a mooring.

The result of Heini's absence from the *Hanse* was that Denise and her friends took to taking the boat without his knowledge, resulting in Heini being subjected to the indignity of having to fax the boat's captain to discover where it was and who was on board. He often suffered the additional insult of failing to receive any response.

* * *

Despite the jewellery, jets and yachts, by 1973 Denise was bored and had taken a lover. In fact, Heini claimed that ever since their marriage she had never been faithful: 'She used to have affairs with members of my staff; even one of the crew on the *Hanse*. She was always very open about it, as she wanted to prove that I was so much in love with her that I wouldn't do anything about it.'

The arrival of the Roman playboy, Franco Rapetti, at Villa Favorita changed their relationship from one of mutually accepted infidelity to a virtual *ménage à trois*. It was not long before Heini accepted the fact that, after a night sitting up drinking wine and playing backgammon, Rapetti then stayed the night and slept with his wife; although Heini admitted that the staff found it somewhat disconcerting serving them breakfast in bed. 'His presence had eventually begun to suit me, as he was the one who had to put up with Denise's tantrums. They had incredible rows.'

Rapetti also used to stay with them on *Hanse* and at their house on Sardinia: 'It was an old house that had been built by an Englishman, well before Karim [Aga Khan] developed the Costa Smeralda in 1963. I bought it through Franco who must have made a huge commission.'

In Sardinia, they would all go out together in Rapetti's black Magnum speedboat. Denise had an identical model in blue. Heini must have bought the house primarily for Denise as he spent most of his time at Alphonso Hohenlohe's Marbella Club, where he built 'Casa Thyssen' and two guest cottages.

The most important influence Rapetti had on Heini's life was in the acquisition of paintings. Although Heini claimed not to have known of the arrangement until its tragic climax, for five years not only did Denise and Rapetti share a bed, but they also shared the commission on the sale of paintings to Heini. Or this is what Heini claimed: 'Franco Rapetti took huge commissions. Not 5 per cent but 25 per cent and even 50 per cent, which the gallery added on to the price.'

Even though the payment of commission is standard procedure, Heini never explained how he could have been unaware of such enormous price hikes, although he would somewhat unconvincingly claim: 'I try not to remember how much I pay for paintings because it spoils my enjoyment of the work.'

Apparently, when he tried to buy from a gallery that had refused to pay their commission, Denise and Rapetti would sit up all night persuading him not to buy the picture in question.

Heini made a number of important acquisitions prior to Rapetti's arrival. In 1971, he purchased 'Christ and the Samaritan woman' by Duccio di Buoninsegna from John D. Rockefeller II for $1.2 million through one of various offshore acquisition companies involved in his art purchases; in this case Internationale Finanz- und Kunsthandels AG, Vaduz.[13] He subsequently claimed to have only paid $400,000. In fact, the only time Heini disclosed how much he had paid for a painting was when he wanted to convince himself that he had paid less than he had.

Among his 1973 acquisitions were 'Old Waterloo Bridge' by André Dérain, for which he paid $290,000, a drawing, 'Pillared walkway with walkers' by Francesco Guardi for SwFr 160,000 and 'Vermuse' by Maurice Estève for SwFr 220,000. This was also the first year he bought work through the Andrew Crispo Gallery in New York. It was the start of an increasing encouragement of Heini's interest in the New York art scene by Denise and Rapetti.

* * *

While Heini's cultural relationship with the US developed, so did his apparent commercial interest in Indian Head, a US conglomerate comprised of fifty-five factories with 18,000 employees making textiles, car parts, plastic tubes and glass vessels. Under the guidance of Bernard Huiskamp, Heini took TBG into America by purchasing the US conglomerate for $50 million by 1974. According to Groenendijk, it was the formation of a holding company in the tax haven of Curaçao around this time that led to the decision to move the management control from Holland to Monte Carlo, where TBG could enjoy total freedom of taxes for transfers of profits and interests from the US. Apparently the Dutch tax authorities, under the socialist head of government Joop den Uyl, had not permitted the Netherlands management of a holding company in Curaçao. Meanwhile, Huiskamp advertised his success by claiming the Group's total profits had risen 54 per cent in 1974 to $39 million on a turnover of $710 million, much of the increase resulting from Indian Head's profitability. By 1975, Heini's 30 per cent share in the profits of the Group amounted to Dfl 25 million and by 1976 to Dfl 35 million.

* * *

In 1974, Denise announced that she was pregnant and on 20 November gave birth prematurely to Wilfrid Alexander August Gabor Thyssen-Bornemisza de Kaszón.

Having tried unsuccessfully to persuade his brother-in-law Ivy Batthyány to arrange for Cardinal Mindszenty, Primate of Hungary, to read a mass for the child so that it could develop in his spirit, Heini then attempted to enhance the child's social status by getting Aunt Ilda to confirm he had royal Hungarian blood in his veins.

In a contradictory but by now predictable development Heini then started to cast doubts on the boy's legitimacy, initially claiming that it was 'highly unlikely' that he was the father before flatly denying any responsibility. But regardless of his father's identity, Heini still accepted Alexander as part of his family and a legitimate heir, despite often referring to him in conversation as 'the cretin' or 'the imbecile'.

* * *

With Dolf gone, Ivy committed to a life of privileged imperial Hungarian exile and Heini's brother and sisters financially secure, they were making fewer financial demands. In 1975, his sisters each unexpectedly accepted a Dfl 500,000 settlement of the 'August Thyssen Bank Berlin affair'. Heini said this was so 'favourable' and the result of such diligence on the part of his accountants that there really was little point in having it checked by the auditors, Klynveld, Kraayenhof & Co.

The next generation of Thyssens would prove less co-operative and more financially demanding. By 1975, Gaby's eighteen-year-old son Steven was already firmly committed, albeit unconsciously, to spending his mother's fortune. Having attended thirteen schools in England, Switzerland and France, he tried and failed to join the French Foreign Legion, toured Israel with a theatre company, spent a year at the Valley Forge US Military Academy and enrolled at Brunel University in London to study economics. He then started a film production company, a magazine publishing company and spent a million pounds on a London West End musical based on the life of James Dean: 'I was never short of money. My mother readily financed my various financial ventures. At the time, the level of investment did not cause any undue concern to her or her advisers.'[14]

By 1977, Steven had begun to take an active role in his mother's financial affairs and persuaded her to invest $5.3 million in two Californian ranches. The first property was a fruit farm and could have been seen as a commercial opportunity. But when Gaby invested in the Diamond H cattle ranch and her son took to wearing a stetson and adopting a Texan accent when speaking from his flat in London's Eaton Square to the ranch managers in California, it became obvious to Gaby's advisers that her son seemed to be dangerously eccentric.

While Heini was prepared to admit that Steven was 'charming, entertaining and good-looking', he was unwilling to allow his nephew to squander his mother's money:

> After he had wasted millions in disastrous business ventures I offered him a guaranteed, index-linked allowance of $5 million a year if only he would stay away from business. I was inviting him to get paid for doing nothing but he refused. I remember when he finally married a fifty-year-old woman I said to Gaby, 'Thank God for that, at least he won't have any heirs'.

Steven's sister Henriette was only marginally less 'eccentric' but by 1967 she had already become someone else's problem when she married one of Britain's richest aristocrats, Spencer Douglas David Compton, Marquess and Earl of Northampton. But even the somewhat relieved Heini recognised that 'Spenny' was also slightly 'dotty' after discovering that every evening around ten o'clock he used to have long conversations with his dead father.

Meanwhile, much to the fury of Ivy, Margit made her own eccentric gesture by developing a relationship with a cruise-ship doctor called Dr Schiefelbein, who had bought himself the title of 'Admiral of the Paraguayan Navy' from Consul Weyer, Göring's godson and an endearing conman.

* * *

By 1974, only five years after McKinsey's damning report, Heini was feeling sufficiently confident to consider a $5 million Grumman Gulfstream II replacement for his Lear Jet to be a prudent investment. The decision may have been in response to pressure from Denise who wanted a plane with longer range and greater capacity for their forthcoming South American tour, the purpose of which was to search for 'business opportunities'. However, following the tour in a plane loaned by the manufacturers, which had included extended visits to Brazil, Argentina and Uruguay, Heini decided not to buy the Gulfstream on the grounds that it was too noisy for Lugano airport.

Negotiations for a replacement jet continued for some years. In 1976, Heini's negotiations extended to a five-year-old, $2.2 million Falcon. Apparently, it had been fitted out with so many extras and such a luxurious interior, which included gold faucets in the toilet, that they had 'slight difficulties' getting it off the ground and Heini was advised to pass on the plane until the runway was extended. Heini didn't buy the plane but he did become involved with Helmut Horten, the owner of a chain of German department stores and Ticino resident, in a DM 364,000 land purchase for a planned runway extension for Lugano airport.

Heini's corporate confidence was no doubt inspired by the management's announcement in 1975 of an increase in the Group's turnover by 83 per cent to DM 1.6 billion with a capital yield of 21 per cent and an intended long-term goal of an annual 5 per cent increase in profits. Meanwhile, in 1976, there was evidence that while TBG then owned more than 90 per cent of the outstanding common shares of Indian Head, they had to withdraw their proposal to make it a wholly-owned subsidiary after stock and warrant holders took TBG to court. According to the *New York Times* of 22 July:

> Thyssen-Bornemisza Inc. agreed yesterday to a settlement of a class-action brought by shareholders protesting the proposed merger of Indian Head with a Thyssen-Bornemisza subsidiary. The settlement calls for payment of more than $32 million to holders of Indian Head debentures, common stock and warrants.

This was deeply embarrassing for Heini and contributed to Bernard Huiskamp's early retirement and his replacement in 1977 by Robert Genillard, an old friend and adviser of Heini's.

In 1976, Heini also established a Monaco residency prior to the introduction of new Ticino tax laws. There was to be income tax, wealth tax, tax on profits from important participations, inheritance and gift tax, resulting in a total tax debt that could rate as high as 64 per cent. According to Article 213, the attorney general could also request an examination for tax evasion even without it being requested by the tax authorities.

Realising that many of the canton's wealthier residents would be unlikely to remain long enough to qualify for such stringent taxation, many Swiss were extremely unhappy about the situation and Dr Franco Masoni, a local lawyer, was not at all pleased that one of his most valued clients appeared to be slipping through his fingers. He was a man with considerable political power in the canton and agreed to represent Heini's interests, which were submitted, indirectly through Masoni, in the form of a carefully crafted letter. In it Heini stressed that he was not in any way expecting 'any special treatment by Ticino', which was of course exactly what he and his father before him had been enjoying since 1932. He also pointed out that his flight to Monaco should not in any way be considered as a means of 'pressurising the local authorities' and invited them to consider his 'closure of his galleries with its detrimental effect on suppliers and employees' in the same light. He also felt sure that his leaving the canton could be achieved 'without any publicity'.

In a reply a Ticino state councillor informed Franco Masoni that the canton would make an exception and exempt Heini from all the new taxes including income and wealth regarding the entire collection on the understanding that the art gallery remained open to the public and he personally resided in the canton for no more than ninety days a year. This was hardly a restriction for Heini, who would rarely have spent anything like this amount of time in Lugano. So not for the first time were the Swiss, or those who ran the canton of Ticino, prepared to accommodate the Thyssen-Bornemiszas while in a will that Heini made before leaving the canton there was among the various gifts in appreciation for services rendered, SwFr 200,000 for the mayor of Lugano.

* * *

Although Heini was quite prepared to take advantage of the principality's undemanding tax laws, due to the power wielded in Monaco by his rival Onassis, he had no intention of actually living there. The fact that Georg, now twenty-six years of age, was prepared to live in Monaco contributed to Heini's decision to encourage him to join the Group. At the same time Heini also made him head of the Kaszony Family Foundation; a symbolic rather than a practical role. It would be another four years before the agreement with his mother was fulfilled and Georg was given a seat on the board. Meanwhile, having read two years of physics and mathematics in Munich before reading law in Zurich, he became Robert Genillard's assistant in Monaco. Heini prepared for Georg's arrival by trying to convince himself that they were compatible, despite their contrasting characters and the fact that they hardly knew each other: 'I had complete confidence in him although he was very cautious and careful. I never had anything to hide in my business life but I may have been somewhat indiscreet, while he has always been very secretive.'

Of course Heini had many things to hide, particularly from his own family, to whom he often avoided telling the truth. But Heini did not like people withholding information from him and even had a telephone system installed at Villa Favorita that enabled him to listen into people's telephone calls. However, in a somewhat contradictory manner, he did not seem to mind if people overheard his conversations. Emil Bosshard remembered Heini quite happily having an intimate telephone conversation in his presence and even waving him back when he rose to leave.

Heini insisted, 'I was very fond of Junior despite the fact that he did not confide in me', but revealed a degree of vulnerability when he confessed: 'We really weren't very close to begin with although we would hug each other, but it was more out of habit than anything else, as we are both very prudish.'

Heini was probably referring to his difficulty with direct physical contact, particularly with men, although his women had also complained about it. In fact, Heini found close relationships of any kind difficult. Many years later, when the effects of red wine were accentuating the maudlin side of his character, he would often display brief moments of regret for his inability to enjoy close relationships with his children: 'When I divorced, I was often unable to look after my children as I would have liked. The best example was Georg, or Heini Junior, who I rarely saw as a child as he continued to live with his mother.'

A common trait amongst the Thyssen-Bornemiszas was their insistence that their offspring would be brought up in such a manner as to avoid the pitfalls of being born into immense wealth. They also claimed to limit staff and services to ensure that their children's effort, motivation and responsibility were maximised and a life of total decadence avoided. Perhaps to the relief of both the children and newspaper columnists, the parents failed miserably and at times seemed determined to set the worst possible examples themselves.

The only exception to this rule was Theresa, who had no intention of allowing the pursuit of pleasure to corrupt her son, who was now in a position of almost unassailable power. Her reaction to Heini's request, back in 1964, to take his son on holiday had been polite, sympathetic but firm. 'She seemed convinced that foreign travel would somehow give him a feeling of superiority. She insisted he was just a sensitive, fourteen-year-old schoolboy who enjoyed simple pleasures and who she wanted to stay that way for as long as possible. I remember her predicting that he was going to have a difficult life and that we should give him every possible support, so that he would be equipped to withstand all the stresses and temptations that he was going to be subjected to'.

It was an admirable, if ironic sentiment, which may have effectively contributed to Georg's sober hyper-normality. Wilhelmus Groenendijk even compared him to his great-grandfather, August Thyssen, but only with reference to his financial austerity and single-minded ambition.

* * *

Having completed an education at Le Rosey, which appeared to involve a great deal of skiing and very little contact with her parents, in 1976, Heini's daughter Francesca followed her mother to London and moved into a small house on Seymour Walk, which was bought for her by her father.[15] Having inherited at least some of her mother's looks, considerable social skills plus a generous allowance and seemingly endless credit, the eighteen-year-old adopted fashionable society with an enthusiasm matched only by her much loved mother who, according to Anthony Price, the fashion designer, 'was just as crazy as Francesca in those days'.

Even Fiona's mother displayed the knowledge, if not the physical stamina, to enjoy the wilder side of life. This became obvious one evening when, having overheard a discreet dinner conversation between Fiona and Francesca concerning a friend's excessive cocaine consumption, she commented: 'You don't have to whisper. I know what you're talking about. We used to call it "happy powder" in my day.'

Francesca was soon enjoying a relationship with the fashion photographer John Swannell and a brief career as a model, before moving on to acting classes and further relationships with Gary Tibbs, Roxy Music's bass guitarist, and Wayne Eagling, principal dancer with the Royal Ballet. Her appreciative 'court' included Dolph Lundgren, Grace Jones, Robert Mapplethorpe, Robert Frazer, Mick Jagger and Julian Schnabel. Having achieved limited public exposure through her work as a fashion model, 'Chessy' developed a far greater ability for achieving press coverage by exposing parts of her naked body to social photographers. It was an activity that, for a while, would ensure her far greater public recognition than any other member of the Thyssen-Bornemisza family.

From an early age it became obvious that Francesca's ambitions were social and creative and that she did not intend to draw attention to the German industrial source of her fortune. Instead she developed a fascination for the Price family and the Bornemiszas and liked it to be believed that she was related to Transylvanian and Croatian royalty. She considered herself an aristocrat and developed friendships with Prince Ernst Hanover and Princess Gloria von Thurn und Taxis, whose outrageous behaviour rivalled her own. The only part of her inheritance for which 'Chessy' displayed any long-lasting appreciation, apart from the money, was her father's art collection and as the only one of his children with any interest in art she always assumed she would eventually inherit its control.

* * *

By 1977, in addition to his homes in Sardinia, Marbella and Jamaica, Heini had bought a new house overlooking St Moritz. He also had an apartment in New York, at 812 Fifth Avenue, and a rented London town house in Chester Square when Rosita, Duchess of Marlborough and friend of Denise, persuaded him to buy a country seat in Oxfordshire from her friends, the Viscount and Viscountess Rothermere, for £600,000. The original, twelfth-century house having fallen into disrepair, it had been replaced by 'Daylesford', a rather unimpressive, six-bedroom manor house in 1800.

Francesca partying with Prince Ernst Hanover, 1980.

Heini would justify the purchase by the fact that the French government decided to impose restrictive foreign exchange laws on Monte Carlo and as a result he moved his tax residence from Monaco to England, although the house in Chester Square would have been more than adequate for his purposes. It was most likely pressure from Denise that persuaded Heini to buy Daylesford. He even jokingly suggested that she wanted it to go with her new Rolls-Royce Corniche.

Daylesford had only recently enjoyed a fourteen-year restoration but that did not prevent Denise from commissioning the Italian interior decorator Renzo Mongiardino to redesign the interior at a cost equal to the purchase price. That was only the start of the ever-increasing peripheral costs: 'I had to invest at least three million pounds. There were several houses on the estate that all needed renovation. We also had to buy the surrounding land, which was very expensive, and more stables had to be built for Denise's horses.'

From buying a place in the country, where they were unlikely to spend more than three weeks a year, Heini soon found himself to be the owner of a 12,000-acre estate: 'We had to get someone to run the farm for us. Then there was the expense of the farm machinery, labour, insurance, bodyguards, drivers, watchmen and household staff. It was endless, and the weather was appalling, so we only went in the winter, because at least we knew what to expect.'

* * *

Heini did not like staying in his London house alone and on the evening of 8 June 1978 he was staying at Niarchos's apartment at Claridges.

> I had been to the theatre with Princess Feryal of Jordan. Then, we had dinner at Marks Club. When we got in, Denise had called from New York to say that Rapetti had died. She told me that he had been trying to open a window on the fifth floor but due to the effect of the sedatives he had taken, he fell out and was killed.

News of Rapetti's death spread fast and it was not long before some of Heini's more imaginative friends were suggesting that he had been pushed out of a 10th floor window. Others insisted he had committed suicide while Nona Summers, wife of the art dealer Martin Summers and a close friend of Denise, appeared to encourage the implication of Heini: 'He was grinning from ear to ear when he walked into the Waldorf. I've never seen someone so happy as Heini when Rapetti died.'[16]

Later, Heini fanned the flames of conspiracy by insisting 'He didn't even fall onto the sidewalk underneath the window. His body was found on the other side of the street with only a pair of underpants on.'

Marco Grassi had yet another theory; he thought the Italian's death was the result of gambling debts which Rapetti had incurred in Rome. He also, rather ominously insisted that, shortly before the accident, Heini had sworn never to do another deal with Rapetti which led to the rumour that Heini paid the gambling debts on the understanding that the Romans took care of Rapetti. Certainly there had been no shortage of motives and many years later, in one of his more bibulous moments, Heini even made a tearful confession to me and claimed to have been responsible for Rapetti's death.

The only problem had then been what to do with the body and how to avoid an investigation. But Heini had obviously already thought of that:

> There was no police inquiry after Rapetti's death, because he was a foreigner. Usually, there is an autopsy when someone falls out of a window. In this case, the Italian Consulate should have been informed but that would have led to endless formalities. That's why Denise said we should remove the body straight away. So we got a private ambulance to take him to the airport, where I had a chartered plane to fly Denise and the coffin back to Europe. I don't know where she buried him.

But the plan was not quite as seamless as Heini liked to pretend and events were soon assuming farcical proportions. The plane Heini had chartered belonged to his friend Helmut Horten who was rich enough to afford his own Gulfstream jet with a greater range and carrying capacity than Heini's Lear. Through a leasing company, Heini had an option to lease Horten's plane and vice versa but the agreement did not cover the transportation of corpses.

Having been discovered, Heini was refused permission to continue his use of the plane while the crew were ordered to unload and return to Switzerland immediately. Heini was then left with the problem of what to do with Rapetti, as a replacement jet was unavailable until the following day. Not wishing to recall the ambulance, he slid the coffin into his stretch limousine and proceeded to enjoy a night out in New York. His claim to have entertained himself by repeatedly asking his friends if they wanted to meet his wife's lover, before opening the coffin to reveal Rapetti, would continue to amuse him many years later.

Unfortunately, Horten remained unamused by Heini's behaviour, particularly his unwillingness to pay for the aborted charter, and on 6 November 1978 successfully took the case to court in Zurich for the payment of SwFr 153,302 plus interest.

It was around this time that Heini took to drinking red wine after his doctor had forbidden him to drink any more whisky.

* * *

Heini had hoped that Denise would slow down when Rapetti died: 'On the contrary, she went on having lovers and as far as her art dealing was concerned, she soon replaced Rapetti with her brother Roberto'.

As far as Heini's art collecting was concerned, the triumvirate of Ketterer, Heinemann and Grassi would soon be largely replaced by that of Denise, Roberto Shorto and Andrew Crispo; the latter being quite prepared to continue selling Heini paintings, with or without Rapetti who had originally introduced them. Roberto Shorto, while maybe not having achieved the level of creative influence that he often claimed when insisting that he was responsible for the creation of the Thyssen-Bornemisza Collection, certainly had a considerable influence over its modern content. There is no evidence that his influence owed anything to his appreciation of either the aesthetics or the history of art but the next generation of dealers whom the twenty-four-year-old Roberto could influence tended to deal in the work of contemporary painters, so Roberto had to persuade Heini to invest in more modern paintings. But his claim to have introduced Francis Bacon to Heini was somewhat far-fetched, as Heini had bought 'Portrait of George Dyer in a Mirror' in 1971, and his second 'Small Triptych' in 1977. Predictably, Denise gave her own role far greater importance: 'As a collector, Heini had stopped at German Expressionists when I met him. We built up the whole modern collection together.'[17]

Heini refused to accept Denise's claim but it is actually difficult to repudiate. Even he admitted susceptibility to her powers of persuasion and, during their marriage, he purchased an astonishing 800 pictures. These purchases transformed the collection by the inclusion of modern masters but unfortunately, while the collection grew, the quality, direction and focus did not improve and the number of exceptional works purchased remained relatively small.

In 1974, Heini had bought two paintings by Georgia O'Keeffe, 'From the Patio no. II' and 'Near Abiquiu / New Mexiko', each for $50,000, but he never displayed any particular enthusiasm for her work. He was even introduced to her in New York, which was possibly the first time that he ever met the creator of paintings in his collection. But when asked what they talked about, he could only yawn and say: 'I can't remember.'

The same year Heini received his first invoice from the Andrew Crispo Gallery in New York for $207,000 for pictures bought in 1973. Among the list were Andrew Wyeth's 'Fire Wood' for $26,000; 'Love, love, love – Homage to Gertrude Stein' by Charles Demuth for $55,000; and Maurice Prendergast's 'Autumn' for $50,000. The latter was considered of particular importance as signalling his new interest in the nineteenth-century American painters. Heini claimed to have a particular affinity with and appreciation for them but when he moved half the collection to Spain in 1992, he left many of them hanging in the gallery at Villa Favorita.

On 24 January 1974, he also paid $340,000 for a Joan Miró, 'Catalan peasant with a guitar', whose authenticity was initially questioned but subsequently confirmed by Heini's own experts to be an 'early surrealist Miró', despite a suspicious lack of provenance.[18] In March, Heini bought a Schiele, 'Boy in sailor's outfit', from Ketterer for DM 95,000. It was followed by a Max Ernst, 'Untitled. Dada', for $150,000, which may have signified a genuine appreciation for Ernst's work, as Heini already had seven of them.

In May, Andrew Crispo convinced Heini of the importance of buying the Rauschenberg 'Express' for the good of the collection. But Heini's failure to appreciate Rauschenberg ensured that there were no further acquisitions of his work. Richard Lindner's 'Moon over Alabama' was almost certainly in the same category. Another painting that was unlikely to have appealed to him was 'Abstraction' by Willem de Kooning, predictably bought through Crispo from Christie's for $31,000. More in Heini's style were a Renoir, 'Woman with a parasol in a garden', bought from Christie's for £204,550 and a Sisley, 'The Flood at Port Marly'.

Among the mystery purchases of 1974 were five works by Charles Beauchamp, all bought at the same time. The mystery was not the works, but why Heini bought them. He would never admit that it had been the 'next thing in the catalogue' after a failed bid, although Simon de Pury would subsequently admit this was not an unusual occurrence.

In the case of the twenty-three superb theatre and costume designs by Leon Bakst, bought between 1974 and 1984, the reason Heini gave for buying them was so endearingly simple as to be quite possibly genuine – 'I found them pretty' – although, as if to cover up this rather vulnerable display of camp appreciation, he quickly added: 'But they weren't very expensive at the time.'

* * *

In 1974, Hanna Kiel, one of the curators at Villa Favorita, produced a catalogue of the 'Thyssen-Bornemisza Collection of Modern Masters', which indicated that Heini considered that he had by now gathered sufficient modern works to justify such a statement. A catalogue could still not improve the quality of his paintings and even, in many cases, exposed the paucity of their provenance but his collection of modern art was now of sufficient size and importance to enable him to increase his new acquisitions' value by publishing their inclusion in the Thyssen-Bornemisza Collection.

Meanwhile, in September 1975 in New York he bought two Rembrandts, 'Portrait of a man', for $1.5 million and 'Portrait of a man in a white brimmed hat' for $750,000. Neither of them was accepted as genuine by the Rembrandt Commission in Holland and Heini was convinced that the Commission was conspiring against him and adamant it would change its opinion after he had put the paintings back on the market. However, having insisted, 'The art trade is the most corrupt business in the world', he had difficulty remembering if he had included the details of the pictures' doubtful authenticity in the sale catalogue.

The pressure on Heini to continue buying remained constant. In October when he returned to New York and fell ill with a cold, Crispo sent a note to his hotel offering Heini a doctor, some medication and 'a very very important Rosenquist and Edward Hopper's "Hotel window", which is here at the gallery at a price of $265,000. Far less than you have been quoted. I also have a Léger which is the definitive of the "L'Aviateur series".' Heini was sufficiently pressurised to buy the Hopper although he eventually sold it back to Crispo in 1980 for $580,000, by which time he had bought two more Hoppers.

Considering the indiscriminate manner in which Heini collected art, it was difficult to explain why he bought seven works by Lyonel Feininger between 1963 and 1977, unless it was to please Ketterer.

Due to the sheer quantity of purchases, Heini often experienced difficulties in remembering where and when they had been made. But in the case of Cézanne's 'Portrait of a farmer', it was difficult to believe that he apparently 'forgot' having bought the painting for $1.5 million: 'I neither remember where nor from whom I bought it, nor any story related to it, only that I always wanted to have a Cézanne and I believe I bought it in Paris.'

* * *

It is also difficult to believe that Heini could not remember the 100th painting that he bought in 1976. It was recorded to be 'The Bath' by Auguste Renoir, yet he claimed to have absolutely no knowledge of the painting's existence, where it may have come from or where it went. It did not seem to concern him that a Renoir could so easily have slipped through his hands.

The next purchase of note was a Delacroix, 'The Duke of Orléans unveiling his lover to the Duke of Burgundy', which Heini bought in March 1977 for $133,000 and which was notable for its total lack of any form of provenance. This is not unusual in the Thyssen-Bornemisza Collection but it was when it came through the London-based Martin Summers and the Lefèvre Gallery.

Another mystery was a Picasso, 'Negro Dancer', which Heini bought from the Art Council Establishment of Vaduz, for $400,000 through Marco Grassi but later claimed, 'I have no idea where that went.'

Francesca indulging her love of extravagance with Philip Niarchos in St Moritz.

While he seemed quite prepared to accept the fact that he had so little influence over the choice of his acquisitions and occasional divestments, there were inevitably times when Heini wanted the freedom to make his own decisions:

> The acquisition of the Monet was incredible. I had to run away from Rudolf Heinemann in New York to be able to get to the gallery of the Hungarian, Sam Salz, where the Impressionists used to be exhibited. I was accompanied by Gianni Agnelli, who didn't buy anything while I bought two; one work by Berthe Morisot, 'The cheval-glass', for which I paid $250,000 and the Monet 'The Thaw at Vétheuil' for $300,000. This painting became very famous because it appeared in so many exhibitions. But in spite of the precautions I had taken to escape from Heinemann, even to the point of changing cars, he soon worked out where we had gone and made it obvious that he strongly disapproved of what I had bought. Just like my father, Rudolf used to think that all modern paintings were meaningless extravagance.

Heinemann certainly would not have approved of the next Kandinsky, 'Ludwigskirche in Munich', which Heini bought for $250,000, claiming it to be 'interesting because it's a picture from his first period, and shows the place where Hitler made many of his speeches'. He was more likely to have grudgingly accepted 'The Fruit Garden' by Paul Cézanne, which was Heini's ninety-seventh purchase in 1977. Being somewhat vague about the price probably meant that he paid too much, as he had no difficulty remembering that it was valued at $4.5 million when it was inherited by his son Lorne.

* * *

The year 1978 started off in similar style but considerably greater cost, with the purchase of a Dégas, 'At the Milliners', for $1.5 million from Mrs Leeman through Thomas Gibson Fine Art in London. Heini agreed that it was a very expensive picture, but he had developed an accompanying anecdote to cheer himself up: 'The day they went to collect it, the people who were in charge of the removal crossed the whole museum, picked up the picture and took it to the lorry without alerting anybody and nobody said anything to them. Of course you have to have a clear conscience to succeed in such a move'.

However, it would not generally be a good year for acquisitions or the acquirer. Of note were a Grosz, 'Nude', for DM 128,725; a Pollock, 'Untitled', for $100,000; a Gris, 'The Smoker', for $450,000, a price that would have caused Heini considerable concern, and another Grosz, 'Metropolis', for an even more punishing $550,000. Yet again, Heini felt compelled to give some form of justification for this expenditure: 'The picture is something unique, which I bought in New York. I'm very proud of it, because it shows Berlin in 1916.'

It was a somewhat fatuous qualification for a picture that had originally been confiscated and sold by Hitler's government as degenerate art at an auction held in the Fischer Gallery in Lucerne on 30 June 1939.

* * *

Around December 1978, Georg officially started to work at TBG and Heini insisted that he was 'capable, intelligent and careful'. But it soon became obvious from one of Robert Genillard's periodic reports that there were problems with Georg, which he found difficult to express without causing offence: 'Georg is very intelligent and so highly engrossed in the business that he does not seem to have any other meaningful interests in life.'[19]

According to Heini, Georg was also coming under immediate attack from Denise. With little chance of any further challenge or revelations concerning Alexander's true father and fully aware of the power of Georg's position, Denise set about mounting a palace coup: 'She wanted me to make Alexander my sole heir, insisting that he was the only one of my children displaying any interest in furthering the Thyssen-Bornemisza dynasty.'

As Alexander was only six years old at the time, it would have been, by any stretch of the imagination, somewhat difficult to tell what his predilections might be. Nevertheless, Denise continued with her apparent intention to advance Alexander's position within the family: 'It was a nightmare, but I really couldn't face another divorce, so I became increasingly involved with my collection.'

Heini's aversion to another divorce may also have been the result of his fear that it could cost him as much as 50% of the Group and the art collection.

Collecting art was not his only distraction. Having decided against divorce, he took a mistress in the shape of a beautiful Italian girl, whose brother was a friend of Gianni Agnelli. Although she came from Florence, she was very Neapolitan, with long black hair, huge brown eyes and full breasts. She was emotional, exciting and dangerous. Even more dangerous was her brother, who encouraged the relationship and sought Heini's assistance in opening a private bank in Geneva. Josi Groh found the affair highly amusing, even when Heini used the Grohs' holiday home in Porto Santo Stefano to hide his new girlfriend from Denise. But when Heini appointed Groh to be the manager of their new bank and no one could tell him where the huge amounts of money involved were coming from or going to, he became somewhat less amused. Josi was quite convinced the Italians were Mafia and when the brother was finally arrested and jailed he was very relieved.

Meanwhile, Heini continued to have relationships with a number of other women, including Mercedes Kellogg, while his hysterical wife continued in her attempt to either overthrow Georg or at least get her son Alexander an assurance of some future position on the board. In the speech he gave to the board of the Thyssen Bornemisza Group in Divonne on 6 June 1979, Heini even gave the impression that his resistance may have been weakening: 'It is up to my family to ensure continuity. Already out of the fourth generation, my eldest son is now working in the Group and will join the supervisory board next year. My younger children will, I expect, follow the same path.'

* * *

Heini was not the only one experiencing family problems. His sister Gaby was having difficulties retrieving a SwFr 1.5 million loan from her former lover Ion Ratiu. Both her London solicitor and her junior counsel, Michael Crystal, warned Gaby:

> Unfortunately, it is not possible to have the hearing conducted in secrecy, so one cannot guarantee that no report would ever appear, although there is nothing in the title 'Regent House Properties *v.* Cortivo Holding Fribourg' to

alert anyone to your involvement. Really it seems you have to decide at this stage whether the risk of possible publicity is more important than recovering the loan and interest from Mr Ratiu.

The risk that Ratiu would reveal the details of their relationship proved a sufficient deterrent and Gaby settled out of court to Ratiu's advantage. She found the whole procedure so fatiguing that Professor Paul Millier certified: 'Madame Bentinck, given her general state of exhaustion and for medical reasons, must take a total rest and must only take part in meetings or receptions which are shorter than one or two hours.'

It was a condition that Gaby would soon find sufficiently appealing to adopt on a permanent basis, despite no shortage of invitations. She managed dinner with Ted Heath at Klosters in 1980, but turned down Harold Macmillan. She also promised to visit Marc Chagall 'as soon as my health gets better'.

But it would not and by 1982 Gaby had less convivial events bidding for her attention. By then her son admitted that the total invested in the ranches had risen from $5.3 million to $10.5 million, at a time of 'rapid collapse in the US agriculture industry'. But Steven was quite capable of acting out more than one fantasy at a time: 'My mother had during the same period from 1977 to 1982 given me gifts totalling $4.5 million, which I had invested in highly speculative ventures in publishing, theatrical production, music recording and movies, made due to a youthful enthusiasm for the arts.'

It was hardly surprising that Mich Pruszynski should devote so much time and effort to protecting Gaby from her son's extravagance. Finally, in 1982, she approved the establishment of the Gaby Bentinck Trust, for the benefit of Steven and Henriette but most of all for her own protection. The trust would have her lawyer, Dr Peter Hafter, Heini and her lover Pruszynski as its trustees and would provide Gaby with an annual allowance and Steven and his sister with SwFr 500,000 per annum. This would prove far short of the money needed to fund her son's extravagance and by 1983 his mother had approved 'the transfer of a further $5.75 million dollars to her companies under Steven's management'.

* * *

In 1969 McKinsey had advised Heini against the excessive complication of TBG's structure, yet ten years later there had been no simplification of the astonishingly complex web of foundations, trusts and companies. Under Heini's ownership, either directly or through the Kaszony Foundation, there was a network of interconnected 'holding' organisations based in the Dutch Antilles, Bermuda, Switzerland, the British Virgin Islands, Panama, Luxembourg, Liberia, the Bahamas, Liechtenstein and Holland. They in turn owned the operating companies in Germany, Holland, the United States, Australia, New Zealand, Brazil, South Africa, Argentina, Britain, Greece and probably in places long since forgotten.

Meanwhile, TBG remained an organisation rich in the services of lawyers and tax avoidance specialists. On 3 May 1979 a number of them met in London to discuss Heini's tax and domicile position. There were the considerable expenses involved in getting everyone there and putting them up in hotels and while they discussed the possibility of his domicile being moved to the Bahamas, Heini would have been running up an impressive hospitality bill at Claridges, Marks Club and Annabel's. No one ever seemed to heed McKinsey's advice and work out if it was cheaper for Heini to pay his taxes.

He was obviously a willing participant in his advisers' organisation and methods and neither the cost nor the morality of the process appeared to concern him. Apart from the fact that he strongly objected to the payment of tax, he also considered its avoidance to be another form of anti-establishment rebellion and an essential part of his self-styled persona as a capitalist agitator. One evening as the sun went down and Heini summoned Giorgio for another bottle of wine, he announced with considerable pride: 'I am a tax evader by profession. If you wanted to be correct, I should be in jail.'

The discussion concerning his possible Bahamian residency could also have been considered somewhat premature as Josi Groh was still trying to justify to the authorities Heini's new residential status in Britain: 'He wishes to educate his son Alexander in England. Also London is the ideal transport hub for his many international trips. Thirdly, he wishes to extend his art collection and wants to go to the auctions and continue his study of art.'

Heini certainly enjoyed London's privileged social life and its convenience, while Britain's contribution to his tax avoidance would prove questionable. But the country's most important contribution to his plans would be in its enabling Heini to divorce Denise under British law while the extravagance of his international existence remained undiminished. This was evident in the logistics involved in getting him and his guests to the *Hanse* for a short winter escape from the inclement British climate:

> Your trip to Port of Spain has now been arranged in detail. You will fly by Concorde on 19 December 1980 and land in Caracas at 7 pm. You will be collected from the plane, taken through customs so that you can then be flown from Caracas on a private Cessna Citation jet to Port of Spain. Our

Agent will await you in Trinidad at 9:15 pm with two limousines and drive you directly to the 'Hanse'. The yacht has been given a nice work-over and I hope everything will be to your satisfaction.

In the opinion of Marco Grassi, at this time the extravagance of both Heini and Denise reached its peak: 'For example, she would send Heini's private plane to fetch a dress she had left somewhere. A normal man would have refused and said it was a company plane, but Heini never said a word.'

* * *

Tita liked to give the impression that she and Heini met in 1980 or even earlier and even though she had admitted he was not the father of her son Borja, who was born in July 1980, she would subsequently encourage the possibility.

According to Tita, she had been invited to go with some friends to Sardinia on a yacht. At the same time, Heini and Denise were also there with Fred Horowitz. Maybe it was coincidental that Tita was invited to Fred's for dinner but she certainly knew that Heini was going to be there and had been told that 'he was very lonely because his wife was always playing around with other men'.

Horowitz, who was working for Harry Winston, also knew the Thyssens' relationship was rocky and while jewellers rarely profit from divorce, they certainly do from engagements; especially if they make the introduction and particularly in the case of Heini Thyssen. Tita said it was 'destiny' when their eyes met and they went 'boom' and Heini invited her to lunch at his place the following day. When she arrived, Denise appeared totally unconcerned and remained chatting on the phone, while Heini and Tita went swimming before a lobster lunch, where, Heini 'didn't let her out of his sight'. Then, that night, he took her aboard the *Hanse* where, according to Tita he kissed her in the moonlight and Fred Horowitz's dreams came true. The only time Denise showed any concern was when Tita ate half her pizza at lunch the following day: 'I was very hungry from all that swimming. Denise was coming in and out and in and out, never sitting down to have her pizza. So I cut it in half and gave it to Heini. When she saw half of her pizza had gone, Denise went ballistic.'

The sixty-year-old Heini was smitten: 'The truth is, Tita dazzled me as no other woman before her. It was like the dawn of a new life.'

No one, though, could remember exactly when it was that the sun came up. It was certainly not on the *Hanse* because Tita claimed that when Heini had offered to show her his cabin, she had told him: 'I don't know you well enough yet.'

* * *

Heini's romantic activities had no effect on the rate of his acquisitions, which would certainly suggest that Denise and her collaborators had no intention of encouraging any interruptions in 'their' development of the collection.

Before the end of 1978 there had even been a degree of support for the old master section of the collection with the purchase of a 'Portrait of Thomas Cromwell' by Hans Holbein the Younger for $250,000. Heini's attention was then returned to more modern work with a Braque for $375,000 and another Wyeth for $350,000. A Picasso, 'Still life: glasses and fruit', for which Heini paid $105,000 was perhaps most remarkable for having previously been owned by Gertrude Stein and Nelson Rockefeller. A Rothko, 'Untitled', in tempera on paper mounted on linen for $100,000 would hardly have been bought for aesthetic reasons; or certainly not by Heini Thyssen.

In November, he returned to Fischer Fine Art in London where he bought a Schiele, 'Houses on the river. The Old town', admitting that the deal had been 'negotiated' by Roberto Shorto. Then he went back to Crispo for Lichtenstein's, 'Girl in Bath', for $300,000.

It looked as if 1979 was to be an equally abundant year for both Heini and Roberto Shorto when, in January, Heini purchased Freud's 'Last Portrait' for what would now be considered a miserly £25,000 from Marlborough Fine Art, while the collection's profile was no doubt enhanced by his acquisition of a Cézanne for FrFr 3.8 million. As in many impressionist paintings the subject matter, 'Bottle, Carafe, Jug and Lemons', could hardly have been considered inspiring.

* * *

Until 1979, the Thyssen-Bornemisza Collection had been looked after by Marco Grassi and Sandor Berkes but around this time someone obviously explained to Heini the value of a full-time professional curator who could increase the perceived value by organising international exhibitions and publishing catalogues while filling in provenance gaps and authenticating pictures. It was a task ideally suited to someone in the upper echelons of an auction house.

While Heini remained vague about his reasons for choosing Simon de Pury, he admitted that there may have been certain mutual, financial advantages in choosing a Swiss national who had been running Sotheby's in Monaco. This would become obvious when, after establishing the Thyssen-Bornemisza Collection's international reputation, de Pury would rejoin the firm in 1986 as managing director for Europe and Chairman of Sotheby's in Geneva. De Pury claimed to have been taken by surprise at being offered the job:

He came into Sotheby's one day and invited me to lunch. I had met him but didn't know him at all ... When he offered me the job as curator, it took me completely by surprise. He makes up his mind very quickly ... But what impresses me most, aside from his fantastic knowledge [of art and enormous feeling for quality], is his energy and his disciplined use of time, plus the fact he never takes any of it too seriously.[20]

Or that was certainly the image of Heini that he liked to portray. But it could also have been an extremely diplomatic means of describing Heini's bibulous excesses, for Simon de Pury was no stranger to the art of flattery. He was also the perfect choice for the job and within the year the first major exhibition of the Thyssen-Bornemisza Collection would take place. The show, titled 'Old Master Paintings from the Collection of Baron Thyssen-Bornemisza', included among the fifty-seven paintings work by El Greco, Goya, Rembrandt, Rubens and Titian and began a two-year American tour in November 1979 with a show at the National Gallery of Art in Washington. After that the paintings were put on display in Detroit, Minneapolis, Cleveland, Los Angeles, Denver and Fort Worth. But such an extravagant exhibition is not mounted without ensuring some guarantee of critical approval and judging by the response from Hilton Kramer of the *New York Times*, who had originally seen the show in Washington, de Pury's efforts had been embarrassingly successful:

The Thyssen Bornemisza Collection is said to be the greatest private art collection now in existence anywhere. On the basis of the fifty-seven paintings selected for the present display, one is not inclined to dispute the claim. Much that we see here represents the art of painting at the highest level the human mind has yet conceived. Only the greatest of public museum collections can rival the quality of such paintings.

* * *

Although it was the US show that made the headlines, de Pury had actually put together another touring exhibition at almost the same time entitled 'America & Europe, a Century of Modern Masters from the Thyssen-Bornemisza Collection' for Australia and New Zealand. After days and nights of cultural hospitality, speeches and presentations in both countries, Heini and Denise crossed the Pacific to join the Old Masters tour in Los Angeles. There they were exposed to people to whom the name Thyssen was more familiar in connection with Fritz's financial support of Hitler than extravagant art exhibitions. But having been warned of this risk, Heini had prepared various appeasing statements concerning the healing power of art:

> I tried to unite people and nations through art. Art helps to develop the best qualities in people and those qualities are not only incompatible with war but they help many people in such a way that their actions prevent the development of conditions which result in war. The Nazis are to be blamed for the whole world hating the Germans. That has affected me although I have always been against the Nazis and I am not even German.

But a contingent from the local Jewish community arrived in front of the museum to boycott the opening of the exhibition. Heini was 'sure that there was a misunderstanding, so I phoned Cutler, my lawyer who was also Jewish. He advised me to talk with Dr Simon Wiesenthal, the Nazi hunter, who knew who had been a Nazi and who had not.'

Although Dr Wiesenthal could not confirm any such conversation, Heini recalled that half an hour later, presumably having been assured that he was 'not a Nazi', 'Everything was resolved and all the Jews attending the opening changed their banners saying "Nazi Thyssen", into apologies and flowers.'

Having been exposed to the risk of such accusations, it seems strange that in 1987 Heini should have risked commissioning Hitler's favourite sculptor, Professor Arno Breker of Düsseldorf, to create busts of both himself and Tita.

* * *

Over the next few years, several further travelling exhibitions followed without any social or political criticism. While Heini displayed no intention of reducing his rate of acquisition, he was left with minimal time for research or discovery and his knowledge of art remained, as one close to the collection described it, 'anecdotal'. When giving speeches at the opening of his exhibitions, Heini's ignorance could result in mild amusement or deep embarrassment on the part of his audience; depending on the amount he had drunk. But the power of his chequebook overcame any criticism from the dealers or auction houses.

On 31 March 1979 another Picasso, 'Le petit ver', was acquired for $700,000 and another O'Keeffe, 'White Iris', for $230,000. Meanwhile, Heini bought from Mr Pallessi in Rome a painting by Rubens, 'Portrait of a lady with a rosary', for $690,000. The painting then went to Paris, where it received 'four original expert opinions'. While no record of their assessment remains in the archives, the painting was subsequently sold to Spain as a work of the master.

In November 1979, via Swiss and Liechtenstein companies, Heini spent

$450,000 on 'Allées et venues, Martinique', even though it was only 'attributed' to Paul Gauguin. When it was eventually inherited by Tita, the 'attribution' had been replaced by a confirmation of originality and its value increased to an astonishing $7 million. On a more direct level, he also spent $2.2 million in the same month on Picasso's 'Harlequin with a Mirror', and later remembered the purchase while exemplifying the challenge still presented to him by Cubism: 'I was at Lefèvre in 1979 when two people were arguing over the price while I quietly outbid them. It is a very good painting with a normal face. Picasso normally paints such crooked faces.'

* * *

In 1980, Heini Junior celebrated his thirtieth birthday and as far as the inheritance contract was concerned, he came of age and inherited a seat on the supervisory board of the Thyssen Bornemisza Group. The date of the eighty-third meeting of the TBG Supervisory Board was made to coincide with Georg's birthday on 19 March 1980 and, to mark the occasion, was held at Landsberg Castle.

It was also the year when Heini liked to give the impression that he retired from the Group to devote most of his time and effort to his collection and his 'artistic endeavours'. But in reality there appeared to have been little change and Heini continued to attend many of the major meetings, while others continued to buy paintings on his behalf.

Apart from Hopper's 'The Martha McKeen of Wellfleet' which was acquired for $435,000, the most important addition to the collection in early 1980 was Tintoretto's 'Paradise' which was hailed by *Zeit Magazine* as 'a brilliant coup': 'He bought the almost five-metre-long sketch for the Doges Palais mural in Venice for DM 11 million. He paid three-quarters of the sum with a dozen paintings from his collection, among which was a Rembrandt that experts today say is a fake. Heini, however, is still convinced that it's a true Rembrandt.'

By now it was becoming obvious that Heini was perhaps beginning to overreach himself financially. To acquire Picasso's 'Woman at Fountain' for $2 million from Crispo he had to sell Picasso's 'Le petit ver' for $850,000, Hopper's 'Hotel lobby' for $580,000 and use a $300,000 deposit already received for a Poussin with the $270,000 balance to be paid between November 1980 and February 1981.

But regardless of his obvious cash shortage, Heini made no perceptible attempt to reduce his rate of acquisition. Like a fog-blind driver with his foot pressed down hard on the accelerator, he seemed supremely confident he would see the stoplights before the inevitable crash. Crispo was less optimistic and two days before Christmas, when he sent Heini an invoice for seven pictures

Francesca and Georg ('Heini Junior') at a formal reception at Villa Favorita.

including Winslow Homer's 'Waverly Oaks' for $650,000, he demanded 'immediate payment' of the $2.2 million total. He recognised the fact that it was not so much the money Heini was paying for individual works, as the rate at which he was spending that was becoming unsustainable.

Perhaps Heini should have seen the significance in his next, $2.5 million acquisition from the Kennedy Galleries in New York, because he certainly knew what Winslow Homer's 'The signal of distress' was about: 'It is about a ship which is about to sink in a very rough sea.'

1 A contract involving Ruhrkohle AG, Thyssen-Bornemisza Group Amstelveen/BV Maatschappij vor Belegging en Beheer Francesca and Thyssen Asset Management Düsseldorf, a company representing the interests of Counts Federico and Claudio Zichy-Thyssen, was signed in December 1981. Records from 1997 show interest on the lease payable from Ruhrkohle Bergbau AG to Thyssen Asset Management of DM 802,483 for a period of six months (TBG Archives).
2 *Sunday Telegraph,* 4 May 1969.

3 *Daily Express*, 20 November 1967.
4 Note to the files from the federal prosecutor, Mr Wütherich, dated 8 July 1948 (Swiss Federal Archives).
5 Letter from Franz von Marosy to Heini Thyssen-Bornemisza, dated 9 March 1968 (TBG Archives).
6 Higham, p. xvii. The Rockefeller-controlled Chase National Bank and the Bank of the Manhattan Company merged to form the Chase Manhattan Bank in 1955.
7 *Der Spiegel*, no. 25, 1972.
8 Ketterer, pp. 197 ff.
9 Ibid.
10 *New York Times*, 15 October 1981.
11 *Apollo*, p. 21.
12 Author's conversations with Baron Steven Bentinck, 1975–2003.
13 Invoices of art purchases and 1992 distribution list of art works (TBG Archives).
14 From a statement made by Baron Steven Bentinck in his libel case against the *Daily Mail*'s Nigel Dempster in 1995 (Bentinck Archives).
15 Le Rosey is an exclusive Swiss boarding school which operates in Rolle on Lake Geneva during the summer and in Gstaad during the winter.
16 *Vanity Fair*, August 2002.
17 Ibid.
18 See Irene Martin's foreword to the Thyssen-Bornemisza Collection catalogue '*The European Avant-gardes*', compiled by Christopher Green in 1995.
19 Thyssen *v*. Thyssen, Supreme Court of Bermuda, 13 October 1999.
20 *Town & Country Magazine*, March 1984.

Chapter IX
1981–1988

Enter Tita... The Spanish connection

*It is a truth universally acknowledged,
that a single man in possession of a good fortune,
must be in want of a wife.*
Jane Austen

If, as Tita would later claim, she was welcomed into Heini's life as a temporary, diversionary tactic by Georg and the TBG management to lure him away from Denise and her potential danger to the organisation, it certainly succeeded. Even before the paint had a chance to dry on the scene of Heini and Tita's moonlit romance and he slipped away on his private jet, he had whispered in her ear, 'I will wait for you in Lugano; please be my guest. Please come and visit me. Denise will stay on the yacht.'

Once again Heini was in love and acting like a character in a romantic melodrama.

> Tita gave me two things that had never lasted very long for me, love and happiness; at a time when I thought that my romantic life had come to an end. She arrived at a moment when I was feeling helpless, weak and unhappy. Then, without warning, she appeared like a tornado of vitality and joy. I fell in love and once again everything seemed possible to me.

For three days and nights in his lake-side palace their love became passion; before he invited her to fly with him to New York and a suite at the Waldorf.

* * *

Despite Heini's avowed commitment to the new woman in his life, somewhere between the mountains of Switzerland and the concrete canyons of Manhattan, he somewhat surprisingly chose to spend a few days in Jamaica on board the *Hanse* with Denise. It was there that he received the first indication that his brother was dying. The news came from Josi Groh in a telex to the yacht: 'Sad news. Your brother Stephan is in the intensive care unit of St Clare's Hospital with a fever of 106 degrees. He has a lung infection and may have also suffered a heart attack.'

The rest of the telex consisted of news concerning the political situation in Poland and how it might affect their ship-building programme, the avalanches in St Moritz and the movement of paintings. Having been dropped off at Alligator Head, Heini displayed no inclination to visit his brother in New York. Instead he chose to lie in the sun and telex the captain of the *Hanse* concerning such pressing matters as Gianni Agnelli's arrival on board, and whether the 'MS August Thyssen' launch dinner at Bremer Vulkan scheduled for 9 March should be followed by music and dancing. There is no evidence of any further communication concerning Stephan who, at 11.20 on 22 January 1981, died at the New York Hospital in Manhattan aged seventy-three. Heini displayed his typical lack of emotion when he recounted the story:

> My brother died of an overdose of vitamins. He never ate any food and his only source of nourishment was vitamin tablets. After a while, his body refused to absorb anything and he lost twenty kilos in a week. He looked like a skeleton and spent all day in bed. He was living in a hotel that had him sent to a clinic. However, it was not very good. When I found out, I sent several physicians to see him. They managed to get him on his feet again, but the strain was too much for his heart. Denise very kindly attended the funeral on my behalf. I hate going to funerals and having to talk to all those people.

Denise had in fact kept in regular contact with Stephan, whose company she enjoyed and intelligence she admired. By contrast, it appeared that, like Heini, Gaby and Margit had also made no attempt to visit their brother in hospital or attend his funeral. The only other evidence of any remorse for Stephan's death was contained in a poignant letter to Heini from his favourite Aunt Ilda in Ticino:

> Stephan's death has touched me enormously because it brought back memories of my youth. I was eleven years old when Stephan was born in Rechnitz and my parents and I lived in the castle. Right from the start, Stephan had been an unlucky fellow who lived in constant fear. Your parents did not provide him with any homely warmth. He was beaten a lot; excuses were always found to do so. This is why he started telling lies, but they were unconvincing, so that they only led to more beatings.

He was incarcerated in the ghostly part of the castle, from which he tried to escape. At one time he managed to do so by forcing his way through a glass door and ending up bleeding under my father's bed. I still see this unfortunate child whose life went from one disaster to the next. His stay in America was a complete failure. The money gave him a lot of options and he got married to a Texan girl. When his father found out about it, he lost his apanage and he ended up without money, going from house to house selling bibles. His marriage experiment was dissolved and he came home with a sort of lyre that he was playing.

Then came the stay in Budapest and the shooting of his alleged girlfriend through carelessness followed by the unfortunate marriage with the salesgirl from Gerbeaud. Everything he did failed and he lived in fear. During the Hitler years he was in Hanover where we visited him. He was divorced from his wife and it appears that he had promised her many things, which he could not keep. You well know how unhappy his second marriage was and how badly he was treated. It is no surprise that he became an 'outsider'. Now he has been released from this joyless life and one can only be grateful to God that it happened the way it did. In his last letter he wrote that his feet were bleeding. In his childhood, he had a similar condition and his mother used to bind his feet. Your childhood and youth was of course completely different.

Otherwise known as Princess Matilda Sapieha, through her third marriage, Ilda also died quite soon afterwards, on 19 July 1981. Heini, and subsequently Georg, would continue to support Stephan's surviving wife and daughter, albeit with a conspicuous lack of sympathy or spirit of generosity. This was made painfully evident in a letter from Heini to Inge:

Following Stephan's sudden death, I have consulted my files to find out what my obligations are that derive from my old agreements with him. According to our contract I still owe him a monthly payment of $2,000 until 1 June 1989 deriving from his share in the inheritance of our mother. It was his wish that following his death, this payment should be made to you and your daughter. I have decided to double this sum voluntarily until the final payment on 1 June 1989. Furthermore, Indian Head have paid Stephan's medical and hospital bills and those of the funeral institute and made several cash amounts available to you. The total amounts to $50,000 and I will reimburse Indian Head this amount. Yours sincerely . . .

* * *

By the summer of 1981, it was obvious that his relationship with Tita was going to lead Heini to yet another divorce. He was also aware that under Swiss inheritance law and in the absence of a pre-nuptial agreement, Denise could make an alimonial claim of up to 50 per cent of his entire fortune, including the Thyssen Bornemisza Group, unless of course, ownership of the Group was transferred to a protective trust. As a result, Heini and Robert Genillard decided to recruit a specialist British lawyer called Jack Moore who arrived at TBG in August and set to work with Genillard and Georg in planning the protective 'Trust Project'.

While all the heirs were aware that any reduction in the family fortune would have a negative effect on their inheritance, Georg's involvement in the creation of such a trust had a somewhat greater degree of vested interest. His mother having negotiated his inheritance as part of her alimony agreement in 1954, Georg's eventual 43.75 per cent share of the Group through what was to become known as the Thyssen-Bornemisza Continuity Trust provided sufficient motivation for him to protect his own interests and minimise his father's extravagance.

Georg's intention was that the trust arrangement would not only protect his father and TBG from Denise but would also make it impossible for his father's fortune to be squandered on some future relationship. The latter proviso no doubt being a reaction to Heini's rapidly developing relationship with Carmen Cervera. No one remarked on the irony that Heini was accepting advice from a son from his first marriage, the divorce from which could be seen to have cost him the control of the family business.

According to Moore, the creation of the Continuity Trust Agreement was constrained by both their ever-present tax avoidance strategy and the circumvention of Swiss inheritance laws: 'We are preparing a series of protective and long-term measures for the settlor's estate . . . One of these measures is the creation of an irrevocable offshore trust in an English common law jurisdiction.'[1]

The use of the British legal system by a Swiss national for such a purpose would always be questionable, particularly in view of his reliance on the even more questionable Swiss Kaszony Foundation. Georg inherited the Thyssen aversion to the payment of taxes and while he was a resident of Monaco, his domicile was a private address in Schaan, Liechtenstein. To assist in organizing the trust arrangement, Georg enrolled the services of the South-African-born Eric Pfaff. An international trust lawyer, working out of offices in Luxembourg and the Isle of Man, he collaborated with Moore and Genillard in the preparation of the Thyssen-Bornemisza Continuity Trust.

* * *

Chapter IX: 1981–1988

Whether the survival of the Group had more to do with Heini relinquishing control than Georg assuming it, was open to conjecture but Heini continued to give the impression that the choice of his successor was based on merit and personal affection:

> In 1984, I made one of the most important decisions of my life when I decided to formally hand over the reins of power [while remaining President for life] in the family business to my son Georg Heinrich in just the same way that my father had done when I was only twenty-three years old.

One of Heini's favourite stories was how, in 1979, he had appointed Georg chairman of the supervisory board of the troubled Bremer Vulkan shipbuilding company. Heini said the job was a test of his abilities, which one of the managers likened to giving trainee surgeons terminally ill patients to practise on.

Any testing of his abilities was largely superfluous as there was no other suitable candidate and the 1954 inheritance contract had given Georg sufficient advantage for it to be quite impossible for Heini to set up the Continuity Trust without his co-operation.

On 13 July 1979, Robert Genillard had formally announced Georg's arrival on the board and the commencement of his own replacement:

> Our chairman recently announced that his son will be joining our supervisory board next year. It is nearly a year that Heini Junior [Georg] has been working in our midst. This has given him a good knowledge of the Group's business and has afforded the organisation an opportunity to get to know and appreciate the eldest member of the next generation of ownership. It is in that capacity that Heini Junior will continue working here, perfecting his knowledge of the Group and in particular of its general management process. To this end, he has a standing invitation to attend management, business and staff meetings and I would appreciate your making sure that copies of all relevant background material and communications are addressed to him so that he is properly briefed.[2]

Like his father, Georg had displayed no interest in mechanical or industrial studies and according to Michael Crystal, the British QC:

> Georg was very interested in trusts and in the uses to which they could be put. He researched trusts. He attended seminars about trusts. He wrote papers about trusts . . . He spent weeks at university studying the family and inheritance laws of Switzerland during his studies for his law qualifications.[3]

Lorne Thyssen-Bornemisza at the Mayfair Hotel in 1983, shortly after his arrival in London (photo: Michael Dyer).

Gradually, as Georg and Heini spent an increasing amount of time together, Heini became reliant on his son's legal abilities and in 1982, Georg negotiated and agreed terms with BHF-Bank concerning the assumption of Heini's personal debt of around DM 80 million:

The new trust, being the sole future shareholder of Thyssen-Bornemisza NV, will assume responsibility for all private debt of Baron Thyssen to BHF-Bank. Furthermore, the trust will agree with the bank a firm repayment schedule. The necessary cash flow will be provided out of profits Thyssen-Bornemisza NV will pay to the trust. Dividends will, on average, amount to 30 per cent of net income of TBNV.[4]

The yearly dividend amounted to around Dfl 40 million, which meant that almost half of it would go towards servicing the debt. Apparently all this was explained to Heini on 8 December 1982 at a meeting in Monaco at which he was finally presented with the proposed structure of the Continuity Trust although he later disputed that he understood its terms. Only Josi Groh remained wary of the trust concept and as early as 3 September 1981 he sent a memo to Heini warning him: 'If you transfer the assets irrevocably to a trust, you are no longer the owner of them.'

Josi Groh had also displayed sufficient loyalty to warn Heini that the legal structure of the original Kaszony Foundation, which had been designed to fulfil a similar function, appeared highly doubtful under Swiss law, pointing out that 'a family foundation is not subject to any regulatory authority. Nobody checks whether the provisions of the statutes are compatible with the applicable law. It is thus possible to find foundation provisions that have been accepted and used, although the question of their validity appears more than doubtful.'

* * *

Having set about protecting itself from Denise, the Thyssen Bornemisza Group had next to solve the problem of what to do with Heini's beloved Bremer

Vulkan. Having already sold 25 per cent of the yard and suffering badly from Far East competition and the ignominy of being caught trying to fund his yacht with taxpayers' money, the last thing TBG needed was a bad case of basic mismanagement. They should probably have sold the yard when they had the chance, but Heini had a weakness for ship-building. So when he was offered the chance to build a luxury ocean liner to be called the *Europa*, common sense deserted him. He was not alone.

In partnership with Krupp's AG Weser yard, with a DM 15 million loan from the Bremen Senate, the order seemed secure. But Krupp pulled out after Vulkan failed to agree labour costs. The error cost the yard DM 300 million. A similar mistake in the construction of six frigates for the German Ministry of Defence resulted in a loss of DM 400 million.

Eventually TBG was left with no other option but to assist the government in nationalising the yard, the details of which Heini had difficulty recounting with any degree of consistent accuracy. One day he would claim: 'We sold Bremer Vulkan because of mismanagement that led us to lose DM 100 million. The shares were worthless and we got DM 1 as a token payment.' But when he was feeling more expansive he would claim: 'I finally sold Bremer Vulkan for DM 100 million.'

Whatever the truth of the matter, it was a sad and lack-lustre end to the ownership of such a legendary shipyard and, despite its wartime activities, an integral part of Germany's industrial heritage.

Amid this disaster and perhaps as a result of it, in 1982 Robert Genillard was 'obliged' to place the leadership of the Thyssen Bornemisza Group in the inexperienced hands of Georg. According to Frank Holze of *Manager Magazine*, Georg would have preferred to have remained on the supervisory board for a few more years but Heini insisted that he accept the post of Chief Executive Officer, even though some of the management were far from happy with the decision. They failed to appreciate how a shy, tennis-playing, confirmed bachelor, with a flat above the office and no experience apart from his time spent with TBG and one month's work placement with the Chase Manhattan bank in London, could possibly demand sufficient respect to assume control of the organisation. The only qualification apart from his law degree and the fact that he was the owner's son, was his undeniable commitment to his work and lack of enthusiasm for the development of any extravagant social life.

While Georg apparently remained uninterested in girls, it failed to discourage the more determined or even their parents. Following a private dinner party, the American Malcolm D. Crawford sent Georg a note extolling the attractions of his daughter Chandler and her apparent enthusiasm for presentable young heirs to financial fortunes. While he reminded Georg of his daughter's exceptional beauty, there was no evidence of any further social, let alone romantic interaction. His continued existence as a bachelor made the production of a future son and heir appear increasingly unlikely.

Georg's brother Lorne displayed no such inability to enjoy a rich social life or relate to the opposite sex. Having completed his schooling in Switzerland, he arrived in London and took up residence with his Alsatian dog in the house next door to his sister Francesca on Seymour Walk. While Lorne was genuinely interested in academia and sufficiently intelligent to justify enrolling at Edinburgh University to read politics and philosophy, his over-indulgence in the town's social attractions eventually curtailed his academic ambitions.

* * *

Heini's schedule of social and cultural engagements increased considerably after he relinquished control of TBG. His 1982 diary contained details of lunch with Jacques Chirac in Paris, followed by an exhibition opening at the Petit Palais, dinner in Regensburg with Prince Johannes Thurn und Taxis, then back to Paris

Heini's audience with Pope John Paul II. (photo: Pontificia Fotografia, Rome).

Chapter IX: 1981–1988

for a dinner the following day with the American Ambassador John Galbraith before flying down to Rome in his new Falcon 50 for a 'work session' with Simon de Pury and a representative from the Kennedy Gallery, as well as visits to the Sistine Chapel and the Vatican Museum. This was followed by a birthday dinner in Munich before he flew to Amsterdam for the notarisation of his signature on some documents regarding an art trust. Then back to Paris for yet another opening at the Petit Palais. There followed another dinner with the American Ambassador given in Versailles by the Smithsonian Institution, followed a few days later by a dinner at the Jockey Club in honour of the National Board of Smithsonian Associates. Then he was off to visit Agnelli in Turin and giving an interview to Swiss Italian television before heading back to Paris for dinner with Niarchos and on to Berlin for an exhibition opening. Heini then headed to the US for a press breakfast and briefing tour with de Pury and Fred Cody, before lunch at the National Gallery of Art in Washington, then off to the Houston Museum of Fine Art for a private view, before a 'Blue Jeans Dinner' at the ranch of Alanzo Dunn and back to London for drinks with Lucian Freud at Claridges.

Heini's busy social schedule also involved a great deal of drinking which, according to Dr H. C. Goldman of Upper Wimpole Street in London, was becoming critical:

> My dear Baron, I think your liver is not in a very good state. Please stop alcoholic drinks altogether as soon as you receive this letter. If you cannot do it on your own, I shall be very pleased to put you into a clinic for a fortnight to get your condition out of the danger line. Please try to do it on your own if you can. Whatever you do, take my letter seriously.

There followed visits to various clinics and even the odd period of abstinence but Heini continued to drink. As a result of his wealth and power, those around him remained deferentially amused and accepted his odd naked appearance or display of head-stands and mimicry of dogs, the latter of which, according to his assistant Fred Cody, often took place at business meetings when Heini became bored. It involved him getting down on all fours, obliging the sober Fred Cody to follow suit, while they proceeded to bark at each other.

The Spanish writer José Luís de Vilallonga told of a social occasion when Heini, having been retired to bed by his long-suffering butler, returned to the party, stark naked and accused the wife of the Philippine Ambassador of trying to steal his Gauguin; an event that Heini claimed he could not remember.

* * *

Heini with one of his two Lucian Freud portraits (photo: Alan Davidson).

Heini rarely had the time to view paintings, still preferring to select his purchases from catalogues or photographs. This method certainly enabled him to maintain his break-neck rate of acquisition but did little to improve the overall standard of the collection. Heini continued to buy paintings with the random intensity that defied the existence of any overall plan. A typical example of his knee-jerk style of acquisition occurred while he was being driven to the US diplomatic mission in Paris for a dinner given by Ambassador Galbraith in 1982. He proudly claimed that while leafing through a Sotheby's catalogue, he saw that Piet Mondrian's 'Grey/Blue Composition' was to be sold in London that evening, so as soon as he arrived at the Embassy, he telephoned Sotheby's and asked to be kept on the line throughout the auction. To the annoyance of his fellow diners whom he was doubtless trying to impress, between courses he bid for a picture he had only seen in a catalogue a few hours previously. How much such impulsive and un-researched purchases were the result of Heini's alcohol consumption is unclear but it was certainly unlikely to have improved his critical faculties.

Heini's excessive spending had reached a peak in 1980 when he spent approximately $23 million on paintings. He spent some $13 million in both 1981 and 1982 and only $7 million in 1983. By now there appeared to be other reasons, apart from the pressure of his schedule, why Heini was becoming increasingly unprepared to visit galleries. This was obvious from a letter he received from the Galerie Gmurzynska in Cologne:

> A few days ago, we spoke to Mr Guscetti concerning payment for the paintings by Sonia Delaunay and Moholy-Nagy and he told me that this payment could only be made at the end of the year. Unfortunately, we urgently need finance right now and we would be enormously grateful if you could make a disposition in this respect.

But his cash crisis had little effect on his extravagance. In 1982, Heini bought a watercolour by Maurice Prendergast, 'The Racetrack', for a remarkable $375,000; Dégas's 'Two Dancers' for $400,000; Klee's 'Revolving House' for $200,000; Chagall's 'House in Grey' for $750,000; 'The Card Game' by Balthus for SwFr 1.7 million; Picasso's 'Man with a Clarinet' from Berggruen for $4 million, which was payable in fourteen instalments, and 'Senolassa' by Lucian Freud, bought directly from the artist for £70,000.

The latter painting disappeared from the records, being either sold on or back to Freud as part of the payment for Heini's portrait. Started in July 1981 and completed in October 1982 after 150 hours of sitting, it was a feat of perseverance on the part of both men. Denise, who did not like Lucian Freud, criticised the work for being 'too small', while Heini enjoyed reminding people: 'You know, Freud was born in Berlin and his family came from Leipzig, so he is more German than I am.'

The cost of these portraits, for there would eventually be two, was claimed to be in the order of a million dollars each. According to Heini, when Freud was short of money, he would even suggest a third.

On 18 December 1982, Heini also bought a Rothko, 'Green on Maroon', for $250,000 from the artist's estate through the Marlborough Gallery in New York. Some years later, a cleaner accidentally damaged the painting and Heini made a successful insurance compensation claim of $102,000 which enabled Emil Bosshard to repair the damage. Considering Emil was quite capable of creating an identical painting in an afternoon with a bill for canvas, stretcher and paints unlikely to exceed $5,000, the payment may have been somewhat excessive, although Heini refused to admit it. He reacted with a remarkable lack of humour, when asked if he thought a 'Damaged Rothko' created by a cleaning lady should be considered more or less valuable than 'An erased de Kooning drawing' created by Robert Rauschenberg.

* * *

Between 1979 and 1990, the Thyssen-Bornemisza Collection formed the basis of ten major international exhibitions. But one of the greatest milestones in the history of the collection's creation did not involve the acquisition or sale of a picture, but the temporary exchange of 120 of Heini's Old Masters for 80 Impressionist paintings from Russia in 1983; eight years before the dissolution of the Soviet Union and the end of the Cold War. It was a triumph for Heini and Simon de Pury.

The story began at a dinner party in Bonn where Vladimir Semjonov, the Soviet Ambassador to West Germany and something of a collector himself, reminded Heini of the rarely seen Impressionist paintings in the Soviets' possession and successfully proposed an exchange.

In 1983, more than 260,000 visitors saw Russia's superb Cézannes, Gauguins, van Goghs, Matisses and Picassos at the Villa Favorita, while tens of thousands flocked to see the Baron's Old Masters amid the splendour of the Pushkin Museum in Moscow where Heini and Tita were treated like heads of state. Tita enjoyed the celebrity status and VIP treatment and got on extremely well with the Russians; particularly with the Ambassador to Germany:

> Semjonov was a great admirer of art. His wife was very 'healthy' and they also had a painter friend with them when they invited us to dinner. She was a very good hostess and we sampled food and drink from many different areas of Russia and mixed lots of different spirits. It was a fantastic evening. We were dancing and drinking while their friend was painting us at the same time. When we wanted to leave, it turned out our driver had disappeared. He was probably drunk. In Moscow you have to be careful. If you get lost, you freeze to death. Outside on the street, Heini hailed a taxi but there was another man who wanted it at the same time. Heini punched him out of the way and said that he must have the cab because he had a lady with him and we finally arrived back at the hotel in the early hours of the morning.
>
> That day, we were supposed to have lunch with the American Ambassador and his wife. Of course, we were very badly hungover. Suddenly, there was a knock on the door, and the telephone went at the same time. I was crawling on my hands and knees, trying to decide what to answer first. When I opened the door, I found two bottles of beer and a bowl with two eggs in it. When I answered the phone it was Madam Semjonov saying: 'Did you get my babys?' She told us that this was the best hangover cure, to have a raw egg and wash it down with beer. So we did and we felt fine.

Chapter IX: 1981–1988

Heini always liked to give the impression that the arrangement with the Russians, including several more exhibitions over a five-year period, was based on his cultural generosity with no commercial interests involved. He also insisted that he had never been to Russia before 1972, when, he said, he had gone to Moscow to work out a trade agreement. In fact, Heini had been there as early as 1967, when his itinerary included travelling to Leningrad, the Caucasus, Tashkent, Samarkand and Irkutsk in Siberia. When he returned to organise the exchange of pictures, he was equally non-committal concerning the reason why his son Georg and a group of his senior managers accompanied him, although the *New York Times* would eventually hint at rumours of a 'lucrative trade accord'.

In Paris in 1997, Heini boastfully admitted: ' Junior got a top deal out of the Russians. He acquired a monopoly on Russian oil but then there was some kind of problem at the Riga ports and they couldn't get the oil out, so they had to sit on it for a while. Meanwhile, the price of oil rocketed, and by the time he took delivery we were able to sell it on at an enormous profit.'

With the help of de Pury, Heini also brokered an auction agreement between the Russian Minister of Culture and Sotheby's. He obviously gained considerable satisfaction from exploiting the communists, but his favourite story was rather more personal and reflected less favourably on his character and arguably his respect for authenticity: 'An old friend of mine had asked to borrow some money but I don't like lending money, so I bought a piece of jewellery from him for quite a lot more than it was worth. Then, on one of our trips to Russia, I put it in a Tiffany's box and gave it as a present to Raissa Gorbachev. She was very impressed and later I saw her on television wearing it.'

* * *

The organisation of the exchange had not been without its problems, most of which, according to Heini, appeared to have been the result of Denise, her pathological dislike of communists and the fact that Heini decided to hang the Impressionists in the Villa rather than the Gallery. It was an arrangement affected by his tax situation, reinforcing the fact that he was theoretically no longer resident in Lugano:

> I remember when the Russian experts arrived to visit me at Villa Favorita, there was a tremendous fight with Denise. She reproached me for making a mess of our rooms and filling them up of with 'all those communist pictures'. Then she provoked our guests by lounging around in all her jewellery. She

was impossible. So impossible that I had to tell Irina Antonova, the expert of the Russian group, 'I am very sorry about my wife insulting you, but very soon she will be my ex-wife because I am going to divorce her'. I also said to Mr Shuslov, the leader of the group, 'I am very sorry, but you won't see her again. I promise you.'

But after fifteen years of marriage, Denise could not have been expected to have left either empty-handed or in good humour from the home that they had shared for so long. Her mood was not improved by Heini's flaunting of his new mistress or his accusation that Denise had filled a truck with looted art and jewellery before she left. He also accused Groh and Guscetti of assisting her, choosing to ignore the fact that Josi Groh and his wife had developed a close friendship with Denise and could hardly have been expected to have stood idly by while she packed her belongings.

Denise's insistence that she only took what Heini had given her seemed far more justifiable than his claim that he wanted 'the jewels to stay in the family as an investment to fall back on in times of hardship'. But that did not prevent him from accusing her of theft which resulted in her being arrested and imprisoned in Vaduz.

In an attempt to gain her release, Denise sent a note to Gaby who, lacking the knowledge of how to 'spring' someone from jail, sent her a box of chocolates which, predictably, did little to improve her sister-in-law's humour. Fortunately the court was not convinced that Heini's claim was legitimate and Denise was freed without charge.

* * *

Three weeks after the Russians shot down the Korean KL007 airliner and ten days after the opening of the Thyssen-Bornemisza exhibition in Moscow, the *US Daily News* picked up the story of Heini's matrimonial problems and announced: 'Sticky divorce for one of the world's most bejewelled women. Her perfect diamonds are the size of ice cubes.'

Heini had commenced divorce proceedings against Denise in Switzerland on 11 April 1983 but she had answered by petitioning in England, where, by achieving greater press coverage of Heini's affairs, she hoped to persuade him to award her a higher settlement.

Tita welcomed this filing for divorce as legally her status had, for the last two years, been that of concubine and while both she and her ever-present mother had been treated with extreme generosity by Heini, she had no legal inheritance rights. But despite the resentment and opposition of his children, by now it should have been obvious that she was going to be the next Baroness Thyssen-Bornemisza.

In the meantime, Denise continued her fight for the legal right of possession of her various liberated assets. Apparently, armed with a court order for possession, she leapt into a car and headed for Daylesford, where she scaled the wall and literally 'dropped in', so avoiding the guards on the gate. According to the *Daily News*, there she stayed for some weeks, while Heini saw to it that all the phone lines were cut.

After she had filed for divorce in the UK, Denise somehow managed to organise a Caribbean cruise on board the *Hanse* before, according to Heini, leaving the boat with yet more boxes and suitcases. But what Denise was after were bigger things than sheets and towels. What she really wanted was half of Heini's estimated $1.4 billion fortune.

Fortunately for Heini, any chance of Denise claiming half his fortune was curtailed when on 18 April 1983, between 9 and 12 o'clock, he, Georg and a posse of legal advisers signed the Continuity Trust Agreement in Hamilton, Bermuda. There followed a lunch at the Lobster Pot restaurant, where a great deal of red wine was drunk, at least by Heini, in celebration of the new ownership of the Thyssen Bornemisza Group by a faceless Bermudan trust.

Denise would have been even angrier if she had known that Heini had taken Tita with him to Bermuda for the signing. Only the lawyers could have predicted that Heini and Georg had in fact signed a series of agreements which would form the basis of a subsequent $150 million court battle back on the same tropical paradise some sixteen years later.

Georg must have despaired when, despite his efforts to protect the family fortune, his father headed straight for New York to impress the new woman in his life with his spending power. Having bought a John Singer Sargent in April for $500,000, he returned in May to purchase a Jawlensky for $190,000, a Mondrian for $1.5 million, a Morris Lewis for $360,000, a Matisse for $775,000, and a Gainsborough for $510,000.

Shortly afterwards Guscetti warned Heini: 'With regard to the paintings which you purchased on the occasion of your US trip in May, having a value of $4.575 million, this sum will not be available until March 1985.'

He also reminded the Baron that his ongoing expenses were still running at $550,000 per month and warned him that his annuity was likely to remain limited through 1984 to 1986, advising him to raise capital by selling the 'Star of Peace' diamond. Unfortunately, he was too late.

Even before Heini had commenced the legal battle with Denise for the return of what he claimed to be $80 million worth of jewellery, he had presented Tita with the pear-shaped 'Star of Peace' diamond. Valued at $3.8 million, he would later describe his gift as 'a token of my esteem to her, to her love and the understanding she has for the recognition of the continuity of my life work in business and art'.[5]

Many similar tokens would follow and by the time he had divorced Denise and married Tita in 1985 he would have presented her with $14,274,481-worth of jewellery – much of it from Harry Winston. It is estimated that during the following seventeen years of their marriage, Heini would spend at least $30 million on jewellery for Tita, while failing to retrieve any from Denise. In fact, the only piece of jewellery that he did manage to retrieve was Nina's engagement ring. Having come up for auction at Sotheby's, it had already been sold by the time it came to the notice of Heini and Tita. Not one to let a flawless, blue-white solitaire diamond the size of a New York roach slip through her fingers, Tita contacted D. D. Brooks, who was then head of the jewellery department and told her that if she did not cancel the sale, Heini would stop using Sotheby's. Miraculously, the diamond was retrieved from its new owner and repurchased by Heini for an undisclosed premium to decorate the hand of his new Baroness. It went with her sapphire and diamond earrings that were of such outrageous size that they required gold hooks over the top of her ears to support their weight.

* * *

The Thyssen-Bornemisza Continuity Trust Agreement was an immensely complicated, 48-page document intended to ensure the continuity and stability of the Thyssen Bornemisza Group beyond Heini's death and protect it from divorce settlements while he was alive. Heini later claimed: 'The documentation which I signed to create the Continuity Trust and place TBG into it was extremely complex. I do not believe that I ever had a full understanding of its details.'[6]

He also insisted that Georg, Moore and Pfaff were responsible for its creation and that he had relied on Georg to keep him informed. But Heini already had considerable knowledge of such ownership cloaking, although he later claimed that Georg had told him that nothing would change in his lifetime in relation to TBG as a result of the trust's existence.

Heini presumably understood the agreement that he would receive 30 per cent of the profits with a base annuity of Dfl 45 million payable on 1 May of each year and that any 'shortfall' would be carried over to the following year. However, there would be considerable confusion concerning the effect of Heini's debt repayment schedule on the 'net available income'.

On Heini's death, this annual share of the Group's profits would be divided between Georg, Francesca, Lorne and Alexander. Georg would receive the lion's share but for the following sixty years neither they nor their offspring would be entitled to the capital value of TBG. Meanwhile, as 'chairman of the Protector' (a Guernsey company called Tornabuoni), Georg inherited control of the Group from his father. For reasons of Swiss law, Heini himself was not officially a direct beneficiary but, via several offshore financial organisations, Tamara Corporation (Bermuda) was created to look after his annuity arrangements while his loans with BHF-Bank were dealt with in the Annuity Agreement to prevent him from emulating his father and leaving huge debts for his heirs.

In addition to the conventional board of directors, the Thyssen Bornemisza Group retained the customary German supervisory board while Heini claimed to have been lulled into the false belief that he still had some control, particularly concerning his income, by being made its chairman. There was also a provision made for the upkeep of the collection that involved the 'discretionary distribution of trust income or capital to the Thyssen-Bornemisza Collection Trust in amounts that are reasonable and necessary for the maintenance and continuity of its art collection, which at present is exhibited in the Pinacoteca of the Villa Favorita, Lugano' for thirty years following Heini's death.

Heini also expected the trust to cover the costs of any necessary enlargements to the gallery.

Three months after the signing of the trust papers, at the hundredth TBG supervisory board meeting, attended by the board members Umberto Agnelli and Freddy Heineken, Heini finally announced the trust deal. In his speech he specifically referred to the fact that he, as 'the owner', would in future not be involved in the running of TBG, although it would later be claimed that he 'only intended the Protector [Georg] to start enforcing those objectives on his death. In the meantime, he was supposed to be able to do with TBG as he wished.'[7]

Unfortunately, despite claims to the contrary by Heini's lawyers, the Continuity Trust did not comply with Swiss inheritance law, first because it tied up the family property for sixty years and second, because it failed to provide for the widow who, under Swiss law, was entitled to as much as half of her husband's estate. The agreement also excluded adopted children from becoming heirs, another factor contradictory to Swiss law and presumably aimed specifically at Tita's son Borja.

*   *   *

As Heini's divorce from Denise gathered momentum and she became increasingly aggressive, he asked Tita if he could go and stay with her in Spain for a few weeks at her house Mas Mañanas in Sant Feliú de Guixols on the Costa Brava.

Having been advised by her mother: 'If you want the pictures to end up in Spain, first you will have to get him to come and live in your country; you will have to make a home in which he will be comfortable,' Tita accepted her good fortune and eagerly agreed. Meanwhile Heini would joke about his fear of Denise's wrath when she discovered that on 17 July 1983, he had signed her disinheritance papers from Tita's bed.

During the next fourteen years, Heini prepared seven wills and six codicils. On 12 May 1987 he created two on the same day. He could not remember who had angered him but admitted, with some giggling, that a family quarrel was the most likely reason. Meanwhile, he was willingly subjected to a new experience; that of living with a woman on far more equal terms than he was used to. Not only did the house belong to Tita but, unlike his previous wives, she had already been married twice and given birth to a son. She also remained very strongly influenced by an ever-present and extremely 'forceful' mother.

Tita's parents, like Heini's, had separated when she was still very young, but unlike him she had retained the affection of both her mother and her father as well as that of her grandparents. Voted Miss Spain in 1961, she was introduced to Lex Barker by her mother in 1963 and married him in Barcelona in 1965. Best known for his role as Tarzan, he had only embarked on a career as a screen actor after qualifying as an architect and in celebration of his fifth marriage he designed and built Mas Mañanas nine years before he died of a heart attack in New York. Tita never fully recovered from the loss and the house remains full of his memorabilia.

Before Lex, Tita had already met Sinatra, Monroe, Newman and Hudson when she visited Hollywood and starred in two movies. After Lex she married a Venezuelan movie producer called Espartaco Santoni whom she admitted was totally irresponsible but 'the best fun ever. If he didn't have money, he took it from you but if he did, he gave it to you.' Eventually Santoni was jailed and they separated.

Heini's marriage to Tita was never something even considered a possibility by his family: 'They certainly didn't plan on my replacing Denise permanently.

Groh had said to Georg, "Ah, Mrs Barker, we use her up until Denise has gone. As soon as the divorce is done, she will be out!" '

Groh must have started to doubt the accuracy of his prediction in November 1983 when the three-year-old Borja was baptised at the St Patrick's Cathedral in New York. His godparents were Heini's friends, the Duke of Badajoz, Ann Getty and Alexander Papamarkou. The following year, Borja was given the somewhat confusing surname of Bornemisza-Cervera and it soon became evident that they had all underestimated 'Mrs Barker'.

It had always been all too easy to write her off as an ex-beauty queen but Tita had influential friends and contacts beyond the world of show-business. She had developed a close and personal relationship with the Las Vegas real estate tycoon Kirk Kerkorian. She also formed a friendship with Gordon White, Lord Hanson and his wife Geraldine. Acutely aware of the potential of the Thyssen Bornemisza Group and Georg's lack of entrepreneurial spirit, she even suggested an amalgamation with Hanson, which, despite the restrictions of the Continuity Trust, would have been possible. Unfortunately, Georg found them 'rather brash' and did not like their style, so the idea did not receive his support; a reaction that Heini came to regret.

* * *

Heini's excessive expenditure continued to be a problem but Simon de Pury saw the situation as an ideal opportunity to encourage the 'pruning' of the collection by selling works of 'lesser quality', a policy which had also been recommended by Emil Bosshard. Unfortunately, according to de Pury, Heini was not easily convinced: 'The idea of selling had infinitely less appeal to the Baron than the one of acquiring [while] things that gradually get superseded in quality by new acquisitions end up in [TBG] offices.'[8]

Heini was equally ill-disposed towards admitting his inability to pay his bills; preferring to delegate the responsibility to Simon de Pury who was obliged to explain to Mr Berggruen: 'Due to various financial commitments, we have to inform you that we have to postpone the eight monthly instalments of $30,000 each that were due for Picasso's "Man with a Clarinet" from August 1983 to March 1984 by five months each'; and to the Wittgenstein Gallery: 'You will no doubt have received the first payment of $45,000 for the Everdingen. Due to other financial commitments, we are sadly in a position of having to delay the second payment.'

De Pury doubtless found Tita's influence over Heini and the collection increasingly difficult to accept but the embarrassment of the financial restrictions must have eventually contributed to his decision to resign as curator of the collection.

The situation was aggravated by the Group's continuing under-performance which resulted in Georg warning Groh that Heini's dividend would have to be reduced from Dfl 45 million to 35 million and advising him to adopt 'prudent financial planning'. But while Guscetti was quite capable of creating a 'liquidity plan', Groh confessed to Georg that he was at a loss to know, 'how I can work on your father to get him at last to realise the seriousness of the situation'.

By 1984, despite telling Denise's divorce lawyers that he was worth between $780 million and $930 million, Heini was suffering a personal liquidity shortfall of $7 million. He also had a debt of $30 million divided between BHF-Bank and Nederlandse Credietbank; both incorporating banks he had once owned. Despite considerable 'restructuring', Guscetti pointed out that he was still $1 million short in paying for a Gauguin, even after selling a Dégas.

The suggested restraint proved no more effective than de Pury's advice on the collection and by now the family were also becoming concerned that a major part of their inheritance was represented by the collection. The fear that their interests might be under threat from Tita was no doubt the catalyst for the establishment, in 1986, of the Bermudan Thyssen-Bornemisza Collections Trust (the Art Trust) designed to ensure the 'continuity' of the collection in the same way that the Thyssen-Bornemisza Continuity Trust did for the Group.

* * *

According to the 1983 Annual Report, the Thyssen Bornemisza Group had corporate headquarters in Amstelveen, New York, Monaco and Curaçao with three strategic units: Higher Technology, Trade and Services and Engineered Products. The group employed 17,100 people in 226 locations in 27 countries with sales of $1.6 billion and Georg predictably appeared to remain optimistic about the future:

> The Higher Technology Unit, which comprises ITG and Electrical Sciences, will be our main building block; the Trade and Services Unit with Interpool [a container leasing system] and Vulcan will expand selectively into 'know-how' intensive services and trading in energy resources; and the Engineered Products Unit, which comprises Terpa, Sterling Fluid Products, Metal and Automative Products and InCon Packaging, will continue to provide a strong industrial core and be a cash generator.

TBG also had a 50 per cent share in Mundogas and a 50 per cent share in

Eurogas, a Dutch company with Europe's largest terminal at Vlissingen, which stored liquefied petroleum gas. They also owned a shipping line that transported and marketed LPG and claimed to be the largest firm in the sector.

The other market leader was InCon Packaging, which, much to Heini's amusement, dominated the egg-packaging business with 85 per cent of the world market in that sector. Surprisingly, their largest clients were the Middle East, Algeria, Egypt and India.

But according to Germany's *Manager Magazine*, both the Group and Georg remained remarkably unimpressive:

> What became of this company which wrote German industrial history? Rue Louis Auréglia, Monaco. No sign on the door. Not exactly a luxurious boss's office. Twenty-five square metres of jumbled up furniture and a worn-out fifties desk. Thirty-four year old Georg Heinrich Thyssen-Bornemisza presides over the DM 5 billion business of the family conglomerate but experts think his father's collection is actually already more valuable than the Group which made DM 110 million in 1983 and since the sale of the German Thyssengas company in 1981, holds DM 500 million in cash.

In 1985, the business press were still producing negative reports: 'Profits have stagnated during the past three years at his private holding company, TBG Holdings NV; it earned $37.1 million last year on sales of $1.75 billion ... TBG's return on equity has slumped to about 11 per cent. Its profits have not moved during the past three years, despite a growth in sales.'[9]

* * *

Before he relinquished all managerial control of TBG, Heini made one last error of judgement that would nearly cost him his Dfl 45,000 annual director's fee and certainly damage a very valuable friendship. On 30 November 1983, Freddy Heineken and his chauffeur were kidnapped. For many years, Heini and Freddy had shared an enthusiasm for women and alcohol and had served as directors on each other's boards. On hearing of the kidnap, Heini and Tita immediately flew to Holland where he became involved in the three weeks of negotiations with the kidnappers and authorised the payment of the Dfl 30 million ransom demand. But before the kidnappers had a chance to enjoy their success, the police liberated Heineken. Far from being grateful for Heini's manifest concern for his well-being, Heineken was furious with what he considered Heini's ill-judged business decision and a waste of company money.

* * *

Tita could hardly have been impressed with either Heini's or Georg's business skills but the Trust barrier prevented her from having any influence over the running of the Group. So she remained far more inspired by the collection and active participation in its continued development. For her the collection also offered considerable social advantages: 'Without the paintings, I was only one more wife, married to a rich man. Through them, I meet the most important people in the world.'

Although Heini would never again buy as many paintings as he did with Denise, with Tita's encouragement he spent at least another $100 million on paintings before he died. It would only buy him half the number of works but this was more a result of the rise in prices than any increase in quality.

It was obvious, especially to the art critics, that the continual increase in the size and value of the collection was doing nothing to improve its quality or Heini's knowledge or aesthetic appreciation. In 1984, in a foreword to a catalogue for the exhibition of Modern Masters from the Thyssen-Bornemisza Collection at the Royal Academy of Arts in London, the English novelist Anthony Burgess wrote: 'The Baron loves art without pretensions to a profundity of historical or technical knowledge.'

Two paintings purchased during this period illustrated Heini's far greater concern with value than style or content. Regardless of the number of times he retold the story of how he had managed to increase the value of a second-rate Gauguin, 'Mata Mua', from $3.8 million to $22 million in five years, it never became any less confusing. But after some years and numerous bibulous explanations, it appeared that he had originally bought the painting with a South American friend in 1984 for $3.8 million. They then auctioned it through Sotheby's New York in 1989 with a reserve of $22 million. Then Heini, represented by Agnews in London and apparently bidding against his co-owner, whom he insisted had subsequently reimbursed him, bought the painting back for the agreed reserve; thus establishing its new value. It was hardly surprising that 'Mata Mua' retained a very special place in his heart but it was undoubtedly the perceived value rather than the painting itself that excited Heini.

The second example was 'The Lock', which may be a fine example of the work of John Constable but his somewhat schmaltzy style had been considered deeply unfashionable for some time. It was therefore suspicious that in 1990, when the art market was in recession and Sotheby's was desperately in need of a major sale to re-establish confidence in the investment value of fine art, one of its own directors should suddenly pay a record £10.8 million for 'The Lock'. While the full weight of Sotheby's publicity department ensured a remarkable amount of media exposure, details of who Heini may have been bidding against were conspicuous by their absence. Until 2006, it remained the highest price paid for a British Old Master.

* * *

As Heini's wedding to Tita drew closer and his spending on the new love of his life escalated, the tension between the protective Georg and his stepmother increased. All too aware of the power and influence wielded by Georg's mother, Tita had soon developed a particularly vitriolic dislike for the woman. The funeral for Ivy Batthyány in 1985 supplied her with what was to become one of her favourite anecdotes:

> We were at this lunch with Margit, all dressed in black, very serious. And when we were having coffee and cookies, with Junior and Groh, Theresa appeared. She was wearing a mini-skirt! It was turquoise with big white dots like this and a transparent shirt in white nylon. Then Margit got up from the table and said, 'What is that woman doing here, dressed like a whore? She is not invited to my house.'

The only reason for the lengthy delay in his marriage to Tita was Heini's ongoing legal battle with Denise to obtain a decree absolute and some form of alimonial settlement, neither of which she was in any hurry to facilitate. But in November 1984, after eighteen months of legal conflict, Judge Eastman granted Denise a decree nisi on the grounds of Heini's adultery with Carmen Cervera and several other women while she had admitted adultery with Franco Rapetti and later with Mariano Hugo Prince zu Windisch-Graetz. Although she said their sex life was unsatisfactory due to Heini's flagging interest, she denied that anyone but Heini was the father of Alexander.

The settlement remained unresolved while Denise contested Heini's claim for the return of the jewellery, which *The Times* followed with predictable interest:

> Baroness demands details of Thyssen fortune in $80 million jewellery dispute. She has rejected his claim that his wealth amounted to £400 million. She told the Court of Appeal in London yesterday that the Baron was worth £1.2 billion. The Baroness said the jewellery was worth a total of under $25 million. If they had remained married and she had inherited, she would have been entitled to a life interest in half his wealth. But because of the divorce she has lost that entitlement and had to be compensated. The Baron is claiming the return of the Manhattan apartment valued at $4.5 million, objets d'art

Heini and Tita on their wedding day in Gloucestershire (photo: Alan Davidson).

and other silver valuables he claims she took from the home at Chester Square, Belgravia. The Baron, in the ancillary relief claim, seeks a return of diamonds, emeralds, rubies, sapphires, and pearls. Eight pieces are valued at $32.3 million. Other jewellery bought, he claims for investment, is valued at $45 million but he says she can keep 124 pieces valued at $4.4 million. The hearing continues.

Denise finally gained a decree absolute on 18 July 1985 through the English High Courts of Justice after Heini had agreed to a highly complicated settlement, which included property in Marbella and Sardinia and an apanage and expenses for the eleven-year-old Alexander exceeding SwFr 1 million and including the cost of a butler. The battle for the return of the jewellery continued while Denise would eventually settle in Paris, Rome and Sardinia with her son in the style, if not the spirit, of Arndt Krupp and his mother.

Alexander never displayed any enthusiasm for becoming involved in gainful employment although, like Lorne, he spent a brief period working for the family firm in Monaco. Neither of them was encouraged to stay, for reasons which, according to Lorne, may have had more to do with sibling rivalry than motivation or ability.

* * *

On 16 August 1985 the sixty-four-year-old Heini married the forty-two-year-old Maria del Carmen Cervera at the town hall in Moreton-in-Marsh, near Daylesford in England.

> Our friends, the Duke of Badajoz, the brother-in-law of King Juan Carlos, and Anne Getty, were our witnesses. We also held a big party at Daylesford in September, when people had returned from their holidays, with hundreds of friends from everywhere. We had a Magyar band playing popular gypsy

music from my native Hungary. The wild violins and short wailing notes always remind me of my Hungarian blood. Every time I have celebrated an important occasion in life I have had gypsy music. When Tita walked in, the gypsies played 'Granada' in tribute to Carmen and to Spain. She wore the glittering 170-carat 'Star of Peace' which I gave her for our engagement.

The party would also prove to be the swan-song for Daylesford. The following year they sold it to Sir Anthony Bamford, replacing it with a house bought from Christina Onassis's ex-husband Thierry Roussel in Paris, where Tita enjoyed shopping.

Before they bought the house they stayed at the Plaza Athénée. One day, while various friends and relatives roamed around their palatial suite, ordering more champagne and unwrapping bags of Christian Lacroix, Heini insisted on showing colourful Polaroid pictures of his recent intestinal operation while giggling at their embarrassment. Tita, totally ignoring everyone else in the room, rapidly leafed through a huge pile of magazines, pausing intermittently to tear a page from their binding. Her mother, dressed in an ankle-length, tiered skirt, fringed shawl and a mantilla the height of a bishop's mitre, stood by her side and clucked encouragement. Fascinated by her total commitment to the task a friend asked Heini what she was doing. With world-weary affection he replied: 'Shopping.'

For Tita, acquisition was a pilgrimage, purchase merely a time-consuming inconvenience which she could now get others to do for her, using the torn pages as a visual shopping list.

*   *   *

Despite most of Heini's extended family turning up for his wedding, his children were not all happy with their father's new bride or his adopted son whom they saw as a threat to their future inheritance. Some of those close to Heini found their loyalty severely challenged.

Josi Groh had worked with Heini for forty years and, superficially, his resignation letter in 1986 appeared to be nothing more than a formalised retirement notice. But his decision may not have been voluntary: a letter from Heini accused Groh of 'comments made to third parties about myself and persons in my immediate circle'. It was a charge that the deeply embittered Hungarian lawyer would eventually admit:

> I left because of Tita. Everything was fine until Heini divorced Denise, then I got fired. I remember when they arrived in my house. Tita was very

friendly. But as soon as he married her, the friendliness stopped. Maybe it was because I spoke badly about her and about her mother. They get $30 million to $40 million a year to live on but that's still not enough for Tita.

He was quite correct. Tita had not waited five years to marry Heini only to have her enjoyment of his extravagant lifestyle curtailed by Josi Groh. Obviously frustrated by his inability to exercise his customary financial control, he resorted to accusations of social inferiority.

I remember at a Goya exhibition, Tita's mother made claims that she was from an old Spanish aristocratic family, which is totally untrue. Tita has very good relations with the King's sister, whose husband I first met on the *Hanse*, when I was in the Caribbean with my wife. He was very nice. But the Queen was absolutely against Tita. The whole of the Spanish aristocracy is against her.

Heini's account of the events leading up to Groh's dismissal displayed an even greater degree of vitriol and highlighted his inability to control or limit the effects of his previous unsuccessful relationships on his staff and business affairs:

I had complete confidence in Josi and our relationship worked very well. But he was always involved when I got divorced and interfered on both sides. He and his wife were good friends of Nina and also with Theresa. They called each other every day to discuss what was going on at the Villa. Later, I discovered all sorts of things, namely that he had been taking a commission on everything, even on silly things like air fares. Groh told Tita I was completely impotent and that he was the stud as I didn't do anything with the women. He also told everyone I was an alcoholic and that he looked after my business and had put the collection together.

* * *

The criticism of Heini's marriage to Tita by his various ex-wives and their children had no effect on the financial support he accorded them. At the time, Lorne was receiving an apanage of SwFr 45,000 plus an extra SwFr 135,000 'voluntary payments' while Francesca was apparently getting much the same. But according to Heini, he was constantly obliged to increase their generous allowances which included rates and service charges on the houses he had bought for them. This did not prevent them from living beyond their means resulting in a stream of hotel bills, doctor's bills and travel invoices landing on his accountant's desk. He claimed his patience, if not his sense of humour, had been sorely tested when Francesca justified a dentist's bill by insisting that her inheritance of his bad teeth was her father's responsibility.

Heini's children were not the only ones who required financial support. He also claimed to be providing allowances of around SwFr 300,000 each for two of his ex-wives, SwFr 105,000 for Gunhilde, SwFr 87,000 for Inge and Birgit, plus various voluntary payments for old friends and ex-girlfriends. Nonetheless, he continued to spend. Having bought another house in Marbella for $900,000 and spent SwFr 2 million on its refurbishment, he then bought a small palace in La Moraleja on the outskirts of Madrid for 96 million pesetas (£3.5 million) in 1987.

La Moraleja is the Cap Ferrat or Beverly Hills of Madrid, an area of extravagant villas and hissing lawn sprinklers. The Thyssens' house is one of the most spectacular, overlooking a lake-sized swimming pool and appearing to extend horizontally under the weight of a vast blue-green, ceramic-tiled pagoda roof.

After spending a small fortune on renovations, they inaugurated their new home with a glittering dinner on 15 July 1988 at which King Juan Carlos and his father Don Juan, Count of Barcelona, were the chief guests. By now it was becoming obvious that the collection, in some shape or form, would be moving to Spain and Heini and Tita were honoured by the Spanish government with the Great Cross of King Charles III and Queen Isabella Catholica.

There were rumours of more formal accolades but the idea was dropped, according to José Luís de Vilallonga, after the entire Spanish court threatened to renounce their titles if Tita was honoured with aristocratic status.

* * *

While Heini facilitated his wife's rise, if not into the aristocracy, certainly into the top echelons of Spanish society, he was also financing his daughter's involvement in the no less competitive social hierarchy of the Tibetan Buddhist court. Within a remarkably short time, Heini had agreed to sponsor a Tibetan Cultural Exhibition to be shown in Paris, London and the United States and organised by his daughter. He also made a contribution that was of more immediate, if contradictory, value, for which 'his holiness' was apparently appreciative: 'Dear Baron von Thyssen. I would like to thank you for your gold coin which I recently received. The inscription which it bears, "virtue surpasses riches", is meaningful. Thank you so much.'

Meanwhile, Heini also funded Chessy's regular trips to the Tibetan Buddhist ashrams in India where many of the monks appeared to be more excited by the sexual potential of visiting Western women than any desire to impart any long-term spiritual enlightenment.

While his sister was enjoying her Indian adventures, Lorne persuaded his father to fund his stage career which he decided would be better pursued in New York. Having generated some critical appreciation, he then rented a large apartment in Paris, converted to Islam and spent an increasing amount of time in Lebanon – a country that would eventually become both the subject and the location of his first movie, entitled *The Labyrinth*.

* * *

In 1988, Heini had persuaded his sister Gaby to bring her affairs under the protective guardianship of Franco Masoni, his Lugano-based lawyer. But his nephew, Steven Bentinck, was still investing vast amounts of his mother's money in his abortive business schemes and by 1991 managed to get rid of Masoni by changing his mother's domicile to an alternative Swiss canton.

While Masoni challenged the decision and fought for his fee for a number of years, Count Pruszynski accused 'Steffi' of having consumed two-thirds of his mother's fortune or an estimated $60 million. This was later neatly documented by Dr Hubert Achermann of KPMG Lucerne, who had been appointed to Gaby as the last in a series of guardians. But Steven managed to persuade his mother to abandon Pruszynski, a man who undoubtedly had both Steven's and his mother's best interests at heart.

By now Henriette was beginning to realise that her mother's fortune and her own inheritance were under very real threat from her brother's 'megalomaniac ambitions' and begged Heini to take action against him. This resulted in a long-drawn-out legal case, before a testamentary pact was signed by Gaby, Henriette and Steven in October 1994. Henriette was left with sufficient millions to give her and her family comfortable financial security for the rest of her life. The same could have been said for her brother and mother. However, Steven's extravagance continued and by the time his mother died in January 1999, the family fortune was almost gone, while his second wife Lisa Hogan, who had been one of the few women on earth to survive a crash in a Lear Jet unscathed, bore him two daughters and one heir.

Gaby died at Casa Melchett, her house in Mallorca, alone except for 'Pussy', her devoted maid Silvia and José her butler. Her son and daughter only turned up for her funeral and burial, which was not next to her husband in Paris or her beloved father in Landsberg but alone in Klosters. A far more bizarre and tactless location for a funeral was Rechnitz, where in 1989 a funeral mass was held for Margit by her family; seemingly impervious to the appalling memories that her name still evoked among the local population.

Chapter IX: 1981–1988

In fact, the last person to take up permanent residence at Landsberg before Heini would be his cousin Countess Anita Zichy-Thyssen whom 'old' August would not even have considered a Thyssen. According to Heini, her family appeared to have adopted some of the Thyssen's more unpleasant characteristics. While continuing to enjoy Anita's immense Thyssen fortune and adopt the title of their long forgotten father, neither Federico nor Claudio turned up for their mother's funeral in Munich in 1990 or her burial at Landsberg Castle, next to her parents Amélie and Fritz. After her death, having become increasingly critical of the management, her sons were reported to have sold most of their shares in Thyssen AG, although Claudia Thyssen-Guerreschi, daughter of Federico, would later deny the claim. Certainly the brothers remained largely divorced from the Thyssen-Bornemisza family.

Apart from regular visits to Europe, Count 'Piggy' Zichy's sons continued to live in Argentina, married and divorced a number of Brazilian women and sired twelve children between them. Federico proudly reprinted his grandfather's book, *I Paid Hitler*, and included a note from the Paraguayan printer describing Fritz as:

> This exemplary man who, like a revived kind of German divinity, emerges from the iron forests created in the Ruhr and he alone defies the arbitrariness of the force, the rage of prepotency and the injustice of the men and their delusive tribunals. I can figure him as a white giant, blue eyes and golden hair, which, if it were not because of his Christian devotion, it would be possible to say that he is to be the personification of some god in the old mythology of the fatherland.

Federico also bought a stud farm in England but the portrait of Fritz Thyssen, in full military uniform complete with Iron Cross, hanging in the main entrance hall, apparently failed to impress the Newmarket trainers and owners and he moved on.

* * *

While Heini gave a certain degree of assistance to his sister in retaining her fortune, it is doubtful that he would have done so had he not been persuaded by his favourite niece, Henriette. He displayed no greater degree of concern towards his brother's widow, who was forced at one point to write begging for financial help:

> Dear Heini, I am very sorry for having to disturb you today. I have been

completely devastated since your office in Lugano told me the awful news that no more payments will be made, for which we were always so grateful as we live off them. I therefore would like to kindly ask you, dear Heini, to be so kind and help us along. We are so dependent on your kind help, which we need so much in order to carry on. Unfortunately, life is getting more and more difficult. I have not been able to sleep at night, because of all the worries. Thank God Birgit is always with me and as I have unfortunately got older, she always handles everything for the two of us. In a few days time, Stephan would already be celebrating his 82nd birthday. We miss him a lot. Dear Heini, please have the kindness and answer my plea.

It is understandable that Heini should have been angered by his brother's failure to provide for his widow and daughter but there was nothing admirable about Heini's lack of grace and his inability to honour Inge with a personal reply:

Dear Baroness Thyssen-Bornemisza, Baron Thyssen has received your letter dated 21 July and thanks you for it. Baron Thyssen is prepared to continue paying you on a voluntary basis during the next five years $4,000 per month. After the end of the five years, he will decide once again what should happen with these monthly payments. The Baron wishes you and your daughter all the best.

While Heini tried to concentrate on his art collection and continued to be subjected to the various financial demands of his dependants, Georg continued to encourage a reduction in his expenditure. This included anything he considered an unnecessary extravagance, including gems, boats, planes, palatial villas and art collections. Ironically, it was largely as a result of Georg's lack of interest in art and desire to avoid the running costs of Villa Favorita that Heini and Tita would immortalise the name Thyssen-Bornemisza; not in the annals of industrial achievement, but in the world of art.

1 Memorandum from Jack Moore to Slaughter & May, London (Thyssen *v.* Thyssen, Supreme Court of Bermuda, 20 October 1999).
2 Note from Robert Genillard to the members of the board of management of Thyssen-Bornemisza NV and to the executives of the Monegasque service company Thyssen-Bornemisza SAM (ibid., 12 October 1999).
3 Thyssen *v.* Thyssen, Supreme Court of Bermuda, 12 October 1999.
4 Memorandum from Baron Heini Thyssen-Bornemisza to the administration of BHF-Bank, Frankfurt, dated 9 November 1982 (TBG Archives).
5 Letter from Baron Heini Thyssen-Bornemisza on 18 October 1985 in Lugano (Thyssen *v.* Thyssen, Supreme Court of Bermuda, 25 January 2001).
6 Evidence statement of Baron Heini Thyssen-Bornemisza (Thyssen *v.* Thyssen, Supreme Court of Bermuda, 1 December 1999).
7 Pleading by Baron Heini Thyssen-Bornemisza's leading QC Michael Crystal (ibid., 6 February 2001).
8 *Apollo*, p. 79.
9 *Wall Street Journal*, 25 June 1985.

Chapter X
1983–1993

By royal appointment...
The $600 million art sale

*Art is art, isn't it? And water is water
and east is east and west is west
and if you take cranberries and stew them
like apple-sauce, they taste much more
like prunes than rhubarb does.*
Groucho Marx

Heini was an intelligent man but by no stretch of the imagination could he have been considered an inspired businessman or industrialist. However, he was responsible or, at the very least, partially responsible for one deal of such brilliance that it overshadowed all his previous commercial disasters. While the original concept may not have been his, the technique certainly was. Most conjurers rely for their success on the use of rapid sleight of hand. Heini would rely on a completely different and entirely original technique. He would create his illusion by moving so slowly and with such confusing legal deliberation that for seven years an entire kingdom appeared to be unaware of what they were agreeing to.

Neither Tita nor her mother liked Lugano. It was damp, cold and grim in the winter and hot and humid in the summer. Apart from the treasures housed there, Villa Favorita offered few attractions and far too much tangible evidence of Heini's ex-wives. It was also easily accessible to his children, none of whom had displayed any enthusiasm for his marriage to 'that Spanish beauty queen'.

Even Heini had no great affection for the place. As he got older, his failing health combined with the 'Mahlerian' atmosphere of the lake only served to increase his sense of foreboding.

Georg also disliked Villa Favorita. It cost far too much to maintain and was also the home from which both he and his mother had been banished when he was only four years old.

By now the collection had outgrown the gallery and Georg was constantly criticising the cost of its upkeep. But while Heini had agreed in principle to Tita's suggestion of moving it to Spain, they were both aware that if they were to gain the family's co-operation and avoid accusations that Tita was stealing their inheritance, Heini had to present them with an offer they could not afford to refuse. However, the most difficult part of the negotiation was going to be selling the deal to Spain, for while Tita and her mother undoubtedly had power and influence, they lacked the necessary diplomatic skills. They needed someone of sufficient social status to have the ear of Spain's ruling elite.

Court advisers recommended Luís Goméz Acebo, the Duke of Badajoz, the brother-in-law of Juan Carlos and husband of Infanta Doña Pilar de Borbón. He was the perfect choice, as Heini had known him since the 1960s through various social and business connections. Heini also had other social connections with the Spanish Royal family:

> I had met Juan Carlos in St Moritz before he became King. He stayed with Ferdinand and Imelda Marcos and we used to ski together. I also saw him at the wedding of General Franco's granddaughter Carmen, who married Alfonso de Borbón. I got to know his father, Don Juan, when he lived in Switzerland during the war.

Heini and Tita had also been introduced to a Spanish lawyer called Jaime Rotondo Russo, who would represent Tita and be granted a place in her inner court of friends and confidants, becoming a vital player in the fulfilment of their ambitions. Another important introduction was that of Heini to Alfred Taubman. In 1983, Taubman, having bought the auction house Sotheby's, set about embellishing its board with glamorous-sounding outside directors, particularly those with titles. By March 1984, Heini was being courted by 'Big Al' in New York, and shortly afterwards both he and Doña Pilar were invited to join the board of Sotheby's. For Heini the £6,000 per annum fee plus generous expenses would represent little more than a token payment. For Doña Pilar, who was better known for her equestrian skills than her knowledge of the auction business, the financial reward would have been a welcome contribution to the Borbón coffers. In return, Sotheby's would be of invaluable assistance in advising Heini and valuing his collection.

* * *

Meanwhile, Tita continued to encourage the growth of the collection through Heini's auction room activities. She also promoted international awareness of the collection, which Simon de Pury had so successfully developed through the travelling exhibitions. But while major international exhibitions undoubtedly increase the value of paintings, there is a constant risk of scrutiny by art critics. When his Twentieth Century Masters exhibition opened at the Metropolitan Museum of Art in New York in 1983, the critic John Russell was profoundly unimpressed:

> No shape, no concentration, no strong personal taste. A little bit of this, a little bit of that never made a great collection even if some of the little bits were very good . . . We are perfectly well able by now to distinguish between a collector and an accumulator . . . Nor does the present show display as yet the kind of judgement that might cause this assessment to be revised upward in the future. This visitor could not help thinking in case after case that better pictures of the same kind can be found in other private collections without leaving Manhattan Island . . . We may wonder if its arrival at the Metropolitan Museum of Art is not premature.[1]

Emil Bosshard, Heini's brilliant Swiss restorer and curator, confirmed Heini's limitations as a collector:

> I like Heini and had some wonderful times with him but I would have to say that his knowledge of art was more anecdotal than academic and his buying was often random and apparently thoughtless. If he failed in a bid for one picture he would often just try the next one in the catalogue. He bought so many he was bound to gather some good work, but he did buy an enormous amount of rubbish, particularly towards the end of his purchasing career. He was also quite tight-fisted in his purchasing, which often prevented him from buying the best works.[2]

The actual choice, quality and authenticity of the collection never appeared to be of any great interest to the public. The interest was in its size and its value as a manifestation of wealth. There appeared to be little concern for the collection's flaws, while Heini continued to deny that it was worth $2.5 billion; for denying specific facts in the media is an accepted means of establishing rumours. The fact that the paintings were being exhibited at the Metropolitan Museum of Art in New York overrode any doubts as to their legitimacy.

* * *

Chapter X: 1983–1993

In November 1986, after barely a year of marriage and the guarantee of financial security through Tita's signing of a 'testamentary pact' or inheritance agreement, their fast-living lifestyle was brought to an abrupt halt while Heini and Tita's relationship underwent a dramatic shift in the balance of power. He remembered the event with fearful clarity:

> We were staying at the Ritz-Carlton in Washington. It was quarter to eight in the morning and I had fallen over in the bathroom. I remember calling out, 'Tita, can you come here a minute and help me?' I could hardly speak but I managed to raise my voice and conceal my alarm. The left side of my body was completely paralysed. My left arm and leg didn't respond, it was as though they were asleep. I was really frightened but tried to keep calm. She called back, 'What's the matter, Heini?', but her voice sounded distant and preoccupied as she was totally unaware of what had happened. It was a big suite and I was terrified that she would walk into another room and out of earshot, so I called again: 'I've got a little problem, could you come here darling?'
>
> Finally Tita came into the bathroom, went white as a sheet, knelt down by my side and asked me what had happened. I told her I had fallen and couldn't move. For a moment I think she was more frightened than I was, then she pulled herself together and said she didn't want to move me in case I had injured myself in the fall, so she was going to go back into the bedroom and ring for help. She ran out of the bathroom and I could hear her on the phone asking for a doctor and an ambulance but I wasn't going to let someone find me on the floor when they arrived, so using my right arm and leg I start dragging myself across the floor to the bathroom door. When Tita came back and found me crawling out of the door she was terrified and begged me to stop but I reassured her and said, 'It's all right, Tita. I am fine. Help me get to the bed.' Which she did, and once I was on the bed and under the covers we both began to calm down a little but I still couldn't move my left arm or leg.

Eventually Heini was taken to the George Washington Hospital where he was examined by three doctors.

> They reassured me that I was out of danger. After about another two hours I even started to get some movement back in my arm and leg. I also slowly began to realise that it had been a close call, very close. The diagnosis was quite clear. It had been an aneurysm; a tumour that forms in or by an artery

and, depending on its size, can cause an obstruction and produce similar effects to an embolism. I spent a week in the hospital recovering and undergoing more tests, in the room where Ronald Reagan recovered from his gunshot wounds in 1981. Then we went to New York so that I could be seen by two other specialists who confirmed the diagnosis and discovered that I had also suffered two previous attacks.

From then on, I had to monitor my blood pressure, go for regular check-ups and avoid any excesses. It had been a warning. I was sixty-five years old and I was beginning to pay the price for my somewhat excessive lifestyle. Even so, I had no intention of letting life pass me by. I still had a lot to do.

Heini made a good recovery. The only after-effect of his illness was the development of a peculiar and annoying habit. On being asked a question which he either did not wish to reply to, or could not be bothered with, he would clasp his hand to his forehead, cough noisily and say: 'I can't remember.' It was rarely genuine, for Heini had a memory that remained, albeit selective, as unimpaired and remarkable as his eyesight. It would drive lawyers to distraction and cost his family an enormous amount of money.

But as a result of the stroke, Heini had suffered physically and realised that his days of pursuing women were over. Tita was to be his last wife and if he did not want to die alone like his father, he was going to have to accept a far greater reliance on her.

In September 1986, when Simon de Pury must have been aware of Tita's increasing power and influence, particularly in the choice of gallery staff, he resigned, albeit with sufficient grace to further his career at Sotheby's where he returned as director of European operations. He handed over responsibility of curatorship of the Thyssen-Bornemisza Collection to the German art historian Susanne Thesing, formerly of the German National Museum in Nuremberg, ably assisted by Gertrude Borghero. But within eleven months, both women had also left.

* * *

In 1986 Heini caused great excitement in both the world of international architecture and fine art museums by publicly admitting that Villa Favorita was too small to house his collection of over 1,500 works of art, and that his gallery either had to be enlarged or the collection moved to a more suitable location.

Heini, who was also aware that Spain's entry into the European Community was likely to result in massive subsidies, particularly in the cultural infrastructure

Tita Cervera and Francesca at a Villa Favorita reception.

of the country, had meetings with Spain's Director General of Fine Art and his lawyer Don Rodrigo Uría. The result of these meetings was the setting-up of a Spanish Thyssen Art Trust, financed by the Spanish government. This was followed by meetings in Barcelona with Pasqual Maragall, the Mayor, Jordi Pujol, the President of the regional government of Catalonia and Juan Antonio Samaranch, chairman of La Caixa savings bank and head of the International

Olympic Committee. The result of all this activity was the signing of an agreement to lend Barcelona 150 paintings from the Thyssen-Bornemisza Collection.

The influence of Tita's pressure and Badajoz's diplomacy was beginning to bear fruit.

Meanwhile, Europe's cultural elite, subtly forewarned of the strengthening of the relationship between the Baron and Spain, began to display an increasing interest in the collection. Although Heini would subsequently admit how much he enjoyed being the centre of cultural attention, the prime purpose of his continued international negotiations was the maintenance of Spain's enthusiasm, as he had yet to negotiate the conditions for the relocation of his collection. How anyone could have imagined the collection moving to any other country was difficult to comprehend when Heini and Tita had houses in Madrid, Barcelona, Sant Feliú de Guixols, Palma de Mallorca and a chalet called 'Mata-Mua' at the Marbella Club.

But Heini had to give the impression that his intentions were based on admirable human emotions rather than commercial principles: 'Probably the wish of every collector is to keep intact the fruits of a life devoted to collecting. To immortalise one's collection. My dream was to keep the whole collection together in one place, as it had been for my father when he originally bought Villa Favorita.'

He also motivated the international architectural world and further promoted his collection by organising a competition for the design of a new and enlarged gallery in Lugano. Then, having chosen a design by the British architect Sir James Stirling, he revealed his grand plan at the Palazzo di Congressi in Lugano where he also suggested to the cantonal authorities that they should devote public funds to the project. After all, Heini insisted, the local traders had profited from the tourists and art connoisseurs who had been drawn to the town by his collection for nearly forty years. But then he privately contradicted his intentions: 'Even with the planned extension the gallery was not going to be big enough.'

Ignoring Emil Bosshard's suggestion that they could extend the gallery by including the already interconnected villa, Heini continued to criticise the Swiss and explain why he considered Favorita to be so 'impractical':

> All attempts to involve the Swiss in any kind of investment or co-operation ran into Helvetian incomprehension. They couldn't understand the importance that Switzerland, let alone Lugano and the canton of Ticino, would gain from retaining the entire collection in their country. When President Mitterrand

came on an official visit to discuss Switzerland's possible entry into the Common Market, he asked for the meeting to take place in Lugano. It was very difficult for the Swiss to comprehend why Mitterrand found it so important to visit the Thyssen-Bornemisza Collection.

While it was quite possible that Mitterrand chose Lugano specifically so that he could view the collection, it is somewhat more likely that he was persuaded to visit Villa Favorita by Heini's daughter Francesca, whose friend Marie Jaoule de Pontcheville was a discreet but extremely close and personal friend of the French President. Certainly both girls were present during his brief visit to Villa Favorita.

Heini would continue to claim that the Swiss refused to offer him any financial incentive for the retention of the collection in Lugano. In fact, the Swiss canton of Ticino made an offer of some SwFr 40 million towards the cost of the extension of the existing gallery, plus a major contribution towards the running costs. They also offered Heini further gallery space at Villa Ciani. But presumably because they did not value the collection as highly as Heini, they refused to become involved in any form of direct investment.

However, Heini's lawyer Paul Coleridge noted that there were collateral benefits to be gained from their ongoing negotiations: 'Regarding tax enquiries in Ticino, all is completely quiet. There has been no specific mention of it since the beginning of the year, and I suspect it is being overwhelmed by the discussions about the foundation and the new gallery.'

* * *

The exit of Simon de Pury and Tita's successful lobbying of the Spanish option had resulted in her increased enthusiasm and involvement in the collection, although she was, initially at least, disarmingly frank concerning her limited knowledge of fine art:

> I had no formal training either practically or theoretically, but I've always been involved with paintings, because my father painted as a hobby and I had many painter friends. My mother also used to love the nineteenth-century Spanish painters. But when I went to museums before I met Heini, I only really looked at the obvious. In the Louvre, I saw the Mona Lisa and maybe some of the more famous impressionists. Here, at the Prado, it was impossible to ignore our great masters Velàzquez and Goya. But the first trip I made to Lugano, Heini and I had lunch and afterwards he took me around the gallery, and I saw all the paintings. I had never seen anything like it. So much incredible work all together. I couldn't believe it. To see them in

a modern museum is one thing, but there in Villa Favorita, where I could touch them and see them so close, it was incredible!

The first indication of Tita's taste in art emerged, two months after they got married, at Sotheby's New York on 1 November 1985 when, through her new 'tax efficient' fine art investment organisation Nautilus Trustees and presumably with Thyssen money, she acquired Ignacio Zuloaga y Zabaleta's, 'Bullfight in Eibar' for $1,075,000. Despite being one of the better examples of the 'genre', it soon became obvious that, unlike Heini, there was nothing random about Tita's choice and that her taste for popular, clichéd paintings was quite genuine: 'I have always been in love with nineteenth- and twentieth-century Spanish painting and no one, not even museums, has collected these paintings seriously.'

Tita was referring to a particular style of nineteenth- and twentieth-century Spanish painting which, despite often being technically superb, many believed did not warrant 'serious collection'. The Spanish magazine *Antenna* was wonderfully diplomatic in its criticism: 'Genre scenes are particularly prone to sliding into the chocolate box league, and the Baroness admits her enthusiasms are for people and colour.'

And slide they did. For when Tita began to buy paintings on her own initiative, she not only continued to buy chocolate box art but often bought cheap examples; their only redeeming feature being their possible qualification as kitsch.

By 1985 she had not accumulated sufficient knowledge or developed sufficient aesthetic appreciation to have been considered anything other than an enthusiastic amateur, yet she still managed to influence Heini's choice of paintings. However, she had to be admired for not only accepting her own lack of knowledge but for using every available opportunity to familiarise herself with the world's great collections. With Heini as a guide this was not as simple a task as she made it sound: 'I went all over the world with him, visiting all the great museums and learning about painting. Heini is very good to go to museums with, because he immediately focuses on the good paintings and ignores the rest.'

The latter comment was no doubt a reference to Heini's habit of viewing paintings at break-neck speed; only pausing briefly to look at works which he owned, had owned or hoped to own. In later years when he was confined to a wheelchair, the sight of Heini urging his butler to push ever faster while Tita, Borja and assorted friends ran to keep up, astonished visitors to the Picasso museum in Barcelona.

* * *

Chapter X: 1983–1993

In anticipation of the collection's relocation, Heini had given Georg the task of creating a new inheritance agreement to circumnavigate the Swiss inheritance rules. It was at this point that Tita began to realise the possible dangers ahead and probably sensed that Heini did not entirely trust her.

> Heini asked me if, as his wife, I would renounce my interest in the collection, as all his heirs were being asked to do, so that he could transfer ownership to a new trust called the Thyssen-Bornemisza Collections Trust, which had been set up in Bermuda and was administrated by the Swiss Thyssen-Bornemisza Art Foundation. I obviously agreed but I also felt uneasy about it. Following my consent in 1986, we went to Zurich with Lorne and Francesca to sign the new agreement which had been prepared by Junior and his team of advisers and included a testamentary pact or inheritance agreement.

But Tita's reassurance was short-lived:

> While we were signing it, I remember Francesca saying, 'Well, we shouldn't really be signing this, because none of us have actually read it.' It was like a book of 363 pages that none of us, including Heini, had ever seen before or had the time to read. But Junior told us what was in the agreement and we didn't have a lot of time, so we all signed it.

Heini claimed that some months after the signing Georg had turned up at Villa Favorita and informed him they were going to have to start selling paintings and create a fund to maintain the collection. To which Heini replied: 'Why? I thought the Swiss Foundation was going to pay for the maintenance of the collection, with or without us. Almost for ever, or at least until the year 2040.'

According to Heini and Tita, Georg then reminded his father: 'The papers you signed in Zurich also included an acceptance of the renunciation of the Continuity Trust funding of the Swiss Foundation, so we have to get the money from selling paintings to pay for the upkeep of the collection.'

What Georg was actually trying to do was to get Heini to pay for his new acquisitions and eventually Tita's, rather than using TBG's funds or taking out further loans. It is highly unlikely that Heini's claimed ignorance was the result of both he and Tita having failed to read the entire testamentary pact agreement. It seems more likely that, having had little choice but to accept Georg's stringent new policies, Heini had chosen not to inform Tita, who as yet appeared to be unaware of her husband's liquidity problems.

* * *

Once Georg had achieved his and possibly his mother's ambition of controlling TBG and the collection, he began to proceed with a programme of rationalisation. The enormous cost of maintaining Daylesford was the first to come under scrutiny, though without any serious opposition from Heini, for whom the place had lost a great deal of its attraction after the Inland Revenue had become regular visitors and Denise had used it as her alimony fortress. Predictably, Tita hated the rain-soaked English countryside, regardless of whether it was grey or green and so its disposal became inevitable. The rationalisation of Daylesford was followed by further cost cuttings to which Tita reacted with a mixture of suspicion, displeasure and apparent bewilderment: 'Why would a son who owed his father so much treat him with such disrespect?'

Actually, respect had little to do with it, as Georg had no intention of allowing his father, and particularly Tita, to continue using the family firm to pay for the upkeep of his private jet and a small transatlantic liner with a captain and twelve crew. Heini would have probably agreed but Tita had no intention of letting her beloved *Hanse* be taken away from her: 'Heini loved the *Hanse*. He had created it and it was very special for both of us. Every winter we had the boat taken to the Caribbean by the captain and we would fly out in the plane to join it for about a month. Then in the summer he used to bring it back to the Mediterranean.'[3]

There is no evidence to suggest that at this time Heini spent a month in any one place, let alone aboard the *Hanse*, and while he had already admitted how quickly he became bored by life on board, it was actually Tita who eventually revealed Heini's increasing fear of being taken ill while at sea.

Ownership of the Falcon 500 private jet, regardless of its leasing income, also became increasingly difficult to justify, as Heini used it so rarely; preferring to travel in the relative peace and tranquillity of a scheduled flight, while Tita led her entourage of mother, brother, son, fourteen yapping dogs and six screeching parrots on board his private jet to the same destination. The extra cost of this somewhat extreme form of travel arrangement was not always limited to the running cost of the plane. Heini's scheduled flight to Madrid in July 1989 involved him in considerably more expense than the cost of a standard fare, when Italian customs confiscated the $68,000 that he was carrying in his briefcase. But he displayed remarkably little concern, even when asked if he thought it would ever be returned: 'What does it matter? If they don't take it, Tita will only spend it.'

Heini had also decided to stay at the Villa Magna Hotel, rather than share their house at La Moraleja with 'the circus' and an army of painters and decorators. But I saw that even at the hotel, life was not without its financial perils.

Chapter X: 1983–1993

Having waited impatiently for his limousine to take us to lunch, he decided to take a cab, which he stopped after travelling less than fifty metres when he spotted his errant car entering the gates. Having paid off the taxi with a fist full of cash that his bodyguard had given him only minutes before and without waiting for the change, we climbed into the waiting limousine before sweeping past the astonished cab driver. It was some minutes before the anxious bodyguard realised Heini had given him the entire roll of bills, which amounted to 1 million pesetas (or £4,000). But Heini, perhaps in order to impress my girlfriend, appeared to remain philosophical: 'Don't stop or we'll be late for lunch. He's just a very fortunate cab driver.'

*   *   *

In 1989, Georg also visited Heini in Madrid and told him that the company's profits were so low that there would be further shortfalls in his agreed annuity. If Tita had been aware of the massive cash reserves Georg was building up in the company, the legal battles might have started much earlier. But Tita had other concerns at the time:

> I was privately suspicious of the influence that Junior's mother, Theresa, had over her son. I'm sure she saw me as nothing more than an encouragement for Heini to spend money which she considered part of her son's inheritance. Perhaps Junior was just trying to affect his father's life in a way that he thought would encourage me to go off and find another man with more available funds.

Rather than abandoning Heini, their interdependence was about to become even stronger, as Heini's health gave yet further cause for concern when his doctors recommended surgery to correct another aneurysm that was in danger of blocking an artery. Heini's hospitalisation did nothing to inhibit his plans for the collection, which he was now suggesting to be the result of Georg's ever-increasing financial constraints:

> The desire of all collectors is to see their entire collection permanently on show to the public in an ideal setting; safe from the economic pressures that affect private collections and particularly those now imposed upon me by my own son. After a great deal of thought it became obvious that the only means of achieving my ambition may be through some form of controlled sale. My achievement of this ambition would be as much the result of Tita's efforts as that of good fortune.

At this stage in a collector's life, most people either build their own permanent museum with an endowment trust to pay for the collection's upkeep or they donate their collection to a national museum in return for some form of commemorative inscription. But Heini was reluctant to admit that he intended to sell the collection and had no intention of donating it to anyone. To avoid being accused of such an uncharitable, materialistic attitude, he gave more acceptable excuses for failing to take up offers that did not include a suitably attractive purchase price.

The German government proposed several sites for the collection. Stuttgart was the most appealing suggestion but the conditions weren't particularly good. They proposed to finance the purchase of both the collection and the building through income from the casinos and lottery, with additional contributions from Daimler-Benz and Bosch. It didn't seem a very reliable method to me. In Berlin, I discovered from the local authorities that the government was going to deduct the cost from aid allocated to the rebuilding of the city. I did not consider this a good idea and I felt sure that the Berliners would agree with me. But it was Helmut Kohl himself who finally put me right off the idea. He had the cheek to say that one of the reasons Germany was interested in the collection was that they needed a museum to keep visiting Head of States' wives entertained! I bit my tongue and simply replied that that wasn't exactly what I had in mind as the purpose of my collection.

France also showed an interest in the collection, although they didn't make a firm offer. Baladur, as Chancellor of the Exchequer, visited Lugano to explain that they didn't really have the necessary funds available, although they suggested that they may be prepared to house the collection at Le Petit Palais. This may be an architectural jewel but it is also a protected building and, due to the inflexibility of French legislation in that respect, couldn't possibly undergo the necessary conversion into a permanent fine art museum. It would have been almost impossible to get permission to put a nail into a wall let alone make major alterations.

Eventually the most serious offer we received came from the British. The United Kingdom was the only party to draw up a complete, detailed proposal and submit it for my approval. But I had already signed a provisional contract with the Spanish authorities.

Certainly the most impressive part of the British offer was the status of its representatives:

Tita and I met Margaret Thatcher twice to discuss the proposal. On the first occasion at 10 Downing Street we discussed several location possibilities but they all had drawbacks. Even so, the 'Iron Lady' kept trying and even invited us to lunch at her private residence. There, she tried to persuade us once again that the collection should be housed in Britain.

Prince Charles's visit to Villa Favorita on 14 May 1988 was also too late and only lasted for two hours. His humour was not improved when, having insisted on piloting his plane, he overshot Lugano's notoriously short runway. Fortunately, the only casualty was Wales's pride while Heini found it difficult to hide his amusement in the fact that the Prince's 'prat-fall' had provided the worldwide publicity he sought for his collection. After the royal visit, there came an abrupt but less publicised withdrawal of Britain's offer. The whole affair probably did little to help Heini and Tita's subsequent attempts to sell Prince Charles their house in Palma de Mallorca. Their offer was politely declined by the Prince's equerry: 'His Royal Highness is sorry that you have been led to believe that he might wish to acquire a property in Mallorca. Much as he enjoys visiting the island, he has no plans to purchase a property. This is simply one of those rumours which seem to follow His Royal Highness around.'

* * *

The international courting of Heini only served to increase his arrogance and he became somewhat abrupt in his dealings with the various suitors. The Spanish, on the other hand, were becoming increasingly flattered and excited by the fact that they appeared to be winning this cultural contest against the three leading nations of Europe.

While Heini was busy in Europe, the Duke of Badajoz had given the proceedings a transatlantic flavour by discussing the collection's future with the Getty Foundation in California. But as the King of Spain's brother-in-law, it is difficult to believe that he had not been aware of Heini's intention from the beginning, or perhaps it would be more accurate to say Tita's intention; particularly if her relationship with the King was as close as was rumoured. Even Heini would rather proudly support my observation concerning Borja's resemblance to Juan Carlos by replying: 'Are you surprised?'

However, Heini and Tita could not be seen to be publicly negotiating directly with the King, which was part of the reason why the Duke had been enrolled. But it would have been unthinkable for him to have assumed such a position without the King's full knowledge, understanding and approval. Though while

Heini and Tita in Marbella, during the early, happier years.

he may have been fully aware of Tita's intentions, it is possible that, at least initially, he was unaware of the extent of Heini's financial ambitions.

There was even evidence to suggest that the Duke was on Heini's payroll as a partner in Pensa Oil, a company owned by TBG via a familiar tax avoidance route through Jersey and Bermuda. Predictably, Heini denied any form of financial reward and liked to give the impression that the Duke was motivated by nothing more than friendship and his love of art. But Badajoz could not have afforded such indulgence as his family, unlike the British extended royal family, received no stipend or financial contribution from an equivalent of the Privy Purse. The Duchess of Badajoz, Doña Pilar, also denied any business relationship between Heini and her late husband: 'No, never. He was the soul of the negotiations and they knew he was loyal to them but at the same time he thought it was a very good thing for Spain to have the collection. To get seven-hundred and fifty pictures of this quality.'[4]

Although she would never make any critical comments concerning either the quality of the collection or its value to Spain, the Duchess could not help but point out that the Prado's treasures had been based on the individual collections of Charles V, Phillip II, Phillip IV and Isabella II: 'The whole of the Prado was paid for by my ancestors', she would say with a smile.

Doña Pilar was also aware that her family were not mere collectors but true patrons of the arts who supported Spain's greatest painters: 'I mean Velázquez, for example, lived in the palace. He had his own apartment there. But nowadays there are many people who are much richer than the King who can afford to be patrons of the arts.'

*   *   *

Having gained royal approval, the project still needed the support of the government. Early in 1987, the Duke of Badajoz, in the company of Tita, first discussed the possibility of acquiring the Thyssen-Bornemisza Collection for Spain with Javier Solana, the Minister of Culture in Felipe González's government. Predictably, they received a positive reaction.

It was also the Duke who sent the formal letter of proposal, in response to which Felípe González gave Javier Solana the go ahead to commence negotiations. It was no doubt as a result of the Duke's power and influence that in April 1987 Heini was presented with a formal letter from the Spanish government accepting the basis of his proposals.

Heini then tried to convince the rest of his family that Tita was innocent of their charges of complicity:

> Tita was obviously delighted that the collection might be moving to Spain but she was not blinded by the love for her country. Nor was she under any illusion that achieving my ambitions would be a simple matter of acceptance. She doesn't fit the Spanish stereotype. She was educated at foreign institutions and has travelled all over the world. She is very cosmopolitan and certainly doesn't suffer from outdated patriotism.

In fact, Heini was just as aware as anyone who knew Tita that she was devoted to her country and fiercely nationalistic. But patriotism was not a familiar concept to Heini. For having accused Switzerland of not supporting the collection, despite their multi-million-dollar offer and the fact that without Switzerland's wartime protection, it is unlikely there would have been a collection to inherit, he once again turned on Germany:

> Tita had worked at my side on the study of other offers; accompanied me on my trips to Germany and the UK and even quite liked the idea of California as a home for the collection, as she had spent many years there and loved the country. She only expressed her dislike of one offer, that of Germany. It wasn't really a political issue but like me she suspected their motives and lack of aesthetic appreciation.

Considering the collection had been founded in Germany by a German industrialist from a German family who had made their money from German industry, armaments, shipping and banking, and that Heini was to be laid to rest, at his request, in German soil, it was a somewhat hypocritical statement, to say the least. But he was fearful of drawing attention to both his own and the collection's German origin. This was also the only explanation for flatly denying his acceptance of a gold Johann Wolfgang von Goethe medal in 1992, awarded him by the Toepfer Foundation in Hamburg in recognition of his cultural contributions to European society. In 2005, the French theatre director Ariane Mnouchkine refused the same prize, citing concerns over Dr Alfred Toepfer's wartime activities.

Despite an increasing number of admissions, as Heini approached the end of his life, he still maintained some of his denials. Particularly concerning Tita:

> Naturally she was in favour of her own country but was just as aware as I was of what a long hard ride it would be and showed no particular interest in convincing me that Spain's offer was any better than anyone else's. The legal problems alone would require a small army of lawyers to sort out, whichever country the collection went to. The largest obstacle being achieving an acceptance of the sale by all my heirs.

In fact, the largest obstacle would be that of persuading a socialist government to pay one of the world's richest capitalists hundreds of millions of dollars for a collection, which they could hardly justify. The Prado already had a far superior collection of Spanish Old Masters, four times more paintings than it could display and desperately needed any spare money to repair, modernise and expand their existing building.

*   *   *

Heini insisted that it was the Spanish lawyer Rodrigo Uría, who came up with the idea of a trial period during which the collection would be on loan to Spain. In fact, the word loan was rather an inaccurate description of the arrangement as it suggested some form of benevolence. 'Lease' may have been a more accurate description, as Heini would be charging the Spanish government $5 million a year, to be paid annually in advance, for the honour of looking after his pictures, while not advertising the financial terms to the Spanish public. Officially, this period would be said to give both sides the opportunity to test their relationship while negotiations proceeded and the legal complexities were untangled. It was in fact a very clever way of giving the Spanish public the pleasure and satisfaction of possession while Heini continued to negotiate the cost of ownership.

When Heini suggested the idea to Georg, he received a positive reaction. Although Georg would no doubt have preferred to have raised more money by selling the pictures individually on the open market, with a temporary loan agreement in place, at least the upkeep would become the responsibility of the Spanish government.

Francesca, Lorne and Alexander would be convinced of the wisdom of the proposal by the simple expedient of threats and bribery. They were warned that if they failed to accept their proportion of the sale proceeds and sign the release, Heini might be tempted to allow the pictures to remain in Spain beyond the period of the 'loan' agreement; after which they would automatically become the property of the Spanish nation and the heirs might lose a major part of their inheritance. The loan period was actually set for nine-and-a-half years; six months short of the period beyond which the Spanish could claim ownership, giving Heini an escape clause if his plans were not accepted.

Having agreed to the lease agreement, the Spanish government continued to negotiate discreetly with Heini concerning the final purchase of the collection, although it was not until May 1988 that they signed a joint 'document of intention' and Heini once again began the process of valuation.

> First we applied to Sotheby's for a valuation of each piece of work that made up the collection – not an easy task by any means, as the art market is constantly fluctuating. What can never be calculated is the value of the work as part of a collection. However, we eventually received a full valuation of the collection from Sotheby's in May 1988 being some $1.2 billion.

Sotheby's valuation represented a 300 per cent increase in the value of the collection since 1983 but it was generally believed that the art market boom was nearing its end. On the night of 11 November 1987, Alan Bond bought Van Gogh's 'Irises' for $49 million, a record price, which, albeit paid for with a 50 per cent loan from the auction house, fuelled yet another boom on what was already a major bull market. But the story was far from over: in the spring of 1990, Ryoei Saito bought Van Gogh's portrait of Dr Gachet from Christie's in New York for $82.5 million and Renoir's 'Au Moulin de la Galette' from Sotheby's for $78.1 million (sold a few years later by his creditors for less than a third of the original sale price). It could not last and that summer the art market collapsed. It was hardly an auspicious time to be negotiating the sale of a collection.

If the Spanish legal advisers had foreseen the complications involved in ownership and control of the collection, the sale might never have been agreed. Sir Timothy Lloyd QC, who represented Heini, was surprisingly sympathetic: 'The agreement would become unbelievably complicated. The Spanish had originally assumed that the whole deal could be written down on two pages of foolscap.'[5]

Heini suffered no such illusions: 'The parties concerned were the Spanish government and Favorita Trustees Limited, which represented the official ownership of the collection. This company with its head office in Bermuda came under British legal jurisdiction and comprised myself and my future heirs. The very nature of this company with no definite position made it difficult to deal with.'

This was a huge understatement as the actual ownership of the collection involved yet another network of several trusts, foundations and companies based in countries where exposure to the payment of tax was minimal and everything was designed by lawyers and accountants to maximise their financial return in the event of such a proposed change in ownership.

> I had divided my inheritance amongst my heirs before death through a separate contract within a Trust and this company represented their interests. The main problem was that I was forced to negotiate with each of them and their lawyers individually with regard to compensation for renouncing what would have been their inheritance.

The brilliance of Heini's plan was that, in doing so, he would actually be paying a large part of his heirs' inheritance as well as the cost of his collection's housing, maintenance and preservation with Spain's money. It was difficult not to be impressed. The problem was that Heini and Georg had created a web of such protective complexity that even Heini had doubts that the negotiations would succeed:

> It was a very complex situation, as my children all came under different judicial systems, with differing legal ages of majority. This was further complicated by the fact that the inheritance was divided into different proportions for each individual heir. The first thing that had to be done was to establish the legitimate rights of each one. In my desire to protect the ownership of the collection, I had accepted the advice of Junior in creating a tight network of trusts and foundations, within which even I found it difficult to move. But over the following months we began to find ways of overcoming these difficulties, with the help of nearly as many lawyers as it had originally taken to create the whole protective system.

The legal team consisted of twelve lawyers, with six on each side; Sir Timothy heading the team of British lawyers, while Rodrigo Uría led the Spanish team.

* * *

Barcelona, not Madrid, had initially been chosen as a home for the collection but King Juan Carlos knew that such an arrangement would fuel the existing bad feeling between the Madrid-based Spanish establishment and the Catalans. As compensation to Tita, whom he knew would be furious at the snub to what she claimed to be her hometown, the Villahermosa Palace in Madrid was suggested as a suitable location for the collection. Heini was impressed and happily agreed that the King was right. Tita was not convinced, sensing correctly that she would never be accepted by Madrid's aristocratic elite.

In fact, while Tita considered Barcelona the more vibrant and fashionable city, she did not speak Catalan and in 2004 it would be revealed that she actually grew up with her grandmother in Los Arcos, a tiny village in Navarra.

With the Spanish monarchy offering an elegant, spacious and soon to be renovated palace to house 775 of Heini's Old and Modern Masters, he graciously accepted. It also left him with 700 paintings to distribute between Tita and his heirs, contradicting his original claim that he had only canvassed a sale as a means of keeping his entire collection together.

Having been informed that the King was not prepared to compromise on the location, Tita was left with little choice but to accept, while Heini encouraged her acquiescence by promising to support the development of her own collection.

> Tita also accepted Madrid as the main location, but it was agreed that part of the collection would remain on show in Barcelona. We negotiated with Maragall, the Mayor of Barcelona, and finally agreed on a permanent exhibition of seventy-five paintings at the Monasterio de Santa Maria de Pedralbes. The building is a convent for the order of St Clare, founded in 1326 by Elisenda de Montcada, Queen of Catalonia and Aragon, who lived there from 1327 until she died in 1364.
>
> My panels and oil paintings exhibited there date from the end of the thirteenth century to the middle of the eighteenth century and were chosen by Tomas Llorens, the eventual head curator of my Spanish collection.

Much of the ground floor area was still used by the nuns for worship. It somehow seemed rather incongruous that while the Thyssen-Bornemisza pictures were housed amidst $8 million-worth of climatically controlled, renovated areas on the first floor, downstairs on the walls of the nuns' chapels the only surviving frescoes by the Catalan painter Ferrer Bassa (*c.*1285–1348) were left unrestored, unprotected and open to the elements.

Oriol Bohígas, an architect and Barcelona's cultural commissioner in 1992, was reported as being more specific in his criticism. He considered the monastery of far greater interest than the seventy-five Thyssen-Bornemisza paintings housed there and described the Bassa frescoes as being 'amongst the most important

Gothic paintings in Europe. These alone are more valuable than the Thyssen Collection.'[6]

Heini was horrified when it was suggested that he might want to make some contribution to their restoration and protection: 'Then they'd start asking me for money for everything else,' he told me on the way back from visiting the monastery in 1998.

*   *   *

A month after the signing of the 'document of intention', a reshuffle in Felipe González's cabinet meant a change in Minister of Culture. Heini was delighted when Jorge Semprún was chosen: 'He is a well-known author and intellectual with whom I felt a close affinity, despite the fact that he was a communist, although he was expelled from the party in 1964 for "revisionist tendencies".'

The son of a Spanish diplomat, Jorge Semprún, according to his autobiography, joined the French resistance in Paris during the war before being incarcerated in Buchenwald from 1943 to 1945. After the war, he became a militant of the Communist Party and fought in the resistance against General Franco, eventually returning to Paris where he wrote novels and screenplays for directors such as Costa-Gavras and Alain Resnais. 'One of Semprún's first duties on being made Minister of Culture was to visit the gallery at Villa Favorita which is where we met. Fortunately we got on very well and had no difficulties continuing with the negotiations.'

Semprún and his family had actually been invited to the Villa for the week-end to be lavishly entertained by Heini and Tita in a transparent charm offensive. 'Our first official contact occurred some time later in Madrid at a lunch in the Ministry's private dining room. The Duke of Badajoz, Tita and I were invited and on behalf of the government, Semprún was wily enough to invite two old friends, Rodrigo Uría and Miguel Satrústegui who had become under-secretary at the Ministry.'

According to Heini, he had already entertained these men at Daylesford when they had previously been in England representing the Spanish state in the repurchase of a Goya which had come up at auction in London.

So despite the changes, the presence of Uría and Satrústegui gave the negotiations a certain continuity and there was an immediate feeling of mutual understanding. One of the first areas for discussion was the restoration of the Villahermosa palace which, in principle, was destined to be run as an extension of the Prado Museum. This decision caused me problems for a while, because its director wrote many articles against the installation of my museum, to the extent that he had to be restrained by his superiors.

Perez Sánchez had already displayed his animosity on another occasion, during the Goya exhibition at Villa Favorita. The Spanish Ministry of Culture had lent us a Goya and Sánchez voiced his opposition to a picture owned by the state being exhibited in a private house.

But Heini refused to accept the generally accepted definition of public ownership: 'I told him that he was wrong, as it was a public gallery and even the Soviets had loaned me pictures.'

The fact that the Duke of Badajoz was so obviously assisting Heini while retaining his position as head of the Friends of the Prado cannot have improved Sánchez's humour.

Meanwhile, regardless of the critics and opponents, negotiations continued and with Semprún's help they finally succeeded in creating and signing the loan contract in December 1988, only four months after he had taken office. It was the first official agreement between the Spanish government and Favorita Trustees Ltd. One Catalan lawyer described it as the most complicated and intricate agreement that he had ever encountered in fifty years of practice. Amid all the legal complexities, the most important difference between the simple original letter of intent and the finalised 113-page loan contract appeared to be that the annual payment of $5 million was to be made outside Spain and free of tax.

Heini originally claimed to have worked day and night to achieve his goals but subsequently admitted that it was the lawyers who were working with 'such due diligence' while Heini lay in the Jamaican sun watching the hummingbirds drink 'his' nectar and Tita spend his money redecorating the house.

> I remember the final negotiations, which involved the annual fee, were carried out over the phone between Madrid and Jamaica. Around this time we also created a private, non-profit-making, Spanish cultural foundation called the Thyssen-Bornemisza Collection Foundation which would represent both sides of the equation; endowed by myself with the loan of the paintings and by the Spanish monarchy who would freely give to the foundation the right to use the Villahermosa Palace in Madrid. The Spanish government contributed 9,000 million pesetas ($34 million), committed themselves to the renovation of the building and agreed to follow the contractual details concerning how the pictures should be hung and stored. They also guaranteed the return of the works in their entirety on completion of the loan period and the payment of shipment and insurance.

* * *

After two years of negotiations Heini remembered, with notable clarity, the most critical part of the proceedings:

> On 3 February 1989, Semprún invited us to Madrid's finest restaurant called Zalacain. Here, he got me against the ropes and said: 'Very well, Mr Thyssen, the negotiations between Spain and yourself will now resolve the various problems with the agreement but what figure do you really have in mind for the eventual purchase of the collection?' Not a very diplomatic question but a subject which had to be broached at some stage. So I replied: '$400 million; the same amount we were negotiating with the Getty Museum in California.'
>
> 'And couldn't you see your way to giving us a discount?' he asked with a smile on his face.
>
> My son Georg Heinrich and I had touched on the subject of price on one occasion. Heini Junior felt that the purchase price should be based on the amount I had invested in the collection since the war and not on its total market value.

It must therefore be assumed that the only purpose of Sotheby's valuation was to convince Spain that it was getting a bargain while Heini appeared to have forgotten to point out that Georg's calculation was for the entire collection and the Spanish would only be acquiring half of it.

> This amount was what my heirs would have received if I had not become an avid collector and therefore was the amount I should offer in compensation. I was in complete agreement and Georg calculated the amount as approximately $350 million. So I told Semprún: 'Well, how about 350 million?'
>
> 'Done', he replied and I took him at his word.
>
> 'Do you realise that you've just got a discount of $50 million for your country?' I joked.
>
> 'Yes, it'll be my contribution to the project.'

Despite this incentive, it seemed ironic that a former communist member of the French resistance movement, who spent much of the war in a Nazi concentration camp, should be encouraging the payment of $350 million to a family whose fortunes helped bring the Nazis to power and who had profited from the resulting war.

It was also difficult to understand why the Spanish did not commission an independent valuation.

While the price had been agreed, or at least the purchase part of it, there was still a considerable amount of legal negotiation to be completed before a sale agreement could be finalised. Of particular concern was the threat presented by the inevitable inheritance disagreements. 'The Spanish authorities, quite rightly, wanted a guarantee that the agreement with Favorita Trustees Ltd would be final and that none of the heirs would be able to contest the agreement at a later date.'

Even though this assurance would be given, it was in fact something that neither Heini nor his lawyers could guarantee.

* * *

In March 1991, a new Spanish Minister of Culture was appointed; Jordi Solé Tura, a renowned jurist who had collaborated on drawing up the Spanish Constitution in 1978, taking Spain along the path of transition from dictatorship to democracy. Although he did not have the same contacts in the art world as his predecessor Semprún, he was clear about one thing: the achievement of the 'Art Triangle'. It was to be something like the 'Museum Island' in Berlin and would form the cultural centre of Madrid; ready for the emblematic year of 1992.

The first and unquestionable point of the triangle would be the Prado Museum, the second, the Reina Sofia Centre of Contemporary Art (which was the Queen's pet project), and the third would be the Thyssen-Bornemisza Museum in the Villahermosa Palace. In 1992, all eyes would be on Spain with the Universal Exhibition in Seville, the Olympics in Barcelona, and Madrid as the European Capital of Culture.

Heini welcomed the Spanish government's intentions, as he was all too aware that the deadline imposed offered a fortuitous incentive to complete negotiations and so he did everything within his power to assist:

> With this objective in mind, the Minister pushed forward the restoration work on Villahermosa. Originally, Semprún had suggested that Tita and I visited the Museum of Roman Antiquities in Merida before deciding on an architect. He wanted us to see the work of Rafael Moneo, an internationally renowned architect who had spent five years as a professor at Harvard. His work at the Palace of Cinema at the Lido in Venice or the Museum of Modern Art in Stockholm erased any doubts we might have had.
>
> Despite the many well-publicised disagreements between Tita and Moneo, such as their difference of opinion on choice of wall colour, work was completed

in May 1992. Predictably, Tita won the colour battle and managed to persuade Moneo that her inspired choice of pale sienna was far more interesting and in keeping with Spain than his somewhat clichéd choice of 'art gallery white'.

Unfortunately, not all her choices were so inspired. At the entrance to the museum, four of the most awful, kitsch, life-size, full-length portraits, painted by Ricardo Macarrón, an artist friend of Tita's, face each other across the hallway. On one side are the portraits of Heini and Tita, while on the opposite side of the entrance are a matching pair of equally frightful portraits of the King and Queen of Spain; giving the impression that both couples are of equal social significance. Heini thought they were very funny and agreed that they may have been a form of subtle revenge for the King insisting that the collection was housed in Madrid rather than Barcelona but this theory was dispelled when it was revealed that Tita liked the portraits and considered Macarrón an important painter. And so they remain as a wonderful tribute to her total disregard for social and aesthetic convention.

Meanwhile, both the press and the public awaited the great day with ever-increasing excitement; partly, no doubt, due to Tita's regular, if hardly culturally stimulating coverage in ¡Hola! magazine.

While Tita had been constantly accused by the family of bringing undue pressure to bear on Heini to move the collection to Spain, an equal degree of responsibility for the Cervera-Thyssen 'joint venture' could undoubtedly be attributed to Tita's mother. For although Heini had managed to persuade her to take a somewhat less obtrusive role in their lives, her power and influence were in no way diminished. Her physical presence, in traditional long tiered dress and black lace mantilla, may have been reduced but her omnipotent leadership of Tita's court was something over which Heini had little influence. In full flight she resembled, both in character and form, some incredible reincarnation of Goya's Queen Maria Luisa of Parma.

In a cruel trick of fate, Tita's mother would be unable to share in the pride and pleasure of her daughter's triumph, for on 22 February 1992, eight months before the inauguration of the Thyssen-Bornemisza Museum in the Villahermosa Palace, she succumbed to a stroke. Tita was devastated. Her mother's death was far more than the end of a truly remarkable woman's life. It was also the end of an odd and complicated relationship between a mother and her daughter: 'She fulfilled a far greater position in my life than purely that of mother. She was also my best friend, in the same way that I was hers. She was my refuge and my protector.'

She was also almost entirely responsible for the upbringing of Tita's son Borja, and there was no doubt that she applied tremendous pressure on her daughter to succeed. Some would even accuse her of using her daughter to achieve her own ambitions. It is therefore possible that her death may have proved to have been somewhat of a relief to her daughter. Certainly, Tita displayed no obvious tributes to her mother's memory or any evidence of her existence at either Madrid or Sant Feliú, despite the fact that she had lived with them in both houses.

* * *

Meanwhile, negotiations for the permanent installation of the collection in Spain were drawing to a close. Three months before the opening of the refurbished Villahermosa Palace, on 30 June 1992, a secret purchase agreement in the form of yet another declaration of intent was signed. The official reason given for the secrecy was that it was intended to protect the Spanish people from considering nine-and-a-half years of loan a second-class prize, if an agreement on the sale failed to be reached. But it also had the effect of hiding the huge cost of the purchase from the public until after it had taken place.

Only one original was signed which was then deposited with a notary with specific instructions that he should destroy it on 1 September 1993. The intention apparently being that either the sale would be completed by that date or the loan agreement would remain in place. Why they could not have continued negotiating for the full term of the loan agreement was never explained. Perhaps no one wanted to remind Heini of his mortality. Certainly, it was a somewhat forceful, if effective, means of applying a time limit and there was no doubt that inch by inch Heini was getting closer to his goal.

The Minister of Culture, Solé Tura, was also achieving his objectives. The Reina Sofia Centre of Contemporary Art had been opened by the Queen in September 1992 which only left the final point of the triangle, the Thyssen-Bornemisza Museum, to open its doors. The official opening was due to take place in Madrid on 8 October 1992. But before it could open an amazingly complicated piece of cultural logistics had to take place in the form of the transportation of 845 pictures from Lugano to Madrid; a process that Heini found particularly fascinating.

> They arrived by plane and the largest in lorries, to occupy their chosen places. I think that the painting 'Portrait of Sara Buxton' by Thomas Gainsborough must hold the record as the most travelled painting in my collection. Before I acquired it in 1983, it had crossed the Atlantic four times as it changed owners. I imagine that paintings such as this must be especially grateful for finding a permanent home at last.

A group of experts, including Miguel Satrústegui, José Manuel Pita Andrade, who was the curator for the period 1988 to 1990, and his successor, Tómas Llorens, had chosen the paintings.

The selection criteria were based on Sotheby's valuation. The works had been listed and divided into five categories in order of importance (A–E). The commission chose all category A and B paintings, some 445; most of C and some from D and E based on their importance to Spain. They chose 447 Old Masters and 328 Modern Masters, while 70 paintings belonging to Heini and Tita would remain on permanent loan to the Museum. This was the case with 'The Lock' by Constable, and 'Mata Mua' by Gauguin.

The transport of what was to become the Spanish collection was not the only challenge. Many of the paintings were still of questionable authenticity, although Emil Bosshard was more diplomatic:

> It's a grey area. One can run the whole gamut from completely genuine to completely fake with various shades of authenticity in between. A picture may be genuine, but the signature may not. Or it may have been signed later. You can have a replica of a master artist's painting, which was actually painted by another master. Or a replica by his own school which the master signed. But while a picture restorer can make a picture more genuine or less fake, it is in the catalogue that much of the work has to be done if a collection is to withstand public scrutiny.

It was therefore hardly surprising that, in anticipation of the sale, Heini should have commissioned Emil's wife Veronika to re-catalogue the paintings or 'clean-up' their provenances. But even then, forty pictures still defied any provenance apart from having become the property of the Thyssen Collection, with no explanation as to their previous ownership.

As far as Emil's work was concerned, he preferred not to comment, apart from admitting that the degree and style of restoration was the Baron's responsibility. Given that Heini once admitted that he 'liked them all to match', regardless of their age, Emil, who was without doubt a world-class restorer, must have often found Heini's instructions somewhat challenging. 'I want all my pictures to look alike, not one yellow, the other brown, and so on.'

Unfortunately, this policy tended to destroy the character of the paintings and give them the appearance of being contemporary reproductions or the work of the restorer rather than the artist.

*   *   *

Once the conversion of the building was completed, the museum was to be opened in October by the King and Jordi Solé Tura; the third Minister of Culture to have been involved since the negotiations began. But before the great day dawned, Heini's daughter Francesca created somewhat of a publicity diversion by announcing, on 26 September 1992, her engagement to Karl Habsburg or, as she liked him to be known, 'His Imperial and Royal Highness Archduke Karl von Habsburg', pretender to the crown of the Austro-Hungarian Empire and son of Archduke Otto von Habsburg, Euro MP and Honorary Town Councillor of Benidorm.

It was a time when Chessy was at her most disagreeable; particularly towards Tita. Refusing to sign the collection trust sale agreement, she no doubt still harboured ambitions of representing her father's collection in place of her stepmother. It was a situation that Tita would use Francesca's forthcoming marriage to rectify, by reminding the prospective in-laws of their obligations:

> Karl's father Otto had supported his family for years by persuading Heini and people like him to contribute to his political ambitions. As they obviously hadn't got any money of their own, I decided that it was only fair to point out that if they were hoping to profit from the fortunes of their new daughter-in-law, it may be a good idea to persuade her to be more co-operative with her father before they awarded her the title of Archduchess.

Persuading Francesca to co-operate was not the only problem facing Otto in his attempt to replenish the Habsburg coffers at the Guzwiller Bank in Basel. According to the Austrian *News* magazine: 'Almost all forty male members of the Habsburg family condemn the liaison and say they will not recognise Karl as future head of the family. It would mean their children would not be archdukes and would not inherit the position.'

They believed that the Habsburgs should continue to adhere to the marital guidelines on noble birth laid down in 1839 by Prince Metternich, the Austro-Hungarian chancellor. The current head of the family, Karl's father Otto, overcame the problem by the simple expedient of changing the family law. In his eyes at least it made the wedding possible and gave his grandchildren the right to their appropriate titles, though it did not alter the fact that, as Austria no longer recognised aristocratic titles, the whole process was somewhat academic.

* * *

The opening, on 8 October 1992, was attended by the King, who officially inaugurated the museum, the Queen and all the governmental authorities as well as various members of the Thyssen family. Heini was delighted:

The night of the opening, Tita organized a dinner for two hundred guests in the museum itself and another for five hundred at the Palace Hotel opposite. The days leading up to the opening were also extremely busy. One day was devoted to a preview for the Spanish press, one for the international press and another for friends and family.

Tita even claimed to have tried to retain a convivial relationship with Heini's ex-wives by inviting them to her triumphal opening. But in the case of Theresa, her good intentions failed spectacularly.

I have tried all my life to keep good relations with people, so I told Heini: 'You should invite all your former wives. This is a major event. Invite them all! Denise, Fiona, everybody.' And then Junior said: 'No, no, no, no. None of his other ex-wives are to be invited. Only my mother.' And I said 'Fine'. But she came wearing a dress that if I was twenty years old I would not wear. I mean, her body was OK, but it was a skin-tight dress, *tight*. I put her on the table with Doña Pilar, a good table. It was a special dinner in the museum. There was the Prime Minister, the King, the Queen and other people from the government. Nobody else could get in. Aznar, who eventually became the Prime Minister of Spain, could not get in to this dinner. Yet this idiotic woman was invited to this kind of event! And not even a thank-you letter.

Theresa could have certainly afforded to be a little more gracious, for despite marrying a Fürstenberg, inheriting another fortune and giving birth to three further children, she continued to receive alimony from Heini, something Tita considered an unjustified privilege.

Around the time of the opening, there was a lot of public criticism about the way in which the collection had come to be in Spain, which was not helped by the fact that the sale contract had still not been made available for public scrutiny. A commercial loan agreement was unheard of in the art world and not considered the correct way of doing things. At the time, most people were unaware that it was simply an instrument used to gain time in order to proceed with the sale, and negotiations for the purchase of the collection took their course, despite various obstacles caused by family objections and changes within the Spanish government. Meanwhile, Heini continued to promote the magnificence of his collection and justify Spain's investment. But as Emil Bosshard noticed, the extra space unfortunately did little to improve its quality. 'When his collection was housed at the Villa Favorita, there was only enough space for the best works. Unfortunately, they can now show everything and everything is not worth showing.'

But Heini's dream, or at least part of it, had come true. With his Thyssen-Bornemisza Collection now on permanent exhibition, he had achieved cultural immortality, financed by the Spanish. However, he was still not entirely satisfied: 'When I look through the leaflet prepared for visitors to the Thyssen-Bornemisza Museum, it surprises me to see the work of two generations of collectors summed up in a few short lines.'

> The collection has been hung following a historical route. The numerical order of the rooms indicate the suggested itinerary, starting on the second floor keep right round the central patio, you'll find the Renaissance as Classic tendencies from Duccio and Giotto's disciples to eighteenth century Venetian painting. There are also important sections dedicated to Flemish and German paintings and examples of French and Spanish painting. You'll find the first two rooms at the end of this route dedicated to Dutch painting, here shown with their most Italian influence. The rest of the Dutch work, a highlight of the museum, is on the first floor; the main style being Realism, from Frans Hals in the eighteenth century to Max Beckmann in the twentieth century. Here you'll find Impressionist and Post-Impressionist work with two of the most important parts of the collection, nineteenth century painting, from Cubism and the most Avant-garde movements from the early part of the twentieth century to Pop Art.

'My life's passion is contained in nothing more than this succinct description of the museum.'

Perhaps what he was expecting was a monument to his brilliance as a collector but what he got was his family name on the front of a national museum and $350 million.

Not for the first time was I reminded that despite Spain's hospitality and generosity, in private Heini was still quite capable of displaying xenophobic opinions. Once, in answer to my questioning his lack of knowledge of the Spanish language as we walked round the pool together, he giggled and said: 'I will only learn to speak Spanish when they have something intelligent to say.'

* * *

In February 1993, Francesca finally appreciated the wisdom, both for her own future and that of the Habsburgs, in signing the family agreement to permit the sale of the collection, before marrying Karl in a little village in Austria called Mariazell and subsequently settling down in a $6.25 million palace in Salzburg which Heini had paid for. But that was only after she had given Heini a written undertaking that she would not give away or sell his wedding present and Karl had signed a pre-nuptial agreement. Heini then stole the show by dressing up in a distinctly operatic Hungarian Hussar's dress uniform, complete with fur-trimmed cape and knee boots: 'The wedding and the palace which I had to buy for them to live in had cost me millions and I thought the least I could do was to tease the Habsburgs a little by making fun of all their Austro-Hungarian Empire nonsense.'

He forgot to mention his own reliance upon the same Austro-Hungarian Empire for his questionable title. Perhaps that was the real reason why he went to all the trouble of flying to Hungary to get a distant relative, Gloria von Berg, to design and make him the uniform which Tita claimed to have been his father's. It was in a vain effort to try and convince those among the Habsburgs who still doubted the suitability of his daughter, that he was a Hungarian aristocrat and not just a 'bloody German'.[7]

Unfortunately, the majority of the Habsburgs were anything but convinced and once again the media appeared delighted to reveal their lack of acceptance: 'The Habsburg family and young aristocracy are shunning the wedding. Otto's four brothers decided not to attend. "It is a demonstrative sign of protest, to make known our feelings of rejection for Francesca".'

The *Sunday Times* also picked up on the story: 'Austrian royalty rages against "vulgar" bride. Their objection is not only that the Thyssens are commoners, but that they are vulgar as well.'

Even the long-suffering Otto admitted that there had been forty-three written objections from members of the family. The only positive information appeared to be the guest list which included Gianni Versace with the wedding dress, the Princess Gloria von Thurn und Taxis, with her bodyguard, Mick Flick and his wife who looked bored but rewarded the press by being spotted escaping to a near-by bar, Eliette von Karajan, Rolf and Maja Sachs, Prince Eugen of Bavaria, Friedrich Wilhelm of Prussia, François de Bourbon, Prince Andreas of Sachsen Coburg Gotha, Yasmin Khan (daughter of Rita Hayworth), Prince Friedrich Schwarzenberg, Princess Moulay Rachid of Morocco, Prince Fumihito Ayanomiya of Japan, Victor Emanuel of Savoy, Prince Ernst August von Hanover who also went to the bar, Oliver Porsche, Rafael de Casanova, Eckbert von Bohlen und Halbach, Count Ladislaus Batthyány, Count Windisch-Graetz, Portugal's ex-King Don Duarte de Braganca, the Crown Prince of Hohenzollern and Fürstenberg, attended by ninety waiters, fifteen chefs, fifty policemen, two bomb disposal experts, twenty bodyguards, Vienna's Arch-bishop Cardinal Hans Herman Groer, various bishops representing Hungary,

Romania and Croatia, plus twelve assorted priests, which confirmed Francesca's belief that she was finally achieving full aristocratic status.

* * *

Back at the negotiating table, the problems were far from over and the secret sale agreement that expired in March 1993 had to be extended, initially to 1 May, then to 1 July. Then an economic crisis caused some friction between the Ministry of Culture and the strict budgets of the Ministry of Trade. The change in the representatives involved in the negotiations did not help matters, while even darker clouds appeared on the horizon when a general election was called for 6 June.

In May 1993, an agreement had been signed between the foundation and the Ministry of Culture, where the latter assumed liability for any losses incurred in the running of the museum. It was also fortunate that the new Minister of Culture, Solé Tura, wanted to complete the operation as quickly as possible but his enthusiasm only increased the workload of the twelve lawyers who were already putting in eighteen-hour days. The cost of the legal bills for the entire project was never disclosed.

The main obstacle was still the signing of the agreement by all the individual heirs. Lorne had never been a problem, while Georg had by now fully appreciated the financial advantages to the family of the Spanish sale. After Francesca, the person most reluctant to sign had been Denise, who was acting for Alexander. Under Swiss law he did not attain his majority until 1994, when he would be twenty years old and was therefore ineligible to sign himself. Eventually, the lawyers found a way round Denise by getting Alexander to formally commit to signing his agreement when he came of age. This he eventually did. In the meantime, Heini's legal advisers warned Heini that if Alexander chose to challenge the inheritance agreement at some time in the future, they could not guarantee that he would not succeed. But it was a risk Heini was prepared to take.

Finally, on 18 June 1993, Royal Decree Law 11/1993 was signed by King Juan Carlos and ratified by the government of Felípe González, which granted the finance for the purchase of the Thyssen-Bornemisza Collection by the Spanish Thyssen-Bornemisza Collection Foundation. The foundation has twelve trustees; eight nominated by the Spanish government and four by Heini. The position of senior patron would be taken up by the King, while the Baron was appointed honorary president for life and the actual presidency was reserved for the Minister of Culture who, as of July 1993, was Carmen Alborch. Tita was appointed vice-president while the rest of the group was made up of the Under-Secretary at the Ministry of Culture, the Director General of Budgets, the Director General of National Heritage, the managing director of the museum and head curator Tomàs Llorens, Infanta Pilar de Borbón, Miguel Satrusteguí, Luís Angel Rojo, Oriol Bohígas, Simon Levie and Heini's son Georg.

On 21 June 1993, the Kingdom of Spain finally and formally purchased half the Thyssen-Bornemisza Collection and the following week in Zurich, Heini's heirs, Tita, Georg, Francesca and Lorne, signed various valuation waivers and yet more inheritance agreements for the tax-free $350 million. Then they and their lawyers had a celebratory lunch at the Pavilion Restaurant of the Hotel Baur au Lac. Considering they were celebrating the sharing of $350 million, it was a somewhat anti-climactic lunch. Heini was grumpy because he was drunk and not being sufficiently praised for his generosity and brilliance. Tita was annoyed because Heini was drunk and seething because the family had refused to accept Borja as an heir. Francesca was angry because she had not been offered a position on the board of the Spanish foundation. Georg was angry because Tita had prevailed and was blaming him for taking Francesca's seat on the board and Lorne was angry because he was having to sit through a ridiculous lunch rather than be given a cheque there and then and allowed to return to his lady friend who was waiting for him at a local hotel. The only happy guests were the lawyers.

* * *

There were many Spanish journalists who praised their government for stealing a march on other, less culturally appreciative European neighbours. There were others, particularly those briefed by the Thyssen-Bornemisza Museum press office, who credited Heini with having pulled-off the art deal of the century and an absolute masterstroke. But not everyone approved of the arrangement. Many felt hoodwinked by both the Thyssens and the Spanish government. Francesco Umbral wrote in *El País*, 'It's just a crude business deal', while in the same paper Picasso's biographer John Richardson was predictably more forthright: 'It's the messiest way to dispose of one's collection that I have ever heard of.'

José Luís Vilallonga was also sceptical: 'One day Spain is going to wake up and realise how much it really paid and how much it will cost to maintain this collection.'

Certainly, many museums and art galleries were already fearful that the Baron had set a costly financial precedent. But it was too late for objections to have any effect. Heini's defence against his critics would do little to justify his supporters' claims of his generosity towards Spain:

Chapter X: 1983–1993

The collection cost the Spanish $350 million, minus the loan agreement payments, plus the cost of the renovation of two buildings [not forgetting the cost of the palace, plus transport, seven years of legal fees and limitless running expenses], while the valuation carried out by Sotheby's in 1988 valued the collection at some $1,200 million. More than double the amount paid. The collection may not have been 'donated' to Spain, but one could hardly say it was a profit-making deal. I only wanted to satisfy my heirs, my intention was never to make money on the arrangement.

Heini had once again forgotten to mention that the Spanish had only acquired half his collection while admitting that the real cost was closer to $600 million than the generally accepted $350 million. Considering the state of the art market, it could hardly have been considered an act of philanthropy. There also remained the question of what Spain had actually paid for.

One late summer afternoon in Sant Feliú de Guixols, when Heini was lying back on his lounger, wine in hand, staring out across the deep blue Mediterranean, I asked him: 'If the positions had been reversed and you had been in charge of Spain's fiscal budget, would you have done the deal?'

'No', he said, 'I wouldn't,' and giggled into his wine glass.

'But the thing I find most remarkable about the deal is that having paid $600 million for your collection, they still don't actually own it.'

'Of course they do,' said Heini, grumpily.

'No they don't. If you own something, it's yours to do what you like with. To be more specific, "to sell, swap or trade without lien or encumbrance" and they can't do any of those things. You have actually charged them $600 million to look after your paintings, for ever. They don't actually "own" the pictures, do they, Heini?'

He giggled into his glass again: 'No, I suppose not.'

* * *

After the money had disappeared for a few days en route from Spain, via Switzerland and Brussels, and Tita had accused Georg of stealing it, the $350 million finally arrived at the Morgan Bank in New York before being divided between each of the heirs' individual sub-trusts, each of which was named after a painter whose initial matched the appropriate heir: Caravaggio, Ghirlandaio, Fragonard, Leonardo and Antonello. Once Heini's $64.4 million art-purchasing loan had been paid off, Tita received 39 per cent ($108.9 million), Georg 19 per cent ($53 million) while Chessy, Lorne and Alexander each received 14 per cent ($39 million). It had also been determined, by means of the new family agreement, that the remaining unsold pictures would be divided among the heirs in proportion to their share of the money.

The value of the paintings seemed to be the deciding factor in their division as there was little evidence of any patterns of personal choice apart from Alexander whose rather camp persona was reflected in his choice of theatrical set and costume designs by Bakst, Exter, Gontcharova, Manuel, Tirloff, Erte, Bertaux and José de Zamora. Even Stanley Spencer's 'Love Letters' reflected an appropriate degree of whimsy, while Lucian Freud's 'Still Life with Quinces' was hardly lacking in 'quaint humour'.

He also displayed sufficient aesthetic appreciation to choose two works by Edward Hopper and the delightfully unchallenging 'Gallows Island' by Winslow Homer. 'No. 11' by Jackson Pollock, valued at $2.25 million, was totally out of character and suggested the influence of his mother and the fearsome Uncle Shorto or even Heini who was rumoured to have curtailed Alexander's luxury of choice as punishment for his refusal to sign the inheritance agreement.

Meanwhile, Francesca's choice displayed remarkably little inspiration for someone who professed such commitment to art. It appeared to lack any direction, although it did include two Noldes, 'A Young Couple' valued at $250,000 and 'A Flower Garden' at $800,000, plus 'The Olive Trees' by Maurice Vlaminck. However, 'Portrait of Baron, Man in Chair' by Lucian Freud was doubtless the most genuinely personal choice made by any of the heirs.

For someone who would publicly admit that her favourite picture was the 'Mischievous Model' by Raimundo de Madrazo y Garreta, it was even more remarkable that Tita's choice would contain 'The Martha McKeen of Wellfleet' by Edward Hopper and Georgia O'Keeffe's 'New York with Moon' valued at $900,000.

In addition to the paintings there were also sculpture, carpets, fabrics, tapestries, furniture, ceramics, gold, silver and ivory 'objets d'art' whose value in 1992, according to Sotheby's, amounted to $81,125,640; all of which had to be divided.

Due to the fact that he had taken such a small share of the paintings, Georg was entitled to the largest share of the objects. Valued at $26 million, this mainly comprised a collection of ivory and Renaissance jewellery.

Lorne claimed the only other collection to remain undivided, which consisted of forty-eight snuff-boxes; the most precious being designed in gold and decorated in diamonds. It was valued at $1.45 million. He also claimed two of the Rodin marbles which he would later sell to Tita, so that Tita would have four and Francesca two.

The greatest missed opportunity was Heini's refusal to sell his and his father's superb collection of seventy carpets and nine textiles to the New Museum of Islamic Art in Qatar. Tita had greatly amused Heini by reacting to the bid by asking, 'What funny country is that?' He preferred to allow it to be divided among his unappreciative family. Even Lorne chose to ignore its survival in favour of snuff-boxes, allowing the two stars of the collection, the Braganza valued at $97,500 and the Behague Saguszko valued at $187,000, to go to Tita and Francesca respectively. Before the collection was broken up, Tita was using the carpets, of which she had the largest share and for which she admittedly displayed the greatest appreciation, as floor covering. In one case she even used them to cover unfinished tiling, on the night of her inaugural party at La Moraleja.

Any kind of personal choice or cultural appreciation had little to do with the fact that the additional value of the paintings and objects would raise the total value of each of the heirs' collection inheritance to $175 million for Tita, $65 million for Georg, and $80 million for each of the others.

* * *

Heini assumed that any mortal would be pleased with such rewards and appreciative of their father and stepmother's achievement; particularly his children who had done nothing to earn such wealth. But even within this spectacular arrangement, there would be cause for ill-feeling.

Until Heini's demise the heirs' share of the collection would remain in Switzerland, controlled by the Bermudan Thyssen-Bornemisza Collection Trust and administrated by the Swiss Thyssen-Bornemisza Foundation, while some specific works would continue to grace the walls of the gallery at Villa Favorita. Other paintings were also lent to the Spanish Art Foundation for various exhibitions but when they failed to return, some of the heirs accused Tita of being responsible. Meanwhile, she had her own 'bone of contention'.

The family agreement had specified that while she received a far larger proportion of Heini's collection, or the proceeds, she would, unlike his children, not inherit any share entitlement in the Thyssen Bornemisza Group. It was a thorn in her flesh of equal proportion to the one caused by the heirs' refusal to accept Borja's inclusion in the division of the inheritance. If, as Heini sometimes claimed, Francesca was his only legitimate offspring, it seemed to be a remarkably unreasonable attitude on the part of the heirs. Perhaps it was their paranoid response to the conditions of inheritance that included the proviso that the share of any heir who died, through natural or unnatural means, be distributed among the remaining heirs.

1 *New York Times*, 2 September 1983.
2 Author's conversations with Emil Bosshard (†), 2000–2005.
3 The yacht was sold to Tiny Rowlands (né Roland Furhop), head of Lonrho. Its next owner was Paul Allen, co-founder of Microsoft.
4 Author's interview with the Infanta Doña Pilar de Borbón, 1999.
5 Author's interview with Sir Timothy Lloyd, 1998.
6 Kim Bradley in *Art in America,* New York, February 1992.
7 Heini Thyssen-Bornemisza's description of himself in a frank moment during a conversation with the author on 3 August 1998.

Chapter XI

1993–2001

Thyssen *v.* Thyssen ...
The $150 million court case

*Money isn't everything, but it sure
keeps you in touch with your children.*
John Paul Getty

The relationship between Georg and Tita was like a festering sore, which never gave any indication of healing. In 1994 it became so poisonous that it was obvious the limb was going to need severing before it infected the whole body.

According to a lawyer's report made in July 1993, two days before the signing of the second part of the Testamentary Pact or family agreement, after Heini's death the income of the Continuity Trust was to be distributed to give Georg 43.75 per cent while Chessy, Lorne and Alexander were to receive 18.75 per cent each. Tita was not eligible as she had already received 39 per cent, or the largest share, of the Spanish art sale money, which was safely invested in the Thyssen-Bornemisza Fund, based in the British Virgin Islands. In the early 1990s, none of the heirs, including Tita, received any income from this 'Art Fund', the interest being continually reinvested.

Tita's dissatisfaction with this arrangement, as well as her deep dislike of Georg and objection to what she considered his arrogant attitude, would become increasingly evident during the following year, despite the fact that she was also due to receive a further 39 per cent of Heini's personal estate, which had been valued at $132 million. Georg was to get 32.86 per cent and all the others 9.38 per cent.

Tita's frustration was aggravated when, despite Genillard's recommendation that TBG should not become involved in running family affairs, Georg objected to Heini's intention to make Tita an immediate beneficiary of both the capital and income of her Caravaggio art sub-trust.

Meanwhile, Georg also objected to Tita signing an undertaking with Spain that would lead to yet more of the remaining paintings being made available for loan to the Spanish Art Foundation. According to Heini, every time Tita organised art exhibitions Georg would advise his siblings against loaning her any of their pictures. Heini was infuriated and replied with a formal letter to the trust's protectors, saying how he had full confidence in Georg to run the business but that he wanted Tita to run the art: 'These two areas should be separated and a new arrangement along these lines should be formed when we meet in Paris. This would strengthen the family.'

By this time Tita had no intention of limiting her involvement to art and sent her own warning letter to Georg, which she copied to the rest of the family. In it she accused him of setting up the Continuity Trust without her knowledge; ensuring that she could never participate in the business trust. She also questioned both the trust's legal validity and Georg's translation of its powers.

Tita complained that he had too much power, being the main beneficiary of the Continuity Trust and also its protector and that after nine years of marriage to Heini, she had still not seen a single paper relating to the Continuity Trust. She also thought it was about time she was given some respect as Heini's wife and have her art sub-trust administrated by people who had her full confidence in a correct manner.

Although Francesca, Lorne and Alexander had little more respect for their stepmother than their elder brother, they were obviously sympathetic towards her insistence that they should be allowed some income from their art trusts. Heini, too, saw no good reason for Georg's insistence that for 'tax reasons' everyone should wait for their father's demise; especially as the resulting income would reduce their financial dependence on him.

* * *

On 16 May 1994, there was a family meeting at the Plaza Athénée in Paris, attended by a mass of protectors, trustees, lawyers and accountants. There, Georg and his supporters bowed to pressure and agreed that everyone should receive their share of 3.5 per cent of the fair market value of the TB Fund at the beginning of each year. To minimise their exposure to tax, yet more companies were formed to receive the funds.

The proposal meant that around $10.5 million were available each year to be divided between them: Tita got $4 million a year, Georg $2 million while Lorne, Chessy and Alexander would be entitled to $1.5 million each. However, Alexander had yet to sign the family agreement, so he could not claim his entitlement, while Tita, with the support of Heini, finally managed to have her capital released and placed under her own control.

There were further arguments concerning the distribution of the remaining pictures, which theoretically was not due to happen until after Heini's death; but due to general mistrust and the fact that Heini had already given Tita so many, there was increasing pressure to at least determine the division of the paintings, even if they had to wait to be awarded the right of sale.

The constant references to his death and their inheritance could hardly have imbued Heini with a generous attitude towards his offspring, particularly on the eve of his imminent return to the Salpetrière hospital for yet further cardio-vascular surgery. Tita appeared to be the only one particularly concerned with the inherent dangers involved in his latest operation: 'I knew how critical the operation was but no one seemed to understand how important it was for him to be in a relaxed state of mind.'

The following day, when Heini failed to return from the operation, Tita became distressed:

> Finally I went to see Professor Kiefer who was responsible for the operation and I said 'What happened?' He said, 'Well, he has had a little thrombosis. He has a little mark on his brain that could have happened during the operation or before, but it is there. Now he is in a coma and has to be on a machine.' It was terrible. He was unconscious for twelve days.

Tita claimed to have been appalled by the lack of respect for Heini, insisting that during this period the heirs, who understandably may have doubted that he was likely to recover, apparently continued to discuss the distribution of the $120 million worth of paintings that they may have assumed they were about to inherit. Apparently they also tried to persuade Alexander to sign the family pact, so that the Art Trust could give the Spanish authorities a guarantee that there would be no challenge after Heini's death. But Alexander refused to co-operate, as long as Heini continued to demand the return of his mother's jewellery.

Regardless of the alleged squabbling, Heini appeared to respond to Tita's prayers and after almost two weeks came out of his coma, was taken off the life support machine and moved to a recovery room. According to Tita's version of events, Georg having declined to comment, what followed was a scarcely believable farce. Having been informed that contrary to her wishes, Georg planned to have Heini moved to a hospital more suitable for his convalescence, she decided to kidnap her husband and take him back to Spain:

First I got an ambulance and a private plane on standby, with a doctor on board. I then ordered another ambulance from the hospital to take Heini to the airport. Then, on the day he was due to leave, I said to the nurse, 'Where is the ambulance for my husband that I reserved two days ago?' She said, 'Oh, the doctor has cancelled it.' I said, 'Oh yes? Well, I would like to speak to the doctor.' In the meantime I said to the people who were with me: 'Get Heini out and put him into my ambulance while I go and keep the doctor talking.' It was like a movie. Then the doctor told me Heini would not be going to the airport but to another clinic (the one recommended by Junior) and I just said, 'Oh yes! How sweet of you to organise everything.'

Meanwhile, Heini was already on his way to the plane and Genillard and Junior were calling everywhere: 'Where is my father? He has left!' They were so furious that I had taken him out of the hospital that I thought they may have been capable of accusing me of anything, so I made sure that Heini was very well taken care of in the plane and Professor Kiefer had signed a paper saying that Sant Feliú would be a very good place for Heini to recuperate.

* * *

While his offspring may well have been infuriated by Tita's apparent kidnap of their father, they may also have appreciated the fact that the challenging role of caring for their father had been accepted by their stepmother. Tita did not see her role as limited to Heini's physical well-being. Apparently with his blessing, she also became increasingly involved in the administration of his financial affairs. This, in addition to trying to get Borja a seat on the board of TBG and her decision to start her own Carmen Thyssen-Bornemisza Collection, would do little to improve her relationship with the family and particularly Georg. His constant criticism of her involvement in his father's affairs was becoming increasingly annoying to Heini: 'Georg had a whole support cast of lawyers, accountants, management, advisory board members and no doubt his mother, yet at the first sign of my reliance upon my wife's support they accused Tita of manipulating me.'

In her new role, Tita's knowledge of Heini's financial position increased and it was not long before she had discovered the reason for the dramatic curtailment of his spending power: at the annual meeting of the trustees and protectors of the Continuity Trust held in Bermuda on 3 October 1994, it was announced that the shortfall in Heini's annuity had risen to \$65 million.[1] When Tita complained to Genillard he came up with an even more dramatic revelation:

After I had asked why Heini was always so broke and why the company was so broke it couldn't pay Heini's annuity in full, Mr Genillard eventually told me, 'Oh, but the company isn't broke, there is a great deal of money accumulated in the company.' So I asked him how much and was totally shocked by his reply. Apparently there was $371 million in bonds and short-term equities in what was called the Corporate Liquidity Fund. I didn't want to make a big scene in case I forewarned them into moving the money somewhere where it was less accessible, so I just said, 'Oh, really?' and then asked him, 'Can we have a meeting in Monaco?' He said, 'Oh, yes! I will arrange it.'

Although Heini pretended to be surprised, he must have known of the ever-increasing value of the liquidity fund, due to the fact that it had been started in 1983 and its value recorded annually in the company reports. The shortfall in Heini's annuity had never been a particular problem in the past. According to Michael Crystal QC, the barrister who would be recruited to lead the legal bloodletting that was about to take place, and who some twenty years earlier had represented Heini's sister Gaby in her dispute with her lover Ion Ratiu: 'The shortfall gradually continued to mount. However, on two occasions, first in 1987 and then again in 1992, the Baron insisted on receiving further payments from the Group, and on each occasion millions of dollars were paid to him.'[2]

* * *

Initially, it was difficult to tell why Heini allowed the conflict to develop. He would certainly have been aware of the dangers involved in a direct confrontation between Tita and Georg in Monte Carlo. Most of his extended family and friends held Tita responsible but it was not something she would have done without his support and encouragement.

Although there was no specific reason to doubt her genuine affection, there was little evidence that either Tita or his dysfunctional and largely illegitimate family wanted to spend any more time with Heini than was absolutely necessary. Then, one afternoon, when the wine had made him maudlin, Tita was away in Barcelona and the sleeping servants were not answering his bell, he said to me: 'The problem with being rich is that it condemns you to a life of loneliness.'

The following morning, as he sat alone on the hill, his comment was reinforced when I paid my customary visit to the cavernous Casino bar on the seafront of Sant Feliú, where the air was full of the sound of slapping cards on wet tables and old men laughing and arguing with their friends, while from time to time a son or daughter arrived with an adored grandchild to be cooed over. Then, as I enjoyed their noisy company, the reason why Heini was prepared to go to war with his son suddenly became obvious. It was certainly not for financial reasons, for, apart from the cost of his servants, medical treatment and an endless supply of rather poor quality 'vino tinto', his needs were no longer very extravagant. Loneliness and mortality were of far greater concern to Heini.

What he wanted was to give his wife and family an incentive to keep him alive while ensuring he had some form of regular social contact. When the opportunity presented itself to achieve his objectives while directing the spectacle of his selfish family tearing itself apart in their battle for his inheritance, it was a last great game which the old 'capitalist agitator' just could not resist. The social contact would arrive in the shape of a posse of British barristers who would make regular visits to report on their progress, take Heini's instructions and share his red wine.

* * *

Predictably, Tita's visit to Monaco on 14 November 1995 did not go well. Having failed to meet her at the airport and tried to avoid discussing the matter at his office by delegating responsibility to the unfortunate Robert Genillard, Georg proceeded to criticise Heini and Tita's extravagance: 'He talked as if Heini didn't know what he was doing and treated me as if I had no business to ask.'

Tita claimed that Georg refused to discuss the shortfall, while subsequently accusing her of threatening him with legal action to take the Trust apart if he failed to organise a special dividend. He no doubt annoyed her even further by suggesting he paid a visit to Madrid to discuss the matter with Heini.

Three months later, Georg arrived in Madrid but refused to pay off the shortfall. Despite the group's enormous cash reserves, his best offer was that the Trust paid off $20 million of his father's debts by means of a loan. Tita was furious while Heini fanned the flames by demanding that Borja be made a beneficiary of the Continuity Trust. By now Heini considered legitimacy to be a very flexible concept and when Georg replied that Borja was not a natural child of the Baron, Heini mysteriously stated 'the Baroness could say that he would be'.

By 13 April 1996, relations were reaching a critical level and Heini's seventy-fifth birthday party in Lugano ended in the type of physical violence normally associated with the films of Pedro Almodóvar.

Georg, having resigned from the Spanish art board, announced his decision to be replaced by Francesca. Heini forcefully reminded him that he, not Georg, decided who was appointed to the board and that he had no intention of appointing a Habsburg. By his authority Georg would be replaced by Alexander. According to Tita, who had presumably added her opinion, it was at this moment that Francesca lost control, screaming at the top of her voice and things threatened to get physical (the accusation was later theatrically modified to include the unlikely use of a knife). Francesca then left and with her any chance of peaceful negotiation. It would be the last family meeting without lawyers present.

Physical confrontation between Heini and his children was not unusual. Previously, Francesca had admitted that a very large black eye had been the result of a fistfight with her father. There had also been rumours that Heini's wine-fuelled violence had, from time to time, been directed at his wives.

* * *

Tita had already recruited the services of Robert Ham QC, a leading British trust barrister, when she negotiated the release of her art trust funds. Apparently he had also assured her that with the right legal team, including the highly paid barrister Michael Crystal QC, he could break the Continuity Trust.

Heini then reminded Conyers, Dill & Pearman, the trustees' solicitors in Bermuda, that when he signed the Continuity Trust agreement in 1983, it had certainly not been his intention to reduce his income, change his lifestyle or limit his acquisition of paintings. In May 1996 he sent them a demand that the annuity shortfall (which had now reached $69 million) be paid in full before the end of the year. Georg responded with two conciliatory letters. Largely due to the fact that they contained criticisms of Tita, whom he constantly referred to as 'your wife', they only succeeded in aggravating the situation.

On 5 June 1996, Heini's accountant, Riccardo Guscetti, resigned. Georg complained it was a decision that Guscetti had been 'obliged' to take, leaving the way free for Tita to take control of Heini's personal finances. Soon afterwards, when Giorgio approached the lunch table with some documents, it became obvious that this had already happened. While Tita was guiding his hand, Heini asked what he was signing and with a big smile she answered: 'Nothing to worry your old head about, my darling. Just some little old powers of attorney.'

Georg also raised objections to Tita's exhibition, 'From Canaletto to Kandinsky', at the Villahermosa Palace. She claimed it consisted of paintings from her collection, but, as Georg pointed out, while Heini was still alive, the paintings were not yet technically hers. Tita retaliated by accusing Georg of selling off more than a million dollars-worth of paintings in 1995, which she claimed should have been kept in the art trust. By this time, it was clear that Georg was obsessed with Tita and incapable of any degree of diplomacy. It was an attitude which Heini found totally predictable and caused Tita's eyes to sparkle with the excitement of revenge. By September she could resist the temptation no longer and offered the story to the press, who reacted enthusiastically.

Lorne said that Heini wished to throw Junior off TBG's board, while Tita threatened to have him charged with embezzlement and fraud. She had also gone public with claims that Junior was the son of Ivy Batthyány, an accusation Lorne did not seem to think was beyond the bounds of possibility due to the fact that it was generally accepted in the family that Francesca was Heini's only legitimate offspring. Apparently, Georg was less sanguine about the accusation:

> He wants to nail Tita for slander, tax evasion and damages. But the directors and members of the supervisory board are planning to take out a half-page advertisement to put the record straight. One of them has described Heini and Tita's attack as the result of a 'marriage between insanity and senility'.

* * *

On 10 December 1996, Heini wrote to the trustees and protectors concerning his 'supposed' son, who, he suggested, had not been respecting his wishes. Because of Georg, Tita's interest in the Continuity Trust had been restricted, while Heini had been paid 'only part of the amounts due to me, pretending that TBG could not afford more, while accumulating a cash hoard in TBG of over $370 million'. He claimed this had obliged him to sell a major part of his collection to Spain. He also suggested that Georg may have been assuming that his father's demise would take place prior to his collection of the annuity claim, which would also result in Georg's total control of both TBG and the liquidity fund.

Meanwhile, Heini intended to sue Georg for the annuity shortfall, to remove him from control of TBG and to ensure that Tita would inherit the maximum legal quota under Swiss law. He also encouraged people to believe that it was Tita, not him, who was responsible for the hostilities.

On 6 January 1997, with the aid of QCs Crystal and Ham and a breathtakingly expensive team of barristers, Heini commenced legal proceedings, including a claim against Georg for compensation for equitable fraud in excess of $1.5 billion. Then Heini and his team created LRT Trustee (PVT) Ltd, otherwise known as the 'Vlaminck Trust', whose purpose was to receive the retrieved funds and enable Tita to continue the action in the event of his death.

On 20 January 1997 a writ of summons was entered by Appleby, Spurling & Kempe in the Supreme Court of Bermuda between the two plaintiffs, Hans

Heinrich Thyssen-Bornemisza and LRT Trustee (PVT) Ltd and the one personal defendant, Georg Heinrich Thyssen-Bornemisza, and three corporate defendants (Favorita Holding Ltd, Thybo Trustees Ltd and Tornabuoni Ltd). The ninety-four-page document consisted of a plea to set aside the trust and claim compensation or damages from Georg in the amount of the present value of shares in Favorita, which were estimated to be worth between $1 billion and $2.8 billion. In addition there was a $147 million claim for compensation or damages for the breach of the annuity agreement.

Instead of accepting the legal challenge, Georg might have been better advised to seek what would undoubtedly have been the more cost-effective assistance of a witch or anyone versed in the black arts. Tita is a deeply superstitious woman, who goes to considerable lengths to avoid even minor confrontation with a gypsy or anyone she considers in any way capable of summoning the forces of evil. According to a member of her staff, her refusal to attend the hairdressers was not, as many thought, the result of meanness but of fear that her hair and nail clippings might be used in the preparation of curses. She regularly took the same precautions with Heini and the sight of him seated on a chair in the middle of the lawn with a towel round his shoulders while Tita cut and dyed his hair was one of the more bizarre pre-lunch sights at Mas Mañanas.

Predictably for a man who had studied law, Georg chose to defend himself with what he obviously considered an appropriate, if marginally less extravagant, legal team who would take two and a half years to prepare a defence. While the delay may have frustrated Tita, it did not cause Heini any concern, nor apparently Georg.

Despite the confidence of his lawyers, Georg displayed a degree of insecurity when, less than two months after the writ had been issued, he presented his supervisory board with a report that celebrated his achievements. He started by reminding them how his timely exit from Bremer Vulkan had prevented the group suffering from serious financial strain.

He also spoke of the reduction in debt and the importance of the Corporate Liquidity Fund: 'TBG now has a very strong financial position and high liquidity reserves, particularly important for a privately owned company without access to public financial markets.'

However, Georg failed to explain why the organisation needed to maintain such a high level of reserves and proportionally low level of growth. He also glossed over the costly mistakes involved in Interpool Leasing and Greenland agricultural machinery and claimed they were 'vastly offset by the strategic success of building one of the world's most prominent electronic information groups and largest pump groups with today very substantial unrealised values for TBG'.

He then concluded, 'TBG has moved from a centralised old fashioned management style to a highly decentralised entrepreneurial style', choosing not to elaborate on the details of his 'entrepreneurial style'.

* * *

Four months after the plaintiffs had filed their first writ, there was still no evidence of a defence. In May, both parties appeared in chambers in front of Chief Justice Ward at the Supreme Court in Bermuda who gave the defendants six more weeks to complete the preparation of their defence. When the case had first been entered, the Attorney General appreciated that it could take a considerable amount of time to settle and as she was already being faced with another similarly time-consuming case, they were going to require more court space if the island's judicial process was not to be brought to a halt. It was therefore decided that a Salvation Army chapel should be purchased and the $270,000 cost of conversion into two courts divided between the plaintiffs. In addition, another Judge was apparently needed to handle the Thyssen case.

Denis Mitchell was a Scots-born Irish QC who had been working in Hong Kong and only considered the job as a means of getting his dog back into

Heini, the Von Bergs and Pusch (second from right) at Mas Mañanas, on his seventy-seventh birthday.

The 'Archduke' Karl and the 'Archduchess' Francesca with their Habsburg heir Ferdinand Zvonimir and his sister Eleonore.

England without it having to serve six months quarantine. He would be recruited for the post by Jeffrey Elkinson, an Irish barrister and close friend of Mitchell and his wife. It was a relationship that Elkinson would deny until he was reminded that Mitchell had been an invited guest at his wedding in Hong Kong. This denial may have been the result of the fact that Elkinson was also part of Georg Thyssen's legal team.

Another element, which no one seemed particularly keen to discuss, was the official time allotted for the trial. While, off the record, both Ham and Crystal had been happy to admit that the trial could last for five years before appeal and anything up to twenty-five years with appeals, they were very hazy when asked what the trial had been set down for. Two years later it was revealed by the court registrar that the allotted time had been one year. As Mitchell was only employed on a three-year contract and he had assured the Department of Justice that he was prepared to serve one term, it should have been obvious to everyone on the claimants' side, including Tita, that the trial might never be completed.

However, regardless of Justice Ward's deadline for the filing of a defence, for two years no one appeared to be in any hurry to get the trial started; nor were the barristers in any rush to move to Bermuda, particularly in the case of Michael

Crystal and Robert Ham who continued to voice their dislike of the island. Presumably they preferred to earn their doubtless well-earned, multi-million pound fees from the comfort and convenience of their London Chambers.

* * *

As we awaited developments high up above the sea with the wind sighing in the pines and the cicadas still singing their one-note song, Heini appeared to enjoy our company and, when he was not being grumpy, Caroline and I enjoyed his. While he told us the story of his life, the most we saw of Tita was her running across the lawn, pursued by her pack of yapping dogs shouting: 'Big kiss, my darling. I will see you later, my darling', as she sped by. Later Heini would ask Giorgio where she had gone and when she would return. It was invariably Barcelona or Madrid and sometimes she would return for lunch or dinner. Sometimes the same day. Sometimes the next day or the day after that. Sometimes, having phoned to say she was stuck in Barcelona, she would return unannounced to eat in the kitchen with the staff where we could hear her talking and laughing.

Heini never commented although, from time to time, he would become very ill-tempered and snap at her when she arrived breathless to join us for coffee and cigarettes. This anger was often the result of her indiscretions; particularly when she told us a story of General Pinochet's daughter asking them for help to get money out of Chile using art.

The question of Tita's whereabouts was complicated by what appeared to be a secret entrance from the property next door to her quarters on the next terrace down, where the guard dogs slept and the parrots shrieked. Both she and Heini denied any knowledge of the demolition of the house next door and its replacement by what was obviously to be a very grand palazzo, despite the fact that from time to time Tita could plainly be seen directing the building work, following which the dogs in her quarters would start barking in greeting before Tita reappeared before us. The process also worked in reverse and one day when she assured Heini she would be joining us for lunch but 'just needed to go downstairs for a little shower', lunch was held for two hours while we awaited her return. Finally, Heini summoned the reluctant Giorgio to help him downstairs where we heard him kicking the door and screaming with rage. Lunch was served on his return, while no mention was made of Tita's absence.

One night, Tita arrived with a group of over-excited friends from Barcelona, who were far more representative of her real social circle than any of Heini's friends and acquaintances. They appeared as if from a Fellini movie or a Lindsay Kemp stage production. Of indeterminate sex, they included a television priest, the Catalan composer of a musical called 'The Virgin of Guadaloupe', a transsexual whom Tita claimed to be one hundred years old, a fat lady called Pucci who made a pass at Heini and a charming, even fatter jeweller who worked for Chaumet. When they disappeared downstairs to Tita's quarters, Heini giggled, shook his head in disbelief and said: 'What do you think they are all doing down there?'

* * *

Apart from the lawyers, Pusch was one of the few visitors whose presence Heini encouraged. From time to time, another of his old friends would telephone and Tita would try and get him to take the call but he rarely did. There was no evidence to support his children's claim that Tita kept them away while Heini insisted they only ever came to see him when they wanted money. He displayed remarkably little interest even when Chessy's first son Ferdinand Zvonimir was born in July 1997, though the fact that in her pursuit of Habsburg glory he was named after a Croatian King and she continued to claim Croatian lineage obviously amused Heini.

He also managed to replace his own family with a far more appreciative group consisting of the devoted Baroness Ildiko von Berg, whose mother was Heini's cousin Maximiliane, her three charming children, as well as Baroness Gloria von Berg, who lived in Budapest and entertained Heini with her Hungarian anecdotes. Other members of the small group who turned up for Heini's birthday and Christmas celebrations, which were invariably recorded by a group of journalists and photographers from ¡Hola! magazine, included Professor Marco Marcoff, an old friend from his university days, who assisted Heini in validating his somewhat theatrical academic record. Pusch remained a regular visitor as did the petulant Alexander, who sat with him in silence for hours with the most wonderfully bored and superior expression on his face; sighing quietly when Heini asked him, in German, whether he was ever going to do anything useful with his life. Meanwhile, Heini complained that he never saw enough of Borja, who was usually with his mother.

On the rare occasions when Tita shared time with us, during the three years of our regular visits, she enjoyed talking about her life with Lex Barker and keeping us updated with news of the legal battle. This was usually the result of a visit from the barristers whose morning meetings with Heini, Tita was apparently not invited to attend. The lawyers stayed at the five-star 'La Gavina', where their main source of entertainment seemed to be the competitive consumption of the hotel's most expensive wines. Although this was a male reserve, from time to time they were accompanied by their wives and a lunch would be organised at Mas Mañanas. It was during one such visit that we all met for lunch on the terrace, when Juanita, Heini's toothless but protective Yorkshire terrier, attempted to savage Alicia Crystal as she descended the steps. While there was no evidence of any physical damage, there was obviously a degree of injured pride.

When a toast was made, Alicia rather pointedly made hers 'Shalom', to which Heini responded with an equally pointed 'Glückauf'.[3] Some time later when we had gone out for the evening with Tita and the question of the nationality of the Thyssen fortune was raised, Michael insisted it was Dutch, not German. Presumably this made it easier for him to accept their money.

* * *

Tita continued to put time and energy into the building and maintaining of her collection, with the full support of the Thyssen-Bornemisza Museum staff and facilities. On 30 September 1999, she would sign a statement of intent with the Ministry of Education and Culture that her paintings would also be housed in an enlarged Thyssen-Bornemisza Museum in Madrid by 2002. To most of the visitors attending her travelling exhibitions, the two collections were already indistinguishable, particularly in the case of the Chinese to whom Tita had presented her 'From Zurbaran to Picasso' exhibition, consisting of 'Masterpieces from the Collection of Carmen Thyssen-Bornemisza'.

Despite the curatorship of Tomàs Llorens and the appearance of Tita with her jewellery and nineteen pieces of Louis Vuitton luggage, the exhibition must have created considerable confusion among the Chinese concerning the meaning of the word 'masterpiece'. For while it contained some very second-rate works by Picasso, Monet, Gauguin, Pissarro and Toulouse-Lautrec, the exhibition consisted mainly of Tita's decorative Spanish pictures and a large selection of 'luminous' nineteenth-century American landscape paintings.

Unlike Villa Favorita, where one was invariably surrounded by prime examples of the collection's original star attractions, this was certainly not the case at Mas Mañanas where, apart from a large N. C. Wyeth, whose frame was being enthusiastically devoured by woodworm, the drawing-room and terrace were dominated by a vast, anonymous naval battle, originally the property of Lex Barker. Neither of them knew anything about the picture and Tita later admitted that Heini had never discussed the content or subject matter of any picture with her.

However, it quickly became obvious that one thing they would discuss was price. One day, they purchased a painting of a Dutch interior by telephone for

$60,000 from Christie's in New York but the subsequent logistics of value development were of far greater interest to Heini than the subject matter of the painting. The day after the purchase, the *Herald Tribune* ran a half-page arts review, describing the purchase as an inspired discovery in an otherwise uninspired auction. But what followed was even more revealing, as Heini explained that the news feature announcing the painting's new owner would double the value of the picture, while every travelling exhibition of which it formed part would further enhance its value.

* * *

As Heini got closer to the end of his life, he became increasingly moody and difficult. But his sense of humour always returned, though by now it was often accompanied by a degree of sadness.

He became particularly unhappy when Giorgio, his butler for some thirty years, finally announced his retirement. He wanted to return to his family in Lugano but he was also painfully aware that Heini would soon be better cared for by a nurse.

The loyal Giorgio generously accepted Heini's bad humour but in a wonderful display of his appreciation of irony, he presented Borja with a parting gift of small boxes of tissue-wrapped visiting cards which for the first time since his formal adoption, included the title of 'Baron'. Heini refused to be amused by the fact that Borja had been given his title by the butler.

The 'Baron' Borja Thyssen-Bornemisza.

Some weeks later, Heini was confined to a wheelchair and attempts were made to reduce his wine consumption to two glasses a day. Initially, Tita denied any deterioration in his condition despite his obvious frailty, occasional confusion and difficulty in communicating; our conversations being further hindered by the noise from the rapidly encroaching building site, which she was finally forced to admit, in a conspiratorial whisper, was going to be an arts centre.

Heini's general well-being was not improved by a letter that he claimed to have received from Francesca, which he insisted constantly referred to his death and displayed a far greater degree of concern for her inheritance than his health and welfare. Apparently her lawyer had informed her that if the court case were to be successful, on Heini's death all shares in TBG would pass to Tita who she was not confident could be relied upon to act in his heirs' best interests.

This was from a daughter who, as Heini pointed out, had already inherited some $80 million from the collection; a legacy which Tita had been partially responsible for achieving.

While the Archduchess had been questioning her father's intentions and Tita's integrity, her husband, the Archduke Karl, had been involved with an Austrian charity from which fifteen million Schilling had disappeared. Karl was reported to have resigned from his position on the board of World Vision but the Austrian *News* magazine considered that the Habsburgs deserved little sympathy: 'All hell has broken lose in the phantom empire. Imaginary thrones are threatened to tumble. It's the biggest crisis for the house of Habsburg since 1918.'

They accused Francesca of referring to herself as the 'Archduchess of Austria' and inviting people to address her as 'Royal Highness' in a country that, until 1966, forbade the Habsburgs' return and where royalty and titles remained prohibited. The magazine also alleged that their marriage 'now only exists on paper'.

There followed further allegations claiming the charity's involvement in the laundering of money from arms dealing. Eventually, Karl told a Viennese court that he had to 'recognise with great sadness that monies intended for children in the Third World went into my political campaign'. Karl was a member of the European Parliament at the time and the scandal brought about a dramatic termination of his political ambitions. It also terminated his and his father's plans to restore the Austro-Hungarian Empire and Francesca's dreams of becoming an Empress.

The story overshadowed Judge Mitchell's arrival in Bermuda on 28 November 1998 and that of his dog Ban's arrival in January 1999 – the latter being arguably the most pivotal event in the whole process of the Thyssen *v.* Thyssen trial.

* * *

Bermuda doesn't have an airport, it has an aerodrome called Kindley Field, not much changed from the days when aeroplanes had propellers and landed on grass. The sky is usually blue and the sea the colour of a Winslow Homer painting. Pastel-coloured houses are surrounded by flowers that look as if they

Chapter XI: 1993–2001   411

had been designed by Georgia O'Keeffe with tropical foliage by Rousseau. Everyone smiles, waves and honks their horns in greeting to each other despite the fact that the direct descendants of the black slaves share the same surnames with their surviving white owners and the British Governor still drives around in a tired old Daimler with a hole in the exhaust and a crown instead of letters and numbers on its licence plate.

It is an island that has played host to the extravagance of the Vanderbilts, Rockefellers, Chaplins, Pickfords and Astors. But even those families never rivalled the Thyssen-Bornemiszas' level of legal indulgence. Headlined in the press as a '$3.5 billion dollar inheritance battle', none of the family ever bothered to attend.

The press predicted the case to be in danger of becoming the most expensive civil action in legal history while they also posed the question: 'One wonders why a seventy-eight-year-old man in poor health would want to regain control of the family firm. Equally confusing is why his son would go to such lengths to avoid reaching an agreement with his father, when the Group admits cash reserves of some $350 million.'[4]

While the Bermudans had been quite prepared to profit from this situation, they were puzzled by the Thyssens' apparent intention to wash their dirty linen in public and far from happy that, in the process, the island's offshore financial services were likely to be brought into disrepute. They were even less happy that both the challenge and the defence should be carried out by ten very highly paid QCs and barristers from London's Inns of Court, who did little to hide their dislike of the island and disdain for what they described as its 'immature' legal profession. Crystal criticised their employment of substandard judges; particularly Denis Mitchell, whom he described as a 'failed silk'.

After nearly two-and-a-half years of preparation, the discovery and submission of thousands of documents, the exchange of hundreds of letters, eighty days of interlocutory hearings and a false start, the Thyssen *v.* Thyssen court case commenced on the morning of 11 October 1999.

Before the judge arrived, the atmosphere was generally relaxed, good-humoured and informal. Greetings were exchanged and travel arrangements discussed. Apart from their position in the court, there was nothing to indicate whom they were representing or that they were not all on the same side. It was only when the judge entered that they all immediately assumed their appointed roles.

After some discussion concerning the procedure, Michael Crystal formally addressed the court for the first time. 'Good morning, my Lord. As your Lordship is aware, the current estimate for the length of this trial is more than one year.'

The fact that the first sentence of his opening speech should appear so astonishingly imprecise and that Judge Mitchell chose not to demand clarification should have been an indication of the manner in which the trial was to proceed. 'Before starting on the process of introducing the Court to the relevant events and the voluminous documentation in detail, could I try to shortly summarise, at risk of over-simplification and some technical inexactitude, what the Plaintiffs say this case is about and how it has come about?'

And so, for the next nine months, at a cost of millions of dollars, four QCs, eight barristers and junior barristers, five solicitors and a judge supported by two clerks and three computer operators listened to Crystal's 'short summary'.

* * *

By day three, Judge Mitchell was complaining that he was having difficulty understanding some of the finer points of Michael Crystal's introduction and requested that he slow down. In response, Crystal proceeded to take the whole morning to explain the translation of one document, pushing home the point with 'asides' and theatrical winks to his fellow barristers. Far from chastising such impudence, Justice Mitchell gave every indication of being amused by Crystal's performance.

Mitchell obviously decided to extend the proceedings further by indicating his intention to minimise the number of hours that he was prepared to spend examining his notes to Crystal's opening in his own time. This news was greeted with lots of nodding heads and obvious approval, while Crystal continued to entertain the court with schoolboy humour and involve himself in what was to become a regular exchange with Alan Boyle QC, the defendants' barrister: 'I was drawing attention to a passage written in Italian by Mr Derek Davies a well-known academic trust lawyer and who used to teach at my learned friend Mr Boyle's old college at Oxford.'

Boyle replied: 'Unfortunately he did not teach me because I was not reading law.'

Then Crystal turned to the court and with a theatrical flourish announced: 'It is not for me to say whether or not it shows.'

Crystal then returned to the purpose of the case by insisting that Georg was the instigator of the whole trust gambit and had persuaded Heini that it was the answer to all his problems without pointing out that it would lead to his relinquishing the control of the Thyssen Bornemisza Group. He also said that Georg had denied ever advising his father on trust matters, insisting that Dr Groh and Dr Masoni had been responsible. But the most important statement of the day and one of the most remarkable of the whole trial, was a comment from the Baron's evidence statement claiming: 'It cannot therefore be assumed that simply because I signed a document I must have read it, let alone read it closely or understood its implications.'[5]

It was an admission that appeared, to the public gallery at least, to make the trial somewhat untenable. It also transpired that his statement was to be his only form of evidence, due to the fact that he had already managed to avoid any form of personal court appearance and thus cross-examination by claiming he was unfit to travel.

Meanwhile, Heini continued to reveal yet more contradictions. He claimed that he had only created the Continuity Trust in order to avoid the type of domestic friction which followed his father's death. Friction that, he failed to mention, was largely the result of his own greed. He also stated: 'I wanted whatever steps were taken to comply with Swiss law', in the full knowledge that the prime reason for creating such an inadmissible trust was to avoid the necessity of adhering to Swiss law.

* * *

The court developed a regular schedule whereby it sat at 10.30 am, rose for lunch between 1 and 2 pm and 'adjourned' at 4.15 pm. There were also intermittent breaks when certain subjects deemed unsuitable for public consumption were discussed in chambers or in letters between the plaintiffs and the defendants that were never revealed to the public.

Meanwhile, the already leisurely schedule was obviously still proving too demanding and on Thursday, 14 October Mitchell announced: 'I am minded not to sit tomorrow. It may become a pattern.'

Apparently, he was finding that the amount of homework that he was obliged to undertake was beginning to overwhelm him and needed to take Friday off to catch up. This was a particularly convenient policy that would facilitate the barristers' weekend visits to the UK, though everyone went to great pains to put it on record that this was only a temporary arrangement. But it was not and from then on the court sat for only four days a week. In order for their clients not to get the impression that they were taking the day off, Fridays were henceforth known as 'working days out of court'.

The judge's decision to reduce the hours that the court sat may also have been affected by the difficulty that many of those present appeared to be having in remaining awake. The computerised LiveNote facility which recorded every word for instant recall and display on individual screens in front of everyone in the court proved useful to those who succumbed to the occasional doze. The value of Crystal's theatrical presentation, in keeping the barristers awake, soon became apparent but it did not prevent Elkinson from accusing him of trying to win the case by what he described as 'trial by boredom'.

It was soon all too easy to miss the occasional statement that was worthy of attention. One such morsel was contained in Heini's statement when in answer to questions posed by his own lawyers as to whether he had read a particular report he answered, 'Well I may have done', which appeared to be almost more pointless than his claim of not being able to remember.

Equally easy to miss was Mitchell's apparent lack of knowledge of the Swiss legal system and his equal lack of any attempt to disguise his ignorance. It seemed a remarkable admission considering its relevance to the case he was judging. Crystal reminded him: 'Your Lordship is going to have to consider in due course whether the Continuity Trust offended Swiss law because it was, or was essentially the same as a family foundation.'

Ignoring the question concerning Swiss law, Mitchell responded by pointing out that it was Heini who had instructed Georg to set up such a trust which would be valid for two generations descending from the Baron, only benefit blood relatives and would be irrevocable. Crystal replied with another memorable line: 'Well, my Lord, the Baron does not remember that level of detail.'

In an attempt to prevent the judge from returning to the subject, Crystal then managed to bring the day's proceedings to a close: 'We have gone over the time your Lordship normally rises.'

But before they rose, Crystal also managed to slip in one of his best understatements: 'This opening is going to last for a little while.'

* * *

The following day, the judge displayed a somewhat more positive approach to the proceedings and reminded Crystal of Jack Moore's notes relating to the trust meeting in Monaco, which pointed out that the trust was to be 'irrevocable' and that the settlor, i.e. Heini, was to have no power over the protector, i.e. Georg. Apparently Heini had confirmed this in his evidence statement, which left Crystal with little choice but to agree before throwing in a wonderfully confusing claim: 'But this has nothing to do with control mechanisms so as to ensure that nothing changed in his lifetime.'

Then, before Mitchell had a chance to decide what he meant, Crystal opened his case against the air-conditioning: 'Would your Lordship mind if I sucked a lozenge? My Lord, I'm sorry. I am finding this slightly difficult, because the air conditions have deteriorated in the courtroom and it makes it more difficult to concentrate. I might ask your Lordship to rise because this is quite complex stuff.'

Rather than suggest that he might wear more suitable clothing, open the doors and windows and turn the air-conditioning off or question why Crystal was the only one complaining, the judge agreed to break for lunch. That afternoon was filled with circuitous arguments concerning the relevance of 'personal opinion', the objection by the defence to Crystal's refusal to adhere to the pleadings and whether Mr Ham was going to be 'dealing with pleading or law'.

Fortunately for Michael Crystal, Mitchell was soon once again replacing his interest in the law with an interest in Earl Grey tea and Chocolate Oliver biscuits, and Crystal's suggestion that it may be a 'convenient time' to rise for the day was met with approval.

The following day, Crystal introduced what was to become another time-consuming feature of his summary. It consisted of detailed readings of the Baron's travel plans and to the public gallery their relevance proved difficult to appreciate. The fact that Jack Moore, TBG's International Counsel and Secretary of Corporate Management, was in London on a particular day, may have been a marginally important piece of information. But did Mitchell really need to know that he was staying at The Churchill Hotel or went to 'Le Dodo Gourmand'? Crystal underlined the irrelevance of the latter by commenting: 'We don't know if this was a play or a restaurant.'

Crystal then went into a long, drawn-out re-numbering of a whole mass of diary and travel notes. It seemed scarcely believable that while commanding fees in excess of five million dollars a year, he should be acting the role akin to filing clerk.

* * *

Before they rose for the afternoon, Mitchell had another subject on his mind. Apparently there was some documentary evidence concerning Heini's health, but for some inexplicable reason Crystal did not want it to appear on screen and preferred that the whole matter was left until the following day. The defendants also seemed to be in no greater haste to make any comment concerning the Baron's health.

Thursday, 21 October 1999, was only the eighth day of the trial and already three weeks of adjournment were being agreed between Crystal and Mitchell to 'facilitate domestic arrangements' and 'prepare for appeals'. This pause in the proceedings would then be followed by the Christmas recess. Having discussed and agreed the adjournment, Crystal was obliged to reveal the contents of a document dated 1977 concerning Heini's health that Mitchell had brought to the court's attention the previous afternoon. It appeared to be a defendants' evidence document, which they had all seen but were attempting to avoid being made public. However, Mitchell insisted it was read out. The succinct note was written on Claridges headed paper: 'Dear Bob [Genillard], I will be two or three weeks in the Wellington hospital to stop drinking. Regards Heini.'

No further questions were asked or answers given concerning Heini's drink problem. It was understandable that Crystal should not wish to dwell on this subject, less understandable on the part of the judge and a total mystery as to why the defence never used it to their advantage.

* * *

The fact that while Judge Mitchell listened to the ridiculously extended opening, his wife Jeannette spent her time playing golf and bridge was both predictable and irrelevant to the case. But her indiscreet comments concerning the case and her attacks against members of Bermuda's political leadership would have severely limited the chances of her husband's contract being sufficiently extended to enable him to complete the trial. She did not consider this to be a problem as she insisted they only intended to stay on the island until their dog was eligible for return to the United Kingdom.

She also openly predicted that the trust would never be overturned and that the Thyssen-Bornemisza family would eventually come to the conclusion that the whole thing was quite 'ridiculous' and that they would settle. She blamed 'Carmen' for being 'behind the whole case' considered the barristers to be earning excessive fees.

The fact that she hated Bermuda because there was 'absolutely nowhere to shop and nothing to buy' was also predictable. What was of far greater concern was Jeannette's open antipathy towards black people which she expressed over lunch at The Royal Bermudan Yacht Club. This had probably been aggravated by the fact that when Mitchell had accepted the post, a white government had been in power. But by the time he and his wife had arrived on the island they had been replaced. Not only was she quite openly opposed to the new black government and the black judges but she also made her disdain of any black women who held a political position particularly obvious by describing both the president and the leader of the opposition as 'black, racist dykes'.

* * *

Day nine and Crystal continued with his claim that prior to signing the Continuity Trust agreement, Heini had received no outside advice, even though he had already admitted that he was in constant contact with Moore and Georg and that all of them had received advice and guidance from American, British and Bermudan law firms. What Crystal was trying to suggest was that Heini had been entirely reliant on his son.

He claimed that Moore had not been a legal adviser but Georg's assistant. He also returned to the tired claim that Heini had been given the impression that the trust agreement was revocable. Then, before anyone could comment, Crystal complained once again about the air-conditioning and suggested to Mitchell that the court rise.

The following Monday, Crystal returned to the Baron's travel plans. But this time Mitchell questioned the relevance: 'What do you invite me to conclude from the fact that he travelled a great deal?'

To which Crystal replied: 'That he left the creation of what becomes the Continuity Trust entirely to Georg.'

But from the travel plans it was also obvious that Heini's life was shambolic and things were not done when they should have been done, or where they were claimed to have been done. This all sounded quite normal for a family for whom the day-to-day pressures of financial survival did not exist.

Crystal would subsequently admit that he and his team were all too familiar with the difficulties of trying to adhere to any schedule with Heini and more so with Tita and he would have had no reason to doubt that this had always been the case. Heini had once claimed that Tita was an improvement on Denise: 'At least she turns up on the right day, even if she is four hours late.'

* * *

On the tenth day of the trial, things looked up a little when the actual amount of Heini's yearly remuneration was brought to Mitchell's notice. Apparently this amounted to $15 million or 'at least 30 per cent of net operating income', which Mitchell accepted was a great deal of money.

What no one saw fit to point out was that while the legal battle dragged on, Heini continued to be paid and even received a reduction in his shortfall, which increased his annuity from $15 million to $27 million per year. It seemed equally incongruous that Heini should also grant his eldest son permission to use $6 million capital from his art trust, for the private purchase of a property in Provence, while continuing to do battle with him in the Bermudan court.

That afternoon, Crystal reflected a major difference between the characters of Heini and Georg when he quoted a member of TBG's financial department who had been asked to value the organisation: 'Given a diversified industrial group concentrated in basic industries, ten to twelve times maintainable earnings at the low point is reasonable and would give a value of approximately Dfl 1 billion on a going concern basis.'

It was the type of Joycean corporate style of communication which suited Georg but bored Heini and was the major cause of him getting down on all fours and barking like a dog during meetings.

Despite Mitchell's questioning of their relevance, Crystal once again referred to the travel schedules to analyse the general logistics of the trust meetings in St Moritz. The questions of why Georg should have chosen such an unlikely and inconvenient location for business meetings or why they took place in his mother's house were not raised. Even more ridiculous was the fact that because the meetings were held at Theresa's house, Heini refused to participate but chose to throw lavish lunches round the corner at his own house, which they all attended before returning, without the by now inebriated Heini, to conclude their meeting. Then, later in the afternoon, they had all trooped back again to get Heini to sign various trust documents over yet more drinks.

* * *

The following day, Wednesday 27 October, Mitchell attempted to clarify the witness situation by asking for confirmation that neither the Baron nor Riccardo Guscetti would be appearing in court. Crystal agreed and reminded him that as he could not examine his own witnesses, he intended to rely on cross-examining the defence witnesses. Otherwise, the plaintiffs apparently intended to rely on Evidence Act Statements in which, according to Crystal, the Baron made himself quite clear.

Mitchell reminded himself what a farce the whole case was when he replied: 'Yes, that he doesn't remember.'

As if to confirm how little the judge's opinion concerned him, the following day Crystal continued with his reading of Heini's travel plans which included visits to London, Zurich, Madrid, Edinburgh, London, Paris, Frankfurt, London, Paris, Hamburg plus dinner with Mr Douglas Cooper, the art collector and friend of Picasso's, most of which had little to do with the case, but which Mitchell failed to criticise or question. A Scottish Justice of the Peace travelling through Bermuda, who decided to pass an hour or two in the public gallery, was astonished and said he had never seen such blatant time-wasting being accepted by a judge.

Crystal then invited the judge to return to the Baron's Evidence Act Statement but Mitchell was obviously still not impressed by this document: 'The Baron does not really help me too much, does he? He says he has no recollection of the meeting but he thinks it is possible he spent part of the meeting of 8th December 1982 with Georg, Pfaff and others and then had lunch with them. So it is possible he may have spent part of the morning?'

To which Crystal replied: 'That is as far as the Baron's recollection carries him and he is not embarking upon a process of dangerous reconstruction, unlike some of the other statements we have seen.'

Incredibly, Mitchell asked: 'You are telling me this is his genuine recollection and that is as far as it goes?'

'My Lord, that is my submission, yes.'

Thus Crystal succeeded in giving Heini's claimed failure to remember legal status, before making a rather puzzling statement:

> My Lord, the next exercise will take a number of days, because there is a fair amount of paper to go through. My Lord, in my very respectful submission, having regard to the fact that we have got to the end of 1982, and that is in a sense a watershed in terms of calendar years, my very respectful suggestion to your Lordship is it may be more useful, given that your Lordship will not be sitting next week, for your Lordship to consider the documents that your Lordship has had available today in your Lordship's notes and come to any further provisional conclusions that your Lordship wants in 1982 rather than for me to embark this afternoon on 1983, where I will not be able to get very far and where the picture which will be presented, having regard to the length of the break, will be a most disjointed one and in my submission of less assistance to your Lordship. I am very much in your Lordship's hands as to which course you want to take.

It actually took a few minutes to understand what he was saying before the judge realised that he was suggesting an adjournment. It worked and after only two hours, the court closed at 12 noon on a Thursday, giving everyone, particularly Mitchell a long week-end prior to having to cope with the rigours of two weeks of bridge, golf and playing with Ban, his beloved animal and presumably, going over his court notes.

*   *   *

Having taken three weeks off for a two-day appeal, Crystal returned to make one of his sillier statements: 'The Baron certainly appears to have been at such a meeting, if there was one, because he takes the chair and signs the documents.'

It would emerge from Crystal's coverage of what did or did not happen in Bermuda between 19 and 22 January 1983, that it was a mess of document signing involving amendments, valuations, dividends, company and trust creations, sale and transfer of shares, promissory notes, loan agreements, option agreements and assignments of claims, involving most of TBG's management team, a posse of solicitors, lawyers, accountants and tax advisers as well as numerous lunches, drinks and dinners, particularly at the Lobster Pot and the Yacht Club. The latter activity no doubt being participated in with a great deal more enjoyment than the former by Heini who was being enthusiastically courted by 'Mrs Barker' in her endeavours to assume the mantle of Baroness Thyssen-Bornemisza. In fact, when the court sat again on 23 November 1999, it was evident that lunch at the Lobster Pot had been one of the few events that Heini was prepared to recall with any clarity.

Among the documents signed on the afternoon of 21 January 1983 in Bermuda were a Deed of Sale, Deed of Addition and Deed of Revocation, all of which Heini claimed he 'did not believe he drafted', although he would later admit 'I appear to have signed', to which Mitchell responded: 'Can I take it that when the Baron is saying he signed a document but did not draft it, if he is silent as to the accuracy of its contents, he is accepting the accuracy of its contents, because on other occasions he does correct documents and points out that they are inaccurate?'

Crystal experienced considerable difficulty answering this question and called for a lifeline: 'I will have to take instructions on this.'

Then, before Mitchell got the chance to ask any more embarrassing questions, Crystal reminded him that he had other public duties the following day and that as that was a Thursday, perhaps he would like to take Friday off to write up his notes and they could all relax until Monday? Before they rose Crystal still deemed it necessary to say to the judge: 'We will complete the first part of the opening before Christmas in any case.'

There could not have been anyone in the court who believed that anything was likely to be completed by Christmas but no comment was made.

By day sixteen, Crystal was describing all the meetings that Georg presumably had evidence to prove took place as 'alleged', regardless of whether he was questioning them or not. He also continued to deny that the Baron was given sufficient written information to enable him to fully appreciate what he was signing but persistently failed to explain why he signed.

The following day Crystal continued to spin out his re-reading of the plaintiffs' pleadings, until Mitchell sighed wearily and pointed out: 'You showed me that yesterday.'

That did not stop Crystal going over the same details at exactly the same pace.

*   *   *

On Wednesday, 8 December, Robert Ham QC was finally introduced to the proceedings: 'May it please your Lordship, it is now for me to open the law.'

His role was to analyse the law in relation to the points raised in Crystal's opening. To do this, he intended to go over all the ground covered by Crystal, while illustrating points of law by drawing on previous cases or precedent, which he referred to as 'authorities'. This would be a particularly time-consuming and uniquely British process; the continental systems sensibly rely on far more time-efficient principles of law, based on civil codes.

Ham also intended to show that what Heini signed was not what he meant to sign. The principle was that if competent independent advice was absent and the transaction could be proved not to be fair or righteous, then the transaction had to be set aside.

By 9 December, Ham's analysis of the law appeared to require far greater intellectual abilities than Crystal's narrative but he lacked the theatrical flair needed to give his ponderous 'authorities' any life beyond their conceptual value.

But as with Crystal, to the innocent observer it often appeared that Ham was intent on using the maximum amount of time to explain even the simplest legality. Having already explained the circumstances of a specific court case, he then commented:

> My Lord, this is a case where Lord Denning sought in his judgment to propound a unifying principle for a number of categories of cases. The principle which he put forward being inequality of bargaining power which he said was something which would give the court power to intervene to set aside transactions. My Lord, as I say that principle is not one that I think has survived. It was a brave effort, but like a number of Lord Denning's brave efforts, it has not prevailed.

So the question as to why he appeared to have been wasting the court's time explaining such an apparent irrelevance remained unanswered.

While the intellectual opportunities may have entertained Mitchell and Ham, the press were interested in far less cerebral details such as the estimated cost of the trial, which had by now risen to £60 million. They were also interested in the

£10,000 a month Bermudan mansion that Crystal and Ham shared. At a Christmas party, hosted by the two QCs, they booked a jazz band and disco and, in a spirit of conviviality, invited the lawyers representing the defendants. But at the eleventh hour, a Chamber's memorandum went round suggesting such obvious fraternisation with the opposition would not be appreciated. It meant that Alan Boyle and Nicholas Patten missed out on a poolside party, which began serving £30 bottles of champagne at 2 pm and was still popping them in the early hours of the morning.

Apart from champagne parties, it was sometimes difficult not to imagine that the QCs' main area of entertainment might have been the competitive presentation of pointless information. Ham would certainly have been awarded a considerable number of points when, on day forty, he introduced an 'authority' concerning the Duchy of Cornwall granting a lease in 1799 on land which was inhabited by a large number of rabbits. There seemed to be some dispute as to whether the lessee had the right to the land as well as the rabbits. Then there was 'an agreement for an exchange of properties, which proceeded on the basis that the conveyance carried the soil as well as the right to the rabbits'. This was apparently inadmissible but ignorance was claimed and Mitchell seemed quite content to let a grown man, who was paid millions of dollars, stand up in court and recount the story on the grounds that it illustrated acquiescence, 'inferred or implied', which apparently related to the case in court.

* * *

Heini continued to enjoy the barristers' irregular visits, while Tita reflected Crystal's constant, evangelical euphoria which he transmitted every time the court rose, insisting that the defendants were 'rattled, worried, on the run' or displaying some form of emotion which apparently signified the imminent collapse of their entire defence. Presumably in an effort to reinforce this positive message, Tita was regularly presented with huge bundles of the LiveNotes with the salient points marked with yellow Post-its. While she often carried them around with her, we never saw her reading them and her knowledge of the actual mechanics of the case often appeared somewhat confused; which may have been why Tita remained convinced that they were 'winning' and the whole ridiculous court case was justified.

By now observers were also beginning to think that maybe the slow progress and mounting costs were a ploy designed to frighten Georg into a settlement; until counsel for the defence appeared to be adopting the same policy. Perhaps it was just a matter of who blinked first.

Francesca and Lorne remained equally convinced that Heini and Tita would lose, while Lorne's actual knowledge of the process also remained sketchy and he appeared ignorant of the fact that, apart from the cost of their individual legal advisers, all the heirs were also paying for the court case. In fact, in 1999 the art sub-trusts alone were contributing to the legal fees in Bermuda, at the rate of $300,000 each for Chessy, Lorne and Alexander and $400,000 for Georg.

While Tita continued to dream of unimaginable wealth, the development of the Carmen Thyssen-Bornemisza Collection and its future was of more immediate interest. On 4 March 2000, Vice-President Rajoy signed an agreement about the cession to Spain of her collection. Not everyone in Spain approved of this move or even the original sale. *El Mundo* quoted a description of Tita as being 'cold and calculating, for whom money is like a sixth sense without which the other five can't operate.'[6] It also seemed quite certain that the heirs would challenge the Spanish sale of their father's collection, particularly if Georg won the case.

Meanwhile, the barristers were claiming that the value of Heini's annuity shortfall, which in May 1999 amounted to US$55.8 million or US$100 million when interest was included, had by now risen to $259 million, due to the guilder/dollar conversion, loss of purchasing power, repayment of bank borrowing, waiver of interest on promissory notes and incentive compensation payments to Georg.

On the fifty-eighth day in court, Michael Crystal announced that in the unlikely event of anyone needing to know, his favourite painting in the Thyssen-Bornemisza Collection in Madrid was the Tornabuoni, and in another display of truly remarkable irrelevance he added: 'David Alexander's is the Carpaccio.'

It seemed fitting that around this time we should return to Madrid to help a by now old and confused Heini celebrate his seventy-ninth birthday in an equally surreal style by his Olympic-sized swimming pool, where we drank champagne and ate a cheap birthday cake, while a Tex-Mex Mariachi band played and the highly emotional staff sang 'Happy Birthday' in English. Pusch,

Heini celebrating his seventy-ninth birthday at La Moraleja in Madrid.

Alexander, Tomàs Llorens and Jaime Rotondo were also present, but no other members of his family or friends, although Tita insisted Denise had intended to come:

> Oh, Denise is driving us absolutely crazy at the moment. She wanted to come for Heini's birthday, so I said fine. Then she wanted to come for lunch, but was worried there were going to be other people. I told her that it would just be her and Alexander and Heini and myself. I didn't really want her in my house, so I proposed lunch at some restaurant. Then she was giving Mrs Stirnimann a mouthful that she insisted on coming to the house. I said fine. Then she said she couldn't make lunch, but it had to be dinner. OK. Then, she says she wants to have dinner with Heini alone. She gave Inmaculada another mouthful. Inmaculada nearly cried, because Denise had been calling her an idiot... Then Denise called Fatima in the kitchen. How she has the direct number for the kitchen I don't know, anyway. Fatima is in hysteria because she thinks it's now her responsibility if Denise turns up. So we tried to contact Alexander to see what his plans were. I mean, it really is too much! She is nuts, really! I have only been surrounded by nuts for the last twenty years!

*   *   *

Sometimes it was difficult to believe that the court case had not been dramatised by Lewis Carroll or perhaps even Groucho Marx. After yet more adjournments and delays, on 19 June 2000, Crystal and Ham having finally completed their opening, Alan Boyle QC rose to his feet. Within minutes it became obvious he had no intention of presenting the defence any more economically than his 'learned friend' had delivered his plea.

Boyle immediately started to run through large sections of Crystal's opening while Mitchell tried to stop him reading out documents that he was quite capable of reading himself. Boyle then busied himself mounting an attack against Crystal's application to amend his pleadings and the court was reminded that on day sixty-eight, nine months after Crystal first started his opening, the trial proper had yet to begin. Only three court days later, on 7 July, after various appeals had been announced and Mitchell had asked, 'When is this case ever going to finish if everybody keeps going off to the appeal court?', he agreed to adjourn the court until 20 September, so that an amended pleading and an amended defence could be prepared.

Everyone seemed to think this was an excellent idea, particularly Nicholas

Patten QC, who had reminded everyone that they all needed a good holiday, especially his children, while Michael Crystal QC could not resist criticising Judge Mitchell for allowing the defendants so much time to prepare their defence.

* * *

Sitting in the garden of the Hotel La Gavina, I waited to have breakfast with Michael Crystal. As I listened to the cooing doves, a single white feather floated down a beam of golden sunlight and Robert Ham, swathed in white towelling, tottered down the hill towards the beach. Having eventually arrived and spent some time bragging with Ham and David Alexander about their previous night's oenophilistic exploits, Crystal then insisted that Heini wanted to settle and for the case to finish. When I pointed out that the whole future of the case was dependent on the judge remaining in Bermuda for a second term, he insisted that this would not be a problem due to Mitchell's deep sense of 'social responsibility' which would apparently oblige him to apply for a second term.

Meanwhile, up the hill at Mas Mañanas, Heini was becoming increasingly frail. The previous day as he shuffled away from the lunch table, supported by his new butler, his shorts suddenly dropped around his ankles. Despite the good-humoured response from Tita, there was something very poignant about an old man, his backside exposed, vulnerable and powerless even to retrieve his own shorts. It was becoming obvious that he was tired of the struggle both to stay alive and to continue a legal battle that had successfully served its purpose. But settlement was not on Tita's agenda, although she appeared to be becoming increasingly suspicious that she was not being kept fully informed of the case's progress and sensed it was not going well: 'What does it mean, to amend the pleadings?' she asked.

'It means to change the basis of your case against Georg.'

'At one time, Crystal was going to amend them because of what Heini and Crystal discussed together. I don't know what they discussed. I don't know a lot of the time what the discussions are between the two of them. When Crystal comes here, Crystal and David Alexander and Ham, usually they come the three of them together and the first thing they do is to have a meeting with Heini. They go on for several hours. Then afterwards Heini has the physio and then we have lunch. So, I'm never around until lunchtime and then only as the hostess.'

She laughed but it sounded hollow and not very confident. Perhaps sensing that it might not be long before she was left to face Georg on her own, her attitude appeared to be softening: 'I have nothing against Junior, in a way. I don't hate him, it's funny, but I don't hate him! He hates me. I think Junior is a victim. In a way, Junior is a victim of Genillard and of Pfaff. It was Genillard's fault that I found out about the shortfall.'

Her view was that having profited from their part in the creation of the Continuity Trust, they were now profiting from a conflict whose encouragement could be seen as keeping them gainfully employed.

* * *

By 26 September, everyone but Patten had returned to Bermuda. Having been appointed to the High Court as a judge, he had been replaced on Junior's team by Trevor Philipson QC. At this point Crystal asked Mitchell for two further weeks to consider the amended defence and twenty-eight days in which to serve the re-amended pleadings. In his view, the defendants could then respond with rejoinders and surrenjoinders which would take things up to 1 December.

The plaintiffs suggested there could then be inspection and preparation of documents which would take them up to 11 December. A Christmas break was planned for the end of that week and so Crystal recommended 15 January 2001 as the next date for a progress report with no guarantee of a date for a return to court.

During this break, Denis Mitchell committed himself to an action that would have by far the greatest effect on the continuation of the case; on 13 December, he went to see the Governor of Bermuda to warn him that he probably would not be able to see the case out. There is no public record of Thorold Masefield's reaction to what was likely to save the island from the embarrassment and possible financial damage of a challenged trust.

The case was thus beginning to show the first signs of unravelling but any settlement was unlikely to be amicable. Francesca was quoted in the press as saying: 'It is the evil stepmother syndrome, who has destroyed an untold number of families. My father's latest wife is not very excited right now about respecting previously settled family arrangements.'[7]

Tita then hit back on the pages of ¡Hola! magazine: 'Of all his five wives, I am the one who has looked after him best. As far as I know, Francesca has been no Cinderella. She hasn't called him in over a year. Not on his birthday, nor at Christmas and that would no doubt have quite an impact on any father. Francesca cannot know much about her father's health if she thinks he had a heart attack.'

In fact, Francesca's diagnosis was not that wide of the mark. Shortly beforehand Heini had suffered cardiac problems that resulted in him having a pacemaker fitted.

* * *

Both sides continued despite Mitchell's intentions to leave Bermuda and on 15 January 2001 Crystal started to open his amended pleading which mainly consisted of Heini's new statement.

Then Boyle proceeded to explain how he intended to open the defence and the technical, logistical and communicative methods he intended to use. Most of the information was unworthy of comment but Boyle made one announcement that caused Heini some considerable concern. Apparently the defendants were intending to start their story from 1926, which indicated that their opening for the defence may easily last longer than Crystal's introduction. Of far greater importance was the risk that particularly sensitive information, such as the wartime banking and industrial activities of the 'Konzern' might be revealed in open court.

It seems highly likely that the risk of such exposure was a contributing factor to the eventual outcome of the Thyssen *v.* Thyssen court case. But before the announcement of any further revelations, Boyle applied for what now appeared to be an obligatory week's adjournment, which Mitchell wearily granted. The next time the court sat, Boyle kept the flame of animosity alight by claiming:

> Tita is the person for whose benefit the litigation is being substantially conducted. The Baron himself makes no secret of the fact that a primary purpose of the litigation is to rearrange the interests of his heirs in her favour. It was she who first threatened legal proceedings. My Lord, the truth is that the Baron himself has started the inheritance war during his own lifetime.

He then entertained the court with an ever increasingly detailed explanation of the Continuity Trust and TBG, which he seemed intent on presenting in an almost ethereal light; an organisation beyond that created or run by mere mortals. Having prostrated himself before the greatness of the supervisory board, it was interesting that he failed to mention what the Thyssen-Bornemisza group of companies did and Mitchell never saw fit to ask.

Boyle also had difficulty explaining the annuity concept, even when questioned by the judge, and had to admit that it was neither intended to be exactly, approximately nor an average of 30 per cent of TBG's net available income over five years, though he got close to admitting 'an average' before pointing out that it should not be considered an 'exact average'.

Boyle insisted that the 30 per cent figure was flexible as long as the trustees and protectors considered any increase constituted 'sound business policy'. When he stated that the Baron could no doubt have got more money out of the company if he had asked for such in 1995 'in a proper manner', Mitchell could contain himself no longer: 'So why on earth are we here?'

Boyle's long-winded, whinging explanation may have justified the need for a degree of arbitration but certainly not a multi-million-dollar court case. The defence also illustrated their ability to rival the plaintiffs in making fatuous claims when Boyle said: 'There was no actual proof that Heini saw or understood the draft but there was also no evidence that he didn't.'

Some days later Mitchell asked Boyle why, when Tita visited Monte Carlo in 1995, Georg had not agreed that the trustees increase Heini's annuity percentage. Obviously not wishing to admit that the defendants were trying to stop Tita spending all Heini's money including Georg's inheritance, Boyle's convoluted explanation appeared to translate as, 'Because she didn't ask!'

Boyle also denied that Georg brought any influence to bear in making himself the major recipient of TBG's profits.

The following day, Mitchell encouraged a similar response in answer to his question: 'In effect you are saying it is not in the true interest of the Baron for him to do what he wants?'

'Yes, and that was his own view.'

The defence pleaded that Georg's professional responsibility was to the company rather than his father. But Mitchell failed to appreciate this concept: 'So he did not and could not have a duty to act single-mindedly and with loyalty to his father?'

'Exactly, my Lord. Exactly. His father could not have asked him to undertake that duty. It is part of the basic fallacy that underlies the plaintiffs' whole approach to this case.'

*   *   *

On day ninety-two, Boyle introduced a welcome element of reality into the proceedings when he challenged the charge of 'presumed undue influence' by Georg over his father by claiming that to uphold the charge one had to prove 'manifest disadvantage'. As the case of Thyssen *v.* Thyssen was a victimless crime where, regardless of the outcome, none of the protagonists was in any danger of losing their qualification as multi-millionaires, any form of material disadvantage may have been difficult to prove.

Of considerably greater concern to the heirs was Boyle's warning of their vulnerability to yet further litigation in the future. Apparently the defendants' Swiss law expert had pointed out that Tita could question the Continuity Trust arrangement on Heini's death in her pursuit of her compulsory share of his estate under Swiss law and he could not guarantee that she would not be successful.

While the barristers continued to complain about the hardships involved in living in a tropical, tax-free paradise, surrounded by pink beaches and emerald green sea, Boyle continued with his opening with only a week's adjournment and the relentless increase in their bank balances to relieve the boredom, until 14 March 2001, when Judge Mitchell suddenly stopped the case dead in its tracks when he announced:

> As you know, my jurisdiction as a judge in Bermuda ends on 30 November of this year. I have today been informed by the Governor that he does not propose to offer me employment beyond that date and has asked me to plan my personal affairs accordingly. It follows that the time available to me for this case ends in November. That is something you may wish to consider. That is all. If you wish me to rise for a short time.

It must have been obvious that Mitchell's announcement signalled the end of the case, for as all the barristers and solicitors were well aware, another judge could not take over a case in progress; it would have to start all over again; just as it had done in 'old' August's case against his son August Junior.

Michael Crystal then gave a short address blaming the Governor whose decision he considered both irrational and unjustifiable. Alan Boyle also voiced his regret, though he neither posed questions nor apportioned blame. Denis Mitchell said he would return the following morning, having decided whether or not to continue, although both sides obviously realised that the case could not be completed or even continued to the point where any outcome could be reached.

The following morning, Judge Mitchell proceeded to give an explanation as to why he had decided to withdraw from the case by stating the obvious. Apparently, by December it had become clear to him that:

> There was a serious danger that the case might last beyond my contract, so I went to the Governor on 13 December 2000 and alerted him to the potential danger. I never had any intention of staying here beyond my current contract. It would have been ludicrous for anyone to imagine that I would have wanted to sign up for another three years. Why a judge on a short-term contract was put on a long-term case, or at least on a case with an obvious potential to be long-term, is one question but having done so, to then fail to find a solution to the problem and reject the judge's attempts

at a solution without communication or comment to the judge is again something I do not understand.

Mitchell made no mention of why neither he nor any of the barristers had failed to publicly question the situation at an earlier opportunity. He also failed to point out that he had agreed to consider another term if he was offered sufficient remuneration and had been asked by the Governor to name his price. Mitchell had suggested a suitable fee would be $1,500 per day in court plus a $100,000 settlement if the case continued after his contract period but the proposal had been refused.

What really angered the judge was that the Bermudan government made no further attempts to negotiate with him. His wife would subsequently admit that their demands were also affected by an element of bitterness which resulted from the disproportionate rewards received by those involved in the case; particularly one individual whom she referred to as 'that nasty little faggot', while her husband continued his explanation in court, on a somewhat less personal level: 'The amount of money which must have been wasted in this case is positively obscene. To be blunt, I've had enough.'

Apparently impervious to the accusation of financial obscenity, Crystal then somewhat unconvincingly thanked the judge for the 'care, consideration and commitment' and informed the court: 'The Plaintiffs propose to prepare to be ready to re-open this case before another judge at the earliest opportunity.'

Boyle also voiced his regret, but no doubt aware that the trial would never restart, refrained from making any such claims. Mitchell's last words in court were, 'So be it', while Crystal's were, 'I am much obliged'.

Somewhat of an understatement, considering the fact that, having made millions, the judge's decision was one of the very few options available to the barristers for closing the case and returning to London with minimal loss of face or professional credibility.

1 Representatives of the Protector of the Continuity Trust present were Georg Thyssen-Bornemisza, Casimir Prince Wittgenstein, Donald Perkins and Warren Hume. Representatives of the Trustee of the Continuity Trust present were Arne Hovdesden, Eric Pfaff, Riccardo Guscetti, Frank Mutch and Cummings V. Zuill.
2 Thyssen *v.* Thyssen, Supreme Court of Bermuda, 11 October 1999.
3 'Glückauf' is the traditional good luck greeting of German miners.
4 *The Times* (London), 15 October 1999.
5 Thyssen *v.* Thyssen, Supreme Court of Bermuda, 13 October 1999.
6 *El Mundo (Azul y Rosa)*, 2 April 2001.
7 *Bermuda Royal Gazette*, 15 January 2001.

Chapter XII

2001–2006

The fall of the House of Thyssen-Bornemisza

*May you get to heaven half an hour
before the devil knows you are dead.*
Irish proverb

Many in the family seemed ignorant of the fact that the appointment of a new judge would necessitate restarting the case from the beginning, rather than picking it up from where Mitchell had abandoned it. Michael Crystal insisted, 'It's going to be a fight to the death' which, albeit unintentionally, may have given them the impression that the lack of a judge was a mere inconvenience, the consequences of which his clients were insured against. Ham even announced that a new judge had been found.

But Heini was becoming very tired. The legal battle had served its purpose and he was ready to put his house in order and close the books, while Tita began to realise that four years and $150-million worth of legal conflict may have served little purpose other than prolonging Heini's life and enriching the lawyers. *The Lawyer* magazine did nothing to improve her ill-humour by asking: 'Should the most expensive case in legal history now be dubbed the biggest farce?'

Fortunately, she could still take a degree of comfort from the fact that she was already worth comfortably in excess of $200 million and the Thyssen-Bornemisza Museum was proceeding with a €38 million extension to the Villahermosa Palace to house her collection which they would lease on a remarkably similar arrangement to that which had preceded Heini's outright sale.

It soon became obvious to Georg that his father had no intention of continuing the fight and in June 2001 he dispatched Lorne to Sant Feliú with what he claimed to be 'a very generous offer'. But Tita was furious when she realised that the offer was considerably less than the previous $100 million settlement that they had been advised to refuse some eighteen months previously and Georg was threatening further reductions in the event of another refusal. So it was hardly surprising that less than a month later Heini agreed, at least in principle, to the suggested settlement.

According to Lorne the draft settlement agreement stated that there would be no alteration in the ownership of the Thyssen Bornemisza Group but that the control vested in the supervisory board would be increased. Tita would inherit the $60 million shortfall, which would be paid out in two or three annual instalments, while Heini would continue to receive his annuity. Following his death and the completion of the shortfall payments to Tita, the annuity would be divided among the heirs. Meanwhile, Heini and Tita would also have to pay 75 per cent of Georg's outstanding legal costs which amounted to some $14 million and all of their own.

Heini's various properties formed part of his personal estate, which theoretically he could do with as he saw fit. Tita was to inherit Villa Favorita while Chessy would retain ownership of her property in London's Holland Park. Heini would also agree to sell her Alligator Head for $1.3 million, which for three houses and an island constituted a considerable discount and resulted in equivalent demands by the other heirs.

The Monaco headquarters of the Thyssen-Bornemisza Group on Boulevard Princesse Charlotte.

The draft agreement also stated that the art sub-trusts would be unlocked so that the heirs would be free to use the capital from the Spanish art sale. The only one to remain closed would be Alexander's. Due to his refusal to sign the inheritance agreement, he had been denied access to both the capital and the interest of his Antonello sub-trust, which had been reinvested. However, assuming he would eventually sign, it was stipulated that before he could enjoy the fruits of ten years of his sub-trust's uninterrupted growth, he would have to pay back some $1 million that he had 'borrowed' in the intervening years

* * *

Despite the imminent settlement, there was no indication of any reduction in family intrigues. These included the fact that, much to the family's astonishment, not only had Georg found himself an extremely aristocratic girlfriend called Katharina von Meran but despite the fact that they were not married, she had also presented him with a son who was to be called Simon.

Theresa, who many thought may have been involved in bringing the couple together, claimed they were 'as good as married', regardless of the fact that von Meran already had an 'ex'-husband and two children and the inevitable alimonial and prenuptial agreements could take years to finalise. Meanwhile his timely paternal achievement did not prevent Georg from squabbling with Tita over Borja's legal adoption status.

Then Georg informed Heini's solicitors that TBG had suffered financially since 11 September and thus the settlement offer that had been on the table was to be reduced still further. Tita apparently reacted with hysterical rage while Heini sent everyone an impatient note saying how the time had come to reach a conclusion.

As Crystal had predicted, an acceptable, amended offer was not received before 14 February 2002, when the court sat once again in Bermuda but this time in the chambers of Justice Wade-Miller, with only the trustees present. Apparently they needed the court's approval to change the terms of the trust so that a settlement could go ahead. With minimal fuss and no suggestion of any delay, the changes were agreed and the signing was scheduled to take place in Zurich the following day.

With thirty barristers, lawyers and solicitors in attendance, complications and delays were inevitable. So it could hardly have come as a surprise when it was decided, for some technical reason, that they could not use the Zurich notary. The signing was cancelled and the whole circus had to move to Basel. Even then there were obstacles to be overcome.

Having started at 8.30 am, by 1 pm the Basel notary announced that he was not prepared to continue with the proceedings, as he had insufficient confidence in Heini's soundness of mind and was unsure that he was capable of forming his own opinions. Tita burst into tears while Georg, having pointed out that it was probably the last chance for the family to reach any form of agreement, persuaded the notary to talk with Heini alone, with no outside influence.

While Heini may not have convinced the notary of his soundness of mind, by the time they returned he had certainly persuaded him that he knew what he was doing and the notary had agreed to witness the signing. But because he had been warned that before too long the heirs would contest the agreement, or perhaps as a compliance with the last breath of Heini's humour, the notary insisted on reading everything out before anyone was authorised to sign anything.

Finally, after hours of reading hundreds of documents to an obviously bored but powerless audience, everyone signed the settlement agreement except Alexander who chose, or was persuaded by his mother, not to sign, thus remaining free to challenge the trust and the inheritance arrangements.

* * *

On 18 February the family issued a press release which announced the settlement but contained little specific information.

> The family very much regrets that misunderstandings have led to legal proceedings, which today are all dismissed or withdrawn and also that the family, its members and professionals who have worked with the family were subjected to adverse media coverage connected with such misunderstandings. The Baron is very pleased that the Baroness, Heini Junior, the Archduchess, Lorne and Borja have reached a full and final agreement with him as to the distribution of his remaining estate in accordance with his wishes and he is grateful to them all for doing so. He said, 'The priority for the family today is to build on its many achievements and to support the contributions of its members to lasting success'.

According to Lorne what the announcement failed to reveal was that Tita was to receive the current annuity shortfall which was to be paid by TBG over the following four years, during which time none of the other heirs would be entitled to any income from the organisation.

Tita would not only retain the proceeds of her art sub-trust but also all the gifts Heini had given her, while Borja was to have no official inheritance status other than that which he received through his mother. Georg's legal expenses were to be paid by the Thyssen Bornemisza Group while Heini and Tita were to pay their own.

Alexander had lost his seat on the Spanish art trust to Francesca who had insisted that this was a precondition for her signing the settlement, as was the replacement of Pierre Rosenberg by Norman Rosenthal from London's Royal Academy, whose wife Manuela Mean was a curator at the Prado. It was an arrangement that would inevitably lead to future conflict with Tita. Meanwhile, the ownership title of all the pictures, sculpture, furniture and objets d'art that had previously been shared out was to be transferred to the individual heirs and they would be free to do with them as they wished.

Georg had also insisted that all the family and business archives be moved to Monte Carlo; a move that was obviously designed to hinder any further legal challenges.

* * *

One month after the signing, on 15 March, Heini had a heart attack, which left him very weak and affirmed his remarkable sense of timing.

The following month he had his second heart attack and died at one o'clock on the morning of 27 April; alone, except for Juanita. The following day, with a haste that suggested some prior arrangement, Tita organised an extremely discreet funeral at the tiny La Ermita de Sant Elm Chapel in Sant Feliú at which no relatives were present apart from Alexander. She claimed to have been unable to invite any other members of the family due to the fact that they all had their mobile phones switched off, although she had managed to summon a photographer from ¡Hola!.

Three days later there was another, equally secretive funeral and burial at the miserably cold, wet and windy Landsberg Castle. Once again it was organised at extremely short notice, which was the excuse given for the lack of invitations. Many staff and friends were not informed and while all Heini's surviving ex-wives attended, there was no evidence of any representatives from the Batthyány, Bentinck, Zichy-Thyssen or the Joseph Thyssen side of the family, the latter of which Georg would describe with some degree of envy as: 'A tight-knit family of very ordinary, normal, successful professional people.'

There was also no indication that Inge or Birgit Thyssen-Bornemisza had been invited, although the one common denominator among those who did attend was that they all had a financial interest in Heini's fortune, either through inheritance or annuity. It was a qualification that resulted in little love being lost between any of them despite the fact that Georg, presumably on the instructions of his father, had already confirmed that all annuities, retainers and alimony allowances would continue to be paid until the demise of their recipients.

As the final resting-place of the last direct male descendant of August Thyssen, the family vault was suitably cheerless, with its 'late gothic crucifix, walls of yellowish-brown travertine, ceiling of richly coloured mosaic work, floor in dark green marble, sarcophagus-like tomb chest and life-sized bronze cast figure of 'old' August'.[1]

But on the front of the funeral programme Baron Hans Heinrich Thyssen-Bornemisza de Kaszón, wearing the full theatrical dress uniform of a Hungarian aristocrat, was still pretending that he was something he was not and denying his German ancestry, despite his insistence on being laid to rest in the Thyssens' Walhalla; that palace of bliss for the souls of industrial heroes.

* * *

On 14 June a delightful memorial service was held for Heini in Lugano attended by old friends and staff. Afterwards there was a reception in the gallery following which, according to witnesses, Tita and the heirs stripped the place of everything; her assistants even levering stone carvings off the walls. She also tried to take the doors of the gallery until she was reminded that there were still pictures inside that needed protecting from the elements.

The path to Villa Favorita.

Prior to the memorial service, Tita had offered the villa to the children but when they all declined she had announced her plans to sell. After the press accused her of callous behaviour, she temporarily reversed her decision.

Meanwhile, the children proceeded to 'cash in' by selling works of art. Georg was the quickest off the mark, seemingly unconcerned by the resulting low prices he obtained in what one of the family described as a 'car boot sale'. Francesca was next with six paintings including a Pissarro being put up for auction through the Baron's old curator Simon de Pury at Phillips de Pury & Luxembourg, whose board she had joined. Subsequently she also tried to mount an exhibition in Salzburg of her siblings' remaining, unsold pictures but it ended in huge fights and yet another legal battle before their collection was renamed Omin GMBH, with no mention of Thyssen-Bornemisza.

Alexander had yet to receive his share of the remaining, unsold collection, due to his refusal to sign the trust agreements, despite the fact that his brothers and sister were threatening to take him to court in Bermuda in order to apply for his entitlement to be shared out between them. But in 2004 he surprised everyone by finally signing the inheritance agreement. They were even more surprised when they discovered that the thirty-year-old confirmed bachelor had also found himself a girlfriend. But, predictably, by the following year the relationship had come to an end and Alexander reverted to spending most of his time in the company of his mother.

* * *

Considering the amount of time and money that had been spent in Bermuda creating and protecting the Thyssen-Bornemisza Continuity Trust and despite the fact that Georg's decision was undoubtedly in the heirs' best interest, it is not difficult to imagine what his father's reaction would have been to the news that only months after the settlement and Heini's death, Georg would be announcing his intention to break up and sell off a large part of the Thyssen Bornemisza Group.

Information Handling Services (IHS), a US-based software company, responsible for 70 per cent of TBG's profits, was to be taken public and the heirs awarded shares from which they would receive an annual premium.

They were also assured that the proceeds from the sale of the rest of the group would then be invested in Thyssen Asset Management, a $650 million fund run by Georg that had regularly posted annual profits of 10 per cent. Surprisingly, the organisation's existence had never been mentioned during the trial despite the fact that it presumably held the $370 million 'liquid assets' that had proved so inflammatory to Tita.

On 2 November 2005, it was reported in the Swiss press that Georg had created yet further tax-efficient financial instruments, this time in Cyprus, in the form of Urvanos Investments Limited for himself and his son, and Urpasis Investments Limited as a holding company for Francesca, Lorne and Alexander.

Meanwhile, Veronika Bosshard had been informed by her hairdresser that

Georg was beginning to display a previously repressed flamboyance and had taken to driving a yellow Lamborghini around Monte Carlo. He had also admitted to other members of the family that he was considering semi-retirement so that he could spend more time with his son.

It was then alleged that a fight had broken out between Georg and Francesca concerning the legitimacy of their respective offspring. This seemed quite likely as even in death Heini had managed to encourage his offsprings' antagonism by including in his inheritance agreement the quite staggeringly hypocritical condition that only 'legitimate' grandchildren should be qualified to inherit. As it became increasingly unlikely that Simon's mother would agree to marry Georg and legitimise their child, Georg tried to persuade the rest of the family to accept a modification to Heini's conditions of inheritance.

While Francesca recruited lawyers to assist in her conflict with Georg, Robert Ham settled his dispute with Tita over non-payment of £500,000 in fees after issuing a High Court writ which also claimed £24,017 interest, increasing by £98.24 a day. In case Tita was suffering from any illusion that she could expect any degree of appreciative loyalty for the many millions that he had already received, he had also frozen her Andorran bank account.

* * *

Tita's self-proclaimed success and influence as an art collector continued to grow with an emphasis on Spanish and Catalan painters. In 2003, it was reported that she had formally agreed with the autonomous government of Catalonia and the city council of Sant Feliú to 'the formation of a consortium which will be charged with the creation and promotion of the Museum Carmen Cervera Thyssen Bornemisza', a branch of the Centro de Arte Nacional de Cataluña. Also called the Colección Thyssen de Pintura Catalana, this was planned to house 350 paintings in the refurbished building of the old hospital in Sant Feliú de Guixols.

On a national level, her negotiations continued with a press release from the Thyssen-Bornemisza Museum in Madrid confirming: 'Both parties have continued to express the desire to arrive at an agreement in the future which will consolidate the presence of the Baroness's collection in the Museum on a permanent basis, once the loan period has expired.'

Then, on 8 June 2004 their Majesties the King and Queen of Spain inaugurated Tita's extension to the Thyssen-Bornemisza Museum in Madrid housing an initial 300 of her paintings, while the Thyssen-Bornemisza Collection at the Monasterio de Pedralbes in Barcelona was transferred to a room at the Museo Nacional de Arte de Cataluña.

Chapter XII: 2001–2006

By May 2005 the press were suggesting that negotiations for the sale of Tita's collection to Spain were imminent by announcing: 'The Parliamentary National Audit Commission asks that the definitive establishment of the collection of Tita Cervera in Spain be negotiated.'

Rumours suggested the price would be somewhere between €150 to €200 million for under half of her collection of paintings and sculpture. The National Audit Office had already admitted that the cost of the museum's extension would exceed the original €38 million budget.

In return, Tita had apparently assured the Commission that she intended to keep her assets in Spain, a promise that was remarkably similar to that made to Switzerland by both Heini and his father and by his Uncle Fritz to the Belgians. But the real reason why Spain was prepared to pay so much money, not once but twice, for a collection that the *New York Times* described as containing 'the minor works of major artists and the major works of minor artists' and that many may consider tainted by the Thyssens' profiteering from the Third Reich, remains a mystery.

Shortly after the announcement, Rodrígo Uría, the leader of Spain's original negotiation team, resigned from the Thyssen-Bornemisza Museum board as did Thomàs Llorens, the chief curator who was to be replaced by Guillermo Solana. Tita claimed to have wept when she was informed of Llorens's departure, despite the fact that five years previously she had been celebrating rumours of his imminent dismissal.

Meanwhile, Francesca decided to continue her battle with Tita, who understandably wanted Borja to inherit her place on the board of the Spanish Art Foundation. Apparently Chessy also wanted to fill the position of vice chairman, despite the fact that she was busy developing T-B A21, her own well-publicised contemporary art collection in Vienna. But while the fighting continued and the press speculated over the future of her marriage, her brother Lorne quietly married his girlfriend Fifi, continued to build his collection of snuff-boxes, planned his next movie and awaited the birth of their first child.

Not to be out-done, in the summer of 2006, the sixty-three-year old Tita adopted two three-week-old babies in America. Proudly insisting that Maria del Carmen and Guadalupe Sabina are naturally blond, she refers to them as her 'little angels'.

* * *

There appeared to be little chance that Heini's dying wish would be granted and peace would reign as, with few exceptions, the Thyssen-Bornemiszas remained a dysfunctional family, held together by wealth and divided by greed. A family who had denied its past and whose past ThyssenKrupp AG continued to deny. A family whose fake aristocratic status remained little more than a memory, while the legacy of their great-grandfather remained purely financial.

They were and are typical of many such families who, despite Scott Fitzgerald's claim that they are 'different from us', are really not. However, they can afford to indulge all the more unpleasant characteristics of the human race and one or two of the nicer ones.

In my role as Heini Thyssen's confessor, it was a family I had become part of and would no doubt continue to do so. I would, also, never raise a glass of red wine to my lips without thinking of him.

*

*Stories never really start or end,
they are just observed for a while
as they pass by.*

Count Maximilian Schosberger

---

1 Knopp, p. 50.

Sources

GENERAL BOOKS AND ARTICLES

Adlon, Hedda, *Hotel Adlon. Das Berliner Hotel, in dem die grosse Welt zu Gast war*, Wilhelm Heyne Verlag, Munich, 1997.
Arnst, Dr Paul, *August Thyssen und seine Werke*, Gloeckner Verlag, Leipzig, 1925.
Ashby Turner Jr, Henry, *German Big Business and the Rise of Hitler*, Oxford University Press, Oxford, 1985.
Bagyinszki, Zoltán, *Szaz magyar kastely. A Hundred Hungarian Castles and Mansions. Einhundert Ungarische Schlösser*, Tóth Könyvkereskedés és Kiadó FFT, Debrecen, Hungary, 2001.
Ball, Hermann & Graupe, Paul, *Die Sammlung Erich von Goldschmidt-Rothschild, Handkatalog und Textband, eingeleitet von L Schnorr von Carolsfeld, Versteigerung durch Hermann Ball und Paul Graupe*, Berlin, 1931.
Baumann, Carl-Friedrich, *Schloss Landsberg und Thyssen*, Thyssen AG, Duisburg, and August Thyssen Foundation Schloss Landsberg, Mülheim a.d. Ruhr, 1993.
Bayerisches Nationalmuseum München, *Sammlung Fritz Thyssen, Ausgewählte Meisterwerke*, Hirmer Verlag, Munich, 1986.
Berkes, Sandor, *Collection Bentinck-Thyssen, Peintures et Objets d'Art, Catalogue*, Ascona, 1987.
Bornemann, Manfred, *Geheimprojekt Mittelbau. Vom zentralen Öllager des Deutschen Reiches zur größten Raketenfabrik im Zweiten Weltkrieg*, Bernard & Graefe Verlag, Bonn, 1994.
Bower, Tom, *Blood Money. The Swiss, the Nazis and the Looted Billions*, Macmillan, London, 1997.
Craig, Gordon, *Germany 1866–1945*, Oxford University Press, Oxford, 1988.
Däbritz, Professor Walter, 'August Thyssen', *Stahl und Eisen*, no. 32, 1942.
Eglau, Hans Otto, *Fritz Thyssen – Hitlers Gönner und Geisel*, Siedler Verlag, Berlin, 2003.
Fear, Jeffrey Robert, *Thyssen & Co., Mülheim (Ruhr), 1871–1934: The Institutionalisation of the Corporation*, PhD Dissertation, Stanford University, California, August 1993.
Finestone, Jeffrey, *The Last Courts of Europe*, J. M. Dent, London, 1981.
Fischer, Klaus P., *Nazi Germany. A New History*, Constable, London, 1995.
Fraser, Nicholas, Jacobson, Philip, Ottaway, Mark and Lewis, Chester, *Aristotle Onassis*, Weidenfeld and Nicolson, London, 1977.
Garlinski, Józef, *Hitler's Last Weapons. The Underground War against V1 and V2*, Julian Friedman Publishers, London, 1978.

Goebbels, Joseph, *The Early Goebbels Diaries*, ed. Helmut Heiber, Weidenfeld and Nicolson, London, 1962.
Heiber, Helmut, *Adolf Hitler: A Short Biography*, Oswald Wolff (Publishers), London, 1961.
Higham, Charles, *Trading with the Enemy. An Exposé of the Nazi-American Money Plot*, Robert Hale, London, 1983.
Hitler, Adolf, *Mein Kampf*, trans. Ralph Manheim, Pimlico, London, 2004.
Hotwagner, J., Mandl, A., Mandl, W. and Stampf, O., *Rechnitz. Chronik einer Gemeinde*, Community of Rechnitz/Austria, 2000.
Jarski, Rosemarie, *The Funniest Thing You Never Said*, Ebury Press, London, 2004.
Jungbluth, Hermann, *Stammtafel der Familie Thyssen=Thissen, Nach urkundlichem Material bearbeitet*, Aachen, 1934.
Kabelac, Robert, *Aus meinem Leben*, manuscript in TBG archives, 1962.
Kaszón, Baroness T. B. de, *Six Weeks under 'The Red Flag', Being the Thrilling Experiences of a Well Known Hungarian Lady During the Revolution of 1918–1919*, W. P. Van Stockum, The Hague, 1920.
Ketterer, Roman Norbert, *Dialoge. Stuttgarter Kunstkabinett Moderne Kunst*, Belser Verlag, Stuttgart and Zurich, 1988.
Kielinger, Thomas, 'Amélie Thyssen', in Joachim Fest (ed.), *Die grossen Stifter*, Siedler Verlag, Berlin, 1997
Knopp, Gisbert, *Schloss Landsberg*, Thyssen AG, Duisburg, and August Thyssen Foundation Schloss Landsberg, Mülheim a.d. Ruhr, 1993.
Köhler, Eva, *Rüdersdorf. Die Kalkhauptstadt am Rande Berlins*, Stapp Verlag, Berlin, 1994.
Lacey, Robert, *Sotheby's. Bidding for Class*, Little, Brown, London, 1998.
Lampert, Catherine, *Rodin. Sculpture & Drawings*, Arts Council of Great Britain, London, 1986.
Mann, Vivian and Cohen, Richard (eds.), *From Court Jews to the Rothschilds. Art, Patronage, and Power 1600–1800*, Prestel Verlag, Munich and New York, 1996.
Matschoss, Conrad, *August Thyssen und seine Werke*, Association of German Engineers and Springer Verlag, Berlin, 1921.
Moore, Sara, *Peace without Victory for the Allies, 1918–1932*, Berg Publishers, Oxford and Providence, RI, 1994.
Price, Louise, *Memoirs of Baron Thyssen-Bornemisza's Grandmother* (written in the 1930s) manuscript in Bentinck Archives.
Pritzkoleit, Kurt, *Die Thyssens – Werk und Familie*, 30-page article in unidentified Ruhr magazine, published ca. 1965, in TBG Archives.
Rodríguez, Conxa, *Los Thyssen, por amor al arte*, Ediciones B, Barcelona, 1997.
Rother, Thomas, *Die Thyssens – Tragödie der Stahlbarone*, Campus Verlag, Frankfurt and New York, 2003.
Rüsges, Dr Wolfgang, *August Thyssen und Eschweiler*, Historical Society of Eschweiler, 1983.

Schatzmann, Paul-Émile, *The Bentincks*, Weidenfeld and Nicolson, London, 1976.
Schifano, Laurence, *Luchino Visconti. The Flames of Passion*, Collins, London, 1990.
Schneider, Georg, *Dossier-Sonderbericht, Januar 1962 (Thyssen-Konzern)*, Georg Schneider, Idar-Oberstein, 1962.
Schweizerisches Institut für Kunstwissenschaft, *Die Kunst zu sammeln. Schweizer Kunstsammlungen seit 1848*, Zurich, 1998.
Stern, Fritz, *Gold and Iron. Bismarck, Bleichröder, and the Building of the German Empire*, George Allen and Unwin, London, 1977.
Thyssen, A., *Correspondence between August Thyssen and Auguste Rodin, 1905 to 1912*, TBG Archives.
Thyssen, A., *Korrespondenz von August Thyssen mit seinem Sohn Heinrich sowie ergänzende Briefe 1919 bis 1926*, nach den Originalen aus dem Familienarchiv Thyssen-Bornemisza, trans. and ed. Dr Carl-Friedrich Baumann, Duisburg, 1996/97. (These letters are held in the TBG Archives in Monte Carlo, Monaco, and in the ThyssenKrupp AG Archives, Duisburg, Germany.)
Thyssen, Fritz, *I Paid Hitler*, Cooperation Publishing Co., New York, and Hodder and Stoughton, London, 1941; Foreword by Federico Zichy-Thyssen, 1990, reprinted Asuncion, Paraguay, 1996.
Thyssen, Stephan (Erster Assistent der Abt. für Erdölforschung der Shell-Petroleum Corp. W. R. III., USA), *Der Elementare Kohlenstoff im Lichte Moderner Theorien (Ferner einiges über Erdölbildung und Thermochemie)*, Königliche Ungarische Universitätsdruckerei, Budapest, 1932.
Thyssen, Dr Stephan von, Hannover, 'Mitteilungen über die neuere Entwicklung des Thyssen-Gravimeters', Sonderdruck aus der *Zeitschrift für Geophysik*, Jahrgang 11, Heft 3, 1935.
Thyssen, Dr Stephan von, 'Messungen mit einem statischen Schweremesser in Norddeutschland, Vortrag gehalten im Geophysikalischen Kolloquium von Professor Dr H Reich am 31.01.1935 in der Technischen Hochschule Berlin', Sonderdruck aus *Beiträge zur angewandten Geophysik*, Bd. 5, Heft 2 (1935), Herausgegeben von V. Conrad, Wien, J Koenigsberger, Freiburg i. Br. und H Reich, Berlin, Akademische Verlagsgesellschaft mbH, Leipzig, 1935.
Th. Bornemisza, Stephen, *The Explanation of Life. The Real Background to Nature*, Rascher Edition, Zurich, 1948.
Thyssen-Bornemisza, Dr Stephan, 'Oscillatory Sliding Friction (The Frictionless Bearing)', reprinted from *Microtecnic (International Review for Measuring and Gauging Technique, Optics and Precision Mechanics)*, Vol. II, no. 6, 1948 and Vol. III, no. 1, 1949.
Thyssen-Bornemisza, Dr Stephan von, 'Gravitational Compass, A New Gravity-Measuring Instrument', *Microtecnic*, Vol. II, no. 4.
Treue, Wilhelm, *Die Feuer verlöschen nie. August Thyssen Hütte 1890–1926 (Volume 1) and 1926–1966 (Volume 2)*, Econ-Verlag GmbH, Düsseldorf and Vienna, 1966.
Uebbing, Helmut, *Wege und Wegmarken. Hundert Jahre Thyssen, 1891–1991*, Thyssen AG Duisburg at Wolf Jobst Siedler Verlag, Berlin, 1991.

von der Heydt, Eduard and von Rheinbaben, Werner, *Auf dem Monte Verità. Erinnerungen und Gedanken über Menschen, Kunst und Politik*, Atlantis Verlag, Zurich, 1958.
Wagner, Jens-Christian, *Das KZ Mittelbau-Dora. Katalog zur historischen Ausstellung in der KZ-Gedenkstätte Mittelbau-Dora*, Herausgegeben im Auftrag der Stiftung Gedenkstätten Buchenwald und Mittelbau-Dora, Wallstein Verlag, Göttingen, 2001.
Watson, Peter, *From Manet to Manhattan*, Random House, New York, 1992.
Weitz, John, *Hitler's Banker. Hjalmar Horace Greeley Schacht*, Little, Brown, New York, 1997.
Wessel, Horst A. (ed.), *Thyssen & Co. Mülheim a.d. Ruhr. Die Geschichte einer Familie und ihrer Unternehmung*, Franz Steiner Verlag, Stuttgart, 1991.
Willing, Martin, Die Thyssens, *Westdeutsche Allgemeine Zeitung*, Dinslaken/Ruhr, 1967–68.
Winkelmann, Edgar, *Versuch einer Darstellung der geschichtlichen Entwicklung der August Thyssen Bank AG*, 1972/73, manuscript in TBG Archives.
Wright, Christopher, *The Art of the Forger*, Gordon Fraser Gallery, London and Bedford, 1984.

VARIOUS FINANCIAL, LEGAL AND OTHER REPORTS

Berliner Handels- und Frankfurter Bank, *Report on the Financial Year 1996; Profile, Performance, People 2000 (BHF-Bank, Member of the ING Group); Annual Report 2002 ('ING-BHF Bank')*, Frankfurt and London.
Foreign & Commonwealth Office, General Services Command, *History Notes. Nazi Gold: Information from the British Archives*, FCO Historians, London, 1996.
Fritz Thyssen Stiftung, *25 Jahre, Sonderdruck aus Jahresbericht 1982/83*, Cologne.
Fritz Thyssen Stiftung, *Jahresbericht 1992/93*, Cologne.
Imperial War Museum, London and Duxford, Anglo-American intelligence reports, post-Second World War:
BIOS 1621: British Intelligence Objectives Sub-Committee, *German Shipbreaking Methods*.
CCFG: Control Commission for Germany, *Report Memorandum of Party Visiting Germany nominated by the Shipbuilding Conference and sponsored by the Admiralty, September 1945*.
CIOS XXVI–32: Combined Intelligence Objectives Sub-Committee, *August Thyssen Hütte AG, Hamborn (Metallurgy)*.
CIOS XXXII–101: *Investigation of Bremen Vulcan Schiffbau- und Maschinenfabrik, Vegesack*, Reported on behalf of US Technical Industrial Intelligence Committee.
CIOS XXXII–119: *German Iron & Steel Industry, Ruhr & Salzgitter Areas*.
GED: German Economic Department, Control Office for Germany & Austria, February 1946, *The Vereinigte Stahlwerke AG Complex*.
LiveNote computerised court transcripts of Thyssen v Thyssen, Supreme Court Bermuda, 1999–2001, produced by LiveNote Reporting (Bermuda) Ltd, Smith Bernal International, Fleet Street, London.

McKinsey and Co., Inc., *Evaluation of Current Position and Organisation Needs, The Thyssen-Bornemisza Group*, December 1969.
Queen's Bench: Bank voor Handel en Scheepvaart N.V. versus Charles Alan Slatford and another, 1953, [1950, B. No. 3010.], Queen's Bench Division, Judge Devlin, 27 June to 30 July 1951; 6 to 8 October and 3 to 4 November 1952.
Stiftung F.V.S. zu Hamburg, *Johann-Wolfgang-von-Goethe-Medaille in Gold 1992, Verleihung an Hans Heinrich Baron von Thyssen-Bornemisza am 9. November 1992 in Hamburg*.
Thyssen AG Duisburg, *Findbuch zu den Beständen Vereinigte Stahlwerke AG und Bergbau- und Industriewerte GmbH*, 2 volumes, Duisburg, 1996.
Thyssen AG Duisburg, *Findbuch zum Bestand Friedrichs Wilhelms-Hütte (1811–1969)*, Duisburg, 1997.
Thyssen AG Duisburg, *Findbuch zu den Beständen der Ruhrstahl-Gruppe*, Duisburg, 1998.
Thyssen-Bornemisza, Hans Heinrich, *The History of the Thyssen Family and their Activities*, a speech held at a TBG board meeting in Divonne, Switzerland, on 6 June 1979.
Thyssen-Bornemisza Group, *Annual Report, 1972*; *A Company Profile, 1982*; *Annual Report, 1983*; *Annual Report, 1985*; *Annual Review, 1990*; *TBG Holdings N.V. Corporate Book Six Months, 1998*.

BOOKS & MAGAZINES ON THE THYSSEN-BORNEMISZA COLLECTION

Alvarez Lopera, José, *Modern Masters; Thyssen-Bornemisza Museum*, Fundación Colección Thyssen-Bornemisza, Madrid, 1992.
Beattie, May H., *The Thyssen-Bornemisza Collection of Oriental Rugs*, Conzett and Huber, Zurich, 1972.
Borghero, Gertrude, *Collezione Thyssen-Bornemisza*, Catalogo ragionato delle opere esposte, a cura di Gertrude Borghero, Electa International, Milan, 1986.
Bowlt, John E. and Misler, Nicoletta, *The Thyssen-Bornemisza Collection: Twentieth-century Russian and East European Painting*, General Editor Irene Martin, Sotheby's Publications, Philip Wilson Publishers, London, 1993.
Boskovits, Miklós, *The Thyssen-Bornemisza Collection: Early Italian Painting 1290–1470*, General Editor Irene Martin, Sotheby's Publications, Philip Wilson Publishers, London, 1990.
de Peverelli, Maria (ed.), *Thyssen-Bornemisza Foundation, Villa Favorita*, Guidebook, Thyssen-Bornemisza Foundation, Lugano, Skira editore, Milan, 1997.
Eisler, Colin, *The Thyssen-Bornemisza Collection: Early Netherlandish Painting*, General Editor Simon de Pury, Sotheby's Publications, Philip Wilson Publishers, London, 1989.
Feulner, Adolf, *Stiftung Sammlung Schloss Rohoncz, 3. Teil, Plastik und Kunsthandwerk*, Lugano-Castagnola, Villa Favorita, 1941.
Fondazione Thyssen-Bornemisza, *Expressionism and Modern German Painting from the Thyssen-Bornemisza Collection*, Electa, Milan, 1989.

Gaskell, Ivan, *The Thyssen-Bornemisza Collection: Seventeenth-century Dutch and Flemish Painting*, Sotheby's Publications, Philip Wilson Publishers, London, 1990.

Green, Christopher, *The Thyssen-Bornemisza Collection: The European Avant-gardes*, General Editor Irene Martin, Sotheby's Publications, Philip Wilson Publishers, London, 1995.

Heinemann-Fleischmann, Rudolf J., *Stiftung Sammlung Schloss Rohoncz, 1. Teil, Beschreibung der Gemälde*, foreword by M. J. Friedländer, Lugano-Castagnola, Villa Favorita, 1937.

Heinemann-Fleischmann, Rudolf J., *Stiftung Sammlung Schloss Rohoncz, 2. Teil, Abbildungen der Gemälde*, Lugano-Castagnola, Villa Favorita, 1937.

Heinemann-Fleischmann, Rudolf J. (ed.), *The Thyssen-Bornemisza Collection, Illustrations of the Paintings*, Lugano-Castagnola, Villa Favorita, 1969.

Kiel, Hanna, *The Thyssen-Bornemisza Collection of Modern Paintings*, Villa Favorita, Lugano-Castagnola, 1974.

Lasarte, Mercedes, *Mercedes Lasarte in the Collection of Carmen Thyssen-Bornemisza*, Lunwerg Editores, Barcelona, 1999.

Levin, Gail, *The Thyssen-Bornemisza Collection: Twentieth-century American Painting*, General Editor Simon de Pury, Sotheby's Publications, Philip Wilson Publishers, London, 1987.

Llorens, Tomàs, Borobia, Maria del Mar, Vela, Concha, *Guide of the Thyssen-Bornemisza Museum*, Fundación Colección Thyssen-Bornemisza, Madrid, 1994.

Lübecke, Isolde, *The Thyssen-Bornemisza Collection: Early German Painting 1350–1550*, Sotheby's Publications, Philip Wilson Publishers, London, 1991.

Marias, Fernando, Luca de Tena, Consuelo, *Thyssen-Bornemisza Collection, Monastery of Pedralbes*, Fundación Colección Thyssen-Bornemisza, Barcelona, 1993.

Müller, Hannelore, *The Thyssen-Bornemisza Collection: European Silver*, General Editor Simon de Pury, Sotheby's Publications, Philip Wilson Publishers, London, 1986.

Novak, Barbara, *The Thyssen-Bornemisza Collection: Nineteenth-century American Painting*, General Editor Simon de Pury, Sotheby's Publications, Philip Wilson Publishers, London, 1986.

Pita Andrade, J. M. and Borobia Guerrero, M. M., *Old Masters; Thyssen-Bornemisza Museum*, Fundación Colección Thyssen-Bornemisza, Madrid, 1992.

Radcliffe, Anthony, Baker, Malcolm, Maek-Gérard, Michael, *The Thyssen-Bornemisza Collection: Renaissance and Later Sculpture*, General Editor Irene Martin, Sotheby's Publications, Philip Wilson Publishers, London, 1992.

Schouvaloff, Alexander, *The Thyssen-Bornemisza Collection: Set and Costume Designs for Ballet and Theatre*, General Editor Simon de Pury, Sotheby's Publications, Philip Wilson Publishers, London, 1987.

Somers Cocks, Anna and Truman, Charles, *The Thyssen-Bornemisza Collection: Renaissance Jewels, Gold Boxes and Objets de Vertue*, Sotheby's Publications, Philip Wilson Publishers, London, 1984.

Sotheby's London, *Old Master Paintings and Works of Art from the Bentinck-Thyssen Collection*, Sale December 1995.
Spuhler, Friedrich, *The Thyssen-Bornemisza Collection: Carpets and Textiles*, Sotheby's Publications, Philip Wilson Publishers, London, 1998.
Sutton, Denys (ed.), 'The Thyssen-Bornemisza Collection', *Apollo Magazine*, no. 257, July 1983.
Vergo, Peter, *The Thyssen-Bornemisza Collection: Twentieth-century German Painting*, General Editor Irene Martin, Sotheby's Publications, Philip Wilson Publishers, London, 1992.
Williamson, Paul, *The Thyssen-Bornemisza Collection: Medieval Sculpture and Works of Art*, Sotheby's Publications, Philip Wilson Publishers, London, 1987.

THYSSEN-BORNEMISZA COLLECTION (AND VISITING) EXHIBITION CATALOGUES (*in chronological order*)

Sammlung Schloss Rohoncz, Ausstellung Neue Pinakothek, foreword by Dr F. Dörnhöffer, Munich, 1930.
Sammlung Thyssen-Bornemisza (Schloss Rohoncz), 110 Meisterwerke der Europäischen Malerei des 14. bis 18. Jahrhunderts, Museum Folkwang, Essen, 27 January to 20 March 1960.
From Van Eyck to Tiepolo, Pictures from the Thyssen-Bornemisza Collection, National Gallery, London, 2 March to 30 April 1961.
Moderne Kunst aus der Sammlung Thyssen-Bornemisza, Kunsthalle Bremen, 2 February to 30 March 1975.
The Origin of the 20th Century in The Collection Thyssen-Bornemisza – The World of Abstract and Surrealist Painting, Prefectoral Museum of Ishikawa, Japan, 27 August to 15 September 1976.
La Collection Thyssen-Bornemisza – Tableaux Modernes, Musée d'Ixselles, Brussels, 14 October 1977 to 15 January 1978.
La Collection Thyssen-Bornemisza, Tableaux Modernes, Musée d'Art Moderne, Paris, 21 February to 20 May 1978.
Collezione Thyssen-Bornemisza – Arte Moderna, Villa Malpensata, Lugano, 1 September to 5 November 1978.
America and Europe – A Century of Modern Masters from the Thyssen-Bornemisza Collection, Art Gallery of Western Australia, Perth; Art Gallery of South Australia, Adelaide; Queensland Art Gallery, Brisbane; National Gallery of Victoria, Melbourne; Art Gallery of New South Wales, Sydney; National Art Gallery, Wellington; Auckland City Art Gallery, Auckland; Robert McDougall Art Gallery, Christchurch, 1979–1980.
Old Master Paintings from the Collection of Baron Thyssen-Bornemisza, National Gallery of Art, Washington; Detroit Institute of Arts, Detroit; Minneapolis Institute of

Arts, Minneapolis; Cleveland Museum of Art, Cleveland; Los Angeles County Museum of Art, Los Angeles; Denver Art Museum, Denver; Kimbell Art Museum, Fort Worth, 1979–1981.

Collection Thyssen-Bornemisza – Maîtres Anciens, Palais des Beaux-Arts, Paris, 7 January to 28 March 1982.

Nineteenth-century American Landscape Painting Selections from the Thyssen-Bornemisza Collection, Museum of Fine Arts, Houston; Oklahoma Art Center, Oklahoma City; Joslyn Museum of Art, Omaha, 29 October 1982 to 19 June 1983.

20th Century Masters: The Thyssen-Bornemisza Collection, National Gallery of Art, Washington; Wadsworth Atheneum, Hartford; Toledo Museum of Art, Toledo; Seattle Art Museum, Seattle; San Francisco Museum of Modern Art, San Francisco; Metropolitan Museum of Art, New York, 30 May 1982 to 2 March 1984.

Capolavori Impressionisti e Postimpressionisti da Musei Sovietici, Collezione Thyssen-Bornemisza, Villa Favorita, Lugano, 14 June to 15 November 1983.

Maestri Americani della Collezione Thyssen-Bornemisza, Musei Vaticani, Rome, 15 September to 15 November 1983.

Modern Masters from the Thyssen-Bornemisza Collection, Tokyo; Kumamoto; London; Nürnberg; Düsseldorf; Firenze; Paris; Madrid; Barcelona, 19 May 1984 to 17 August 1986.

Capolavori da musei ungheresi, Collezione Thyssen-Bornemisza, Villa Favorita, Lugano, 15 June to 15 October 1985.

Meisterwerke des 15.–20. Jahrhunderts aus der Sammlung Thyssen-Bornemisza, Nationalgalerie, Budapest; Neue Galerie, Szombathely, 3 October 1985 to 9 February 1986.

Gold and Silver Treasures of the Thyssen-Bornemisza Collection, Moscow; St Petersburg, 1986.

Ori e Argenti Dall 'Ermitage, Collezione Thyssen-Bornemisza, Villa Favorita, Lugano, 3 June to 2 November 1986.

Goya nelle Collezioni private di Spagna, Collezione Thyssen-Bornemisza, Villa Favorita, Lugano, 15 June to 15 October 1986.

Old Master Paintings of the Thyssen-Bornemisza Collection, Moscow; St Petersburg, 1987.

Fabergé Fantasies, Collezione Thyssen-Bornemisza, Villa Favorita, Lugano, 14 April to 7 June 1987.

Capolavori Impressionisti e Postimpressionisti da Musei Sovietici II, Collezione Thyssen-Bornemisza, Villa Favorita, Lugano, 9 August to 15 November 1987.

Gold and Silver Treasures from the Thyssen-Bornemisza Collection, Center of Fine Arts, Miami; Joslyn Art Museum, Omaha; Indianapolis Museum of Art, Indianapolis; Kimbell Art Museum, Fort Worth; Dixon Gallery and Gardens, Memphis, 7 November 1987 to 26 March 1989

Maestros Antiguos de la Collección Thyssen-Bornemisza, Real Academia de Bellas Artes de San Fernando, December 1987 to March 1988.

Mestres Americans del Segle XIX de la Cooleccio Thyssen-Bornemisza, Palau de la Virreina, Barcelona, 6 April to 19 June 1988.

Old Master Paintings from the Thyssen-Bornemisza Collection, Royal Academy of Arts, London, 18 March to 12 June 1988.
Arte Rivoluzionaria dai Musei Sovietici, Collezione Thyssen-Bornemisza, Villa Favorita, Lugano, 12 June to 2 October 1988.
Paintings 16th– 18th Century of the Thyssen-Bornemisza Collection, Novosibirsk, 1988.
Modern Paintings of the Thyssen-Bornemisza Collection, Moscow; St Petersburg, 1988.
Wege zur Abstraktion – 80 Meisterwerke aus der Sammlung Thyssen-Bornemisza, Villa Vauban, Luxembourg; Haus der Kunst, Munich; Museum des 20. Jahrhunderts, Vienna, 30 April 1988 to 15 January 1989.
Meisterwerke der Sammlung Thyssen-Bornemisza – Gemälde des 14.–18. Jahrhunderts, Staatsgalerie Stuttgart, 10 December 1988 to 5 March 1989.
Ori e Argenti dalla Collezione Thyssen-Bornemisza, Villa Favorita, Lugano, 30 April to 16 July 1989.
Espressionismo. Capolavori dalla Collezione Thyssen-Bornemisza, Villa Favorita, Lugano, 30 July to 29 October 1989.
Expressionism and Modern German Painting from the Thyssen-Bornemisza Collection, National Gallery of Art, Washington; Kimbell Art Museum, Fort Worth, Texas; Fine Arts Museum of San Francisco, San Francisco, 19 November 1989 to 14 January 1990.
Impressionism and Postimpressionism: The Thyssen-Bornemisza Collection, Villa Favorita, Lugano, 1 April to 8 July 1990.
American Impressionism, Collezione Thyssen-Bornemisza, Villa Favorita, Lugano, 22 July to 28 October 1990.
Espressionismo, Capolavori della Collezione Thyssen-Bornemisza, Da Van Gogh a Klee, Roma, Palazzo Ruspoli, 12 December 1990 to 12 February 1991.
Two Hundred Years of American Painting from the Thyssen-Bornemisza Collection, Hyogo Prefectural Museum of Modern Art, Kobe; Nagoya City Art Museum, Nagoya; Bunkamura Museum of Art, Tokyo; Hiroshima City Museum of Contemporary Art, Hiroshima, 5 January to 25 August 1991.
Manifestatori delle cose meravigliose, Collezione Thyssen-Bornemisza, Villa Favorita, Lugano, 7 April to 30 June 1991.
Svizzera Meravigliosa, Collezione Thyssen-Bornemisza, Villa Favorita, Lugano, 27 July to 27 October 1991.
Europa e America, Collezione Thyssen-Bornemisza, Villa Favorita, Lugano, 2 April to 22 June 1993.
Khara Khoto, Collezione Thyssen-Bornemisza, Villa Favorita, Lugano, 25 June to 1 November 1993.
Europa e America, Collezione Thyssen-Bornemisza, Villa Favorita, Lugano, 1 April to 30 October 1994.
The St Petersburg Murakka, Collezione Thyssen-Bornemisza, Villa Favorita, Lugano, 28 June to 2 October 1994.
Europa e America, Collezione Thyssen-Bornemisza, Villa Favorita, Lugano, 14 April to 29 October 1995.

Da Bagdad a Isfahan, Collezione Thyssen-Bornemisza, Villa Favorita, Lugano, 4 June to 7 August 1995.

Aus der Thyssen Sammlung, Steirische Landesausstellung, Mariazell; Neuberg an der Mürz, Austria, 4 May to 27 October 1996.

Gold and Silver Treasures from Dubrovnik, Collezione Thyssen-Bornemisza, Villa Favorita, Lugano, 27 September to 3 November 1996.

From Canaletto to Kandinsky, Masterworks from the Carmen Thyssen-Bornemisza Collection, Palacio de Villahermosa, Madrid, 20 March to 8 September 1996 (in particular the chapter by Le Normand-Romain, Antoinette on *'August Thyssen, Commissioner of Auguste Rodin'*).

Rodin, Les Marbres de la Collection Thyssen, Musée Rodin, Paris, 8 October 1996 to 5 January 1997.

From Zurbaran to Picasso, Masterpieces from the Collection of Carmen Thyssen-Bornemisza, Shanghai Museum; China National Art Gallery, Beijing, 12 October 1996 to 9 March 1997.

60th Anniversary of the Picture Gallery at the Villa Favorita, Masterworks from the Carmen Thyssen-Bornemisza Collection, Thyssen-Bornemisza Foundation, Lugano, 5 September to 2 November 1997.

El Paisatgisme Catala del Naturalisme al Noucentisme dins la col.leccio Carmen Thyssen-Bornemisza, Sala d'Exposicions del Govern, Andorra, 18 October 1997 to 11 January 1998.

The Spirit of the Place, Masterworks from the Carmen Thyssen-Bornemisza Collection, Frick Collection, New York; Wadsworth Atheneum, Hartford, Connecticut, 17 September 1997 to 15 March 1998.

Theater of Reason / Theater of Desire, The Art of Alexandre Benois and Leon Bakst, Thyssen-Bornemisza Foundation, Villa Favorita, Castagnola, 5 June to 1 November 1998.

Aspectos de la Tradición Paisajistica en la Colección Carmen Thyssen-Bornemisza, Salas de Exposiciones del Palacio Episcopal, Malaga, 12 July to 5 September 1999.

El Greco. Identidad y Transformacion. Creta, Italia, Espana, Museo Thyssen-Bornemisza, Madrid; Palacio de Exposiciones, Rome; Pinacoteca Nacional-Museo Alexandros Soutzos, Athens, 3 February 1999 to 17 January 2000.

ARCHIVES AND OTHER ORGANISATIONS

Aachen Town Archives, Aachen, Germany. (Dr Adam Oellers, Dr Hermann Viktor Johnen)

Bentinck Archives, London, UK.

Berliner Handels- und Frankfurter Bank Archives, Frankfurt, Germany (Werner Bendix).

Bildarchiv Preussischer Kulturbesitz, Berlin, Germany (Dr Hanns-Peter Frentz)

Bundesarchiv, Berlin, Germany (Dr Friederich Kahlenberg, Gregor Pickro, Dr Jürgen Real)
Bundesarchiv, Berne, Switzerland (D. Bourgeois, Mr Lauener, H. von Ruette).
Fritz Thyssen Foundation, Cologne, Germany (Professor Hans Kerche).
German Historical Institute, London, UK (Barbara Bültmann).
Hamburgisches Welt-Wirtschafts-Archiv, Hamburg, Germany.
Hello Ltd, London, UK.
Kamer van Koophandel en Fabrieken voor Amsterdam, Haarlem, The Netherlands.
Imperial War Museum, Duxford and London, UK (Stephen Walton)
Instituut voor Maritieme Historie (formerly Deutsches Realgymnasium), The Hague, Netherlands.
Mauritshuis Museum, The Hague, Netherlands (Helma Nederend).
New York Public Library, New York, USA (Peter Craus).
News Magazine Archives, Vienna, Austria (Arno Gattermann).
Nordhausen Town Archives, Nordhausen, Germany (Dr Peter Kuhlbrodt).
Public Record Office (now National Archives), Kew, UK.
Russian State Archives, Moscow, Russia.
Schloss Landsberg Foundation, Mülheim an der Ruhr, Germany (Marion Zorn).
Staatliche Museen zu Berlin, Berlin, Germany (Anne Schäfer-Junker).
The Art Newspaper, London, UK (Melanie Folkes).
The British Library, Newspaper Library, London, UK.
The European (Newspaper) Ltd, London, UK.
The Institute of Contemporary History and Wiener Library, London, UK.
Thyssen AG (now ThyssenKrupp AG) Archives, Duisburg, Germany (Dr Manfred Rasch).
Thyssen-Bornemisza Group (TBG) Archives, Monte Carlo, Monaco.
Thyssen-Bornemisza Museum, Madrid, Spain (Tomàs Llorens Serra, Botoa Lefé).
Universitätsarchiv Ludwig-Maximilians-Universität, Munich, Germany (Ursula Lochner).
Universitätsarchiv Ruprecht-Karls-Universität, Heidelberg, Germany (Mrs Hunerlach).
Universitätsbibliothek Humboldt-Universität, Berlin, Germany (Dr W Schultze).
University of London Library, London, UK (Nicholas Jeffs).
US National Archives, Washington, USA.
Vogue, Condé Nast Publications, Paris and London (Michele Zaquin, Georgina Knight).

Index

Achermann, Dr Hubert 354
Adenauer, Chancellor Dr Konrad 229, 236–7
Agnelli
   Gianni 8, 119, 255, 277, 279, 315, 317, 328, 335
   Umberto 343
Agnew, Thomas & Sons Ltd 348
Aguirre, Dr Ernesto 192
Aktiengesellschaft (AG)
   für Hüttenbetrieb Duisburg–Meiderich ('AGHütt') 47
   Weser shipyard 333
Akzo Chemical Company 193, 203, 220, 292
Albarda, Dr H. 219
Alborch, Carmen 389
alcoholism 8, 11, 21, 62–3, 67–8, 75, 95, 114, 140, 154, 188, 267, 272–3, 279–81, 286, 291, 294, 312, 323, 335–6, 352, 415–6
Alexander QC, David 407, 423, 425
Allen, Paul 394
Alsum harbour, Rhine river 31
Alvensleben, Captain Wichard von 178
Andorra 438
Annigoni, Pietro 253
Ansiaux, Pierre 227
anti-Semitism 23, 54, 60, 65, 86, 89, 104–8, 123, 138, 150–1, 154, 158, 173, 179–82, 191, 195, 223–4, 257
Antonello Trust 391, 423, 433
Antonova, Irina 340
Appleby, Spurling & Kempe 402
ARCH Foundation (Art Restoration for Cultural Heritage) 9
Ardeck of Hesse Barchfeld, Princess Annie, *née* Annie Price 23–5
Argentina 84, 108, 116, 119, 121, 136, 139, 151, 159, 167, 173–4, 188, 191–2, 194–5, 215, 229–30, 234, 236, 250, 262–3, 281, 305, 355
armaments & munitions production 47–50, 53, 55–6, 68, 71, 79, 83, 91, 110, 112, 114, 123–4, 135, 143–6, 151–2, 160–1, 163, 167, 186, 195, 207, 218, 228–30, 267
Art Council Establishment, Liechtenstein 315
August Thyssen
   Bank AG ('ATB') 80, 84, 87, 110, 116, 124, 135–6, 143, 153, 157, 159, 160, 165–7, 169, 175–7, 186–7, 192–5, 199, 202, 209, 211, 238–9, 250, 252, 265, 267–8, 271, 293–4, 303
   Hütte AG (August Thyssen smelting works, 'ATH') 25, 70–1, 79–80, 83, 131, 136, 144, 152, 183, 188, 194, 201–2, 208, 210, 224, 227–9, 236–7, 251, 260, 271, 273, 282–3
Aznar, José Maria 386

B

Bacon, Francis 312
Badajoz
   Infanta Doña Pilar de Borbón y Borbón, Duchess of 352, 359, 372, 390
   Luís Gómez Acebo, Duke of 345, 350, 352, 359, 364, 371–3, 378–9
Baden-Baden 24, 60
Badgastein 48, 131
Bad Homburg 38, 109
Badrutt, Andrea & Caprice 231, 255, 275
Bakst, Leon 313, 392
Baladur, Edouard 370
Ball & Graupe auctioneers, Berlin 89
Balthus (Balthasar Klossowski de Rola) 337
Bamford, Sir Anthony 351
Banco de Montevideo 234
Bankhaus von der Heydt 34, 50

Bank
- of London and South America 159
- voor Handel en Scheepvaart NV, Rotterdam ('BVHS') 55–8, 60, 62, 65–8, 71, 75, 80–1, 86–7, 99, 103, 114, 127–8, 130–2, 135, 143–4, 154, 157–60, 165–7, 174, 193, 198–9, 201–4, 207, 209, 211, 219, 222, 228, 230, 233, 239, 267, 272, 292–4
  - BVHS *v.* Slatford 115, 137–8, 159, 191, 222–3, 228, 237–8

Barker, Lex 6, 7, 344, 407–8
Bassa, Ferrer 377
Batthyány de Németujvár
- Count Ivan Junior 298
- Count Ivan Senior ('Ivy') 10, 89, 123, 170–1, 179–182, 204, 212, 215, 230–1, 238, 262, 271, 303–4, 349, 402
- Countess Margit, *née* Baroness Margit Thyssen-Bornemisza ('Margit Junior') 44–5, 58, 68–9, 73, 75, 81, 89, 96, 104, 123, 154–5, 161, 171, 179–82, 190, 200, 204–6, 209, 212, 215–6, 218–21, 230, 234, 238–9, 262–3, 271–2, 296, 303–4, 328, 349, 354

Beaton, Cecil 253, 266
Beauchamp, Charles 313
Beaulieu, Chales de 261–2
Beck, General Ludwig 222
Becker, Gustav 16
Beiglböck, Stefan 181
Beisteguci, Carlo 232
Belgian Custodian Office (Office des Sequestres) 225, 227
Bentinck-Thyssen Collection 93, 132, 221–2
Bentinck van Schoonheten
- Ambassador Baron Adolphe ('Dolf') 54, 125–6, 164–5, 189–90, 193, 198, 200, 203, 205–7, 209, 212, 213, 215–6, 223, 233, 238–9, 263, 265, 271, 297–8, 303
- Baroness Alice 354
- Baroness Elisabeth Junior 354
- Baroness Elisabeth Senior, *née* Elisabeth Hogan 354
- Baroness Gabrielle, *née* Baroness Gabrielle Thyssen-Bornemisza ('Gaby') 9, 44, 53–4, 58, 68–9, 72–5, 81, 89, 92–3, 96, 104, 116–7, 124–6, 132, 155, 161–2, 164–5, 197, 200, 202–6, 209, 212, 215–9, 221, 230, 238–9, 263–4, 271–2, 297–8, 303–4, 317–8, 328, 340, 354–5, 399
- Baron Steven 132, 221, 263, 265, 297–8, 304, 318, 354
- Baron Wolf 354

Berenson, Bernard 85
Berg
- Baroness Gloria von 388, 404, 407
- Baroness Hedwig von, formerly Baroness Hedwig von Neufforge, *née* Hedwig Thyssen ('Hedwig Junior') 23, 25, 27–33, 37–8, 47, 136–7, 190, 259–60
- Baroness Ildiko von 404, 407
- Baroness Maisie von, *née* Maisie Price 23–5
- Baron Maximilian ('Max') von 25
- Baroness Maximiliane von 407

Berggruen, Heinz 345
Berkes, Sandor 102, 115, 122, 127, 152–3, 188, 206, 212–3, 248, 321
Berliner
- Handelsgesellschaft 267–8
- Handels- und Frankfurter Bank ('BHF'-Bank) 268, 293, 332, 343, 346

Bicheroux
- Balbina, *née* Balbina Thyssen 14, 20, 28
- Désiré 14–5, 20
- Toussaint 14–5

Birnbaum, Rafael 106–7
Bismarck-Schönhausen, Reich Chancellor Otto von 19, 20, 22, 25, 34
Blass, General Director Heinrich 151
Blohm & Voss 257–8

Bochum Cast Steel Manufacturers 152
Bockamp, Dr Kurt 144
Böhler, Julius 127
Bohígas, Oriol 377, 390
Boissevain, Henriette, formerly Henriette Compton, Lady Northampton, *née* Baroness Henriette Bentinck 263, 265, 297–8, 304, 318, 354–5
Borcke, Adrian von 120, 133, 154–5, 262–3
Borghero, Gertrude 362
Bormann, Martin 110
Bornemisza de Kaszón 43–4, 309
    Baron Gabor 24–5, 38–9, 43–4, 328–9
    Baroness Louise, *née* Louise Price 23–5, 32, 8–9, 41–5, 53, 89, 96, 328
    Baroness Mae 25, 38
Bosshard, Emil 307, 337, 345, 360, 364, 384, 386
Boucher, François 295
Boyle QC, Alan 412, 422, 424, 427–30
Braque, Georges 321
Brassert, Hermann A. 151
Brazil 48, 188, 195, 215, 250, 287, 289–90, 305, 355
Breker, Professor Arno 323
Bremer Vulkan AG shipyard ('BV') 71, 80, 110, 123–4, 143–4, 163–4, 166–7, 177, 186, 230, 258–9, 272, 298, 301, 328, 331–3, 403
Brooks, D D. 342
Brouwer, Adriaen 92
Brown
    Bros Harriman & Co, New York 66, 158–9
    House (Nazi headquarters), Munich 87
Brüning, Reich Chancellor Heinrich 88
Buch
    Diana von 274, 276, 278, 281–2
    Max von 281–2
Burgess, Anthony 348
Bush, Prescott S. (grand-father of George W.) 66, 157

C
Canaris, Admiral William 222
Caravaggio
    Michelangelo Merisi, called 111
    Trust 391, 395–7, 434
Carmen Thyssen-Bornemisza Collection 7, 51, 366, 377, 397–8, 401, 408, 423, 431, 438–9
Carnegie, Andrew 227
Carpaccio, El Vittore 111, 219
'Cartier diamond' 299
Cassirer Gallery, Berlin 221
Castro, Fidel 255–6
catholicism 14, 16, 20, 29, 30, 36, 76–7, 138, 150, 244–7, 297, 334
Cehandro (Centrale Handels Vereeniging NV Rotterdam) 192
Cervera Fernandez, Maria del Carmen 340, 344, 351–2, 358–9, 365, 368, 382–3
Cézanne, Paul 314–6, 321, 338
Chagall, Marc 295, 318, 337
Chase
    Manhattan Bank 293, 326, 333
    National Bank 66, 79, 158, 326
Chemical Bank 79
Chirac, Jacques 334
Christie's 313, 409
Clarkson, Elizabeth 82, 329
Class, Heinrich 65
Clay, General Lucius D. 211
Clubs
    Annabel's, London 319
    Carroll's Nightclub, Paris 126, 244
    Coral Reef Club, Bermuda 267
    Corviglia Club, St Moritz 231, 244
    Gezira Club, Cairo 164
    Industry Club, Düsseldorf 98
    Jockey Club, Paris 335
    Marks Club, London 310, 319
    Park Club, Budapest 42
    St James Club, Cairo 164
    Turf Club, Cairo 164
    Union Club, Berlin 121–2, 166

Coca-Cola Company 289–90
Cody, Frederick 335
Coert
    Dr J. Junior & Katherine 201–2, 220
    Dr J. Senior 202–3
Colamina SA, Buenos Aires 159
Coleridge QC, Paul 365
Companhia Thyssen do Brasil 289–90
concentration camps 195
    Buchenwald 161, 176–7, 250, 378
    Dachau 178–80
    Dora / Mittelbau 160–1
    Jamlitz 176
    Sachsenhausen 151, 160, 177
Constable, John 348, 384
Conyers, Dill & Pearman 401
Coolidge, President Calvin 67
Cossa, Francesco del 249
Crawford, Malcolm D. 333–4
Credit Suisse 151, 159, 173, 191, 291
Cripps, Stafford 228
Crispo, Andrew (Gallery, New York) 299–300, 302, 312–4, 321, 324–5
Crystal QC, Michael 317–8, 331, 399, 401–2, 405–8, 411–2, 414–27, 429–31, 433
Csutak, Gabor 44
Cuba 234–6, 255–7
Curaçao 303, 318, 346
Czaky, Countess Ilyana 42
Czaitha Estate, near Rechnitz 96
Czartoryska-Borbon, Princess Eleonora, *née* Eleonora de Picciotto (later Baroness Nora Bentinck) 304

D
Dalai Lama of Tibet, His Holiness, the fourteenth 353
Dalí, Salvador 113
Dawes Plan 67–8, 84
Daylesford, Gloucestershire 309–10, 341, 350–1, 368, 378
Dégas, Edgar 316, 337, 346

Delacroix, Eugène 315
Delaunay, Sonia 337
Demuth, Charles 313
Dérain, André 302
Deutsche
    Bank 50, 64
    Edelstahlwerke AG 210
Dezsö, Dr Sztehlo 172
Dietrich
    Dr Hermann 88
    Sepp 110
Dillon Read 79
Dinkelbach, Dr Heinrich 188
Dixon, Palmer 209
Domestic Fuel Corporation ('DFC') 124, 159, 182, 199, 214
Duccio di Buoninsegna 302
Dütting, Hans D. 273
Dulles
    Allen 199
    John Foster 199, 238
Dunamis (Handelsvereeniging Dunamis NV) 132, 209
Duncan, Sir Frederic and Lady 42

E
Einbeck estate, near Hanover 109, 160
Eisenhower, President Dwight D. 238
El Greco, Domenicos Theotocopoulos called 92, 252
Elkinson, Jeffrey 405, 414
Ellscheid, Dr Robert 208, 223, 260
Erlenhof
    racing stables and stud farm 108–9, 120–2, 124, 154–5, 166, 261–3, 298
    GmbH 122, 124, 262–3
Ernst, Max 313
Erzberger, Matthias 49, 53–4
Esser, Director (Bremer Vulkan AG) 124
Esso Company 272–3
Estève, Maurice 302
Eurogas 347

Index 457

F
Faminta (Familien-Interessen AG), Glarus 87, 116, 130–1, 209, 226
Farouk, King of Egypt 164
Favorita
    Holding Ltd, Bermuda 403
    Shipping Ltd, Bermuda 265
    Trustees Ltd, Bermuda 376, 379, 381
Feininger, Lyonel 314
Fernandez, Jorge 234–5
Firth, Sir William 137, 191
Fischer
    Fine Art, London 321
    Gallery, Lucerne 316
    Harry 295
Flensburger Shipbuilding Company (Flensburger Schiffsbaugesellschaft, 'FSG') 71, 80, 124, 135, 166–7, 259, 272, 298
Flick
    Friedrich 88, 136, 188
    Friedrich Christian ('Mick') 388
Foerster, Baroness Marie 96–7
forced labour 50, 135–6, 143, 152, 160–1, 163, 165, 167, 171, 174–5, 177, 179–182
Foster MP, John 224, 228
Fragonard Trust 391, 423, 433
Francesco di Giorgio Martini 296
Franco, General Francisco 197, 244, 359, 378
Freud, Lucian 321, 335–7, 392
Frick, Wilhelm 137
Friedländer, Dr Max 85
Fritz Thyssen
    Asset Management AG (Vermögensverwaltung AG) 237
    Collection (Sammlung) 442
    Foundation (Stiftung) 250–1
Fromen, Maria 37, 78
Fürstenberg
    Crown Prince Joachim zu 246
    Prince (Hugenpoet Castle) 70
    Prince Friedrich zu 245–6, 290
    Princess Theresa zu, formerly Baroness Theresa Thyssen-Bornemisza, née Princess Theresa zu Lippe Bisterfeld Weissenfeld 3, 10, 146, 169–71, 187–90, 193, 201, 204, 206, 209, 212, 225, 230–2, 244–7, 252, 255, 262, 274, 277, 290, 307–8, 349, 352, 359, 368–9, 386, 418, 433
Funk, Dr Walther 87, 212

G
Gainsborough, Thomas 341, 383
Galbraith, Ambassador John 279, 335–6
Galerie Gmurzynska, Cologne 337
Gauguin, Paul 324, 335, 338, 346, 348, 384
Geestse Shipping Company 301
Gelsenkirchener Bergwerks AG 50
Genillard, Robert L. 265, 305–6, 316, 330–1, 333, 395, 398–400, 416, 426
Germany
    Second Reich
        Centre Party 21
        Reich Economy Ministry 50, 174
        Reich Finance Ministry 50, 104, 174
        Reichsbank 50, 174
        Reich War Ministry 49
    Weimar Republic 65, 79, 81, 85, 150
        Franco–German Conciliation Committee 83
        Freecorps 54, 59
        German National People's Party ('DNVP') 66
        National Socialist German Workers' Party ('Nazi Party') 64–6, 75, 79, 80, 87, 91–2, 98, 104, 107–8, 115, 119–20, 127, 131–2, 136, 138–40, 144–5, 148, 150, 152–3, 157, 165, 167, 171–2, 175–6, 182, 186–8, 191–3, 195, 198–9, 206–7, 211–2, 215, 222–5, 228, 230, 236, 267–9, 323
        Pan–German League 65, 150

Storm detachment ('SA') 64–5, 108, 150, 163
Third Reich 99, 102, 110, 124, 143, 163, 169, 175, 186, 191, 195, 198, 229–30, 293
  Counter Intelligence Services ('Abwehr') 87, 173, 187, 192, 195, 241
  Foreign Exchange Control Office 87, 116, 130–1, 133, 137, 143, 182, 226
  German Economic Council 98
  Hitler Youth 105, 107
  Institute for Corporate Affairs 107
  Navy High Command 124
  Reich Ministry for Armaments and War Production 151
  Reichs Association Iron 183
  Schutzstaffel ('SS') 123, 140, 151, 154, 161, 163, 167, 177–81, 187, 192, 206, 257
  Secret State Police ('Gestapo') 98, 139, 149, 176–7, 180
Allied Military Government of Germany / British Military Government / Office of Military Government US (OMGUS) 132, 175, 182, 236
  Allied High Commission 229, 239, 242
  Control Commission for Germany (British Element) 132, 242
  German Restitution Agency 236
  Inter Allied Reparation Agency 224
  International military tribunal, Nuremberg 188, 230, 240
  Internment camp, Kornwestheim 190
  Interrogation centre, Kransberg 191, 240
  North German Coal Control 186, 188
  Property Control & External Assets Branch 77, 218, 242
  Steel Trustees Administration 188

US Group Control Council 132, 191, 240
Federal Republic Bundesbank 267
Getty
  Ann 345, 350
  Foundation 370–1, 380
Gewerkschaft Deutscher Kaiser ('GDK') 25–6, 30–1, 47–50, 81, 284
Ghirlandaio
  Domenico 111
  Trust 391, 423, 433
Goalen, Barbara 275
Goebbels, Joseph 97–8, 157, 250
Goerdeler, General Carl 222
Göring
  Reich Marshal Hermann, 87–8, 97–8, 108, 110, 114, 116, 119, 122, 131, 136–8, 146, 151, 153, 157, 165, 187, 192, 194, 209, 212, 224, 226, 250, 267, 304
  Emmy 119, 137, 192
Goldman Sachs 68, 77, 151
Goldschmidt, Dr Jakob 227
Goldschmidt-Rothschild, Erich von 89
Goldstein, Dr Robert 130, 216
González, Felipe 373, 378, 386, 389
Goodchild, R C R. 218, 242
Gorbachev, Mikhail & Raissa 339
Goudstikker Gallery, Amsterdam 92–3
Goya y Lucientes, Francisco José de 111, 277, 352, 378–9, 382
Grassi
  Arturo 296
  Luigi 296–7
  Marco 282, 296–7, 311–2, 315, 320–1
Gris, Juan 316
Groenendijk, Wilhelmus 188, 203, 267, 292, 303, 308
Groeninger, Johann G. 157, 203–4
Groh, Dr Joseph ('Josi') 10, 44, 101, 107, 147, 179, 195–8, 211, 248–50, 254, 264, 291–2, 317, 319, 328, 332, 340, 345–6, 349, 351–2, 412

Grosz, Georg 316
Guaranty Trust Bank 158
Guardi, Francesco 302
Gueydan, Father Edouard 146, 170–1
Guscetti, Riccardo 10, 265, 337, 340–1, 346, 401, 418, 430
Guttmann, Max 132, 134, 195
Guzwiller Bank 385

H
Haberstock, Karl 127
Härle, Dr Carl 70, 78, 163
Hafter, Dr Peter 318
Halcyon Lijn (Thyssen trans-Atlantic shipping line) 48, 71, 80, 124, 230
Hals, Frans 111, 219, 221
Ham QC, Robert 401–2, 405–7, 415, 421–2, 424–5, 431, 438
Haniel von Rauch, Mrs Richard 172
Hanomag 151
Hanover, Prince Ernst 309, 388
'Hanse', motor yacht 300–2, 319–20, 327–8, 341, 352, 368, 394
Hanson plc (Lord & Lady Hanson) 345
Hardman, Phillips and Mann 222
Harlan, Samuel (Harlan & Hollingsworth) 23–4, 158
Harriman
    E. Roland 157
    William Averell 66, 157, 206
Harry Winston Jewellers 320, 342
Hatzfeld, Lutz 21
Heath, Edward 318
Heida, Ede Homme 99
Heineken, Freddy 343, 347
Heinemann, Dr Rudolf J. 85, 89, 92–3, 95, 103, 111, 115, 127, 227, 249, 269–70, 294, 312, 315
Hendy, Sir Philip 269
Hess, Rudolf 86–7
Hesse, Prince Philipp of 178
Himmler, Heinrich 110, 157, 177, 187, 267

Hindenburg, Field Marshal Paul von 104, 191
Hintzen, Dr H C. 219–20
Hitler, Adolf 64–5, 74, 83–4, 88–9, 91–3, 97–9, 104–8, 110, 112, 122, 127, 131, 137–8, 140, 149–50, 152, 157, 165, 168, 172, 179, 187–8, 191–2, 218, 224, 230, 315–6, 322–3, 329
Hohenlohe, Prince Alfonso 302
Holbein, Hans the Younger 111, 249, 269, 321
Holland American
    Investment Corporation ('HAIC') 77, 80, 124, 202, 209, 219, 233, 239, 272
    Trading Corporation ('HATC') 77, 80, 124, 159, 183, 209
Hollandsch Trust Kantoor ('HTK') 108–9, 124, 209, 298
Homer, Winslow 325, 392
Hoppegarten race course 109, 154, 166, 298
Hopper, Edward 314, 324, 392
Horowitz, Fred 299, 320
Horten, Helmut 305, 311
Horthy, Admiral Miklós 55, 178
Hotel
    Adlon, Berlin 45, 61, 82, 86, 90, 165, 211
    Astoria, Brussels 225
    Baur au Lac, Zurich 130, 143, 390
    Bristol
        Berlin 149, 162
        Vienna 42, 96
    Carlton, Cannes 113, 139, 237, 249
    Claridges
        London 310, 319, 335, 416
        Paris 113
    Continental
        Cairo 164
        Munich 167
    Crillon, Paris 138
    de Paris, Monte Carlo 138
    Eden Roc, Cannes 249
    Fürstenhof, Dortmund 56

Grand Hotel
  Lucerne 94–5
  Pupp, Karlsbad 118, 133
  Vienna 24
La Gavina, S'Agaro, Spain 112, 407, 425
Metropole, Monte Carlo 220, 222, 234
Nacional, Havana 234–6, 256–7
Palace
  Davos 104, 141, 143, 169
  Madrid 386
  St Moritz 75, 130, 193
Park Hotel, Düsseldorf 98
Plaza Athénée, Paris 351, 396
Queen Elizabeth, Paris 248
Ritz-Carlton, Washington 361
Royal, Lausanne 142–3
Sacher, Vienna 24
Shepherd's Hotel, Cairo 164
Splendide, Lugano 129, 140, 264, 283
Vierjahreszeiten, Munich 290
Waldhaus (Waldhotel), Flims 143, 149, 154, 188, 216
Waldorf Astoria, New York 310, 327
Hotel Drouot auction house, Paris 127
Hotwagner, Dr Josef 179–181, 184
House of
  Bourbon
    Don Juan, Count of Barcelona 143, 353, 359
    Juan Carlos, King of Spain 9, 143, 350, 353, 359, 371–2, 376–7, 382, 385–6, 389, 438
    Sofia, Queen of Spain 352, 381–3, 385–6, 438
  Habsburg 9, 10, 25, 39, 53–5
    Archduchess Eleonore von 405, 438
    Archduke Ferdinand Zvonimir von 405, 438
    Archduchess Francesca von, *née* Baroness Francesca Thyssen-Bornemisza ('Chessy') 3, 5, 7–9, 264, 274, 278–9, 287, 290, 308–9, 334, 352–3, 365, 367, 375, 385, 387–93, 395–6, 400–1, 405, 407, 410, 423, 426, 432, 434–9
    Archduchess Gloria von 438
    Archduke Karl von 385, 387–8, 405, 410
    Archduke Otto von 9, 385, 388
    Archduke Rudolph von 9–10
    Franz Joseph I, Emperor of Austria 25, 39, 43, 53
  Hohenzollern 30, 50, 54, 244
    Leopold, Prince of Prussia 95, 102, 178
    Wilhelm II, German Emperor 46–7, 49 54, 56, 59
  Orange 57, 75, 143, 165, 193, 203–4
    Bernhard, Prince of the Netherlands, *né* Prince Bernhard zu Lippe Bisterfeld Weissenfeld 170, 190, 211, 220
    Hendrik, Prince of the Netherlands, *né* Duke Heinrich von Mecklenburg-Schwerin 58, 74
    Juliana, Crown Princess of the Netherlands 202, 211
    Wilhelmina, Queen of the Netherlands 58, 74, 144, 194
    William III, Prince of Orange 125
  Saxe-Coburg-Wettin
    Albert II and Paola, King and Queen of the Belgians 274
  Saxe-Coburg-Windsor
    Charles, Prince of Wales 371
    Edward VIII, Duke of Windsor 74
Huchzermeier, Hans Martin 301
Hugenberg, Dr Alfred 82–3
Huiskamp, Gerard Bernard 300, 303, 305
Hutton, Barbara 112, 237
Hyde, Henry B. 199–200, 207, 209, 225, 227, 233, 238
Hynning, Clifford 191, 240

Index

I
'I Paid Hitler' 138, 150–1, 156, 223, 229, 243, 355
IG Farben 79, 160
InCon Packaging 346–7
Information Handling Services ('IHS') 437
Indian Head 303, 305, 329
ING-Bank 284
Internationale Finanz- u. Kunsthandels AG, Liechtenstein 302
Interpool Leasing 346, 403

J
Jacke, Dr Fritz 32, 95
Jaipur, Maharaja of 291
Jamaica 251–2, 264–5, 267, 278, 309, 327–8, 379, 432
Jaoule de Pontcheville, Marie 365
Jawlensky, Alexei von 341
J. H. Stein Bank 136, 163
J. Henry Schroeder Bank 79
Jungbluth, Franz 51, 76

K
Kabelac, Dr Robert 123, 134, 144, 163, 177, 186
Kahn, Otto 111
Kammler, SS-Brigadeführer Dr Ing Hans 161
Kamphuisen, Professor P W. 193, 220
Kandinsky, Wasily 315
Karajan, Herbert & Eliette von 275, 290, 388
Kaszony
  Family Agreement (Thyssen-Bornemisza family inheritance agreement) 204–6, 212–7, 220–22, 238–9, 271–2
  Family Foundation, Schwyz 81, 87, 143, 167, 171, 173, 198, 206, 217–8, 221, 233, 239, 271–2, 298, 306, 318, 330, 332
Kellogg, Mercedes 317
Kennedy Galleries, New York 325, 335
Kerkorian, Kirk 345
Ketterer, Roman Norbert 269–70, 295, 312–4
Khan
  Karim (Aga Khan) 290, 302
  Princess Nina, formerly Baroness Nina Thyssen-Bornemisza, *née* Nina Sheila Dyer 3, 244–9, 251–4, 277, 342, 352
  Prince Saddrudin 252–3
Kiel, Dr Johanna 313
Kirdorf, Emil 34, 50, 86, 104
Klee, Paul 337
Klönne, Carl 50
Knoedler Gallery, New York 127
Kohl, Chancellor Dr Helmut 370
Kooning, Willem de 313, 337
Kornfeld and Klipstein auctioneers, Berne 295
Kornis, Count Karl 42
Kouwenhoven, Henrik Jozef 75, 81, 99, 143–4, 157–8, 193, 200, 203, 215–6
KPMG (formerly Klynveld, Kraayenhof & Co.) 167, 217, 241, 303, 354
Kraayenhof, Jacob 193, 198
Kredit, P H. 250
Krupp of Essen 68, 71, 151–2, 283, 333
Krupp von Bohlen und Halbach
  Alfried 183, 188, 283
  Arndt 283, 350
Kun, Bela 54–5

L
Landsberg, Mülheim-Kettwig/Germany Castle 35–42, 54, 60, 62, 65, 69, 76, 79, 92, 98, 151, 162–3, 174, 185, 212, 236, 238, 269, 324, 354–5, 435–6
Castle Foundation 78, 269
Landsberg-Velen auf Steinfurt, Baron Ignaz von 35
Lefèvre Gallery, London 315, 324
Léger, Fernand 314

Leonardo Trust 391, 423, 433
Levie, Simon H. 93, 390
Lichtenstein, Roy 321
Lieftinck, Pieter (Dutch Finance Minister) 203, 207
Lieven, Prince 39
Lievens, Jan 86
Lievense, Cornelis 75, 157–9, 215
Limberger, Gisela 192
Lindner, Richard 313
Lippe Bisterfeld Weissenfeld, Prince Alfred zu 170, 204, 209, 232
Llorens Serra, Tomàs 377, 384, 390, 408, 424, 439
Lloyd QC, Sir Timothy 375–6
Loeb, Louis Carl (Loeb Bros) 208–9
Lowatschek, Dr Erwin 200
Ludendorff, Field Marshal Erich von 65, 224
Lübke, Heinrich 135, 143–4, 152–4, 166–7, 169, 175–7, 212, 238, 241, 250

M

MABAG (Maschinen- und Apparatebau AG, Nordhausen) 146, 160–1, 167, 201
Macarrón, Ricardo 382
MacDonald, Ramsay 48
Macmillan, Harold 318
Madrazo y Garreta, Raimundo de 392
Mafia 234, 317
Malleray, Pierre de 232
Malone, US Senator George W. 227
Mann, Professor Francis 198, 222
Mannesmann AG 21, 286
Maragall, Pasqual 363, 377
Marbella 302, 309, 350, 353, 364
Marcoff, Professor Marco 407
Marini, Marino 277
Marlborough
    Fine Art, London 321
    Gallery, New York 337
    Rosita, Duchess of 309
Marling, Lord (British Ambassador to The Hague) 58
Marosy, Franz von 291
Marquand, Christian 247
Marshall Plan 224, 226
Maschinenfabrik Thyssen & Co. 47
Masefield, Thorold (Governor of Bermuda) 426, 429–30
Masoni, Dr Franco 306, 354, 412
Marcos, Ferdinand & Imelda 359
Massachusetts Institute of Technology 82, 256
Matisse, Henri 295, 341
May, Erwin G. 159, 183
McCloy, John J. 242
McKinsey & Co Inc. 291–3, 300, 305, 318–9
Mdivani, Prince Alexis 112–3
Memling, Hans 127
Meran, Countess Katharina von 433, 438
Metallgesellschaft 208
Metropolitan Museum of Art, New York 249, 360
Meynen, Johannes 292
Mindszenty, Cardinal 303
Miró, Joan 313
Mitchell, Judge Denis 404–5, 410–22, 417–21, 424–31
Mitterrand, President François 364–5
Mittler, Anton 17, 37
Mobil Oil 257–8
Moholy-Nagy, László 337
Mojert, Director Dr. (Reich Commissary, The Hague) 154
Monasterio de Santa Maria de Pedralbes, Barcelona 377–8, 438
Monchy, Dr S J R de 219
Mondrian, Piet 336, 341
Moneo, Rafael 381–2
Monet, Claude 277, 315, 408
Moore, Jack 330, 342, 414–5, 417
Morgan Bank 391
Morgan Library Collection 111

Morisot, Berthe, 315
Munch, Edvard 294
Mundogas 346
Murillo, Bartolomé Esteban 295
Museo Nacional de Arte de Cataluña 438
Museum Carmen Cervera Thyssen Bornemisza (Colección Thyssen de Pintura Catalana) 438
Mussolini, Benito 59, 84, 111

N
Nachtsheim, Joseph 132
Nathan, Dr Fritz 220
National
   City Bank 79, 158–9
   Gallery
      London, 269
      Washington 102, 322, 335
nationality / residency / identity
   Germany 4, 39, 55, 72–3, 87, 93, 102, 106, 114, 116, 119, 121–2, 129, 131, 137, 140, 152, 158–9, 162, 165, 170, 175, 185–6, 188, 190, 194–7, 201–2, 208–9, 211–2, 215, 218, 220, 223, 225–6, 228, 235, 238, 269, 273, 282, 308, 323, 337, 355, 373, 388, 408, 436
   Hungary 39, 43, 45, 48, 54–5, 58, 60–1, 73, 75, 82, 87, 94–5, 99, 102, 104, 113, 121–2, 128–9, 139–40, 145, 147–8, 157, 162, 165, 170–2, 189–90, 194–8, 203, 209, 211, 215, 218, 222, 228, 238, 291, 303, 351, 388, 407, 436
   Switzerland 87, 116, 129, 148, 152, 157, 162–3, 165, 167, 170–1, 173, 192–4, 197, 200, 217–9, 225–6, 228–30, 251, 259, 265, 278, 294, 306, 330, 332, 343, 354, 364, 373, 402, 413–4, 428–9
   The Netherlands 55, 57–8, 61, 73, 75, 81, 87, 89–91, 104–7, 121, 127–8, 157, 159, 162, 165, 171, 188, 194–5, 211, 251, 294, 303, 408
Nautilus Trustees Ltd, Cook Islands 366

Nederlandse Credietbank ('NCB') 293, 346
Netherlands Petroleum Company (Nederlands Artoilje Maatschappij, 'NAM') 272
Neubabelsberg sanatorium (Dr Richard Sinn) 139, 149
Neufforge, Baron Ferdinand von 30–1
Neuter, Hedwig de, formerly Hedwig Thyssen, *née* Hedwig Pelzer ('Hedwig Senior') 16, 20, 23, 26–8, 30, 34, 37–8, 41, 137–8, 153–4, 191, 217
New Museum of Islamic Art, Qatar 393
Niarchos
   Philip 315
   Stavros 255, 257–9, 270–1, 278, 301, 310, 335
Niederrheinische
   Gas- und Wasserwerke GmbH 298
   Hütte AG 210
Nolde, Emil 269–70, 392
Northampton, Spencer Compton, Earl of 297–8, 304

O
Oberbilker Steelworks (Oberbilker Stahlwerk AG, 'OSW') 80, 124, 135, 143, 160, 167, 201
O'Keeffe, Georgia 312, 323, 392
Oldenburg, Hans Joachim 180–1
Omin GmbH 437
Onassis
   Alexander 279
   Aristotle 8, 257–9, 270, 279, 301, 306
   Christina 351
   Jackie 279
Oppenheimer
   Elsa 108
   Emma 263
   Moritz James 108–9, 263
   Paula 283
   Dr Walter 283

Oppersdorff, Count Eduard 83
Oppikofer, Dr Hans 211
Osa, Emilio de la 235

P
Palffy, Count Janos (John) 146, 170
Papamarkou, Alexander 345
Paris Exhibition 34, 36, 110
Patten QC, Nicholas 422, 424–6
Pelzer Family Foundation, Glarus 88, 115, 130, 137–8, 143, 191, 209, 222, 251
Pennington, H D. 157
Pensa Oil 372
Perez Sánchez, Antonio 378–9
Petit Palais Museum, Paris 334–5, 370
Pfaff, Eric 265, 330, 342, 419, 426, 430
Philips 203–4, 220
Phillips, Luxembourg & de Pury 437
Phoenix-Rheinrohr AG 210
Picasso, Pablo 315, 321, 323–4, 337, 345, 408
Piero della Francesca 112
Pilkington, Elizabeth 264
Pinakothek Museum, Munich 93–4
Pinochet, General Augusto 406
Pintsch Bamag AG 287, 293
Pita Andrade, José Manuel 384
Pless, Prince 70
Podezin, Franz 180–1
Poensgen, Ernst 64
Pollock, Jackson 270, 316, 392
Portland, Hans Willem Bentinck, first Earl of 125
Poussin, Nicolas 324
Prado, Madrid 365, 372, 378–9, 381, 435
PRAKLA (Gesellschaft für praktische Lagerstättenforschung) 110
Prendergast, Maurice 313, 337
Press- and Rolling Works Reisholz AG (Press- und Walzwerk Reisholz AG, 'PWW') 80, 135, 143, 167, 239, 241, 272, 286

Price
  James 23–4, 158
  Margaret 23
  Sarah, *née* Harlan 23–4, 158
  Thomas 23
Price Waterhouse & Co. 209
Priestley, H R. 182, 242
Pruszynski, Count Mieczyslaw ('Mich') 164–5, 264, 318, 354
Puchhof Castle, Bavaria 283
Pujol, Jordi 363
Pury, Simon de 295, 313, 321–2, 335, 338–9, 345–6, 360, 362, 365, 437
Pusiol, Giorgio 6–8, 10, 11, 282, 319, 366, 401, 406, 409

Q
QQI 87

R
Rabes, Dr Carl 68
Railey, Marie-France 164
Rapetti, Franco 301–2, 310–2, 349
Ratibor, Prince 124–5
Ratiu, Ion 263–4, 317–8, 399
Rauschenberg, Robert 313, 337
Reagan, President Ronald 362
Regent Shipping Line 264
Reichlin, Dr Albert 99
Reina Sofia Centre of Contemporary Art, Madrid 381, 383
Rembrandt
  Commission 314
  Harmensz van Rijn 86, 92–3, 314, 322, 324
Renoir, Auguste 296, 313–4, 375
Reves, Emery 138
Reynolds, Shelley 276–8
Rhein-Elbe-Union 50
Richardson, John 390
Riefenstahl, Leni 91
Rijksmuseum, Amsterdam 93

Rilke, Rainer Maria 40
Ritter
    Curt 110, 176, 186, 192–4, 202, 211–2
    Klaus 110
Robinson Collection, Edward G. 259
Rockefeller
    David 267, 326
    John D. 302
    Nelson 321
Rodin, Auguste 34, 39, 40, 51, 76, 85, 268–9, 392
Roelen, Dr J. Wilhelm 135, 143–4, 152–4, 166–7, 173–7, 186, 188–9, 201, 212–3, 227, 229, 260
Rohland, Dr Walter 151, 183
Rohoncz (Hungary, later Rechnitz/Austria)
    Art Foundation, Schwyz 99, 206, 218, 221
    Castle 32, 43–5, 53–5, 58–60, 62, 68, 96, 104, 122–3, 154, 179–82, 184, 328–9, 354
Rosenberg, Pierre 435
Rosenquist, James 314
Rosenthal, Norman 435
Rothenberger family 109
Rothermere, Viscount and Viscountess 309
Rothko, Mark 321, 337
Rotondo Russo, Jaime 359, 424
Rotterdamsch Trustees Kantoor ('RTK') 66, 134
Royal Dutch Shell 193, 203, 207, 233, 272–3, 300
Rowlands, 'Tiny', né Roland Furhop 394
Royal Academy of Arts, London 249, 348, 435
Rubens, Sir Peter Paul 92, 323
Rüdersdorf Limestone and Cement Works 46, 80, 124, 193
Ruhrgas AG 273
Ruhrkohle AG 285, 325
Ruspoli of Italy, Prince 83

S

Sal. Oppenheim Bank 25, 283
Salpetrière hospital, Paris 397–8
Salz, Sam 315
Samaranch, Juan Antonio 363
San Remo 42, 112, 140
Sapieha, Princess Matilda, née Matilda Bornemisza ('Aunt Ilda') 25, 38, 75, 77, 114, 303, 328–9
Sardinia 132, 302, 309, 320, 350
Sargent, John Singer 341
Satrústegui, Miguel 378, 384, 390
Schacht, Dr Hjalmar 37, 48, 50, 97–8, 104, 178
Schiefelbein, Dr 304
Schiele, Egon 313, 321
Schlessiger, Kurt 176
Schleusener, Dr Alfred 110
Schmidt-Engel, Hannelore ('Pusch') 90–1, 116–9, 141–2, 148–9, 156, 161, 168, 404, 407, 423
Schmidt-Rottluff, Karl 295
Schönborn-Buchheim, Countess Francesca 204
Schröder, SS-Brigadeführer Baron Kurt von 136, 143
Schumacher, Kurt 242
Schwab, Charles 227
Schwartzkoppen, Eduard von 283
Seamless Steel Equipment Corporation ('SSEC') 124, 159, 182, 214
Seherr-Thoss, Count Theo von 122, 166
Seismos GmbH 109–11, 143, 145, 160–1, 167, 201, 233
Semjonov, Vladimir 338
Semprún, Jorge 378–81
Sert, Russie, née Russie Mdivani 112–3
Shorto, Roberto 289–90, 312, 321, 392
Siemens AG 281
Simon Hirschland Bank 150
Sisley, Alfred 313
Six Bart, Dr P Th. 220

'Six Weeks Under The Red Flag' 54
Smith, Jennifer (Premier of Bermuda) 416
Socec, Captain Alexander & Susie, née Susie Price 23–5
Sohl, Dr Hans-Günther 165, 183, 273
Solana
   Guillermo 439
   Javier 373
Solari, Dr Guido 173
Solé Tura, Jordi 381, 383, 385, 389
Soteria AG, Maienfeld 192, 194
Sotheby's 132, 221–2, 295, 321–2, 336, 339, 342, 348–9, 359, 366, 362, 375, 380, 384, 391–2
Soviet Union 165, 172, 173–81, 184, 186, 193, 202–3, 230, 234, 238, 240–1, 250, 288, 338–340
Spann, Othmar 98
Speer, Albert 151, 160, 269
Spencer, Charles James (Earl, Viscount Althorp) 111
Spencer, Stanley 392
Spritzer, Ralph S. 77, 182–3
Stahlwerk Thyssen, Hagendingen/Lorraine 35, 47, 55–6
Standard Oil 220
Stappert, Dr Albert 153, 172, 198, 241
'Star of Peace' diamond 299–300, 341–2, 351
Stauffenberg family, von 178
Steel Union Sheet Piling Company ('SUSPC') 124, 158, 182, 195, 199
Stein, Dr. Heinz-Gerd 268
Stengel, Barbara von 109, 120
Stinnes, Hugo 50, 68
Stirling, Sir James 364
St Moritz 10, 125, 141, 185, 231, 253, 255, 271, 274, 277, 290, 309, 328, 359, 418
Suisse Outremer 259
Sukarno, Dewi 255
Sullivan and Cromwell 199
Summers, Martin & Nona 310, 314

Swart, Colonel Dirk M A. 202–3, 220, 267
Swiss Bank Corporation 114, 153, 212, 245
Switzerland
   Compensation Office 183, 218
   Foreigner Police 103, 116, 127, 148, 170, 172–3, 225
   Justice Department 148, 229, 288
   Political Department 129, 134, 217, 229
Szapary, Count Paul 42
Szechenyi, Count 115
Szombathely, Hungary 73, 180

T

Tamara Corporation, Bermuda 343
Taubman, Alfred 359
taxation 59, 81, 83–4, 86–7, 116, 132, 134, 137, 143–4, 146, 163, 207, 211, 213, 215–6, 219, 226, 239, 249, 251, 254, 259, 261–2, 264–5, 292, 294, 303, 305–6, 310, 319, 330, 333, 339, 365–6, 368, 372, 376, 379, 390, 396, 402, 437
T-B A21 (Thyssen-Bornemisza Art Contemporary) 439
Terboven, Gauleiter Josef 136
Thatcher, Prime Minister Margaret 371
Themis Finanzgesellschaft, Zug 193
The Netherlands
   Board for Administration of Enemy and Collaborators' Property ('Beheer Institute') 193, 198, 201–4, 211, 216, 219
   Foreign Exchange Institute 174
   'Operation Juliana' 176, 182, 186, 192, 202–4, 209, 211
Thesing, Susanne 362
Thomas Gibson Fine Art, London 316
Thurn und Taxis, Prince Johannes & Princess Gloria von 309, 334, 388
Thybo Trustees Ltd, Bermuda 403
Thyssen
   Amélie, née Amélie zur Helle 30, 33, 47, 69, 84, 87, 89, 98, 119, 136–9, 146, 149, 151, 159–60, 162, 177–9, 190,

208, 218, 223, 225, 229, 236–7, 247, 250, 257–61, 269, 282–3, 355

August ('Old August') 13–23, 25–42, 45–9, 52, 55–72, 76–81, 88, 144, 150, 162–3, 174, 185, 190, 224, 227, 268–9, 272, 282–3, 285–6, 293, 308, 355, 436, 440

August ('August Junior') 20, 26, 28–30, 32–3, 37–8, 41, 45–7, 59, 69, 76, 81–3, 96, 113, 125–6, 132, 155, 163, 167–8, 222, 231, 233

Friedrich Junior 17–8

Friedrich Senior 13–15, 17, 20

Fritz 20, 26–31, 33, 37–8, 41, 46–7, 49, 52–60, 62–71, 73, 76, 78–84, 86–9, 91–2, 97–9, 104–10, 114, 116, 119, 130–1, 135–40, 143–4, 146, 149–53, 156–60, 162, 165, 177–9, 187–8, 190–2, 194–5, 200, 207–9, 218, 222–7, 229–30, 234, 236–7, 240, 251, 258–61, 269, 283, 286, 322, 355, 439

Gertrud, *née* Gertrud Schmid-Scharrer 38, 68–9

Hans 28–9, 38, 47–8, 52, 55, 59, 68–70, 76, 80, 84, 132, 146

Isaac Lambert 13

Josef 13–4, 19, 20, 22, 26–9, 35, 38, 47–8, 52

Jula, *née* Jula Rintelen 38, 76

Julius 28–9, 38, 47, 52, 55, 59–60, 69–70, 76, 80, 132, 146, 165

Katharina 13, 17, 20, 38

Klara, *née* Klara Bagel 20, 28–9, 38–9, 52

Kurt-Ferdinand 165

Thyssen
AG 4, 25, 183, 208, 268, 271, 273, 283, 286, 355
Asset Management 325, 437
Bank, Eschweiler 13–4, 17

Thyssen-Bornemisza
Art Foundation
Spain 10, 379, 389–90, 393, 396, 400, 435, 439
Switzerland 365, 367, 393
Art Fund, British Virgin Islands 395–6
Collection (formerly Schloss Rohoncz Collection) 4, 6, 40–1, 85–6, 88–9, 92–5, 99, 101–3, 107, 111–2, 115, 126–7, 153, 166, 174, 199, 206–8, 211, 215–22, 225, 233, 235, 239, 249, 252, 256–7, 259, 268–70, 282, 287, 294–7, 302, 306, 309, 312–7, 321–5, 336–41, 343, 345–9, 352, 356, 360, 362–87, 389–93, 402, 408, 410, 423, 437–9
Collection Trust, Bermuda 343, 367, 385, 393
Continuity Trust, Bermuda 9, 265, 330–2, 341–6, 348, 367, 376, 395–6, 398, 400–2, 413–4, 417, 426–8, 437
Corporate Liquidity Fund 399–400, 402–3
de Kaszón
Baron Alexander 7, 10, 296, 303, 316–7, 319, 343, 349–50, 375, 389, 391–3, 395–7, 401, 407, 423–4, 433–7
Baroness Alexandra, *née* Alexandra Wright 439
Baroness Birgit 145, 161, 220, 234–6, 256–7, 329, 353, 356, 435
Baron Borja 9, 320, 344–5, 366, 368, 371, 382, 390, 393, 398, 400, 407, 409, 433–4, 439
Baroness Carmen, formerly Carmen Barker, *née* Carmen Cervera ('Tita') 3, 5–11, 171, 300, 320, 323–4, 327, 330, 340–2, 344–53, 356, 358–74, 377–9, 382–3, 385–6, 388–93, 395–403, 405–10, 416–7, 420, 422–8, 431–9
Baroness Denise, *née* Denise Shorto 3, 10, 287–91, 299, 301–3, 305, 309–12, 316–7, 319–22, 327–8, 330, 332, 337, 339–42, 344–6, 348–51, 368, 386, 389, 397, 417, 424, 437

Baroness Fiona, *née* Fiona Campbell–Walter 3, 8, 10, 253–6, 258–9, 262, 264, 270–1, 273–81, 287, 308, 386
Baron Georg Heinrich ('Heini Junior') 7, 9–10, 196, 198, 231, 245, 268, 290, 293, 306–8, 316–7, 324–5, 327, 329–34, 339, 341–3, 345–9, 356, 358–9, 367–9, 374, 376, 380, 386, 389–93, 395–405, 411–4, 417–20, 422–3, 425–6, 428, 431–8
Baroness Gunhilde, *née* Gunhilde von Fabrizius 113–4, 116, 124, 129–30, 153–5, 161–2, 172, 196, 206, 213, 216, 221, 230, 237–8, 353
Baroness Guadalupe Sabina 439
Baron Hans Heinrich ('Heini') 3–11, 26, 39, 44–5, 50, 55, 58, 61, 65, 68–70, 72–5, 80–1, 84, 86, 89–94, 96–7, 101–2, 104–7, 109, 111–2, 115–9, 121, 123–30, 135–6, 139–49, 153–4, 156, 159, 161–3, 167–72, 174, 177, 179, 182, 185–90, 193–202, 204–9, 211–40, 244–65, 267–82, 285–325, 327–56, 358–428, 431–40
Baron Heinrich, *né* Heinrich Thyssen 20, 23, 26–34, 37–9, 41–8, 52–63, 66–76, 78, 80–2, 84–99, 101–4, 107–16, 118–131, 135–7, 140, 143–4, 146, 152–4, 156–7, 160–2, 165–8, 170–5, 177, 180, 185–9, 192–8, 200–1, 204–7, 209, 211–23, 228, 230, 234, 237, 263, 267, 269, 282, 285, 298, 328–9, 343, 362, 388, 393, 439
Baroness Helena, *née* Ilyana Kugler–Andrassy 97, 109–10, 145–6, 160, 167, 329
Baroness Ingeborg ('Inge'), *née* Ingeborg Müller 145, 161, 220, 234–6, 256–7, 329, 353, 355–6, 435

Baroness Julia 439
Baron Lorne 7, 274, 276, 278, 287, 316, 334, 343, 350, 352, 354, 367, 375, 389–93, 395–6, 402, 423, 431–2, 434, 437, 439
Baroness Maria del Carmen 439
Baroness Maud, *née* Maud Feller 73, 95, 99, 101, 103–4, 111–3, 121, 130, 271
Baron Simon 433, 437–8
Baron Dr Stephan 44–5, 58–9, 61, 68–9, 72, 75–6, 81–2, 89, 95–8, 109–111, 145–6, 160–3, 167–8, 200–1, 206–7, 209, 213–5, 217, 218–23, 225, 230, 233–6, 238–9, 255–7, 271, 298–9, 303, 328–9, 356
Group ('TBG') 7–9, 109, 152, 167, 171, 177, 182, 186, 188–9, 193–4, 196–9, 201, 204, 209, 214–6, 225, 227–8, 230, 238–40, 245, 260, 265, 268, 271, 286, 290–3, 300, 303, 305–6, 316–9, 324–5, 327, 330–4, 341–3, 345–8, 368, 372, 393, 395, 398, 402–4, 410–2, 415, 418, 420, 427–8, 432–5, 437
Holdings NV, Amstelveen 293, 325, 332, 346–7, 357
Inc., New York 303, 305, 346
Museum, Madrid 7, 86, 94, 111, 221, 313, 323, 381–7, 408, 431, 438–9
SAM, Monaco 305–6, 346, 357, 432
Thyssen & Co. 15–22, 25–6, 30–1, 33–4, 36–8, 45–50, 52–3, 55–6, 60, 62–3, 65–8, 146
  Eisen und Stahl AG 152
  Gas and Waterworks (Thyssensche Gas- und Wasserwerke, later Thyssengas AG) 71, 80, 124, 135, 144, 154, 163, 171, 174–5, 180, 224, 233, 239, 271–2, 293, 298, 347
  -Gravimeter 110
  -Guerreschi, Claudia 355
  Krupp AG 4, 119, 132, 268, 283, 440

Lametal SA (Thyssen Companía Industrial y Mercantil & Thyssen Limitada Lametal, Buenos Aires) 84, 173–4, 191–2, 194–5
Participations AG (Thyssen AG für Beteiligungen) 237
Schachtbau GmbH (Thyssen mine shaft drilling company) 32
v. Thyssen
    Germany (1910s) 30, 45–6, 429
    Bermuda (1990s) 8–10, 342–4, 410–35
Tintoretto, Jacobo Robusti, called 296, 324
Toepfer Foundation, Hamburg 374
Toninelli Arte Moderne, Milan 270
Tornabuoni Ltd, Guernsey 343, 403
Toulouse-Lautrec, Henri 294–5
Transylvania 24, 44, 309
Trappe, Dr (Seismos GmbH) 109
Troesch, Rita 147
Tschirschky und Bögendorff, Count Heinrich von 118, 133

U
Übersee Trust, Liechtenstein 159, 191
UFA film company 83
Ugolino di Nerio (aka Ugolino da Siena) 296–7
Unilever 203
Union
  Banking Corporation, New York ('Union Bank', 'UBC') 66, 71, 75, 115, 124, 137, 143, 157–9, 167, 195, 199–200, 206, 212, 215, 222, 250
  Bank of Switzerland 245
United Kingdom
  Bank of England 137
  Board of Trade 222, 228
  Foreign Office 183, 211, 218, 223, 228, 241–2
  High Courts of Justice 238, 350
  Trading with the Enemy Department 218

United States of America
  Alien Property Custodian 167, 182–4
  Central Intelligence Agency ('CIA') 199, 220, 238
  Department of Justice 242
  External Assets and Intelligence Branch 209, 226, 241
  Foreign Economic Administration 192, 240
  Office of Strategic Services ('OSS') 199
  Steel Corporation ('US Steel') 70, 79
  Trading with the Enemy Department 51, 209, 241
  Treasury Department (Foreign Funds Control Division) 157, 159, 183, 194
Uría, Rodrigo 363, 374, 376, 378, 439
Urpasis Investments Ltd, Cyprus 437
Uruguay 234, 251, 305
Urvanos Investments Ltd, Cyprus 437

V
van
  Aken, Dr Roberto 116, 153, 170, 172, 189–90, 194, 198, 206–7, 209, 212, 217, 219, 223, 225, 229, 239, 254, 264–5, 271
  der Weyden, Rogier 103
  Dyck, Sir Anthony 221–2
  Elden, Dr W. 220
  Gogh, Vincent 338
  Karnebeek, Dick 189–90
  Meegeren, Hans 221
Velàzquez, Diego de Silva 111, 372
Vereinigte
  Berliner Mörtelwerke ('VBM') 124, 193
  Stahlwerke AG (United Steelworks, 'Steel Trust', 'VSt') 70–1, 79–80, 87–8, 104, 114–5, 130–2, 136, 146, 151–2, 158, 165, 188, 191–2, 194–5, 224, 236–7
Verlohr, Conrad 35, 64
Vermeer, Jan 221
Vilallonga, José Luís de 182, 335, 353, 390

Villa Favorita, Lugano 10, 95, 99, 101–4, 114–5, 124, 129, 140, 143, 152–3, 162, 167, 174, 185–6, 196, 204, 206, 212, 216, 220, 231, 254, 264, 274, 290, 301, 307, 313, 327, 338–40, 343, 352, 356, 358–9, 362, 364–7, 371, 378–9, 386, 393, 408, 432, 436
Villa Monte Verità, Ascona 84, 103
Villahermosa Palace, Madrid 377–9, 381–3, 401, 431
Villegas, Luís 146–7
Vinassa, Professor Walter 220
Vlaardingen port, Rotterdam 48
Vlaminck
    Maurice 392
    Trust (LRT Trustee (PVT) Ltd) 402–3
Vlissingen harbour, North Sea 347
Vögler, Dr Albert 87, 104, 136
Volz, Edda 73–5, 89, 104–5, 117, 119, 129, 148, 168
von der Heydt
    Bank AG 84–5
    Baron August 50
    Baron (Freiherr) Eduard 34, 54, 57, 84–5, 88, 95, 98–9, 103, 125, 143, 195, 241
Vulcaan
    (London) Co Ltd. 132, 209
    NV, Handels en Transport Maatschappij, Rotterdam ('HTMV') 48, 71, 80, 124, 132, 194, 219, 230
Vulcan Inc. 346
Vulkan GmbH 48, 71, 124

W

Walsum coal mine 80, 114, 124, 135, 143, 153, 163, 169, 175, 247, 249, 260, 268, 272, 285, 293
Watteau, Jean Antoine 102
Werenwag Castle, Beuron/Germany 245–6
Wettstein von Westersheimb
    Baron Janos 61, 73, 75, 104, 117, 128–9, 139, 189, 198, 208
    Baroness Margit, formerly Baroness Margit Thyssen-Bornemisza, née Margit Bornemisza ('Margit Senior') 25, 38–9, 41–46, 53–4, 58, 61, 67–9, 71–5, 81, 94, 96–8, 104, 114, 117, 128–9, 140, 200, 206, 221, 287, 298, 328
Whicker, Alan 273–4
White, Gordon 345
Wiesenthal, Dr Simon 323
Wilson, Harold 228
Windisch-Graetz, Prince Mariano Hugo zu 349
Winterhalder, Guillermo 260
Wittgenstein
    Casimir Prince 430
    Gallery, New York 345
Woodroffe, G B W. 242
Wyeth
    Andrew 313, 321
    N C. 6, 408

Z

Zamora, José de 392
Zettel, Dr Waldemar 109–10, 145
Zichy de Zich et Vásonkeö
    Count Gabor 87, 89, 119, 121, 130, 136, 355
    Countess Anita, née Anita Thyssen 47, 69, 84–5, 87, 89, 116, 119, 121, 136, 151, 159, 191, 208, 236–7, 250, 258, 260, 262, 283, 355
    Count Claudio 89, 121, 258, 260, 325, 355
    Count Federico 89, 119, 121, 136, 243, 258, 260, 325, 355
Züblin, Dr Albert 212–3
Zuill, Cummings V. 430

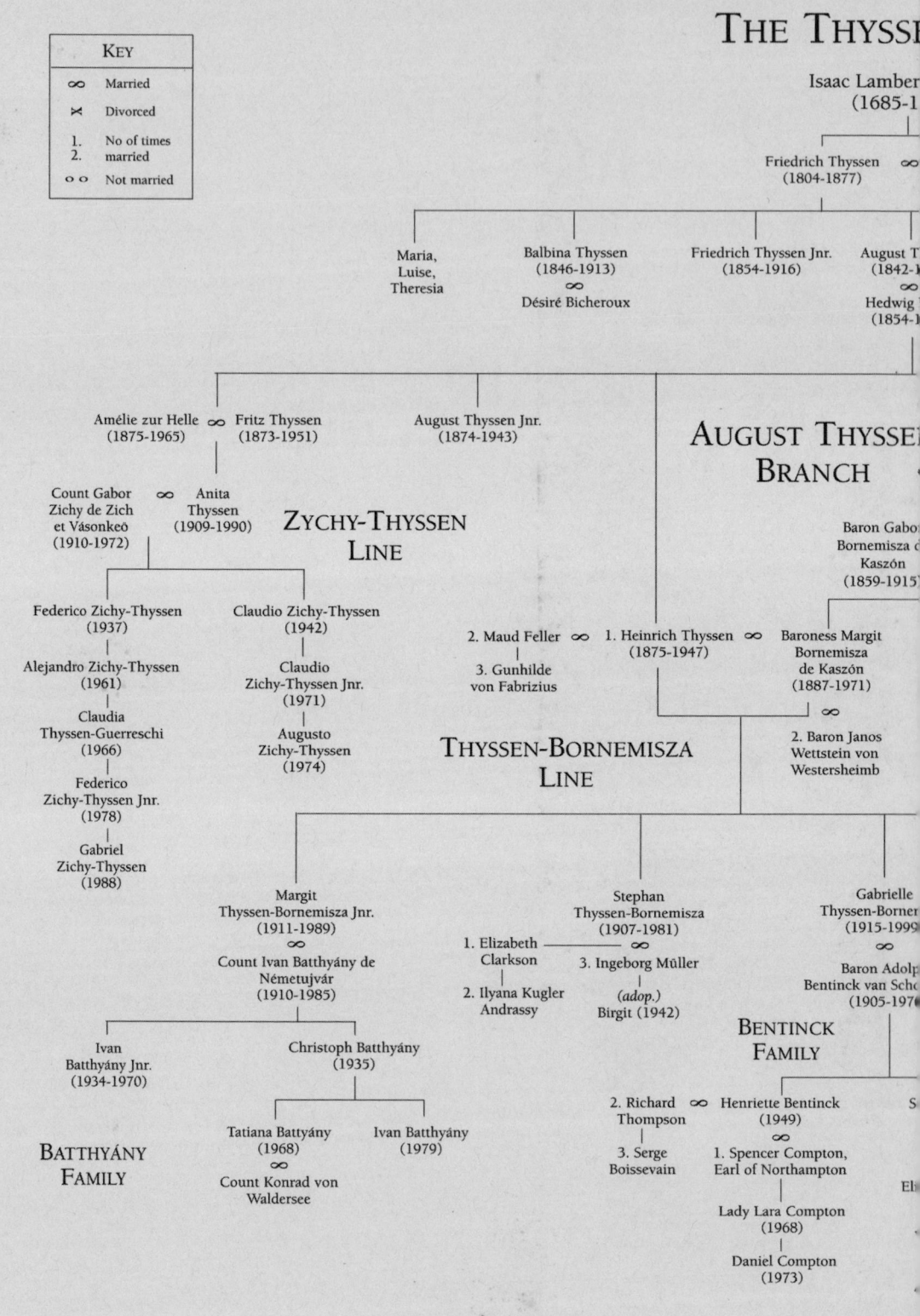